THE GRACE AWAKENING

THE GRACE AWAKENING

CHARLES R. SWINDOLL

WORD PUBLISHING
NASHVILLE
A Thomas Nelson Company

PUBLISHED BY WORD PUBLISHING

DALLAS, TEXAS.

Unless otherwise indicated, Scripture quotations used in this book are from the
New American Standard Bible (NASB) © 1960, 1962, 1963, 1968, 1971,
1972,1973, 1975, 1977 by The Lockman Foundation.
Used by permission.

32530 60545 4451

Other Scripture quotations are from the following sources:
The Amplified Bible (AMP). Copyright ©1965
Zondervan Publishing House. Used by permission.
The Living Bible (TLB) t 1971 by Tyndale House Publishers,
Wheaton, IL. Used by permission.
The New English Bible (NEB), Copyright © the Delegates
of the Oxford University Press and the Syndics of the Cambridge
University Press, 1961, 1970. Reprinted by permission.
The Holy Bible, New International Version (NIV).
Copyright © 1973, 1978, 1984 International Bible Society.
Used by permission of Zondervan Bible Publishers.
The New King James Version (NKJV). Copyright © 1979,
1980, 1982, Thomas Nelson, Inc., Publisher.
The New Testament in Modern English (PHILLIPS) by J. B. Phillips, published
by The Macmillan Company © 1958, 1960, 1972 by J. B. Phillips.

Book design by Mark McGarry
Set in Perpetua

Library of Congress Cataloging-in-Publication Data:
Swindoll, Charles R. The grace awakening / Charles R. Swindoll.
p. cm.
ISBN 0-8499-0769-1 (original edition)
ISBN 0-8499-1323-3
1. Grace (Theology) 1. Title.
BT761.2.S94   1990   234—dc20
90-36943   CIP

Printed in the United States of America

9   BVG   5 4 3 2 1

234
761.2894
SWIN
6/16/03
MB

It is with great affection I dedicate this book to
Paul and Sue Sailhamer
and
Howie and Marilyn Stevenson
whose lives and ministries radiate grace.
Because of our close friendship,
I know better what it means
to be free.

CONTENTS

PUBLISHER'S PREFACE

WE LIVE IN A CHANGING WORLD. PERHAPS NO ERA IN history has seen so many dramatic changes in such a short time as our own. Freedom has broken out in Eastern Europe and the former Soviet Union; social and political events in Palestine and Central Europe are changing the world's landscape. As a result, we are witnessing a tremendous explosion of interest in spiritual matters throughout all segments of society. Today, the Christian faith is going through one of the greatest periods of growth in modern times.

When *The Grace Awakening* first appeared in 1990, Chuck Swindoll wanted to address what he perceived as "grace killers" . . . people who restrain and limit the dynamic potential of the Christian life. Among the most visible and vicious are those who criticize, condemn, and crush our hopes of joyful living. Chuck warned that legalism in the church—hiding behind the mask of orthodoxy or piety—was stealing the happiness of believers and holding faith hostage. What we needed at that hour was awakening.

Within days of the book's release, the responses began flooding in. Letters, cards, and reviews came from grateful pastors, teachers, and other Christians all over the country. Some said they had often felt imprisoned in their faith until they recognized their own need for a "grace awakening." Suddenly they understood the reality of the regeneration that Christ had meant for us to enjoy. If we are "new creatures in Christ," they asked, why aren't we rejoicing more and worrying less? Tragically, some Christian leaders had lost the battle, became weary of the assaults, and resigned from positions they had once occupied.

Chuck Swindoll had pointed out that Paul gave us the right perspective in his letter to the church at Ephesus, when he wrote: "For by grace you have been saved through faith; and that not of yourselves, it is the gift of God; not as a result of works, that no one should boast" (Eph. 2:8–9). Most are quick to adopt a grace-based salvation, but how often, the author asked, have we fallen into the trap of a works-related Christian life? And how often have we traded the freedom and spontaneity of our walk of faith for a manmade code of "do's and don'ts"? Nothing so stifles our faith, he insisted, as the cold scowl of legalism, which brings with it a critical and judgmental spirit.

On numerous occasions since this book was released, Chuck Swindoll has been stopped by total strangers to listen to stories of an individual's transforming awakening of grace. One such occasion occurred at an airport when a woman walked up and asked if he happened to be the author of "the best book I ever read on grace" (her exact words). After the two introduced themselves, she told of how it had not only changed her life—but the lives of everyone in her entire family.

Her husband had been a pastor of an extremely legalistic church in a denomination known for its rigidity and judgmental spirit. In fact, he had been reared and schooled in that kind of stifling, demanding, religious atmosphere. It was all he knew. Performance lists were common as those in charge spelled out what was expected of all who wished to please God. The pressure mounted, especially in that pastor's home.

Not only did the teenage children begin to rebel, the pastor's wife became disenchanted with the whole system of "works theology." Instead of graciously and carefully teaching the Word of God, her husband—and all who filled his pulpit—harassed and threatened the flock. She became depressed, seeing no hope of change and no way of escape. It was then she came upon *The Grace Awakening,* which she "devoured in a few days," even though it was not among the books her denomination approved.

Seeing his wife's enthusiasm and joy returning led her husband to read the book as well. Before he finished it, he began to see how twisted and misguided he had been. He had the courage to go public and admit from the pulpit that an awakening of grace had so changed him, he could no longer promote the legalism, hypocrisy, and joyless religion that was so much a part of their church and denomination. He refused to continue filling the role of a grace killer.

His resignation was met with cold stares . . . the family was virtually ostracized by those who had been long-time "church friends." But this man, his wife, and even their teenagers now know a joy and relief in their relationship with each other (and with their Lord) they never dreamed existed. Their Christian walk, now based on grace, has been literally revolutionized. As Chuck put it, "She is radiant with a joy that is contagious. I've rarely seen a person who exudes the love and grace of Christ so naturally, so enthusiastically. Grace has truly awakened within her!"

Since the release of the book, the world has continued its dramatic changes. In addition to the political changes in Europe and Asia, there have been startling moral and ethical revolutions as well—an awakening of conscience and character of amazing proportions. Christianity has been breaking out around the world.

We have witnessed prayer movements ushered in by open confession of sin and repentance on college campuses. Outpourings of the Spirit have called congregations and even denominations back to their first love for Christ. We have witnessed the birth of a Christ-centered men's movement that has already touched more than seven hundred thousand men with strong admonitions and biblical teaching on the importance of character, integrity, fidelity, facing their pressures, and keeping their promises. Chuck Swindoll has been a part of this movement, not only by speaking at several Promise Keepers events around the nation, but through the ongoing ministry of this important book.

It is clear now that *The Grace Awakening* was prophetic in many ways. So many of the signs of liberation that the author described in these pages have come to fulfillment. And that is the reason for this new edition, re-packaged and re-presented for another generation of believers. It is our hope that the timeless message of *The Grace Awakening* may now begin to touch the lives of a whole new group of Christians, and to encourage men and women everywhere in their walk of faith.

Even though the message of this book has already had a dramatic impact on our thinking about the Christian life, the wisdom and counsel contained in these pages is needed today more than ever. The challenges in the world around us are greater than ever, but the need for Christians who will live out their witness in freedom and compassion is even greater.

Paul writes in Romans 12:6 that "since we have gifts that differ according to the grace given to us, let each exercise them accordingly. . . ." Indeed, each one of us has gifts, but it is the hope of this book that we should become a generation of believers, molded into the image of Christ, walking boldly in the freedom of faith that our Lord intended. For when that occurs, *The Grace Awakening* is not simply a book worth reading but a life worth living.

ACKNOWLEDGMENTS

I AM A GRATEFUL MAN. I HAVE EVERY REASON TO BE. It is my joy to have numerous people surrounding me with encouragement, affirmation, honest feedback, and an abundant supply of fresh hope to stay at tough tasks. I consider them more than friends; they are partners with me, true to the end. To say that they have been helpful in seeing this book to completion is a gross understatement of the fact.

Contrary to a recurring rumor, I have no writing staff or team of researchers who provide me with historical and illustrative material or serve as my "ghost writers." Every word comes from my own pen through the age-old process most authors still use: blood, sweat, tears, sleepless nights, lengthy stares at blank sheets of paper, unproductive days when everything gets dumped into the trash, and periodic moments when inspiration and insight flow. My method is so obsolete I don't even use a word processor, and I have a thick, pen-worn callous on my finger to prove it.

But what I do have are these faithful partners who believe in me enough to pray for me while I'm in the midst of giving birth to a book. They do more than pray, however. Some make suggestions. Others offer ideas and toss out warnings as well as goad me with questions. One types, another edits, several read, and many patiently listen. Because I am a pastor, having served the same church since 1971, I also have a lot of ears who hear the things I later put into a book. They help me hone my words by responding to what I have said with comments that are often poignant. And then there are those who serve with me on the same pastoral staff—my closest colleagues— with whom I have an enviable and rare relationship. As I acknowledge their value in my life and their contribution to my writing, I could not be more sincere or grateful. So much for all my unnamed yet eminently appreciated "partners."

Specifically, I am indebted to Byron Williamson of Word Publishing for his tireless enthusiasm over this book. His support has been relentless since its inception. In addition, Kip Jordon and Ernie Owen, both long-time friends of mine at Word, have given me great encouragement, being convinced that my perspective and convictions on grace deserved to be published so all could read what we have discussed and agreed on for years. While acknowledging my appreciation for those in the Word family, I dare not forget to mention my editor, Beverly Phillips, with whom I have worked for over a decade. She continues to model the qualities an author needs most in an editor—a discerning eye, a sensitive spirit, wise counsel, accuracy mixed with flexibility, penetrating questions that make me think, and a kind of convincing criticism that forces me to reevaluate and (ugh!) rewrite.

My list would be incomplete if I failed to mention Sealy Yates, who supplied invaluable assistance behind the scenes. Being the man of integrity that he is, his advice and suggestions rang true and proved to be best. I am grateful that he cared more about *The Grace Awakening* project than his own schedule, and when my patience wore thin he demonstrated the kind of grace I write about. And, of course, I must again express my profound thanks to Helen Peters, whose diligence knows no bounds. With tireless determination she proofread the manuscript numerous times, corrected my spelling, typed every word, secured approval for my quotations and illustrations, adapted her personal calendar to meet the demands of my deadlines, put the final copy into perfect form ahead of schedule—in itself, a minor miracle—and all without one word of exasperation or complaint. Helen could sit for a portrait of amazing grace.

Finally, I acknowledge the support of my entire family, whose attitudes and expressions of grace (especially over the past two years) have been nothing short of incredible. In spite of the storms we have weathered and the pain we have endured together, not once have I felt anything but their unconditional love and absolute support. Rather than being pulled apart, we have bonded closer than ever. So thank you, Cynthia, Colleen, and Chuck . . . thank you, Curt and Deb, Byron and Charissa, along with Ryan, Chelsea, Landon, Parker, and Heather . . . and thank you, too, Luci, my dear sister, for your unfailing loyalty and love.

> 'Tis grace hath brought us safe thus far
> And grace will lead us home.[1]

INTRODUCTION

A NEW MOVEMENT IS ON THE HORIZON.

It is a movement of freedom, a joyful release from the things that have bound us far too long. More and more Christians are realizing that the manmade restrictions and legalistic regulations under which they have been living have not come from the God of grace, but have been enforced by people who do not want others to be free. It is not an overstatement to describe this movement as an awakening that is beginning to sweep across the country. Nothing could please me more. This awakening to freedom is long overdue. It fits the times in which we are living.

The world has been witnessing an astounding political awakening to freedom in Eastern Europe. The wide-eyed smiling faces of East Germans tell their own story as many in this generation are tasting liberty for the first time. The cry of *Freiheit* has been shouted at border gates and in the streets of Budapest, Prague, Bucharest, and East Berlin. Not since the liberated victims of German concentration camps caught their first glimpse of hope back in the mid 1940s have so many enjoyed the reality of being released. After years of enforcement, they are free . . . *free at last.* We who live in "the land of the free" applaud their liberation. Free people find delight in others' freedom. Only the politically enslaved resist it.

The same is true spiritually. But as much as I would like to say that all are in support of our pursuit of grace-awakening freedom, I cannot. Be warned, there are grace killers on the loose! To make matters worse, they are a well-organized, intimidating body of people who stop at nothing to keep you and me from enjoying the freedom that is rightfully ours to claim. I know whereof I speak; I was once numbered among them. Legalism was my security, and making certain that others marched to my cadence was a major part of my daily agenda. No longer. For years now, I have become increasingly aware of an awakening of grace in my own life . . . and nothing has brought me greater relief or, for that matter, more intense criticism. It was safer back then, but since when have we been commanded to take the safe route? Christ certainly didn't. His revolutionary message and methods, as we shall see, resulted in regular confrontations with the organized religious bureaucrats of His day. They were among those who ultimately pinned Him to a cross, I might add. Following such a Leader is not safe. Freedom movements never have been safe.

When the sixteenth-century European Reformers brandished the torch of freedom and stood against the religious legalists of their era, grace was the battle cry: salvation by grace alone . . . a walk of faith without fear of eternal damnation. The church hated them and called them heretics. When the eighteenth- and early nineteenth-century revival spread across Great Britain and into America, preached fervently by John Wesley, Jonathan Edwards, George Whitefield, and a handful of other risk-taking spokesmen for God, it was again grace that led the way. And there was again strong resistance from those who frowned upon their message of freedom in Christ. Interestingly, that sweeping movement came to be known as "The Great Awakening." What I am sensing these days is yet another awakening in the genre of those history-making movements. Perhaps it is best defined as "The Grace Awakening," a message whose time has come.

Scarcely a day passes when I am not reminded of the need for a book emphasizing the full extent of grace, giving people permission to be free, absolutely free in Christ. Why? Because so few are! Bound and shackled by legalists' lists of do's and don'ts, intimidated and immobilized by others' demands and expectations, far too many in God's family merely exist in the tight radius of bondage, dictated by those who have appointed themselves our judge and jury. Long enough have we lived like frightened deer in a restrictive thicket of negative regulations. Long enough have we submitted to the do's and don'ts of religious kings of the mountain. Long enough have we been asleep while all around us the grace killers do their sinister nighttime work. No longer! It is time to awaken. The dawn is bright with grace.

Too many folks are being turned off by a twisted concept of the Christian life. Instead of offering a winsome and contagious, sensible and achievable invitation of hope and cheer through the sheer power of Christ, more people than ever are projecting a grim-faced carica-ture of religion-on-demand. I find it tragic that religious killjoys have almost succeeded in taking the freedom and fun out of faith. People need to know that there is more to the Christian life than deep frowns, pointing fingers, and unrealistic expectations. Harassment has had the floor long enough. Let grace awaken.

> You may be able to compel people to maintain certain minimum stan-dards by stressing duty, but the highest moral and spiritual achievements depend not upon a push but a pull. People must be charmed into righ-teousness.[1]

I am convinced that nothing will strengthen the magnet of charm like freedom, for which the Bible has a great word:

grace . . . liberating grace . . . revolutionary grace . . . amazing grace . . . *awakening* grace.

If you find yourself yearning to be committed to something beyond yourself, looking forward eagerly to the dawn of each new day, truly liberated from those who would hold you captive, free to be free and to challenge the world to embrace grace's liberties, all I ask for is your time and attention. Before too many chapters, I hope your heart will be as ablaze as mine has become. But I should warn you, once the smoldering embers burst into full flame, you'll not be able to extinguish them. Having joined the ranks of this freedom movement, you will never again be satisfied with slavery.

Having become a part of *The Grace Awakening*, your long-awaited freedom will encourage you and charm others for a lifetime.

Chuck Swindoll
Fullerton, California

1

Grace: It's Really *Amazing!*

~

> [The] moralizing and legalizing of the Gospel
> of God's grace is a dull heresey peddled to
> disappointed people who are angry because
> they have not received what they had no good
> reason to expect.
>
> RICHARD J. NEUHAUS

THERE ARE KILLERS ON THE LOOSE TODAY. the problem is that you can't tell by looking. They don't wear little buttons that give away their identity, nor do they carry signs warning everybody to stay away. On the contrary, a lot of them carry Bibles and appear to be clean-living, nice-looking, law-abiding citizens. Most of them spend a lot of time in churches, some in places of religious leadership. Many are so respected in the community, their neighbors would never guess they are living next door to killers.

They kill freedom, spontaneity, and creativity; they kill joy as well as productivity. They kill with their words and their pens and their looks. They kill with their attitudes far more often than with their behavior. There is hardly a church or Christian organization or Christian school or missionary group or media ministry where such danger does not lurk. The amazing thing is that they get away with it, day in and day out, without being confronted or exposed. Strangely, the same ministries that would not tolerate heresy for ten minutes will step aside and allow these killers all the space they need to maneuver and manipulate others in the most insidious manner imaginable. Their

3

intolerance is tolerated. Their judgmental spirits remain unjudged. Their bullying tactics continue unchecked. And their narrow-mindedness is either explained away or quickly defended. The bondage that results would be criminal were it not so subtle and wrapped in such spiritual-sounding garb.

This day—this very moment—millions are living their lives in shame, fear, and intimidation who should be free, productive individuals. The tragedy is they think it is the way they should be. They have never known the truth that could set them free. They are victimized, existing as if living on death row instead of enjoying the beauty and fresh air of the abundant life Christ modeled and made possible for all of His followers to claim. Unfortunately, most don't have a clue to what they are missing.

That whole package, in a word, is *grace*. That's what is being assaulted so continually, so violently. Those who aren't comfortable denying it have decided to debate it. Similar to the days of the Protestant Reformation, grace has again become a theological football kicked from one end of the field to the other as theologians and preachers, scholars and students argue over terms like frustrated coaches on opposite sides trying to gain advantage over each other. It is a classic no-win debate that trivializes the issue and leaves the masses who watch the fight from the stands confused, polarized, or worst of all, bored. Grace was meant to be received and lived out to the fullest, not dissected and analyzed by those who would rather argue than eat. Enough of this! It's time for grace to be awakened and released, not denied . . . to be enjoyed and freely given, not debated.

Grace received but unexpressed is dead grace. To spend one's time debating how grace is received or how much commitment is necessary for salvation, without getting into what it means to live by grace and enjoy the magnificent freedom it provides, quickly leads to a counter-productive argument. It becomes little more than another tedious trivial pursuit where the majority of God's people spend days looking back and asking, "How did we receive it?" instead of looking ahead and announcing, "Grace is ours . . . let's live it!" Deny it or debate it and we kill it. My plea is that we claim it and allow it to set us free. When we do, grace will become what it was meant to be—*really* amazing! When that happens, our whole countenance changes.

"NO" FACES . . . "YES" FACES

Dr. Karl Menninger, in a book entitled *The Vital Balance*, at one point discusses the negativistic personality. That's the type who says no to just about everything. Calling these sad folks "troubled patients," Menninger (no doubt with tongue in cheek) mentions several of the things that characterize their lives: They have never made an unsound loan, voted for a liberal cause, or sponsored any extravagances. Why? He suggests it is because they cannot permit themselves the pleasure of giving. He describes them in vivid terms: ". . . rigid, chronically unhappy individuals, bitter, insecure, and often suicidal."[1]

I would add one further description—they have never given themselves permission to be free. Still imprisoned behind the bars of petty concerns and critical suspicions, they have learned to exist in a bondage that has hindered their ability to see beyond life's demands. Lacking grace, they have reduced life to the rules and regulations essential for survival. Their God is too small, their world is too rigid, and therefore their faces shout "No!"

Candidly, I know of nothing that has the power to change us from within like the freedom that comes through grace. It's so amazing it will change not only our hearts but also our faces. And goodness knows, some of us are overdue for a face change! Were you reared by parents whose faces said "No"? Or are you married to someone with a "No" face? If that is true, you envy those who had "Yes"-face parents or are married to "Yes"-face mates. All of us are drawn to those whose faces invite us in and urge us on.

During his days as president, Thomas Jefferson and a group of companions were traveling across the country on horseback. They came to a river which had left its banks because of a recent downpour. The swollen river had washed the bridge away. Each rider was forced to ford the river on horseback, fighting for his life against the rapid currents. The very real possibility of death threatened each rider, which caused a traveler who was not part of their group to step aside and watch. After several had plunged in and made it to the other side, the stranger asked President Jefferson if he would ferry him across the river. The president agreed without hesitation. The man climbed on, and shortly thereafter the two of them made it safely to the other side. As the stranger slid off the back of the saddle onto dry ground, one in the group asked him, "Tell me, why did you select the president to ask this favor of?" The man was shocked, admitting he had no idea it was the president who had helped him. "All I know," he said, "is that on some of your faces was written the answer 'No,' and on some of them was the answer 'yes.' His was a 'Yes' face."[2]

Freedom gives people a "Yes" face. I am confident Jesus had a "Yes" face. I have never seen Him, but I've determined from what I've read about Him that this was true. What a contrast He must have been! He was surrounded by lettered men, religious, robed, *righteous,* law-quoting, professional men whose very demeanor announced "NO!" Pious without, killers within . . . yet none of their poison seeped into His life. On the contrary, He revolutionized the entire direction of religion because He announced "Yes" while all His professional peers were frowning "No." That has intrigued me for years. How could it be? What was it that kept Him from getting caught in their grip? In one word, it was grace. He was so full of truth and grace, He left no inner space for their legalistic poison.

While thinking back on his days with Jesus, John (one of The Twelve) remembers there was something about Him that was like no one else, during which time His disciples "beheld His glory." His uniqueness was that incredible "glory," a glory that represented the very presence of God. In addition, this glorious One was "full of grace and truth." Pause and let that sink in. It was His glory mixed with grace and truth that made Him different. In a world of darkness and demands, rules and regulations, requirements and expectations demanded by the hypocritical religious leaders, Jesus came and ministered in a new and different way—He alone, full of grace and full of truth, introduced a revolutionary, different way of life.

Remembering that uniqueness, John adds, "For of His fullness we have all received, and grace upon grace" (John 1:16).

Don't miss the tie-in with John 1:14. Initially, John wrote, "We beheld His glory," and then he added, in effect, "We received His fullness." John and the other disciples became marked men as a result. Grace heaped upon grace rubbed off, leaving them different. His style became theirs. His tolerance, theirs. His acceptance, love, warmth, and compassion were absorbed by those men, so much so it ultimately transformed their lives. By the end of the first century the ministry of those same men had sent shock waves throughout the Roman world.

John puts the capstone on his introductory remarks by summing up the difference between contrastive styles of ministry: "For the Law was given through Moses; grace and truth were realized through Jesus Christ" (John 1:17).

With the Mosaic Law came requirements, rules, regulations. With those exacting demands came galling expectations, which fueled the Pharisees' fire. By adding to the laws, the Pharisees not only lengthened the list, they intensified everyone's guilt and shame. Obsessed with duty, external conduct, and a constant focusing only on right and wrong (especially in others' lives), they promoted a system so demanding there was no room left for joy. This led to harsh, judgmental, even prejudicial pronouncements as the religious system they promoted degenerated into external performance rather than internal authenticity. Obedience became a matter of grim compulsion instead of a joyous overflow prompted by love.

But when "grace and truth were realized through Jesus Christ," a long-awaited revolution of the heart began to set religious captives free. Fearful bondage motivated by guilt was replaced with a fresh motivation to follow Him in truth simply out of deep devotion and delight. Rather than focusing on the accomplishments of the flesh, He spoke of the heart. Instead of demanding that the sinner fulfill a long list of requirements, He emphasized faith, if only the size of a mustard seed.

The change spelled freedom, as the Lord Himself taught, ". . . you shall know the truth, and the truth shall make you free" (John 8:32). Rigid, barren religion was, at last, replaced by a grace-oriented, relationship—liberating grace. His followers loved it. His enemies hated it . . . and Him. Without a doubt, the earliest grace killers were the Pharisees.

GRACE: LET'S UNDERSTAND THE TERM

What exactly is grace? And is it limited to Jesus' life and ministry? You may be surprised to know that Jesus never used the word itself. He just taught it and, equally important, He lived it. Furthermore, the Bible never gives us a one-statement definition, though grace appears throughout its pages . . . not only the word itself but numerous demonstrations of it. Understanding what grace means requires our going back to an old Hebrew term that meant "to bend, to stoop." By and by, it came to include the idea of "condescending favor."

If you have traveled to London, you have perhaps seen royalty. If so, you may have noticed sophistication, aloofness, distance. On occasion, royalty in England will make the news because someone in the ranks of nobility will stop, kneel down, and touch or bless a commoner. That is grace. There is nothing in the commoner that deserves being noticed or touched or blessed by the royal family. But because of grace in the heart of the queen, there is the desire at that moment to pause, to stoop, to touch, even to bless.

The late pastor and Bible scholar Donald Barnhouse perhaps said it best: "Love that goes upward is worship; love that goes outward is affection; love that stoops is grace."[3]

To show grace is to extend favor or kindness to one who doesn't deserve it and can never earn it. Receiving God's acceptance by grace always stands in sharp contrast to earning it on the basis of works. Every time the thought of grace appears, there is the idea of its being undeserved. In no way is the recipient getting what he or she deserves. Favor is being extended simply out of the goodness of the heart of the giver.

I vividly remember my last spanking. It was on my thirteenth birthday, as a matter of fact. Having just broken into the sophisticated ranks of the teen world, I thought I was something on a stick. My father wasn't nearly as impressed as I was with my great importance and new-found independence. I was lying on my bed. He was outside the window on a muggy October afternoon in Houston, weeding the garden. He said, "Charles, come out and help me weed the garden." I said something like: "No . . . it's my birthday, remember?" My tone was sassy and my deliberate lack of respect was eloquent. I knew better than to disobey my dad; but, after all, I was the ripe old age of

---

thirteen. He set a new 100-meter record that autumn afternoon. He was in the house and all over me like white on rice, spanking me all the way out to the garden. As I recall, I weeded until the moonlight was shining on the pansies.

That same night he took me out to a surprise dinner. He gave me what I deserved earlier. Later he gave me what I did not deserve. The birthday dinner was grace. He condescended in favor upon this rebellious young man. That evening I enjoyed what a proper theologian named Benjamin Warfield called "free sovereign favor to the ill-deserving."[4] I enjoyed grace.

One more thing should be emphasized about grace: It is absolutely and totally free. You will never be asked to pay it back. You couldn't even if you tried. Most of us have trouble with that thought, because we work for everything we get. As the old saying goes, "There ain't no free lunch." But in this case, grace comes to us free and clear, no strings attached. We should not even try to repay it; to do so is insulting.

Imagine coming to a friend's house who has invited you over to enjoy a meal. You finish the delicious meal and then listen to some fine music and visit for a while. Finally, you stand up and get your coat as you prepare to leave. But before you leave you reach into your pocket and say, "Now, how much do I owe you?" What an insult! You don't do that with someone who has graciously given you a meal. Isn't it strange, though, how this world is running over with people who think there's something they must do to pay God back? Somehow they are hoping God will smile on them if they work real hard and earn His acceptance; but that's an acceptance on the basis of works. That's not the way it is with grace.

And now that Christ has come and died and thereby satisfied the Father's demands on sin, all we need to do is claim His grace by accepting the free gift of eternal life. Period. He smiles on us because of His Son's death and resurrection. It's grace, my friend, amazing grace. That is enough to give anybody a "Yes" face!

GRACE: A MANY SPLENDORED THING

We use grace to describe many things in life:

- · A well-coordinated athlete or dancer
- · Good manners and being considerate of others
- · Beautiful, well-chosen words
- · Consideration and care for other people
- · Various expressions of kindness and mercy

Those statements remind me of Christ. What a perfect illustration of grace! Think of several examples with me. He stood alongside a woman caught in adultery. The Law clearly stated, "Stone her." The grace killers who set her up demanded the same. Yet He said to those self-righteous Pharisees, "He who is without sin, let him cast the first stone." What grace! Under the Law they had every legal right to bury her beneath the rocks in their hands . . . and they were ready. There they stood with self-righteous fire in their eyes, but He intervened in grace.

When His friend Lazarus died, Martha met Him on the road and Mary later faced Him in the house. Both blamed Him for not coming earlier: "If You had been here, my brother would not have died!" There is strong accusation in those words. He took them in grace. With the turn of His hand, He could have sent them to eternity; but He refused to answer them back in argument. That is grace.

When He told stories, grace was a favorite theme. He employed a gracious style in handling children. He spoke of the Prodigal Son in grace. As He told stories of people who were caught in helpless situations, grace abounded . . . as with the Good Samaritan. And instead of extolling the religious official who spoke of how proud God must be to have him in His family, Christ smiled with favor on the unnamed sinner who said, "God, be merciful to me, a sinner." Even from the cross He refused to be angry toward His enemies. Remember His prayer? "Father, forgive them . . ." No resentment, no bitterness. Amazing, this grace! Remarkable, the freedom and release it brought. And it came in full force from the only One on earth who had unlimited power, the Son of God.

My plea is that we not limit it to Him. We, too, can learn to be just as gracious as He. And since we can, we must . . . not only in our words and in great acts of compassion and understanding but in small ways as well.

Sir Edward C. Burne-Jones, the prominent nineteenth-century English artist, went to tea at the home of his daughter. As a special treat his little granddaughter was allowed to come to the table; she misbehaved, and her mother made her stand in the corner with her face to the wall. Sir Edward, a well-trained grandfather, did not interfere with his grandchild's training, but next morning he arrived at his daughter's home with paints and palette. He went to the wall where the little girl had been forced to stand, and there he painted pictures—a kitten chasing its tail; lambs in a field; goldfish swimming. He decorated the wall on both sides of that corner with paintings for his granddaughter's delight. If she had to stand in the corner again, at least she would have something to look at.[5]

And so it is with our Lord. When we do the things we should not, He may administer discipline, sometimes quite severely, but He never turns His back . . . He doesn't send His child to hell! Neither do we fall from grace and get slammed behind the iron bars of the Law. He deals with His own in grace . . . beautiful, charming, unmerited favor. It is really amazing!

There will always be some—as those who glared at the woman taken in adultery—who will urge us to be stern, rigid, and cold-hearted. Yes, there are always a few who prefer stoning to forgiving, who will vote for judgment rather than tolerance. But my hope is that we might join the swelling ranks of those who decide that Christlike grace (with all its risks) is so much more effective, we opt for it every time. God honors such an attitude.

SOME PRACTICAL EXPECTATIONS

Most of you are familiar with the story of Rip Van Winkle, the man in the children's fairy tale who went to sleep for twenty years and awoke to a very different world from the one he had known before his two-decade slumber. All the while he was asleep, wonderful changes were taking place around him about which he was totally ignorant. Like Rip Van Winkle, many of us are slumbering under the oppressive opiate of those who would keep us from experiencing the marvelous grace-filled life available to those of us who would be made fully alive to its liberating potential. Wake up! Sleep no longer! *The Grace Awakening* is upon us. And what can you expect upon rising from your uninformed stupor? Let me close this first chapter by mentioning four practical expectations you can anticipate as you get a firm grasp on grace.

First, *you can expect to gain a greater appreciation for God's gifts to you and others.* What gifts? Several come to mind. The free gift of salvation (which we shall consider in depth in the next chapter). The gift of life. The gift of laughter, of music, of beauty, of friendship, of forgiveness. Those who claim the freedom God offers gain an appreciation for the gifts that come with life.

Second, *you can expect to spend less time and energy critical of and concerned about others' choices.* Wouldn't that be a refreshing relief? When you get a grasp on grace — when you begin to operate in a context of freedom — you become increasingly less petty. You will allow others room to make their own decisions in life, even though you may choose otherwise.

Third, *you can expect to become more tolerant and less judgmental.* Externals will not mean as much to you by the time you've finished the book. You'll begin to cultivate a desire for authentic faith rather than endure a religion based on superficial performance. You will find yourself so involved in your own pursuit of grace, you'll no longer lay guilt trips on those with whom you disagree.

Fourth, *you can expect to take a giant step toward maturity.* As your world expands, thanks to an awakening of your understanding of grace, your maturity will enlarge. Before your very eyes, new vistas will open. It will be so transforming, you will never be the same.

That reminds me of something that happened to me when I was about ten or eleven years old. If you can believe it, I had never seen a football game . . . I mean an official high school, college, or professional football game played in a stadium. My world was incredibly small because my knowledge of life outside our little home in East Houston was so limited. We did not own a television set as I grew up, which also restricted my awareness. One weekend, while visiting friends in Austin, the father of that family asked all of us kids if we would like to go to a University of Texas football game. I wasn't sure what he meant, but if it had to do with football, I was interested since I played sandlot ball almost every afternoon.

Was I in for a surprise! As we walked up the ramp at the stadium, my eyes must have been the size of saucers. And when we stepped into the bleachers, I literally could not believe the scene that stretched before me. Warming up down on the field stood Bobby Layne, who later that day went on to lead the Longhorns to a one-sided victory. The immediate outcome was great—winning is always fun—but the ultimate change in my life was enormous. In one brief afternoon my world exploded! I had had a taste of the excitement, the color, the competition of big-time football, and I would never be the same. I would not have returned even if I could. The exposure resulted in my taking a giant step toward growing up.

Trust me, once you have tasted the big-time freedom that grace provides, you will never again be satisfied with sandlot living . . . and I really mean *never*.

2

The Free Gift

FOR THE NEXT FEW MINUTES LET'S THINK about heresy. To begin with, answer this question: What would you consider *the most dangerous heresy on earth?* Stop and think before you answer. The one I have in mind is not so bold and ugly that it would make angels blush. This one is subtle, rather attractive. For a long, long time it's been a favorite of many. Actually, it has been around since the Garden of Eden. Let me give you a few hints:

· It is a philosophy found in numerous self-help books, many poems, and most rags-to-riches biographies.
· It is a recurring theme in political speeches and commencement addresses. It flourishes in academia.
· It feeds our pride, it fuels our self-centered bent, it pleases our flesh.

In a word, it's humanism.

William Ernest Henley, born in Gloucester, England, in 1849 — crippled since childhood—was among the early humanists. He wrote a piece that is commonly quoted by valedictorians at high school graduations all across America.

INVICTUS

Out of the night that covers me,
   Black as the Pit from pole to pole,
I thank whatever gods may be
   For my unconquerable soul.

In the fell clutch of circumstance
   I have not winced nor cried aloud.
Under the bludgeonings of chance
   My head is bloody, but unbowed.

Beyond this place of wrath and tears
   Looms but the Horror of the shade,
And yet the menace of the years
   Finds and shall find me unafraid.

It matters not how strait the gate,
   How charged with punishments the scroll,
I am the master of my fate;
   I am the captain of my soul.[1]

Pretty heady stuff, isn't it? Makes you want to get at it, to dig in deeper and try harder, right? After all, if you and I have souls that are unconquerable, the sky's the limit. If we really are our own master and captain, watch out, world!

WARNING: HERESY ON THE LOOSE

You've heard words like that, haven't you? If you're like me, you've heard them since you were just a child. They sound so right, so inspiring. "Just reach down real deep and pull up hard on your own boot-straps, and you can make it all on your own. You can endure whatever. Nothing is out of reach, so press on . . . climb higher! You can make anything of yourself. You can even attain heaven!" (Or, as in Luther's day, at least buy a quicker way to heaven for someone else.)

What seems so right is, in fact, heresy—the one I consider the most dangerous heresy on earth. What is it? *The emphasis on what we do for God, instead of what God does for us.* Some are so convinced of the opposite, they would argue nose to nose. They are often the ones who claim that their favorite verse of Scripture is "God helps those who help themselves" (which doesn't appear in the Bible). Talk about killing grace! The fact is, God helps the helpless, the undeserving, those who don't measure up, those who fail to achieve His standard. Nevertheless, the heresy continues louder now than ever in history. Most people see themselves as "masters" of their own fate, "captains" of their own souls. It's an age-old philosophy deeply ingrained in the human heart. And why not? It supports humanity's all-time favorite subject: self.

Let me show you one of the first times it reared its head back in the earliest days of the Scriptures. Many, many centuries before Christ, even before there were multiple languages and dialects, tribes and nations, the people of the earth lived in an area called Shinar and spoke the same universal language. By unanimous vote they agreed to build an enormous structure—a tower, whose top would reach into heaven itself. The biblical account puts it this way:

> Now the whole earth used the same language and the same words. And it came about as they journeyed east, that they found a plain in the land of Shinar and settled there. And they said to one another, "Come, let us make bricks and burn them thoroughly." And they used brick for stone, and they used tar for mortar. And they said, "Come, let us build

for ourselves a city, and a tower whose top will reach into heaven, and let us make for ourselves a name. . . ." (Gen. 11:1–4)

The Living Bible calls this construction project "a proud eternal monument to themselves." Doesn't that sound appealing? Doesn't that sound like a project that would attract everyone's attention? I mean, nobody could resist! This was the choice opportunity of a lifetime. I can just imagine the Shinar Chamber of Commerce promoting the new slogan, "Glory to man in the highest," as they recruited workers. Everybody pitched in.

This tower has intrigued me for years, especially its top that would "reach into heaven." I remember as a little boy in Sunday school seeing pictures of the Tower of Babel. Each picture of the tower portrayed its top far up in the clouds. I assumed in my little mind that the top literally went right up to the heavens into the very throne room of God. But there was no way such an immense, towering structure could have been erected. Sizable construction projects were possible, but certainly nothing that tall.

Several years ago I went back and did a little extra digging in the Genesis text and discovered some helpful information. I found that a crucial part of verse 4 reads literally, "whose upper part is with the heavens." The little preposition "with" is a preposition of accompaniment or representation. Somehow the topmost part of the tower was designed and constructed so that it would "represent" the heavens.

In my study I also learned that an extensive excavation took place in the land of Shinar numerous decades ago. Not just one tower, but many of these ziggurats (cone-shaped structures built with a spiral road around them for journeying up and down) were constructed. And among all the cone-shaped dwellings in this particular area, one tower stood above all the rest. Chances are good that the tallest was the tower referred to in Genesis 11. What is most interesting is that they discovered in that particular tower the signs of the zodiac etched into the stonework up toward its peak. Signs and symbols that represented the stellar spaces, which are commonly called "the heavens," appeared at the top. It was like an ancient religious shrine up there . . . almost as if they were saying, "Good old God. He's looking down on our city and is pleased with our efforts. Just think of the fame that will come our way as we make a name for ourselves. God can't help but bless us for all we have achieved." It was humanism's finest hour.

The question is, What *did* God think of this original building constructed for and dedicated to the glory of man? To begin with, He immediately saw through their thinking:

> And the Lord came down to see the city and the tower which the sons of men had built. And the Lord said, "Behold, they are one people, and they all have the same language. And this is what they began to do, and now nothing which they purpose to do will be impossible for them." (Gen. 11:5–6)

Make no mistake about it. Human effort can accomplish incredible feats. No one should underestimate the ability of human beings. God himself acknowledges such when He says, in effect, "This is just the beginning of a lifetime of such thinking. There's no limit. Whatever they purpose to do, they will do." Realizing that, He quickly put a stop to the project.

> Come, let Us go down and there confuse their language, that they may not understand one another's speech. (Gen. 11:7)

(Read the next two verses carefully. Notice that God never destroyed the Tower of Babel; the workers deliberately left it unfinished.)

> So the Lord scattered them abroad from there over the face of the whole earth; and they stopped building the city. Therefore its name was called Babel, because there the Lord confused the language of the whole

earth; and from there the Lord scattered them abroad over the face of the whole earth. (Gen. 11:8–9)

One wonders how many generations traveled through Shinar and stared at that city as time slowly deteriorated those towers. Candidly, the answer is *not enough*. Humanity failed to learn the lesson Babel was designed to teach. Instead, we seem to have restored and enshrined what God attempted to erase. Too many of us continue to believe that doing what we want to do will result in being what we ought to be. "I want to build a tower," one announces. Why? "Because I want to be famous. I want to have a name. I ought to be great. And I need that sense of accomplishment, the feeling of pride that comes from making a name for myself. I'll do it my way!" God steps in and says, in effect, "There's no way." But still the self-made towers continue to be erected. After all, "God helps those who help themselves," the workers confidently proclaim. But their self-centered efforts represent heresy . . . a gospel of works, a grace killer in its worst form.

James Russell Lowell was a contemporary of William Ernest Henley. They were separated by the Atlantic Ocean geographically and by an even larger distance theologically. Lowell, an American, wrote in his work "The Present Crisis" of a philosophy that was much different from the one in Henley's "Invictus":

> Truth forever on the scaffold,
> Wrong forever on the throne—
> Yet that scaffold sways the future, and,
> behind the dim unknown,
> Standeth God within the shadow,
> keeping watch above His Own.[2]

DEFENDING: TRUTH ON THE SCAFFOLD

While most people in the world are busy building towers with highest hopes of making a name and gaining fame, God's truth sets the record straight. On the basis of God's Book, His Holy Word, it is my plea that we simply admit our need and claim God's grace. Instead of striving for a manmade ticket to heaven based on high achievement and hard work (for which we get all the credit), I suggest we openly declare our own spiritual bankruptcy and accept God's free gift of grace. "Why?" you ask. "Why not emphasize how much I do for God instead of what He does for me?" Because that is heresy, plain and simple. How? By exalting my own effort and striving for my own accomplishments, I insult His grace and steal the credit that belongs to Him alone.

Let's leave the land of Shinar with its city of towers and turn to a man who lived shortly thereafter. His name was Abraham . . . a man who, in himself, had quite a name, not to mention an impressive reputation. Yet, when it came to his being righteous before God, he had nothing in himself that earned God's acceptance. All this is clearly stated in Romans 4:1–2:

> What then shall we say that Abraham, our forefather according to the flesh, has found? For if Abraham was justified by works, he has something to boast about; but not before God.

That closing statement is worth pursuing. Anyone who has a lot of accomplishments to his credit has something to boast about before the public. People are impressed with human achievement. They will applaud you. They will give you credit. They will honor your name. They may even build a statue out of bronze or name schools and streets after you. You have something to boast about before others on earth, no question. But according to the statement in Romans 4, there is no room for boasting before God. Not even a great man like Abraham could earn God's favor and blessing.

In the final analysis, it was not the result of Abraham's hard work that caused him to find favor with God, it was the result of God's great grace. Apart from anything Abraham owned or earned, bought or achieved, God declared the man righteous. He "justified" Abraham.

> The day came when, in the accounting of God, ungodly Abraham was suddenly declared righteous. There was nothing in Abraham that caused the action; it began in God and went out to the man in sovereign grace. Upon a sinner the righteousness of God was placed. In the accounting the very righteousness of God was reckoned, credited, imputed. The Lord God Himself, by an act of grace moved by His sovereign love, stooped to the record and blotted out everything that was against Abraham, and then wrote down on the record that He, God, . . . credited . . . this man Abraham to be perfect even at a moment when Abraham was ungodly in himself. That is justification.[3]

How could anyone say a great man like Abraham was "ungodly"? Well, when you look behind the scenes of his life (or any life) you find out. Deep within Abraham was a hollow emptiness. Spiritual death. Behind all of the possessions and human greatness there was a background of idolatry (according to the Old Testament book of Joshua, chapter 24). He had been reared by an idolater. He had married a woman who had come from the same region of idolatry. He was by birth, by nature, and by choice a sinner. However, God in sovereign grace penetrated through all of that. And when he heard Abraham say, "I believe," God, in grace, credited perfect righteousness to the man's account. The Scriptures call this "justification."

May I suggest a definition? Justification is the sovereign act of God whereby He declares righteous the believing sinner—while he is still in a sinning state. Even though Abraham (after believing and being

justified) would continue to sin from time to time, God heard
Abraham when he said, "I believe . . . I believe in You." And God credited divine righteousness to his account. This occurred even though
Abraham was still in a sinning state. But never again would the man
have to worry about where he stood before his God. He was, once
and for all, declared righteous. He received what he did not deserve
and could never earn. Once again I remind you, that's grace. But is
Abraham unique? The answer is in the next two verses:

> Now to the one who works, his wage is not reckoned as a favor
> but as what is due. But to the one who does not work, but believes in
> Him who justifies the ungodly, his faith is reckoned as righteousness.
> (Rom. 4:4–5)

Most people I know look forward to payday. You do too, right? For
a week, or perhaps a two-week period, you give time and effort to
your job. When payday arrives, you receive a hard-earned, well-
deserved paycheck. I have never met anyone who bows and scrapes
before his boss, saying, "Thank you. Oh, thank you for this wonderful, undeserved gift. How can I possibly thank you enough for my
paycheck?" If we did, he would probably faint. Certainly, he would
think, *What is wrong with this guy?* Why? Because your paycheck is not
a gift. You've earned it. You deserve it. Cash it! Spend it! Save it! Invest it! Give it! After all, you had it coming. In the workplace, where
wages are negotiated and agreed upon, there is no such thing as
grace. We earn what we receive; we work for it. The wage "is not
reckoned as a favor but as what is due."

But with God the economy is altogether different. There is no wage
relationship with God. Spiritually speaking, you and I haven't earned
anything but death. Like it or not, we are absolutely bankrupt, without eternal hope, without spiritual merit; we have nothing in
ourselves that gives us favor in the eyes of our holy and righteous

heavenly Father. So there's nothing we can earn that would cause Him to raise His eyebrows and say, "Um, now maybe you deserve eternal life with Me." No way. In fact, the individual whose track record is morally pure has no better chance at earning God's favor than the individual who has made a wreck and waste of his life and is currently living in unrestrained disobedience. Everyone who hopes to be eternally justified must come to God the same way: on the basis of grace; it is a gift. And that gift comes to us absolutely free. Any other view of salvation is heresy, plain and simple.

So much for Abraham. Our next stop-off is Romans 5. It will help me explain how this free gift flows over into our lives and the lives of all who will believe.

> Therefore having been justified by faith, we have peace with God through our Lord Jesus Christ. (Rom. 5:1)

Study those words carefully. We, being justified by faith, not works, get the one thing we've longed for—peace with God. Is it through our merits? Not at all. The verse states we've been justified by faith. It is through Jesus Christ our Lord who paid the absolute, final payment for sin when He died in our place at the Cross. Sin against God required the payment of death. And Jesus Christ, the perfect Substitute, made the ultimate, once-and-for-all payment on our behalf. It cost Him His life. As a result, God gives the free gift of salvation to all who believe in His Son.

Because this is foundational to an understanding of grace, I have set aside this second chapter as a declaration and explanation of God's free gift. Once we grasp its vertical significance as a free gift from God, much of horizontal grace—our extending it to others—automatically falls into place. Once we accept the seldom-announced fact that we have nothing to give God or impress God with that will prompt Him to credit righteousness to our account, we will be ready to take His free gift.

This sounds so simple. And it is—except for one troublesome barrier. It is the problem of sin. No amount of education, no amount of reading, no amount of church-going will take away our problem; we are contaminated with sin.

> Therefore, just as through one man sin entered into the world, and death through sin, and so death spread to all men, because all sinned. (Rom. 5:12)

Learn a little theology. It is vital to understanding and appreciating grace. We were born wrong with God. The same sin that Adam introduced has polluted the entire human race. No one is immune to the sin disease. And no human accomplishment can erase the internal stain that separates us from God. Because Adam sinned, all have sinned. This leads to one conclusion: We all need help. We need forgiveness. We need a Savior.

So . . . how do we get out of this mess? Read the next two verses slowly and carefully.

> So then as through one transgression there resulted condemnation to all men, even so through one act of righteousness there resulted justification of life to all men. For as through the one man's disobedience the many were made sinners, even so through the obedience of the One the many will be made righteous. (Rom. 5:18–19)

Wonderful! Marvelous reassurance!

"You're telling me, Chuck, that by simply believing in Jesus Christ I can have eternal life with God, my sins forgiven, a destiny secure in heaven, all of this and much more without my working for that?" Yes, that is precisely what Scripture teaches. I remind you, it is called *grace*. It's what the Protestant Reformation was all about. Salvation is offered by divine grace, not by human works. Do you want a classic scriptural example? How about a man who was breathing his last? The man I have in mind is one who was dying on a cross, hanging next to Jesus at our Lord's crucifixion. Remember the scene?

He was saying, "Jesus, remember me when You come in Your kingdom!" Those are words of faith, the simple statement of a man who has been an unbeliever all of his life. Suddenly, with his last sigh (unable to do one religious deed . . . couldn't even be baptized!), he turns to Christ, hanging helplessly on a cross, and he believes. He states his faith in Christ, "Lord . . . remember me." And Jesus answers with this promise: "Truly . . . today you shall be with Me in Paradise." The man's faith without works, without conditions, was rewarded with Jesus' grace.

Once again, back to Romans 5, verse 20, where we read, "And the Law came in that the transgression might increase. . . ." Did it ever! Some misread that and assume there's something wrong with the Law if it brings an increase in transgression, an inaccurate assumption. Let me put it this way. When the Law came in, our transgression was identified and our guilt was intensified. By reading for the first time "Thou shalt not . . . thou shalt not . . . thou shalt not . . . ," we realized what sin was. God's demands are right, His commands are pure and clean. They are God's expectation of a holy people. The Law came, declaring what it took to measure up to God's standard of righteousness—but we couldn't do it. The Law kept hammering away, "Don't . . . don't . . . don't!" But mankind still failed. The Law gave us the demands of perfection, but no assistance, no encouragement. The best thing the Law did was identify sin and intensify our guilt. As a matter of fact, it still does so. To this day, the Law makes us painfully aware of our wrong.

I remember back when I was in my early teens, one of my earliest jobs was throwing a paper route. I threw the *Houston Press* for a couple of years during junior high school. It was a good job and kept me out of mischief, but it got tiring.

After a long afternoon of folding about two hundred papers, throwing my route, and returning toward home on my bike, I remember coming to the backyard of a large lawn at the corner across the street from our house. I thought to myself, *I'm tired . . . no need to go all the way down to the end of the street and around this big yard. I'll just cut across and be home in a jiffy.* It was a quick-and-easy shortcut. The first time I did that I entertained a little twinge of guilt as I rode my bike across that nice, plush grass. You need to understand, this was a beautiful yard. To make matters worse, our neighbor was very particular about it. I had watched him manicure it week after week. Still, I figured it wouldn't hurt just this once. Late the next afternoon I came tooling down the same street, thinking, *I wonder if I ought to use that same shortcut?* I did . . . with less guilt than the first time. Theoretically, something told me I shouldn't; but practically, I rationalized around the wrong.

In less than two weeks my bicycle tires had begun to wear a narrow path across the yard. By then, I knew in my heart I really should be going down and around the corner, but I didn't. I just shoved all those guilt feelings down out of sight.

By the end of the third week, a small but very obvious sign appeared near the sidewalk, blocking the path I had made. It read: "Keep Off the Grass—No Bikes." Everything but my name was on the sign! I confess, I ignored it; I went around the sign and rode right on over my path, glancing at the sign as I rode by. Admittedly, I felt worse! Why? The sign identified my sin which, in turn, intensified my guilt. But what is most interesting, the sign didn't stop me from going across the yard. As a matter of fact, it held a strange fascination. It somehow prodded me on into further wrong.

It's like a "Wet Paint" sign. I have touched more wet paint just because somebody put a sign there, haven't you? I've thought that if they just wouldn't identify it as wet, I wouldn't touch it. But when it says "Do Not Touch," I have to touch it. Something inside me forces my fingers onto wet paint. It's called sinful depravity. Signs don't help a bit.

One of my close friends told me about a trip he took to San Francisco, during which time he saw a most unusual sign. It read "*Try* to Keep Off the Grass." My point? When you see a sign, the sign has no power whatsoever to make you obey. It certainly identifies the sin in us, and it intensifies the guilt when we ignore it, but it offers no power to restrain us.

And so it is with the Law. The Law came and in bold letters etched by the finger of God it read, "This is holiness! Honor My Name by keeping My Law!" But the fact is, nobody could keep it, which explains the statement in Romans 5:20 that says "sin increased." The Law arouses sin but never arrests it. So how can the tailspin stop? What hope is there? The answer is found in the same verse: ". . . but where sin increased, grace abounded all the more." Isn't that great! Grace overshadowed sin, it outranked it and thereby brought hope.

Let me amplify the scriptural statement even more. Where sin overflowed, grace flooded in. Where sin measurably increased, grace immeasurably increased. Where sin was finite, grace was infinite. Where sin was colossal, grace was super-colossal. Where sin abounds, grace superabounds. The sin identified by the Law in no way stopped the flow of the grace of God. Jesus' death on the cross was the sufficient payment for sin, putting grace into action that was not simply adequate but *abundant*.

Augustus Toplady wrote it this way:

> The terrors of Law and of God
> with me can have nothing to do;
> My Savior's obedience in blood
> hide all my transgressions from view.[4]

EXPLAINING: GRACE FOR THE SINFUL

For the next few moments, graze slowly over this paragraph of truth recorded by Paul in the letter to the Ephesians. Take your time. Don't hurry.

> And you were dead in your trespasses and sins, in which you formerly walked according to the course of this world, according to the prince of the power of the air, of the spirit that is now working in the sons of disobedience. Among them we too all formerly lived in the lusts of our flesh, indulging the desires of the flesh and of the mind, and were by nature children of wrath, even as the rest. But God, being rich in mercy, because of His great love with which He loved us, even when we were dead in our transgressions, made us alive together with Christ (by grace you have been saved), and raised us up with Him, and seated us with Him in the heavenly places, in Christ Jesus, in order that in the ages to come He might show the surpassing riches of His grace in kindness toward us in Christ Jesus. For by grace you have been saved through faith; and that not of yourselves, it is the gift of God; not as a result of works, that no one should boast. (Eph. 2:1–9)

Pay close attention to ten single-syllable words, "by grace . . . through faith . . . it is the gift of God."

One of my greatest anticipations is some glorious day being in a place where there will be no boasting, no namedropping, no selfishness. Guess where it will be? Heaven. There will be no spiritual-sounding testimonies that call attention to somebody's supercolossal achievements. None of that! Everybody will have written across his or her life the word "Grace."

"How did you get up here?"

"Grace!"

"What made it possible?"

"Grace."

"What's your name?"

"Grace."

There will be more graces up there than any other name. Every-where, Grace, Grace, *Grace!*

When I was in seminary, one fellow who struggled with academics—I mean really struggled—was grateful just to get through school. I can still remember going to the mail room where everybody got their tests back. Invariably, there would be a handful of guys in the corner, asking, "What did you get on Number 4?"

"Well, I got so and so."

"Really? I wrote the same thing and he counted me wrong on 4."

But one dear guy never did any of that nonsensical comparison stuff. He would quietly open his box, pull out his test booklet, and before he ever looked at his grade, he wrote in big bold letters across the front of the test "G-R-A-C-E." If he did poorly: "Grace." If he did well: "Grace!" If he passed, that was sufficient: "Grace!" I learned a valuable lesson from my friend. That's all any of us have to claim.

> Nothing in my hands I bring,
> Simply to Thy Cross I cling.[5]

And when grace is our only claim, who gets the glory? The One who went to the Cross.

Now for the big question: Can you understand why the grace kill-ers would attack this great truth? Of course! It cuts the heart out of do-it-yourself-and-get-the-glory religion. As they did in Luther's day, they appear in every generation with convincing arguments, saying, "You know, you have to try real hard." Or, "You need to give up such and such." Or, "You need to start doing so and so." Or, "You must prove the sincerity of your faith." Or, "Before God can do this in your life, you must earn it by doing such and such." Forget it! God, in grace, offers you the free gift of forgiveness. All you can do is take it. Once you take it, you will be given the power to give up, to put on, to take off, to quit, to start—whatever. But don't confuse the issue of salvation. It is yours strictly on the basis of God's free gift. In spite of all the stuff you may hear to the contrary, the emphasis is not on what we do for God; instead, it is on what God has done for us.

Some time ago, while digging deeply into this subject of God's amazing grace, I happened upon a piece by Dorothea Day, in which she answers Henley's "Invictus" with words that cut to the heart of his humanistic philosophy. She calls it "My Captain."

MY CAPTAIN

> Out of the light that dazzles me,
>   Bright as the sun from pole to pole,
> I thank the God I know to be
>   For Christ the conqueror of my soul.
>
> Since His the sway of circumstance,
>   I would not wince nor cry aloud.
> Under that rule which men call chance
>   My head with joy is humbly bowed.
>
> Beyond this place of sin and tears
>   That life with Him! And His the aid,
> Despite the menace of the years,
>   Keeps, and shall keep me, unafraid.
>
> I have no fear, though strait the gate,
>   He cleared from punishment the scroll.
> Christ is the Master of my fate,
>   Christ is the Captain of my soul.[6]

Can you honestly say that Christ is the Master of your fate, the Captain of your soul? Trust me, His name is the only name that will take you from earth to heaven when you die. And it won't be your achievements or your fame or your fortune that will get you there. You will be granted entrance because you accepted the free gift of eternal life—nothing more, nothing less, nothing else.

There is one and only one password for entering heaven: Grace.

3

Isn't Grace Risky?

BY NOW SOME OF YOU MAY BE THINKING,
The reason you are emphasizing grace so much is because you're from California.

That kind of comment always makes me smile inside. Being from California means you have to tolerate the looks and comments from those who think all Californians are like the stereotype image—sun-tanned surfers who sport a casual, carefree look, think shallow thoughts, and operate on a rather relaxed mentality. Which, when interpreted, means Californians live near the edge of extremes and conduct themselves in a questionable lifestyle. As my sister Luci and I were discussing this recently, she laughed and added, "Just living in California means we live on the fault line in more ways than one." Too bad, but I suppose it comes with the territory (pun intended).

Not too long ago I received a strongly critical letter from one of my radio listeners. Among several things the lady unloaded on me, she had a bone to pick about my family's picture that appears on the back of the jacket of one of my books. We were all there—kids, grandkids, our dog Sah Sha—the whole tribe. She said that she didn't like it, that we all looked "so *Californian*." And then she added, "Even your *dog* looks Californian!" What are we supposed to look like, *Latvian*? I mean, can Sah Sha help it if her thick coat of fur is snow white? It's pretty difficult to find a Samoyed puppy with black or red fur these days.

At the risk of sounding a lot like former President Richard Nixon, *I want to make something perfectly clear.* I believed in the grace of God before I ever stepped foot into the state of California. I was, in fact, reared in a family that believed in grace. I studied at a seminary that upheld grace. I have loved and taught the importance of living by grace in every place I have lived—Texas, the Orient, New England, and now on the West Coast. It is a message that is welcomed because it fits any geographical location: the Midwest, the Deep South, the great Northwest, the sun-drenched Southwest, the islands, the Third World, *anywhere*. Everywhere I have even visited I have observed one common denominator: Most people yearn to be free. They hate living under bondage. They want liberty, yet many have no idea where or how to find it. There is nothing like an accurate understanding of God's matchless grace to help make that happen. One of my joys in life is doing just that.

But isn't it risky? Won't some people take it to an extreme? In California—or anywhere—doesn't a minister run the risk that some in his flock may take unfair liberties if he presents the message of grace with the same gusto that I'm emphasizing in this book? Couldn't an awakening of grace lead to an abusing of grace?

Before I answer those questions, I invite you to travel with me across the Atlantic Ocean. Of all the countries in the world, England has to be considered among the most understated. In my travels I have observed that very little is flaunted in the British Isles. And when it comes to Christianity, *evangelical* Christianity that is, perhaps it is as conservative there as it is anywhere around the globe. And to go one step further, few evangelical British ministers would qualify as being more conservative than the late Martyn Lloyd-Jones, pastor of Westminster Chapel for decades. As a staunch Calvinist of the Puritan school of thought Dr. Lloyd-Jones was a biblicist of the first order. His expositions represent a conservative position to the ultimate degree. I mention all that so you will understand that this man I am about to quote was one who would be the farthest removed from the popular (albeit erroneous) stereotype of a Californian mentality.

Twelve years before his retirement and until the day he completed his ministry, the man taught the book of Romans from the historic Westminster Chapel pulpit. His expositions would be considered tedious by some, but no one could ever say they were casual or loose. And yet, in no uncertain terms Martyn Lloyd-Jones (of all people!) states that preaching grace is not only risky, but the fact that some take it to an unwise extreme is proof that a minister is indeed preaching the true grace of God. Hold on to your surfboards as you read his remarks concerning Paul's question at the beginning of Romans 6: " . . . Are we to continue in sin that grace may increase?"

> . . . If it is true that where sin abounded grace has much more abounded, well then, 'shall we continue in sin, that grace may abound yet further?'
>
> First of all let me make a comment, to me a very important and vital comment. The true preaching of the gospel of salvation by grace alone always leads to the possibility of this charge being brought against it. There is no better test as to whether a man is really preaching the New Testament gospel of salvation than this, that some people might misunderstand it and misinterpret it to mean that it really amounts to this, that because you are saved by grace alone it does not matter at all what you do; you can go on sinning as much as you like because it will redound all the more to the glory of grace. That is a very good test of gospel preaching. If my preaching and presentation of the gospel of

salvation does not expose it to that misunderstanding, then it is not the gospel. Let me show you what I mean.

If a man preaches justification by works, no one would ever raise this question. If a man's preaching is, 'If you want to be Christians, and if you want to go to heaven, you must stop committing sins, you must take up good works, and if you do so regularly and constantly, and do not fail to keep on at it, you will make yourselves Christians, you will reconcile yourselves to God, and you will go to heaven'. Obviously a man who preaches in that strain would never be liable to this misunderstanding. Nobody would say to such a man, 'Shall we continue in sin, that grace may abound?', because the man's whole emphasis is just this, that if you go on sinning you are certain to be damned, and only if you stop sinning can you save yourselves. So that misunderstanding could never arise. . . .

. . . Nobody has ever brought this charge against the Church of Rome, but it was brought frequently against Martin Luther; indeed that was precisely what the Church of Rome said about the preaching of Martin Luther. They said, 'This man who was a priest has changed the doctrine in order to justify his own marriage and his own lust', and so on. 'This man', they said, 'is an antinomian; and that is heresy.' That is the very charge they brought against him. It was also brought against George Whitefield two hundred years ago. It is the charge that formal dead Christianity—if there is such a thing—has always brought against this startling, staggering message, that God 'justifies the ungodly'. . . .

That is my comment; and it is a very important comment for preachers. I would say to all preachers: If your preaching of salvation has not been misunderstood in that way, then you had better examine your sermons again, and you had better make sure that you really are preaching the salvation that is offered in the New Testament to the ungodly, to the sinner, to those who are dead in trespasses and sins, to those who are enemies of God. There is this kind of dangerous element about the true presentation of the doctrine of salvation. [1]

To Martyn Lloyd-Jones grace was not only risky, it was downright dangerous. He was clearly convinced it could be easily misunderstood. Meaning what? Well, some people will take advantage of it. They will misrepresent it. They will go to such an extreme that they will promote the erroneous idea that you can go on sinning as much as you like. To all fellow ministers I must add my voice to that of Martyn Lloyd-Jones: If you claim to be a messenger of grace, if you think you are really preaching grace, yet no one is taking advantage of it, maybe you haven't preached it hard enough or strong enough. I can assure you of this: Grace-killing ministers will never have that charge brought against them. They make sure of that!

THE REALITY OF THE RISK

All this brings me to the reality of the risk. I ask again, is grace risky? You bet your life it is. There is great risk in the book I am writing. I am well aware that this issue of grace is indeed controversial, especially when I am calling for a new awakening to the freedom Christians have in Christ. A few will take what I write and go crazy with it. Others will misread what I write, and misquote me, misunderstand me, and charge me with caring little about the holiness of God because (they will say) I give people the freedom to sin. On the other hand, some in the camp of carnality will thank me for relieving their guilt, because in their misunderstanding they now think it is okay for them to continue in their loose and carefree lifestyle. I wish these things would not occur, but that is the chance I'm willing to take by holding nothing back in order that the full message of grace be set forth. Yes, grace that is presented in all its charm and beauty is risky. It brings grace abusers as well as grace killers out from under the rocks!

Statement of Clarification

Let's return to a verse of Scripture we looked at in the previous chapter, Romans 5:1: "Therefore having been justified by faith, we have peace with God through our Lord Jesus Christ."

In order for anyone to stand securely and be at peace before a holy and just God, that person must be righteous. Hence, our need for justification. Remember the definition of justification? It is the sovereign act of God whereby He declares righteous the believing sinner while still in his sinning state. It doesn't mean that the believing sinner stops sinning. It doesn't even mean that the believing sinner is *made* righteous in the sense of suddenly becoming perpetually perfect. The sinner is *declared* righteous. God sovereignly bestows the gift of eternal life on the sinner at the moment he believes and thereby declares him righteous while the sinner still lives a life marked by periodic sinfulness. He hasn't joined a church. He hasn't started paying tithes. He hasn't given up all to follow Christ. He hasn't been baptized. He hasn't promised to live a sacrificial, spotlessly pure life. He has simply taken the gift of eternal life. He has changed his mind toward Christ (repentance) and accepted the free gift of God apart from works. Period. Transaction completed. By grace, through faith alone, God declares the sinner righteous (justification), and from that moment on the justified sinner begins a process of growth toward maturity (sanctification). Day by day, bit by bit, he learns what it means to live a life that honors Christ. But immediately? No way.

Please understand, to be justified does not mean "just as if I'd never sinned." I hear that often and it always troubles me. In fact, it weakens the full impact of justification. Justification really means this: Even though I still sin periodically and have found myself unable to stop sinning on a permanent basis, God declared me righteous when I believed. And because I will continue to sin from time to time, I find all the more reason to be grateful for grace. As a sinner I deserve vengeance. As a sinner I'm afraid of justice. And so, as a sinner, my only hope for survival is grace. In its purest form, it makes no earthly sense!

Let's imagine you have a six-year-old son whom you love dearly. Tragically, one day you discover that your son was horribly murdered. After a lengthy search the investigators of the crime find the killer. You have a choice. If you used every means in your power to kill the murderer for his crime, that would be *vengeance*. If, however, you're content to sit back and let the legal authorities take over and execute on him what is proper—a fair trial, a plea of guilty, capital punishment—that is *justice*. But if you should plead for the pardon of the murderer, forgive him completely, invite him into your home, and adopt him as your own son, that is *grace*.

Now do you see why grace is so hard to grasp and to accept? Very few people (if any) who are reading this page right now would happily and readily do that. But God does it *every day*. He takes the guilty, believing sinner who says, "I am lost, unworthy, guilty as charged, and undeserving of forgiveness," and extends the gift of eternal life because Christ's death on the cross satisfied His demands against sin, namely, death. And God sees the guilty sinner (who comes by faith alone) as righteous as His own Son. In fact, He even invites us to come home with Him as He adopts us into His forever family. Instead of treating us with vengeance or executing justice, God extends grace.

Allow me to repeat my earlier statement: To believe grace to that extreme and to live grace at that extreme means some will take advantage of it. Count on it. Some of you have had wonderful experiences in your homes with your children as they were growing up. You've dealt with them graciously and maturely. You have given them room to learn, to grow, even room to fail, as you've loved them, taught them Scripture, and encouraged them. You have raised the kids by grace, as, hopefully, we have in the Swindoll home. And yet some of you are going through desperate times right now, though you did many things right. You gave your child proper freedom and let out the reins when it seemed right to do so. And yet, when your youngster reached an age of independence, he or she turned on you and, surprisingly, still remains in that state of mind. The enormous battle you have is the guilt that goes with it. My prayer is that God might help every one of you going through such a time. I have observed that most parents have no reason whatsoever to live with such guilt. You may struggle with some shame and embarrassment as well, though it is undeserved and inappropriate. In reality, your grown child has made a decision and is living in the wake of the consequences, but unfortunately it impacts you. It grieves you. You fear you may have been too gracious.

It's that same fear that causes many a minister to stay away from grace lest the congregation misinterpret his message and think of it as "cheap grace," a term we learned from Dietrich Bonhoeffer. Frankly, I'm glad he introduced those words to us. But we need to understand exactly what he meant by them. "Cheap grace" justifies the sin rather than the sinner. True grace, on the other hand, justifies the sinner, not the sin. Let me encourage you not to be afraid of true grace because some have misrepresented it as cheap grace. In spite of the very real risks, grace is worth it all.

Alternatives to Grace

If I choose not to risk, if I go the "safe" route and determine not to promote either salvation by grace or a lifestyle of grace, what are the alternatives? Four come to my mind, all of which are popular these days.

1. *I can emphasize works over grace.* I can tell you that as a sinner you need to have a stronger commitment to Christ, demonstrated by the

work you do in His behalf, before you can say that you truly believe. My problem in doing so is this: A sinner cannot commit to anything. He or she is spiritually dead, remember? There is no capacity for commitment in an unregenerate heart. Becoming an obedient, submissive disciple of Christ follows believing in Christ. Works *follow* faith. Behavior *follows* belief. Fruit comes *after* the tree is well-rooted. Martin Luther's words come to mind:

> No one can be good and do good unless God's grace first makes him good; and no one becomes good by works, but good works are done only by him who is good. Just so the fruits do not make the tree, but the tree bears the fruit. . . . Therefore all works, no matter how good they are and how pretty they look, are in vain if they do not flow from grace . . . [2]

2. *I can opt for giving you a list of do's and don'ts.* The list comes from my personal and/or traditional preferences. It becomes my responsibility to tell you what to do or not to do and why. I then set up the conditions by which you begin to earn God's acceptance through me. You do what I tell you to do . . . you don't do what I tell you not to do, and you're "in." You fail to keep the list, you're "out." This legalistic style of strong-arm teaching is one of the most prevalent methods employed in evangelical circles. Grace is strangled in such a context. To make matters worse, those in authority are so intimidating, their authority is unquestioned. Rare are those with sufficient strength to confront the list-makers. I have much more to say about this alternative later in the book.

3. *I leave no room for any gray areas.* Everything is either black or white, right or wrong. And as a result, the leader maintains strict control over the followers. Fellowship is based on whether there is full agreement. Herein lies the tragedy. This self-righteous, rigid standard becomes more important than relationships with individuals. We first check out where people stand on the issues, and then we determine

whether we will spend much time with them. The bottom line is this: We want to be *right* (as we see it, of course) more than we want to love our neighbor as ourselves. At that point our personal preferences eclipse any evidence of love. I am of the firm conviction that where grace exists, so must various areas of gray.

4. *I cultivate a judgmental attitude toward those who may not agree or co-operate with my plan.* Grace killers are notorious for a judgmental attitude. It is perhaps the single most un-Christlike characteristic in evangelical circles today.

A quick glance back through the time tunnel will prove beneficial. Jesus found Himself standing before the brain trust of legalism, the Pharisees. Listening to Him were also many who believed in Him. He had been presenting His message to the crowd; it was a message of hope, of forgiveness, of freedom.

> As He spoke these things, many came to believe in Him. Jesus there-fore was saying to those Jews who had believed Him, "If you abide in My word, then you are truly disciples of Mine; and you shall know the truth, and the truth shall make you free." (John 8:30–32)

He spoke of the liberating power of the truth. Even though the official grace killers rejected His message, He assured them it could make them free. All who embrace grace become "free indeed."

Free from what? Free from oneself. Free from guilt and shame. Free from the damnable impulses I couldn't stop when I was in bond-age to sin. Free from the tyranny of others' opinions, expectations, demands. And free to what? Free to obey. Free to love. Free to for-give others as well as myself. Free to allow others to be who they are—different from me! Free to live beyond the limitations of human effort. Free to serve and glorify Christ. In no uncertain terms, Jesus Christ assured His own that His truth was able to liberate them from every needless restriction: "If therefore the Son shall make you free, you shall be free indeed" (John 8:36). I love that. The possibilities are unlimited. Return with me to Romans 6, where we started this chapter:

> Knowing this, that our old self was crucified with Him, that our body of sin might be done away with, that we should no longer be slaves to sin; for he who has died is freed from sin. Now if we have died with Christ, we believe that we shall also live with Him, knowing that Christ, having been raised from the dead, is never to die again; death no longer is master over Him. For the death that He died, He died to sin, once for all; but the life that He lives, He lives to God. Even so consider yourselves to be dead to sin, but alive to God in Christ Jesus.

> Therefore do not let sin reign in your mortal body that you should obey its lusts, and do not go on presenting the members of your body to sin as instruments of unrighteousness; but present yourselves to God as those alive from the dead, and your members as instruments of righteousness to God. For sin shall not be master over you, for you are not under law, but under grace.

> What then? Shall we sin because we are not under law but under grace? May it never be! (Rom. 6:6–15)

When we were without Christ, we were like ancient slaves on the slave block, consumed by the hopelessness of our depravity, lost, chained to sin, joyless, empty, spiritually bankrupt. All we could do was say to God, "Have mercy. Guilty as charged. I am enslaved to my passions. I am not free to obey my Savior." But once Christ took charge, He overthrew our old master and freed us to obey. Before conversion, all of us were in bondage to sin. After conversion, we were set free . . . free to obey. That is grace.

THE INESCAPABLE TENSION

All the above brings us back to that same issue of risk. Because of grace we have been freed from sin, from its slavery, its bondage in our attitude, in our urges, and in our actions. But having been freed and now living by grace, we can actually go too far, set aside all self-control, and take our liberty to such an extreme that we again serve sin. But that isn't liberty at all, that's license. And knowing of that possibility, many opt for legalism lest they be tempted to live irresponsibly. Bad choice. How much better to have such an awesome respect for the Lord we voluntarily hold back as we apply self-control.

I remember when I first earned my license to drive. I was about sixteen, as I recall. I'd been driving off and on for three years (scary thought, isn't it?). My father had been with me most of the time during my learning experiences, calmly sitting alongside me in the front seat, giving me tips, helping me know what to do. My mother usually wasn't in on those excursions because she spent more of her time biting her nails (and screaming) than she did advising. My father was a little more easygoing. Loud noises and screeching brakes didn't bother him nearly as much. My grandfather was the best of all. When I would drive his car, I would hit things . . . *Boom!* He'd say stuff like, "Just keep on going, Bud. I can buy more fenders, but I can't buy more grandsons. You're learning." What a great old gentleman. After three years of all that nonsense, I finally earned my license.

I'll never forget the day I came in, flashed my newly acquired permit, and said, "Dad, look!" He goes, "Whoa! Look at this. You got your license. Good for you!" Holding the keys to his car, he tossed them in my direction and smiled, "Tell you what, son . . . you can have the car for two hours, all on your own." Only four words, but how wonderful: "All on your own."

I thanked him, danced out to the garage, opened the car door, and shoved the key into the ignition. My pulse rate must have shot up to 180 as I backed out of the driveway and roared off. While cruising along "all on my own," I began to think wild stuff—like, *This car can probably do 100 miles an hour. I could go to Galveston and back twice in two hours if I averaged 100 miles an hour. I can fly down the Gulf Freeway and even run a few lights. After all, nobody's here to say "Don't!"* We're talking dangerous, crazy thoughts! But you know what? I didn't do any of them. I don't believe I drove above the speed limit. In fact, I distinctly remember turning into the driveway early . . . didn't even stay away the full two hours. Amazing, huh? I had my dad's car all to myself with a full gas tank in a context of total privacy and freedom, but I didn't go crazy. Why? My relationship with my dad and my granddad was so strong that I couldn't, even though I had a license and nobody was in the car to restrain me. Over a period of time there had developed a sense of trust, a deep love relationship that held me in restraint.

After tossing me the keys, my dad didn't rush out and tape a sign on the dashboard of the car, "Don't you dare drive beyond the speed limit" or "Cops are all around the city, and they'll catch you, boy, so don't even think about taking a risk." He simply smiled and said, "Here are the keys, son, enjoy it." What a demonstration of grace. And did I ever enjoy it! Looking back, now that I'm a father who has relived the same scene on four different occasions with my own children, I realize what a risk my father had taken.

There are many joys of being liberated that some of you have never known because you haven't given yourself permission to operate under grace. I don't mean this to sound insulting, but I am convinced that some Christians would be terrified if they were completely on their own. Because they have been told what to do so many years, freedom is frightening. There are people who want to be told what to do and when . . . how to believe and why. And the result is tragic—perpetual adolescence. Without being trusted, without being freed, maturity never happens. You never learn to think on your own.

Someone on our staff at our Insight for Living office informed me several months ago that a woman had called the ministry office to find out what my "official position" was on a certain gray area. When she was told that it's not my policy to make "official" public statements on such issues, she was bewildered . . . actually, a little irritated. She asked, "How are we to know what to decide on this issue if Chuck doesn't tell us?" Some may find her question amusing. Frankly, I find it a little frightening. I thought, "Have we created that kind of Christian, where the minister must make statements in areas that are a matter of personal preference?" There is a fine line between responsible leadership and dogmatic control. All risks notwithstanding, people need to be informed, and then released to come to their own convictions. Why must a minister constantly issue public edicts and decrees? Seems awfully popelike to me. Have we wandered that far from grace?

You will never grow up as long as you must get your lists and form most of your opinions from me or some Christian leader. It is not my calling as a minister of the gospel to exploit a group of loyal listeners or dictate to everyone's conscience. It is my responsibility to teach the truths of Scripture as accurately as I am able and to model as best I can a lifestyle that pleases God (regardless of whether it pleases others) and allow others the freedom to respond as God leads them. That has worked well for me, and I plan to continue doing so. Seems to me that was the style Joshua modeled when he told the Hebrews they needed to decide where they stood when he said, "But as for me and my house, we will serve the Lord." Pretty risky, but it worked.

It still does.

I like the way some saint of old once put it: "Love God with all your heart . . . then do as you please." The healthy restraint is in the first phrase, the freedom is in the second. That's how to live a grace-oriented, liberated life. Some of the joyous benefits of such a life? I can think of several. You are:

· No longer helplessly bound by impulse and desires.
· Free to make your own choices.
· Able to think independently without the tyranny of comparison or the need to control.
· Able to grow more rapidly toward greater maturity and flexibility, becoming the person you were meant to be.

And while I mention growing up, perhaps this is a good time to say to all parents, I hope you aren't continuing to look for ways to control your adult children. Release them. Toss 'em the keys. Let them be. Most therapists I know spend too many hours of their day dealing with people's struggles with their parents' messages. It has them all bound up. Let's give our grown kids a lot of room, parents, and let's give them a break. In fact, I would suggest writing each one of them a letter stating their independence, saying, "Now that you're on your own, I want you to know that my trust is in you. My confidence is in God to guide you. And I respect you. You're an adult."

One of the best ways to handle the tension of letting go is to maintain a balance, realizing that some will take their liberty to an unwise extreme. We all admit that grace is risky. Let's also admit that some will live irresponsibly. You can detect such irresponsibility rather quickly.

1. There is a lack of love for others . . . little care about anybody else.
2. There is rationalization of out-and-out sin.
3. There is an unwillingness to be accountable.

4. There is a resistance to anyone's getting close enough to give them wise advice.

5. There is a disregard for one who is a new convert and there fore weak in the faith.

Scripture calls such a person a "weaker brother." (We need to be careful here; some people are "professional weaker brothers." Those folks are not weaker brothers at all, they are hardcore legalists who play the role of weaker brothers.)

A balance is necessary. Because grace is risky, self-imposed restrictions are important. It is necessary that we monitor those two things, isn't it? You can't be afraid of the heights if you're going to walk on the tightrope of grace. But at the same time you have to watch out for the strong gusts of wind that will occasionally blow like mad.

PRACTICAL SUGGESTIONS FOR
GUARDING AGAINST EXTREMES

Three suggestions come to mind as I think about living with risks and putting all this into balanced living.

First, *guard against extremes if you want to enjoy the freedom grace provides.* Try your best to keep balanced, then enjoy it. No reason to feel guilty. No reason to be afraid. Try this first: Simply give yourself permission to be free. Don't go crazy . . . but neither should you spend time looking over your shoulder, worrying about those who "spy out your liberty," and wondering what they will think and say. I will write more about that in chapter 5.

Second, *treat grace as an undeserved privilege rather than an exclusive right.* This will also help you keep a balance. Live gratefully, not arrogantly. Have fun, but don't flaunt. It is all in one's attitude, isn't it? It has nothing to do with financial status or where you live or what clothes you prefer or which car you drive. It has everything to do with attitude.

Third, *remember that while grace came to you freely, it cost the Savior His life.* It may seem free, but it was terribly expensive when He purchased it for us. And who wouldn't want to be free, since we have been purchased from the horrors of bondage?

The Killing Fields is quite a movie. It is the true story of a *New York Times* reporter who was working in Cambodia during a time of awful bloodshed. His closest assistant was a Cambodian who was later captured by the Marxist regime, the Khmer Rouge, a totalitarian group known for its torturous cruelty. What the Cambodian assistant endured while trying to find freedom is beyond belief. If you reacted as I did when you watched the film, there were times you couldn't help but gasp.

The plot of the story revolves around the assistant's escape from the bondage of that terrible regime. It isn't a movie for the squeamish. There are things he sees and endures that defy the imagination. He is brutally beaten, imprisoned, and mistreated. Starving, he survived by sucking the blood from a beast in the field. He lives in the worst possible conditions. Finally, he plans his escape. He runs from one tragic scene to another. On one occasion, while fleeing, he sinks into a bog only to discover it is a watery hellhole full of rotting flesh and human bones and skulls that foam to the top as he scrambles to climb out. It's enough to make you sick! Fleeing from one horror to another, he is surprised as he stumbles into a clearing.

Having endured the rigors of the jungle while being chased by his captors, he finally steps out into a clearing and looks down. To his utter amazement, he sees the Cambodian border. Down below him is a small refugee camp. His eyes catch sight of a hospital and a flag. And on that flag, a cross. There, at long last, hope is awakened! At that point the music builds to a climax. Light returns to his weary face, which says in a dozen different ways, "I'm free. I'm free!" The joys and the delights of his long-awaited freedom are his once again. Ultimately, he makes it to America and enjoys a tearful reunion with his friend—all because he is free. Free at last!

Grace is God's universal good news of salvation. The tragedy is that some continue to live lives in a deathlike bog because they have been so turned off by a message that is full of restrictions, demands, negativism, and legalism. You may have been one of those held in bondage, victimized by a system that has stolen your joy and snuffed out your hope. If so, I have some wonderful news. You've gotten very close to the border. There's a flag flying. And on that flag is a cross. And if you come into this camp of grace beneath the cross, you'll never have to be in that awful bog again.

You will be free . . . *free at last.*

4

Undeserving, Yet Unconditionally Loved

TO MANY PEOPLE, GRACE IS NOTHING
more than something to be said with heads bowed
before dinner. But that idea, simple and beautiful as
it may be, is light-years removed from the depth of
meaning presented in Scripture regarding grace. This biblical concept
of grace is profound, and its tentacles are both far-reaching and life-
changing. Were we to study it for a full decade we would not come
close to plumbing its depths.

I never knew Lewis Sperry Chafer, the founder of the seminary I
attended. He had died a few years before I began my theological studies in 1959. Some of my mentors and professors, however, knew him
well. Without exception they still remember him as a man of great
grace. He was an articulate defender of the doctrine and an authentic model of its application throughout his adult life, especially during
his latter years. I sincerely regret never having known Dr. Chafer.

I love the story one of my mentors tells of the time when this dear
man of God had concluded his final lecture on grace. It was a hot afternoon in Dallas, Texas, that spring day in 1952. The aging professor (who
taught that particular semester from a wheelchair) mopped the perspi-
ration from his brow. No one in the class moved as the session ended.

It was as though the young theologues were basking in what they had heard, awestruck with their professor's insights and enthusiasm about God's matchless grace. The gray-haired gentleman rolled his chair to the door, and as he flipped the light switch off, the class spontaneously broke into thunderous applause. As the beloved theologian wiped away his tears, head bowed, he lifted one hand, gesturing them to stop. He had one closing remark as he looked across the room with a gentle smile. Amidst the deafening silence, he spoke softly, "Gentleman, for over half my life I have been studying this truth . . . and I am just beginning to discover what the grace of God is all about." Within a matter of three short months, the stately champion of grace was ushered into his Lord's presence at the age of eighty-one.

I seldom sing John Newton's eighteenth-century hymn "Amazing Grace" without remembering those final words of that giant of grace:

> Amazing grace! how sweet the sound
> That saved a wretch like me!
> I once was lost, but now am found,
> Was blind, but now I see.[1]

Nobody—not Lewis Sperry Chafer, not even John Newton—ever appreciated grace more than Paul, the first-century apostle. From a past of Pharisaic pride, cruel brutality, and religious unbelief, he was changed from a zealous persecutor of the church to a humble servant of Christ. And what was the reason? The grace of God. Hear his own testimony:

> For I am the least of the apostles, who am not fit to be called an apostle, because I persecuted the church of God. But by the grace of God I am what I am, and His grace toward me did not prove vain; but I labored even more than all of them, yet not I, but the grace of God with me. Whether then it was I or they, so we preach and so you believed. (1 Cor. 15:9–11)

Whatever he became, according to his own statement, Paul owed it all to "the grace of God." When I ponder the words from that grand apostle, I come up with what we might call his credo. We can reduce it to three single-syllable statements, the first consisting of only eight words; the second, ten words; and the third, twelve. Occasionally, it helps to take a profound, multifaceted theological truth and define it in simple, nontechnical terms.

First statement: *God does what He does by His grace.* Paul's first claim for being allowed to live, to say nothing of being used as a spokesman and leader, was "by the grace of God." Paul deserved the severest kind of judgment, but God gave the man His grace instead. Humanly speaking, Paul should have been made to endure incredible suffering for all the pain and heartache he had caused others. But he didn't, because God exhibited His grace.

That leads us to the second statement: *I am what I am by the grace of God.* It is as if he were admitting, "If there is any goodness now found in me, I deserve none of the glory; grace gets the credit."

In our day of high-powered self-achievement and an overemphasis on the importance of personal accomplishments and building one's own ego-centered kingdom, this idea of giving grace the credit is a much-needed message. How many people who reach the pinnacle of their career say to the *Wall Street Journal* reporter or in an interview in *Business Week,* "I am what I am by the grace of God"? How many athletes would say that kind of thing at a banquet in his or her honor? What a shocker it would be today if someone were to say, "Don't be impressed at all with me. My only claim to fame is the undeserved grace of God." Such candor is rare.

There's a third statement, which seems to be implied in Paul's closing statement: *I let you be what you are by the grace of God.* Grace is not something simply to be claimed; it is meant to be demonstrated.

It is to be shared, used as a basis for friendships, and drawn upon for sustained relationships.

Jesus spoke of an abundant life that we enter into when we claim the freedom He provides by His grace. Wouldn't it be wonderful if people cooperated with His game plan? There is nothing to be compared to grace when it comes to freeing others from bondage.

Some, it seems, are like the cartoon character I saw recently. A dominant, aggressive type is philosophizing alongside his friend, who happens to be quieter and more passive. With unhesitating boldness, the stronger one says to the weaker one, "If I were in charge of the world, I would change EVERYTHING!" A bit intimidated, the friend who is forced to listen says rather meekly, "Uh, that wouldn't be easy. Like . . .where would you start?" Without a hesitation he looks directly back and says, "I would start with YOU!" No grace. You and I have been around a few grace killers like that, haven't we? With that notorious "No" face, they frown, "You need changing, so I'm going to start with you."

There are those who seem to be waiting for the first opportunity to confront. Suspicious by nature and negative in style, they are determined to find any flaw, failure, or subtle weakness in your life, and to point it out. There may be twenty things they could affirm; instead they have one main goal, to make sure you never forget your weaknesses. Grace killers are big on the "shoulds" and "oughts" in their advice. Instead of praising, they pounce!

Jackie Hudson is a good friend. She is the talented lady who has the dubious distinction of trying to teach me to snow ski, and she has the scars to prove it. What a beautiful model of patience! She wrote a book called *Doubt: A Road to Growth*, from which the article "People Grow Better in Grace" was adapted by *Worldwide Challenge* magazine in April 1988. In it she illustrates what I'm getting at:

> Early in my career, I had a boss who held to numerous spoken and

unspoken rules. One was that I needed to have my lights out by 11 P.M. so I wouldn't be tired on the job the next day. His house wasn't far from mine, and if he noticed my lights on after 11, I heard about it the next morning.

I remember my first compliment from him—a full year after I'd been on the job. I'd been given a project, and I worked night and day to make it perfect and, thus, win his approval.

The day of the event he wanted all the other employees to arrive an hour early to help with the preparations. Even after I explained that it wouldn't be necessary, he insisted. After the employees stood around for an hour with nothing to do, the program began. I couldn't have been more pleased with the event. The project was flawless.

Afterwards, my boss walked up to me, looked down at the floor, and out of his mouth came the long-awaited words: "Well done, Miss Hudson." My year in this environment brought on a remarkable response: rebellion. I was hardly growing in grace. Grace is fertile soil. . . .

Grace focuses on who God is and what He has done, and takes the focus off ourselves. And yet it's so easy to think we need to do something to earn God's favor, as though grace is too good to be true.[2]

Many (dare I say, most?) Christians live their lives as though they're going to be graded once a year by a God who stands there frowning, with his hands stuck in the pockets of his robe. (I don't know why, but probably most people usually think of God with a robe on, never in sweats or cutoffs or a swimsuit . . . He's always wearing a beard and this white robe). Glaring, He says, "Well, Johnson, that gets a C–." And, "Dorothy, you ought to be ashamed!" And, "Smith? Not bad. Could've been better, though." What heretical imaginations we have.

Why do we think like that? Who is responsible for such horror-images of the Almighty? Where did we pick up the idea that God is mad or irritated? Knowing that *all* of God's wrath was poured out on His Son at His death on the cross, how can we think like that? As a matter of fact, the reason he brought Jesus back from the grave is that He was satisfied with His Son. Ponder this: If the Father is satisfied with His Son's full payment for sin, and we are in His Son, by grace through faith, *then He is satisfied with you and me.* How long must Christians live before we finally believe that? Perhaps our problem is that we will forever have bosses and friends and pastors and parents who will give us lists. There will always be those who will give us more and more and more to live up to. These are grace killers whether they know it or not. But using guilt trips, shame techniques, and sneaky manipulations, they virtually drive us to distraction! But never God. He's the One who assures us that if we are anything, it is by His marvelous, infinite, matchless grace. And once we truly get hold of it for our own lives—once we experience *The Grace Awakening*—it's amazing how we want to share it. We delight in letting others be what they are by the same grace of God.

In a fine little book titled *The Liberty of Obedience*, Elisabeth Elliot writes about a young man eager to forsake the world and to follow Christ closely. *What is it I must forsake?* he asks himself.

She records the following response and in doing so illustrates the foolishness of trying to please God by keeping man-made rules and legalistic regulations. What must he give up? Try not to smile:

> Colored clothes, for one thing. Get rid of everything in your wardrobe that is not white. Stop sleeping on a soft pillow. Sell your musical instruments and don't eat any more white bread. You cannot, if you are sincere about obeying Christ, take warm baths or shave your beard. To shave is to lie against Him who created us, to attempt to improve on His work.[3]

"Does this answer sound absurd?" she asks. Then she surprises us with this statement:

> It is the answer given in the most celebrated Christian schools of the second century! Is it possible that the rules that have been adopted by many twentieth-century Christians will sound as absurd to earnest followers of Christ a few years hence?[4]

Before we cluck our tongues or laugh out loud at second-century grace killers, we had better ask ourselves questions like: What message are we delivering to our brothers and sisters in the family of God? What list of do's and don'ts have we concocted and now require of others? What must they do to earn their way into the circle of our conditional love so that they can feel more accepted? And I must add this final question: Who gave us the right to give someone else the rules to live by?

If the great apostle had no list, if he was what he was by the grace of God, considering himself undeserving, I can assure you, we are all in the same camp, equally unqualified, undeserving, yet unconditionally loved by our Father. For there to be true maturity, people must be given room to grow, which includes room to fail, to think on their own, to disagree, to make mistakes. Grace *must* be risked or we will be stunted Christians who don't think, who can't make decisions, who operate in fear and without joy because we know nothing but someone else's demands and expectations. When will we ever learn? God *delights* in choosing those most unworthy and making them the objects of His unconditional acceptance.

CONSIDERING AN EXAMPLE OF GRACE

For the next few minutes let's leave our modern world and step into the time tunnel. Travel back with me three thousand years as we return to the days of ancient dynasties and the kings of Israel. It's a brutal era when all those in the family of the previous king were exterminated once a new dynasty took control. Naturally, all members of the former monarch's family had every reason to live in fear once the new king took the throne.

In the case I'm thinking of, King Saul and his son Jonathan had died following a battle. When word of the dual tragedy reached David's attention, it grieved him; nevertheless, he was the Lord's choice as Saul's successor. Knowing that David was now Israel's new king, the members of Saul's family fled for their lives, erroneously thinking that David would treat them like all the other monarchs of eastern dynasties. The scene portrayed in Scripture is one of pandemonium and panic.

> Now Jonathan, Saul's son, had a son crippled in his feet. He was five years old when the report of Saul and Jonathan came from Jezreel, and his nurse took him up and fled. And it happened that in her hurry to flee, he fell and became lame. And his name was Mephibosheth. (2 Sam. 4:4)

In the haste of escape, Saul's little grandson suffered a permanent injury. Not having medical help available and not knowing where to turn for such assistance, the boy never recovered from the fall. He lived the balance of his life lame in both his feet. We leave him as a five-year-old on the pages of the ancient record. Nothing more is said regarding Mephibosheth for fifteen to twenty years.

A Question Asked

Chapter 9 of 2 Samuel provides a link to the continuing story. Years have passed. Mephibosheth is now an adult, living out his days with a severe handicap. He is still crippled in both his feet. David has not only taken the throne, he has won the hearts of the people. The entire nation is singing his praises. As yet there is not a blemish on his integrity. He has expanded the boundaries of the United Kingdom of the Jews in Palestine from approximately six thousand to sixty thousand square miles. The military force of Israel is stronger than ever in its history. Enemy nations now respect this powerful new country. David is healthy and happy. He has not known defeat on the battlefield, which means his immediate world is relatively peaceful. His economy and diplomacy are a refreshing change from Saul's. There was not only a chicken in every pot, there were grapes on every vine. It is a rare scene of incredible prosperity and God-given peace.

Overwhelmed by the Lord's goodness and grace, the middleaged king muses over all his blessings. While doing so, he must have enjoyed a nostalgic moment, remembering his former friendship with Jonathan, which prompts him to ask:

> . . . "Is there yet anyone left of the house of Saul, that I may show him kindness for Jonathan's sake?" (2 Sam. 9:1)

It's a question of grace asked by a grateful man.

Those of you who find yourself at a similar time in your own life know there are occasions when you will do that kind of reflecting. You think back and remember with fondness some pleasant relationship . . . some individual who played a significant role in your being where you are today. You smile, you wish there were some special way you could show your appreciation, but perhaps your long-time friend or mentor is dead.

This is precisely where we find David. Most likely he remembers the tender moment in his past when he and Jonathan agreed to preserve and protect one another, no matter what.

> ". . . And may the Lord be with you as He has been with my father. And if I am still alive, will you not show me the lovingkindness of the Lord, that I may not die? And you shall not cut off your lovingkindness from my house forever, not even when the Lord cuts off every one of the enemies of David from the face of the earth." So Jonathan made a covenant with the house of David, saying, "May the Lord require it at the hands of David's enemies." And Jonathan made David vow again because of his love for him, because he loved him as he loved his own life. (1 Sam. 20:13–17)

While lost in his memory, David has a flashback. Recalling that promise, he seeks a way to make it good. I don't want you to miss the importance of one term David used:

> . . . "Is there yet anyone left of the house of Saul, that I may show him kindness for Jonathan's sake?" (2 Sam. 9:1)

It's the Hebrew word *chesed,* often rendered mercy, lovingkindness, or grace in the Old Testament. *Is there anyone still living in the family of Saul to whom I could demonstrate the same kind of grace that God has demonstrated to me?* That's the idea turning over in David's mind.

I love the question for what it does not ask. It does not ask, "Is there anyone who is deserving? Is there anyone who is qualified? Is there anyone who is sharp, whom I could use in government matters . . . or in good shape whom I could add to my army?" No, he simply asks, "Is there anyone?" It is an unconditional desire, a question dripping with grace. "I'm wondering if there is *anybody* out there?"

David has a "Yes" face at this nostalgic moment. But something tells me that the servant he calls in has a "No" face. His name is Ziba. Listen to his answer and feel the "No" in his voice.

> Now there was a servant of the house of Saul whose name was Ziba, and they called him to David; and the king said to him, "Are you Ziba?" And he said, "I am your servant." And the king said, "Is there not yet anyone of the house of Saul to whom I may show the kindness of God?" And Ziba said to the king, "There is still a son of Jonathan who is crippled in both feet." (2 Sam. 9:2–3)

Can't you feel the "No" in his response, even though it was affirmative? Of course. "King David, I know of someone . . . but I really doubt that you'd want him around. You see, he's crippled. He just doesn't fit in. He isn't kingly." Which, being interpreted in unmasked pride, sniffs, "He's not like the rest of us."

I love the response of King David. Rather than "Oh, really? How badly is the man crippled?" David responds, "Where is he? If there's somebody, anybody . . . let's get him in here." What grace! Perhaps a bit surprised, "Ziba said to the king, 'Behold, he is in the house of Machir the son of Ammiel in Lo-debar'" (2 Sam. 9:4).

Lo-debar, interestingly, in Hebrew, means "a barren place." In English, the name of the place could be translated "no pasture land." It's as if the servant is saying that Jonathan's son is living in a place of stark barrenness—a place where there are no crops, a wilderness . . . a wasteland. There is not a moment's hesitation. David had heard enough to put a plan into action.

A Cripple Sought

Then King David sent and brought him from the house of Machir the son of Ammiel, from Lo-debar. And Mephibosheth, the son of Jonathan the son of Saul, came to David and fell on his face and prostrated himself. And David said, "Mephibosheth." And he said, "Here is your servant!" And David said to him, "Do not fear, for I will surely show kindness to you for the sake of your father Jonathan, and will restore to you all the land of your grandfather Saul; and you shall eat at my table regularly." (2 Sam. 9:5–7)

The crippled man was obviously frightened when he arrived at the king's palace in Jerusalem. The watchword of his life since he was a little boy had been anonymity. He never wanted to be found, certainly not by the king who succeeded his grandfather. To do so would mean sure death. And yet there was no way he could say no when David sent for him. Before he knew it, he was whisked away in a chariot provided for him; and before he could believe it, there he stood before the king.

All that explains why David's words must have stunned Mephibosheth. They fit David, however. When grace is in your heart, your hope is to release others from fear, not create it.

Let me interrupt this wonderful story to ask you a question about Jesus, the One who was "full of grace and truth." Do you know what was the most often-repeated command from His lips? Most people I ask are unable to answer that question correctly. Our Lord issued numerous commands, but He made this one more than any other. Do you happen to know what it was? It was this: "Fear not." *Isn't that great?* "Do not fear." Naturally, the most common reaction when someone stood before the perfect Son of God would have been fear. And yet Jesus, great in grace, repeatedly said, "Do not be afraid." He didn't meet people with a deep frown, looking down on them and swinging a club. He met them with open arms and reassuring words, "Don't be afraid." Those are the words David used before Mephibosheth. They drip with grace.

Mephibosheth's first reaction must have been the fear of a spear in his belly. Small wonder he says, "Here is your servant!" as he falls on his face before the king. "Don't be afraid," says David, but the crippled man cannot stop shaking. It is as if David wants to say, "I haven't sought for you to punish you for something you've done or not done. I have good in mind for you, not harm. I want to lift you up, not tear you down." The secret of David's entire message to the man could be stated in seven words, "I will surely show kindness to you."

A Privilege Provided

Don't miss something that's terribly important in the overall message of grace. David wanted to show kindness not because of Mephibosheth (he didn't even know the man before they met that day), but to show kindness "for the sake of your father Jonathan . . ." Mephibosheth still can't believe what's happening. "Again he prostrated himself and said, 'What is your servant, that you should regard a dead dog like me?'" (2 Sam. 9:8). In calling himself "a dead dog" he uses the most descriptive words he could think of for a contemptuous, despicable, worthless creature. "I'm just a dead dog, living in Lo-debar. Why not just leave me alone in my misery?"

Remember when you said that to God? Has it been that long since you and He met? Or could you have already forgotten? Candidly, this is one of my all-time favorite stories in the Old Testament because its portrayal of grace is so powerful. Here is a man who is unknown, of no consequence to the king, and is crippled in both his feet. He can give nothing of benefit to the kingdom so far as physical strength is concerned. There was absolutely zero personal appeal; but David stooped in grace. Due to a relationship David had with his long-time friend Jonathan, the king is going to provide Mephibosheth the privileges and benefits he would have given his own son.

Swiftly and completely, the king kept his word. Watch it transpire . . . it's wonderful!

> Then the king called Saul's servant Ziba, and said to him, "All that belonged to Saul and to all his house I have given to your master's grandson." (2 Sam. 9:9)

Ziba must have shaken his head in amazement.

> And you and your sons and your servants shall cultivate the land for him, and you shall bring in the produce so that your master's grandson may have food; nevertheless Mephibosheth your master's grandson shall eat at my table regularly. . . ." (2 Sam. 9:10)

Four separate times in the biblical account we read that the cripple would eat at the king's table—verses 7, 10, 11, and finally verse 13: "So Mephibosheth lived in Jerusalem, for he ate at the king's table regularly. Now he was lame in both his feet" (2 Sam. 9:13).

What a scene! What grace! From that time on he was welcome at the king's table of continual nourishment and uninterrupted provisions. Undeserving . . . yet unconditionally loved. Mephibosheth's head must have swirled for days as he forced himself to believe his new situation wasn't a dream.

Imagine a typical scene several years later. The dinner bell rings through the king's palace and David comes to the head of the table and sits down. In a few moments Amnon—clever, crafty Amnon—sits to the left of David. Lovely and gracious Tamar, a charming and beautiful young woman, arrives and sits beside Amnon. And then across the way, Solomon walks slowly from his study; precocious, brilliant, preoccupied Solomon. The heir apparent slowly sits down. And then Absalom—handsome, winsome Absalom with beautiful flowing hair, black as a raven, down to his shoulders—sits down. That particular evening, Joab, the courageous warrior and David's commander of the troops, has been invited to dinner. Muscular, bronzed Joab is seated near the king. Afterward, they wait. They hear the shuffling of feet, the clump, clump, clump of the crutches as Mephibosheth rather awkwardly finds his place at the table and slips into his seat . . . and the tablecloth covers his feet. I ask you: Did Mephibosheth understand grace?

Were he living today I think He would quickly identify with the words from the hymn by John Newton:

> Through many dangers, toils, and snares
> I have already come;
> 'Tis grace hath brought me safe thus far,
> And grace will lead me home.[5]

SEEING THE ANALOGIES OF GRACE

Maybe you have already noticed some of the analogies between the grace demonstrated to Mephibosheth and the grace extended to you and me. I find no fewer than eight:

1. Once Mephibosheth enjoyed fellowship with his father. And so did the original couple, Adam and Eve, in the lovely Garden of Eden.
2. When disaster struck, fear came, and Mephibosheth suffered a fall that crippled him for the rest of his life. And so it was when sin came, humanity suffered a fall which has left us permanently crippled on earth.

3. David, the king, out of unconditional love for his beloved friend Jonathan sought out anyone to whom he might extend his grace. In like manner, God the Father, because of His unconditional acceptance of His one and only Son's death on the cross, continues to seek anyone to whom He might extend His grace.

4. The crippled man had nothing, did nothing, and deserved nothing. He didn't even try to win the king's favor. All he could do was humbly accept it. So we—sinners without hope and totally undeserving, in no way worthy of our God's favor—humbly accept it.

5. The king restored the cripple from his miserable existence . . . a place of barrenness and desolation . . . to a place of fellowship and honor. God, our Father, has done the same for us. From our own, personal "Lo-debar" of brokenness and depravity, He rescued us and brought us into a place of spiritual nourishment and intimate closeness.

6. David adopted Mephibosheth into his royal family, providing him with uninterrupted provisions, nourishment, and blessings. We, too, have been adopted as sons and daughters into His royal ranks, surrounded by ceaseless delights.

7. The adopted son's limp was a constant reminder of the king's grace. Our imperfect state keeps us from ever forgetting that where sin abounds, grace *super*abounds.

8. When Mephibosheth sat at the king's table, he was treated as one of David's own sons—no less than Absalom or Solomon. When we feast one day with our Lord, the same will be true.

There we shall sit alongside Paul and Peter, Lydia and Priscilla, Mary and Phoebe, James, John, Barnabas, and Luke . . . martyrs, monks, reformers and evangelists, seminary presidents and professors, ministers and missionaries, authors and statesmen alike, with no emphasis on rank or title . . . no special regard for high achievement.

Why? Because we are all so undeserving, every one of us. Cripples all! And oh, how we'll sing God's praise.

> When we've been there ten thousand years,
>   Bright shining as the sun,
> We've no less days to sing God's praise
>   Than when we first begun.[6]

All our praise will go to the One who came and died, arose and lives. His name is Jesus; His message is grace. Few have ever pictured Him and His message more clearly than John Bunyan:

> Thou Son of the Blessed,
> what grace was manifested in Thy condescension
> Grace brought Thee down from Heaven;
>   grace stripped Thee of Thy glory;
>   grace made Thee poor and despised;
>   grace made Thee bear such burdens of sin,
>   such burdens of sorrow,
>   such burdens of God's curse as are unspeakable.
> O Son of God!
> Grace was in all Thy tears;
>   grace came out of Thy side with Thy blood;
>   grace came forth with every word of Thy sweet
>   mouth;
>   grace came out where the whip smote Thee,
>   where the thorn pricked Thee,
>   and where the nails pierced Thee.
> Here is grace indeed!
> Grace to make angels wonder,
>   grace to make sinners happy,
>   grace to astonish devils.[7]

Gathered with the people of God at that great Marriage Feast of the Lamb, the tablecloth of His grace will cover all our crippling needs.

5

Squaring Off
Against Legalism

LIBERTY IS ALWAYS WORTH FIGHTING for. It is the main reason Americans have laid down their lives for their country. If we were to interview any of those people who have fought in battle and ask, "Why did you live in those miserable and dangerous conditions?" or "What was it that kept you out there fighting for your country?" the response would probably include words like, "Well, our liberty was at stake . . . I love my country, and our freedom was being threatened by the enemy. I wanted to defend it, and if necessary, I would still fight to the death for it."

Back in our earliest days as a nation, a determined thirty-nine-year-old, radical-thinking attorney addressed the Virginia Convention. It was on March 23, 1775, a time of great patriotic passion. And his patriotism refused to be silenced any longer. Sounding more like a prophet of God than a patriot for his country, he announced:

> If we wish to be free we must fight! . . . I repeat it, sir, we must fight! An appeal to arms, and to the God of hosts, is all that is left us. It is vain, sir, to extenuate the matter. The gentlemen may cry "Peace, peace!" but

there is no peace. The war has actually begun! . . . Our brethren are already in the field. Why stand we here idle? . . . Is life so dear or peace so sweet as to be purchased at the price of chains and slavery? Forbid it, Almighty God. I know not what course others may take, but as for me, give me liberty or give me death![1]

What a soul-stirring speech! We applaud the courageous passion of Patrick Henry to this day. Because of it he remains in our minds as one of our national heroes.

Not quite ninety years later we were fighting one another in our country's worst bloodbath. And again I remind you, it was for the cause of liberty. The issue was slavery versus freedom. The black people of our nation were not free. It was the conviction of the United States government that they should be free, and if necessary we would take up arms against those who opposed their liberation from slavery.

Charles Sumner did a masterful job of summing up the issue of the Civil War in a speech he made on November 5, 1864: "Where Slavery is, there Liberty cannot be; and where Liberty is, there Slavery cannot be."[2]

I find it more than strange. Actually, I find it amazing that we as a nation will fight other nations for our national liberty, and that we as a people will, if necessary, fight one another for the freedom of those within our borders, but when it comes to the living out of our Christianity, we will give up our liberty without a fight. We'll go to the wall and square off against any enemy who threatens to take away our national freedom, but we'll not be nearly so passionate as Christians under grace to fight for our rightful liberty. Let enough legalists come aboard and we will virtually give them command of the ship. We will fear their frowns, we will adapt our lives to their lists, we'll allow ourselves to be intimidated, and for the sake of peace at any price (even though it may lead to nothing short of slavery), we will succumb to their agenda.

This is nothing new. As far back as 1963, S. Lewis Johnson, one of my seminary professors, wrote an excellent article titled "The Paralysis of Legalism." In it he put his finger on the crux of the problem.

> One of the most serious problems facing the orthodox Christian church today is the problem of legalism. One of the most serious problems facing the church in Paul's day was the problem of legalism. In every day it is the same. Legalism wrenches the joy of the Lord from the Christian believer, and with the joy of the Lord goes his power for vital worship and vibrant service. Nothing is left but cramped, somber, dull, and listless profession. The truth is betrayed, and the glorious name of the Lord becomes a synonym for a gloomy kill-joy. The Christian under law is a miserable parody of the real thing.[3]

Though he wrote decades ago, Dr. Johnson described the church of the 1990s and on into the twenty-first century. If you want to find a group of "cramped, somber, dull, and listless" individuals, just visit many (I'm trying hard not to write *most*) evangelical churches today. It is with a deep heartache and great disappointment that I write these words. If I were asked to name the major enemies of vital Christianity today, I'm not sure but what I wouldn't name legalism first! As I have stated from the beginning of this book, it is a killer. It kills congregations when a pastor is a legalist. It kills pastors when congregations are legalistic. Legalistic people with their rigid do's and don'ts kill the spirit of joy and spontaneity of those who wish to enjoy their liberty. Strict legalistic people in leadership drain the very life out of a church, even though they may claim they are doing God a service.

If you have never been under the thumb of legalism, you are rare . . . you don't know how blessed you have been. If you have been under bondage and have broken free (as I have), you know better than most what a treasured privilege freedom really is. It's worth fighting for!

I have my Bible beside me opened to the fifth chapter of the letter to the Galatians. Galatians is what some have correctly called the Magna Charta of Christian liberty. In fact, the first verse in this chapter contains the single command that, if believed and obeyed, would go a long way in putting a stop to legalism.

> It is for freedom that Christ set us free; therefore keep standing firm and do not be subject again to a yoke of slavery. (v. 1)

Nothing disturbs the legalist like the liberating truth of grace. Paul, far back in the first century, is writing to Christians who knew better than to let it happen, but they had allowed themselves to fall under the paralyzing spell of grace killers. J. B. Phillips, in a paraphrase of Galatians 5:1, renders it:

> Do not lose your freedom by giving in. . . . Plant your feet firmly therefore within the freedom that Christ has won for us, and do not let yourselves be caught again in the shackles of slavery.

If Patrick Henry had the courage to say, "Give me liberty or give me death," then the Christian ought to have the courage to say, "Give me freedom because of Christ." Bondage is bondage, whether it be political or spiritual. Give me the liberty that He won at Calvary or I am still enslaved. Death is to be preferred to bondage . . . so grant me the liberty He won or I should die! To live in slavery is to nullify the grace of God.

DEFINING TWO SIGNIFICANT TERMS

Without becoming needlessly academic, I want to define a couple of the terms that I've been tossing around. First of all, What do I mean when I declare that the Christian has *liberty?* And second, What does it mean to say that *legalism* puts people under bondage?

Liberty

Essentially, liberty is freedom . . . freedom from something and freedom to do something.

Liberty is freedom from slavery or bondage..It is initially freedom from sin's power and guilt. Freedom from God's wrath. Freedom from satanic and demonic authority. And equally important, it is freedom from shame that could easily bind me, as well as freedom from the tyranny of others' opinions, obligations, and expectations.

There was a time in my life without Christ when I had no freedom from the urges and impulses within me. I was at the mercy of my master Satan and sin was my lifestyle. When the urges grew within me, I had nothing to hold me in check, nothing to restrain me. It was an awful bondage.

For example, in my personal life I was driven by jealousy for many miserable years. It was consuming. I served it not unlike a slave serves a master. Then there came a day when I was spiritually awakened to the charming grace of God and allowed it to take full control and almost before I knew it the jealousy died. And I sensed for the first time, perhaps in my whole life, true love; the joy, the romance, the spontaneity, the free-flowing creativity brought about by the grace of a faithful wife, who would love me no matter what, who was committed to me in faithfulness for all her life. That love and that commitment motivated me to love in return more freely than ever. I no longer loved out of fear that I would lose her, but I loved out of the joy and the blessing connected with being loved unconditionally and without restraint.

Now that Christ has come into my life and I have been awakened to His grace, He has provided a freedom from that kind of slavery to sin. And along with that comes a freedom that brings a fearlessness, almost a sense of invincibility in the presence of the adversity. This power, keep in mind, is because of Christ, who lives within me.

In addition, He has also brought a glorious freedom from the curse of the Law. By that I mean freedom from the constancy of its demands to perform in order to please God and/or others. It is a freedom from the fear of condemnation before God as well as from an accusing conscience. Freedom from the demands of other people, from all the *shoulds* and *oughts* of the general public.

Such freedom is *motivated*—motivated by unconditional love. When the grace of Christ is fully awake in your life, you find you're no longer doing something due to fear or out of shame or because of guilt, but you're doing it through love. The dreadful tyranny of performing in order to please someone is over . . . forever.

Grace also brings a freedom *to do* something else—a freedom to enjoy the rights and the privileges of being out from under slavery *and* allowing others such freedom. It's freedom to experience and enjoy a new kind of power that only Christ could bring. It is a freedom to become all that He meant me to be, *regardless of how He leads others*. I can be me—fully and freely. It is a freedom to know Him in an independent and personal way. And that freedom is then released to others so they can be who they are meant to be—different from me!

You see, God isn't stamping out little cookie-cutter Christians across the world so that we all think alike and look alike and sound alike and act alike. The body has variety. We were never meant to have the same temperaments and use the same vocabulary and wear the same syrupy smile and dress the same way and carry on the same ministry. I repeat: God is pleased with variety. This freedom to be who we are is nothing short of magnificent. It is freedom to make choices, freedom to know His will, freedom to walk in it, freedom to obey His leading me in my life and you in your life. Once you've tasted such freedom, nothing else satisfies.

Perhaps I should reemphasize that it is a liberty you will have to fight for. Why? Because the ranks of Christianity are full of those who compare and would love to control and manipulate you so you will become as miserable as they are. After all, if they are determined to be "cramped, somber, dull, and listless," then they expect you to be that way, too. "Misery loves company" is the legalists' unspoken motto, though they never admit it.

Legalism

Now is a good time for us to become better acquainted with the staunch enemy of liberty. Legalism is an attitude, a mentality based on pride. It is an obsessive conformity to an artificial standard for the purpose of exalting oneself. A legalist assumes the place of authority and pushes it to unwarranted extremes. As Daniel Taylor states so well, it results in illegitimate control, requiring unanimity, not unity.

> The great weapon of authoritarianism, secular or religious, is legalism: the manufacturing and manipulation of rules for the purpose of illegitimate control. Perhaps the most damaging of all the perversions of God's will and Christ's work, legalism clings to law at the expense of grace, to the letter in place of the spirit.
>
> Legalism is one more expression of the human compulsion for security. If we can vigorously enforce an exhaustive list of do's and don'ts (with an emphasis on external behavior), we not only can control unpredictable human beings but have God's favor as well. . . .
>
> Legalistic authoritarianism shows itself in the confusion of the Christian principle of unity with a human insistence on unanimity. Unity is a profound, even mystical quality. It takes great effort to achieve, yet mere effort will never produce it; it is a source of great security, yet demands great risk.
>
> Unanimity, on the other hand, is very tidy. It can be measured, monitored, and enforced. It is largely external, whereas unity is essentially internal. Its primary goal is corrected behavior, while unity's is a right spirit. Unanimity insists on many orthodoxies in addition to those of belief and behavior, including orthodoxy of experience and vocabulary. That is, believers are expected to come to God in similar ways, to have

similar experiences with God, and to use accepted phrases in describing those experiences.[4]

In so many words, legalism says, "I do this or I don't do that, and therefore I am pleasing God." Or "If only I could do this or not do that, I would be pleasing to God." Or perhaps, "These things that I'm doing or not doing are the things I perform to win God's favor." They aren't spelled out in Scripture, you understand. They've been passed down or they have been dictated to the legalist and have become an obsession to him or her. Legalism is rigid, grim, exacting, and lawlike in nature. Pride, which is at the heart of legalism, works in sync with other motivating factors. Like guilt. And fear. And shame. It leads to an emphasis on what should *not* be, and what one should *not* do. It flourishes in a drab context of negativism.

Few people have ever described legalism better than Eugene Peterson does in his fine book *Traveling Light*, where he contrasts the healthy walk of faith with legalism.

> The word *Christian* means different things to different people. To one person it means a stiff, uptight, inflexible way of life, colorless and un-bending. To another it means a risky, surprise-filled venture, lived on tiptoe at the edge of expectation.
>
> Either of these pictures can be supported with evidence. There are numberless illustrations for either position in congregations all over the world. But if we restrict ourselves to biblical evidence, only the second image can be supported: the image of the person living zestfully, explor-ing every experience—pain and joy, enigma and insight, fulfillment and frustration—as a dimension of human freedom, searching through each for sense and grace. If we get our information from the biblical material, there is no doubt that the Christian life is a dancing, leaping, daring life.
>
> How then does this other picture get painted in so many imaginations? How does anyone get the life of faith associated with dullness, with caution, with inhibition, with stodginess? We might fairly suppose that a congregation of Christians, well stocked with freedom stories—stories of

Abraham, Moses, David, Samson, Deborah, Daniel—would not for a moment countenance any teaching that would suppress freedom. We might reasonably expect that a group of people who from infancy have been told stories of Jesus setting people free and who keep this Jesus at the center of their attention in weekly worship, would be sensitive to any encroachment on their freedom. We might think that a people that has at the very heart of its common experience release from sin's guilt into the Spirit's freedom, a people who no longer lives under the tyranny of emotions or public opinion or bad memories, but freely in hope and in faith and in love—that these people would be critically alert to anyone or anything that would suppress their newly acquired spontaneity.

But in fact the community of faith, the very place where we are most likely to experience the free life, is also the very place where we are in most danger of losing it.[5]

Be honest, how many congregations do you know who are "dancing, leaping, daring" congregations—congregations whose individual grace awakenings are motivating people to live out their freedom in Christ? I'm afraid the number is much fewer than we might guess. Let's get specific. How many Christians do you know who exercise the joy and freedom to be a person full of life, living on tiptoe, enjoying spontaneous living—as opposed to the numberless hundreds of thousands who take their cues from the legalists and live life accordingly? Isn't it surprising to anyone who has been set free that anybody would ever want to return to bondage? I suggest that you ponder the final sentence in Peterson's quote once more. As usual, he is right on target. The one place on earth where we would most expect to be set free is, in fact, the very place we are most likely to be placed into slavery: the church. Surely, that must grieve our God.

What happened in the first century can surely happen in the twentieth. Paul writes the Galatians of his surprise: "You were running well; who hindered you from obeying the truth?" (5:7).

Allow me to amplify his thought—"When I was with you, some of you were into the 100-meter dash, others were doing the 440 with ease. Still others were into much longer distances . . . you were marathoners. The truth freed you and I distinctly recall how well you were running as well as how much joy you demonstrated. Who cut in on your stride? Who took away your track shoes? Who told you that you shouldn't be running or enjoying the race? Some of you have stopped running altogether" (Swindoll paraphrase).

That isn't all. Back in chapter 3, verses 1–3, Paul is even more assertive. His opening salutation is borderline insulting: "You foolish Galatians." (You won't like to read this, but J. B. Phillips calls them "idiots.") He writes:

> O you dear idiots of Galatia, who saw Jesus Christ the crucified so plainly, who has been casting a spell over you? I shall ask you one simple question: Did you receive the Spirit of God by trying to keep the Law or by believing the message of the Gospel? Surely you can't be so idiotic as to think that a man begins his spiritual life in the Spirit and then completes it by reverting to outward observances?

The apostle says, in effect, "When I was there, teaching you the truth, I presented a Savior who paid the full penalty for your sins. The death that He died and His subsequent resurrection from the grave was God's final payment for sin. *Paid in full!* All you have to do is believe that He died and rose again from the dead for you. He was publicly displayed for all to see and now the truth can be declared for all to believe. You believed that once upon a time, and you were gloriously free. Not now. Who bewitched you? Who caused you to transfer allegiance from the glory of God to the opinions of man, from the work of the Spirit to the deeds of the flesh? When did you start running scared?" It's that idea.

The Living Bible renders this first verse: "Oh, foolish Galatians! What magician has hypnotized you and cast an evil spell upon you?" In other words, Have you gone completely crazy? Who stole your mind? Paul is beside himself. Who had hypnotized the once fully "awake" Galatians?

Earlier in Galatians 1:6, he admits his amazement: "I am astonished that you are so quickly deserting the one who called you by the grace of Christ and are turning to a different gospel" (NIV).

It could be compared to your rearing your children in a healthy environment. They grow up in your home and because it is a good home, they develop a security and a stability as they pick up your authenticity and unguarded lifestyle. They communicate openly and freely. They learn how to confront and handle problems. In short, they learn the basics of real living . . . which includes knowing Christ and loving God and walking with Him and relating well to one another—all those things that represent integrity, vulnerability, authenticity.

Once they grow up, they move far away. Time passes and you begin to miss them, so after three or four years you go visit them. You're shocked! You find them living cramped, closed, dirty, and emotionally crippled lives. You're amazed to find them struggling with problems, evidencing negative attitudes; they're even suicidal. Naturally you ask, "Who got to you? Who twisted your mind? What's happened over these past few years." It is with that same kind of passion that Paul writes his concern to his Galatian friends.

Think, now . . . what's he fighting for? Liberty! "You were once freed. But now, my friends in Galatia, you are enslaved. I want to know what's gone wrong." The answer is not complicated; the grace killers had invaded and conquered.

IDENTIFYING THREE TOOLS OF LEGALISM

Let's get down to brass tacks. What are the inroads most legalists make on a life, on a church, on a missionary outreach, or on a denomination? How do legalists get in? Who are they? Furthermore, why are they effective? As a result of studying the first and second chapters of Galatians, I'm prepared to identify at least three different tools used by century-one legalists: those of doctrinal heresy, ecclesiastical harassment, and personal hypocrisy.

First, let's consider *those who disturb and distort by interjecting doctrinal heresy*. Scripture says it plain and simple; legalists were twisting truth among the Galatian assembly.

> I am amazed that you are so quickly deserting Him who called you by the grace of Christ, for a different gospel; which is really not another; only there are some who are disturbing you, and want to distort the gospel of Christ. But even though we, or an angel from heaven, should preach to you a gospel contrary to that which we have preached to you, let him be accursed. As we have said before, so I say again now, if any man is preaching to you a gospel contrary to that which you received, let him be accursed. For am I now seeking the favor of men, or of God? Or am I striving to please men? If I were still trying to please men, I would not be a bond-servant of Christ. (Gal. 1:6–10)

Legalists were disturbing others and distorting the truth as they spread doctrinal heresy. Their heretical message was that the Galatian Christians should let Moses finish what Christ began. In other words, salvation is not by faith alone . . . it requires works. Human achievement must accompany sincere faith before you can be certain of your salvation. We continue to hear that "different gospel" to this day and *it is a lie*. A theology that rests its salvation on one ounce of human performance is not good news, it is bad information. It is *heresy*. It is antithetical to the true message that lit the spark to the Reformation: *Sola fide*—faith alone.

A salvation that begins with God's love reaching down to lost humanity and is carried out by Christ's death and resurrection results in all the praise going to God. But a salvation that includes human achievement, hard work, personal effort, even religious deeds distorts the good news because man gets the glory, not God. The problem is, it appeals to the flesh. Paul's twice-repeated reaction to the one who introduced that doctrinal heresy is "Let him be accursed!" This is Paul's way of saying the person is *doomed!* The original word is *anathema!* It is the strongest single Greek term for condemnation.

Nevertheless, the heresy goes on. Most every cult you could name is a cult of salvation by works. It appeals to the flesh. It tells you, if you will stand so long on a street corner, if you will distribute so much literature, if you will sacrifice so much of life, if you will be baptized, if you will contribute your money, if you will pray or attend numerous meetings, then your good works and hard effort will cause God to smile on you. Ultimately, when the good is weighed against the bad on the Day of Judgment, you will finally earn His favor. The result in that, I say again, is man's glory, because you added to your salvation.

Grace says you have nothing to give, nothing to earn, nothing to pay. You couldn't if you tried! Remember what we learned in chapter 2? Salvation is a free gift. You simply lay hold of what Christ has provided. Period. And yet the heretical doctrine of works goes on all around the world and always will. It is effective because the pride of men and women is so strong. We simply *have* to *do* something in order to feel right about it. It just doesn't make good humanistic sense to get something valuable for nothing.

Please allow me to be absolutely straight with you: Stop tolerating the heretical gospel of works! It is legalism. Wake up to the fact that it will put you into a bondage syndrome that won't end. The true gospel of grace, however, will set you free. Free forever.

Let's take a closer look at Galatians 1:10: "For am I now seeking the favor of men, or of God? Or am I striving to please men? If I were still trying to please men, I would not be a bond-servant of Christ."

You wonder what Paul's life was like before Christ? He tells us; he was a man-pleaser. He says, "If I were *still* trying to please men. . . ." He was a legalist back in his years as a Pharisee. His goal, among other things, was to please people.

When he realized Christ was who He claimed to be and His death was effective and sufficient to provide the complete payment for sin, he was crushed to the bone when he realized the enormity of his guilt before God. He was stunned in meeting Christ on the road to Damascus. He learned then (and in subsequent years) that you cannot try to please people or live your life being afraid of people. There is only One to please and to fear on this earth and that is God.

I want to add something here especially for pastors and Christian leaders. Those who seek to please God only are invincible from within. Not only that, but when we stop striving to please people, we are also unintimidated from without. The church of Jesus Christ needs more invincible, unintimidated pastors. We put a lot of effort into training men and women for ministry. But there isn't equal effort in training congregations for ministers. That is most unfortunate. Church congregations need to know when to let a pastor lead, how to respect his judgment, and the importance of following him with confidence. Yes, he needs to be deserving of such respect and he needs to be accountable . . . no question. But the tragedy is that there are numerous ministers who "seek the favor" and "strive to please" at any price. I don't know of a quicker way to ruin a ministry or, for that matter, to be consumed with anxiety. True spiritual leadership cannot occur as long as the leader runs scared of what people may think or say.

I can remember an experience that taught me this lesson permanently. I was pastoring a church in another state over twenty years ago. A particular issue arose that divided the leadership right down the middle. It was a volatile issue, and I realized it had the possibility of splitting the church. Adding to my pressure was the inescapable reality that my vote on the board of elders was the "swing vote." Our board of strongminded men was equally divided on each side, and my vote was needed to break the tie. All eyes would ultimately be on me. The climactic meeting was set for a Thursday evening. I was relatively young and looking back, I was still too interested in pleasing people—I now admit to my own embarrassment.

I told Cynthia I had to be alone overnight to think everything through. I got into my 1969 Volkswagen early Wednesday morning, turned onto the highway that led out of town, and rested my New Testament on the steering wheel as I drove along. I opened to Galatians, chapter 1, and began reading aloud, glancing up onto the road then back down at my Bible. Suddenly, verse 10 leaped off the page like a tiger with sharp claws, ". . . am I striving to please men? . . ." Yes, it was the same verse of Scripture we have been analyzing, but that day I saw it for the first time. I immediately pulled to the side of the highway, turned off the engine and read the words aloud again and again and again. *What a rebuke!* I not only had my answer, I had stumbled upon a life-changing principle. Within a very few minutes, confidence replaced fear. I lost the nagging desire to please a group of men. My one goal was to please God. I was freed from the awful clutches of "striving to please men."

I did a U-turn, drove back home to the surprise of my wife, who was not expecting to see me until the next day, and told her of the discovery. She smiled in agreement. She had noticed my insecurity earlier that morning. The following night I openly declared my convictions, which displeased some of the board members but resulted in what proved to be the best decision. A few left the church . . . yet for the first time in my ministry I experienced a fresh surge of

freedom. Invincible and unintimidated, I displayed a calm assurance
in my leadership style that has stayed with me; thank God. And what
a difference it has made. I was liberated from the bondage of striving
to please people.

Perhaps that is one of the reasons I write with such passion about
the importance of being free—why I plead with you so earnestly to
allow the quickening power of God's grace to awaken within you a
hunger for liberty. Those who let freedom be taken from them not
only embrace heresy, they live under the thumb of grace killers who
love to control and intimidate.

The second tool I find legalists using is ecclesiastical harassment;
they are *those who spy and enslave*.

> Then after an interval of fourteen years I went up again to Jerusalem
> with Barnabas, taking Titus along also. And it was because of a revelation
> that I went up; and I submitted to them the gospel which I preach
> among the Gentiles, but I did so in private to those who were of repu-
> tation, for fear that I might be running, or had run, in vain. But not even
> Titus who was with me, though he was a Greek, was compelled to be
> circumcised. But it was because of the false brethren who had sneaked
> in to spy out our liberty which we have in Christ Jesus, in order to bring
> us into bondage. But we did not yield in subjection to them for even an
> hour, so that the truth of the gospel might remain with you. But from
> those who were of high reputation (what they were makes no difference
> to me; God shows no partiality)—well, those who were of reputation
> contributed nothing to me. (Gal. 2:1–7)

I know of few scriptures that more boldly expose the damaging
style of legalism. Earlier we analyzed those who disturb and distort
the gospel. Now, we are considering those who spy on and enslave
individuals who wish to be free. In a few sentences let me give you
the background to what Paul wrote about here in Galatians 2.

Fourteen years earlier, the apostle Paul had been given a direct revelation from God that he was called to minister especially to the Gentiles. Peter, you may remember, was called to minister especially to the Jews. A great question grew out of Paul's reaching out to Gentiles: Should a Gentile be circumcised in order for him to be a Christian? There were related questions. Does he need to maintain a certain diet? Does he need to fulfill the requirements of the Mosiac Law? Does he need to become "somewhat Jewish"? In other words, was it necessary for Moses to complete what Christ had begun? Paul emphatically said no. In doing so, he presented the gospel of Christ based on the message of grace. Not surprisingly, the Gentiles responded by the thousands. This caused some of the Jewish believers to get a little nervous, especially those who held to a more legalistic position of salvation. The influx of so many Gentile converts disturbed them no little bit.

The apostle Paul's response was commendable: "Let's let the distinguished church fathers, the pillars of the church, answer this one. We need their seasoned wisdom." And so off he went to Jerusalem where the meeting would be held, taking along with him Barnabas (a circumcised Jew) and Titus (an uncircumcised Gentile), both of whom had believed in the Lord Jesus Christ as Savior. Paul tells us what he did when he arrived: ". . . I submitted to them the gospel which I preach among the Gentiles, but I did so in private to those who were of reputation, for fear that I might be running, or had run, in vain" (v. 2).

This assures us that he came with an open attitude. He said, in effect, "Men, I want you to know that I have been teaching the good news of Christ according to grace. Am I right or do I need to be corrected?" Their answer, in brief, was, "You're right. We approve of this message." Don't miss the third verse: "But not even Titus who was with me, though he was a Greek, was compelled to be circumcised."

You think the legalists took that sitting down? No way:

> But it was because of the false brethren who had sneaked in to spy
> out our liberty which we have in Christ Jesus, in order to bring us
> into bondage. But we did not yield in subjection to them for even an
> hour. . . . (vv. 4–5)

Good for him! Why didn't Paul tolerate their disagreement and submit to their legalistic demands? Because liberty is worth fighting for!
The sneaking legalists were making their move, and he refused to
submit to them for even sixty minutes.

We need to pause and analyze the words "spy out our liberty." The
Greek term *kataskopos* is translated "spy out." A. T. Robertson says it
means "to reconnoitre, to make a treacherous investigation."[6] Why?
That's not difficult to answer: To enslave! There were those who not
only disliked Paul's freedom but who also wanted others to live in the
same bondage they did. (By the way, people like that still exist.)

In verse 4 Paul says they "sneaked in" to bring them into bondage.
In verse 5 he states, "I didn't submit, to make sure you kept free."
Good principle: When there is a sneaking in of legalism, there will
also be the need for those in leadership to stand fast. The strong must
defend the weak. Paul was undaunted, unintimidated, unrelenting in
his determination. With confidence, he pursued the freedom each
one of those Gentile converts had every right to claim. He withstood
legalism, and *so must we*. Trust me, legalists don't get the message if
you're unsure and soft with them. No need to be mean-spirited, but
there is the need to be firm.

Earlier, I quoted Eugene Peterson. Because his words fit what I am
trying to communicate, let's return to one further paragraph:

> There are people who do not want us to be free. They don't want us
> to be free before God, accepted just as we are by his grace. They don't
> want us to be free to express our faith originally and creatively in the
> world. They want to control us; they want to use us for their own pur-
> poses. They themselves refuse to live arduously and openly in faith, but

huddle together with a few others and try to get a sense of approval by insisting that all look alike, talk alike and act alike, thus validating one another's worth. They try to enlarge their numbers only on the condition that new members act and talk and behave the way they do. These people infiltrate communities of faith "to spy out our freedom which we have in Christ Jesus" and not infrequently find ways to control, restrict and reduce the lives of free Christians. Without being aware of it, we become anxious about what others will say about us, obsessively concerned about what others think we should do. We no longer live the good news but anxiously try to memorize and recite the script that someone else has assigned to us. In such an event we may be secure, but we will not be free. We may survive as a religious community, but we will not experience what it means to be human, alive in love and faith, expansive in hope. Conforming and self-congratulatory behavior is not free. But Paul "did not yield in submission even for a moment, that the truth of the gospel might be preserved for you." Every free person who benefits from Paul's courage will continue vigilant in the resistance movement he formed. [7]

Several months ago I was conversing with a man I greatly admire. He is a Christian leader in a position that carries with it heavy and extensive responsibilities. He said he was grieved on behalf of a missionary family he and his wife had known for years. The legalism they had encountered again and again on the mission field from fellow missionaries was so petty, so unbelievably small-minded, they had returned to the States and no longer planned to remain career missionaries. He said it was over a jar of peanut butter. I thought he was joking, to which he responded. "No, it's no joke at all." I could hardly believe the story.

The particular place they were sent to serve the Lord did not have access to peanut butter. This particular family happened to enjoy peanut butter a great deal. Rather creatively, they made arrangements with some of their friends in the States to send them peanut butter every now and then so they could enjoy it with their meals. The problem, is they didn't know until they started receiving the supply of peanut butter that the other missionaries considered it a mark of spirituality that you *not* have peanut butter with your meals. I suppose the line went something like this: "We believe since we can't get peanut butter here, we should give it up for the cause of Christ," or some such nonsense. A basis of spirituality was "bearing the cross" of living without peanut butter.

The young family didn't buy into that line of thinking. Their family kept getting regular shipments of peanut butter. They didn't flaunt it, they just enjoyed it in the privacy of their own home. Pressure began to intensify. You would expect adult missionaries to be big enough to let others eat what they pleased, right? Wrong. The legalism was so petty, the pressure got so intense and the exclusive treatment became so unfair, it finished them off spiritually. They finally had enough. Unable to continue against the mounting pressure, they packed it in and were soon homeward bound, disillusioned and probably a bit cynical. What we have here is a classic modern-day example of a group of squint-eyed legalists spying out and attacking another's liberty. Not even missionaries are exempted.

Would you please give up your list of do's and don'ts for everybody else? Just keep it for yourself. If you're not into peanut butter, that is fine. That's great! In fact, you have every right to take hands off. If that's your thing, you shouldn't eat it! But don't tell me or someone else we can't enjoy it. And don't judge us because we do.

The examples of such harassment are legion. Recently, I heard about a fellow who attended a legalistic college where students were to live according to very strict rules. They weren't supposed to do any work on Sundays. None! Guess what? He spied on his wife and caught her hanging out a few articles of clothing she washed on Sunday afternoon. Are you ready? The guy turned in his wife to the authorities! I'll bet she was fun to live with the next day or two. Candidly, there are days in my life when the pettiness of some people makes me want to scream.

In one of his more serious moments, Mike Yaconelli, editor of *The Wittenburg Door*, wrote strong words concerning pettiness in the church.

> Petty people are ugly people. They are people who have lost their vision. They are people who have turned their eyes away from what matters and focused, instead, on what doesn't matter. The result is that the rest of us are immobilized by their obsession with the insignificant. It is time to rid the church of pettiness. It is time the church refused to be victimized by petty people. It is time the church stopped ignoring pettiness. It is time the church quit pretending that pettiness doesn't matter. . . . Pettiness has become a serious disease in the Church of Jesus Christ—a disease which continues to result in terminal cases of discord, disruption, and destruction. Petty people are dangerous people because they appear to be only a nuisance instead of what they really are—a health hazard.[8]

Yaconelli is correct: Now is the time for the church (and that's you and me, my friend) to acknowledge the need for a "grace awakening" in the land—a new reformation of freedom that proclaims that liberty is worth fighting for.

The third grace killer identified in the book of Galatians is *hypocrisy—those who lie and deceive* (Gal. 2:11–14). This is one of those rare accounts in Scripture where two important church leaders clash. The two are Paul, the apostle, and Peter, here called Cephas. "But when Cephas came to Antioch, I opposed him to his face, because he stood condemned" (v. 11). Question: Why would Paul rebuke Peter? He tells us:

> For prior to the coming of certain men from James, he used to eat with the Gentiles; but when they came, he began to withdraw and hold himself aloof, fearing the party of the circumcision. (v. 12)

The New English Bible says, "He was in the habit of eating his meals with the Gentiles." That went on until the Jews showed up. And when they did . . . "Oh, no thanks, I never eat ham," lied Peter, hoping to make the Jews smile in approval. The problem was that before James and his Jewish friends arrived, ol' Peter could be heard saying to his Gentile cronies, "Sure, serve it up. Add a little bacon while you're at it. I love the taste!" Hypocrite!

I like Ralph Keiper's contemporary paraphrase of Paul's strong rebuke:

> "Peter, I smell ham on your breath. You forgot your Certs. There was a time when you wouldn't eat ham as part of your hope of salvation. Then after you trusted Christ, it didn't matter if you ate ham. But now when the no-ham eaters have come from Jerusalem you have gone back to your kosher ways. But the smell of ham still lingers on your breath. You are most inconsistent. You are compelling Gentile believers to observe Jewish law which can never justify anyone.
>
> "Peter, by returning to the law, you undercut strength for godly living."[9]

Paul saw through the duplicity and exposed the hypocrisy in Peter. In effect, he scolds, "The very idea, Peter, that you would fake it in front of Jews and then turn around and fake it in front of Gentiles. You're talking freedom, Peter, but you're not living it. Then out of the other side of your mouth, you're talking law, but you don't live that either. Get off the fence, Peter."

The problem intensified as others saw their leader and modeled his hypocritical lifestyle:

> And the rest of the Jews joined him in hypocrisy, with the result that even Barnabas was carried away by their hypocrisy. But when I saw that they were not straightforward about the truth of the gospel, I said to Cephas in the presence of all, "If you, being a Jew, live like the Gentiles and not like the Jews, how is it that you compel the Gentiles to live like Jews?" (vv. 13–14)

Why would Paul be so strong? Because people take their cues from their leaders. Sheep follow shepherds. And since legalistic hypocrisy never quietly dies on its own, it must be confronted. Again I remind you, liberty is always worth fighting for.

I know a man approaching sixty years of age today who is still haunted by the memory of being raised by hypocritical parents. It has taken him most of his adult life to face the full truth that he was emotionally and spiritually abused by their deception. Throughout his childhood his family attended a church where they were taught you shouldn't go to the movies. This was so firmly enforced that in Sunday church services people would be called to come forward to an altar and confess that they had done that or some other "sins." The problem is, his family usually went to movies on Friday or on Saturday night, always in secret. But they made it very clear that he shouldn't say anything about it. They drilled it into him, "Keep your mouth shut." Here he is, a little boy, being lectured on the way home from the theater, week after week, "Don't tell anybody on Sunday that we did this." Of course, they went to see the film miles away from the church so church folks wouldn't know. Not until recently has the man come to realize how damaging that hypocrisy was to his walk with Christ. Because they were not straightforward about the truth, no one should be surprised he picked up a lifestyle of deception and lying. Only lately, through the help of a fine Christian therapist, has he been able to sort through his confusion.

You want to mess up the minds of your children? Here's how—guaranteed! Rear them in a legalistic, tight context of external religion, where performance is more important than reality. Fake your faith. Sneak around and pretend your spirituality. Train your children to do the same. Embrace a long list of do's and don'ts publicly but hypocritically practice them privately . . . yet never own up to the fact that it's hypocrisy. Act one way but live another. And you can count on it— emotional and spiritual damage *will* occur. Chances are good their confusion will lead to some sort of addiction in later years.

By the way, before you're tempted to think that you'll never be guilty of hypocrisy, that you're above that sort of temptation, remember what Paul exposed in this letter to the Galatians. A spiritual leader as strong and stable as Peter fell into it. And with him, many others as well, "even Barnabas." Legalism is so subtle, so insidious. I have found that it's especially tempting to those whose temperament tends toward pleasing people, which brings us back to that wonderful verse that frees us, Galatians 1:10:

> For am I now seeking the favor of men, or of God? Or am I striving to please men? If I were still trying to please men, I would not be a bond-servant of Christ.

SPECIFYING FOUR STRONG STRATEGIES

Killers cannot be mildly ignored or kindly tolerated. You can no more allow legalism to continue than you could permit a rattlesnake to slip into your house and hide. Before long, somebody is going to get hurt. So then, since liberty is worth fighting for, how do we do it? Where can our personal grace awakening begin? I can think of four strong strategies:

1. *Keep standing firm in your freedom.* I'm reminded of what Paul wrote in Galatians 5:1: "It was for freedom that Christ set us free; therefore keep standing firm and do not be subject again to a yoke of slavery." Stand your ground. Ask the Lord to give you courage.

2. *Stop seeking the favor of everyone.* This may be a stubborn habit to break, but it is really worth all the effort you can muster. If you're in a group where you feel you are being coerced to do certain things

that are against your conscience or you're being pressured to stop doing things that you see no problem with, get out of the group! You're unwise to stay in situations where your conscience tells you it is not right. That is nothing more than serving men, not God. I don't care how spiritual sounding it may be, stop seeking the favor of every-body.

3. *Start refusing to submit to bondage.* Call it what it is: slavery. It's trying to be "spiritual" by performance. Think of how delightful it would be to get rid of all the anxiety that comes with the bondage to which you have submitted yourself; think how clean you could feel by being real again, or perhaps real for the first time in your adult life.

4. *Continue being straightforward about the truth.* That means live honestly. If you don't agree, say so kindly but firmly. If you are the only one, be true to yourself and stand alone. When you blow it, say, "I blew it." If you don't know, admit the truth. It's okay not to know. And the next time your kids spot hypocrisy, even though you may feel embarrassed, agree with them, "You know what, kids? You're right. I was a first-class hypocrite. What you saw and pointed out is exactly right." Tell them that. It may sound embarrassing to you now, but they will admire and respect your admission. And they won't grow up damaged. Best of all, they will learn to model the same kind of vul-nerability and honesty, even if you are in vocational Christian work . . . *especially if you're in vocational Christian work.* Nobody ex-pects perfection, but they do and they should expect honesty.

We need affirmation and encouragement to be all we're meant to be and because so many are rather delicate within, they need those who are strong to assist them in their fight for liberty. And so, if for no other reason, liberty is worth fighting for so others can breathe freely.

Paul Tournier writes of this in *Guilt and Grace:*

. . . in all fields, even those of culture and art, other people's judgment exercises a paralyzing effect. Fear of criticism kills spontaneity; it prevents men from showing themselves and expressing themselves freely, as they are. Much courage is needed to paint a picture, to write a book, to erect a building designed along new architectural lines, or to formulate an independent opinion or an original idea.[10]

If fighting for liberty sounds too aggressive to you, perhaps too selfish, then think of it as fighting so others can be set free—so others can be awakened to the joys and privileges of personal freedom. Those who do that on real battlefields are called patriots or heroes. With all my heart, I believe those who square off against legalism should be considered the same.

6

Emancipated?
Then Live Like It!

I HAVE NEVER WITNESSED SLAVERY. NOT IN raw reality. I have read about it, and I have seen films, plays, and television docudramas where slavery was portrayed in all its cruelty, but I have never seen it firsthand. I'm glad I haven't. I know of nothing more unjust or ugly. As an American I find it amazing—perhaps a better word is *confusing*—to think that my forefathers were willing to fight for their own freedom and win our country's independence, yet turn around and enslave others without the slightest hesitation. The triangles of such twisted logic are not mentally congruent—free citizens owning slaves.

It took a civil war to break that yoke. It called for a courageous, clear-thinking president to stand in the gap . . . to be misunderstood and maligned and ultimately killed for a cause that was, to him, not only worth fighting for but worth dying for.

At Abraham Lincoln's second inaugural in 1865, only weeks before he was assassinated, he spoke of how both parties "deprecated war," and yet a war had come. He continued:

Neither party expected for the war, the magnitude, or the duration, which it has already attained. . . . Each looked for an easier triumph. . . . Both read from the same Bible, and pray to the same God, and each invokes His aid against the other.[1]

At that point the reelected sixteenth president's voice broke, his feelings showing through. And he spoke of how strange it was "that any men should dare to ask a just God's assistance in wringing their bread from the sweat of other men's faces."[2]

Ultimately, with the adoption of the thirteenth amendment of the United States Constitution, slavery was legally abolished. It was then that black slaves all across America were officially set free. Long before that, however, and even before his second inaugural address, the president had stated his antislavery convictions in a proclamation that won him no favor in the South. It was on New Year's Day 1863 when the Emancipation Proclamation was publicly stated, but it was not until December 18, 1865, that the Constitution made those convictions official. Though dead by then, Lincoln still spoke. At last his dream was realized. The word swept across Capitol Hill and down into the valleys of Virginia and the back roads of the Carolinas and even deeper into the plantations of Georgia, Alabama, Mississippi, and Louisiana. Headlines on newspapers in virtually every state trumpeted the same message: "Slavery Legally Abolished."

And yet, something happened that many would have never expected. The vast majority of the slaves in the South who were legally freed continued to live on as slaves. Most of them went right on living as though nothing had happened. Though free, the Blacks lived virtually unchanged lives throughout the Reconstruction Period.

Shelby Foote, in his monumental, three-volume work on *The Civil War,* verifies this surprising anomaly.

. . . the Negro—locked in a caste system of "race etiquette" as rigid as any he had known in formal bondage . . . every slave could repeat with equal validity, what an Alabama slave had said in 1864 when asked what he thought of the Great Emancipator whose proclamation went into effect that year. "I don't know nothing bout Abraham Lincoln," he replied, "cep they say he sot us free. And I don't know nothing bout that neither."[3]

I call that tragic. A war had been fought. A president had been assassinated. An amendment to the Constitution had now been signed into law. Once-enslaved men, women, and children were now legally emancipated. Yet amazingly, many continued living in fear and squalor. In a context of hard-earned freedom, slaves chose to remain as slaves. Cruel and brutal though many of their owners were, black men and women chose to keep serving the same old master until they died. There were a few brave exceptions, but in many parts of the country you'd never have known that slavery had been officially abolished and that they had been emancipated. That's the way the plantation owners wanted it. They maintained the age-old philosophy, "Keep 'em ignorant and you keep 'em in the field."

Now if you think that is tragic, I can tell you one far worse. It has to do with Christians living today as slaves. Even though our Great Emancipator, Christ the Lord, paid the ultimate price to overthrow slavery once for all, most Christians act as though they're still held in bondage. In fact, strange as it is, most seem to prefer the security of slavery to the risks of liberty. And our slave master, Satan, loves it so. He is delighted that so many have bought into that lie and live under the dark shadow of such ignorance. He sits like the proverbial fat cat, grinning, "Great! Go right on livin' like a slave!" even though he knows we have been liberated from his control. More than most in God's family, the adversary knows we are free, but he hates it. So he does everything in his power to keep us pinned down in shame, guilt, ignorance, and intimidation.

REVIEWING SOME BASIC
THOUGHTS ON SLAVERY

Though some are well-informed about these facts I want to mention
regarding slavery in the spiritual realm, most aren't. Therefore, I
believe a brief review of some basics is necessary. Let's begin in the
"emancipation letter" of Romans.

> . . . as it is written,
> "There is none righteous, not even one;
> There is none who understands,
> There is none who seeks for God;
> All have turned aside, together they have become useless;
> There is none who does good,
> There is not even one."
> "Their throat is an open grave,
> With their tongues they keep deceiving,"
> "The poison of asps is under their lips;"
> "Whose mouth is full of cursing and bitterness;"
> "Their feet are swift to shed blood,
> Destruction and misery are in their paths,
> And the path of peace have they not known."
> There is no fear of God before their eyes."
> Now we know that whatever the Law says, it speaks to those who are
> under the Law, that every mouth may be closed, and all the world may
> become accountable to God; because by the works of the Law no flesh
> will be justified in His sight; for through the Law comes the knowledge
> of sin. (Rom. 3:10–20)

I find in Romans at least three analogies regarding slavery. The first
analogy is grim: *All of us were born in bondage to sin.* You wonder how
bad our slavery really was in our unsaved condition? Look back over
those words and observe for yourself:

- No one righteous
- No spiritual understanding
- No worthwhile achievements before God
- No purity, no innocence, no peace, no hope

On top of all that, we had no escape . . . we were unable to change our enslavement to sin. In that unsaved condition the lost person truly knows nothing about liberty.

The second analogy is glorious: *A day came when Christ set us free.* There came a day when an eternal Emancipation Proclamation was made known throughout the heavens and all the way to the pit of hell—"the sinner is officially set free!" It is the announcement that originated from Christ's empty tomb on that first Easter, the day our Great Emancipator, Christ, set us free. Doctrinally, the word is *redemption.* He redeemed us.

> But now apart from the Law the righteousness of God has been mani-
> fested, being witnessed by the Law and the Prophets, even the
> righteousness of God through faith in Jesus Christ for all those who be-
> lieve; for there is no distinction. (Rom. 3:21–22)

I love those last two words—"no distinction." To qualify for freedom, you don't have to be born in a certain country. You don't have to speak a certain language. Your skin doesn't have to be a certain color. You don't have to be educated or cultured or make a certain amount of money or fulfill some list of requirements. There is absolutely no distinction. Why? Because we were all slaves, slaves of our master and slaves of sin. "For all have sinned and fall short of the glory of God" (v. 23). Therefore, all sinners are "savable," if I may use that word. How? "Being justified as a gift by His grace through the redemption which is in Christ Jesus" (v. 24).

Let me explain this in nontechnical terms, staying with our word picture of slavery. Christ came on the scene and He saw every one of us on the slave block—lost, miserable, spiritually useless, and unable to change ourselves or escape from the bondage of our master. Moved by compassion and prompted by love, He, in grace, paid the price to free us. The price was His death. By doing so, He said to every one of us, in effect, "You don't have to live under your former master any longer. You're free. You're free to serve Me for the rest of your life."

Before Christ came into our lives, we were hopelessly lost in our lust, helpless to restrain our profanity, our glandular drives, our insatiable greed, our continual selfishness, or our compulsions either to please people or to control and manipulate others. While some of those things may have brought us feelings of pleasure and periodic satisfaction, our inability to control them was not without its complications. We were slaves! We were chained to the slave block, and we had to serve the old master. There was insufficient strength within us to live any other way. By "redeeming" us, Jesus set us free. When God raised Jesus from the dead (the crucial act of triumph over Satan), He said, in effect, "No one else need ever live as a victim of sin. All who believe in Jesus Christ, My Son, will have everlasting life and will have the power to live in Me." How could it be that wicked slaves could be given such standing before God? We're back to our favorite word: grace. To use terms everyone can understand, President Grace legally freed us from our lifelong master Sin and his wife Shame. Theoretically, we were freed when we believed in Christ, but practically speaking, our plantation owners do everything in their power to keep us ignorant, afraid, and thinking like a slave.

The third analogy I find in Romans 3 is tragic: *Many Christians still live as though they are enslaved.* When told they are free, some could easily respond like the Alabama slave: "I don't know anything about grace, except they say it set us free. And I don't know anything about that either." As a result of choosing to ignore the freedom Christ won for His own, many still live with a sin-oriented mentality. Most do, in fact.

It comes out in words like, "You know, I just can't help myself. I'm really not worth much; I'm only human." Instead of living above those constant references to failure and inadequacy and shamefulness, Christians too often resemble frightened and unsure religious slaves. Sometimes it emerges in other manifestations. We rationalize around our sin, we act hypocritically, occasionally we lie and cheat and steal. Then with a shrug we say, "Well, you know, man, nobody's perfect." In effect, we are saying, "I'm still enslaved. Sin still overpowers me. I'm so ashamed. But I just can't help it." Nonsense! When will we start living like those who are free? God says to every one of us, "Where sin abounded, grace superabounded. You were once enslaved to a passion, yes, but no longer . . . now you're free from that. You can live above it." Grace awakens, enlivens, and empowers our ability to conquer sin.

Are you ready for a maverick thought? Once we truly grasp the freedom grace brings, we can spend lengthy periods of our lives without sinning or feeling ashamed. Yes we can! And why not? Why should sin gain the mastery over us? Who says we cannot help but yield to it? How unbiblical! You see, most of us are so programmed to sin that we wait for it to happen.

To tell the truth, most Christians have been better trained to expect and handle their sin than to expect and enjoy their freedom. The shame and self-imposed guilt this brings is enormous, to say nothing of the "I'm defeated" message it reinforces. We begin the day afraid of sin. We live ashamed. We go to bed with a long list, ready to confess. If it isn't very long, we fear we've overlooked several "hidden sins." Maybe we've gotten proud.

What in the world has happened to grace? Furthermore, where is the abundant life Christ offered? Are freed people supposed to live such a frightened existence? Are we emancipated or not? If so, let's live like it! That isn't heresy, it's the healthiest kind of theology imaginable.

I can assure you, your old master doesn't want you to read this or think like this. He wants you to exist in the shack of ignorance, clothed in the rags of guilt and shame, and afraid of him and his whip. Like the cruel slave owner, he wants you to think you "gotta take a beatin' every now 'n' then" just so you will stay in line. Listen to me today: *That* is heresy! Because our Savior has set us free, the old master—the supreme grace killer—has no right whatsoever to put a whip to your back. Those days have ended, my friend. You're free. Those of us who are a part of *The Grace Awakening* refuse to live like slaves. We've been emancipated!

UNDERSTANDING THE THEMES OF LIBERTY

Turning a few pages further in the liberating letter of Romans, we arrive at Romans 6, one of the great chapters in all the Word of God. Having spent months studying this one chapter (and loving every minute of it!), I have come to realize it contains the Christian's Emancipation Proclamation. Here, as in no other section of Scripture, is the foundational truth of our liberty—freedom from Satan's intimidation and sin's domination. It is here all young Christians should spend their first hours in the Bible . . . not passages that tell us what to do once we sin (like 1 John 1:9) or how to restore our fellowship, important as those scriptures may be. No, it is *here* the believer discovers his or her freedom from sin's control and how to live on that victorious level above fear, guilt, shame, and defeat.

For the next few minutes, graze gently over the first fifteen verses of Romans 6. Take plenty of time; there is no hurry.

What shall we say then? Are we to continue in sin that grace might increase? May it never be! How shall we who died to sin still live in it? Or do you not know that all of us who have been baptized into Christ Jesus have been baptized into His death? Therefore we have been buried with Him through baptism into death, in order that as Christ was raised from the dead through the glory of the Father, so we too might walk in newness of life. For if we have become united with Him in the likeness of His death, certainly we shall be also in the likeness of His resurrection, knowing this, that our old self was crucified with Him, that our body of sin might be done away with, that we should no longer be slaves to sin; for he who has died is freed from sin. Now if we have died with Christ, we believe that we shall also live with Him, knowing that Christ, having been raised from the dead, is never to die again; death no longer is master over Him. For the death that He died, He died to sin, once for all; but the life that He lives, He lives to God. Even so consider yourselves to be dead to sin, but alive to God in Christ Jesus.

Therefore do not let sin reign in your mortal body that you should obey its lusts, and do not go on presenting the members of your body to sin as instruments of unrighteousness; but present yourselves to God as those alive from the dead, and your members as instruments of righteousness to God. For sin shall not be master over you, for you are not under law, but under grace.

What then? Shall we sin because we are not under law but under grace? May it never be!

Even a casual reading of these thoughts reveals two questions that get the same answer from the apostle. The questions may appear to be the same, but they are not.

What shall we say then? Are we to continue in sin that grace might increase? May it never be! (vv. 1–2a)

What then? Shall we sin because we are not under law but under grace? May it never be! (v. 15)

These two questions introduce two themes related to liberty. The first question addresses *those who fail to claim their liberty and continue to live like slaves*—those who *nullify* grace. (That theme is developed in the opening fourteen verses of Romans 6.)

The second question is addressed to *those who take their freedom too far* (vv. 15–23). In other words, they take advantage of their liberty. They live irresponsibly. Those who do that *abuse* grace (a subject I will address in the following chapter). Now, go back and read Romans 6 again and see if that doesn't make sense and help you understand the chapter better.

Paul, the writer, answers both questions with identical words, "May it never be!" Frankly, he is horrified. We could say what he says in similar ways:

- "By no means!"
- "Away with such a notion!"
- "Perish the thought!"
- "Never, never, never!"
- "What a ghastly thought!"

Paul's summary answer to the first question comes in the form of another question: "How shall we who died to sin still live in it?" (v. 2).

All it takes to appreciate that question is a brief mental trip back to our unsaved days. Many of you may recall that time with misery. Remember how you couldn't get control of your desires? Perhaps you helplessly dropped into bed night after night a victim of a habit that you couldn't conquer for the life of you. You recall the feeling that there was no hope at the end of a tunnel—no light. No matter what, you could not change, not permanently. Your slavery was an addiction at its worst. It was a prison from which no one could escape on his own. Remember how the shame increased and, at times, over-whelmed you? Others may have lived in the realm of freedom so long they've forgotten what it was like to be enslaved in the lost estate. If so, the following words will help:

> It is my earnest conviction that everyone should be in jail at least once in his life and that the imprisonment should be on suspicion rather than proof; it should last at least four months; it should seem hopeless; and preferably the prisoner should be sick half of the time. . . . Only by such imprisonment does he learn what real freedom is worth.[4]

Imagine being thrown in jail on suspicion of a charge, left there, virtually forgotten, while the system, ever so slowly, caught up with you. You get sick. You're treated harshly. Abused. Assaulted. Would you begin to entertain that feeling of lostness and hopelessness?

Back to the question: "How shall we who died to sin still live in it?" Who would volunteer to be dumped in a jail for another series of months, having been there and suffered the consequences of such a setting? His point: Then why would emancipated slaves who have been freed from sin and shame return to live under that same domination any longer?

"Yes, master. Yes, master. Don't hit me, ma'am . . . I'll be a good slave." Why, those words should make one gag, especially former slaves. You say, "I would never say such a thing!" Oh yes you would! We do every time we see ourselves as helpless victims of our urges and sin's tempting thoughts. I call it running scared of a master who no longer has any rights over me. How much better to say, "I refuse to live like that any longer. By the grace of Christ, I will live as a victor, not as a victim." Yes, you can live like that. Most, however, have been programmed to live another way.

I would venture to say that many who are Christians know 1 John 1:9 from memory: "If we confess our sins, He is faithful and righteous to forgive us our sins and to cleanse us from all unrighteousness." And yet, how few could quote Romans 6:13:

> And do not go on presenting the members of your body to sin as instruments of unrighteousness; but present yourselves to God as those alive from the dead, and your members as instruments of righteousness to God.

We have been programmed to think, *I know I am going to sin, to fail . . . to fall short today. Since this is true I need to be ready to find cleansing.* You have not been programmed to yield yourself unto God as those who have power over sin.

How much better to begin each day thinking victory, not defeat; to awake to grace, not shame; to encounter each temptation with thoughts like, *Jesus, You are my Lord and Savior. I am your child—liberated and depending on Your power. Therefore, Christ, this is Your day, to be lived for Your glory. Work through my eyes, my mouth, and through my thoughts and actions to carry out Your victory. And, Lord, do that all day long. When I face temptations, I will present myself to You and claim the strength You give to handle it. Sin has no authority over me any longer.*

Yes, I know there will be times when we may momentarily fail, but they will be the exceptions rather than the rule of our day. We are under new ownership. Prompted by love, we serve a new master, Christ, not the old one who mistreated us. There is something exciting about enjoying a relationship with our new Friend. But we won't until we put our "old man" in his place.

The late J. Vernon McGee told a memorable story when I was a student at Dallas Theological Seminary. He was bringing the Bible lectures on the letter to the Romans. His humorous illustrations were unforgettable, especially this one.

I remember sitting in Chafer Chapel as Dr. McGee was waxing eloquent on Romans 6. He told the story of a lady who lived in the Deep South and had a close relationship with her childhood sweetheart. She fell in love with him and ultimately married him. Their life together was not perfect, but it was rewarding. There was faithfulness and there were times of joy. This continued for years, until he was suddenly taken from her side by a heart attack. Not being able to part with him visibly, she decided to have him embalmed, put in a chair, sealed up in a glass case, and placed immediately inside the front door of their large plantation home. Every time she walked through the door, she smiled, "Hi, John, how are you?" Then she would walk right on up the stairs. Things rocked along as normally as possible month after month. There he sat day after day as she acknowledged his presence with a smile and friendly wave.

A year or so later she decided to take a lengthy trip to Europe. It was a delightful change of scenery. In fact, while in Europe she met a fine American gentleman who was also vacationing over there. He swept her off her feet. After a whirlwind romance, they got married and honeymooned all over Europe. She said nothing about ol' John back on the farm.

Finally, they traveled together back to the States. Driving up the winding road to her home, he decided, *This is my moment to lift my bride over the threshold and to carry her back into her home . . . this wonderful place where we'll live together forever.* He picked her up, bumped the door open with his hip, and walked right in. He almost dropped his bride on the floor!

"Who is this?"

"Well, that is John. He was my old man from—"

"He is *history;* he's dead!"

The new husband immediately dug a big hole and buried her former old man in it, case and all.

That's exactly what Christ has done! However, without realizing the effect, many Christians put the old man in a case and greet him every morning and cater to him every day of their lives. We live as though our "old man" is alive, even though we are dead to him. He has no right to be in our conscious thinking. We serve a new Master who has walked us across the threshold, who has awakened us to new life, new love, a new relationship, and an entirely different future.

Being creatures of habit, we still prefer the security of slavery to the risks of liberty. That is why the slaves stayed on the plantation, and that's why we continue to be sin-conscious . . . even more than Savior-conscious. We know down deep that He lives within us, that He has redeemed us; but most are at a loss to know how to get beyond the fear-failure-shame-confession syndrome. How is it possible to break the habit of serving the old master and start enjoying the benefits of being free under the new One?

CLAIMING OUR FREEDOM FROM
SIN'S CONTROL

In this wonderful sixth chapter of Romans, Paul presents three techniques for living by grace, above sin's domination. I find each one linked to a particular term he uses:

Know—"Or do you not know that all of us who have been baptized into Christ Jesus have been baptized into His death? . . . knowing this, that our old self was crucified with Him, that our body of sin might be done away with, that we should no longer be slaves to sin; . . . knowing that Christ, having been raised from the dead, is never to die again; death no longer is master over Him" (vv. 3, 6, 9).

Consider—"Even so consider yourselves to be dead to sin, but alive to God in Christ Jesus" (v. 11).

Present—"And do not go on presenting the members of your body to sin as instruments of unrighteousness; but present yourselves to

God as those alive from the dead, and your members as instruments of righteousness to God" (v. 13).

In order for us to live free from sin's control, free from the old master, with the power to walk a new kind of life, we have to *know* something, we have to *consider* something, and we have to *present* something.

Candidly, Romans 6 is not easy and entertaining. Understanding it is not Saturday-morning cartoons on the tube; we will have to think. So for the next few minutes I'll do my best to make it clear and keep it interesting as we answer three questions in the balance of this chapter. What is it that you and I have to know? What is it that you and I have to consider? And what is it that you and I have to present?

Let's start with *knowing.*

> Or do you not know that all of us who have been baptized into Christ Jesus have been baptized into His death? Therefore we have been buried with Him through baptism into death, in order that as Christ was raised from the dead through the glory of the Father, so we too might walk in newness of life. For if we have become united with Him in the likeness of His death, certainly we shall be also in the likeness of His resurrection, knowing this, that our old self was crucified with Him, that our body of sin might be done away with, that we should no longer be slaves to sin; for he who has died is freed from sin. (vv. 3–7)

To understand what this is all about, we have to set aside the concept of water baptism and understand that this is a reference to dry baptism. Some baptisms in the New Testament are *wet* and some of them are *dry.* This one is in the latter category.

The word *baptizo* primarily has to do with identification. It was a term that was used in the first century for dipping a light-colored garment into a dye that was, let's say, scarlet. Once the fabric was dipped into the scarlet dye, it would be changed in its identity from its original color to scarlet. The act of dipping it, resulting in changing its identity, was called *baptizo*. It is the Greek term from which we get our English word *baptism*.

Christ died for us on the cross. He was raised from the dead for us at the tomb. When we believed in the Savior's death and resurrection, we were "dipped" into the same scene. Our identity was changed. We didn't feel it, we didn't see it, we didn't hear it, but it occurred, nevertheless. When we came to Christ, we were placed into Him as His death became ours, His victorious resurrection became ours, His "awakening" to new life became our "awakening," His powerful walk became our powerful walk. Before we can experience the benefits of all that, we have to *know* it. The Christian life is not stumbling along, hoping to keep up with the Savior. He lives in me and I live in Him. And in this identification with Him, His power becomes mine. His very life becomes my life, guaranteeing that His victory over sin is mine to claim. I no longer need to live as a slave to sin.

> Now if we have died with Christ, we believe that we shall also live with Him, knowing that Christ, having been raised from the dead, is never to die again; death no longer is master over Him. For the death that He died, He died to sin, once for all; but the life that He lives, He lives to God. (vv. 8–10)

You will meet well-meaning Christians who teach about crucifying oneself. But I have good news for you: That has already been done. You are in Christ. He was crucified once for all. He died for you so you never need to die again. Because we have our identification with Him, we have all the power needed to live the rest of our lives above the drag and dregs of slavery. Death to sin is an accomplished act, a finished fact. Theoretically, it has all been taken care of. A victorious walk begins with our *knowing* this fact. Christ's "Emancipation Proclamation" has put to death the whole idea of slavery to sin. Having died to sin's power, we are now free to serve our new Master.

I love the story of the missionary who sailed from Liverpool to serve Christ along the African coast. He changed vessels at Lagos. He boarded a coastal tugboat to make his way into a fever-infested region where he would invest the rest of his life. While changing vessels, he came upon a cynical old slave trader who looked critically on the man's decision by saying, "If you go to that place, you will die." The missionary, a devoted Christian, replied softly, "I died before I ever left Liverpool."[5]

Not until you and I *know* that we are dead to sin's control and alive to God's power through Christ will we live like victors, not victims.

Next, Romans 6:11 tells us there is something we must *consider:* "Even so consider yourselves to be dead to sin, but alive to God in Christ Jesus." The word *consider* is crucial. It is from a Greek word that means "to calculate, to take into account, to figure." It is a financial term, an accounting term. Rather than meaning "act like it is so," it means "reckon it true. Enter it in the ledger. Record it in the creases of your brain." What exactly are we to calculate? Namely this: We are *in Christ,* dead to sin's power. And Christ is in us, releasing God's *new* power.

And the result of such calculating? "Therefore do not let sin reign in your mortal body that you should obey its lusts" (v. 12).

By calculating (considering) all of this and by taking into account the truth we know to be a fact, we *dethrone* sin and refuse to obey our lusts any longer. The flip side of this truth is equally liberating. Even when we do sin, when we occasionally fail, God's interest is not in flailing us as slaves, screaming, "You ought to be ashamed!" but in forgiving us as His dear children.

While speaking at a week-long conference last year, I was introduced to a twenty-four-year-old woman. She was visibly uneasy and tearful. As we talked it was obvious that she was riddled with guilt, overcome with shame. She could hardly maintain eye contact. I soon learned she had been promiscuous in her past. A couple or three years prior to our meeting, she had become a Christian. As she became increasingly more interested in spiritual things, her past returned to haunt her. Within recent weeks she began to be tortured with shame and the accompanying fear that either God would judge her or she would fall back into that old lifestyle.

The more we talked the clearer it became that she genuinely believed in and loved the Lord . . . but she knew nothing of the truth of Romans 6. Her major problem? She failed to understand grace. She did not realize that her secure position in Christ left her with nothing to fear, absolutely nothing to be ashamed of. I turned to this great section of Scripture and read it to her, pausing periodically and explaining what she needed to "know" and what she needed to "reckon as true." Time and again she interrupted and reminded me of her past, which intensified her feelings of shame. Her face reflected an inner battle. Her old master didn't want to let her go. He stubbornly clung to her, using fear to immobilize her. Each time I reminded her of God's forgiveness in Christ . . . of her new position by grace . . . and of her need to see herself as free, no longer enslaved. I must have said those words a half-dozen times. Finally, the light dawned. She forgave herself (a giant step toward accepting grace) and she claimed her freedom. The woman was aglow with radiance the rest of the week. She had been transformed in her mind from a slave, full of shame and disgrace, to one who was free, liberated from the enemy's oppressive desire to keep her defeated. Instead of beginning each day in dreadful fear, she began to focus on being free from her old master. Rather than thinking, "My sin, my shame, my failure," she remembered, "His forgiveness, His grace, His life." The change in her countenance was nothing short of remarkable. By Friday she had the most obvious "Yes" face at the conference.

In our great state of California there are many picturesque roads and highways through mountainous areas. Though some are narrow and a bit treacherous, all of them lead through sights that are breathtakingly beautiful. Those who have driven the Pacific Coast Highway, Highway 1, can never forget the incredible natural scenes that stretch along the craggy coastline from Los Angeles to San Francisco. A few of the curves are especially dangerous and must be driven slowly and with great care. There are treacherous drop-offs, which add both to the beauty and to the danger of the journey.

It occurred to me that our state could offer two options to travelers along these dangerous mountain roads. First, the state could build very well-equipped clinics at the bottom of those high elevations where the narrow roads twist and turn. Every sharp curve could be provided with a clinic down below. When speeding drivers went over the side and tumbled down the cliff, those in the clinic would be there to rescue and treat them. Second, the state could erect very clear, well-placed signs before each sharp curve, reading *"Danger! Curve Ahead. Drive Slowly.* "You are not surprised to know that the highway department chose the second option, not the first. Smart plan.

We should learn from that decision. First John 1:9 is the corrective clinic at the bottom of the hill. It rescues and treats us, which is wonderful, but it's not the best alternative. Romans 6, on the other hand, is preventive counsel, providing the signs: "No need to crash . . . slow down . . . danger ahead." We must calculate the importance of these spiritual "signs" and reckon them as true.

This brings us to the third crucial term: *Present.*

> And do not go on presenting the members of your body to sin as instruments of unrighteousness; but present yourselves to God as those alive from the dead, and your members as instruments of righteousness to God. For sin shall not be master over you, for you are not under law, but under grace. (vv. 13–14)

Not only must there be intelligent calculation ("consider") based on true information ("know"), there has to be a conscious *presentation* of ourselves to God. Paul spells that out in two simple commands.

Negatively. "Do not go on presenting the members of your body to sin as instruments of unrighteousness." Why? Because we aren't slaves any more. Our bodies are not helpless victims of lustful urges and uncontrollable weaknesses. Those days ended when we became Christians. Remember, we've been emancipated!

Positively: "But present yourselves to God as those alive from the dead. . . . For sin shall not be master over you."

Since we have been emancipated, it is high time we start living like it. I remind you that our adversary doesn't want us to think like this. He would erase grace immediately if he could. But since he cannot, his strategy is to do everything in his power to deceive us into thinking like slaves. Why? Because when we start operating like free men and women, our old "master" can no longer control us.

A NECESSARY WARNING

I would love to tell you that change is easy, but I cannot. Old habits are terribly difficult to break. Thinking correctly takes courage. Furthermore, our adversary, Satan, won't back off easily. Neither will the legalists he uses. If you think the plantation slave owners following the Civil War were determined to keep their slaves, I'm here to tell you that today's grace killers are even more stubborn than they were. Count on it, the enemies of our souls despise this message of freedom. They hate grace, so be warned. In order for you to leave the security of slavery and ignorance and walk out into the new, risky fields of freedom and grace, you will need courage and inner resolve. My prayer is that God will give you an abundance of both. You're not alone in your quest for freedom. There are a lot of us taking this journey with you. There is a "grace awakening" beginning in the hearts of God's people.

The sixteenth president made a comment shortly after the Emancipation Proclamation was passed by Congress early in 1863. Sounding more like Captain Ahab in Melville's novel *Moby Dick* than Abraham Lincoln delivering a speech, he warned:

> We are like whalers who have been on a long chase. We have at last got the harpoon into the monster, but we must now look how we steer, or with one flop of his tail he will send us all into eternity.[6]

The president proved himself a prophet with those words. His proclamation resulted in an escalation of the Civil War. He was absolutely correct. The declaration of freedom brought on even greater struggles and more bloodshed.

Such a warning is necessary. Who knows what battles you will encounter now that you have determined to live emancipated rather than enslaved? But the good news for many of you is this: At last we have gotten the harpoon into the monster. Now we must steer carefully and watch out for that wicked tail.

7

Guiding Others to Freedom

AN UNEXPECTED SHIFT OF ATTENTION occurred during the presidential campaign in the fall of 1988. Instead of the evening news focusing on the Democratic and the Republican candidates, all eyes were on two California whales up in Alaska, trapped in a breathing hole many miles from the ocean.

Strange as it may seem, Bush and Dukakis were upstaged by "Bonnett" and "Crossbeak," the names biologists gave the whales.

It all started when the gentle giants of the sea overlooked the fact that winter arrived early that year in northern Alaska. This mistake left them trapped, stranded inland by the ever-increasing covering of solid ice that prevented them from swimming to freedom.

At first few bothered to notice . . . only a few compassionate Eskimos who decided the creatures needed help. In a rather primitive fashion they hauled their chain saws and dragged long poles to the site and began to gouge out ice holes, enabling the whales to breathe en route to open water. Crude, rugged, and tiresome though the work was, they were determined to work their way toward the open ocean.

The weather wasn't cooperating. During some of the days, the temperature dropped below zero. That meant the small band of rescuers had to add some water-churning devices to keep the surface of the water from freezing over, especially during the screaming winds of the night. Interest in the project intensified once it caught the attention of the media. Other volunteers joined in the rescue efforts. Because the original plan wasn't moving along fast enough, in rolled an "Archimedean Screw Tractor," an enormous eleven-ton vehicle that rode on two screw-shaped pontoons, resembling something taken from a sci-fi movie set. That clumsy behemoth would clear away the ice after it was broken up and push it aside inch by inch, slowly grinding out a pathway to the sea. But that was also too slow and tedious. Next came the National Guard, who brought in two CH-54 Skycrane helicopters that systematically dropped five-ton concrete bashers onto the ice, mile after mile, so the journey to freedom could be accelerated.

If you can believe it, the Soviets arrived next, having dispatched two of their ships to the scene. One was a mammoth twenty-ton, eleven-story-tall icebreaker, and the other a smaller vessel with similar equipment. Interestingly, two flags flew on the stern of the Russian ships. Perhaps for the first and only time, the United States' stars and stripes flew alongside the familiar hammer and sickle. All political contrasts, economic differences, and military conflicts were set aside for this unusual mission . . . so a couple of whales could be free. Eureka! It finally happened at Point Barrow, Alaska. The world cheered as the exhausted creatures silently slipped out to sea.

Frankly, I found it a nice diversion from the presidential race. We got a chance to look at two new faces and see some unusual scenery. Instead of mudslinging, there was ice gouging. Rather than caustic comments, there was mutual cooperation. We felt good inside. There was something gallant and clean and beautiful about the whole thing.

Even though it evolved into an expensive project—over $1.5 million during a three-week period—and even though the sixty-mile pathway was grueling, the shift in emphasis was refreshing.

It occurred to me a few days after the rescue project ended that we had been observing a strange phenomenon. I thought of the contrast between what we are willing to do as human beings for whales and yet what we're not willing to do for one another. There they were, two huge denizens of the deep, with whom we cannot intelligently communicate, yet we will risk life and limb, spend an enormous amount of money, expend tireless energy in subzero weather for as long as it takes so that they can go free—and that is all well and good. What stunned me was how little effort we are willing to put forth to help another human being find freedom in God's family.

When it comes to providing personal freedom so others can breathe free and enjoy an ocean of endless possibilities, we're not nearly so cooperative. Isn't it strange? Most seem to prefer restricting and resisting someone's getting to freedom rather than helping that person along. Nations are willing to set aside vast ideological differences and cooperate in a joint effort to do whatever is necessary to help the natural world breathe free, but when it comes to the Christian community's assisting one of its own to find true freedom, well, that's another story. Cruel as it may sound, there are grace killers throughout this world, who are plugging up breathing holes and trapping people under the ice pack of their manipulations and rigid controls. What is so unbelievably tragic is they continue doing so, even if it cripples or kills the spirit of a fellow human being. We'll free the whales, but not one another.

With all this talk about grace and liberty, perhaps it's time for me to clarify something. Some may be asking: Doesn't liberty have its limits? Shouldn't folks restrain their freedom and occasionally hold themselves in check? Yes, without question. Grace can be—and sometimes is—abused. By that I mean exercising one's liberty without wisdom . . . having no concern over whether it offends or wounds a young and impressionable fellow believer. But I must hasten to add that I believe such restraint is an individual matter. It is not to be legislated, not something to be forced on someone else. Limitations are appropriate and necessary, but I fail to find in Scripture any place where one is to require such restraint from another. To do so is legalism. It plugs up breathing holes. It kills grace. The best restraint is self-restraint that comes from the inner prompting of the Holy Spirit through the person and presence of Jesus Christ in each individual life. It's been my observation over the last thirty years that the vast majority of believers need to be freed, not restrained. Our job is to free people; God's job is to restrain them. God is doing His job much better than we are doing ours.

WONDERFUL TRUTHS REGARDING FREEDOM

I like to think of certain verses in Scripture as those that help us breathe. By that I mean they encourage true freedom. They liberate! I suggest that all who wish to be free—truly free from bondage traps and legalistic prisons—read these verses again and again and again. I would suggest you type them on three-by-five cards and tape them to your bathroom mirror. Read them aloud each morning. They will help awaken grace within you on a daily basis. Here are a few that I often quote and claim.

It was for freedom that Christ set us free. . . . (Gal. 5:1)

For he who has died is freed from sin. (Rom. 6:7)

For the law of the Spirit of life in Christ Jesus has set you free. . . . (Rom. 8:2)

What then shall we say to these things? If God is for us, who is against us? He who did not spare His own Son, but delivered Him up for us all, how will He not also with Him freely give us all things? (Rom. 8:31–32)

"... and you shall know the truth, and the truth shall make you free." (John 8:32)

"If therefore the Son shall make you free, you shall be free indeed." (John 8:36)

More such verses will come to your attention as you begin to see the subject of freedom emerging from Scripture. For example, Paul writes Timothy that God "richly supplies us with all things to enjoy" (1 Tim. 6:17). I can't think of a greater mission in life than helping others know how to *enjoy* the life God has supplied. To be honest, that is one of my life goals . . . to help others *enjoy* life.

Some of you are engaged in a counseling ministry. And unless I miss my guess, helping others relax and enjoy living is one of your constant assignments and delights. I commend you and encourage you to help your counselees find the freedom that they need. Once they have dealt with their sins correctly, urge them to lift the veil of guilt and draw in the rusty anchor of shame that has ensnared them long enough. Such weights become galling, unbearable. They smother. They strangle. They stifle. They ultimately *bury*. Don't stop opening those breathing holes! No matter how long it takes, stay at it, fellow Christian.

You don't have to be a professional counselor to help others. Make it your aim to help your trapped friends to freedom. You may be their only defense and protection from the grace killers. I can tell you without hesitation that one of my major goals for the rest of my years in ministry is to provide more and more breathing holes for fellow ministers who have lost the joy of freedom, who know little of the charm of grace. If anybody needs to breathe free, to join *The Grace Awakening*, those in vocational Christian service do!

There are breathing holes throughout God's Word. I'm thinking of that huge hole Paul broke open in his letter to the Corinthians:

> Eat anything that is sold in the meat market, without asking questions for conscience sake; FOR THE EARTH IS THE LORD'S AND ALL IT CONTAINS. If one of the unbelievers invites you, and you wish to go, eat anything that is set before you, without asking questions for conscience' sake. But if anyone should say to you, "This is meat sacrificed to idols," do not eat it, for the sake of the one who informed you, and for conscience' sake; I mean not your own conscience, but the other man's; for why is my freedom judged by another's conscience? If I partake with thankfulness, why am I slandered concerning that for which I give thanks? (1 Cor. 10:25–30)

First Corinthians 10 centers attention on eating meat. In those days the premier taboo was not going to the movies or wearing cosmetics or dancing or playing cards. Back then the major question was this: Should Christians eat meat that had been offered to idols? That needs some explanation.

In ancient pagan worship, portions of meat were offered to idols. Some of the carcass, however, was left over, which was sold in a meat market. It was perfectly good meat. There were Christians back then who had no qualms about buying that meat in the meat market. Others who were young and recently converted out of an idol-worshiping lifestyle felt they should not do that. They reasoned like this: "That is meat that has been offered to idols. We shouldn't buy it or eat it. Its association with an idol temple and pagan worship contaminates the meat." Paul writes to say, in effect, "Meat isn't contaminated because the other part of the animal was sacrificed on a pagan altar. There's no way that some idol of wood or stone could contaminate a piece of meat." Which explains why he says, "Eat anything that is sold in the meat market. . . ." The apostle felt free to eat it even though others did not.

Look again at verse 27: "If one of the unbelievers invites you, and you wish to go, eat anything that is set before you. . . ." Paul is digging an ice hole. He is setting believers free. They don't have to worry about the meat served in an unbeliever's home. If the unbeliever is going to have barbecued steak, great! Eat up and don't ask questions.

Paul also makes some wise comments about times when it is best to restrain; but the overall general rule is to eat the meat. "The grace of God says you can eat it," implies the Apostle of Grace. So enjoy! Some, however, don't feel the same freedom, but they have no reason to slander those who eat.

And Paul says the same thing here. Look at verse 30: "If I partake with thankfulness, why am I slandered concerning that for which I give thanks?" That's a great question. In asking it he breaks open another breathing hole. And he states his case rather boldly: "Why do you slander me because I happen to enjoy eating the meat that is served? Some go for certain kinds of meat, others for another."

A funny thing happened to me recently. One of the sound-and-light people at the church where I pastor (a real character!) heard me teach on this subject. A couple of weeks later he pulled a gag on me. With an impish grin he said, "You had a birthday recently, didn't you?" I nodded yes. He said, "You're originally from Texas, right?" By now I knew I was in for something! "Yep," I answered. He said, "Well, I have something for you." He put a small can in my hand about the size of a can of snuff. It was a can of armadillo meat. I groaned. The label read, "Pure Texas Armadillo—sun-dried and road-tenderized." The ingredients were printed on the other side: "Pure sun-dried armadillo, run over by a log truck three miles south of Pollok, Texas. Not over twenty percent hair and gravel. May contain foreign matter."

He told me that since I was such a believer in grace, I was free to eat it. I thought, *Whoa! This will gag a maggot!* My point? Because of grace, my friend can eat armadillo and I can eat armadillo. It's okay. It's fine if he wishes to, but it so happens that God has led me *not* to eat armadillo. (It's that "foreign matter" that concerns me.) But if you want to eat armadillo, that's great! Personally, I have my own personal list of dietary don'ts (which includes armadillo). You may not have that on your list, so in good Texas fashion, "git at it." I promise, I will not slander you or judge you as you munch on all that hair and gravel.

What in the world is all this about? Let me give it to you straight. Don't give me your personal list of do's and don'ts to live by! And you can count on this: I will never give you my personal list of do's and don'ts to follow! Being free means you have no reason whatsoever to agree with my personal list; nor should you slander me because it isn't exactly like yours. That is one of the ways Christians can live in harmony. It is called living by grace . . . and it is the only way to fly.

Now you say, "Well, what if we find a list in Scripture?" That is a very different issue! Any specified list in Scripture is to be obeyed without hesitation or question. That's an inspired list for all of us to follow, not someone's personal list. Let me encourage you to guide your life by any and all Scripture with all of your heart, regardless of how anyone else may respond. But when questionable things aren't specified in Scripture, it then becomes a matter of one's personal preference or convictions. I'll say more about that later.

God has given His children a wonderful freedom in Christ, which means not only freedom from sin and shame but also a freedom in lifestyle, so that we can become models of His grace. Being free, enjoying your liberty, and allowing others the same enjoyment is hard to do if you're insecure. It is especially hard to do if you were raised by legalistic parents and led by legalistic pastors with an oversensitive conscience toward pleasing everyone. Those kinds of parents and pastors can be ultra-controlling, manipulative, and judgmental. Frequently, they use the Bible as a hammer to pound folks into submission rather than as a guide to lead others into grace. Sometimes it takes years for people who have been under a legalistic cloud to finally have the courage to walk freely in the grace of God. Unfortunately, some who finally grasp this freedom go so far in it they abuse the grace of God by flaunting their liberty.

That can be just as tragic as those who don't go far enough. To return to one of my favorite words, we need the *balance*.

In the previous chapter, I referred to the first part of Romans 6. In this chapter, let's focus on the second part of that chapter. But first I'd like to look again at the two questions around which Romans 6 revolves. The questions may sound alike, but they are not the same.

First Question

What shall we say then? Are we to continue in sin that grace might increase? (Rom. 6:1)

Earlier, in Romans 5:20, we read "where sin increased, grace abounded all the more." The question that would logically follow such a statement is the one Paul asks in 6:1, which could be paraphrased, "Should we continue living under the domination of sin so that grace might superabound more and more?" And he answers with gusto: "Perish the thought!"

As we've already discovered, the first question has to do with those who fail to live in freedom. They choose sin as their dominating master. Those Christians who live like that every day are overly conscious and sensitive to sin. They fear failing. Shame dominates their thinking. In essence, they focus so clearly on sin that they set themselves up for failure. Instead of concerning themselves with the positive benefits of serving Christ and enjoying the liberty He has provided, they continue living under the domination of their old nature.

By living like that, we develop a "worst-case" mentality. That is like my taking my keys and handing them over to one of my teenagers who just got a driver's license and saying, "Now let me remind you, you're going to have a wreck. So the first thing you need to do is memorize the phone number of our car insurance agent. That way, when you have an accident, you can be sure to call the right number. But here are the keys. Hope you enjoy the drive."

What a weird, negative piece of counsel. Yet that's what we do with young Christians. "Listen, you need to know *you're going to sin.* And so you've really got to watch out. Memorize 1 John 1:9, okay? That way *when* you sin you'll know what to do." How seldom (if ever) young believers are told, "You know what? You no longer have to serve sin. You can actually live several days without it, perhaps a week or more. The reason is you've got a new Master—Christ. And you know what else? You have a power down inside of you, one you never had before, called the Holy Spirit. And you have a set of keys called the Scriptures. So when you engage the key in the ignition correctly, you can enjoy a life like you've never enjoyed before. There may be times when you may have an accident. There will be times when sins do occur. When they do, let me tell you how to handle it. But remember: That's not the norm, that's the exception. The good news is that you have freedom from the old master because of Christ." Grace has set us free! We have been emancipated.

Talk about opening up breathing holes! What if someone had told us that? Could we have grown? Would we have found the ocean? I mean, with people cutting holes like that for us, we would have been swimming free, out in the depths, within a matter of months! When grace awakens, hope and joy dominate our days.

Second Question

What then? Shall we sin because we are not under law but under grace? May it never be! (Rom. 6:15)

This question may look the same, but it is quite different from the first. This one asks, "Shall we deliberately sin now because we're not under law, but under grace?" In other words, why not just go full bore? Pull out all the stops? "Not under law" must mean "I'm strictly on my own. Why not eat, drink, and have a blast? I'm under grace!" Some have misread it to mean just that. As a result, they rationalize their way around deliberate acts of disobedience. I have seen folks go off the deep end so far they convince themselves it is okay to disobey specific scriptural statements or principles, dissolve their marriages, walk away from prior commitments, and choose another partner. When asked how they could justify such irresponsible behavior, almost without exception they refer to grace, as though it is the God-given, pervasive covering for whatever they please. Twisting Scripture to accommodate our desires has nothing to do with grace.

Such rationalization is freedom gone to seed, liberty without limits . . . which is nothing more than disobedience in another dress. Some may see it as amazing grace; I call it abusing grace. Those who do so not only live confused and get hurt, they confuse and hurt others. And that's what the latter half of Romans 6 is about: being so determined to fly free that you abuse the very freedom you've been given. We are wise to think of grace as a privilege to be enjoyed and protected, not a license to please ourselves.

CAREFUL WARNING TO ALL
WHO ARE FREE

Even those who live in a free country need warnings. So we shouldn't be surprised that God gives His own a few warnings lest we abuse our privileges as people under grace. These warnings are set forth in verses 16 through 23 of Romans 6. None of them is complicated, but to grasp each one we'll need to concentrate. For some reason, this information is not commonly heard in many churches today. So we must be taught to handle grace rather carefully.

An overall principle is woven into the words of verse 16:

> Do you not know that when you present yourselves to someone as slaves for obedience, you are slaves of the one whom you obey, either of sin resulting in death, or of obedience resulting in righteousness?

If you were to ask me to give you in one sentence what the balance of chapter 6 is teaching, it would be this: *How we live depends on the master we choose.* "Do you not know that when you present yourselves to someone as slaves for obedience, you are slaves of the one whom you obey. . . ."Why, of course! Submission to a master is tantamount to slavery to the same master. And what are the alternatives?

There are only two: ". . . either of sin resulting in death, or of obedience resulting in righteousness?" Every day we live, we have a choice to do what is right or what is wrong. When we send our young children off to school, we tell them, "Now, sweetheart, you need to know that Mom and Dad won't be there to make your decisions. You will find some kids at school who will encourage you to do what is right and you'll find others who will lead you to disobey and do what is wrong. Make the right choice. Select your friends carefully. Be smart."

We would say in terms of Romans 6, "Serve the right master. Link up with righteousness." You see, before the Savior was present in our lives; we had no choice. We were all trapped under the ice. Breathing free wasn't an option. There was no way we could find freedom, no way to enjoy the ocean depths of righteousness. We were enslaved to wrong, lawlessness, selfishness, wicked choices, and impure motives. When Christ came, He freed us, leaving us with a choice. We can choose Him to be our Master, or we can go back and choose sin to master us.

As J. B. Phillips states it: "You belong to the power which you choose to obey." It's that simple. Each moment of every day we choose whom we wish to follow. If it's the Savior, the benefits are many. If it is sin, the consequences are destructive and miserable. Then where does grace enter in to this equation? Quite simply, grace makes the choice possible.

Before Christ, we had no choice. Sin was our one and only route. All of life was marked by unrighteousness. But once we came to the Cross and gave the Lord Jesus the right to rule our lives, we were granted a choice we never had before. Grace freed us from the requirement to serve sin, allowing us the opportunity to follow Christ's directives voluntarily. So as long as we do this, *we will not sin!* But as soon as you or I compromise with His mastery over us, the old master stands ready to lure us into sin.

I wish I could guarantee all of us full freedom from sin 365 days a year, but that is not possible—not so long as we are earthbound. Perpetual sinlessness (theologians call it "sinless perfection") will not be ours to enjoy until we are given glorified bodies and we are at home in heaven. But the good news is that we don't have to sin on a constant, day-after-day basis. Grace has freed us to obey Christ.

> But thanks be to God that though you were slaves of sin, you became obedient from the heart to that form of teaching to which you were committed, and having been freed from sin, you became slaves of righteousness. (vv. 17–18)

Wonderful, wonderful truth! Choosing righteousness, we enjoy a lifestyle marked by God's blessings, stability, and strength. All of which seem to multiply. But have you discovered, as I have, that when you choose wrong, you adopt a lifestyle that gets increasingly worse? Let me show you from Scripture how true that is. Proverbs 5:21 states: "For the ways of a man are before the eyes of the Lord, / And He watches all his paths."

Let's imagine that Frank is a Christian. Though he knows better, Frank chooses to fall under the dominating sway and authority of his own nature—sinfulness. He deliberately decides to disobey, which he's free to do. Even though the Lord could intervene, He permits Frank, in grace, the freedom to choose. Look at what happens.

> His own iniquities will capture the wicked,
> And he will be held with the cords of his sin.
> He will die for lack of instruction,
> And in the greatness of his folly he will go astray.
>   (Prov. 5:22–23)

What a word picture! We usually think of this situation as applicable only to an unbeliever. But it could just as easily be applied to a Christian who deliberately chooses to disobey his Lord. And instead of seeing the error of his way, he stays in a state of carnality, which grieves the Spirit of God living within him. Carnality occurs when a believer deliberately operates in the strength of his or her own will . . . stubbornly refusing to acknowledge wrong and choosing to walk contrary to the teachings of Scripture. The promptings of God's Spirit are ignored as disobedience becomes a lifestyle. Choosing to live like that is like getting caught in a whirlpool. The wickedness intensifies. It gets more treacherous as Frank goes deeper into it, until he finds himself less sensitive to it, and before long he is sucked into a kind of black hole of waywardness. Like the Prodigal Son, he winds up in misery and filth. And that is exactly where some Christians find themselves today. There aren't many places on earth more miserable. Actually, Frank could die in that condition, tragic as it may be. Some in Corinth did: "For this reason many among you are weak and sick, and a number sleep (1 Cor. 11:30). Yes, some refused to return by confession and repentance, and it resulted in physical death.

Admittedly, many carnal Christians excuse such a lifestyle by saying, "It's all under grace. I can leave my wife and walk away from our children and marry someone else who is more attractive and will love me more passionately. It may not be accepted by some in the Christian community, but under grace I am free to do that. After all, the lady I'm marrying is a Christian, too. We're both under grace!" Or "My preference is to live with this person, not marry him. I'm not into a long-term commitment and vows. Grace gives me the liberty to do as I please!" Wrong! That isn't what grace is about. That is an abuse of grace.

Grace never means we're free to live any way we wish, whatever the consequences. Grace does not mean God will smile on me, regardless. It means I'm free to choose righteousness or disobedience. If I choose the latter I will have to take the consequences: mental anguish, a guilty conscience, hurting and offending others in the Christian community, and bringing reproach to the name of Christ. If righteousness is spurned, sin can multiply much the same way as it did in our unsaved days. The Christian can be temporarily addicted to sin. As I have mentioned before, it is called carnality. I would encourage you to make a serious study of carnality, because you will encounter it throughout your Christian life and you will discover how easy it is to get caught in its trap. As one man writes:

> Sin begets sin. The first time we do a wrong thing, we may do it with hesitation, and a tremor and a shudder. The second time we do it, it is easier; and if we go on doing it, it becomes effortless; sin loses its terror. To start on the path of sin is to go on to more and more. [1]

I am emphasizing this not to be negative, but to sound a necessary warning. We need to pass it on to those we wish to guide into freedom. As we begin to stretch our wings in grace, enjoying new freedom, new depths and new heights, we will be wise never to forget our primary goal in life: to glorify and please God. God grants you grace . . .

So that you may walk in a manner worthy of the Lord, to please Him in all respects, bearing fruit in every good work and increasing in the knowledge of God; strengthened with all power, according to His glorious might, for the attaining of all steadfastness and patience; joyously giving thanks to the Father, who has qualified us to share in the inheritance of the saints in light. (Col. 1 :10–12)

Before we came to the Cross by faith, we couldn't please God. Now that the Cross has cast its shadow over our lives and Christ's blood has cleansed us from our sin, we are gloriously free—free to please Him. But we don't have to. And when we don't, we can get caught in the cords of our sin.

One writer describes the path of continued sin quite vividly:

> One lie has to be covered by a dozen more . . .
> The downward cycle of sin moves from a problem to a faulty sinful response, thereby causing an additional complicating problem which [is] met by . . . additional sinful response. . . .
> Sinful habits are hard to break, but if they are not broken they will bind [you] ever more tightly. [You will be] held fast by these ropes . . . in a downward cycle. . . . At length, [you] become sin's slave.[2]

Need a good warning? A healthy reminder? Never give yourself permission to hide behind grace as a cover for disobedience. Scripture calls that presumption. I've noticed that more and more Christians are prone to do that. Within the past eight or ten years I have heard and seen grace abused in this manner more than ever before in my ministry. One more voice deserves to be heard on the subject. John Henry Jowett wrote words many years ago that still sting with relevance:

> Sin is a blasting presence, and every fine power shrinks and withers in the destructive heat. Every spiritual delicacy succumbs to its malignant touch. . . . Sin impairs the sight, and works towards blindness. Sin benumbs the hearing and tends to make men deaf. Sin perverts the taste,

causing men to confound the sweet with the bitter, and the bitter with the sweet. Sin hardens the touch, and eventually renders a man "past feeling." All these are Scriptural analogies, and their common significance appears to be this—sin blocks and chokes the fine senses of the spirit; by sin we are desensitized, rendered imperceptive, and the range of our correspondence is diminished. Sin creates callosity. It hoofs the spirit, and so reduces the area of our exposure to pain.[3]

Life is like a menu in the Grace Restaurant. In this new establishment you are free to choose whatever you want. But whatever you choose will be served to you and you must eat it. If you choose the wrong food and realize later just how badly your body reacted to it, don't think that grace will protect you from getting sick. There is good news, however. God's grace does hold out the hope of acceptance before the Father. He will welcome you back into His fellowship if you *deal with the wrong, repent of it, and get back on track.*

Since I am a brother in the same family, I may warn you of the harm it will cause you to make the wrong choice, but grace means I take hands off and give you the freedom to choose. God is quite capable of guiding you. He will lead some to live one kind of lifestyle and others to live another . . . some to choose this occupation, others another . . . some, this career, others that one. He will direct some to rear their children this way and others to rear their children another way. You have the freedom to do whichever. You may prefer this kind of music; I may prefer a different kind of music. I may decide to emphasize this in my ministry; you may choose that. One of us may give this amount, another that. Some may live in this kind of house, others in another. Those options are all open to us. Because there are differences of taste or preference, grace frees us to choose. My counsel is this: Let people make their own choices. Accept them as they are. Let's uphold each other's right to have different opinions, convictions, and preferences. By doing so we keep opening up holes in the ice for one another. We all breathe easier.

I heard a fine group of singers several years ago who traveled around Southern California. They called themselves "Gospel State of Mind." Great harmony . . . good spirit . . . wonderful music, much of it original. One of their selections was about grace. As I listened to them and watched the joy with which they sang, I thought, *I like the name of their group. It fits.* As I write these pages on grace, I am reminded of their song, and it occurs to me that what I'm urging is not just tacking grace onto our vocabulary, but cultivating it in each other . . . encouraging a mental framework of grace in one another. My plea is for the body of Christ to have a "grace state of mind." As this transpires an awakening will become obvious to all, even those outside the ranks of Christianity.

IMPORTANT REALIZATIONS

When we read through Romans 6:19–23, we come to several realizations that are important in cultivating this "grace state of mind."

First, we discover the indisputable fact that we need a master. Christ is the ideal one to choose. We don't do well with no one in authority over us. We cannot handle either life's pressures or life's temptations strictly on our own. God didn't create us to live isolated lives without a master. We need Him in charge.

Read the balance of the chapter slowly:

> For just as you presented your members as slaves to impurity and to lawlessness, resulting in further lawlessness, so now present your members as slaves to righteousness, resulting in sanctification. For when you were slaves of sin, you were free in regard to righteousness. Therefore what benefit were you then deriving from the things of which you are now ashamed? For the outcome of those things is death. But now having been freed from sin and enslaved to God, you derive your benefit, resulting in sanctification, and the outcome, eternal life. For the wages of

sin is death, but the free gift of God is eternal life in Christ Jesus our Lord. (Rom. 6:19–23)

As I read those words and try to put what they are saying into simple terms, I come up with two statements. First this passage is teaching us to *make the right choice.* Look again at the first three verses, this time from the New International Version: "I put this in human terms because you are weak in your natural selves. Just as you used to offer the parts of your body in slavery to impurity and to ever-increasing wickedness, so now offer them in slavery to righteousness leading to holiness. When you were slaves to sin, you were free from the control of righteousness. What benefit did you reap at that time from the things you are now ashamed of? Those things result in death!" (vv. 19–21)

And second, I believe it is telling us to *focus on the benefits of our current position in grace.* Again, from the New International Version, read the next two verses: "But now that you have been set free from sin and have become slaves to God, the benefit you reap leads to holiness, and the result is eternal life. For the wages of sin is death, but the gift of God is eternal life in Christ Jesus our Lord" (vv. 22–23).

- Because of God's grace we are freed from sin's mastery.
- By God's grace we are enslaved to God.
- Through God's grace there are benefits to be derived.

What benefits? I can think of at least three: an exciting process of growing up and maturing as a Christian; a guilt-free lifestyle characterized by creativity and freedom; and finally, enjoying the outcome—eternal life. The alternative? A sinful lifestyle that results in "death wages." Several come to mind:

- Instant breakdown of fellowship with God
- Removal of His hand of blessing

· Misery of a guilty conscience . . . knowing how
  much others were hurt
· Loss of personal integrity
· Sudden stoppage of spiritual growth
· Strained relationships with fellow Christians
· Reproach brought to one's family and to the name
  of Christ
· Injury to the testimony of your local church

Yes, in grace you are free to choose either path. It is wise to choose righteousness. If that is your selection, quality life can be yours to enjoy . . . called here "eternal life." The benefits are numerous and all are delightful. But you can also choose the path of disobedience and start cashing in on some "death wages," all of which are awful. Before you yield to the temptation to abuse the grace God extends to you, spend some time considering the consequences. The scars of such a decision could mark you for life. Sins can be forgiven, but some scars cannot be erased.

I knew a fellow in high school who is now gone; he died of a sudden heart attack a couple years ago. What a guy! While in school he was the toughest, vilest, most rebellious kid in the class. He played the meanest game of football imaginable. He was also on the wrestling team (he was never pinned . . . never lost a match), and he played catcher on the baseball team. One of his summer hobbies was racing speedboats in Galveston Bay. He was one of those wild guys who preferred to drive his boat full speed at night. Needless to say, the last thing on his mind was any interest in spiritual things. Nothing any of us could say interested him in the least—until the night God got his attention.

While speeding about sixty miles an hour under a summer moon, his boat hit a large wave near Galveston's west jetties. The boat flipped and soon sank. Although pretty banged up, he was able to swim to some rocks where he grabbed hold. The sharp barnacles began to cut into his arms, chest, stomach, and legs. The waves and swells pulled him up and down, slicing his skin into ribbons, which caused blood to flow rather freely into the water. Realizing that sharks might be near, he was scared for the first time in his life. This led him to do something else he'd never done before: pray. He told God that he didn't deserve it, but he asked to be rescued. Without realizing it, he prayed for grace . . . God's unmerited favor. He told the Lord he would not only become a Christian, he would become a minister (which, to him, was the ultimate, drastic sacrifice—ugh!). God graciously intervened.

It wasn't five minutes before a Coast Guard vessel spotted him with a searchlight and soon had him on board. He looked like raw meat—his arms, belly, and legs were shredded from the razorlike barnacles. In the hospital he did a lot of thinking. During recovery he truly gave his heart to Christ. No conversion was more amazing to those of us who had known him through school. As he healed, long and ragged vertical scars remained on his body, never allowing him to forget his narrow escape from death.

As time passed, however, he forgot his words to God and he chose to return to a carnal lifestyle—drinking heavily, chasing women, cursing, the whole ugly scene. He wasn't happy in his carnal state, but he never let on how miserable he was. Late one night he was driving while intoxicated and struck head-on a concrete column of an underpass. He was thrown through the windshield, leaving his face mutilated and permanently scarred.

Finally, that got his attention. He went on to college, then seminary, and for the remaining years until his death he proclaimed the Savior whom he had ignored and whose grace he had abused. He told me many years ago that every time, after a shower, as he stood in front of a mirror toweling off, those scars he bore silently shouted back at him . . . mute reminders of the wrong choices he had made both before and after his conversion. He was forgiven, but the scars didn't go away.

Yes, grace frees us to choose. We can decide to walk with God and draw strength from Him to face whatever life throws at us. Or we can decide to walk away from God, like my friend, and face the inescapable consequences. The next time you are tempted to yield to your old master, remember this: Grace invites you to return and find forgiveness, but it doesn't automatically erase the scars that accompany sin; some could stay with you for life.

In spite of the terrible consequences sins may bring, I still must emphasize that grace means we allow others the freedom to choose, regardless. To do otherwise abuses as much as those who use their freedom as a license to sin. I am a firm believer in mutual accountability, but grace means I will not force or manipulate or judge or attempt to control you, nor should you do those things to me. It means we will keep on helping others to freedom by providing breathing holes. It means we deliberately let go so each of us can grow and learn on our own; otherwise, we shall never enjoy the liberty of an open sea. For most of us, letting others go is neither natural nor easy. Because we care, it is more our tendency to give people hints or advice. The thought of letting them fail or fall is extremely painful to us, but God treats us like that virtually every day of our lives. We tend to clutch, not release . . . to put people in our frame and not allow them any breathing holes unless and until they accept the shape of our molds.

If you are like that, the following piece (author unknown) is written just for you. It will help you release your grip. Being a person of grace *requires* letting go of others.

LETTING GO

To let go doesn't mean to stop caring,
    it means I can't do it for someone else.
To let go is not to cut myself off,
    it's the realization that I can't control another.
To let go is not to enable,
    but to allow learning from natural consequences.
To let go is to admit powerlessness,
    which means the outcome is not in my hands.
To let go is not to try to change or blame another,
    I can only change myself.
To let go is not to care for,
    but to care about.
To let go is not to fix,
    but to be supportive.
To let go is not to judge,
    but to allow another to be a human being.
To let go is not to be in the middle arranging all the outcomes,
    but to allow others to effect their own outcomes.
To let go is not to be protective;
    it is to permit another to face reality.
To let go is not to deny,
    but to accept.
To let go is not to nag, scold, or argue,
    but to search out my own shortcomings and to correct them.
To let go is not to adjust everything to my desires,
    but to take each day as it comes.
To let go is not to criticize and regulate anyone,
    but to try to become what dream I can be.
To let go is not to regret the past,
    but to grow and live for the future.
To let go is to fear less and love more!

8

*The Grace
to Let Others Be*

GRACE COMES TO US IN TWO DIMENSIONS, vertical and horizontal. Vertical grace centers on our relationship with God. It is amazing. It frees us from the demands and condemnation of the Mosaic Law. It announces hope to the sinner—the gift of eternal life, along with all its benefits. Horizontal grace centers on our human relationships. It is charming. It frees us from the tyranny of pleasing people and adjusting our lives to the demands and expectations of human opinion. It gives relief—the enjoyment of freedom along with all its benefits. It silences needless guilt and removes self-imposed shame.

Few people realize better than non-Christians how guilt ridden many Christians are. A lady in our congregation tells of a conversation she had with a fellow student while the two of them were students at the Berkeley campus of the University of California. He knew she was a Christian, and he made it painfully clear that he had no interest whatsoever in her faith. When she asked why, his answer bore the sting of reality: "Because the most guilt-ridden people I know are Christians. No thanks."

This is a good time for me to ask you two probing questions. Only you can answer them:

1. Do you add to others' guilt or do you lessen it?
2. Are you the type who promotes another's liberty or restrains it?

Both questions have to do with attitude, don't they? We do what we do with others because of the way we think. Our attitude, therefore, is crucial. It is also at our mercy. We have full control of which attitude we shall have: charming and gracious, or restrictive and rigid. Liberty or legalism will be the result. Depending on our attitude, we are grace givers or grace killers.

Dr. Victor Frankl survived three grim years at Auschwitz and other Nazi death camps. In his book, *Man's Search for Meaning,* he reflected back on those dark months and offers this insightful observation:

> We who lived in concentration camps can remember the men who walked through the huts comforting others, giving away their last piece of bread. They may have been few in number, but they offer sufficient proof that everything can be taken from a man but one thing: the last of the human freedoms—to choose one's attitude in any given set of circumstances.
>
> And there are always choices to make, every day, every hour, offered the opportunity to make a decision . . . which determined whether you would or would not submit to those powers which threatened to rob you of your very self, your inner freedom; which determined whether or not you would become the plaything of circumstance, renouncing freedom and dignity to become molded into the form of the typical inmate. . . . even though conditions such as lack of sleep, insufficient food and various mental stresses may suggest that the inmates were bound to react in certain ways, in the final analysis it becomes clear that the sort of person the prisoner became was the result of an inner decision, and not the result of camp influences alone.[1]

True words, and wise indeed. It's those inner decisions, not outer influences, that make us into the kind of people we are. One of my great hopes in writing this book is to encourage others to come to grips with the importance of maintaining a positive attitude that results in extending grace . . . the kind of grace that lets others be whomever and whatever God is leading them to be. Being that kind of person begins with an inner decision to release, to deliberately let go.

TWO STRONG TENDENCIES
THAT NULLIFY GRACE

Located in the greatest doctrinal book of the Bible is a paragraph of intensely practical instruction. It is, in fact, a series of commands that, if obeyed, will turn us into some of the most affirming people imaginable.

> Let love be without hypocrisy. Abhor what is evil; cling to what is good. Be devoted to one another in brotherly love; give preference to one another in honor; not lagging behind in diligence, fervent in spirit, serving the Lord; rejoicing in hope, persevering in tribulation, devoted to prayer, contributing to the needs of the saints, practicing hospitality. Bless those who persecute you; bless and curse not. Rejoice with those who rejoice, and weep with those who weep. Be of the same mind toward one another; do not be haughty in mind, but associate with the lowly. Do not be wise in your own estimation. Never pay back evil for evil to anyone. Respect what is right in the sight of all men. (Rom. 12:9–17)

In a nutshell, those words represent the essence of authentic Christianity. Unless I miss my guess, I think every person who knows and loves Jesus Christ would respond to that list in words similar to these: "I would love to be like that. What a list of resolutions to claim at the

beginning of every new year. My relationships with others would immediately improve. How I would wish all these things were true of me!"

Why don't we treat one another as the Lord instructs us to? Why
do we love with such hypocrisy? What keeps us from being devoted
to one another, from honoring one another, from contributing to
each other's needs, from practicing hospitality? When others are promoted or receive special recognition, or are able to enjoy a few
luxuries we may not have, why don't we applaud their success and rejoice with them? Why do we pay back evil for evil, even though we
know that retaliation will only create greater barriers? The list of why
questions could continue for another page. The inescapable fact is that
more often than not we nullify grace rather than magnify it. We resist
it much more often than we release it. What is it within us that hin-
ders an attitude of horizontal grace from flowing freely?

I have thought about that for many months. While thinking, I have
not only examined my own life, I have also observed others, most of
them Christians. My findings have not been pleasant, but they are
revealing and I think reliable. Most of us fall short when it comes to
letting others be because of two strong and very human tendencies:
We compare ourselves with others (which leads us to criticize or
compete with them) and we attempt to control others (which results
in our manipulating or intimidating them). For a few moments, let's
dissect and examine both of those tendencies that keep grace from
awakening.

To Compare

Christians seem especially vulnerable when it comes to comparison. For some reason, which I cannot fully discern, we are uneasy
with differences. We prefer sameness, predictability, common inter-
ests. If someone thinks differently or makes different choices than we
do, prefers different entertainment, wears different clothing, has

different tastes and opinions, or enjoys a different style of life, most Christians get nervous. We place far too much weight on externals and the importance of appearances, and not nearly enough on individuality and variety. We have "acceptable norms" in which we are able to move freely and allow others the freedom to do so. But heaven help the poor soul who steps beyond those bounds!

We compare musical tastes. We compare financial incomes. We compare marital status. We compare spirituality on the basis of externals. If an individual appreciates hymns and mellow songs, fine. If another prefers jazz or rock, watch out. If someone makes about as much money as we do (or less), we feel comfortable, relaxed, and accepting. If they make a great deal of money, drive a luxury car or two, own their own airplane or a summer home, or take extensive vacations, we consider them extravagant . . . even though we know next to nothing of their giving habits. If someone is married, has several well-disciplined and intelligent children (like ours!), we enjoy being around them. They are "in." If a person is living alone, divorced, or is a single parent, or has never gotten married, well—"something must be wrong with him (or her)." Actually, the only thing wrong is the comparison!

Who wrote the "let's compare" rulebook? Will you please show me from Scripture where God is pleased with such negative attitudes? Why can't a person be spiritual and enjoy expressions of music or art totally different from those you like? Who says it is carnal to have nice things or enjoy a few extravagant luxuries, especially if one's generosity is also extravagant? Why can't people drive any car they can afford or vacation anywhere they please or live in whatever size home they enjoy or wear whatever clothing they prefer? Just because you or I can't or don't choose to or would prefer not to doesn't mean others can't or shouldn't. Comparison fuels the fire of envy within people. It prompts the tendency to judge . . . it makes us prejudiced people. The worst part of all is that it nullifies grace. It was never God's intention for all His children to look alike or embrace identical lifestyles. Look at the natural world He created. What variety! The buzzard and the butterfly . . . the dog and the deer . . . the zinnia and the orchid . . . the wriggling minnow and the sleek shark.

The church is not a religious industry designed to turn out mass-produced reproductions on an assembly line. The Bible wasn't written to change us into cookie-cutter Christians or paper-doll saints. On the contrary, the folks I read about in the Book are as different as Rahab and Esther, one a former prostitute and the other a queen . . . as unusual as Amos and Stephen, fig-picker turned prophet and deacon who became a martyr. Variety honors God, predictability and mediocrity bore Him. And if there is proof that He prefers differences, take a look down the long hall of fame in church history. Some of those folks would never have been welcome in most evangelical churches today: "too extreme . . . too eccentric . . . too liberal!" Can you imagine fiery John Knox in one of today's sophisticated pulpits? Or how about Martin Luther on television! You're smiling if you are familiar with the man's uninhibited, provocative style. He was the one who once admitted that he never preached better than when he was angry.

Before we will be able to demonstrate sufficient grace to let others be, we'll have to get rid of this legalistic tendency to compare. (Yes, it is a form of legalism.) God has made each one of us as we are. He is hard at work shaping us into the image He has in mind. His only pattern (for character) is His Son. He wants each one of us to be unique . . . an individual blend and expression unlike any other person. That is by His design. There is only one you. There is only one me. And the same can be said of each member of His family.

Legalism requires that we all be alike, unified in convictions and uniform in appearance, to which I say, "Let me out!" Grace finds pleasure in differences, encourages individuality, smiles on variety, and leaves plenty of room for disagreement. Remember, it releases others and lets them be, to which I say, "Let me in!" I agree with and often quote the old saying, "Comparisons are odious." Not until we put a stop to them will horizontal grace flourish in the body.

To Control

Another attitude worth changing (if we hope to promote The Grace Awakening in our generation) is the tendency to control others. I find this especially prevalent among those who find their security in religious rigidity. They get their way by manipulating and intimidating. They use fear tactics, veiled threats, and oblique hints to get their way. If you have ever been around a controller, you know exactly what I'm trying to describe. Most often, controllers are insecure in themselves and do not know the first principle of being free, so naturally they are uneasy with your or my being free. Hence, they issue demands and force their will on others in no uncertain terms. You're not around controllers very long before you know it. Subtlety is not their long suit, which can be very intimidating.

I'm reminded of a dialogue between a couple of comic strip characters. One is sitting alone, watching television. In storms the other, demanding that he change the channel to the one she wants to watch, threatening him with her fat little fist in his face. Rather meekly he asks her what makes her think she can walk in and take over. She blurts out: "These five fingers!" which she tightens into a fist. It works. Without a word the little guy responds by asking which channel she prefers.

Naturally, she gets to watch any channel she wants. Slowly, he slips out of the room, feeling like a wimp. He looks at his own five fingers and asks, "Why can't you guys get organized like that?"

Controllers win by intimidation. Whether physical or verbal, they bully their way in as they attempt to manipulate us into doing their

THE GRACE AWAKENING

will. In Christian circles controllers usually are more insidious than the strong-willed little gal was with her wimpy friend. But they are equally determined, count on it. Whatever the method, controlling, like comparing, nullifies grace. If you are given to controlling others, grace is a foreign concept to you.

FOUR BIBLICAL GUIDELINES
THAT MAGNIFY GRACE

Enough about things that nullify grace. What we want most is to magnify it . . . promote it . . . release it, right?

In his letter to the Romans, Paul goes into great detail regarding the issue of personal freedom—greater detail than almost anywhere else in his writings. In the fourteenth chapter, for example, he sets forth four very practical guidelines that can be followed by all who are serious about releasing others in grace. My hope is that we not only learn what they are but, equally important, that we spend our days following them.

The first guideline is based on Romans 14:1–4:

> Now accept the one who is weak in faith, but not for the purpose of passing judgment on his opinions. One man has faith that he may eat all things, but he who is weak eats vegetables only. Let not him who eats regard with contempt him who does not eat, and let not him who does not eat judge him who eats, for God has accepted him. Who are you to judge the servant of another? To his own master he stands or falls; and stand he will, for the Lord is able to make him stand.

Since we have already dealt with the issue of eating meat from a carcass offered to idols, there is no reason for me to explain the background again. But perhaps I should repeat the question that arose from the controversy: Should a Christian eat it or not? Some had no problem whatsoever, while others thought it was wrong to do so, feeling that the one who ate it would be spiritually contaminated by the association with pagan worship. Let's see how this situation can relate to magnifying grace:

Guideline 1: *Accepting others is basic to letting them be.* The problem was not a meat problem, it was a love problem, an acceptance problem. It still is. How often we restrict our love by making it conditional: "If you will (or won't), then I will accept you." Paul starts there: "Accept one another!" In other words, "Let's allow each other the freedom to hold to convictions that are unlike our own . . . and accept them in spite of that difference." Those who didn't eat (called here "weak in faith") were exhorted to accept and not judge those who ate. And those who ate were exhorted to accept and not regard with contempt those who did not eat. The secret lies in accepting one another. All of this is fairly easy to read so long as I stay on the issue of eating meat. That one is safe because it isn't a current taboo. It's easy to accept those folks today because they don't exist!

How about those in our life who may disagree with us on issues that are taboos in evangelical Christian circles today? Here are a few:

- Going to the movies or live theater
- Wearing cosmetics
- Playing cards
- Watching television
- Going to the beach
- Not having a "quiet time" every morning or at least every day
- Going to a restaurant that sells liquor
- Wearing certain clothing
- Driving certain cars
- Wearing certain jewelry

- Listening to certain music
- Dancing . . . square, ballroom, disco—whatever
- Holding a certain job
- Wearing your hair a certain way (assuming you have hair)
- Having lovely and elegant possessions
- Getting a face-lift
- Drinking coffee
- Eating certain foods
- Working out in leotards

There are a dozen other things I could list, some of which would make you smile. But believe me, in various areas of our country or the world some or all of these things may be taboo, and if you cross that boundary, may God help you continue on in the church you're attending. Probably someone will say something. If not, you will be pounced upon by looks and reactionary treatment, revealing attitudes that lack grace. We are masters at that. If you hope to "survive," you had better learn the rules—fast. But don't assume that all areas are identical when it comes to taboos. The list changes from culture to culture even to this day.

I read this past week about a pastors' conference where a group of German Lutherans had gathered. Part of their reception included serving beer. No one thought anything of it because in that culture a mug of beer is absolutely accepted. But if one of the men lit up a cigar, the place would go up in smoke! Strange, isn't it? They shouldn't smoke, but if they choose to enjoy a swig of beer, no problem.

I know of churches where you are frowned on if you go to live theater or attend a movie, no matter what the rating is. Members of these congregations even spy out those places. But some of those same people will sit up late into the night and watch movies on television. Some even have cable TV and may watch movies that are far worse than those at the theaters. Funny, to me movies are movies, no matter where they are viewed. But not to these folks!

One of my favorite stories comes from a man who used to be in our church. He and his wife were close friends of our family, but they have now moved to another part of the country. We really miss their joyful presence. When he was a youth worker many years ago in an ethnic community, he attended a church that had Scandinavian roots. Being a rather forward-looking and creative young man, he decided he would show the youth group a missionary film. We're talking simple, safe, black-and-white religious-oriented movie. That film projector hadn't been off an hour before a group of the leaders in the church called him in and asked him about what he had done. They asked, "Did you show the young people a film?" In all honesty he responded, "Well, yeah, I did." "We don't like that," they replied. Without trying to be argumentative, the youth worker reasoned, "Well, I remember that at the last missionary conference, our church showed slides—" One of the church officers put his hand up signaling him to cease talking. Then, in these words, he emphatically explained the conflict: "If it's still, fine. If it moves, sin!" You can show slides, but when they start movin', you're gettin' into sin. My friend crossed the invisible line and got his hand slapped. He and I still laugh about the incongruity of that logic, but he does not look down on those leaders for their different understanding. (Remember, our goal is acceptance, the basis of a grace state of mind.)

Paul mentions the two most common reactions to such conflicts in Romans 14. First he says, "Let not him who eats regard with contempt him who does not . . ." (v. 3). The words regard with contempt mean "regard as nothing, utterly despise, to discount entirely." That is the normal response of those who feel the freedom to do whatever toward those who are more restrictive and rigid. It is easy to look down on them . . . to "regard as nothing."

The second reaction Paul mentions is that of the other side—"and let not him who does not eat judge him who eats." Judging means to criticize, to view negatively, to make assumptions that are exaggerated and erroneous and even damaging to character. No matter how strongly you may feel about a certain taboo, judging another who may disagree with you is going too far. That kind of thing has been going on for years, actually, ever since the *first* century.

William Barclay writes:

> The Jews had made a tyranny of the Sabbath, surrounding it with a jungle of rules, regulations and prohibitions.[2]

It became a fetish!

Can you imagine making the Sabbath into a fetish? Why, of course! Anything we make too much of easily becomes a fetish, which is the tragedy of it all.

Do you remember Paul's question? "Who are you to judge the servant of another? To his own master he stands or falls. . . ." When we truly accept another person, we remember that the Lord is perfectly capable of directing his or her life. That relieves us from having to be his or her conscience. It's our job to accept others; it's God's job to direct them.

What does acceptance mean? What does it include? Because I cannot say it better than what I read in a periodical many years ago, I'll return to that source for my answer to those two questions:

> Acceptance means you are valuable just as you are. It allows you to be the real you. You aren't forced into someone else's idea of who you really are. It means your ideas are taken seriously since they reflect you. You can talk about how you feel inside and why you feel that way—and someone really cares.
>
> Acceptance means you can try out your ideas without being shot down. You can even express heretical thoughts and discuss them with

intelligent questioning. You feel safe. No one will pronounce judgment on you, even though they don't agree with you. It doesn't mean you will never be corrected or shown to be wrong; it simply means it's safe to be you and no one will destroy you out of prejudice. [3]

Acceptance is basic to letting others be. Consider the next four verses of Romans 14 as we turn to a second guideline:

> One man regards one day above another, another regards every day alike. Let each man be fully convinced in his own mind. He who observes the day, observes it for the Lord, and he who eats, does so for the Lord, for he gives thanks to God; and he who eats not, for the Lord he does not eat, and gives thanks to God. For not one of us lives for himself, and not one dies for himself; for if we live, we live for the Lord, or if we die, we die for the Lord; therefore whether we live or die, we are the Lord's. (vv. 5–8)

Guideline 2: *Refusing to dictate to others allows the Lord freedom to direct their lives.* I especially appreciate the statement at the end of verse 5: ". . . Let each man be fully convinced in his own mind." Give people room to make up their minds. Do you have a few new converts who are a part of your life and ministry? Do you want to help them grow toward maturity? Here is how: Let them grow up differently. Let them learn at their own pace, just like you had to learn, including failures and mistakes. If you really want grace to awaken, be easier on them than others were on you. Don't make up their minds . . . let them! Don't step in and push your weight around . . . give them plenty of space. Whatever you do, don't control and manipulate them to get what you want.

Be an accepting model of grace. Refuse all temptations to be a brother basher or sister smasher. We already have too many of them roaming around the religious landscape. And nothing catches the attention of the unsaved world quicker than those times when we

Christians beat up on one another. Don't think the unsaved world doesn't notice our cannibalism.

Leslie Flynn writes about the time when evangelist Jack Van Impe was closing a citywide crusade in Green Bay, Wisconsin. It was to end on a Sunday afternoon. The very same public arena also featured wrestling on Sunday night. Interestingly, on Monday evening (the following day), Rex Humbard was scheduled to begin a new series of evangelistic meetings. One wonders if the man who set up the sign didn't have his tongue in his cheek when he arranged the letters on the marquee,

JACK VAN IMPE

WRESTLING

REX HUMBARD[4]

Most Christians have a long way to go when it comes to releasing others to the Lord. I love the way Paul provides the right perspective—"We are the Lord's." Few things will keep us from directing others' lives like that reminder. Each one of us belongs to the same Lord. When we stop dictating, it is easier for others to mature as they follow the Lord's directing.

Let's press on to the next four verses in Romans 14:

For to this end Christ died and lived again, that He might be Lord both of the dead and of the living. But you, why do you judge your brother? Or you again, why do you regard your brother with contempt? For we shall all stand before the judgment seat of God. For it is written, "AS I LIVE, SAYS THE LORD, EVERY KNEE SHALL BOW TO ME, AND EVERY TONGUE SHALL PRAISE TO GOD."

So then each one of us shall give account of himself to God. (vv. 9–12)

Guideline 3: *Freeing others means we never assume a position we're not qualified to fill.* This, in one sentence, is enough to stop any person from judging another. We're not qualified. We lack full knowledge. How often we have jumped to wrong conclusions, made judgmental statements, only to find out later how offbase we were . . . then wished we could cut out our tongue.

What keeps us from being qualified to judge?

- We do not know all the facts.
- We are unable to read motives.
- We find it impossible to be totally objective.
- We lack "the big picture."
- We live with blind spots.
- We are prejudiced and have blurred perspective.
- Most of all, we ourselves are imperfect and inconsistent.

In a Connecticut city, fifty-three residents of a certain neighborhood signed a petition to stop reckless driving on their streets. The police set a watch. A few nights later five violators were caught. All five had signed the petition.[5]

I will never forget what happened to me several years ago that illustrated how wrong I could be in judging another. I was speaking at a summer Bible conference for a week. Attending the same conference was a couple I had not seen before. We met briefly the first night. Both were friendly and seemed especially glad to be there. I began to notice as the week wore on that the man fell asleep in every one of the meetings. I mean every one. Normally, that doesn't bother me . . . I often talk in other people's sleep! But this time, for some strange reason, it began to bug me. By Wednesday I felt feelings of irritation. As I mentioned, that has happened to me numerous times . . . but this guy was out within ten minutes after I started to speak. It made no difference if I spoke in the morning or evening—he slept. By the last meeting on Friday evening (through which he slept, of course) I had become convinced it was she who wanted to be there, not her husband. I sized him up as a fella who talked one way but lived another, "probably a carnal Christian," I mused.

She stayed after the crowd and her husband had left. She asked if she could speak with me for a few minutes. I figured she wanted to talk about how unhappy she was living with a man who didn't have the same interest in spiritual things as she. How wrong I was. She said their being there was his idea. It had been his "final wish." I didn't understand. She informed me he had terminal cancer and had only weeks to live. At his request they attended the conference where I was speaking even though the medication he was taking for pain made him sleepy—something which greatly embarrassed him. "He loves the Lord," she said, "and you are his favorite Bible teacher. He wanted to be here to meet you and to hear you, no matter what." I was sincerely stunned. She thanked me for the week and left. I stood there, all alone, as deeply rebuked as I have ever been. I had judged my brother, and I was as wrong as I could possibly have been.

Does this guideline mean we must always agree? It does not. That is the subject of my next chapter, so I'll not attempt to address it at length here. There are any number of people with whom you and I may not agree. That's fine . . . we can still be civil to each other; instead of spending our time putting their faces on a dart board. I'm a lot happier if I accept the fact that others won't always fall in line with my convictions. That's okay. But the main thing you and I must guard against is judging. I repeat, we are not qualified to fill that role. God alone is to be our Judge and Jury.

There is one more guideline that grows out of verses 13–18 in Romans 14:

> Therefore let us not judge one another anymore, but rather determine this—not to put an obstacle or a stumbling block in a brother's way. I know

and am convinced in the Lord Jesus that nothing is unclean in itself; but to him who thinks anything to be unclean, to him it is unclean. For if because of food your brother is hurt, you are no longer walking according to love. Do not destroy with your food him for whom Christ died. Therefore do not let what is for you a good thing be spoken of as evil; for the kingdom of God is not eating and drinking, but righteousness and peace and joy in the Holy Spirit. For he who in this way serves Christ is acceptable to God and approved by men.

Guideline 4: *Loving others requires us to express our liberty wisely.* In other words, love must rule. I'm not my own, I'm bought with a price. My goal is not to please me, it is to please my Lord Jesus, my God. It is not to please you, it is to please my Lord. The same is true for you. So the bottom line is this: I don't adapt my life according to what you may say, I adapt my life according to the basis of my love for you because I answer to Christ. And so do you.

To paraphrase those verses we just read from Romans: "Nothing that is not specifically designated as evil in Scripture is evil—but rather a matter of one's personal preference or taste. So let it be. Even if you personally would not do what another is doing, let it be. And you who feel the freedom to do so, don't flaunt it or mock those who disagree. We are in the construction business, not destruction. And let's all remember that God's big-picture kingdom plan is not being shaped by small things like what one person prefers over another, but by large things, like righteousness and peace and joy."

One of the marks of maturity is the ability to handle liberty without flaunting it. Mature folks don't flaunt their privileges. They enjoy them fully, yet quietly . . . privately . . . with those of like mind, who aren't offended by the liberty.

When our children began to grow up, we (like you) increased their privileges. One of the first privileges our oldest child enjoyed was not having to take a nap and not having to go to bed so early. He could miss his afternoon nap, and he could stay up later with his mom and dad. The problem was, the other three weren't old enough to have the same privilege. So he had to be mature about handling this new freedom. If he flaunted it, chaos would break out. In other words, he couldn't walk by their closed bedroom door and taunt them by shouting, "Na-na-na-na-na . . . I don't have to take a na-ap." Or "Ha! You've got to go to bed early—not me. I'm free to stay up reeeel late!" We warned him about staying quiet and handling his liberty very wisely. Paul cautions you and me to do the same. Otherwise, the grace killers will get ammunition and have reason to load up and fire in our direction. Grace never gives us the right to rub anyone's nose in our liberty. When I see that happening, I realize I'm watching religious childishness in action.

A FEW ACTIONS THAT SIGNIFY GRACE

I want to close this chapter by focusing our final attention on the concluding verses in Romans 14. Read verse 19 slowly and thoughtfully. "So then let us pursue the things which make for peace and the building up of one another." On the basis of that great statement, consider the first of four action steps.

1. *Concentrate on things that encourage peace and assist others' growth.* An idea that works for me is to filter whatever I do through a twofold "grid"—two questions that keep me focused: (a) Is this going to make a lot of waves, or will it encourage peace? (b) Is this going to hurt and offend, or will it help and strengthen my brother or sister? Let's commit ourselves anew to encouragement and affirmation.

2. *Remember that sabotaging saints hurts the work of God.* "Don't tear down the work of God for the sake of food . . ." (v. 20). You sabotage

the saints when you flaunt your liberty, knowing that they have convictions against it. That is not fair. Frankly, that is fighting dirty. Scripture calls it "regarding with contempt," and counsels us against it. Enjoy your liberty with discretion.

3. *Exercise your liberty only with those who can enjoy it with you.* I repeat, that means to keep it private and personal. Remember my story about our oldest child. What others don't know can't hurt them. That's not deception, it's wise and necessary restraint. It isn't prompted by hypocrisy but by love.

4. *Determine where you stand and refuse to play God in anyone else's life.* That may sound simple and easy, but it is tougher than it may seem. Be absolutely sure you are right, then press on, regardless. By letting others be, you free yourself to give full attention to what God is trying to make of you. You have neither the time nor the energy to keep holding on. Love demands that you let go.

Some time ago *The American Scholar* magazine included a piece by Wyatt Prunty that illustrates rather well what I've been attempting to write in this chapter.

LEARNING THE BICYCLE
(for Heather)

The older children pedal past
Stable as little gyros, spinning hard
To supper, bath, and bed, until at last
We also quit, silent and tired
Beside the darkening yard where trees
Now shadow up instead of down.
Their predictable lengths can only tease
Her as, head lowered, she walks her bike alone
Somewhere between her wanting to ride
And her certainty she will always fall.

Tomorrow, though I will run behind,
Arms out to catch her, she'll tilt then balance wide
Of my reach, till distance makes her small,
Smaller, beyond the place I stop and know
That to teach her I had to follow
And when she learned I had to let her go.[6]

9

Graciously Disagreeing and Pressing On

ONE OF THE MARKS OF MATURITY IS THE ability to disagree without becoming disagreeable. It takes grace. In fact, handling disagreements with tact is one of the crowning achievements of grace.

Unfortunately, the older we get the more brittle we become in our reactions, the more tedious and stubborn and fragile. For some strange reason, this is especially true among evangelical Christians. You would think that the church would be the one place where we could find tolerance, tact, plenty of room for disagreement, and open discussion. Not so! It is a rare delight to come across those in the family of God who have grown old in grace as well as in knowledge.

A friend told me of a beautiful example of this—a true story. The minister of a church of a different denomination contacted the pastor of a large downtown Baptist church and made an unusual request. He had several folks who had recently joined his church who preferred to be baptized by immersion rather than by sprinkling, the church's normal mode of baptism. The minister requested not only the use of their baptistry but that the Baptist pastor himself baptize those who

THE GRACE AWAKENING

came. This posed a dilemma—what if those being baptized weren't born again? Since it was the pastor's conviction that only Christians should be baptized, he realized he couldn't with good conscience cooperate with the plan, but he wished to handle his answer with tact so as not to offend the other minister. I understand that he wrote a letter, a masterpiece of grace, in which he included this humorous statement: "We don't take in laundry, but we'll be happy to loan you our tub." Would that all issues of that nature were handled that graciously.

Many a ministry lives on the edge of upheaval and borderline controversy, simply because there is no room for disagreement . . . no freedom to negotiate . . . no open ear to those who hold to a different opinion. I know of some ministers who never read critical mail; it's all screened by their secretaries and quickly discarded. Another has publicly stated that he would have no one on his board who says "No." When I heard that, I couldn't help but wonder about two things: How in the world could he find enough people like that to form his board and how does his wife handle her disagreements? Maybe she mails them in anonymously. Just kidding.

The other side of this matter of criticism needs to be addressed with equal vigor, namely, the importance of stating our disagreements graciously. Because I happen to read most of my critical mail, I am continually aware of how people declare their disagreements. There are a few beautiful exceptions, but the general rule is that criticisms are tactless, blunt, accusatory, and sometimes sarcastic. The most offensive ones are usually left unsigned (a cowardly act) and lack much truth, if any. Talk about grace killers!

I've said for years that people should not read unsigned mail. My problem is that I usually do. I also have said people should not pay any attention to it—"toss it in the trash!" My problem is that I usually

178

memorize it. I know, I know, it isn't healthy, but since when am I a model of perfection? Oh, to practice what one preaches!

All this is to say that I have read enough "hate mail" (strong term but occasionally true) to make this suggestion: *Think before you write your disagreements.* I have found that it helps to pause and put myself in the other person's place and imagine myself opening the letter and feeling the sting of those words. As a result of that little exercise, I have usually torn up my letter of criticism and never sent it.

Trust me, bitter and harsh words stick like pieces of shrapnel in one's brain, even in those you might think of as strong and able to handle it. The critic may soon forget them, but seldom will the one being verbally assaulted. I love the old saying, "Write your criticisms in dust, your compliments in marble."

The last four verses of Ephesians 4 come to mind:

> Let no unwholesome words proceed from your mouth, but only such a word as is good for edification according to the need of the moment, that it may give grace to those who hear. And do not grieve the Holy Spirit of God, by whom you were sealed for the day of redemption. Let all bitterness and wrath and anger and clamor and slander be put away from you, along with all malice. And be kind to one another, tender-hearted, forgiving each other, just as God in Christ also has forgiven you. (vv. 29–32)

No one could say it more succinctly than that. Just be nice, my Christian friend, in whatever you say or write. It costs no more, and it takes only a little more time to express your disagreements in tactful and gracious ways . . . when you don't get your way or when someone holds a different opinion, or even when a correction should be made and reproof is in order. Rudeness is never appropriate. Without exception, kindness is.

THINGS WE AGREE ON
REGARDING DISAGREEMENTS

As much as we may pursue peace, and as positive and tactful as we may be, there will still be occasions when disagreements arise. As one wag put it, "Life ain't no exact science," which brings me to the first of four facts with which everyone (well, most of us) would agree.

1. *Disagreements are inevitable.* Throughout this book, I have emphasized the value of variety and the importance of individuality. The downside of that is it leaves the door open for differing opinions. I say downside only because those inevitable differences can lead to strong disagreements. There will be opposing viewpoints and a variety of perspectives on most subjects. Tastes differ as well as preferences. That is why they make vanilla and chocolate and strawberry ice cream, why they build Fords and Chevys, Chryslers and Cadillacs, Hondas and Toyotas. That is why our nation has room for Democrats and Republicans, conservatives and liberals—and moderates. The tension is built into our system. It is what freedom is all about, including religious freedom. I am fairly firm in my theological convictions, but that doesn't mean you (or anyone) must agree with me. All this explains why I place so much importance on leaving "wobble room" in our relationships. One's theological persuasion may not bend, but one's involvements with others must. Leaders are especially in need of leaving "wobble room" if they hope to relieve steam from inevitable tensions.

2. *Even the godly will sometimes disagree.* When I was younger I had difficulty with this one. I couldn't understand how two people who loved the Lord with equal passion and who believed the Bible with equal zeal could come to different conclusions. In my two-by-four mind I was convinced that all godly minds held to identical conclusions. Not so! To my amazement, I soon discovered that there were not only various opinions on the same subject, but that God had the audacity to bless those who disagreed with me. I believe it was Dr.

Bob Cook, while he was president of The King's College, who wisely said, "God reserves the right to use people who disagree with me." I'll go one step further, for I am now convinced that God is not nearly so narrow as many of His people are. I find that God is much easier to live with than most of His followers . . . far more tolerant, certainly full of more grace and forgiveness than all of us are.

Unlike us, when He forgives, He forgets the transgression and removes it as far as East is from West. Perhaps you have heard of the man who loved the Lord, but he couldn't seem to conquer a particular sin. Time and again through the week he would come before the Lord and confess the same transgression. In all sincerity, he would tell God how much he hated what he had done and how grateful he was for God's grace in forgiving him. Wouldn't you know it, by Saturday of that same struggling week he was back on his knees: "Here I come again, Lord, with the same sin . . . asking Your forgiveness and claiming Your cleansing." To his surprise, he heard God's audible answer: "What sin?"

There will be no denominations in heaven, no categories of Christians—only the vast company of the saints, and only then will there be perfect harmony of heart and complete unanimity of agreement. Until then, count on it, even the godly will disagree.

3. *In every disagreement there are the same two ingredients*: (a) an issue, and (b) various viewpoints. The issue is usually objective and involves principles. The viewpoints are subjective and involve personalities. And therein lies the sum and substance of a clash, which could be defined as a disagreement over an issue because of opposing points of view. I will be candid with you: Every time I have remembered those two basic ingredients in the midst of a disagreement, I have been able to keep calm and think clearly. When I have forgotten them, almost without exception I have failed to negotiate my way through the clash with wisdom. Furthermore, I have regretted something I said in the heat of verbal exchange. Those two simple ingredients have never failed to help me keep cool. Why? The next fact will explain.

4. *In many disagreements each side is valid.* As "liberal" as you may think that sounds, chew on it before you toss it aside. On numerous occasions when I have encountered a brother or sister who felt as strongly as I about the other side of the argument, I came to realize it was not so much an I-am-right-and-you-are-wrong matter as it was an I-see-it-from-this-perspective-and-you-from-that-perspective matter. Both sides of most disagreements have strengths and weaknesses, which means neither side is an airtight slam dunk. Nevertheless, any disagreement can lead to a serious, permanent rift in a relationship . . . and sometimes (this may surprise you) that is God's will. There are times God chooses to spread the good news of His Son rapidly in different directions by having two capable servants of His have a major disagreement. As they separate and minister effectively in two different locations, He accomplishes a greater objective than their being in agreement.

A DISAGREEMENT BETWEEN
TWO GODLY LEADERS

That is exactly what happened between two men who had labored alongside each other for years. I am thinking of Paul—the godly apostle of grace, and Barnabas—the godly servant of compassion. Two more dedicated men could not be found in the first century. Both were effective; both spiritually minded. Neither was selfish or immature. But what an argument! Can you imagine what the media today would have done with the headlines?

RELIGIOUS CO-WORKERS CLASH HEAD-ON

or

EVANGELISTS FIGHT OVER TEAM MEMBER

. . . or some such nonsense. If there is one thing I have learned over the past few years it is this: Be suspicious of the headlines and never expect the media to get the whole story straight. If it can be garbled or exaggerated or slanted, they will do it.

Frankly, I am pleased to read of two men as respected and as full of integrity as Paul and Barnabas wrestling over an issue about which both felt strongly. Too often we Christians resemble the little toy dog sitting in the back window of a car always nodding in agreement. Too many fear that disagreement is tantamount to mutiny. But that's not true; grace leaves room for a few clashes. The late great G. Campbell Morgan agrees:

> I am greatly comforted whenever I read this [disagreement between Paul and Barnabas]. I am thankful for the revelation of the humanity of these men. If I had never read that Paul and Barnabas had a contention, I should have been afraid. These men were not angels, they were men.[1]

One more thought before we get into the specific clash between Paul and Barnabas. No matter how much good may come from such disagreements, they often hurt . . . and I mean hurt deeply. This is especially true when you have to take it on the chin and choose not to strike back. The more heated the disagreement, the more our inner steam tank builds to the breaking point; and it is all we can do to keep a level head through the whole explosive episode. Again, only God's grace can give us sufficient strength to restrain retaliation.

This reminds me of the Quaker who owned an ornery cow. Every time he milked her, it was a clash of two wills. This particular morning she was unusually irritable, but he was determined to endure the session without so much as a cross word. As the farmer began to milk her, ol' Bossy stepped on his foot with all her weight. He struggled silently, groaned a little under his breath, pulled his foot free, then sat back down on the stool. She then swished her tail in his face like a long-string whip. He merely leaned away so it wouldn't be able to reach him. Next she kicked over the bucket, by then half-full of warm milk. He started over, mumbling a few words to himself; but he never lost his cool. Once finished with the ordeal, he breathed a sigh of relief, picked up the bucket and stool, and as he was leaving she hauled off and kicked him against the barn wall twelve to fifteen feet away. That did it. He stood to his feet, marched in front of his cow, stared into those big eyes, and as he shook a long bony finger in her face, he shouted, "Thou dost know that I am a Quaker. Thou dost also know that I cannot strike thee back . . . BUT I CAN SELL THEE TO A PRESBYTERIAN!"

Let's look now into the biblical account and set the stage for how the disagreement arose between Paul and Barnabas. It all started when they took their first missionary journey together. Accompanying these two seasoned veterans of the faith was a young man named John Mark, who was neither seasoned nor strong. Perhaps because he was Barnabas's cousin and because he showed real promise as an up-and-coming young believer, they felt comfortable having him travel with them. For sure, they could use an extra set of hands to help them with what they carried by way of supplies and clothing, not knowing what they would encounter in the primitive and rugged places of their destination. Everything was fine at the start.

> And when they reached Salamis, they began to proclaim the word of God in the synagogues of the Jews; and they also had John as their helper. (Acts 13:5)

But when they crossed over to the difficult area of Pamphylia, they reached a region that was probably tougher to take than the Normandy coastline was in the Second World War. An imposing range of mountains stood before them like rugged giants of stone. It was a mosquito-infested, feverish coastline. To say the least, the honeymoon of adventure was over when they got to Perga in Pamphylia. The excitement and theoretical delight of missionary travel screeched to a halt as the three companions came upon hard times. Finally, it became too much for John Mark, who lost the heart to go any further. "Now Paul and his companions put out to sea from Paphos and came to Perga in Pamphylia; and John left them and returned to Jerusalem" (Acts 13:13).

Don't move too hurriedly over that last statement. The young man's drive weakened. His dream turned into a personal nightmare. No doubt embarrassed, he admitted, "I just can't go any further. I'm leaving." William Barclay calls him "the deserter."[2] Chrysostom says, "The lad wanted his mother."[3] More than a few New Testament scholars refer to him as "the defector." When the going got tough, John Mark up and quit. If my figuring is correct, this was also the time Paul got sick. It may have been a bout with malaria or the beginning of his intense headaches connected with some form of eye disease. Whatever, it was the worst possible time to be deserted. If ever they needed to pull together, it was then. Nevertheless, Paul and Barnabas were faced with no other option than to slug it out on their own. Little did they know the pain awaiting them. It was on this trip, you may remember, that Paul was stoned and left to die. Ultimately, he and Barnabas endured the rigors of the trip, came back, and reported the wonderful results. I have often wondered if John Mark was there in the Antioch church when the report was given. If so, he probably sat in the shadows back out of sight, feeling terribly ashamed.

The Critical Issue

Some time later the thought dawned in Paul's mind, *Let's go back and look things over.* The Acts account picks up the story:

And after some days Paul said to Barnabas, "Let us return and visit the brethren in every city in which we proclaimed the word of the Lord, and see how they are." And Barnabas was desirous of taking John, called Mark, along with them also. (Acts 15:36–37)

"Let's take John Mark. Let's give him another chance." The next verse makes it clear that Paul disagreed: "But Paul kept insisting that they should not take him along." Remember my earlier comment? In every disagreement there are two ingredients: an objective issue and opposing viewpoints. The issue here? Should a person who defects from a mission be given a second chance? Should someone who leaves people in the lurch when they really need him be taken again on a similar mission? And the viewpoints? Paul said, "No, absolutely not." Barnabas said, "Yes, by all means."

The Opposing Viewpoints

There stood two men of God, each fully convinced in his own mind that he was right. Remember Barnabas? He is the model of compassion. I have heard my friend, Howie Hendricks, call him "the man with an oily disposition." Barnabas is the builder-up of men. He is the same one, in fact, who earlier had searched for and found Paul when the other disciples were suspicious of Paul's recent conversion. When one who had been persecuting Christians said, "I've become a Christian," the other Christians sneered, "No, we don't trust that." But it was Barnabas who found Paul, believed in him, vouched for him, and won a hearing for Paul. It was Barnabas who was responsible for introducing him to the Christian community. Giving people a chance was Barnabas's style. Naturally, he felt it would be best to give John Mark another chance.

Not Paul. His style was altogether different. He was the man of great conviction and strong commitment to the truth, the one who founded more churches than anyone in the history of Scripture. Paul was the trailblazer who set the pace for missionary ministries to this day, a man of discipline and determination . . . more of the shape-up-or-ship-out mentality. Paul looked at the issue from the viewpoint of the overall good of the ministry. Barnabas looked at the issue from the viewpoint of the overall good of the man. Barnabas saw it as the classic opportunity to restore John Mark's confidence. It is not an oversimplification to say that Paul was led by his head, Barnabas by his heart. That is why we read, "Barnabas was desirous of taking John, called Mark." He thought, *Why, he could become a great disciple of Christ. We can't leave him here with his memories, licking his wounds, feeling ashamed and badgered by remorse. That would kill him! We've got to bring him along.* Paul strongly disagreed, "There is no way!"

A close reading of the next verse reveals the intensity of Paul's feelings: "But Paul kept insisting that they should not take him along who had deserted them in Pamphylia and had not gone with them to the work" (v. 38). The Greek term translated "deserted" is the term from which we get *apostasized*. In Paul's mind, Mark had done more than back off and bail out . . . the young man had apostasized. "He was unfaithful once, and I've learned in dealing with defectors that you can't trust them once they blow it, certainly not as royally as John Mark blew it." Paul had no room in his future plans for John Mark . . . at least not now.

Unless I miss my guess, you are leaning in favor of Barnabas, right? I understand, and I am tempted to agree. However, I am reminded of a proverb we would be wise to consider: "Like a bad tooth and an unsteady foot is confidence in a faithless man in time of trouble" (Prov. 25:19).

Franz Delitzsch, the late reliable and reasonable German scholar, amplifies the verse to say: "He who, in time of need, makes a faithless man his ground of confidence, is like one who seeks to bite with a broken tooth and one who supports himself on a shaking leg, and thus stumbles and falls."[4]

Before you start feeling too magnanimous and greathearted, let me ask you if you have ever loaned money to somebody who never paid it back. Let's say the debt is still outstanding. My question is this: Would you be desirous of loaning that person money again if you had a chance? Probably not. Suddenly, the issue is clearer.

Why? Because confidence in an unfaithful man in time of trouble is a shaky thing. He stumbled and fell once . . . he's still not paid you back, and chances are good he will do the same again. Paul's reasoning is, what if he defects again and one of us gets hurt . . . or it has an impact on the lost souls we're ministering to? What if his action gains public sentiment and several in the church begin to be persuaded that John Mark has a better plan, leaving the home church polarized? It's risky, no doubt about it.

Paul has a point. If you see only Barnabas' side, chances are good you have never been in a rugged place in ministry and had a partner fail you. Nothing hurts quite like that. I am not saying I vote for Paul or that I vote for Barnabas. I am really saying I see both sides . . . which highlights my earlier comment that both sides have validity.

Was it really a severe argument? Verse 39 states that the conflict resulted in a "sharp disagreement." It is the Greek word *paroxysm*. Interestingly, our English word is a transliterated Greek word. "There arose such a paroxysm." One Webster's dictionary says a paroxysm is "a sudden attack, as in a disease." It is a convulsion, a violent emotion. There arose such a clash of wills the rift could not be mended. The final outcome? They agreed to disagree. As Scripture states, "They separated from one another."

The Permanent Separation

The fact is that the two men never ministered together again. They reached such a stalemate in their argument that one said, "I'm going this way"; the other, "I'm going that way." If you take a map and study where each went you will see they traveled in opposite directions—Barnabas and John Mark took to the sea and traveled to

Cyprus; Paul and Silas (his new partner) stayed on the land and went northeast toward Syria, then swept over toward the west as he came to Cilicia and the other cities.

There was a loss of temper. There was an outburst of unrecorded, strong words. I am glad all the words are not recorded in the passage of Scripture, just like you and I are glad that our words in a violent outburst of a recent paroxysm were not recorded, right? I don't want to diminish the heat of their disagreement. There was a strong, highly charged debate between these two men of God.

One writer offers an imaginary dialogue that could have occurred that day between Paul and Barnabas.

PAUL   John Mark? We can't take him. He failed us last time.

BARNABAS   But that was last time.

PAUL   He's likely to fail us again. He's a deserter.

BARNABAS   He's had time to think it over. We've got to give him another chance. He's got the makings of a great missionary.

PAUL   Tell me, Barnabas, isn't it because he's your cousin that you want to take him again?

BARNABAS   That's not fair. You know I've tried to help many people who aren't related to me. I'm convinced this lad needs understanding and encouragement. He could be a great evangelist some day.

PAUL   We need someone who can stand up to persecution, an angry mob, beatings, perhaps jail. Our team has to be close-knit, thoroughly reliable. How can we trust a lad who failed like John Mark? No, Barnabas. Recall the word of the Master, "No man who puts his hand to the plow and looks back is fit for the kingdom of God."

BARNABAS   I've talked to him about his failure. I'm sure he won't defect again. To refuse him might do spiritual damage at the moment of his repentance. It'd be like breaking a bruised reed, like quenching smoking flax.

PAUL   It's too soon to trust him.

BARNABAS   Paul, remember how soon after your conversion I took a chance on you. The apostles were afraid of you, thinking you were faking your conversion in order to infiltrate the church at Jerusalem. I didn't make you prove yourself first. I'd rather not keep John Mark waiting. I vouch for him now. [5]

It could have been more passionate than that. Keep in mind that these are long-time friends. They had had significant years of ministry together. Their roots went way back. I have wondered if they might have been boyhood friends. Each of them owed the other a great deal. Barnabas stood for Paul, and Paul had stood for Barnabas. In a burst of emotions mixed with conflicting convictions their ministry together screeches to a halt, and they go in opposite directions.

If you have never had this happen, you cannot imagine the pain of it, especially if it happened between you and a coworker in ministry. Don't minimize the conflict. It's painful beyond description. All is not lost, however. I remind you, the upside of it is that this is how new churches or seminaries are sometimes started. This is sometimes how campus ministries are expanded. Disagreements prompt fresh starts, new works, broader visions. The event that caused it to happen isn't good. It is more like a rock hitting a placid lake, creating a sudden wake where there are hurt feelings, at least initially. But the ripples continue on until people are greathearted enough to forget the pain and stop licking their wounds and proceed into new directions.

Who knows what ministries took place in Cyprus and regions beyond, thanks to the new missionary team, Barnabas and Mark?

Furthermore, it was John Mark who wrote the Gospel of Mark. Even Paul stated at the end of his life, ". . . Pick up Mark and bring him with you, for he is useful to me for service" (2 Tim. 4:11). And he later writes favorably of Barnabas as well. Paul was too much of a man of grace to spend the rest of his life nursing a wound.

A. T. Robertson is right: "No one can rightly blame Barnabas for giving his cousin John Mark a second chance nor Paul for fearing to risk him again. One's judgment may go with Paul, but one's heart goes with Barnabas. . . . Paul and Barnabas parted in anger and both in sorrow. Paul owed more to Barnabas than to any other man. Barnabas was leaving the greatest spirit of the time and of all times."[6]

I hope we never forget something that is recorded in the final verse of the Acts 15 account. After Barnabas took Mark and set sail for Cyprus, ". . . Paul chose Silas and departed, being committed by the brethren to the grace of the Lord" (Acts 15:40).

One wonders if someone in the church didn't say, "Now, Paul, don't spend the rest of your life taking shots at Barnabas. You can handle this. Get over it and press on. Get on with it. It will take grace . . . the grace of the Lord."

It is interesting to me that the church does not commend Barnabas but commends Paul. I rather believe that they chose to side with Paul because they committed Paul to the new journey and not Barnabas. Maybe Barnabas left that night. Perhaps he chose not to stay around to negotiate his way through that minefield of opinions in the church at Antioch. The best part of all is that both of these strong-minded men got over the disagreement. That, too, takes enormous grace.

In too many cases the battle goes on and on and on, and the ministry becomes fractured because the opposing parties are not big enough to get over the initial hurt. Many people today emotionally are sitting in dark rooms, eaten up with bitterness because of an argument that they had with someone a long time ago. They feel they were humiliated or they feel they weren't listened to. How many are living out their lives with their spiritual shades drawn, thinking to themselves, *I'll have nothing more to do with the church* because of an argument they witnessed or maybe participated in? We need to be people who can disagree in grace and then press on, even if the disagreement leads to a separation.

A FEW PERSONAL REMARKS

Let me share a few things I have learned over the years that have to do with disagreements and/or relating to those with whom I may not dot the same "I" or cross the same "T" theologically. To save time, I'll be specific and to the point. I'm not a hard-line, five-point Calvinist. However, I have no trouble calling those who do embrace this viewpoint my brothers and sisters in the faith. In fact, I continue to minister with them, and they with me. On more than one occasion I have invited those who represent reformed theology to speak in our pulpit in Fullerton. I have no problem with that whatsoever. I love those folks! I don't see it as an issue worth breaking fellowship over. Grace covers the difference.

Here's another grace-binding example: I'm not a charismatic. However, I don't feel it is my calling to shoot great volleys of theological artillery at my charismatic brothers and sisters. Who knows how much good they have done and the magnificent ministries many of them have? The church I pastor is not a charismatic church. The doctrinal roots of our church are not in that camp—probably never will be. But that does not mean that we break fellowship with individuals who are more of that persuasion or that we take potshots at them. There was a time in my life when I would have done that. Thankfully, I've grown up a little and learned that God uses many of them, in song as well as in writing and in pulpits today. Grace helps to hold us close.

I do not embrace covenant theology, but I have a number of pastor friends who are covenant theologians. Some of them are in my circle of friends in the ministry. We disagree on certain points of doctrine, but we're on the same team. We're going to spend eternity together. We're going to meet the Lord in the air (whether they believe it or not!). So we might as well enjoy each other's company on earth.

I have a friend who jokingly says he is so premillennial he doesn't even eat Post Toasties in the morning. Well, God bless him . . . I'm just not that extreme. I happen to be premillennial and pretribulational in my theological position, but I don't see that as an issue worth breaking Christian fellowship over. The deity of Christ is certainly crucial. And the inerrancy of Scripture as well as a few other crucial issues. But most of the things we would name are not. Let's face it, there are far more things that draw us together than separate us.

The words of C. S. Lewis come to my mind. Following his conversion in 1929, he wrote to a friend: "When all is said (and truly said) about divisions of Christendom, there remains, by God's mercy, an enormous common ground."[7] In light of this, my encouragement for you today is that each one of us should pursue what unites us with others rather than the few things that separate us. The "common ground" is vast. It's high time we focus on that. It will take grace, I remind you.

I speak at a number of different schools, including Christian schools and colleges, seminaries, and secular universities. And even though I would not necessarily endorse or encourage someone to study at some of these schools, it does not mean that I should not speak there or minister there or ask God to use me as I minister there. Grace frees me to disagree and to speak openly of Christ even in places that disagree with me.

There was a time in my life when I had answers to questions no one was asking. I had a position that was so rigid I would fight for every jot and tittle. I mean, I couldn't list enough things that I'd die for. The older I get, the shorter that list gets, frankly.

As I mentioned at the beginning of this chapter, I am learning that growing old gracefully and graciously is an important assignment. If I lose an argument, I should lose it graciously. If I win an argument, I am to accept it humbly. The most important thing is to glorify God—win or lose.

MODELING GRACE THROUGH
DISAGREEABLE TIMES

I close this chapter with several comments that may help you handle future disagreeable times in a gracious manner.

First, *always leave room for an opposing viewpoint.* If you don't have room for an opposing viewpoint, you're not going to do well when you get teenagers. Teens can be among our best teachers. I know ours have been. They haven't always been right, nor have I. However, I have learned in rearing teenagers that they are great at pointing out another point of view, if nothing else than just to make me think, just to challenge me, just to remind me that there is another way of viewing things. I can assure you, it has helped me in my ministry. It has certainly helped me in my relationship with those to whom I am personally accountable. Opposition is good for our humility.

Second, *if an argument must occur, don't assassinate.* An argument—even a strong clash—is one thing, but killing folks is another. I have seen individuals in an argument verbally hit below the belt and assault another's character. I've seen a lot of mud slinging happen in arguments related to the work of the church. I've seen brutal character assassinations occur in the name of religion—in public speaking as well as in writing—and they are all ugly memories. No need for that. If we must fight, let's fight fair.

Third, *if you don't get your way, get over it, get on with life*. If you don't get your way in a vote at a church, get over it. The vote was taken (if the church has integrity, the vote was handled with fairness), now get on with it. Just press on. And don't rehearse the fight or the vote year after year. The work of God slows down when we are not big enough to take it on the chin and say, "We lost!" Having been raised in the South, I didn't know the South lost the Civil War until I was in junior high school . . . and even then it was debatable among my teachers. Be big enough to say, "We lost." Grace will help.

Fourth, *sometimes the best solution is a separation*. There is good biblical support for this, remember. Paul and Barnabas simply couldn't go on together, so they separated. If I can't go on with the way things are in a particular ministry, I need to resign! But in doing so I should not drag people through my unresolved conflicts because I didn't get my way. If separation is the best solution, doing it graciously is essential. If your disagreements are starting to outweigh your agreements, you ought to give strong consideration to pulling out. Who knows? This may be God's way of moving you on to another dimension of ministry.

This chapter has been helpful for me personally. That may seem unusual, but occasionally an author needs to read his stuff with enough objectivity that it speaks directly to him. Over the past several years, disagreements voiced by various sources about matters of opinion have been more intense than usual. Some things especially have been hard to hear and painful to read. Cynthia and I have bitten our tongues on more than one occasion and refused to defend ourselves. In some cases we have been misrepresented and, though we've made a few attempts to correct the perception, misunderstanding persists. Erroneous statements and exaggerated rumors designed to discredit our ministry occasionally resurface. And it's painful. Things have been said against us that have caused some to question our credibility, which makes it difficult to stay silent and go on in grace. But we shall. Our confidence is that God will vindicate our integrity.

I now realize that the pain has been great because grace has been absent in so much of what others have thought, said, and written. But God gives grace for such times as these. What Cynthia and I must do is draw upon it, claim it, and give it in return . . . in abundance. I am convinced that God's grace will see us through those occasions, even when others disagree. It always has.

And so . . . graciously disagreeing, we press on. It's all part of practicing what one preaches, right?

10

Grace: Up Close and Personal

~

BESIDES THE BIBLE, PERHAPS THE GREATEST book ever written was *The Pilgrim's Progress*. Those who are not familiar with this seventeenth-century classic would be surprised to know it was written by a man enduring his third term in jail. The first time he was in for six long years, the second time, for another six. The reason for both of those times behind bars was the same: preaching the gospel of Jesus Christ. When he returned for a third sentence, John Bunyan, a tinker from Bedford, England, was led by God to write his immortal work. Like Handel when composing his musical magnum opus, *Messiah*, Bunyan's pen moved rapidly. As one man described it, ". . . it moved, indeed, with the speed of a dream—and the dream became a book."[1]

The book, published over three hundred years ago, has touched lives literally around the globe. Who can imagine the multiple millions of copies, the numerous translations that have been released? Everywhere I turn I find others who, like me, have worn out more than one copy and still find delight in returning to the volume for personal enrichment. I reserve this endorsement for very few books, but I would say without hesitation that it is a creative masterpiece where biblical truth is made relevant for any generation.

It is the fascinating story of a man called Christian whose pilgrimage from earth to heaven, from sin to salvation, is full of all the struggles and pitfalls life could throw at him. Following his incredible journey, he reaches his long-awaited destination, the "paradise of God." From start to finish, Christian must deal with friend and foe alike, all of whom have descriptive names, like Evangelist, Help, Interpreter—who encourage him in his "progress"—and Pliable, Obstinate, Hypocrisy, Apollyon, a giant named Despair, and many others who hinder him.

Of special trouble to Christian is Legality, whose dwelling, as you would imagine, was Mount Sinai. In the earlier part of his journey, Christian is traveling with a heavy pack on his back (sin) and none of those who worked against him could help relieve him of his burden . . . especially Legality, as one part states:

> This *Legality* . . . is not able to set thee free from the burden. No man was as yet ever rid of his burden by him; no, nor ever is like to be: ye cannot be justified by the works of the law.[2]

Shortly after encountering Legality, Christian is led by Interpreter into a large room full of dust. It had never been swept since the day it was built. Bunyan does a superb job describing how the room was swept and cleaned:

> Then he took him by the hand, and led him into a very large parlor that was full of dust, because never swept; the which after he had reviewed a little while, the *Interpreter* called for a man to sweep. Now, when he began to sweep, the dust began so abundantly to fly about, that Christian had almost therewith been choked. Then said the *Interpreter* to a damsel that stood by, Bring hither the water, and sprinkle the room; the which, when she had done, it was swept and cleansed with pleasure.
> Then said *Christian*, What means this?

The *Interpreter* answered, This parlor is the heart of a man that was never sanctified by the sweet grace of the gospel; the dust is his original sin and inward corruptions, that have defiled the whole man. He that began to sweep at first, is the *Law*; but she that brought water, and did sprinkle it, is the *Gospel*. Now, whereas thou sawest, that so soon as the first began to sweep, the dust did not fly about that the room by him could not be cleansed, but that thou wast almost choked therewith; this is to shew thee, that the law, instead of cleansing the heart (by its working) from sin, doth revive, put strength into, and increase it in the soul, even as it doth discover and forbid it, for it doth not give power to subdue.

Again, as thou sawest the damsel sprinkle the room with water, upon which it was cleansed with pleasure; this is to shew thee, that when the gospel comes in the sweet and precious influences thereof to the heart, then, I say, even as thou sawest the damsel lay the dust by sprinkling the floor with water, so is sin vanquished and subdued, and the soul made clean through the faith of it, and consequently fit for the King of glory to inhabit.[3]

It took *grace*, "the sweet grace of the gospel," to cleanse that room of all its defilements. It still does.

All those familiar with *The Pilgrim's Progress* have no trouble remembering that the pilgrim's name throughout the book is Christian. To my surprise few remember his original name, even though it is plainly stated in the allegory. In the scene where it first appears, the pilgrim is conversing with a porter:

PORTER   What is your name?

PILGRIM   My name is now *Christian*, but my name at the first was *Graceless*.[4]

The same could be said for all of us today who claim the glorious name of Jesus Christ as our Lord and Savior. Our name is now Christian, but it has not always been so. That title was given to us the moment we believed, the day we took God at His word and accepted the gift of eternal life He offered us. Prior to the name change, we were Graceless, indeed.

My question is this: Now that Christ has come into our lives and ripped that heavy pack of sin off our backs, are we now full of grace? Having been *Graceless* for so many years, are we "grace conscious," are we "grace aware," are we experiencing a "grace awakening," are we truly becoming "grace-full"? Models of grace are needed now more than ever.

THE PROCESS THAT LEADS TO
GRACE AWAKENING

Want a boost of encouragement? Our God is working toward that end in all of His children. It is His constant pursuit, His daily agenda, as He points us toward our final destination, "the Celestial City," as Bunyan calls it. Having cleansed our hearts of the debris of inward corruptions and the dust of sin's domination, God is now daily at work awakening grace within us, perfecting our character and bringing it to completion. Let me show you from four New Testament sources why I am so sure of that:

> And we know that God causes all things to work together for good to those who love God, to those who are called according to His purpose. For whom He foreknew, He also predestined to become conformed to the image of His Son, that He might be the first-born among many brethren. (Rom. 8:28–29)

> For I am confident of this very thing, that He who began a good work in you will perfect it until the day of Christ Jesus. (Phil. 1:6)

Who will transform the body of our humble state into conformity with the body of His glory, by the exertion of the power that He has even to subject all things to Himself. (Phil. 3:21)

Do not lie to one another, since you laid aside the old self with its evil practices, and have put on the new self who is being renewed to a true knowledge according to the image of the One who created him. (Col. 3:9–10)

Don't miss those key phrases: "become conformed," "He who began . . . will perfect" (bring to completion), "transform," and "being renewed." We are all engaged in the same process, our own "pilgrim's progress," under God's mighty hand and constant surveillance. He is working for us, not against us . . . and His plans are for good, not evil. His goal for us is clearly set forth: that we might become like His Son, "full of grace and truth."

As I think about our becoming people of awakening grace, I believe at least three things are involved in the process:

First, *it takes time.* Learning anything takes time. Becoming good models of grace, it seems, takes years! Like wisdom, it comes slowly. But God is in no hurry as He purges graceless characteristics from us. But we can count on this, for sure: He is persistent.

Second, *it requires pain.* The "dust" in our room doesn't settle easily. I know of no one who has adopted a "grace state of mind" painlessly. Hurt is part of the curriculum in God's schoolroom.

Third, *it means change.* Being "graceless" by nature, we find it difficult to be anything different. We lack it, we resist it, we fail to show it, but God never stops His relentless working. He is committed to our becoming more like His Son. Remember? "He who began a good work . . . *will* bring it to completion."

SOME EVERYDAY EXAMPLES OF CLAIMING GRACE

In *Mere Christianity* by C. S. Lewis we read:

> The real Son of God is at your side. He is beginning to turn you into
> the same kind of thing as Himself. He is beginning, so to speak, to "in-
> ject" His kind of life and thought, . . . into you; beginning to turn the tin
> soldier into a live man. The part of you that does not like it is the part
> that is still tin. [5]

I am intrigued by the word picture painted by C. S. Lewis. While
pondering the thought of those areas that are "still tin" in my own life,
it occurred to me that *that* is where I must claim the grace of God. All
of us could say the same thing. And so I pulled my concordance off the
shelf, located the word *grace*, and began to study the places in the
New Testament that addressed or illustrated some common everyday
examples of "tin" where most of us are still in need of claiming God's
grace. I found five very tender spots where help is needed from our
Lord: insecurity, weakness, abrasiveness, compromise, and pride. I
realize these are all intensely personal battles, but if grace doesn't
come to our rescue up close and personal, who needs it? And so, for
the next few pages let's allow this soothing oil to touch some of the
"tin" in our lives. Maybe by bringing grace up this close and making
it personal, we'll be able to get rid of a few rusty spots that have been
a plague long enough. I hope it will help accelerate our own pilgrim's
progress toward an awakening of Christlike grace:

1. *Claiming the grace to be what I am* (the "tin" of insecurity).

> After that He appeared to more than five hundred brethren at one
> time, most of whom remain until now, but some have fallen asleep; then
> He appeared to James, then to all the apostles; and last of all, as it were
> to one untimely born, He appeared to me also. For I am the least of the
> apostles, who am not fit to be called an apostle, because I persecuted the
> church of God. But by the grace of God I am what I am, and His grace

toward me did not prove vain; but I labored even more than all of them, yet not I, but the grace of God with me. Whether then it was I or they, so we preach and so you believed. (1 Cor. 15:6–11)

In my years of ministry, during which I have rubbed shoulders with numerous Christians, I have observed that many of God's servants are afraid to be who they are. Granted, I find some who haven't a clue as to their own identity (since they are so busy pleasing people), but the majority are in another category: They know, but they are uncomfortable letting the truth be known. They are concerned about things such as their image, or what someone might think or say, or more often, "If they knew the *real* me, they wouldn't like me."

The scripture I just recorded is helpful. Paul writes candidly of his own poor track record. After listing the gallery of the "greats" to whom the risen Lord appeared (Peter, James, the apostles), he states "last of all . . . He appeared to me." This is not false humility, it's historical fact. But what speaks with vivid eloquence is how Paul refers to himself as "one untimely born." You may be shocked to know the Greek term refers to one born before the full period of gestation— one who was aborted—literally, "the dead fetus." It means one who was totally devoid of spiritual life.

If that isn't enough, Paul sees himself not simply as among the last but "least" of the apostles, having been one who persecuted the church. While those others he names were defending and building up the body, he was hard at work assaulting it, hoping to destroy it. That is Paul's estimation of himself, when he stands alongside those men of God. That could have done a number on the man's self-esteem, but it didn't. While not denying the reality of his dark side, Paul refused to cringe and hide, crippled by feelings of insecurity. Why? The answer is clear: Grace. God's awakening, invigorating grace changed his whole perspective. "But by the grace of God I am what I am, and His grace toward me did not prove vain; but I labored even more than all of them, yet not I, but the grace of God with me" (1 Cor. 15:10).

Grace made him what he was. Grace gave him courage to be who he was. Grace energized him to accomplish what he did. By realizing that he did not deserve and could never earn the privileges given him, Paul was freed to be exactly who he was and do precisely what he was called to do. Grace became his silent partner, his constant traveling companion, his invisible security, since he (in himself) was in no way deserving of the part he played in God's unfolding drama. I cannot help but mention that he refused to compare himself to and compete with his peers. Grace relieves us of all that. I love the way one commentary describes it: "In spite of his unfitness to bear the name, the grace of God has made him equal to it. The persecutor has been forgiven and the abortion adopted."[6]

If insecurity happens to be the "tin" in your life, I suggest large doses of grace applied daily. Bring it up close and personal. You will find it has healing power, bringing soothing relief. If it worked for Paul the persecutor, I can assure you it works for insecure pilgrims today.

2. *Claiming the grace to learn from what I suffer* (the "tin" of weakness).

And because of the surpassing greatness of the revelations, for this reason, to keep me from exalting myself, there was given me a thorn in the flesh, a messenger of Satan to buffet me—to keep me from exalting myself! Concerning this I entreated the Lord three times that it might depart from me. And He has said to me, "My grace is sufficient for you, for power is perfected in weakness." Most gladly, therefore, I will rather boast about my weaknesses, that the power of Christ may dwell in me. Therefore I am well content with weaknesses, with insults, with distresses, with persecutions, with difficulties, for Christ's sake; for when I am weak, then I am strong. (2 Cor. 12:7–10)

Another undeniable struggle all of us live with is our own human weaknesses, which crop up any number of ways again and again. We suffer. We hurt. We fail. We blow it. We feel bad. Medication won't relieve it. Prayer doesn't remove it. Complaining doesn't help it. Our problem? We are just human! Imperfection dogs our steps.

In Paul's case he lived with the "thorn," some form of excruciating pain, which refused to leave except on rare occasions. When it returned it never failed to leave him weak and feeling terribly human. How could he go on in spite of such suffering? The answer is the same as before: Grace.

It was grace that made him "content with weaknesses." And once that contentment came, strength revived within him. Not even insults, distresses, or persecutions could sideline the apostle once grace gave him contentment in weakness.

It works not only for a first-century apostle-missionary, it works for us today. By not hiding or denying our weaknesses, others are made to feel closer to us. Vulnerability invites people in, helps them identify with and feel comfortable around us. Grace enables us to admit our struggles. When we find contentment even in our weaknesses, the anxiety that accompanies keeping up a good front vanishes, freeing us to be real. You don't have to rely any longer on power ties or a certain brand of wristwatch or alligator-skin shoes. How easy for those things to become unspoken grace killers.

I appreciate it when professional athletes don't hide their weaknesses, don't you? When we watch them perform with such dexterity and accuracy, we can easily believe that all parts of their lives are that slick and polished. When we lived in Boston back in the mid-1960s, Bill Russell was the star basketball center for the world-champion Celtics. It was fun watching him and his team play at the Boston Garden. He dominated the boards, and with effortless ease, he seemed to take charge of the whole court once the game got underway. The whole team revolved around his larger-than-life presence. Sports fans watched him from a distance, respecting his command of the sport. Then, in a radio interview, I heard a comment from Russell that immediately made me feel closer to him, though I have never met the man. The sports reporter asked the all-pro basketball star if he ever got nervous. Russell's answer was surprising. He said, in his inimitable style of blunt honesty, "Before every game, I vomit." Shocked, the sportscaster asked what he did if they played two games the same day. Unflappable Russell replied, "I vomit twice." All of a sudden the man no longer seemed like a specimen of athletic perfection . . . he had weaknesses, too.

We have nothing to hide when it comes to the fragile and imperfect areas of our lives. Say it! Admit it! Grace will help you do so. It will get you safely through. Remember John Newton's lines:

> Through many dangers, toils, and snares
> I have already come;
> 'Tis grace hath brought me safe thus far,
> And grace will lead me home.[7]

Not self-effort, not perfectionism. (May God help you who are perfectionists and those who live with you. Both need tons of grace.) I heard the other day that a perfectionist is a person who takes pains and gives them to others. Grace will help you let the cracks of your life show. Let them show! No one can identify with those who give the impression of nothing but flawless performances and slick success. We can all identify with failure and imperfection. And God has ways of honoring those times.

I remember preaching a sermon during which I was struggling with a sore throat and laryngitis. I could not raise my voice above a whisper. So I thought, *I'll save my voice by whispering.* (I learned later that is the worst possible thing I could have done for my voice, but I didn't know it then.) When I finished that sermon, I wanted to run. I felt my delivery was terrible. I thought it was the worst job I had ever done. Then something surprising happened. I don't know how many people contacted me later and said, "You'll never know how that ministered to me." There I was in obvious physical weakness and pain . . . hindered, restrained by something I could not control or stop. Yet it became encouragement to others, especially those who said they wondered if I ever struggled with weaknesses. Immediately, they could identify with me rather than view me from a distance in some sort of unrealistic admiration. I think you see my point: Grace in weakness enables us to become instruments of power in God's hands.

3. *Claiming the grace to respond to what I encounter* (the "tin" of abrasiveness).

> Conduct yourselves with wisdom toward outsiders, making the most of the opportunity. Let your speech always be with grace, seasoned, as it were, with salt, so that you may know how you should respond to each person. (Col. 4:5–6)

This "grace" has to do with our response to people. Have you noticed that life is really a series of responses? We spend our days responding to the lost who do not know the Savior, responding to those who are fellow members of the body, responding to children, to parents, to friends, to those in need, to colleagues at work, and to fellow students at school. In light of that, did you notice what Paul writes about the tendency toward abrasiveness, this "tin man" in all of us? He mentions the need for wisdom, talk seasoned with salt, the right kind of response to others. *Salt* here probably carries with it the idea of good taste, tactfulness, well-timed words. Grace will give us that and much more, like pleasantness. Let your speech always be attractive, charming, winsome, pleasant. When it comes to having words like that, grace is a master.

If I had the power in my hand to touch and heal one part of the body of Christ, I would touch the tongue, certainly including my own. It is the tongue that spreads more diseases in the body than any other organ—specifically, when it lacks grace, which gives needed tact. "Tact is like a girdle. It enables you to organize the awkward truth more attractively."[8] Truth alone can be a bit harsh and abrasive. Occasionally, it is too sharp, sometimes brutal. There is nothing like a nice supply of grace to make the truth attractive. Grace helps us cushion our words so that the truth can be received without needless offense.

> Tactfulness is an approach to another human being which involves being sincere and open in communication while at the same time show-ing respect for the other person's feelings— and taking care not to hurt him unnecessarily. . . . It involves a trust or faith in the other person and communicates this message: I trust you will be able to handle what I'm going to tell you. I respect your feelings and will do my best to guard against my own destructive tendencies so that I don't hurt you unneces-sarily.[9]

While I am on the subject of tact, an antidote for abrasiveness, this is a good time for me to mention the importance of a good sense of humor. If there is anything that will help strengthen the charming magnet of grace, it is the ability to laugh at oneself, to laugh at life, to find humor in everyday encounters with people. Talk about sprinkling salt to enhance the taste! Humor works like magic.

One of my long-term friends and mentors, Howie Hendricks, is a master at this. I have loved him and listened to him for over thirty years! Time and again I've seen him warm up hundreds of people packed in the same room—very few of them knowing each other—by his winsome words, usually spiced with humor. What an ambassador of grace! If I have learned nothing else from the man, I have learned the importance of speaking the truth forcefully and clearly, yet in a nondestructive manner. Have you observed that some communicators virtually bludgeon people with the Bible? Never my friend Howie Hendricks. And it is amazing to see how people open up once they know we care about their feelings. Who was it? Mary Poppins, I think, who said, "A spoonful of sugar makes the medicine go down." If abrasiveness happens to be some of the "tin" you wrestle with, grace added to your speech will help you respond to whatever you encounter.

4. *Claiming the grace to stand for what I believe* (the "tin" of compromise).

> Remember those who led you, who spoke the word of God to you; and considering the result of their conduct, imitate their faith. Jesus Christ is the same yesterday and today, yes and forever. Do not be carried away by varied and strange teachings; for it is good for the heart to be strengthened by grace, not by foods, through which those who were thus occupied were not benefited. (Heb. 13:7–9)

The writer is bringing his thoughts to a close. In doing so he addresses a concern on his heart, namely the tendency on the part of some to give up the faith because times are hard. Persecutions are abounding. Martyrdom is occurring. And some are wondering, *Have I really believed in vain? Should I continue this Christian walk?* Some, in fact, are recanting. And so the writer takes up his pen to encourage them to keep standing for what they believe. "Don't give up! Don't concede. Don't surrender." It is the tendency to compromise that concerns him.

That same tendency is present in every generation, certainly our own. While sitting snugly in church, surrounded by fellow Christians, we feel as strong and determined as a steer in a blizzard. We feel like we would die for our faith. Yet twenty-four hours later, in the midst of our work, we're surrounded by those who hate the faith. It would be eye-opening to find out how many of these faith-haters know we are Christians. In the workplace there is the tendency to concede, to stay quiet when the subject of faith surfaces. Haven't you wondered why? The answer is here . . . we lack grace. Maybe you never realized it before, but grace strengthens us. It strengthens our hearts, awakens in us the courage to stand firm. How? What is it about grace that gives us strength to stand up for what we believe? Maybe it is because grace keeps us from being what we are not. Maybe it is the authenticity it prompts within us. Grace strips away the tin, rips off the masks, helps us to be ourselves, so that when we speak of our faith it rings true. Could it be that you compromise your faith where you work or where you go to school because you've tried to appear to be something you're not? Grace is so relieving, so strengthening, it removes the phony.

So far we have uncovered four areas of "tin" commonly found in ourselves: insecurity, weakness, abrasiveness, and compromise. No one can argue that we need grace up close and personal to come to terms with each. But the list is incomplete without my including a final area that plagues us all.

5. *Claiming the grace to submit to what I need* (the "tin" of pride).

> But He gives a greater grace. Therefore it says, "GOD IS OPPOSED TO THE PROUD, BUT GIVES GRACE TO THE HUMBLE." Submit therefore to God. Resist the devil and he will flee from you. (James 4:6–7)

> You younger men, likewise, be subject to your elders; and all of you, clothe yourselves with humility toward one another, for GOD IS OPPOSED TO THE PROUD, BUT GIVES GRACE TO THE HUMBLE. (1 Pet. 5:5)

Both of those New Testament scriptures find their source in Proverbs 3:34: "Though He scoffs at the scoffers. / Yet He gives grace to the afflicted."

Charles Bridges, a fine nineteenth-century student of the Old Testament, writes: "On no point is the mind of God more fully declared than against pride. . . . A *lowly* spirit—a deep conviction of utter nothingness . . . is a most adorning grace. Nor is it an occasional or temporary feeling . . . but a habit, 'clothing' the man . . . 'from the sole of the foot to the head.' . . . He pours it [grace] out plentifully upon humble hearts."[10]

Few qualities are more stubbornly persistent within us than pride. It is ever present! I find it absolutely amazing that we who deserve to have been left as aborted fetuses and not given life (as Paul put it earlier) should have anything to feel proud about. Nevertheless, pride is always there, ever ready to defend itself. It is also clever. It has the ability to go underground and mask its ugliness in subtle, quiet ways. Because it doesn't fit the Christian life for anyone to be overtly proud, we find our pride in other ways: our work, our salaries, our prestige, the power and influence we wield, our titles, our clothing, our approach to people, our tendency to manipulate. It is all so unattractive, so inappropriate. As powerful as any influence, pride is a classic grace killer.

But let it be understood that God will not bless what springs from pride. As Scripture repeatedly reminds us, He brings His mighty hand down over our lives and presses His sovereign fingers into areas where it hurts. We sigh, we squirm, we struggle, and (hopefully) we lay hold of grace and finally submit. What blessed submission! It is in those hurting areas where we cannot handle it on our own that God does His very best work.

George Matheson of Scotland echoes the discipline of his personal despair in his book *Thoughts for Life's Journey* when he writes:

> My soul, reject not the place of thy prostration! It has ever been the robing room for royalty. Ask the great ones of the past what has been the spot of their prosperity; they will say, "It was the cold ground on which

I once was laying." Ask Abraham; he will point you to the sacrifice of Moriah. Ask Joseph; he will direct you to his dungeon. Ask Moses; he will date his fortune from his danger in the Nile. Ask Ruth; she will bid you build her monument on the field of her toil. Ask David; he will tell you that his songs came from the night. Ask Job; he will remind you that God answered him out of the whirlwind. Ask Peter; he will extol his submission in the sea. Ask John; he will give the palm to Patmos. Ask Paul he will attribute his inspiration to the light that struck him blind. Ask one more—the Son of Man. Ask Him whence has come His rule over the world. He will answer, "From the cold ground on which I was lying—the Gethsemane ground; I received my sceptre there." Thou too, my soul, shalt be garlanded by Gethsemane. The cup thou fain wouldst pass from thee will be thy coronet in the sweet by-and-by. The hour of thy loneliness will crown thee. The day of thy depression will regale thee. It is the *desert* that will break forth into singing; it is the trees of thy silent *forest* that will clasp their hands.[11]

My fellow pilgrim, is the progress more painful than you expected? Thinking you were in for a Disneyland experience, have you been surprised to find yourself on cold, barren ground—lonely, depressed, and broken? Are you beginning to wonder if you are on the wrong road? Trust me, you are not. God is at work in you. His "mighty hand" is above you. His love is around you. His grace is available to you. Awake and claim it.

George Matheson and John Bunyan both would agree: You are in the "robing room for royalty."[12] The tailor's name is Grace . . . and when you are perfectly fitted, the process will end.

11

Are You Really a
Minister of Grace?

THIS CHAPTER IS DEDICATED TO ALL WHO are in ministry.

I realize that statement prompts most of you to think, *Well, that leaves me out. I'm not a preacher, I'm not an evangelist or a missionary . . . I don't work for a church.* Let me clarify that my opening comment has to do with all who are in ministry, not just those in vocational Christian service. By "ministry" I am including anyone who serves some segment of the body of Christ on a consistent basis.

Perhaps you are a teacher of a class, an elected officer in a church, or maybe you're a counselor, a Christian speaker, a musician. Maybe you are involved in Christian education or camping . . . *whatever.* You may or may not earn your living from this source of activity, but you are deliberately and regularly engaged in some form of ministry-related involvement that influences others, most of whom are believers in Jesus Christ. You are the target of my thoughts throughout this eleventh chapter.

Now that I have your attention, I want to ask you a crucial question, which only you can answer: Are you really a minister of grace? This could be asked in a variety of other ways:

- When you do what you do, do you dispense grace?
- Are the people you serve given the freedom to be who they are, or who you expect them to be?
- Do you let others go or do you smother them . . . control them?
- Would folks feel intimidated or relieved in your presence?
- Are you cultivating spontaneous, creative celebrants, or fearful captives?
- Do you encourage, build up, and affirm those to whom you minister?

It's time to take off the gloves, rip off the masks, knock off the rationalizations, and face the truth head-on. Are you one who models and ministers grace or not? Is what you're doing the work of your own flesh energized by your own strength? Are you relying on your charisma to pull it off? Do you often have a hidden agenda? How about your motive? With a captive audience hanging on to your words and following your ministry with unquestioned loyalty, do you exploit them . . . do you use your power for your own purposes? Is the enhancement of your image of major importance to you, or can you honestly say that your work is directed and empowered by the Spirit of God. Is yours a "grace awakening" ministry?

<h2 style="text-align:center">STRONG MESSAGE FROM A
SPIRIT-DIRECTED PROPHET</h2>

To help you appreciate the value of being a minister of grace, I want to introduce you to one of the most obscure men in the Bible. He was a prophet who lived and wrote in the ancient days of the Old Testament. His name is Zechariah. His book is the next to last book of the

Old Testament, just before Malachi. Most folks—even church folks—are not at all familiar with this powerful prophet. Therefore, a little background information is necessary before we can appreciate how he ties in to my earlier questions.

Historical Background

Jerusalem lay in ruins. Her wall of protection had been leveled, nothing more than piles of debris, rocks, and stones scattered across the landscape. The Hebrews' houses had been burned and destroyed years earlier, actually decades ago. Equally tragic, the temple of the Lord lay in ruins. The chosen people lived in captivity in the distant land of Babylon. After seventy years of this existence, some began to make their way back to the city of Jerusalem, back to their beloved Zion. Some returned under Nehemiah's leadership and rebuilt the wall. It proved to be quite a task because many of them who had returned earlier were more interested in constructing their own houses than they were in building a wall of defense around the city. But thanks to Nehemiah's persistence and the people's cooperation, that job finally got finished. In the meantime, the temple had only its foundation laid. There it sat in virtual neglect for fifteen or sixteen years; no one seemed to care. After completing the wall, the Jews went back to their own suburbs and returned to the rebuilding of their own houses. The wall was finished, but not the temple.

That need became a burden to a prophet named Haggai. No more single-minded prophet ever wrote in all the Bible than Haggai (his writings appear just before Zechariah). The man comes with strong, severe, and pungent admonitions. With sharp words and stinging rebukes, including a few sarcastic comments, Haggai communicated that the temple of God needed immediate attention. The late Kyle Yates said that Haggai "tips his arrows with scorn, wings them with sarcasm . . . then speeds them skillfully to the mark. . . . His duty was to take the scattered embers of national pride . . . and kindle the flame anew."[1]

That's an appropriate description of Haggai. But the fact is that folks can stand that kind of preaching only so long. After a while you become apathetic. The shouts and the admonitions, the commands and even the sarcasm lose their bite among the indifferent as apathy returns. So the temple remained unfinished in spite of Haggai's persistent albeit wearisome harassment.

The governor through those tumultuous times was Zerubbabel, who lived with the task of getting the temple project completed. But he relied on the motivation of prophets to stir the citizens into action. Haggai did what he could, but it proved to be not enough. It took another prophet whom God brought on the scene as Haggai departed. That prophet's name was Zechariah; he had the same vision that Haggai had but a much different style of communicating it to the people. His predecessor had been severe and stinging in his reproofs. Not Zechariah. His approach was more colorful and gracious. As we would say today, Zechariah was easier to live with.

Kyle Yates wrote this of Zechariah:

> A serious depression, with crop failures and apparent ruin, faced the Jewish people who had responded to the call of Haggai to build the house of God. Under the pressure of discouragement and want that faced them they found it easy to fall out. The blunt, prosaic hammering that Haggai did had its effect, but a new voice was needed to lift them into the kind of enthusiasm that would keep them working to the finish line. Zechariah came to the rescue to supply the needed help. . . .
>
> He does not rebuke or condemn or berate the people. With striking colors and vivid imagination he paints glowing pictures of the presence of God to strengthen and help. Words of inspiration flow from his lips.[2]

Zechariah is a book of visions—striking, colorful, and at times mystical. There were occasions when not even the prophet himself understood what he saw, which is what we find in the fourth chapter of his book.

> Then the angel who was speaking with me returned, and roused me as a man who is awakened from his sleep. And he said to me, "What do you see?" And I said, "I see, and behold, a lampstand all of gold with its bowl on the top of it, and its seven lamps on it with seven spouts belonging to each of the lamps which are on the top of it." (Zech. 4:1–3)

As the chapter begins, an angel is speaking to him regarding the vision of a lampstand of gold. It has a bowl on the top and seven lamps on it with seven spouts. Then there are two olive trees, a tree on the right side and another on the left. By now Zechariah is wondering what this was all about. In fact, he asks, ". . . What are these, my lord?" (v. 4). The angel answers, "Don't you know?" To which Zechariah honestly responds, "No, my lord." He had seen what God revealed but he didn't know its meaning, its interpretation.

At this moment we come to a most interesting section of Scripture. We are not left at the mercy of an insightful expositor or some Hebrew scholar to tell us what it means. We get the answer directly from the mouth of the angel. The one who revealed the vision now interprets it for the prophet (and all who would later read this) to understand.

Timeless Reminder

The angel addresses Zerubbabel, the governor whose task it is to see the job to completion. Perhaps Zerubbabel has run low on hope in recent weeks. He has become weary as the building project has lingered unfinished. Maybe it seemed as though it would never be finished, hence the angel's words of hope to the governor:

"This is the word of the Lord to Zerubbabel saying, 'Not by might nor by power, but by My Spirit,' says the Lord of hosts. 'What are you, O great mountain? Before Zerubbabel you will become a plain; and he will bring forth the top stone with shouts of "Grace, grace to it!"'" (v. 6, 7)

Let's understand what he is saying. The mountain represents the enormous number of obstacles facing those who would take up the task. For example, there is apathy within the Jewish community in and around Jerusalem. There is opposition from outside the walls of Zion. There is weariness and a fair amount of indifference from those who had lived under the harsh style, the probing, penetrating words of Haggai. In addition, the "mountain" would include a new genera-tion of Jews who don't have a desire for building the temple, along with the tired, old generation who believes they've already paid their dues. The governor is caught in the middle of all this, along with an unfinished temple, and out of the blue comes a message from God that promises "The mountain will become as a plain." Good news! "The obstacles will be taken care of." In other words, "You don't have to shout louder or worry any longer. Trust in the Lord, Zerubbabel, *God is at work!* But before you exhibit all kinds of human ingenuity and creative skills from the flesh, remember, Zerubbabel, it is not by might nor by power." The primary responsibility for completing the temple is God's, not the governor's. It will be done by the Spirit of God as He moves among God's people.

Might and power (v. 6) intrigue me. They are words that describe human effort, another way of saying the energy of the flesh. They ring a familiar bell in the minds of all ministers, for every one of us has been guilty of occasionally doing the work of God in the energy of the flesh.

Theodore Laetsch, in his thorough work on *The Minor Prophets* says:

> The two Hebrew words *might* and *power* denote inner strength . . .
> inherent power, courageous bravery, fortitude, as well as manpower,

large numbers of soldiers, riches, leaders, well-coordinated organizations, good financial systems, etc. The Lord's work, the building of His Temple, the inner growth, the expansion of His Church cannot be carried out by mere external means. Human strength and wisdom alone will fail. My Spirit must do it![3]

Talk about a relevant message for every minister today! It is this one: *Human wisdom and fleshly energy alone will fail.* God's best work is not going to be done by human might or by fleshly power. The work of God, if done for His greater glory, must be accomplished through His gifted leaders. When facing the mountainlike obstacles inherent in every ministry, we tend to rely on fleshly tactics to get a big job done: manipulations, guilt-giving methods, verbal force as well. Wrong! says this scripture. No! says the Spirit of God. Much of that is nothing more than a carnal display of human strength. It will backfire. As one hymn-writer put it, "The arm of flesh will fail you, ye dare not trust your own."[4]

Our tendency to rely on our own strength is compounded by the very real fact that fleshly power gets results. Human ingenuity works. It raises funds. An excessive amount of energy and manipulation and scheming will cause a large number of people to do more and to work harder and to give money to get a project finished. Overnight results will occur. And there is nothing that feeds our instant-gratification hunger like instant results. Only one major problem: In the final analysis the satisfaction will have a hollow ring to it. It will be empty, a study in futility. The work of the flesh will amount to zilch in light of eternity. The glory will belong to the One who made it happen and the rewards will stop there, too.

God has a better idea. In verse 7 the governor is promised a removal of the obstacles by God's power, and rather than his getting the glory, it will all go to God. And the final capstone of the whole project will be "Grace! Grace!" This temple will be completed . . .

this building will be erected because of the grace of God. I appreciate the way Ken Taylor paraphrases this verse in *The Living Bible:*

> Therefore no mountain, however high, can stand before Zerubbabel! For it will flatten out before him! And Zerubbabel will finish building this Temple with mighty shouts of thanksgiving for God's mercy, declaring that all was done by grace alone. (v. 7)

In light of those immortal words from an ancient prophet, several questions emerge. Why are you relying on "might and power" rather than the Spirit of God? What is it that keeps you returning to human effort and manipulative schemes? What will it take to bring us back to a "by-grace-alone" style of ministry? How much longer will we continue in our hurry-worry leadership mode?

A Strong Warning

To all who are engaged in ministry, a warning is appropriate. Every project you undertake can be accomplished your way or God's way. The energy source of human strength is impressive and logical and effective. It works! Initially, folks cannot tell the diVerence. A ministry built by the energy of the flesh looks just like a ministry built by the energy of the Spirit. Externally, I warn you, it looks the same. But internally, spiritually, down deep in the level of motive, you know in your heart God didn't do it; *you did it!* There is no glory vertically. And equally tragic, there is no grace horizontally.

Let me put it to you straight. Restrain yourself from might and power if you are a minister. Deliberately give the Spirit time and room. Consciously hold yourself back from clever ingenuity and reliance on your own charisma. If you don't, you will live to regret it. You will become a "graceless" minister.

To my pleasant surprise, while reading again Spurgeon's *Lectures to My Students*, written over a hundred years ago, I came across a grand discourse on the "graceless pastor." Only Spurgeon could say it so well:

> A graceless pastor is a blind man elected to a professorship of optics, philosophizing upon light and vision, discoursing upon and distinguishing to others the nice shades and delicate blendings of the prismatic colours, while he himself is absolutely in the dark!
>
> He is a dumb man elevated to the chair of music; a deaf man fluent upon symphonies and harmonies! He is a mole professing to educate eaglets; a limpet elected to preside over angels. . . .
>
> Moreover, when a preacher is poor in grace, any lasting good which may be the result of his ministry, will usually be feeble and utterly out of proportion with what might have been expected. [5]

All this brings us back to my opening question: Are you *really* a minister of grace? Is yours a "grace awakening" ministry? Is your leadership characterized by grace? In almost thirty years of ministry I have observed two very noticeable characteristics of those who lack grace and operate in the energy of the flesh. Both could be called grace killers. One has to do with projects and the other with people.

First, I notice that *those who operate in the flesh use human might in order to accomplish visible projects.* There are always telltale signs: Great emphasis is placed on "success." There is no hesitation to use strategies from the world; secular managerial styles are employed, impressive techniques are used, size and numbers mean too much, and manipulative methods are used for raising money. It is extremely important to make a good impression. Without exception, the importance is placed on impressing people, not glorifying God. Weaknesses are hidden. Vulnerability is out of the question. The great hope is to hear people exclaim, "Wow! Look at that." There is a gnawing hunger for a place in the headlines.

Second, I notice that *those with a might-and-power style rely on personality power to get their way with people.* Several ingredients go into this style of ministry: Charisma. Power plays. Pressure. Force. Threats. Control. Intimidation. Deceit, if necessary. Embarrassment, if essential. Rather than encouraging people to pray, to wait, to seek God's mind, and to rely on His Spirit for clear direction, this style of leadership (I have a hard time calling it a "ministry") abuses people, uses them for unfair advantage, bullies them if they get in the way, and discards them once they are no longer "useful."

All who desire to be ministers of grace need the reminder that this counsel is not popular in a day of great emphasis on rapid church growth and highly efficient methods for making things happen. A prophet today who uses words like, "not by might nor by power" is a lonely voice in the wilderness. You will not find it in newspapers or most magazines (secular or Christian), nor will you find it promoted in most churches. Sadly, it isn't overtly taught in most seminaries, either. There, you may learn to handle the text of Scripture or a system for understanding theology, maybe a fairly good grasp of church history, but being a grace-oriented minister? Not likely.

My warning stands: *Anything that does not result in God's getting the glory ought to be enough to restrain our own might and power so His Spirit can do the job, which includes removing the obstacles.* It is easy to forget that not all the grace killers are "out there" trying to get people under the law. Some are "in here," within the ranks of leadership, trying to do God's will their way.

I once knew a very kind college president who framed a small sign and hung it on the wall leading to his office in the administration building on the campus. Only three words appeared, but they spoke with eloquence, inviting students and faculty in:

KINDNESS SPOKEN HERE.

Enough of the negatives and the warnings in this chapter. Let's turn our thoughts from those who are not examples of grace to how we might become better at modeling and promoting it. Hopefully, the things we uncover from the New Testament will be so invigorating and inviting, some who are now grace killers will become grace givers. And speaking of that, what *are* some of the characteristics of a grace-awakening ministry? How would people know if there is grace to be found in your ministry? I've never seen anyone advertise it, at least not in printed form, but there are ways others can know that "Grace Is Shown Here." Five come to mind.

OBVIOUS MARKS OF A
GRACE-AWAKENING MINISTER

The first of these characteristics is *generosity with personal possessions* (absence of selfishness). In the earliest days of the church, the generosity of God's people was notorious.

> And the congregation of those who believed were of one heart and soul; and not one of them claimed that anything belonging to him was his own; but all things were common property to them. And with great power the apostles were giving witness to the resurrection of the Lord Jesus, and abundant grace was upon them all. For there was not a needy person among them, for all who were owners of land or houses would sell them and bring the proceeds of the sales, and lay them at the apostles' feet; and they would be distributed to each, as any had need. (Acts 4:32–35)

There they were, a flock of sheep struggling for survival in a hostile world of Christ-hating citizens and politicians. They had every reason to live frightened, selfish lives of isolation and secrecy. Not so! Do you know why? We just read the answer: Because "abundant grace was upon them all." That prompted a spirit of generosity, a genuine desire to meet needs. Can you believe the results? "There was not a needy person among them. . . ."

An atmosphere of grace creates an absence of selfishness. After all, it isn't your money, it's God's money. So you give it. It isn't your church, it's God's church; so you share it. They aren't your people, pastor, they're God's people; so you release them. It isn't your project, it's God's project; so you rely on Him. Going back to what we learned from Zechariah's vision, it is His work done His way for His glory. Even though you could raise twice the amount in the energy of the flesh, you refuse to do so. You won't do it! You will trust God to work in His way and in His time. Understand, you will present the need and invite a response, but you will refuse to strongarm your own plan.

By the way, I've noticed that words like *mine* and *keep* and *ours* are not heard in ministries of grace. Neither does a suspicious kind of spirit pervade a place where there is grace. Instead, there is openhanded generosity.

I have learned a lot about grace from the flock I have served here in Fullerton, California, since 1971. What models of generosity! Several years ago when a sister church in downtown Los Angeles was struggling for survival—the historic Church of the Open Door—we were moved with compassion. We kept hearing of their plight over television and reading about it in the paper. We began to pray for them. Our pastoral staff and boards unanimously agreed that we should do more than pray, however. One Sunday we announced that we were going to receive an after-church offering, all of which would be sent to that church to encourage them. I will never forget the enthusiasm. Everybody was thrilled to participate. I cannot remember the exact amount, but somewhere around $18,000 was contributed. More recently, the mid-October 1989 San Francisco earthquake took its toll on two of our sister churches in the Bay area. One was greatly damaged, and the other also needed a fair amount of repair. Again, we felt we should do more than pray and write. With only a brief announcement, an after-church offering was collected, allowing us to send over $8,000 to one church and more than $4,000 to the other. Ours is not a wealthy church, but there is an abundance of grace, which brings generosity with personal possessions. Such unselfish joy is contagious.

Another characteristic of a grace-awakening ministry is *encouragement in unusual situations* (absence of predictability). Where grace abounds you will not only find generosity with personal possessions, you will also find *encouragement in unusual settings.* Grace keeps us flexible, willing to adapt.

Some time after the Jerusalem church was established, God's desire was that they take the gospel to the Gentiles. We read in Acts 11 how it happened.

> So then those who were scattered because of the persecution that arose in connection with Stephen made their way to Phoenicia and Cyprus and Antioch, speaking the word to no one except to Jews alone. But there were some of them, men of Cyprus and Cyrene, who came to Antioch and began speaking to the Greeks also, preaching the Lord Jesus. (Acts 11:19–20)

They first went to Jews alone, but later they found themselves surrounded by Greeks, and so they went to the Greeks also. They didn't change their message. They were still preaching the Lord Jesus. But they were flexible with their method. The target changed from strictly Jews to Jews and Gentiles. That took grace.

When the church at Jerusalem heard of the large numbers of Gentiles who were turning to the Lord in Antioch, they sent Barnabas to check it out. Once in Antioch, he witnessed a new setting. Rather than an all-Jewish congregation, there were Greeks everywhere. He saw the grace of God at work, and he applauded it. He encouraged them. There was no legalism, no "you-ought-to-be-grateful" speeches. No place for shame or warnings. He modeled grace in a different setting. He adapted. Likewise, when you and I minister graciously, we have room for a different way of ministering.

Missionaries who do the best job are people of grace. If they minister cross-culturally, they don't try to change people into Western Christians. They don't try to make the American culture the standard for Christian living. When they are in Latin America they minister to Latinos in a context of Latin America. When they are in the Orient, they adapt to the Oriental way of thinking, because the mind of the Oriental is so different from the Western mind. That is grace! There is a lack of predictability, true freedom, willing adaptability—a sense of comfort in other methods of expression. The absence of a narrow, rule-book mentality frees anyone for an open-hearted ministry. It is fun to be around those who minister like that. There is affirmation along with a lot of flexibility. Rather than requiring a predictable style of response, grace-awakening ministries encourage openness, acceptance, and a willingness to go with the cultural flow. Best of all, converts are given plenty of freedom to learn and to grow.

Years ago, when the Jesus-people ministry was meeting needs out here on the West Coast, some of the churches got pretty nervous with the results. Frankly, I admired the outreach of Calvary Chapel under Chuck Smith's competent and wise leadership; it became one of the dominant forces in that era. Interest in spiritual things remained strong, thanks to Chuck (and others, of course) who decided to reach out to those who were disillusioned on the bleak backwash of the Timothy Leary philosophy. Some of the churches flexed back then and as a result became harbors of hope for young men and women who had dropped out of society.

During that same era a young man stumbled into our church one Sunday evening. He was stunned to see a building full of folks, singing and having a great time together. There he stood, barefoot, cutoffs, no shirt, full beard . . . all alone. I watched from the platform as he stared in amazement. We found out later it was the first time in his life he had ever been inside a church among a congregation. He wandered down a side aisle, looking at us like a calf staring at a new gate. One of our members invited him to sit next to him, shared his hymnal, and answered his questions. It was wonderful to see such grace in action. I loved it!

Following that particular evening meeting the young man immediately came down front to talk. He had a dozen or more questions, all of them excellent. I noticed sand still sticking to the hairs on his legs. He was fresh off the beach. He was treated with kindness and respect. No one told him what he "should" wear or how he "should" act. A couple of fellows invited him to have a Coke and a hamburger with them. He was surprised and accepted. Not surprisingly, he was back the next Sunday. And the next. Within a matter of weeks he became a Christian. He spoke of how our love and acceptance won him. He publicly testified of his faith in Christ when he was baptized. The context of grace gave him room to grow, to think, to be himself, to ask questions. That young man later finished his university work, attended and graduated from seminary, and is now in ministry. I think he's even wearing shoes.

Now let me mention a third mark of grace: *life beyond the letter of Scripture.* When there is a grace-awakening ministry, there is an absence of dogmatism and Bible-bashing. I love the way the apostle Paul writes these thoughts in 2 Corinthians 3:

> Not that we are adequate in ourselves to consider anything as coming from ourselves, but our adequacy is from God, who also made us adequate as servants of a new covenant, not of the letter, but of the Spirit; for the letter kills, but the Spirit gives life. (vv. 5–6)

I want to be careful here, lest you misunderstand. Paul's emphasis in this section of Scripture is on a new-covenant (as opposed to an old-covenant) ministry . . . a ministry of grace rather than law, a thought which he spends quite some time developing. Anyone who reads the second and third chapters of his second letter to the Corinthians with an open mind cannot help but observe a marked departure from what could be called a "traditional" type of ministry.

He promotes—

· a lack of professional adequacy (2:16, 3:5)
· the presence of vulnerable authenticity (2:17)
· an emphasis on personal relationships (3:1–4)
· the importance of a servanthood mentality (3:6)

as he pleads for an attitude of grace, which leads to a teachable spirit rather than the hammerlike poundings of a dogmatic style of teaching.

Handling God's Word accurately is essential for those who minister. Only through its being correctly interpreted can it be correctly applied. The disciplines of good hermeneutics (correct method of biblical interpretation) and capable homiletics (clear communication of biblical truth) should be blended together by those who teach God's Book. Care must be taken, however, to interpret and communicate with grace. When grace is present, there is a spirit of openness, an attitude of compassion, which includes an absence of Bible-bashing and dogmatism.

It is not uncommon for me to meet people who have come out of strict fundamentalist ministries where they were bruised and wounded by a grace killer who presented Scripture in such a rapid-fire, harsh manner, they felt beaten by the "letter of the Law" rather than led and comforted by the Spirit of liberty. Having come out of such a climate many years ago, I understand whereof I write. "The letter kills," states Paul. But the Holy Spirit, ministering in a context of freedom mixed with the charm of grace, "gives life."

While we are here in 2 Corinthians 3, I find a fourth characteristic of a grace-awakening ministry: *liberty with creative expression*. When grace is present there is plenty of freedom provided for creative expression. Paul writes of that this way: "Now the Lord is the Spirit; and where the Spirit of the Lord is, there is liberty" (v. 17). This means there is also an absence of expectations.

I really hope you will let these words seep in slowly and permanently guide your ministry: Where the Spirit of the Lord is, there is room—plenty of room—for liberty.

Commenting on the meaning of the liberty of the Spirit in verse 17, one New Testament authority writes:

> He means that so long as man's obedience to God is dominated and conditioned by obedience to a book and a code of laws he is in the position of an unwilling . . . slave. But when it comes from the operation of the Spirit . . . then the very centre of his being has no other desire than to serve and obey God, for then it is not law but love which binds him.[6]

I observe an interesting phenomenon among caring Christians. I notice that most of us are pretty good in evangelism when it comes to grace. Most of us don't require the lost person to clean up his life before he comes to the Savior. We flex, we bend, we forgive, we tolerate *whatever* among the unsaved. But we don't provide nearly as much liberty once folks come to the Savior. We don't care if they blow smoke in our faces while we witness to them. We don't even talk about it. We cough, we smile, and we continue to share Christ with them. "But they had better not blow smoke in my face as a Christian, not if they claim to be converted!"

Why not? What if that part of their life hasn't been dealt with yet by the Spirit of God? Why are we so intolerant of and impatient with our brothers and sisters? Where's the grace? Think of what others have to put up with when it comes to you and me. Think of the things in your life that are not yet cleaned up. Now maybe it isn't one of the "dirty dozen" or the "nasty nine" that is obvious to everyone, but think of the stuff you still have to work through—things I need to be gracious with you about . . . and you with me. I ask you, where is all this wonderful liberty of which Paul writes? Why do we lay such heavy expectations on each other? Furthermore, what makes us so afraid of creativity?

Do you encourage individuality? Do you find delight in a person on your discipleship team who is just the opposite in style from you? Do you live with that graciously? How about the kid in class who is bored? Let's say he is hyperactive . . . his mind is off somewhere else. I know he is a challenge. (Believe me, I understand, I was like that years ago and was a real task for my teachers.) But what an opportunity for us to demonstrate grace in finding creative expressions for those individuals, encouraging them to develop and become all they are meant to be. The creative minds today were quite likely the hyperactives of yesteryear, the ones who were bored stiff twenty years ago.

If the Spirit of the Lord provides liberty, I suggest that the saints of the Lord take their cues from Him and do the same. Rather than reminding people of all the things they are not, how great it would be—how full of grace, actually—to give them all the room they need to fail and recover, to learn and grow.

This reminds me of one more characteristic of a grace awakening ministry: *release from past failures.* A ministry of grace doesn't keep bringing up the past for the purpose of holding it over people. There is an absence of shame. Paul addresses the sin I Timothy 1:12–14:

> I thank Christ Jesus our Lord, who has strengthened me, because He considered me faithful, putting me into service; even though I was for-

merly a blasphemer and a persecutor and a violent aggressor. And yet I
was shown mercy, because I acted ignorantly in unbelief; and the grace
of our Lord was more than abundant, with the faith and love which are
found in Christ Jesus.

You may be surprised to know that the apostle Paul had every reason to feel ashamed. He was one whose past was dreadful: "formerly
a blasphemer . . . persecutor . . . violent aggressor." Then how could
the same man write, "I am not ashamed" (2 Tim. 1:12)? He gives us
the answer here in 1 Timothy 1:14: Grace was more than abundant.
Blasphemy had abounded in his past, but grace superabounded. Violence and brutality had abounded, but grace superabounded.

What if it read "divorcee"? What if it read "homosexual"? What if it
read "addict"? I realize it reads "blasphemer, persecutor, aggressor."
But what if it read "prostitute" or "ex-con" or "financial failure"
or "murderer"? In a grace-awakened ministry, none of those things in
the past are allowed to hold those people in bondage. They are released, forgiven, and the believer is allowed to go on to a new life in
Christ.

Grace releases people, not only from sin but from shame. Do you
do that in your ministry? Or do you make a note of those things and
keep reminding yourself when that particular name comes up, "Well,
you know, you'd better watch her" or "You've gotta watch him." Do
you give people reasons to feel greater shame? Who knows what
battles of shame most folks struggle with. It is enormous.

Two good friends of mine in the Orange County area of Southern
California are therapists . . . and they are excellent in their work.
Marilyn Meberg and Dr. Earl Henslin have both mentioned to me on
separate occasions that one of the most frequent struggles they try to
help people with is the inner struggle with shame. Since both counselors are Christians, many of their clients are too, yet this does not

free them from shame. To be completely candid about it, it usually intensifies the problem. Why? Because many in God's family are better at encouraging shame in others than they are at releasing it.

Before you question that, stop and think how often you have heard the five words, "You ought to be ashamed" or how many times you have received a look that said the same. Shame is not only counterproductive, it is debilitating. It brings a thick, dark cloud of depression over an already hypersensitive conscience, severing what few threads of self-respect remain. It adds disgrace to what has already been done, leaving one to wallow in the mire of failure rather than claim the release that forgiveness can bring. It holds down rather than lifts up; it steals hope instead of offering encouragement. Shame is a classic grace killer.

Christians can be such shamers! We not only make people ashamed of their wrongs, we shame them for being different. I know a few Christians who have been made to feel ashamed because they never married. Others because they had made a lot of money, all of it honestly and through hard work. Some told me they felt ashamed because their sickness didn't go away, others because their depression didn't end quickly. I know one gentleman who is an absolute joy to be around—so much fun. He told me it isn't uncommon for him to get looks as well as letters of rebuke because he has "too much fun in life." A fine Christian wife and mother told me recently that she was told she "should be ashamed" because she worked outside the home. She is in her mid-fifties and all her children are married.

Dr. Henslin often speaks on this subject. In doing so he distributes a small flier that includes the following list of contrasts, which I have found helpful, and I think you will, too:

SHAME-BASED SPIRITUALITY	HEALTHY SPIRITUALITY
1. Having problems is sin.	Problems are a part of my human condition. I can bring them to God and my fellow Christians.
2. Emotions are sinful.	Emotions are neither good nor bad. It's what I do with them. "Be angry and sin not."
3. Compulsive disease is sinful.	There is a difference between disease and sinful behavior.
4. Having fun is sinful.	There are many different ways to delight in God's goodness.
5. Spirituality = Perfection.	Living within grace not legalism.
6. Sexuality = Sin.	Sexuality is a part of who we are as people and is to be enjoyed.
7. Success (or its lack) is sinful.	Prosperity or poverty is not due to deficient spirituality.
8. Becoming a Christian fixes everything within me.	Accepting Christ in my life enables and empowers me to face issues.
9. If I am not healed it is due to my lack of faith.	Having illness is not a sin. I can avail myself of the best treatment possible.
10. Not being able to think of a clever 10th item may mean I'm not being led by God.	God probably likes the number 9 just as well.[7]

A QUICK REVIEW

We have covered a lot of ground in this chapter. Because it has been a bit lengthy, a quick recap might help.

Those who minister grace are essential in this day of graceless legalism and human might-and-power accomplishments. More than ever we need grace-awakening ministers who free rather than bind. These five characteristics are true of those who serve others in grace:

1. Generosity with personal possessions . . . absence of selfishness
2. Encouragement in unusual settings . . . absence of predictability
3. Life beyond the letter of Scripture . . . absence of dogmatic Bible-bashing
4. Liberty for creative expression . . . absence of expectations
5. Release from past failures . . . absence of shame

Do you remember one of Paul's exhortations to Timothy? His words provide the marching orders for all who take these five characteristics seriously: "Be strong in the grace that is in Christ Jesus" (2 Tim. 2:1)! My fellow ministers, stand tall in it. Be firmly committed to it. Make grace your aim, your pursuit, your passion. Model it. Teach it. Demonstrate it.

"Jefferson Starship" is a singing group that rose to the top in the decade of the 1980s with a song that stayed on the popular hit parade for months: "We Built This City on Rock and Roll." Borrowing my idea from that title, I suggest that we do all we can to change whatever is necessary so that it won't be said, "We built this church on might and power," or "We built this relationship on expectations and shame." Such things will not last. They will fade and ultimately fail. How much better to be able to say, "We built this ministry on truth and grace." Like a house built on rock, such a ministry will outlive us.

12

A Marriage
Oiled by Grace

ACTRESS CELESTE HOLM SPOKE FOR ALL of us when she said, "We live by encouragement and we die without it; slowly, sadly, angrily."[1] There is no way to measure how many find themselves in that tragic situation, but we can be sure the number is astronomical.

The lack of encouragement and affirmation is notorious. It is for that reason so many hate to go to work every day. Or cannot wait to get out of school. Or dread facing the demands of a family. Or do not get more involved in community activities. Responsibilities become little more than a series of grinding, grim assignments without the relief provided by encouragement. This means that those who do affirm and encourage others are not only rare, they are remarkable. Almost invariably, I have found they are people of grace. They model the things I have been writing about in this book . . . and they do so in private just as consistently as they do in public. They value relationships even with the unknown and so called "unimportant."

My years in ministry have allowed me a great deal of exposure to the public, which has included a fair amount of travel. I am usually met at the airport by those whose job it is to transport me to a hotel or the place where I will be speaking. One of the things I enjoy about such encounters is the opportunity to spend several miles with these faithful folks who work behind the scenes, those whose faces and names are not generally known, yet they are vital links in the success of the meetings or the event that is about to transpire. Almost without exception I find these people gracious, servant-hearted givers who carry out their tasks with diligence and humility. Therefore, I deliberately do my best to treat them with grace—to express appreciation, to lift their spirits, to affirm the importance of their role in the particular ministry I have the privilege of being a part of.

I cannot tell you how many times such a person has expressed surprise that anyone has bothered to notice or taken the time to encourage. I recall one young man who, after we had gotten better acquainted and enjoyed a few laughs together, spoke candidly of how difficult it had been trying to please some of those he had assisted. He commented on one well-known public figure (whom he did not name) who was such a pain in private. "He griped 'cause I was a few minutes late," he said. "He was discourteous, demanding, and even rude to me. But when he spoke that night, you would think he was Dale Carnegie's twin!" My young friend admitted he had begun to get the impression that apparently that is the way it must be, even though his heart told him otherwise. The truth is, he found himself dying without encouragement—"slowly, sadly, angrily." What really threw him was that all his riders were Christians.

When will we ever learn? Those who make a lasting investment for good on our lives are not necessarily people with a name or people with reputations, but servant-hearted people with grace. People whose kindness is as consistent with a hardworking secretary as with the hand-clapping public. Not people who are guilty of polishing their public presence yet so uncaring about private relationships they are tyrannical and insensitive. The words of Dag Hammarskjold come to mind:

> Around a man who has been pushed into the limelight, a legend begins to grow as it does around a dead man. But a dead man is in no danger of yielding to the temptation to nourish his legend, or accept its picture as reality. I pity the man who falls in love with his image as it is drawn by public opinion during the honeymoon of publicity.[2]

I pity someone else even more—his wife.

What does it take to make a person great . . . not just under the lights or before the camera but behind the scenes as well? What does it take to make one just as charming and thoughtful and encouraging with his or her mate as with those who sit in awe? I have the answer: *It takes grace*—the oil that lessens the friction in marriage, which is precisely what I want to address in this chapter.

We have thought about grace from God, grace that breaks sin's enslavement, grace in the church, grace between friends in times of disagreement, as well as grace among those in ministry. It is now time for us to think about the importance of grace between husbands and wives. In my opinion, it is here—in the privacy of one's home—that grace faces its major test, a test which begins not too many days after the honeymoon ends. As one wag put it, "Every marriage has three rings: engagement ring, wedding ring, and suffering." More times than I want to remember, I have found that it was easier to extend grace to a parishioner or one of the folks on our church staff than it was for me to treat Cynthia with grace. So as I write these things, understand I write as an imperfect learner. We may have been married thirty-five years, but the oil of grace has not always flowed in abundance, certainly not from me. Like many married couples, we have had to admit that a "grace awakening" is just as needed in our home as it is in our church, perhaps more so.

While grazing through the New Testament over the past several years, I have found that marriage is addressed somewhat at length in three separate places, each time mentioning both husbands and wives. Those scriptures are 1 Corinthians 7, Ephesians 5, and 1 Peter 3. As I analyzed each section, I found that the Corinthians reference deals with marital realities that are tough to face, the Ephesians reference deals with marital responsibilities every couple must accept, and the Peter reference deals with the marital roles that need to be fulfilled. In each case, the secret of making it happen as God planned it requires grace.

THE GRACE TO FACE MARITAL REALITIES

As I study the seventh chapter of 1 Corinthians, I find no fewer than three realities (of course, there may be more) to be faced by every married couple. I am so convinced of the significance of each one, that I mention them to every couple I marry. I also have observed that among those I know, whose marriages have not lasted, one or more of these realities was passively ignored or deliberately set aside.

First: *Marriage requires mutual unselfishness.*

> Let the husband fulfill his duty to his wife, and likewise also the wife to her husband. The wife does not have authority over her own body, but the husband does; and likewise also the husband does not have authority over his own body, but the wife does. Stop depriving one another, except by agreement for a time that you may devote yourselves to prayer, and come together again lest Satan tempt you because of your lack of self-control. (1 Cor. 7:3–5)

Paul writes of "duty" and "authority" and "depriving," all terms in this context having to do with sexual intimacy. The application is broader, however. What he is encouraging is unselfishness. What does it take to operate unselfishly? It takes grace. Grace to accept, to overlook, to understand. Grace to forgive. Grace to respect. Grace to yield one's own rights. Grace to affirm. Grace to restrain. Grace to give as well as grace to receive. Marriage requires mutual unselfishness. When I speak to those who are still single, I frequently address the issue of selfishness. I'll often say, "If you tend toward being selfish, if you're the type who clings to your own rights and has no interest sharing with others, please do the world (and certainly any potential mate) a favor and don't marry!" Why do I make such a strong statement? Because marriage, a good marriage, requires mutual unselfishness. It calls for grace to release rights and expect little in return.

There is a second reality: *Marriage means a lifelong commitment.*

> But to the married I give instructions, not I, but the Lord, that the wife should not leave her husband (but if she does leave, let her remain unmarried, or else be reconciled to her husband), and that the husband should not send his wife away. But to the rest I say, not the Lord, that if any brother has a wife who is an unbeliever, and she consents to live with him, let him not send her away. And a woman who has an unbelieving husband, and he consents to live with her, let her not send her husband away. (1 Cor. 7:10–13)

Unless you are ready for a commitment that lasts for life, again I say without hesitation, don't marry. If Paul is writing anything in this paragraph, he is writing this, "When you marry, you marry for life." He has permanence in mind. Did you observe his firm counsel along these lines?

· The wife should not leave her husband (v. 10).
· The husband should not leave his wife (v. 11).
· Let him not send her away (v. 12).
· Let her not send him away (v. 13).

To write it once would be sufficient. Twice would be extremely and unmistakably clear. Three times would be more than enough. But four times? The man means business!

Years ago Cynthia and I took the ugly word *divorce* out of our dialogues. We agreed we would not even store it in the arsenal of our argument vocabulary. No matter how heated our disagreements may be, we'd not threaten each other with that term. It does something to a marriage when you can count on your partner to stick around and hammer out your differences with each other instead of walking away from them.

What does it take to stick it out . . . to be permanently committed to each other? I repeat, it takes grace! There is not a divorcee reading these words who wouldn't agree with that. It takes an enormous amount of grace to negotiate through the minefield of disagreements. It takes grace to forgive and go on. Grace to hang tough even though the same mistake is made over and over or the same sin committed again and again. A marriage well-oiled by grace is durable, long-lasting—protected against the wear and tear of friction.

There's a third reality, just as important to remember as the first two: *Marriage includes times of trouble.*

> I think then that this is good in view of the present distress, that it is good for a man to remain as he is. Are you bound to a wife? Do not seek to be released. Are you released from a wife? Do not seek a wife. But if you should marry, you have not sinned; and if a virgin should marry, she has not sinned. Yet such will have trouble in this life, and I am trying to spare you. (1 Cor. 7:26–28)

Truer words regarding marriage were never written: "Such will have trouble." Every bride who thinks she has found the knight in shining armor who is going to save her from all her disappointments needs to remember, "such will have trouble." Every groom who thinks he has found Wonder Woman, the perfect blend of Mother

Teresa, Betty Crocker, Chris Evert, and Cheryl Ladd, needs to remember, "such will have trouble." I'll go one step further: Marriage and troubles are synonymous!

Without wanting to come across as the Ebenezer Scrooge of wedding bells and lovely ceremonies at the altar, I must say that *troubles are inevitable*. The list is endless. Trouble from calamities. Trouble from disease. Trouble from the old nature. Trouble from children. Trouble from family squabbles. Trouble from differing viewpoints about time, temperature, and trips. Trouble from neighbors. Trouble because of finances. Trouble due to pressure at work you can't turn off. Trouble, trouble, trouble! And it will require grace for the two of you to endure. Grace to accept, grace to forgive . . . to laugh much of it off, grace to keep going, grace to encourage the other in the midst of the periodic paths that lead through conflict and disagreement.

I don't know how many times Cynthia has taken my hand, looked me right in the eye, and said, "Honey, we'll make it through this." That took grace, and it lifted my spirit. On other occasions I had the grace to help her. Without the grace to let each other be, our marriage would be stormy and full of struggles. We have very different temperaments. We also have tastes that don't always agree. Most noticeably, we also have opposite internal thermostats. She is perpetually cold in the winter . . . and often cool in the summer. I'm hot through both! This means that the place in our home that collects the most fingerprints is the thermostat. I regularly push it down, she continually pushes it up. It takes grace for me to live in a sweltering greenhouse . . . and grace for her to survive in a frosty igloo. I sweat, she freezes. I like it to be so cool you could hang meat in the kitchen, she likes it a couple of notches below the Arabian Desert.

But we've finally solved one temperature problem, the electric blanket battle: Dual controls! I prefer my side on Off or, if there's a blizzard outside (which is rare in Southern California), maybe on 1.

She varies between 7 and 9. Actually, I much prefer to sleep on top of the covers. She likes being buried beneath all those layers—it is unbelievable! But the best part comes when her side of the dual-control blanket finally burns out. We just flip that baby over—I take her side that no longer works and she gets mine, which seems like it's brand new—and we get twice the life out of the sucker. Grace not only gives us tolerance, it saves us bucks.

THE GRACE TO ACCEPT
PERSONAL RESPONSIBILITIES

So much for realities; let's focus next on the grace needed to accept responsibilities. That seems to be the emphasis in Ephesians 5:22–33.

I realize as we dig deeper into the subject of marriage that I am treading on delicate ground. To say it is controversial is to put it mildly. Some have taught the subjects of husband-wife responsibilities to such a severe extreme, little room is left to breathe on one's own or to think things through. On the other hand, these (and related verses) have been twisted and altered so much that their original impact has sometimes been neutralized. I want to guard against both extremes. My hope is to help you see two foundational facts: first, the wife's primary responsibility, and second, the husband's primary responsibility. Neither is all that complicated, but for some strange reason, many marriages seem to consistently miss the mark.

The Wife's Primary Responsibility

As we determine the wife's basic responsibility, let's allow Scripture to speak first: "Wives, be subject to your own husbands, as to the Lord. For the husband is the head of the wife, as Christ also is the head of the church, He Himself being the Savior of the body. But as the church is subject to Christ, so also the wives ought to be to their husbands in everything" (Eph. 5:22–24).

These are familiar words to many Christians; therefore, they can easily lose their "punch." To guard against that, let's consider other versions and paraphrases of the same verses.

> Wives, submit to your husbands as to the Lord. For the husband is the head of the wife as Christ is the head of the church, his body, of which he is the Savior. Now as the church submits to Christ, so also wives should submit to their husbands in everything. (NIV)

> You wives must learn to adapt yourselves to your husbands, as you submit yourselves to the Lord, for the husband is the "head" of the wife in the same way that Christ is head of the Church and savior of the body. The willing subjection of the Church to Christ should be reproduced in the submission of wives to their husbands. (PHILLIPS).

> Wives, submit yourselves to your husbands as to the Lord. For a husband has authority over his wife just as Christ has authority over the church; and Christ is himself the Savior of the church, his body. And so wives must submit themselves completely to their husbands just as the church submits itself to Christ. (TEV)

> Wives, submit to your own husbands, as to the Lord. For the husband is head of the wife, as also Christ is head of the church; and He is the Savior of the body. Therefore, just as the church is subject to Christ, so let the wives be to their own husbands in everything. (NKJV)

As I examine these words, I find that *the wife's primary responsibility is to know herself so well and to respect herself so much, she gives herself to her husband without hesitation.*

Let me suggest that you read the previous statement again, this time more slowly and preferably aloud.

In the context of this section of Scripture, there is an atmosphere of sweet harmony. If you take the time to read the verses (vv. 15–21) leading up to the three that are specifically addressed to wives, you will find that Paul emphasizes being wise (v. 15), being filled with the Spirit (v. 18), having a heart that is overflowing with joy (v. 19), giving thanks (v. 20), and possessing a submissive spirit to one another out of respect for Christ (v. 21). It is within that atmosphere of delightful harmony that a wife is best able to know and respect herself so much, she has little difficulty giving herself to her husband. In such a home there isn't a struggle for authority or rights. There is a willingness to release the controls. At the risk of repetition, it is a grace state of mind that prompts such attitudes.

I can hear some answering back, "If you only knew my husband, you would know how much grace it takes!" To which I'd probably agree, you are correct. But that is the challenge of it all. With the Lord Jesus Christ supremely in charge of your life, with the Spirit of God energizing your actions and softening your attitude, your words, and your responses, it is remarkable how powerful grace can be. It isn't called "amazing grace" for nothing! Just as God, in grace, stooped and loved you in an unlovely state, so, too, can His grace awaken within you the desire to stoop and give yourself to another who may be just as unlovely as we all once were.

Suddenly, I am getting the feeling that a few husbands are beginning to feel a little smug as they are reading these pages. And so, for your sake we need to see what God's Word says to the man. Interestingly, He says a lot more to us than He does to our wives, men. Take a look at verse 25 for starters: "Husbands, love your wives, just as Christ also loved the church and gave Himself up for her."

Here's a fresh thought: The wife is told to love her husband so much that she lives for him, but the husband is told to love his wife so much, he would die for her.

The wife is given the analogy of the Savior's life. But the husband is given the analogy of His death. I call that love, men. Each husband is to love his wife enough to die for her.

I can't remember how often, following funerals, I have stood alongside men who have just buried a wife. Almost without exception I've had them fall on my shoulder in tears and say, "Oh, Chuck, why did it take this to stop me and to show me what I had in my wife?"

> Husbands, love your wives, just as Christ also loved the church and gave Himself up for her; that He might sanctify her, having cleansed her by the washing of water with the word, that He might present to Himself the church in all her glory, having no spot or wrinkle or any such thing; but that she should be holy and blameless. So husbands ought also to love their own wives as their own bodies. He who loves his own wife loves himself; for no one ever hated his own flesh, but nourishes and cherishes it, just as Christ also does the church, because we are members of His body. (vv. 25–30)

The Husband's Primary Responsibility

As I examine these words addressed to husbands, I find that *the primary responsibility of the husband is to love his Lord so deeply and to like himself so completely he gives himself to his wife without conditions.* As I asked you to do before, pause and read that again, more slowly and thoughtfully. Our love is to be without conditions. We need to take the word "if" out of our vocabulary. "If you will do . . . If you will say . . . If you will respond, then I will give myself." No, that is not the way our Savior loves us or loves the church. Notice verse 28 once again: "So husbands ought also to love their own wives as their own bodies. He who loves his own wife loves himself."

The next time you wonder if men really love their own bodies, stop by and visit one of the physical fitness clubs. Incredible! There are mirrors everywhere but on the floor . . . and standing in front of them will be men admiring their muscles—really loving themselves.

Knowing how true this self love is for men, Paul uses it as an example of how men should love their wives—no conditions, no reservations. Again, grace is essential, so essential. It doesn't flow easily, however, when there is competition for authority or conditions placed on love. In a book titled *The Pleasers*, with the subtitle *Women Who Can't Say No—and the Men Who Control Them*, Dr. Kevin Leman makes some insightful observations:

> . . . the cost of marriage is higher for wives than for husbands. If you are talking about good mental health and psychological well-being, the men have it better every time.
>
> Despite all of their complaints about marriage, more women than men find marriage a source of happiness. They cling to marriage regardless of the cost.
>
> Down through the centuries women have been the pleasers, men the controllers. Robert Karen, who conducts workshops for men and women on power and intimacy, refers to the "old" and "new" systems of male/female relationships. Our parents and grandparents knew a world that had stabler values and much more clearly defined roles for men and women. Power and responsibility were clearly assigned, and everyone knew where he or she stood. The system was often unfair to women but it did offer them a certain amount of security. If a woman was willing to accept the ground rules and the limits that marriage imposed on her, she could be quite happy.
>
> A woman's job was to keep the home, raise the children, and be there for the whole family. The man's job was to go out and earn the living and "make contributions to society." Men were, in effect, put on a pedestal and wives were relegated to second-class citizenship.
>
> Enter women's liberation in the latter part of the twentieth century, and all this inequality is supposed to be dying out—but is it?
>
> Women are finding that "having it all" is nothing that special. In fact, they are catching up with the men in having heart disease, ulcers, and other stress-related illnesses. Now they are allowed to get good jobs and earn excellent incomes, but the emotional balance of power at home is still much the same.

Most women still do the giving, while the men continue to take. The woman is the one who is more capable of compassion, support, and being there when needed. Men still aren't in touch with their feelings the way women are. They are less capable of reaching out to make emotional contact. But they are very capable of reaching out to take whatever a woman has to offer, and in so doing, they often take advantage.[3]

Dr. Leman uses a vivid word picture in this book. He calls "pleasers" the moths and "controllers" the flame. Men, be awfully careful in making strong statements regarding submission unless you have really done your homework. More often than not (especially in evangelical circles) such statements are a grand power play. When grace awakens in a husband's heart, he cares for the one God gave him and he becomes increasingly aware of her value, her gifts, and her significance. The grace within him frees him to let her be.

I'm honest when I say, the better acquainted I become with the grace of God, the less I concern myself with authority in our home, and the less threatened I feel. The more I become acquainted with the grace of God, the more I want to model servanthood, the more I desire to affirm and release my wife— the less I want to dominate and control her. Grace loves and serves, it gives and forgives. Grace doesn't keep a record of wrongs and then dangle them over our marriage partner's head. As we have learned in previous chapters, grace gives room—room to grow and to be, to discover and to create. And when there is this kind of grace–awakened love, the man loves his wife as he loves himself and the wife respects her husband, which is exactly as God planned it.

Nevertheless let each individual among you also love his own wife even as himself; and let the wife see to it that she respect her husband. (Eph. 5:33)

When that happens, there is no interest in being intimate with someone else. Jealousy and suspicion are also silenced.

Few grace killers are worse in a marriage than jealousy. I married a couple several years ago whom I shall not soon forget. During the premarital counseling sessions, I detected a strong jealous streak in the young man. I mentioned this to both of them, but they passed it off as not that important. He assured me he "used to struggle a little with it," but no more. Following their honeymoon and the first few months of marriage, they returned for some follow-up time—and what a change! Brimming with anger, she blurted out, "This man is so jealous of me, before he leaves for work in the morning he checks the odometer on my car . . . then when he comes home, sometimes even before he comes into the house, he checks it again. If I have driven a few extra miles, he quizzes me during supper. Lacking trust and encouragement, she was dying "slowly, sadly, angrily."

I repeat, the more the grace of God is awakened in a marriage, the less husbands will attempt to control and restrict and the less wives will feel the need to "please no matter what." It makes marriage easier to manage.

· Grace releases and affirms. It doesn't smother.
· Grace values the dignity of individuals. It doesn't destroy.
· Grace supports and encourages. It isn't jealous or suspicious.

I know whereof I speak. For more years than I care to remember, I was consumed with jealousy. I was so insecure and fearful it wasn't uncommon for me to drill Cynthia with questions—petty, probing questions that were little more than veiled accusations. It is amazing she endured it. Finally, we had one of those famous showdown confrontations every married couple has had. No need to repeat it, but she made it painfully clear that I was smothering her, I was imagining things she never even thought of doing . . . and it had to stop. Her words hurt, but she did the right thing. I took her seriously.

I went to work on this ugly side of my life. I confessed my jealousy to Cynthia. I assured her I would never again treat her with such a lack of trust. I asked God for grace to help, for relief from the destructive habit I had formed, for the ability to love and give myself to this woman without all the choking conditions. I distinctly recall how much an understanding of grace helped. It was as if grace were finally "awake" in my life, and I could appropriate its power for the first time. It seemed to free me, first in small ways, and finally in major areas. I can honestly say today that I do not entertain a single jealous thought. Grace *literally* wiped the slate clean.

One final comment before I move on to some concluding thoughts in the chapter. I have found that once Cynthia and I gave grace its proper place in our marriage, the struggles and arguments over submission ceased. It has been years (not an exaggeration) since either one of us has even mentioned the "S" word! I say again, once grace finds its place and brings the freedom only it can bring, a desire to control diminishes and submission is no longer an issue.

Ephesians 5:33 sums up the responsibilities: "Nevertheless let each individual among you also love his own wife even as himself; and let the wife see to it that she respect her husband." The man who genuinely loves his wife finds that he must first have a healthy self-esteem, a strong and secure self-image. It is nothing short of incredible how that opens the gate to let grace flow through his life into his wife's life, which oils all the friction spots. Furthermore, the woman who truly respects her man must first see herself as valuable and significant. As she is given the freedom to grow and become what God meant her to be, her respect for her husband grows.

GRACE TO FULFILL DISTINCT ROLES

We live in a day where domestic roles have become blurred. The home reveals the consequences. Many children grow up not knowing the significance of female femininity or male masculinity. Bonding is short-circuited, thanks to the breakdown of marriages, and kids must opt for surrogate parents.

Traditional and dated though his words may seem, the apostle Peter goes to the heart of the issue and offers a couple of principles that still work . . . if we will only abide by them. He begins his section on the roles of wives and husbands by writing to those wives whose husbands couldn't care less about spiritual things:

> In the same way, you wives, be submissive to your own husbands so that even if any of them are disobedient to the word, they may be won without a word by the behavior of their wives, as they observe your chaste and respectful behavior. (1 Pet. 3:1–2)

Amazing! She wins her husband "without a word." How? She lives in such a convincing manner that he cannot help but notice. Peter selected a wonderful word that is translated "observe." It means "a keen looking into something," as you would watch a replay on a close call in sports. The husband takes careful notice of her winsome behavior and it blows him away. Ultimately, she "wins" him with kindness.

Now, the tendency is to substitute external things for the right kind of attitude and behavior. Peter undoubtedly realized this because he goes on to say, "And let not your adornment be merely external—braiding the hair, and wearing gold jewelry, or putting on dresses" (3:3).

I have heard some use this verse as an opportunity to support their legalistic bias. They say the woman should not have her hair done and she should not wear cosmetics or any form of jewelry. Funny, I have never heard one of them say, "And neither should you put on a dress," even though that is also on the same list. No, this is not a list for legalists to camp on. The secret is in the word *merely*. Don't let your adornment be *merely* external. Don't limit your life to the externals, don't stop there. Don't yield to the tendency to substitute external adornment for internal character.

And that is why verse 4 is so important. It gives us the positive side: "But let it be the hidden person of the heart, with the imperishable quality of a gentle and quiet spirit, which is precious in the sight of God."

This doesn't mean that if you really fall in love with the Lord you can start looking like an unmade bed. I like to warn ladies about abusing this verse by taking it to an extreme. There's no need to look dowdy and plain because your interest is only on the inner person. That is not the idea. There needs to be a balance. There can be, in fact, there needs to be external expressions of feminine beauty, but don't stop there. Guard against letting your external appearance take so much of your time and attention you leave out the charm and loveliness of a beautiful interior. What holds a husband in the long haul is internal character. Externals finally fade. As age creeps in, much of the beauty you may have had as a young woman slips away.

This reminds me of a story I heard recently. During a last minute Christmas rush, a woman hurried up to a perfume saleswoman in a large department store and asked her, "Do you still have Elizabeth Taylor's *Passion?*" The hassled lady behind the counter responded with quick wit: "If I did, do you think I'd be working here?"

Long after external beauty fades, you will still have what really matters.

This brings me to the wife's role: *to model true femininity . . . character traits that are precious to God and impressive to her husband.* God will honor that. Furthermore, it will get results—lasting, satisfying, ful-filling results.

Verse 7 begins, "You husbands likewise . . ." Just as the wife has a role of submission to the Savior and to her husband, so the husband is to be in submission to Christ. Not nearly enough is said about this. We hammer on wives to submit to their husbands, yet we say all too little to husbands about bending their wills and yielding in full sub-mission to their Lord. I've seldom seen an exception—when a husband lives his life in submission to Christ, he finds his wife coop-erative and gracious in return.

> You husbands likewise, live with your wives in an understanding way, as with a weaker vessel, since she is a woman; and grant her honor as a fellow-heir of the grace of life, so that your prayers may not be hindered. (v. 7)

The phrase "live with" means to "be at home with." Not just come in the house after work, choke down supper, stare at a television, say nothing to his wife, and finally drop off to sleep (sound familiar?). To "live with" is to get to know, to be at home with, to make your mu-tual relationship a priority. In fact, Peter goes further. In this same verse he says, literally, "Live with your wife *according to knowledge.*" Really get to know her. Find out what she is really like. What are her innermost thoughts? Discover her deepest hurts, find out her fears. Learn when and where she needs affirmation and encouragement, then give it. You may be surprised to find her dying "slowly, sadly, angrily" without your encouragement and affirmation. She's a weaker vessel, physically. But that does not mean she is weaker emotionally; nor does it mean she is weaker in character. She's a woman, meaning she's not put together like a man. She has different needs, different feelings, entertains different wishes and dreams, sees life from a different perspective. Respect those differences; she will adore you for it. In other words, be a masculine model of grace in your home.

All this leads me to the husband's role: *to model genuine masculinity . . . unselfish and sensitive leadership that strengthens the home and gives dignity to the wife.* Remember how verse 7 concludes: "and grant her honor as a fellow-heir of the grace of life. . . ." If the husband provides genuine masculinity, unselfish and sensitive leadership, it is his way of granting honor to his wife. She will feel supported, affirmed, and treasured.

One of the by-products of a grace-filled marriage is that the kids will have little problem bonding. They will bond correctly. They will grow right. They will feel secure and confident. As they step into the real world as young adults, they will hit the road running. Your son will understand what it is like to be a man, and your daughter will have discovered what it means to be a woman. They will be well on their way to a healthy and happy maturity. And in this day, that is no small accomplishment.

We are also reminded in verse 7 that we are fellow-heirs together of the grace of life. We are mutual heirs of grace. Grace brings the husband and wife together . . . not one reigning over the other, not two separate people doing their own thing regardless of the other. But partners enveloped by grace, operating in grace, thinking with grace, releasing because of grace. Think of it as four enduring benefits:

- · Mutual equality (fellow)
- · Mutual dignity (heir)
- · Mutual humility (grace)
- · Mutual destiny (life)

And I can assure you, the magnet in a home like that is so strong you won't want to be anywhere else.

I've said for years that my favorite place on earth is just inside the door of my home. I absolutely love being home. It is there that I find maximum security and acceptance, fulfillment and accountability, responsibility and harmony, honesty and love. Why? Because we are committed to the same common denominator: Grace.

A FITTING CONCLUSION

How do you bring a chapter like this to a close? I find it especially difficult since we have covered so much territory, all of it important. We have faced several marital realities. We have looked at the primary responsibilities of a husband and a wife. And we have also considered the distinct roles of both. All the way through we have returned to the essential importance of grace in order for these things to happen.

It is my firm conviction that there would not be nearly as many fractured relationships or dysfunctional families destroyed by affairs, abuse, disunity, or divorce if we simply met the needs within each others' lives. These needs are neither mysterious nor complicated, but when they remain unmet, they erode into grace killers, which lead to every form of unhappiness. What are those needs?

Allow me to let another answer that question for me. Dr. Willard Harley has written a fascinating book entitled *His Needs/Her Needs*. It is an in-depth study of extramarital affairs and how to avoid them. Dr. Harley invested more than twenty years of his career counseling married couples, many of whom were engaged in affairs. During those years he gathered over fifteen thousand questionnaires that deal with the sexual history and behavior of his clients. There are exceptions, of course, but generally speaking he has concluded that both women and men have five major needs. By identifying them, I find that it is easier to concentrate direct attention on them, applying the "oil" of grace where needed.

FIVE MAJOR NEEDS OF WOMEN	FIVE MAJOR NEEDS OF MEN
1. Affection	1. Sexual fulfillment
2. Conversation	2. Recreational companionship
3. Honesty and openness	3. An attractive spouse
4. Financial support	4. Domestic support
5. Family commitment	5. Admiration

Dr. Harley states that the key need for the woman is affection—feeling that she is truly prized, loved, and cherished. The key need for the man is sexual expression followed closely by respect.[4]

The words of actress Celeste Holm speak again, with relevance, to all married couples: "We live by encouragement and we die without it; slowly, sadly, angrily."[5] My hope is that these few pages will make a difference first in your life and then in your home. As you apply the oil of grace to those major needs in your mate's life, may you be strengthened with the realization that you could not be engaged in any investment on earth that yields greater dividends. After all, what is more important than rescuing someone who is dying?

13

The Charming Joy of Grace Giving

I HAVE A PERSONAL THEORY ABOUT Christmas. It explains, at least to my satisfaction, the mysterious magic of its magnetism. For years I have wondered what it was that annually draws people into the Yuletide season. Even though we get turned off in mid-October when we see all those fake trees being set up at department stores and in spite of the dreaded commercialism and crowds and "Jingle Bells" played three thousand times in the mall . . . somehow we cannot resist the spirit of the season once we find ourselves enveloped in the sights and smells unique to Christmas. Why?

As beautiful as the colorful lights and decorations may be, they are not the reason. As magnificent as the music and nostalgic memories may be, they aren't either. Neither is it the cakes and candy or the trip to Grandma's house or the parties with friends. My theory, I think, explains it best: Christmas scratches the itch of grace deep within us. It provides us an opportunity each year to deliberately get out of ourselves and do something tangible for someone else with no thought of or interest in being "paid back." It gives us a chance to counteract that selfish streak we all hate in ourselves. In simplest terms, Christmas (like no other annual celebration) prompts us to demonstrate true grace.

Would you like to put my personal theory to the test? Here's how. The next time December 25 rolls around and it is open-the-gifts time around the tree, force yourself to watch the *giver* rather than the one opening the gift. Some of the best photographs we have of the Swindoll family gathered around the tree are those taken of the giver of a certain gift at the time another family member is opening it. There is more than excitement; there is *sheer delight* written all over the face of the giver as he or she is totally absorbed in the charming joy of giving. I've finally figured it out—at that moment we are caught up in the full-on ecstasy of grace. When you stop to think about it, it isn't receiving gifts around the tree that makes Christmas so much fun; it's giving them. It's watching the other person's look of surprise or sensing that special surge of gratitude, which suddenly and without a word makes us feel close.

Last Christmas my wife surprised all of us in the family by giving us matching bathrobes, each one with his or her name monogrammed on the front. She had the most fun of anyone! She brought the gifts in and set each one on the right lap. She told us not to open them until everyone was ready . . . then, "Go!" I deliberately watched Cynthia as one after another opened the package and shouted. She was dancing and laughing and clapping and jumping up and down—yes *she* was! Then she had all of us put them on at the same time and "model" them, with hoods on and hands in pockets. By the time we finished, we looked like a roomful of monks from the Order of St. Michael's, embracing each other and having the time of our lives. But nobody experienced more joy than the one who thought up the idea, pulled it off, then enjoyed the sheer pleasure of watching others take delight in her gift to each member of the family. Our Lord knew what He was talking about when He taught that it is more blessed to give than to receive.

I freely admit that I have racked my brain to find a way to reconstruct that same once-a-year delight throughout the year in this chapter on the joy of grace giving. If I could do that, we would all have our defenses down and we would be on the edge of our seats anticipating what the Bible teaches about giving as God intended us to give. Unfortunately, many people, both within the church and without, honestly feel money is "filthy lucre," so we are better off not even mentioning it. I have actually heard laymen bragging that their minister had never once talked about money during the twelve-or-whatever years he had been their pastor. While I have serious concerns about such silence, I understand how that could happen. I, too, tend to shy away from the subject.

WHAT MAKES US SO DREADFULLY DEFENSIVE

Having been engaged in ministry for about three decades, I can remember times when I could almost hear the groans and feel the sighs as I announced that I'd be speaking on giving that particular Sunday. Why do we feel that way? I think it is a lot like the groans and sighs we release in mid-October when the stores drag out the plastic trees and put Santa Claus in the window. Three specific analogies come to mind.

First, *it seems terribly repetitive.* The subject of giving is seldom approached creatively, and then when it is addressed, the comments are usually overstated and punctuated with guilt-giving remarks. Most often the congregation is not instructed as much as it is exhorted and exploited. Furthermore, there is neither subtlety nor much humor employed . . . only large helpings of hard-core facts mixed with a pinch of panic "because giving has dropped off." It doesn't take a Ph.D. from Yale to sense the objective during the first five minutes: *GIVE MORE!* Same song, ninth verse. The repetitive cycle gets monotonous.

Second, *the whole thing has been commercialized.* Because grace has been separated from giving, greed has come in like the proverbial flood. Mr. and Mrs. Average Christian are punchy, suspicious, and resentful . . . sometimes for good reason. During the latter half of the twentieth century, all of us have been embarrassed, haven't we? We have seen shameful examples of greed employed in the name of religion. Unbelievable techniques have been used to wrench money from the public's pocket and we're fed up with the gimmicks. Everybody wants more, not just religious folks. Enough is never enough.

I recently heard about a guy who gave his girlfriend his lottery ticket . . . and to their surprise, it won three million dollars! But the government taxed *him* for the cash. And then, if that wasn't bad enough, when his ex-wife heard that he was now worth a lot of money, she upped the ante on the alimony payments.

Third, *there always seems to be a hidden agenda.* Just as merchants don't go to a lot of extra expense and trouble getting their stores ready for Christmas simply for the fun of it, neither do most ministers speak on financial stewardship because it is a fun subject. The bottom line is usually uppermost. The emphasis is seldom on the charming joy of grace-oriented giving but rather on the obligation and responsibility to give "whether you like it or not."

This is an appropriate time for me to mention a couple of things, just to set the record straight. How and why we give is of far greater significance to God than what we give. Attitude and motive are always more important than amount. Furthermore, once a person cultivates a taste for grace in giving, the amount becomes virtually immaterial. When those age-old grace killers, Guilt and Manipulation, are not used as leverage, the heart responds in generosity. Giving at that point becomes wonderfully addictive.

Late one year I challenged someone who means a lot to me to be more generous than she had ever been in her life throughout the new year. Because she is not wealthy and because she is unmarried and therefore has only a single source of income, this lady lived under the fear of running out of money if she followed the lead of her heart. Being a true model of grace and having a heart of compassion, she had often been prompted within to be more generous, but her fear restrained her. All she needed was a little encouragement to replace her fear with faith . . . which she did throughout the new year. She told me at the end of that year that she had never given more in one year in all her life nor had she ever been so full of joy. In addition, she said the Lord had abundantly met every one of her financial needs, which motivated her to do a repeat performance in the year to come. That lady who has discovered this new dimension of grace is my sister Luci. I am exceedingly proud of her for taking a giant step of faith as she has trusted God to honor her generosity. Today she is addicted to giving.

WHAT MAKES GIVING SO
WONDERFULLY ADDICTIVE?

It is not my intention to make a saint out of Luci. Neither do I wish to leave the impression that only a few who have some kind of "gift of giving" can know the joy of generosity. That is simply not the case. It is true, God does lead some to be unique examples of extreme generosity, but my thoughts in this chapter are not limited to them. My hope is to help you and others like you to see how grace can liberate you to become a model of unusual and consistent generosity, all the while filling you with inexpressible joy. No, this is not some ideal reserved for a chosen few . . . this is reality for all of God's people to claim.

Now is the right moment to step into the time tunnel and return to the first century. The original church in Jerusalem had fallen on hard times. Unable to pull itself out of a financial slump, thanks to the depressed economy in Judea and other Palestinian regions, those early believers were facing a bleak and barren future.

As is often the case in our own times, while one part of the world was suffering great need, another was flourishing. The Greeks in Corinth were doing quite well, which prompted Paul to urge them to give financial assistance to their fellow Christians in Jerusalem. His words to the Corinthian believers regarding this need are recorded in 2 Corinthians 8 and 9, two of the finest chapters in all the Bible on grace giving.

At the beginning of his charge he mentions the generosity of the struggling churches in Macedonia who gave during days of affliction. In spite of their own poverty, and with great joy, they took delight in giving to those in need. On the basis of their example, Paul urges the Corinthians to follow the example they set. Those words of background information will help you understand the apostle's opening remarks.

> Now, brethren, we wish to make known to you the grace of God which has been given in the churches of Macedonia, that in a great ordeal of affliction their abundance of joy and their deep poverty overflowed in the wealth of their liberality. For I testify that according to their ability, and beyond their ability they gave of their own accord, begging us with much entreaty for the favor of participation in the support of the saints, and this, not as we had expected, but they first gave themselves to the Lord and to us by the will of God. (2 Cor. 8:1–5)

Paul admits that he was surprised. He states that what the Macedonians gave was "not as we had expected." Of greater importance, their gifts did not originate in their purses and wallets. No, "they first gave *themselves* to the Lord" (emphasis mine) and then they gave their money. Grace giving begins in the heart. Grace-oriented generosity is the overflow of a liberated heart. This assures us that it has nothing to do with one's investment portfolio or monthly salary. Whether Macedonian or Corinthian, American or Canadian, Asian or Australian, the challenge is the same; first and foremost, we are to give ourselves to the Lord. When we do, our treasure will follow the leading of our heart.

Returning to my earlier question, What is it that makes all this so addictive?

First, *it helps us keep a healthy balance.* "But just as you abound in everything, in faith and utterance and knowledge and in all earnestness and in the love we inspired in you, see that you abound in this gracious work also" (2 Cor. 8:7).

In many a church there is faith; there is good teaching ("utterance"), a working knowledge of the Christian life; there is zeal, spiritual passion, and a great deal of love . . . but generosity? A superabundant willingness to give? Often, that is the one ingredient conspicuous by its absence. How easy to take, to be blessed, instructed, encouraged, exhorted, affirmed, and strengthened—all those things received in abundance—yet fail to balance the receiving with our giving.

Did you notice how Paul refers to financial support? He calls it "this gracious work" . . . and he exhorts us to "abound" in it. The Christian life takes on a healthy balance when our taking in and giving out stay in step. You and I feel closer to the Savior because that is what He did . . . He gave. "For you know the grace of our Lord Jesus Christ, that though He was rich, yet for your sake He became poor, that you through His poverty might become rich" (2 Cor. 8:9).

Study those words for a moment. Here was someone who was

rich, imminently rich. At his disposal was the wealth of heaven, so mind-boggling it is beyond description. Yet He left it all as He came to give Himself for us. Why? That we, in turn, might pick up the riches of His life and follow His model.

The second reason why giving is addictive is that *in giving we model the same grace of Jesus Christ.* I am impressed that the verse of Scripture doesn't say, "for you know the obligation of the Lord Jesus Christ," or, "You know the sense of duty," though that is true. It was a duty that He come to earth. But Paul doesn't write: "You know the requirement" or "You know the sacrifice." No, he mentions only the grace. When our Lord Jesus left heaven, He didn't leave gritting His teeth and clenching His fists, shouting "Okay . . . OKAY!" It wasn't obligation . . . it was grace that motivated Him to come. It was grace within Him that brought Him to Bethlehem as a little baby. It was grace within Him that allowed His hands and feet to be pierced with nails, and grace within Him to say, "Father, forgive them. They do not know what they are doing." When you give, knowing there will be no gift in return, you have modeled the purest form of the grace of the Lord Jesus Christ. It will help if you think about giving in that way.

Third, giving by grace is addictive because in doing so *we counteract selfishness and covetousness.* Read slowly and carefully the first five verses of 2 Corinthians 9.

> For it is superfluous for me to write to you about this ministry to the saints; for I know your readiness, of which I boast about you to the Macedonians, namely, that Achaia has been prepared since last year, and your zeal has stirred up most of them. But I have sent the brethren, that our boasting about you may not be made empty in this case, that, as I was saying, you may be prepared; lest if any Macedonians come with me and find you unprepared, we (not to speak of you) should be put to shame by this confidence. So I thought it necessary to urge the brethren that they would go on ahead to you and arrange beforehand your previ-

ously promised bountiful gift, that the same might be ready as a bountiful gift, and not affected by covetousness.

Sometime in the past the Corinthians had promised that they would participate in an offering to answer needs in Jerusalem. But for some reason they had left their promise. Their pledge had begun to wear thin. So Paul writes, in effect, "I just want to prod you a little and say you need to finish what you said you were going to do. I don't want your covetousness to get the best of you."

It can, can't it? Have you gotten a raise within the last twelve months? Isn't it easy, when that happens, for covetousness to take charge? Something we had wished we could own is now within reach. We come into a little money, whether it is a nice income-tax refund check or from some unexpected source, and it is easy for greed to cause a pledge to wear thin or a previous promise ("Lord, if I made more, I'd give more!") to be forgotten. And, by the way, this is a good time to insert: It is better to emphasize someone's giving rather than someone's income. I think Americans are enamored over how much people make. Frankly, that's the wrong thing to talk about. If I read the Scriptures correctly, I don't find the Lord's concern resting on what one makes nearly so much as on what one gives.

In an article entitled "Planned Giving—Legalism or Love?" which appeared in *Moody Monthly* magazine, May 1986, Sylvia and John Ronsvalle stated that "the average church member gives only 2.5 percent of his income to the church."[1] I've also heard my longtime friend and financial counselor, Ron Blue, frequently mention in his seminars:

If all Christians were reduced to a welfare income and they tithed on that amount, the church would double its receipts.

In working with our clients, it has been our experience that, with planning, their giving goes up, on an average, about four times what they were giving prior to doing planning.

The problem is not a lack of desire to give, but more so confusion because of the tremendous uncertainty and conflicting advice we live with on a day-to-day basis.[2]

Wise words from a trustworthy source.

In his book, *Human Options*, Norm Cousins mentions a fact that surprised me.

The cash lost each year in the United States amounts to about seventy-five dollars per capita—money that has fallen out of pockets, is misplaced, and so forth. The total average income for most of the human occupants on this planet comes to about sixty-nine dollars per person annually. The average American thus loses more money each year than almost anyone else earns. . . .

The essential problem in a computerized age remains the same as it has always been. That problem is not solely how to be more productive, more comfortable, more content, but how to be more sensitive, more sensible, more proportionate, more alive.[3]

I live in Orange County, adjacent to Los Angeles County in Southern California. One of our local newspapers recently reported some disappointing statistics:

Orange County residents are making more money but sharing less of it with charities, the Orange County Annual Survey found.

Compared with charitable giving elsewhere in the country, the average Orange County resident could pass for Ebenezer Scrooge.

The 1987 survey found the average annual donation in Orange County was $262—"unduly low" for the then-median income of $42,000, according to the survey.

But giving was even less in 1988. The average annual contribution plummeted 30 percent to $182, even though median annual income grew by 5 percent, to $44,000. . . .

The rate of donation declined from 0.6 percent of income in 1987 to 0.4 percent in 1988. A Gallup Poll released in October found that even the least-generous people nationally contributed an average of 1.5 percent of their annual income.[4]

The secret is not *making* more money. No one ever changed his or her giving pattern strictly because of increased income. I repeat, the focus should not be on the amount of money someone makes. Our Lord rarely emphasized that. Rather, His concern is on what one gives and the importance of releasing it in grace. What a wonderful way to counteract selfishness and covetousness. You will find that when grace awakens within you, selfishness will no longer win the day! It will be defeated and finally eclipsed by generosity.

Let me mention a fourth reason generosity based on grace is so addictive. *You can't help but be generous when grace consumes you.* "Now this I say, he who sows sparingly shall also reap sparingly; and he who sows bountifully shall also reap bountifully" (2 Cor. 9:6).

Here is an encouraging verse for anyone who fears that giving more will result in "running out." If I read these words correctly, the bountiful sower becomes that kind of reaper. I cannot explain the magic, the beauty, and the wonder of it all, but this much I know for sure: We cannot outgive our God.

WHAT MAKES GRACE SO ATTRACTIVE?

Beginning in 2 Corinthians 9, verse 6, through the end of the chapter, I discover four things that make grace so attractive, not just at the Christmas season, but all through the year. In verse 7 we are told: "Let each one do just as he has purposed in his heart. . . ."

Here is the first reason grace is so attractive: *Grace individualizes the gift.* When you give by grace, you give individually. You give proportionately to your own income. You have needs and you have an income to meet those needs. That combination is unlike anyone else's on earth. You are an individual. When you give on that basis, your gift is an individual kind of gift. We are not all shoved into a tank, blended together, then "required" to give exactly 10 percent. (Though if everyone gave 10 percent, we would have such an enormous surplus in God's work we would not know what to do with the extra . . . but I'm sure we'd quickly find out.) It is much more individualized than that. Grace, remember, brings variety and spontaneity.

If you are married, how about regularly discussing your giving plans with your mate? Or if you are single and you have a job where your salary is increasing, and you respect your parents and their giving habits, how about talking over with them a game plan for giving during this next year? By discussing it, you can discover ways to individualize your style of giving. Paul puts it this way: "Each *one* do *just* as he purposed in his heart."

You know our problem? Most folks don't "purpose"; they don't plan, they impulsively react. But God says, "Let each one do just as he purposed in his heart." Think of how carefully you would plan a room addition. You leave nothing to chance, making certain not to miss one detail, one electrical socket in your planning, one window placement, or one place where you will or will not use carpet. You purpose and plan exactly how you want to add on to the house. I challenge you to do the same with your giving. Give grace a chance! Start with planning, praying, and thinking it through. Determine the amount and where your gift will go, and when, and then release it with joy.

The second reason grace is so attractive: *Grace makes the action joyfully spontaneous*. ". . . not grudgingly or under compulsion; for God loves a cheerful giver" (v. 7).

I never have been able to understand why everyone in the church looks so serious during the offering. Wouldn't it be great if when the offering plates are passed in church next Sunday instead of grim looks, stoic silence, and soft organ music you heard laughter? I can just imagine: "Can you believe we're doing this?" "Put it in the plate, honey. Isn't this great? Put it in!" . . . followed by little ripples of laughter and applause across the place of worship. Wonderful! Why not? Deep within the heart there is an absence of any compulsion, only spontaneous laughter. The word *cheerful* is literally a Greek term from which we get the word *hilarious*. "God loves a *hilarious* giver."

I have said all through my ministry, and I repeat it again: If your giving isn't done with hilarity, don't bother. Giving is not for the unbeliever or for those who are grim and resentful. Such giving will not be blessed. The best kind of giving has no strings attached.

In an excellent and creative article titled "The Gift of Giving," author Calvin Miller addresses what I'm getting at.

> The wise men started it all, some say. Still, I like the way the Magi gave their gifts, for they presumably returned "to the East" without expecting Mary and Joseph to give them anything in return.
>
> Their gifts were meant for the baby Jesus, but there seemed to be no . . . obligation in their giving. . . .
>
> Often at Christmas, gifts become a subtle power play, resulting in obligation. Such gifts may subtly say, "While my gift appears free, repay me in kind," or "Enjoy this, Joe, but you owe me one now. . . ."
>
> Let me suggest two ways to give a grace gift.
>
> First, be sure it's impossible to measure the cost of your gift. My daughter's Italian mother-in-law has taught her to cook authentic Italian foods. So when my daughter wants to please me most, she fills a bowl with meatballs swimming in her marvelous marinara sauce, and I am content through long winters. . . .
>
> Second, realize that non-material gifts are the best way to say, "Don't try to pay me back." . . .
>
> One friend promised to pray for me all through the Christmas season. Another friend who knows I am fond of Shakespeare gave me a book of Shakespearean quotes from his personal library.[5]

You see, as I write about giving in this chapter, I am not limiting my remarks to money. Don't worry, monetary generosity will fall into place when grace is in place. Money will take care of itself.

Now for a third reason grace is so attractive: *Grace enables us to link up with God's supply line.* Look at verse 8: "And God is able to make all grace abound to you, that always having all sufficiency in everything, you may have an abundance for every good deed." When we possess an attitude of grace, we give. We give ourselves. We give from what we earn. And He, in turn, gives back in various ways, not matching gift for gift, but in an abundance of ways, He goes beyond.

Fourth: *Grace leads to incomparable results.*

> Because of the proof given by this ministry they will glorify God for your obedience to your confession of the gospel of Christ, and for the liberality of your contribution to them and to all, while they also, by prayer on your behalf, yearn for you because of the surpassing grace of God in you. (2 Cor. 9:13–14)

As I read these verses, I find at least three results I would call "incomparable":

1. Others give God the glory.
2. They learn, by example, to be generous.
3. The relationship transcends any gift we give.

Allow me one final bit of counsel: Once you begin to give on the basis of grace, do so *confidentially*. In plain English, keep your mouth closed. Keep the extent of your giving to yourself. Ideally, do so anonymously. And He who rewards in secret will fulfill His part of the bargain.

The "apostle of grace" concludes this lengthy section on giving by announcing, "Thanks be to God for His indescribable gift!" (v. 15). Paul had a pretty good vocabulary, but when he attempted to describe God's gift of Christ he ran out of Greek words. He simply couldn't find a word for it, so he admits it is *indescribable*.

Once again, I am reminded of Christmas . . . God's "indescribable" Gift to us, the greatest example of grace giving in the history of time. Holding nothing back, He cared enough to send the best gift of all. When you stop and think about it, He chose the Gift we needed most.

This past Christmas I received a boost of encouragement through numerous cards, colorful greetings, and meaningful letters. Among them was a simple white sheet of paper—no name, no address, not even a postmark on the envelope in which it came. Printed in beautiful calligraphy on the center of the sheet was a message that captures the essence of God's grace in sending us His Son.

> If our greatest need had been information,
> *God would have sent us an educator.*
> If our greatest need had been technology,
> *God would have sent us a scientist.*
> If our greatest need had been money,
> *God would have sent us an economist.*
> If our greatest need had been pleasure,
> *God would have sent us an entertainer.*
> But our greatest need was forgiveness,
> *so God sent us a Saviour!* [6]

On that first Christmas morning, when Mary first unwrapped God's "indescribable" Gift, grace awakened.

14

Grace: It's Really *Accepting*

～

WHEN I BEGAN THIS BOOK I STATED IN the opening chapter that grace is *really* amazing. As I write the closing chapter, I want to emphasize that grace is *really* accepting as well. It not only gives with joyful generosity, it receives with grateful humility. When a person truly experiences a "grace awakening" and begins to understand and demonstrate the kind of love I have been describing, there is not only the amazing desire to extend encouragement, affirmation, support, and reassurance to others, there is also an accepting attitude that allows others to reciprocate in like manner. As easy and simple as that may sound, it is neither. In fact, it cuts cross-grain against our natural tendency to be self-sufficient and invulnerable. Before you reject that thought, think realistically. Just how open and accepting are you when others extend unexpected and undeserved grace in your direction?

THE FLIP SIDE OF SEVERAL STRENGTHS

We who believe so firmly in the pursuit of strong character often forget that such pursuits have a downside. I can think of four off the top of my head.

First, *with a commitment to excellence there comes an attitude of intolerance.* There is absolutely nothing wrong with pursuing excellence. Those who do are on a warpath against mediocrity, laziness, and incompetence. But the flip side of excellence cannot be denied: the tendency to be intolerant. If you work for an individual whose goal is the pursuit of excellence, you need no convincing. You have found there is little margin for error. To ignore a mistake is out of the question. No flaw is considered too small to correct. No accomplishment is so well done it cannot be improved.

One of the best-selling books of the previous decade was *In Search of Excellence*, in which the authors hailed companies who modeled standards of excellence in eight primary areas. The implication was clear: You wish to be excellent? Do not tolerate anything less. It's the same motto we heard from a professional football coach back in the 1970s: "Winning isn't everything, it's the only thing." The downside of such an intolerant philosophy is that it can be interpreted as rejection by anyone who fails to measure up.

Second, *with a lifestyle of discipline there comes impatience and the tendency to judge.* Unfortunately, both come in the same package. A person who works hard to stay fit by eating better and less, plus maintaining a consistent, rigorous exercise program, tends to be impatient with those who eat too much and refuse to exercise even a little. The overeaters may view themselves as pleasingly plump. But Mr. Atlas and his iron-pumping wife, Wonder Woman, see them as slobs, plain and simple. Such a contrast reminds me of some amazing statistics I came across in a couple of similar sources that paint a statistical portrait of America. Among the things that happen each day in our country:

- Americans purchase 45,000 new automobiles and trucks, and smash up 87,000.

- We eat 75 acres of pizza, 53 million hot dogs, 167 million eggs, 3 million gallons of ice cream and 3000 tons of candy. We also jog 17 million miles and burn 1.7 billion calories while we're at it.[1]
- $2,021,918 is spent on exercise equipment, $3,561,644 on tortilla chips . . . $10,410,959 on potato chips.
- Americans . . . drink 524 million servings of Coca-Cola, are served 2,739,726 Dunkin' Donuts . . .
- 101,280,321 adults are on diets.[2]

My point is this: If you're a jogger who burns off hundreds of calories while clicking off six or seven miles a day, you have no patience with the fella who eats half an acre of pizza and washes it down with a couple quarts of his favorite cola. Discipline and impatience tend to occupy the same body.

Third, *with a broad education and a love for culture and the arts, there is usually the flip side of exclusive sophistication.* Cultural buffs stick together. Art lovers are in their own world . . . and God help any poor soul who prefers country-western and foot-stompin' bluegrass music but finds himself among those who prefer Brahms or Chopin or Tchaikovsky! Because I happen to enjoy most any kind of music other than opera, I smiled when I read Haddon Robinson's admission. "I do not appreciate opera; what is worse, I have several friends who do."[3] As wonderful, delightful, and satisfying as the cultural world may be, none can deny the air of exclusive sophistication that accompanies it.

There is also a fourth flip side that comes to my mind: *With an emphasis on independence and high production, there is the presence of pride.* If you are an independent worker, an independent thinker, or if you have become independently wealthy by nothing other than sacrifice and hard work from ground zero up, chances are good that you have a great deal of pride. You have struggled for every dime you've made.

You took no handouts, got no breaks, and refused all shortcuts to success. Whatever you got, you earned it the "old-fashioned way." Whatever you needed, you dug down deep and refused to quit until you got it. And as a result, you made it to the top, and it is no secret that you're proud of it. Then one day, along comes somebody who wants to do something for you; someone who desires to extend to you a little undeserved, unearned grace. Lots of luck.

Right now, do you know who I'm thinking of? A lovely young woman who was very coordinated, athletic, strong, healthy, capable, independent of spirit, and talented. She loved to ride horseback, in fact, she loved everything about life. She was athletic, popular, and fulfilled. Her name is Joni Eareckson Tada. But, as a result of a fateful dive into the Chesapeake Bay in 1967, her world was suddenly reduced to a wheelchair. Joni, still a delightful and beautiful person, is now a quadriplegic. Once independent, she is now forced to depend on others for survival. Can you imagine the difficulty of such a challenge? What a battle I would have with pride! And let's face it, it would be a struggle for any strong-willed, independent, highly productive person to be forced into a reversal of roles, from independence and achiever to dependence and acceptance.

How difficult it is for those of us who are able to produce a great deal to be accepting and receiving of the grace of others. We are not only determined, we are driven. We set a goal and we achieve it. We meet deadlines because we apply the necessary discipline and we produce. Accompanying all that is an ironlike mind-set and spirit that is so involved in giving, giving, giving that when someone graciously comes to give to us, we are quasi-embarrassed. We may hide it, but we are uneasy, reluctant. To use words we can now understand, we resist grace. Capable and frequent givers find it the next thing to impossible to be grateful and willing receivers.

This especially reveals itself in the individual who has lived a great deal of his or her adult life without Jesus Christ. If you are independent and proud, successful and strong, productive and competent, you are fairly sufficient on your own. Then along comes someone who tells you about the Savior, Jesus Christ, offering you something you don't deserve and cannot earn. The normal response is "No thanks. No help wanted. I've made it this far, I'll make it the rest of the way." It is possible you may cope fairly well with life, but I must remind you that you will not make it beyond death. As Jesus Himself taught, "For what is a man profited if he gains the whole world, and loses or forfeits himself?" (Luke 9:25).

EXAMPLES OF RESISTING AND ACCEPTING GRACE

While reading through the Bible this year, I made a note of several lives that illustrate both resisting grace and accepting grace. Though the people we'll be looking at lived centuries ago, their circumstances, surroundings, and attitudes pulsate with relevance, making it easy for us to identify with each one.

Two Old Testament Examples: Moses and Samson

Exodus 3 records the account of a man who resisted grace when it was offered to him. His name was Moses. As we step into his life in the third chapter of Exodus, he is eighty years old. His life is a study in contrast between his first forty years and his second forty years.

During his first forty years he was remarkable. His resumé was nothing short of impressive. He was the adopted son of Pharaoh's daughter. Raised in elegance. Educated at the Temple of the Sun. Experienced as a warrior. Capable as a speaker. Respected and confident. Josephus, the Jewish historian, suggests that he was what we would call the "Pharaoh-elect." He was being primed to take the throne as the next Egyptian pharaoh. He had won battles fighting Ethiopia and other countries. Perhaps he had a chest full of medals for bravery. He had a polished chariot, and servants available at the snap of his fingers. When he rode through the fields, surely the people shouted, "Bow the knee. Bow the knee!" He was the epitome of nobility, the pride of ancient Egypt.

While in the court of Pharaoh, he was spoken to by his God and was told that he was to deliver the Hebrews from bondage. He determined to obey. One day he happened upon an Egyptian assaulting a Hebrew. Without hesitation, he acted in the Hebrew's defense and murdered the Egyptian. To borrow from the words of the prophet Zechariah, Moses attempted to free the Hebrews by "might and power," rather than doing the deliverance God's way and in God's time. Tragically, he thought he could lead the exodus in the energy of the flesh.

God (as always) put thumbs down on the process. There he was, forty years old, no longer the darling of the nation. Everything for Moses changed . . . almost overnight. Pharaoh had no more use for him. He was instantly humiliated as he ran for his life. His guilt must have been unbelievable. His whole life went "down the tubes." It would be like building, building, building, building all through your adult life, and shortly after you reach the pinnacle of success, doing something stupid financially or ethically or perhaps morally. It destroys your family. It destroys your reputation. It ultimately destroys your business, even ends your career. And you wind up behind bars. (Scripture calls that "sowing the wind and reaping the whirlwind.")

The bars on Moses' jail happened to be the Midian Desert, a sudden and unexpected career change. And for the next forty years Moses' God remained silent. There is no record here or anywhere in Scripture that God spoke to Moses while he was a shepherd working for his father-in-law. Here he is on the stinging sands of the Midian

Desert with a flock of sheep—the same man who had the leadership of a nation in his grip and had blown it! Disqualified, he had escaped to the desert. Guilt and remorse consumed him, leaving him with no other thought than this: *It's all over.* Keep in mind, all of that is the background to Exodus 3.

One morning Moses awakens and leads the flock of sheep to the backside of the desert. He may have been there hundreds of times before, but today was different. Today, the silence of God would be broken, much to Moses' surprise.

> Now Moses was pasturing the flock of Jethro his father-in-law, the priest of Midian; and he led the flock to the west side of the wilderness, and came to Horeb, the mountain of God. And the angel of the Lord appeared to him in a blazing fire from the midst of a bush; and he looked, and behold, the bush was burning with fire, yet the bush was not consumed. (Exod. 3:1–2)

If you have traveled much in the desert, you know that a bush may suddenly, on its own, burst into flames. But of course they always burn up. This one didn't. The flame persisted, but the bush was not consumed. Moses was puzzled. The longer he stood and studied the bush, the more it burned and burned and burned. Abruptly, out of the midst of the bush came a voice he hadn't heard for decades, "Moses! Moses!" Incredible moment! He knew that voice. He remembered it from forty years before. There was no other voice like that one. He thought his life was finished. He had made such a mess of things, he had been convinced he would never hear that voice again. How wrong he was!

Do you know what is in that voice? Grace. Have you heard it? Sitting in a bar some night trying to drown your fears and loneliness, did you hear the voice? Sitting in jail, having ruined your reputation, have you heard that voice? Leaving a divorce court with horrendous memories of what might have been, as you returned all alone to your apartment, did you hear the voice? Having messed up your life through a series of events too shameful to rehearse, did you convince yourself you were through forever? Or have you forgotten the voice? Listen again! That voice comes from God's heart of grace and it is calling your name. You may have been saying for a long time now, "It is over. It is finished. I am through. There is no chance." Grace knows no such restrictions. Let grace awaken! Like the bush that kept burning, grace keeps reaching.

F. B. Meyer writes eloquently of this moment.

> There are days in all lives which come unannounced, unheralded; no angel faces look out of heaven; no angel voices put us on our guard: but as we look back on them in after years, we realize that they were the turning points of existence. Perhaps we look longingly back on the uneventful routine of the life that lies beyond them; but the angel, with drawn sword, forbids our return, and compels us forward. It was so with Moses. . . .
>
> . . . Then, all suddenly, a common bush began to shine with the emblem of Deity; and from its heart of fire the voice of God broke the silence of the ages in words that fell on the shepherd's ear like a double-knock: "Moses, Moses."
>
> And from that moment all his life was altered. The door which had been so long in repairing was suddenly put on its hinges again and opened.[4]

Moses thought he was finished forever. Do you know why? *Guilt. Shame.* Because of those twin grace killers, don't think for a moment that Moses jumped at the chance to lead the Exodus. Remember, he was finished so far as his mind was concerned. But not God's. What we have in the balance of chapter 3 and into chapter 4 is a dialogue, better defined as an argument. God is saying "Go" and Moses is answering "No." God initiates the invitation: ". . . come now, and I will send you to Pharaoh, so that you may bring My people, the sons of Israel, out of Egypt" (Exod. 3:10).

Had he heard that before? For sure. That was four decades ago, back in Egypt, before he impulsively killed the Egyptian, remember? Maybe his mind was playing tricks on him. *It can't be real . . . or is it? God is saying the same thing he said forty years ago—but it can't be God! No way would He give me another chance!*

Examine the argument. Moses answers, "Who am I?" If God had interrupted, He would have said, "You're nothing. But you don't have to be somebody to be used by Me." Grace means God uses nobodies. Grace also means He makes nobodies into somebodies. The problem is this: Our shame screams so loudly and our guilt is so huge, we convince ourselves we're not useful and we think we cannot measure up. After all, you may think, *I have to be somebody special to be useful or important to God.* But the fact is He does great things through nobodies. He does some of His best work with those who think they are finished and, humanly speaking, should be. Moses' words reveal his inability to accept grace. "Who am I, that I should go to Pharaoh, and that I should bring the sons of Israel out of Egypt?"(v. 11).

I love God's answer! ". . . Certainly I will be with you, and this shall be the sign to you that it is I who have sent you: *when* you have brought the people out of Egypt, you shall worship God at this mountain" (v. 12, emphasis mine). Notice God said when, not if. God will get His way. You will look back and say, "I really cannot explain how, but God did it." That is the way it is with grace.

Moses' fear begins to surface.

> Then Moses said to God, "Behold, I am going to the sons of Israel, and I shall say to them, 'The God of your fathers has sent me to you.' Now they may say to me, 'What is His name?' What shall I say to them?" (v. 13)

Dear, anxious Moses! He's already got a worry list started. Listen to him rehearse his "they-may-say" concerns. Don't miss his use of the scare-word, "may." It is typical of all who are afraid of acting on grace. The worry hasn't happened yet. But, you know, "Lord, they may say, 'What is His name?' and I won't have all the answers." God's answer is designed to bring comfort: "You will have all of Me." But the man is still unconvinced. He simply cannot accept God's grace.

The argument continues into Exodus 4. Moses' guilt is enormous! His shame has him pinned to the mat. God hasn't yet convinced him that neither guilt nor shame is appropriate. Moses' answer begins with "What if?" (That is another missile from his arsenal of worry.)

> Then Moses answered and said, "What if they will not believe me, or listen to what I say? For they may say, 'The Lord has not appeared to you.'" (Exod. 4:1)

Moses is saying, in effect, "Lord, I won't have their respect. Some of them may even remember I'm the man who killed the Egyptian. They may say, 'You've got a record. You're a killer!'" God reassures him, "You'll have all of My power. You will have all the power you need." And after God performs a miracle in front of him, using Moses' own hands, He adds, "If I can do that with a staff and with a serpent, believe Me, I can take your power, as little as it is, and I can use it." Moses is still hesitant. "Please, Lord, I have never been eloquent, neither recently nor in time past, nor since Thou hast spoken to Thy servant; for I am slow of speech and slow of tongue" (Exod. 4:10).

Too many years in the hot desert has blurred Moses' memory. When he was younger, "he was a man of power in words and in deeds" (see Acts 7:22). He was once eloquent. But for the last forty years he had just been talking to those woolies in the wilderness. And you don't cultivate your public-speaking skills in the wilderness with the sand stinging your face and the sun turning your skin to leather.

It is survival city out there, nothing more. So he whines, "Lord, I'm not qualified. Those Egyptians are well-trained and well-educated." And he jumps to the conclusion, "I'm not eloquent." In no uncertain terms, the Lord tells him, "You'll have all that is needed." What God wants is an obedient heart and availability.

God commands, "Go, and I'll be with your mouth." Isn't that beautiful? I've claimed that verse on a number of occasions, especially when I have had to stand before audiences I didn't know. I just said, "Lord, You promised Moses You'd be with his mouth, so I ask You to be with mine. I'm satisfied to be Your mouthpiece. My heart's prepared, so please speak through my vocal cords." Time and again, He has "been with my mouth."

In verse 13 Moses is still arguing: ". . . 'Please, Lord, now send the message by whomever Thou wilt.'" That may sound humble, but the man is really trying to get out of the assignment. "Send somebody else." One paraphrase reads, "Send anybody else," which, being interpreted, certainly meant, "Send anybody but me." And the Lord says, "Okay, you have a brother. His name is Aaron. I'll send him." Remember Aaron? He was the one who encouraged the people only weeks later, to build and worship the golden calf. One of the heartaches of Moses' life was his brother. Yet God graciously allowed Moses to have him as his spokesman.

When it comes to accepting grace, the first thing to remember is this: *We resist grace when our guilt and shame have not been adequately dealt with.* Most folks, it seems, are better acquainted with their guilt and shame than with their God. Grace nullifies guilt. It renders shame powerless. Many of you who are reading these lines are better students of what you have done wrong than you are of what God wants to do with you now that you have made things right. And you are using your guilt and shame as a way to stay away from God's best.

One more thought on this. You know the last person on earth we forgive? Ourselves. We can forgive an enemy easier and quicker than we will forgive ourselves. But not until we have fully accepted the forgiveness of the Lord God will we be ready to let His grace awaken in us.

Alexander Whyte writes beautifully of Moses' life and ours:

> Some of you will know what forty years in the wilderness, and at the back of the Mount of God, have done for yourselves. You know how those years have reduced and subdued your too-high temper, and weaned you off from the shams and the sweetnesses of this world, and given you some eyes and some heart to suffer the loss of all things. . . . And if forty years have wrought such a change in such a slow-hearted scholar of God as you are, you will not wonder at the man Moses as he came back from the land of Midian. Any use you are, or are ever likely to be, or have now any hope or any ambition to be—it all has its roots in the great grace of God to you. . . .[3]

I hope you will never forget the following: Any person being greatly used of God is a recipient of God's great grace. Not one deserves it. Not one is adequate for the blessings that he or she is receiving. But God in His sovereign mercy has chosen to give great grace to an imperfect, ill-deserving individual . . . in spite of and in greater measure than his or her guilt and shame.

Judges 16 is our next stop. We have considered Moses. Let's look next at Samson. Those who have been raised in the church know the story of Samson fairly well. I remember as a little boy having a Bible that included colorful pictures. I remember often looking at the picture of how some artist thought Samson looked and trying to imagine what it was like to be that strong. And I didn't understand as a little boy that he was not strong because of something external . . . not because he looked fit or kept himself in shape. He was strong because of the grace of God.

Before the man was even born, his parents asked the Lord to guide them in the rearing of this little boy they would soon have in their arms. He had a godly set of parents who prayed for God's grace to be upon their son. And sure enough, before he was born, God promised, "He will be a Nazarite from birth. He will be set apart unto Me. He will begin to deliver Israel from the hand of the Philistines."

So when the boy was born, Samson's parents set him apart to God as a Nazarite. That means he was never to drink strong drink, he was never to touch a dead animal carcass or a human corpse, and he was never to cut his hair. His hair became long and flowing, representing a secret symbol of his strength. And sure enough, exactly as God predicted, he began to deliver Israel from the Philistines. The problem with Samson, as you may already know, is that he refused to control his lust, resulting in the collapse of his world.

We read in Judges 15:20: "He judged Israel twenty years in the days of the Philistines."

For two continuous decades Samson was in the process of delivering Israel from the hand of the enemy. For twenty years, he did his work. For twenty years he carried out his divine calling. And yet, immediately on the heels of that verse we read that he went in to a harlot (16:1) and shortly thereafter we find him in the valley of Sorek, which is Philistine country, playfully lusting in the lap of Delilah. And the rest is a study in tragedy. The man toys with his relationship with God as he tells Delilah the secret of his strength. And after he falls asleep on her lap, she calls for help from her conspirators-in-hiding, who come and shave his head. When Samson awakens he doesn't even realize both the Lord and his strength have departed from him. Bald, vulnerable, insensitive, he doesn't know how helpless he is. Soon, however, he is at their mercy. One verse tells it all: "Then the Philistines seized him and gouged out his eyes; and they brought him down to Gaza and bound him with chains, and he was a grinder in the prison" (Judg. 16:21).

What a tragic set of affairs! A victim of his lust, Samson became a prisoner of hated enemies. After being brutally blinded, he was led away to live in the excrement and filth of a Philistine dungeon and to labor as a grinder. Here is the once-strong judge of Israel in a place he deserved, humanly speaking. He played with fire and couldn't escape getting burned. In the words of Proverbs 5:22, he was "held with the cords of his sin." And if you and I were to vote as judges on the bench, we would say, "Guilty! Let him live there the rest of his life." Justice had her due. The man got what he deserved, no question.

But God? He never runs out of grace. Read the next verse in case you doubt that. "However, the hair of his head began to grow again after it was shaved off" (Judg. 16:22).

To borrow from the apostle John's words, "Where sin abounded, grace superabounded." If men and women had had their way in that day, they would have said, "May he be bald the rest of his life." But God doesn't operate like that. You think Samson wasn't thrilled the morning he awoke and felt a little fuzz? Talk about grace awakening! You think he didn't check his head *every morning* from then on? With more hair came additional strength. And as his strength returned, so did his determination to fulfill the mandate given by God at his birth: to deliver Israel from the Philistines.

Here's the rest of the story.

> Now the lords of the Philistines assembled to offer a great sacrifice to Dagon their god, and to rejoice, for they said, "Our god has given Samson our enemy into our hands." When the people saw him, they praised their god, for they said, "Our god has given our enemy into our hands. Even the destroyer of our country. Who has slain many of us." It so happened when they were in high spirits, that they said, "Call for Samson, that he may amuse us. . . . " (Judg. 16:23–25)

In other words, they're saying, "We need that Israelite clown in here. Bring him in to make us laugh!"

. . . So they called for Samson from the prison, and he entertained them. And they made him stand between the pillars. Then Samson said to the boy who was holding his hand, "Let me feel the pillars on which the house rests, that I may lean against them." Now the house was full of men and women, and all the lords of the Philistines were there. And about 3,000 men and women were on the roof looking on while Samson was amusing them. (Judg. 16:25–27)

I love what follows! "Then Samson called to the Lord and said, 'O Lord God, please remember me and please strengthen me just this time, O God, . . . '" (Judg. 16:28). Here is a man who certainly does not deserve the attention of God . . . a man who should have forfeited all rights to prayer, but he humbly calls on the name of his God. How could he? GRACE. Maybe you have read this story dozens of times, but you may have never focused on what was happening in the last part of verse 28: ". . . just this time, O God, that I may at once be avenged of the Philistines for my two eyes."

Here is a second principle about receiving grace: *We accept grace when we release all our expectations.* When we no longer feel we deserve special favors, grace awakens deep within us. It flows to and through those who have no expectations.

Every Christmas season I have the pleasure of speaking to the single parents' fellowship in our church in Fullerton. Great folks. The room is always packed. Hundreds of teachable, open, and, yes, broken, humble folks. The thing I love the most about speaking to our single parents is that they have no expectations of me. Do you realize how seldom that happens to me? Can you imagine how wonderful and freeing it is to stand in front of a group and know that you can blow it, and have hundreds of people who understand and even enjoy it! Those folks know what it means to be rejected, shoved aside, forgotten. The remainder of their adult life is being spent, they feel, recovering from failure. Therefore, they have no great expectations of life, in general, or of me, in particular. When I step up to the plate, I don't have to knock a homer. They appreciate it if I just bunt. No big expectations. Actually, they appreciate it just because I suit up and show up.

That word picture gives me an idea. Let's say we're at the World Series and it is the bottom of the ninth. The Los Angeles Dodgers are playing the Oakland A's. It is a game the Dodgers really need to win, and the score is tied. Slugger Kirk Gibson steps up to the plate and he prays for a homer. The next thing we know . . . BOOM! He smashes one over the wall. We all scream, jump up and down, and shout, "There's nobody like Gibson; he's our man!" When it is time to pull out a win in the last inning, Kirk Gibson's the guy.

But let's go further for the sake of illustration. Let's just imagine Tommy Lasorda, manager of the Dodgers, ran out of players (everybody was hurt or something), and he had to use the bat boy in the bottom of the ninth. (I know, I know. You realists won't like this, but go along with me, okay?) Here's this inexperienced bat boy, stepping up to the plate at Dodger Stadium and he prays for a homer. Nobody has any expectations . . . least of all the bat boy. Then, BOOM! He smashes one into the second deck. Now if Butch the bat boy knocks one out, that is grace. If the bat boy saves the game, that is superabounding grace. Our problem is that most of us see ourselves as Gibson the slugger, not as Butch the bat boy. Sluggers expect a homer. Bat boys live their lives surprised.

Samson did not deserve new strength! But *without expectations*, he prayed, "Just this once, Lord, I claim Your grace." He was a washout, a failure, a man with a bad record. No expectations. And God, in grace, granted him his request. There are few grace killers more effective than expectations. Only when we release them are we ready to accept the grace God offers.

Two New Testament Examples: Peter and Paul

John 13 records a third story. The scene portrayed in this chapter took place at the Last Supper, an intimate setting. Jesus is with His men for the last time before His arrest and trial. Actually, it is just a few hours before the crucifixion. Do you know what the disciples were doing before Jesus washed their feet? I am sure that many would think they were praying. On the contrary, according to Luke 22:24–26, they began arguing over who was the greatest. Can you imagine?

"I'm going to sit on Jesus' right."

"No, that's my position. I am confident He will have me sit there."

"Well, I'm at least going to sit on the left."

"You don't deserve the left hand. . . . You don't deserve the end of the table!"

They were arguing back and forth over who would be at the top of the heap in the kingdom.

What most folks don't realize is that all twelve had come into the room for the meal and nobody had washed anybody's feet. If you've ever lived in or visited a home in the Orient, you understand how inappropriate their negligence was. To enter with dirty feet was as improper as coming into the room with your shoes on. In those days, a house servant was normally stationed at the door. And if there was not an appointed servant, it was a self-appointed servant-heart who waited at the door with a towel and a basin and washed feet as people arrived. Not these twelve! They were so busy worrying and arguing over who would be considered top dog they forgot about taking care of their dirty feet.

But Jesus remembered:

[He] rose from supper, and laid aside His garments; and taking a towel, He girded Himself about. Then He poured water into the basin, and began to wash the disciples' feet, and to wipe them with the towel with which He was girded. And so He came to Simon Peter. He [Peter] said to Him, "Lord, do You wash my feet?" (John 13:4–6)

The Amplified Bible renders John's account of Peter's emphatic resistance this way: "Lord, are my feet to be washed by You?" I mean, the audacity! As Peter said that, I would imagine he also pulled his feet up under him. Can't you feel the resistance?

Anyone who has made a study of Peter can understand his reluctance. He was the spokesman for the group, clearly the leader among The Twelve. He normally operated in a rather confident and proud manner. But let's not be too critical. The man was passionately loyal, fervently committed to the mission of Christ. However, being strong and capable, he could not tolerate the thought of admitting need or weakness.

Even when Jesus had told him earlier, "Peter, Satan would sift you as wheat!" the disciple had responded by saying, in effect, "Lord, all the other disciples may turn away, but I will *never* turn my back on You." And yet within a matter of a few hours he lied three times straight: "I don't even know Him. I SWEAR, I don't know Him!"

We should not be surprised at Peter's strong reluctance: "Never shall You wash my feet!" (v. 8). Our Lord had stooped and reached out in grace, but Peter dogmatically refuses. In rather emphatic Greek, John records Peter's statement of independence, "By no means will You wash my feet unto the age." Today we'd say, "No way, Lord . . . never!"

Here we find a third principle about receiving grace: *We resist grace when our pride is still paramount.* Of all the internal killers ready to pounce on grace, none is more assaulting than pride. Each time grace reaches, pride resists. Each time grace offers, pride refuses. Yes, each and every time, pride leaves no room for grace. Awakening grace and a proud heart cannot coexist.

Are you still impressed with your title, your public image, what people think of you? Is your position more important to you than your salvation? Are you still overly impressed with what you're doing? Do you look for subtle ways to pay back when someone gives to you? Or can you simply and graciously say, "Thank you"? If your pride is under proper restraint, you could even be vulnerable enough to say, "You know, I really needed what you gave me. Thank you."

That is hard to do when you are proud, like our friend Peter. Pride holds us back and conveys a false image that says, "I am without need." Haven't you ever looked at someone you really respected and wondered, *Does that person ever have a need? Can that individual imagine what it is like to live in the kind of world I live in?* The truth is that all of us are needy people, it's just that some of us hide it better than others.

If you really want to be a model of grace, get hold of that killer within you named Pride. Force it to the mat. Make it surrender. If your feet are dirty and grace offers to wash them, don't listen to pride for two seconds. Be grateful for cleansing grace.

So far we have looked at three lives. First, Moses resisted grace because his guilt was not sufficiently dealt with. Second, Samson accepted grace because his expectations had been done away with. Third, Peter resisted grace because his pride was still paramount. We're ready now for a fourth and final example—Paul. What a magnificent model! He accepted grace because *he no longer put confidence in the flesh.*

What was his flesh like? What was it like to be in the skin of Saul of Tarsus, a.k.a. the apostle Paul? Read and try to imagine . . . He was "circumcised the eighth day, of the nation of Israel, of the tribe of Benjamin, a Hebrew of Hebrews; as to the Law, a Pharisee" (Phil. 3:5). The consummate Pharisee, to the letter of the Law! You could not find a flaw, not even in his zeal. Continuing his pedigree—"as to zeal, a persecutor of the church; as to the righteousness which is in the Law, found blameless" (v. 6).

Paul says, "That's my record." But God cut him down to size. In the eyes of the world, he was impressive. But before the eyes of God, he was lost and in great need. Look at how he states that fact: "But whatever things were gain to me, those things I have counted as loss for the sake of Christ" (v. 7). A few lines later, he admits:

> Not that I have already obtained it, or have already become perfect, but I press on in order that I may lay hold of that for which also I have laid hold of by Christ Jesus. Brethren, I do not regard myself as having laid hold of it yet; but one thing I do: forgetting what lies behind and reaching forward to what lies ahead, I press on toward the goal for the prize of the upward call of God in Christ Jesus. (vv. 12–14)

Paul says, in effect, "For too many years I went full-speed-ahead in the wrong direction. Now I realize how off-target I really was. Christ alone is worth my zeal and passion! There is no other course worthy of pursuing. There I was on the wrong road earlier in life, but no longer."

You know what I read here? I read the testimony of a humble man who had lost all confidence in his own track record. He has gotten beyond his pedigree and his press clippings. He is now a man who has decided to "put no confidence in the flesh, although I myself might have confidence even in the flesh" (vv. 3–4). Finally, he got his priorities straight. When that happened, everything fell into place.

I repeat, *we accept grace when we no longer put confidence in the flesh.* By "flesh" I mean what we can achieve in our own strength or what we have done or might do for our own glory. The flesh, as I have mentioned several times in this book, is an all-powerful destructive force.

Those who master that inner struggle are wonderful recipients of grace. Do you know what God has for people like that? A future that is magnificent beyond belief, relaxed, full of contentment and relief.

WHAT IT TAKES TO LET GRACE IN

What I have been writing about is letting grace into our lives—being open to it, allowing it to occur, permitting it to permeate us so completely that we awaken others to its glorious freedoms. Rather than resisting it like Moses and Peter did, my plea is that we accept it, like Samson (the undeserving) and Paul (the supercapable).

But how? First, it takes *an admission of humanity*. In other words, an attitude that says in authentic honesty, "I am only human—I'm no prima donna, I can't walk on water, and I won't try to impress you." Grace awakens within folks like that.

Second, it takes *an attitude of humility*. Nothing is so welcomed by grace as true humility, which is nothing more than a realization of one's standing before God (He is tops, number one, preeminent) and a willingness to be cut down to size in order for Him to be exalted and glorified. Humility has learned the hard way that no person can operate in the flesh and produce any good thing, so it prevents us from trying.

What a wonderful future God has for people who accept grace. It is almost too good to be true. When George MacDonald, the great Scottish preacher, was talking with his son about the glories of the future, his little boy interrupted and said, "It seems too good to be true, Daddy." A smile spread across MacDonald's whiskered face as he answered back, "Nay, laddy, it is just so good it must be true!"[6]

It is in accepting grace that we can begin to model amazing grace. Only then do we realize how good grace really is.

CONCLUSION

IT WAS MANY MONTHS AGO THAT I BEGAN WRITING
this book on grace. Little did I realize what would transpire between
my starting and my finishing the volume.

I stated at the outset that this is essentially a book about
freedom . . . claiming it for ourselves and extending it to others. By
now you understand what I meant by that statement. I had no idea
that before I arrived at the conclusion of the book the world would
have witnessed the most powerful example of freedom one could
imagine: the fall of the Berlin Wall.

While I was writing on the importance of letting grace
awaken—which necessitates our pursuing freedom at any and all
cost—the daily newspaper, the magazines, and the television screen
have been pulsating with the same message. One remarkable scene
followed another . . . story after story, all of them representing one
of the greatest of all words: Freedom. I watched, as you did, and I
wept and sang as they did. I shouted as one section after another of
the infamous wall tumbled to the ground, giving renewed hope to
people who often wondered if they would ever know the thrill of

being liberated from social, economic, and religious bondage. Now they do. Now they are free indeed.

The stones and the steel, the barbed wire and the guards, that once separated East from West and dream from reality, are now, for all practical purposes, gone. The people of East Berlin no longer awaken each dawn to face another grim and bleak day of colorless existence due to enforced restrictions. *Now free at last*, they awaken to the glorious new dawn of liberty.

One of the most moving scenes I watched on television was a group of men taking turns with a sledge, pounding away on one section of the wall. One would grab the massive sledge and strike the stone with all his might. After ten or fifteen blows, another would step in and do the same. While one blasted with the sledge, the others stood near, singing, cheering, and occasionally dancing in circles. Although I was half a world removed, I felt a knot in my throat as I smiled along with those men I have never met. All were deliriously happy. Finally, at long last, the stones loosened and they could see daylight through the hole.

There is another wall that is now being torn down. Because it is invisible it is all the more insidious. And because it has been standing for centuries instead of decades, it is far more overpowering and stubborn. The stones that comprise the wall are formidable, intimidating, and thick. They would hold us back from all the things that God intended His people to enjoy. They still keep untold millions in bondage. I have identified many of them throughout these pages; from without: legalism, expectations, traditionalism, manipulation, demands, negativism, control, comparison, perfectionism, competition, criticism, pettiness, and a host of others; and from within: pride, fear, resentment, bitterness, an unforgiving spirit, insecurity, fleshly effort, guilt, shame, gossip, hypocrisy, and so many more . . . grace killers, all!

My hope has been to create an appetite for grace that is so strong nothing will restrain us from pursuing the freedom and spontaneity it can bring—a longing so deep that a new spiritual dawn, a "grace awakening," if you will, cannot help but burst through the wall of legalism. Since I am a Christian minister, much of my involvement and exposure is in the realm of the church and Christian organizations. It has been my observation that even here most folks are not free; they have not learned to accept and enjoy the grace that has come to us in Jesus Christ. Though He came to set us free, it saddens me to say that many still live behind the wall of bondage. Regrettably, the stones of constraint are everywhere to be found. Instead of being places of enthusiastic, spontaneous worship, many churches and Christian ministries have become institutions that maintain a system of religion with hired officials to guard the gates and to enforce the rules.

In vain I have searched the Bible, looking for examples of early Christians whose lives were marked by rigidity, predictability, inhibition, dullness, and caution. Fortunately, grim, frowning, joyless saints in Scripture are conspicuous by their absence. Instead, the examples I find are of adventurous, risk-taking, enthusiastic, and authentic believers whose joy was contagious even in times of painful trial. Their vision was broad even when death drew near. Rules were few and changes were welcome. The contrast between then and now is staggering.

The difference, I am convinced, is grace. Grace scales the wall and refuses to be restricted. It lives above the demands of human opinion and breaks free from legalistic regulations. Grace dares us to take hold of the sledge of courage and break through longstanding stones. Grace invites us to chart new courses and explore everexpanding regions, all the while delighting in the unexpected. While others care more about maintaining the wall and fearing those who guard it, grace is constantly looking for ways to freedom. Grace wants faith to fly, regardless of what grim-faced officials may say or think or do.

Thank you for walking with me through the pages of this journey. It has been a stimulating challenge to write these thoughts. In many ways, I feel as though I have been plowing new ground, blazing new trails. Not much has been written on personal, liberating grace from an evangelical perspective . . . at least I have not found much along these lines. Perhaps this book is enough to encourage you to join the movement and get you started on your own venture. I hope so. But as you strike out on your own, beware. As surely as Bunyan's hero encountered every test and temptation en route to the Celestial City, you will come up against one legalistic stone after another, each existing for the same purpose: to keep you from the freedom you have in Christ.

Whatever you do, don't quit! Press on. It is worth all the effort. The good news is that you are not alone.

There is a "grace awakening" loose in the land. Will you become a part of it? While you take your turn with the sledgehammer and pound away, a host of us are standing near, and some of us may be half a world away, cheering you on. Don't think of it as a lonesome, isolated task. You are breaking through to freedom, and no one is more delighted than the Lord Jesus Christ, who has promised you His grace. Never forget His words: "If therefore the Son shall make you free, you shall be free indeed." Stay at it. By the grace of Almighty God, the new movement will someday sweep across every continent and the longstanding wall that has kept people in bondage for centuries will come tumbling down. And we shall all, at last, be free indeed.

NOTES

ACKNOWLEDGMENTS

1   John Newton, "Amazing Grace" (1779).

INTRODUCTION

1   Reinhold Niebuhr, "Well-Intentioned Dragons," *Christianity Today*, 1985, 63.

CHAPTER 1   Grace: It's *Really* Amazing!

1   Dr. Karl Menninger, M.D., with Martin Mayman, Ph.D., and Paul Pruyser, Ph.D., *The Vital Balance* (New York: Viking Press, 1963), 204–205.
2   Ibid., 22.
3   Donald Grey Barnhouse, *Romans, Man's Ruin*, vol. 1 (Grand Rapids: Wm. B. Eerdmans Publishing Company, 1952), 72.
4   Benjamin Warfield, in *Great Quotes & Illustrations*, compiled by George Sweeting (Waco, TX: Word, 1985), 133.

5   Sir Edward C. Burne-Jones, in *Let Me Illustrate* by Donald Grey
Barnhouse (Westwood, NJ: Fleming H. Revell Company, 1967),
145–146.

CHAPTER 2   The Free Gift

1   William Ernest Henley, "Invictus," in *The Best Loved Poems of the American People*, selected by Hazel Felleman (Garden City, NY: Garden City Books, 1936), 73.
2   James Russell Lowell, "The Present Crisis" [1844]. Taken from 15th ed. of *John Bartlett's Familiar Quotations*, 567.
3   Donald Grey Barnhouse, *Romans, God's Remedy*, vol. 3 (Grand Rapids, MI: Wm. B. Eerdmans Publishing Company, 1954), 208.
4   Augustus Toplady, as cited in *Romans: The New Man, An Exposition of Chapter 6* by Martyn Lloyd-Jones (Grand Rapids, MI: Zondervan Publishing House, 1973), 19.
5   Augustus Toplady, "Rock of Ages" (1776).
6   Dorothea Day, "My Captain," in *The Best Loved Poems of the American People*, selected by Hazel Felleman (Garden City, NY: Garden City Books, 1936), 73–74.

CHAPTER 3   Isn't Grace Risky?

1   Martyn Lloyd-Jones, *Romans: The New Man, An Exposition of Chapter 6* (Grand Rapids, MI: Zondervan Publishing House, 1973), 8–9.
2   Reprinted from *What Luther Says* (vol. 2 p. 614), copyright © 1959, Concordia Publishing House. Reprinted with permission from CPH.

CHAPTER 4   Undeserving, Yet Unconditionally Loved

1   John Newton, "Amazing Grace" (1779).
2   Jackie Hudson, "People Grow Better in Grace," *Worldwide Challenge* Magazine, April 1988, 11–13, an adaptation from her book *Doubt. A Road to Growth*.
3   Elisabeth Elliot, *The Liberty of Obedience* (Waco, TX: Word, 1968), 32.
4   Ibid., 33.
5   John Newton, "Amazing Grace" (1779).

6   Ibid.

7   John Bunyan, cited in *The Grace of God* by William MacDonald (Walterick Publishers, 1960), 30.

CHAPTER 5   Squaring Off Against Legalism

1   Patrick Henry, in a speech in Virginia Convention, Richmond [March 23, 1775]. Taken from 15th ed. of *John Bartlett's Familiar Quotations*, 383.

2   Charles Sumner, "Slavery and the Rebellion"; speech at Cooper Institute [November 5, 1864]. Taken from 15th ed. of *John Bartlett's Familiar Quotations*, 539.

3   S. Lewis Johnson, "The Paralysis of Legalism," *Bibliotheca Sacra*, A Theological Quarterly Published by Dallas Theological Seminary, 120, no. 478 (April–June 1963): 109.

4   Daniel Taylor, *The Myth of Certainty* (Waco, TX: Word, 1986), 34–36.

5   Eugene H. Peterson, *Traveling Light* (Colorado Springs, CO: Helmers & Howard, Publishers, Inc., 1988), 57–58.

6   A. T. Robertson, *Word Pictures in the New Testament*, vol. 4 (Nashville, TN: Broadman Press, 1931), 284.

7   Eugene H. Peterson, *Traveling Light*, 67.

8   Mike Yaconelli in *The Wittenburg Door* (Dec. 1984/Jan. 1985), issue 82. Reprinted with permission, *Wittenburg Door*, 12245 Greenfield Drive, El Cajon, CA 92021.

9   Ralph Keiper, cited in *When the Saints Come Storming In* by Leslie B. Flynn (Wheaton, IL: Victor Books, a Division of Scripture Press Publications, Inc., 1988), 42.

10 Paul Tournier, *Guilt and Grace* (New York: Harper & Row, Publishers, 1962), 98.

CHAPTER 6   Emancipated? Then Live Like It!

1   Abraham Lincoln, in his second inaugural address, March 4, 1865, cited in *Abraham Lincoln: The Prairie Years and the War Years* by Carl Sandburg (New York: Harcourt, Brace & World, 1954), 664.

2   Ibid.

3   Shelby Foote, *The Civil War, A Narrative*, vol. 3 (New York: Vantage Books, 1986), 1045.

4   Gordon S. Seagrave, cited in *Quote Unquote* compiled by Lloyd Cory
     (Wheaton, IL: Victor Books, a division of Scripture Press Publications,
     Inc., 1977), 123. World rights reserved.
5   Donald Grey Barnhouse, *Romans, God's Freedom*, vol. 6 (Grand Rapids,
     MI: Wm. B. Eerdmans Publishing Company, 1961), 34. All rights
     reserved under International and Pan-American and Universal Copyright
     Conventions.
6   Abraham Lincoln in Washington, D.C., Aug. 26, 1863, as cited in *The Life,
     Public Service and State Papers of Abraham Lincoln* by Henry Raymond (New
     York: Darby and Miller, 1865), 752.

CHAPTER 7   Guiding Others to Freedom

1   William Barclay, *The Daily Study Bible, The Letter to the Romans* (Edinburgh:
     The Saint Andrews Press, 1957), 92. Used by permission.
2   Jay Adams, *Competent to Counsel* (Nutley, NJ: Presbyterian and Reformed
     Publishing Company, 1970), 145.
3   John Henry Jowett, *The Epistles of St. Peter*, 2nd ed. (London: Hodder and
     Stoughton, 1906), 93.

CHAPTER 8   The Grace to Let Others Be

1   Victor Frankl, *Man's Search for Meaning* (New York: Pocket Books, 1980),
     104–105.
2   William Barclay, *The Daily Study Bible, The Letter to the Romans* (Edinburgh:
     The Saint Andrews Press, 1957), 200. Used by permission.
3   Gladys M. Hunt, "That's No Generation Gap!" *Eternity Magazine*,
     October 1969, 15.
4   Reprinted with permission from Leslie Flynn, *When the Saints Come
     Storming In* (Wheaton, IL: Victor Books, a Division of Scripture Press
     Publications, Inc., 1988), 37.
5   Ibid., 44.
6   Wyatt Prunty, "Learning the Bicycle" (for Heather), *The American
     Scholar*, 58, no. 1 (Winter 1989): 122. Used by permission of
     the author.

NOTES

CHAPTER 9   Graciously Disagreeing and Pressing On

1   G. Campbell Morgan, *Acts of the Apostles* (Old Tappan, NJ: Fleming H. Revell, 1924), 369.
2   William Barclay, *The Acts of the Apostles* (Edinburgh: The Saint Andrew Press, 1964), 107. Used by permission.
3   Chrysostom, cited in *The Acts of the Apostles* by William Barclay, 108.
4   Franz Delitzsch, *Commentaries on the Old Testament, Proverbs of Solomon*, vol. 2 (Grand Rapids, MI: Wm. B. Eerdmans Publishing Company, n.d.), 165.
5   Leslie Flynn, *When the Saints Come Storming In* (Wheaton, IL: Victor Books, a Division of Scripture Press Publications, Inc., 1988), 64–65.
6   A. T. Robertson, *Word Pictures in the New Testament, The Acts of the Apostles*, vol. 3 (Nashville, TN: Broadman Press, 1930), 241.
7   C. S. Lewis, in the preface to *Christian Reflections* and cited in *A Mind Awake: An Anthology of C. S. Lewis*, ed. Clyde S. Kilby (New York: Harcourt Brace Jovanovich, 1980), 128.

CHAPTER 10   Grace: Up Close and Personal

1   William MacDonald, *The Grace of God* (Kansas City, KS: Walterick Publishers, 1960), 54.
2   John Bunyan, *The Pilgrim's Progress* (New York: The Heritage Press, 1942), 28.
3   Ibid., 35–36.
4   Ibid., 54.
5   C. S. Lewis, *Mere Christianity* (New York: Macmillan Publishing Co., 1964), 162.
6   Archibald Robertson and Alfred Plummer, *The International Critical Commentary, A Critical and Exegetical Commentary on the First Epistle of St. Paul to the Corinthians* (Edinburgh: T. & T. Clark, 1961), 341.
7   John Newton, "Amazing Grace" (1779).
8   Taken from *Quote Unquote*, compiled by Lloyd Cory (Wheaton, IL: Victor Books, a division of Scripture Press Publications, Inc., 1977), 319.
9   Sven Wahlroos, *Family Communication* (New York: New American Library, Inc., a Subsidiary of Pearson, Inc., 1983), 159.

10 Charles Bridges, *A Commentary on Proverbs* (Carlisle, PA: The Banner of Truth Trust, 1846), 41–42.

11 George Matheson, *Thoughts for Life's Journey* (London: James Clarke & Co., 1907), 266, 267.

12 Ibid., 266.

CHAPTER 11   Are You Really a Minister of Grace?

1 Kyle Yates, *Preaching from the Prophets* (Nashville, TN: Broadman Press, 1942), 201.

2 Ibid., 205, 206.

3 Theodore Laetsch, *Bible Commentary, The Minor Prophets* (St. Louis, MO: Concordia Publishing House, 1956), 428.

4 George Duffield, "Stand Up, Stand Up for Jesus" (1858).

5 Charles Haddon Spurgeon, *Lectures to My Students* (Grand Rapids, MI: Zondervan Publishing House, 1954), 9, 8.

6 William Barclay, *The Daily Study Bible, The Letter to the Corinthians* (Edinburgh: The Saint Andrew Press, 1963), 216–217.

7 Earl Henslin, Psy.D., "Shame-based and Healthy Spirituality," an unpublished chart. All rights reserved. Used by permission.

CHAPTER 12   A Marriage Oiled by Grace

1 Celeste Holm, *Reader's Digest Treasury of Modern Quotations*. Taken from *Reader's Digest*, February 1974 (New York: Reader's Digest Press, 1985), 484.

2 Dag Hammarskjold, *Markings* (New York: Alfred A. Knopf, 1964), 66.

3 From *The Pleasers: Women Who Can't Say No—and the Men Who Control Them* by Kevin Leman (pp. 287–288). Copyright © 1987 by Kevin Leman. Used by permission of Fleming H. Revell, Company.

4 Willard F. Harley, Jr., *His Needs/Her Needs* (Old Tappan, NJ: Fleming H. Revell, 1986), 10.

5 Celeste Holm, *Reader's Digest*, 484.

CHAPTER 13   The Charming Joy of Grace Giving

1 Sylvia and John Ronsvalle, "Opinion," *Moody Monthly* (May 1986): 12.

2   From a lecture by Ronald W. Blue, president of Ronald Blue & Co., 1100
    Johnson Ferry Road, Suite 600, Atlanta, Georgia 30342.
3   Norman Cousins, *Human Options* (Berkley Publications, 1983), 103.
4   Carroll Lachnit, "OC residents make more but give away less," *The Orange
    County Register*, 6 December 1988, A6.
5   Calvin Miller, "The Gift of Giving," *Moody Monthly* (December 1988):
    23–25. Used by permission of the author.
6   Source unknown.

CHAPTER 14   Grace: It's *Really* Accepting!

1   From *On an Average Day . . .* by Thomas N. Heymann. Copyright © 1988
    by Thomas N. Heymann. Reprinted by permission of Ballantine Books, a
    Division of Random House, Inc.
2   Tom Parker, *In One Day: The Things Americans Do in a Day* (Boston:
    Houghton Mifflin Co., 1984).
3   Haddon Robinson, *Biblical Preaching, The Development and Delivery of
    Expository Messages* (Grand Rapids, MI: Baker Book House, 1980), 31.
4   F. B. Meyer, *Moses, the Servant of God* (Grand Rapids, MI: Zondervan
    Publishing House, 1953), 33–34.
5   Taken from *Whyte's Bible Characters from the Old Testament and the New
    Testament* by Alexander Whyte. Copyright © 1952, 1967 by Zondervan
    Publishing House. Used by permission. Alexander Whyte, *Bible Charac-
    ters*, vol. 1, The Old Testament (London: Oliphants Ltd., 1952),
    139–140.
6   Greenville MacDonald, *George MacDonald and His Wife* (a reprint of a
    1924 ed.) (New York: Johnson Reproductions, a subdivision of Harcourt,
    Brace Jovanovich, n.d.), 172.

About the Author

CHARLES R. SWINDOLL serves as president of Dallas Theological Seminary. He is also president of Insight for Living, a radio broadcast ministry aired daily worldwide. He was senior pastor at the First Evangelical Free Church in Fullerton, California for almost twenty-three years and has authored numerous books on Christian living, including the best-selling *Laugh Again* and *Flying Closer to the Flame*.

HOPE AGAIN

Publications by Charles R. Swindoll

BOOKS

Active Spirituality

The Bride

Come Before Winter

Compassion: Showing We Care in a Careless
  World

Dear Graduate

Dropping Your Guard

Encourage Me

The Finishing Touch

Flying Closer to the Flame

For Those Who Hurt

The Grace Awakening

Growing Deep in the Christian Life

Growing Strong in the Seasons of Life

Growing Wise in Family Life

Hand Me Another Brick

Improving Your Serve

Intimacy with the Almighty

Killing Giants, Pulling Thorns

Laugh Again

Leadership: Influence That Inspires

Living Above the Level of Mediocrity

Living Beyond the Daily Grind, Books I and II

Living on the Ragged Edge

Make Up Your Mind

Man to Man

Paw Paw Chuck's Big Ideas in the Bible

The Quest for Character

Recovery: When Healing Takes Time

Sanctity of Life

Simple Faith

Standing Out

Starting Over

Strengthening Your Grip

Stress Fractures

Strike the Original Match

The Strong Family

Three Steps Forward, Two Steps Back

Victory: A Winning Game Plan for Life

You and Your Child

MINIBOOKS

Abraham: A Model of Pioneer Faith

David: A Model of Pioneer Courage

Esther: A Model of Pioneer Independence

Moses: A Model of Pioneer Vision

Nehemiah: A Model of Pioneer
  Determination

BOOKLETS

Anger

Attitudes

Commitment

Dealing with Defiance

Demonism

Destiny

Divorce

Eternal Security

Fun Is Contagious

God's Will

Hope

Impossibilities

Integrity

Leisure

The Lonely Whine of the Top Dog

Moral Purity

Our Mediator

Peace . . . in Spite of Panic

Prayer

Sensuality

Stress

Tongues

When Your Comfort Zone Gets the Squeeze

Woman

Hope Again

Charles R. Swindoll

WORD PUBLISHING

NASHVILLE

A Thomas Nelson Company

WORD PUBLISHING
1996

Unless otherwise indicated, Scripture quotations used in this book are
from the New American Standard Bible NASB © 1960, 1962, 1963, 1968, 1971, 1972,
1973, 1975, 1977 by The Lockman Foundation. Used by permission.
The King James Version of the Bible (KJV). *The Living Bible* (TLB),
copyright 1971 by Tyndale House Publishers, Wheaton, Ill. Used by permission.
The Message (MSG). Copyright © 1993. Used by permission of NavPress
Publishing Group. The Holy Bible, New International Version (NIV).
Copyright © 1973, 1978, 1984 International Bible Society. Used by
permission of Zondervan Bible Publishers. J. B. Phillips: The New Testament
in Modern English, Revised Edition (PHILLIPS). Copyright © J. B. Phillips
1958, 1960, 1972. Used by permission of Macmillan Publishing Co., Inc.

Book design by Mark McGarry
Set in Monotype Dante

Library of Congress Cataloging-in-Publication Data
Swindoll, Charles R.
Hope Again / Charles R. Swindoll
p. cm.
ISBN 0–8499–1132–X (hardcover)
ISBN 0–8499–3994–1 (foreign edition)
1. Suffering — Religious aspects — Christianity.   2. Hope — Religious
aspects — Christianity.   3. Consolation.   4. Bible. N.T. Peter,
1st — devotional literature.   I. Title.
BV4909.S95   1996   248.8′6 — dc20
96–8962
CIP

Printed in the United States of America.

9 0 1 2 3 4   BVG   9 8 7 6 5 4 3 2 1

I dedicate this book to two of my closest colleagues and
faithful friends on the leadership team at
Dallas Theological Seminary:

Dr. Wendell Johnston
and
Dr. Charlie Dyer

Without their invaluable assistance, there is no way these
recent years could have been so satisfying and
rewarding. These men have given me
fresh encouragement to press on . . . to finish strong
. . . to hope again.

Contents

Acknowledgments

I WANT TO ACKNOWLEDGE, with great gratitude, my longstanding friendship with several important people.

First, my friends on the leadership team at Word Publishing: Byron Williamson, Kip Jordon, Joey Paul, and David Moberg. There are others I could name, but these four have been especially encouraging and helpful on this particular project. Thank you, men, for continuing to believe in me and for knowing how to turn dreams into books.

I also want to express my gratitude to writer Ken Gire for his excellent work many years ago on our Insight for Living study guide on 1 Peter. I found several of his insights and illustrations helpful as I worked my way through this volume.

Judith Markham has again proven herself invaluable to me as my editor. Her ability to transform my primitive lines and disjointed phrases into understandable sentences and meaningful paragraphs is something to behold! I am especially grateful for her wise and seasoned counsel throughout this process. Without her help this book would have been twice as long and half as interesting.

Although I've already mentioned them in my dedication, I want to repeat my thanks to Wendell Johnston and Charlie Dyer for giving me hope again and again on numerous occasions since I began my work as president of Dallas Theological Seminary back in the summer of 1994. The Dallas heat during that July was enough to wilt the most stouthearted, but there they were right from the start, smiling, serving, and sweating alongside me, giving constant affirmation and providing plenty of wind beneath my wings. Without their whole-hearted commitment and assistance, rather than soaring like an eagle, I would have wandered around those halls like a turkey wondering where to roost. So thank you, men, for your faithful and supportive presence.

Finally, I want to acknowledge the encouragement of my wife, Cynthia, and express my thanks for her unswerving loyalty and compassionate understanding. We have been through a whale of a transition (we're still in it!), but because I haven't had to travel alone, the journey hasn't been nearly as difficult as it could have been. Having her by my side and knowing she is always in my corner and excited about my work has freed me up to finish what I started, regardless of the time and effort required. Thanks to her, I never felt the challenging task of finishing another project this extensive was hopeless.

CHUCK SWINDOLL

DALLAS, TEXAS

The Old Fisherman's Letter

HOPE IS A wonderful gift from God, a source of strength and courage in the face of life's harshest trials.

- When we are trapped in a tunnel of misery, hope points to the light at the end.
- When we are overworked and exhausted, hope gives us fresh energy.
- When we are discouraged, hope lifts our spirits.
- When we are tempted to quit, hope keeps us going.
- When we lose our way and confusion blurs the destination, hope dulls the edge of panic.
- When we struggle with a crippling disease or a lingering illness, hope helps us persevere beyond the pain.
- When we fear the worst, hope brings reminders that God is still in control.
- When we must endure the consequences of bad decisions, hope fuels our recovery.

- When we find ourselves unemployed, hope tells us we still have a future.
- When we are forced to sit back and wait, hope gives us the patience to trust.
- When we feel rejected and abandoned, hope reminds us we're not alone . . . we'll make it.
- When we say our final farewell to someone we love, hope in the life beyond gets us through our grief.

Put simply, when life hurts and dreams fade, nothing helps like hope.

Webster defines hope: "Desire accompanied by expectation of or belief in fulfillment . . . to desire with expectation of obtainment . . . to expect with confidence." How vital is that expectation! Without it, prisoners of war languish and die. Without it, students get discouraged and drop out of school. Without it, athletic teams fall into a slump and continue to lose . . . fledgling writers, longing to be published, run out of determination . . . addicts return to their habits . . . marriage partners decide to divorce . . . inventors, artists, entertainers, entrepreneurs, even preachers, lose their creativity.

Hope isn't merely a nice option that helps us temporarily clear a hurdle. It's essential to our survival.

Realizing the vital role hope plays in life, I decided several years ago to do a serious, in-depth study on the subject. To my surprise, one of the best sources of information was a letter located toward the end of the New Testament that was written by the old fisherman himself, Peter. He should know the subject well, having found himself in great need of hope at a critical moment in his own life—when he failed miserably.

And so . . . here it is, a book for all who sincerely search for ways to hope again . . . when your life hurts and when your dreams fade.

1

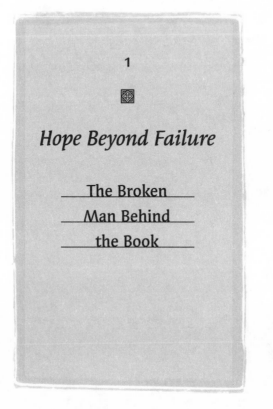

Hope Beyond Failure

The Broken
Man Behind
the Book

THIS IS A BOOK ON HOPE. *Hope.* It is something as important to us as water is to a fish, as vital as electricity is to a light bulb, as essential as air is to a jumbo jet. Hope is that basic to life.

We cannot stay on the road to anticipated dreams without it, at least not very far. Many have tried—none successfully. Without that needed spark of hope, we are doomed to a dark, grim existence.

How often the word "hopeless" appears in suicide notes. And even if it isn't actually written, we can read it between the lines. Take away our hope, and our world is reduced to something between depression and despair.

There once lived a man who loved the sea. Rugged, strong-willed, passionate, and expressive, he did nothing halfheartedly. When it came to fishing, he was determined—and sometimes obnoxious. But he was loyal when it came to friendships . . . loyal to the core, blindly courageous, and overconfident, which occasionally caused him to overstate his commitment. But there he stood, alone if necessary, making promises with his mouth that his body would later be unable to keep.

As you probably realize by now, the man's name was Peter, not just one of the Twelve, but the spokesman for the Twelve (whether they liked it or not). Once he decided to follow Christ, there was no turning back. As time passed, he became all the more committed to the Master, a devoted and stubborn-minded disciple whose loyalty knew no bounds.

Ultimately, however, his commitment was put to the test. Jesus had warned him that Satan was hot on his heels, working overtime to trip him up. But Peter was unmoved. His response? "Lord, with You I am ready to go both to prison and to death!" (Luke 22:33). Jesus didn't buy it. He answered, "Peter, the cock will not crow today until you have denied three times that you know Me" (Luke 22:34). Though that prediction must have stung, Peter pushed it aside . . . self-assured and overly confident that it would never happen.

Wrong. That very night, Jesus' words turned to reality. The loyal, strong-hearted, courageous Peter failed his Lord. Deliberately and openly he denied that he was one of the Twelve. Not once or twice but three times, back to back, he turned on the One who had loved him enough to warn him.

The result? Read these words slowly as you imagine the scene.

> And the Lord turned and looked at Peter. And Peter remembered the word of the Lord, how He had told him, "Before a cock crows today, you will deny Me three times." And he went out and wept bitterly. (Luke 22:61–62)

No longer loyal and strong, far from courageous and committed, the man was suddenly reduced to heaving sobs. What guilt he bore! How ashamed he felt! Words cannot adequately portray his brokenness. Emotionally, he plunged to rock bottom, caught in the grip of hopelessness; the effect on Peter was shattering. Every time he closed his eyes he could see the face of Jesus staring at him, as if asking, "How could you, Peter? Why would you?" That look. Those words. The man was haunted for days. The Savior's subsequent death by crucifixion must have been like a nail driven into Peter's heart.

The one thing he needed to carry him on was gone . . . gone forever, he thought. *Hope.* Until that glorious resurrection day, the first Easter morn, when we read not only of Jesus' miraculous, bodily resurrection from the dead but also those great words of grace, "Go, tell His disciples and Peter . . . " (Mark 16:7). *And Peter!* The significance of those two words cannot be overstated.

They introduced hope into the old fisherman's life . . . the one essential ingredient without which he could otherwise not recover. Upon hearing of his Savior's resurrection and also his Savior's concern that *he* especially be given the message, Peter had hope beyond his failure. Because of that, he could go on.

And, not surprisingly, he would later be the one who would write the classic letter of hope to those who needed to hear it the most . . . those who were residing "as aliens, scattered" across the vast landscape of the Roman Empire (1 Pet. 1:1).

Between his earlier failure and his writing this letter, Peter had been used of God as the catalyst in the formation of the early church. But having been broken and humiliated, his leadership was altogether different than it would have been without his failure. Now that he had been rescued by grace and restored by hope, he had no interest in playing "king of the mountain" by pushing people around. Rather, he became a servant-hearted shepherd of God's flock.

I like the way Eugene Peterson describes Peter in his introduction to 1 and 2 Peter:

> The way Peter handled himself in that position of power is even more impressive than the power itself. He kept out of the center of attention, he didn't parade his power, because he kept himself under the power of Jesus. He could have easily thrown around his popularity, power, and position to try to take over, using his close association with Jesus to promote himself. But he didn't. Most people with Peter's gifts couldn't have handled it then *or* now, but he did. Peter is a breath of fresh air.[1]

I cannot speak for you, but I certainly can for myself—this is a time when I could use some of Peter's "fresh air" in the form of a big dose of hope! These past two and a half years of my life and ministry have been anything but relaxed and settled. Having left a thriving, flourishing church where I had ministered for almost twenty-three years with a staff many would consider among the best in the country, and having stepped into a whole new arena of challenges—including endless commuting, facing the unknown, and accepting responsibilities outside the realm of my training, background, and expertise—I have found myself more than ever in need of hope. Solid, stable, sure hope. Hope to press on. Hope to endure. Hope to stay focused. Hope to see new dreams fulfilled.

And so it follows naturally that a book with this title has begun to flow from my pen. I trust that you who once smiled with me as we learned to laugh again by working our way through Paul's words to the Philippians are ready to travel with me through Peter's words as we now learn to hope again.

The journey will be worth the effort, I can assure you. We'll find hope around the corner of many of life's contingencies: hope beyond suffering and temptation . . . hope beyond immaturity and bitterness and the realities of our culture . . . hope beyond our trials and beyond times of dissatisfaction, guilt, and shame, to name only a few.

Best of all, we'll be guided on this journey by one who knew hopelessness firsthand, thanks to his own failures . . . and who experienced, firsthand, what it was like to hope again and again and again.

If that sounds like the kind of journey you need to take, read on. It will be a pleasure to travel with you, to be your companion on a road that leads to the healing of hurts and dreams fulfilled.

A Prayer for Hope Beyond Failure

Dear Father, every person reading these words, including the one writing them, has experienced failure. It has left us broken and disappointed in ourselves. And there are times when a flashback of those failures returns to haunt us. How sad it makes us when we recall those moments! Thank You for the remarkable transformation made possible by forgiveness. Thank You for understanding that "we are but dust," often incapable of fulfilling our own promises or living up to our own expectations.

Renew our hope—hope beyond failure—as we read and reflect on the words of Peter, with whom we can so easily identify. Remind us that, just as You used him after he had failed repeatedly, You will also use us, by Your grace.

May we find fresh encouragement from his words and new strength from his counsel as we journey together with Peter as our guide. We look to You for the ability to hope again, for You, alone, have the power to make something beautiful and good out of lives littered with the debris of words we should never have said and deeds we should never have done.

Our only source of relief comes through Your grace. Bring it to our attention again and again as we discover the truths You led the old fisherman to write so many years ago. In the gracious name of Jesus, I ask this.

AMEN

2

Hope Beyond Suffering

How We Can
Smile Through
Suffering

WE DON'T LOOK ALIKE. We don't act alike. We don't dress alike. We have different tastes in the food we eat, the books we read, the cars we drive, and the music we enjoy. You like opera; I like country. We have dissimilar backgrounds, goals, and motivations. We work at different jobs, and we enjoy different hobbies. You like rock climbing; I like Harleys. We ascribe to a variety of philosophies and differ over politics. We have our own unique convictions on child-rearing and education. Our weights vary. Our heights vary. So does the color of our skin.

But there is one thing we all have in common: We all know what it means to hurt.

Suffering is a universal language. Tears are the same for Jews or Muslims or Christians, for white or black or brown, for children or adults or the elderly. When life hurts and our dreams fade, we may express our anguish in different ways, but each one of us knows the sting of pain and heartache, disease and disaster, trials and sufferings.

Joseph Parker, a great preacher of yesteryear, once said to a group of aspiring young ministers, "Preach to the suffering and you will never lack a congregation. There is a broken heart in every pew."

Truly, suffering is the common thread in all our garments.

This has been true since the beginning, when sin entered the world and Adam and Eve were driven from the Garden. It shouldn't surprise us, therefore, that when the apostle Peter wrote his first letter to fellow believers scattered throughout much of Asia Minor he focused on the one subject that drew all of them together. Suffering. These people were being singed by the same flames of persecution that would take the apostle's life in just a few years. Their circumstances were the bleakest imaginable. Yet Peter didn't try to pump them up with positive thinking. Instead, he gently reached his hand to their chins and lifted their faces skyward—so they could see beyond their circumstances to their celestial calling.

> Peter, an apostle of Jesus Christ, to those who reside as aliens, scattered throughout Pontius, Galatia, Cappadocia, Asia, and Bithynia, who are chosen according to the foreknowledge of God the Father, by the sanctifying work of the Spirit, that you may obey Jesus Christ and be sprinkled with His blood: May grace and peace be yours in fullest measure. (1 Pet. 1:1–2)

The men and women Peter wrote to knew what it was like to be away from home, not by choice but by force. Persecuted for their faith, they had been pushed out into a world that was not only unfamiliar but hostile.

Warren Wiersbe, in a fine little book entitled *Be Hopeful*, says this about the recipients of the letter:

> The important thing for us to know about these "scattered strangers" is that they were going through a time of suffering and persecution. At least fifteen times in this letter, Peter referred to suffering; and he used eight different Greek words to do so. Some of these Christians were suffering because they were living godly lives and doing what was good and right. . . . Others were suffering reproach for the name of Christ . . . and being railed at by unsaved people. . . . Peter wrote to

encourage them to be good witnesses to their persecutors, and to remember that their suffering would lead to glory.[1]

Take another look at the beginning of that last sentence: "Peter wrote to encourage them to be good witnesses to their persecutors." It is so easy to read that. It is even easier to preach it. But it is extremely difficult to do it. If you have ever been mistreated, you know what a great temptation it is to retaliate, to defend yourself, to fight back, to treat the other person as he or she has treated you. Peter wants to encourage his fellow believers to put pain in perspective and find hope beyond their suffering.

While most of us are not afflicted by horrible persecution for our faith, we do know what it means to face various forms of suffering, pain, disappointment, and grief. Fortunately, in the letter of 1 Peter we can find comfort and consolation for our own brand of suffering. Just as this treasured document spoke to the believers scattered in Pontius or Galatia or Cappadocia or Asia, so it speaks to us in Texas and California, Arizona and Oklahoma, Minnesota and Maine.

The first good news Peter gives us is the knowledge that we are "chosen by God." What a helpful reminder! We aren't just thrown on this earth like dice tossed across a table. We are sovereignly and lovingly placed here for a purpose, having been chosen by God. His choosing us was *according to His foreknowledge, by the sanctifying work of the Spirit, that we may obey Jesus Christ, having been sprinkled with His blood.* Powerful words!

God has given us a purpose for our existence, a reason to go on, even though that existence includes tough times. Living through suffering, we become sanctified—in other words, set apart for the glory of God. We gain perspective. We grow deeper. We grow up!

Can you imagine going through such times without Jesus Christ? I can't. But frankly, that's what most people do. They face those frightening fears and sleepless nights in the hospital without Christ. They struggle with a wayward teenager without Christ. Alone, they endure the awful words from a mate, "I don't want to live with you any longer. I want my freedom. I don't love you any more. I'm gone." And they go through it all without Christ.

For souls like these, life is one painful sting after another. Just imagining what life must be like without Christ, I am surprised that more people who live without hope don't take their own lives. As appalled as I am by Jack Kevorkian and his death-on-demand philosophy, I am not surprised. What surprises me is that more people don't simply put an end to it all.

Yet if we will only believe and ask, a full measure of God's grace and peace is available to any of us. By the wonderful, prevailing mercy of God, we can find purpose in the scattering and sadness of our lives. We can not only deal with suffering but rejoice through it. Though our pain and our disappointment and the details of our suffering may differ, there is an abundance of God's grace and peace available to each one of us.

These truths form the skeleton of strong doctrine. But unless the truths are fleshed out they remain hard and bony and difficult to embrace. Knowing this, Peter reminds his readers of all they have to cling to so that they can actually rejoice in times of suffering, drawing on God's grace and peace in fullest measure.

Rejoicing Through Hard Times

As I read and ponder Peter's first letter, I find six reasons why we as believers can rejoice through hard times and experience hope beyond suffering.

We Have a Living Hope

> Blessed be the God and Father of our Lord Jesus Christ, who according to His great mercy has caused us to be born again to a living hope through the resurrection of Jesus Christ from the dead. (1 Pet. 1:3)

As difficult as some pages of our life may be, nothing that occurs to us on this earth falls into the category of "the final chapter." That chapter will not be completed until we arrive in heaven and step into the presence of the living God. Our final meeting is not with the antagonist in our life's story but with the author Himself.

"Who can mind the journey," asks the late, great Bible teacher James M. Gray, "when the road leads home?"

How can we concern ourselves that much over what happens on this temporary planet when we know that it is all leading us to our eternal destination? Peter calls that our "living hope," and he reminds us that it is based on the resurrection of Jesus Christ. If God brought His Son through the most painful trials and back from the pit of death itself, certainly He can bring us through whatever we face in this world, no matter how deep that pit might seem at the time.

Do you realize how scarce hope is to those without Christ? One cynical writer, H. L. Mencken, an American newspaperman during the early half of this century, referred to hope as "a pathological belief in the occurrence of the impossible."

To the unsaved, hope is nothing more than mental fantasy, like wishing upon a star. It's the kind of Disneyland hope that says, "I sure hope I win the lottery." . . . "I hope my boy comes home someday." . . . "I hope everything works out OK." That's not a living hope. That's wishful thinking.

But those who are "born again" in the Lord Jesus Christ have been promised a living hope through His resurrection from the dead.

So if you want to smile through your tears, if you want to rejoice through times of suffering, just keep reminding yourself that, as a Christian, what you're going through isn't the end of the story . . . it's simply the rough journey that leads to the right destination.

"Hope is like an anchor," someone has said. "Our hope in Christ stabilizes us in the storms of life, but unlike an anchor, it does not hold us back."

We Have a Permanent Inheritance

Blessed be the God and Father of our Lord Jesus Christ, who according to His great mercy has caused us . . . to obtain an inheritance which is

HOPE AGAIN

imperishable and undefiled and will not fade away, reserved in heaven for you. (1 Pet. 1:3–4)

We also can rejoice through suffering because we have a permanent inheritance—a secure home in heaven. And our place there is reserved under the safekeeping, under the constant, omnipotent surveillance of Almighty God. Nothing can destroy it, defile it, diminish it, or displace it. Isn't that a great relief?

Have you ever had the disconcerting experience of finding someone else in the theater or airplane seat you had reserved? You hold the proper ticket, but someone else is in your seat. At best it's awkward; at worst it can lead to an embarrassing confrontation.

Have you ever made guaranteed reservations at your favorite hotel for a "nonsmoking" room and arrived late at night to find they have given it to someone else? What a disappointment! You give them your guaranteed reservation number and they punch endless information into the computer, then they look at you as though you've just landed from Mars. Your heart sinks. You force a smile and ask to speak to the manager. He comes out, stares at the same computer screen, then gives you the same look with a slightly deeper frown. "Sorry," he says. "There must be some kind of mistake."

Well, that's not going to happen in glory! God will not look at you like, "Now, what did you say your name was again?" The living God will ultimately welcome you home to your permanent, reserved inheritance. Your name is on the door.

I don't know what that does to you, but it sure gives me a reason to rejoice. The more difficult life gets on this earth, the better heaven seems.

We Have a Divine Protection

[We] . . . are protected by the power of God, through faith for a salvation ready to be revealed in the last time. (1 Pet. 1:5)

Under heaven's lock and key, we are protected by the most efficient security system available—the power of God. There is no

16

way we will be lost in the process of suffering. No disorder, no disease, not even death itself can weaken or threaten God's ultimate protection over our lives. No matter what the calamity, no matter what the disappointment or depth of pain, no matter what kind of destruction occurs in our bodies at the time of death, our souls are divinely protected.

Our world is filled with warfare, with atrocities, with terrorism. Think of those men and women, especially those precious, innocent children, whose lives were shattered in an instant on that April 1995 morning in Oklahoma City when the world blew up around them. What happens in such times of tragic calamities? Is our eternal inheritance blown away with our bodies? Absolutely not. Even through the most horrible of deaths, He who made us from the dust of the earth protects us by His power and promises to deliver us to our eternal destination.

"God stands between you and all that menaces your hope or threatens your eternal welfare," James Moffatt wrote. "The protection here is entirely and directly the work of God."

Two words will help you cope when you run low on hope: *accept* and *trust*.

Accept the mystery of hardship, suffering, misfortune, or mistreatment. Don't try to understand it or explain it. Accept it. Then, deliberately *trust* God to protect you by His power from this very moment to the dawning of eternity.

We Have a Developing Faith

In this you greatly rejoice, even though now for a little while, if necessary, you have been distressed by various trials, that the proof of your faith, being more precious than gold which is perishable, even though tested by fire, may be found to result in praise and glory and honor at the revelation of Jesus Christ. (1 Pet. 1:6–7)

Here is the first of several references in Peter's letter to rejoicing. The words "even though" indicate that the joy is unconditional. It does not depend on the circumstances surrounding us. And don't overlook the fact that this joy comes *in spite of* our suffering, not because of it, as some who glorify suffering would have us believe. We don't rejoice because times are hard; we rejoice in spite of the fact that they are hard.

These verses also reveal three significant things about trials.

First, trials are often necessary, proving the genuineness of our faith and at the same time teaching us humility. Trials reveal our own helplessness. They put us on our face before God. They make us realistic. Or, as someone has said, "Pain plants the flag of reality in the fortress of a rebel heart." When rebels are smacked by reality, it's amazing how quickly humility replaces rigidity.

Second, trials are distressing, teaching us compassion so that we never make light of another's test or cruelly force others to smile while enduring it.

How unfair to trivialize another person's trial by comparing what he or she is going through with what someone else has endured. Even if you have gone through something you think is twice as difficult, comparison doesn't comfort. It doesn't help the person who has lost a child to hear that you endured the loss of two.

Express your sympathy and weep with them. Put your arm around them. Don't reel off a lot of verses. Don't try to make the hurting person pray with you or sing with you if he or she is not ready to do that. Feel what that person is feeling. Walk quietly and compassionately in his or her shoes.

Third, trials come in various forms. The word *various* comes from an interesting Greek term, *poikolos,* which means "variegated" or "many colored." We also get the term "polka dot" from it. Trials come in a variety of forms and colors. They are different, just as we are different. Something that would hardly affect you might knock the slats out from under me—and vice versa. But God offers special grace to match every shade of sorrow.

Paul had a thorn in the flesh, and he prayed three times for God to remove it. "No," said God, "I'm not taking it away." Finally Paul said, "I've learned to trust in You, Lord. I've learned to live with it." It was then God said, "My grace is sufficient for that thorn." He matched the color of the test with the color of grace.

This variety of trials is like different temperature settings on God's furnace. The settings are adjusted to burn off our dross, to temper us or soften us according to what meets our highest need. It is in God's refining fire that the authenticity of our faith is revealed. And the purpose of these fiery ordeals is that we may come forth as purified gold, a shining likeness of the Lord Jesus Christ Himself. That glinting likeness is what ultimately gives glory and praise and honor to our Savior.

We Have an Unseen Savior

And though you have not seen Him, you love Him, and though you do not see Him now, but believe in Him, you greatly rejoice with joy inexpressible and full of glory. (1 Pet. 1:8)

Keep in mind that the context of this verse is suffering. So we know that Peter is not serving up an inconsequential, theological hors d'oeuvre. He's giving us solid meat we can sink our teeth into. He's telling us that our Savior is standing alongside us in that furnace. He is there even though we can't see Him.

You don't have to see someone to love that person. The blind mother has never seen her children, but she loves them. You don't have to see someone to believe in him or her. Believers today have never seen a physical manifestation of the Savior—we have not visibly seen Him walking among us—but we love Him nevertheless. In times of trial we sense He is there, and that causes us to "greatly rejoice" with inexpressible joy.

Some, like the struggling, reflective disciple Thomas, need to see and touch Jesus in order to believe. But Jesus said, "Blessed are they who did not see, and yet believed" (John 20:29). Even though we can't see Jesus beside us in our trials, He is there—just as He was when Shadrach, Meshach, and Abednego were thrown into the fiery furnace.

We Have a Guaranteed Deliverance

> . . . obtaining as the outcome of your faith the salvation of your souls. (1 Pet. 1:9)

How can we rejoice through our pain? How can we have hope beyond our suffering? Because we have a living hope, we have a permanent inheritance, we have divine protection, we have a developing faith, we have an unseen Savior, and we have a guaranteed deliverance.

This isn't the kind of delivery the airlines promise you when you check your bags. ("Guaranteed arrival. No problem.") I'll never forget a trip I took a few years ago. I went to Canada for a conference with plans to be there for eight days. Thanks to the airline, I only had my clothes for the last two! When I finally got my luggage, I noticed the tags on them were all marked "Berlin." ("Guaranteed arrival. No problem." They just don't guarantee when or where the bags will arrive!) That's why we now see so many people boarding airplanes with huge bags hanging from their shoulders and draped over both arms. Don't check your bags, these folks are saying, because they probably won't get there when you do.

But when it comes to spiritual delivery, we never have to worry. God guarantees deliverance of our souls, which includes not only a deliverance from our present sin but the glorification of our physical bodies as well. Rejoice! You're going to get there—guaranteed.

Rejoicing, Not Resentment

When we are suffering, only Christ's perspective can replace our resentment with rejoicing. I've seen it happen in hospital rooms. I've seen it happen in families. I've seen it happen in my own life.

Our whole perspective changes when we catch a glimpse of the purpose of Christ in it all. Take that away, and it's nothing more than a bitter, terrible experience.

Nancy and Ed Huizinga in Grand Rapids, Michigan, know all about this. In December 1995, while they were at church rehearsing for the annual Christmas Festival of Lights program, their home burned to the ground. But that wasn't their only tragedy that year. Just three months earlier, Nancy's long-time friend, Barb Post, a widow with two children, had died of cancer. Nancy and Ed had taken her two children, Jeff and Katie, into their home as part of their family, something they had promised Barb they would do. So when Ed and Nancy's house burned to the ground just before Christmas, it wasn't just their home that was lost; it was the home of two teenagers who had already lost their mother and father.

As circumstances unfolded, irony went to work. The tragedy that forced the Huizingas from their home allowed Jeff and Katie to move back to theirs. Since their home had not yet been sold following their mother's death, they and the Huizinga family moved in there the night after the fire.

On the following Saturday, neighbors organized a party to sift through the ashes and search for anything of value that might have survived. One of the first indications they received of God's involvement in their struggle came as a result of that search. Somehow a piece of paper survived. On it were these words: "Contentment: Realizing that God has already provided everything we need for our present happiness."

To Nancy and Ed, this was like hearing God speak from a burning bush. It was the assurance they needed that He was there . . . and He was not silent.

Nancy's biggest frustration now is dealing with insurance companies and trying to assess their material losses. Many possessions, of course, were irreplaceable personal items such as photographs and things handed down from parents and grandparents. But her highest priority is Jeff and Katie, along with her own two children, Joel and Holly. The loss has been hardest on them, she says.

"They don't have the history of God's faithfulness that Ed and I have. We've had years to make deposits in our 'faith account,' but they haven't. We've learned that if you fail to stock up on faith when you don't need it, you won't have any when you do need it. This has been our opportunity to use what we've been learning."

While the world might view this as a senseless tragedy, deserving of resentment, Nancy and Ed have seen God reveal Himself to them and refine them through this fire as He pours out a full measure of grace and peace.[2]

Suffering comes in many forms and degrees, but His grace is always there to carry us beyond it. I've lived long enough and endured a sufficient number of trials to say without hesitation that only Christ's perspective can replace our resentment with rejoicing. Jesus is the central piece of suffering's puzzle. If we fit Him into place, the rest of the puzzle—no matter how complex and enigmatic—begins to make sense.

Only Christ's salvation can change us from spectators to participants in the unfolding drama of redemption. The scenes will be demanding. Some may be tragic. But only then will we understand the role that suffering plays in our lives. Only then will we be able to tap into hope beyond our suffering.

A Prayer for Hope Beyond Suffering

Lord, mere words about hope and encouragement and purpose can really fall flat if things aren't right in our lives. If we're consumed by rage and resentment, somehow these words seem meaningless. But when our hearts are right, we hear with new ears. Then, rather than resisting these words, we appreciate them, and we love You for them.

Give us grace to match our trials. Give us a sense of hope and purpose beyond our pain. And give us fresh assurance that we're not alone, that Your plan has not been aborted though our suffering intensifies.

Help those of us who are on our feet right now to maintain a compassion for those who aren't. Give us a word of encouragement for others living in a world of hurt.

Let us never forget that every jolt in this rugged journey from earth to heaven is a reminder that we're on the right road.

I ask this in the compassionate name of the Man of Sorrows who was acquainted with grief.

AMEN

3

Hope Beyond
Temptation

Staying Clean
in a
Corrupt Society

WOULDN'T IT BE wonderful if God would save us and then, within a matter of seconds, take us on to glory? Wouldn't that be a great relief? We would never have any temptations. We would never have to battle with the flesh. We would never even have the possibility of messing up our lives. We could just be whisked off to glory—saved, sanctified, galvanized, glorified! Trouble is, I have a sneaking suspicion that many, if not most, would wait until fifteen minutes before takeoff time to give their lives to Christ and then catch the jet for glory.

Since that's not an option and since it's clearly God's preference that we prove ourselves blameless and innocent and above reproach, we obviously have to come up with an alternative route. Some have suggested sanctification by isolation, believing the only way to keep evil and corruption from rubbing off on you is to withdraw from the world. After all, how can you walk through a coal mine without getting dirty? The logic seems irrefutable.

But God, in His infinite wisdom, has deliberately left us on this earth. He has sovereignly chosen to give many of us more years *in* Christ than *out* of Christ—many more years to live for Him "in the midst of a crooked and perverse generation, among whom you appear as lights in the world" (Phil. 2:15). Or, as one of my mentors, the late Ray Stedman, so succinctly put it, "Crooked and perverse simply means we are left in a world of crooks and perverts." That's the kind of world God left us in on purpose.

Don't think for a minute, however, that the Lord has made a mistake leaving us here. We are His lights in a dark world. In fact, just minutes before Jesus' arrest and ultimate death on the cross, He prayed this for His disciples and for us:

> I have given them Thy word; and the world has hated them, because they are not of the world, even as I am not of the world. I do not ask Thee to take them out of the world, but to keep them from the evil one. (John 17:14–15)

Think about that. "I'm not asking You to take them out from among the midst of a crooked and perverse generation," Jesus said. "But I do ask You to guard them, to protect them." Jesus doesn't ask the Father to isolate His disciples from the world but to insulate them, "to keep them from the evil one."

He has left us in the world on purpose and for His purpose. In a world where the majority are going the wrong way, we are left as lights—stoplights, directional lights, illuminating lights—as living examples, as strong testimonies of the right way. We are spiritual salmon swimming upstream.

The Seductive Cosmos Mentality

Few things are more awesome than pictures of earth the astronauts have taken from space. Our big, blue-and-white marble planet stands out so beautifully against the deep darkness of space. However, that's not the "world" Jesus has in mind here. He's not talking about the visible planet named Earth; He's talking about a philosophy that envelopes earthlings. It's not a place but a system—a system that finds its origin in the Enemy himself. It's a figure of speech that encapsulates the mind-set and morality of the unregenerate. It's what John calls the *cosmos*.

> Do not love the world, nor the things in the world. If anyone loves the world, the love of the Father is not in him. For all that is in the world [the *cosmos*], the lust of the flesh and the lust of the eyes and the boastful pride of life, is not from the Father, but is from the world. And the world is passing away, also its lusts; but the one who does the will of God abides forever. (1 John 2:15–17)

The physical world upon which we have our feet planted is visible. It can be measured. It can be felt. It has color and odor and texture. It's tangible . . . obvious. What is not so obvious is the system that permeates and operates within lives on this earth. It is a world-system manipulated by the pervasive hand of Satan and his demons, who pull the strings to achieve the adversary's wicked ends. If we are ever to extricate ourselves from those strings, we must be able to detect them and understand where they lead.

So what is this system? What is its philosophy? What is the frame of reference of the *cosmos*—its thinking, its drives, its goals?

The first thing we need to know is that it is a system that operates apart from and at odds with God. It's designed to appeal to us, to attract us, to seduce us with its sequined garb of fame, fortune, power, and pleasure. God's ways are often uncomfortable, but the world-system is designed to make us comfortable, to give us pleasure, to gain our favor, and ultimately to win our support. The philosophy of the world-system is totally at odds with the philosophy of God.

Greek grammarian Kenneth Wuest wrote:

> *Kosmos* refers to an ordered system . . . of which Satan is the head, his fallen angels and demons are his emissaries, and the unsaved of the human race are his subjects. . . . Much in this world-system is religious, cultured, refined, and intellectual. But it is anti-God and anti-Christ.

. . . This world of unsaved humanity is inspired by "the spirit of the age," . . . which Trench defines as follows: "All that floating mass of thoughts, opinions, maxims, speculations, hopes, impulses, aims, aspirations, at any time current in the world, which it may be impossible to seize and accurately define, but which constitutes a most real and effective power, being the moral, or immoral atmosphere which at every moment of our lives we inhale, again inevitably to exhale."[1]

You want to know what we are inhaling? Pay close attention to the commercials on television and observe what they're advertising and how virtually every word, picture, and sound is designed to pull you in, to make you dissatisfied with what you have and what you look like and who you are. The great goal is to make you want whatever it is that is being sold.

But it's not just on television. The world-system, the cosmos philosophy, is everywhere. It's going on all the time, even when you can't see it, and especially when you're not thinking about it. It's whistling its appeal, "Come on. Come on. You'll love it. This is so much fun. It'll make you look so good. It'll make you feel so good." It motivates us by appealing to our pride and to that which pleases us, all the while cleverly seducing us away from God.

And over all this realm, don't forget, Satan is prince.

A Challenge to Be Different

The pull of the world is every bit as strong and subtle as gravity. So invisible, yet so irresistible. So relentlessly there. Never absent or passive.

Unless we realize how strong and how subtle the world's influence really is, we won't understand the passion behind Peter's words.

Living in Holiness

Therefore, gird your minds for action, keep sober in spirit, fix your hope completely on the grace to be brought to you at the revelation of Jesus Christ. As obedient children, do not be conformed to the former lusts which were yours in your ignorance, but like the Holy One who called you, be holy yourselves also in all your behavior; because it is written, "You shall be holy, for I am holy." (1 Pet. 1:13–16)

Reading these statements, we can't help but catch something of Peter's assertive spirit. He seems to be saying that this is no time to kick back; this isn't a day to be passive. In fact, I think Peter really bears down with his pen at this point. Look at the forcefulness of his phrases: "gird your minds for action" . . . "keep sober" . . . "fix your hope." He spits them out in staccato form. Today we might say, "Straighten up!" . . . "Get serious!" And then the clincher command from God, saying, in essence: "Be holy like I am."

It's easy to let the world intoxicate us and fuzz our minds. But if we're to shake ourselves out of that dizzying spell, we must resist the power it exerts on us.

I think Peter is saying, "You have to realize that even though you're living in the cosmos, your mind, your eyes, *your focus* must be beyond the present." Kenneth Wuest suggests this: "Set your hope perfectly, unchangeably, without doubt and despondency."

That goes back to what we were thinking about in the previous chapter. No matter how bad things get, fix your mind beyond what's happening around you and what's happening to you. Otherwise you'll erode into the cosmos mentality.

I love the way verse 14 begins, "As obedient children. . . ." Isn't that affirming? Rather than coming down on his fellow believers, assuming they're disobedient, Peter assumes just the opposite here. "You're obedient children."

Through the years, my wife, Cynthia, and I found that if we referred to our children as good kids, obedient kids, kids we were proud of, that attitude instilled in them a sense that Mom and Dad had confidence and trust in them. And that's the attitude Peter employs when he tells the believers scattered throughout the ancient world: "As obedient children, do not be conformed." This also reminds me of Paul's words to believers in Romans 12:2: "And do not be conformed to this world, but be transformed. . . ."

How easy it is to allow the world, the cosmos, to suck you into its system. If you do, if you conform, then you are adopting the kind of lifestyle that was yours when you were in ignorance, when you didn't know there was another way to live. That was back when the cosmos was your comfort zone.

Have you been in Christ so long that you have forgotten what it was like to be without Him? Remember, He has called us to follow in His footsteps—to be *holy* "like the Holy One who called you, be holy yourselves also in all your behavior; because it is written, 'YOU SHALL BE HOLY, FOR I AM HOLY.'" We have a Father who is holy, and as His children, we're to be like Him.

But what does it mean to be *holy*? That's always a tough question to answer. Stripped down to its basics, the term *holy* means "set apart" in some special and exclusive way. Perhaps it will help if we think of it in another context. In holy matrimony, for example, a man and a woman are set apart, leaving all others as they bond exclusively to each other.

When I was a young man and a young husband serving in the marines, I was eight thousand miles away from my wife. I knew Cynthia existed. I could read her letters and occasionally hear her voice on the phone, but I couldn't see her or touch her. I had only the memory of our standing together three years earlier before God and a minister who had pronounced us husband and wife, setting us apart exclusively to each other for the rest of our lives. We were wed back in June 1955, but regardless of how long ago it was, we stood together and committed ourselves to a *holy* intermingling of our lives. To be intimate with another woman would break that holy relationship, that exclusive oneness. Remembering that helped keep me faithful to my wife while we were apart those many months . . . and it still helps over forty-one years later!

Church ordinances or sacraments, such as baptism and communion, are often called *holy*. In Holy Communion, for example, the bread and wine are set apart from common use and set aside to God alone. The same meaning lies behind the word *sanctify* in 1 Peter 3:15: "But sanctify Christ as Lord in your hearts." I love that. We are to "set Him apart" as Lord in our hearts.

What a successful way to deal with the cosmos! To begin the morning by saying, "Lord, I set apart my mind for You today. I set apart my passion. I set apart my eyes. I set apart my ears. I set apart my motives. I set apart my discipline. Today I set apart every limb of my body and each area of my life unto You as Lord over my life." When we start our day like that, chances are good that temptation's winks will not be nearly as alluring.

Walking in Fear

> And if you address as Father the One who impartially judges according to each man's work, conduct yourselves in fear during the time of your stay upon earth. (1 Pet. 1:17)

Another secret of living a godly life in the midst of a godless world involves the way we conduct ourselves hour by hour through the day. Peter says we are to do it "in *fear*." We don't hear much about the *fear* of God today, and when we do, some may think only of images of a fire-and-brimstone preacher pounding a pulpit. We need a better perspective. Perhaps the word *reverence* gives us a clearer picture of what Peter means here. In fact, the New International Version translates this phrase "live your lives as strangers here in reverent fear." The point is, if we're going to address God as Father, then we should conduct ourselves on earth in a way that reflects our reverence for Him as our Father.

Also, if you're going to address Him as your Father, if you're going to have a one-on-one relationship with Him in fellowship and in prayer, then conduct yourself as one who knows that you will someday have to account to Him for your life. Why? Well, in case you didn't know, "each one of us shall give account of himself to God" (Rom. 14:12).

When we die, we will be brought before the judgment seat of Christ where we will independently account for our lives before God. He will see us as our lives pass in review, and He will reward us accordingly. It's not a judgment to see if we get into heaven. That's taken care of. As we saw in the previous chapter, we can't lose our salvation. We can, however, lose our reward. At the judgment seat, Christ will judge our works and determine whether they were done in the power of the Spirit or in the energy of the flesh. We will all give an account of the deeds we have done in this life, and God will "test the quality of each man's work" (1 Cor. 3:13). That thought, alone, will instill a big, healthy dose of the fear of God in us!

We don't know how God is going to do this, but it helps me to put it into an everyday image we can understand. So I picture myself in the future standing there all alone before my heavenly Father. Along comes an enormous celestial dump truck, piled high with stuff. The truck backs up, the bed lifts up, and the whole load is dumped out in front me. The Lord and I talk about all the wood, hay, and stubble that's piled there, and then He begins digging through it. "Oh, there's a piece of gold," He says. "Hmm, here's some silver." With that He begins setting aside all the precious and permanent stuff. Then, *whoosh!* The wood, hay, and stubble are gone, instantly consumed by fire. Only the gold, silver, and precious stones that remain are rewarded.

In the 1988 Summer Olympics in Seoul, South Korea, Ben Johnson of Canada won the one-hundred-meter dash, setting a new Olympic record and a new world record. Our American contender, Carl Lewis, came in second, and most were shocked that he hadn't won the gold. After the race, the judges learned that Johnson had had an illegal substance in his body. He ran the race illegally, so the judges took away his medal. Though he ran faster and made an unforgettable impression, he did not deserve the reward.

Though the world and even our fellow Christians may be impressed with and applaud our deeds, let's not forget that God is the final judge! He searches our hearts; He alone knows our motivation. And He will be the One to say, "This deserves a reward. Ah, but that does not."

That's why we conduct ourselves in fear. That's why we walk in reverence. Because we know that He is checking for illegal substances. He knows whether down deep inside we have gotten sucked into the cosmos, whether we have bought into the system. He knows whether our noble acts and deeds are done out of pride and self-aggrandizement or whether they have been carried out in the power of the Spirit. He knows whether our inner, unseen thoughts and motives match our external words and works. He is pleased when our lives honor Him—inside and out. He is grieved when they do not. And it is *His* smile we want. It is *His* reward, not the reward of this world, not the applause of those around us, not the superficial spotlight of fame or fortune or power.

This Christian life is a tough fight. Earlier in this century, Donald Grey Barnhouse, a well-known minister and radio preacher, wrote an entire book on this subject, *The Invisible War*. This conflict is not a war fought with Uzis or tanks or smart bombs or ground-to-air missiles. The land mines, ambushes, and traps set by our enemy are much more subtle than that—and even more deadly, for they aim at the soul. And they are everywhere.

But with the pride and pleasures of the cosmos so alluring, how can weaklings like us run the race without being disqualified and forfeiting our reward? How can we win the battle over an enemy we can't see? The solution to that problem rests within our minds.

Focusing Your Mind

. . . knowing that you were not redeemed with perishable things like silver or gold from your futile way of life inherited from your forefathers, but with precious blood, as of a lamb unblemished and spotless, the blood of Christ. For He was foreknown before the foundation of the world, but has appeared in these last times for the sake of you who through Him are believers in God, who raised Him from the dead and gave Him glory, so that your faith and hope are in God. (1 Pet. 1:18–20)

I'm convinced that the battle with this world is a battle within the mind. Our minds are major targets of the Enemy's appeal. When the world pulls back its bowstring, our minds are the bull's-eyes. Any arrows we allow to become impaled in our minds will ultimately poison our thoughts. And if we tolerate this long enough, we'll end up acting out what we think. So the third technique for counteracting that poison, for dealing with the seduction of the cosmos, the world around us, is to focus our minds on Christ. We can do this by remembering what our Savior has done for us. Or, to paraphrase 1 Peter, "remember what your inheritance cost your Savior."

The first thing Christ did for us was to deliver us from slavery—slavery to a "futile way of life." Whether we knew it or not, we were trapped in a lifestyle that had only empty pleasures and dead-end desires to offer. We were in bondage to our impulses spawned from our sinful nature. In such a condition, we were hopelessly unable to help ourselves. The only way for us to be emancipated from that slavery was to have someone redeem us. That ransom price was paid by Christ, not with gold or silver, but with His precious blood. In doing so, He broke the chains that bound us to this world. He opened the door and said, "Now you're free to live for Me and serve Me." That single emancipation proclamation made possible a life of hope beyond temptation.

The second thing Christ did for us was to come near and make Himself known; He "appeared in these last times for the sake of you who through Him are believers in God . . . so that your faith and hope are in God" (vv. 20–21). That makes the whole thing personal, doesn't it? He realized the enormity of our earth-born emptiness. He knew our inability to free ourselves. And He willingly stepped out of His privileged position in heaven to pay the ransom . . . for us! He gave Himself, not only so we could become free, but so we could be secure, with our faith and hope resting not precariously on our own shoulders but securely on His.

What is life like without Christ? Look at 1 Peter 4:3–4.

> For the time already past is sufficient for you to have carried out the desire of the Gentiles, having pursued a course of sensuality, lusts, drunkenness, carousels, drinking parties and abominable idolatries. And in all this, they are surprised that you do not run with them into the same excess of dissipation, and they malign you.

That's a pretty vivid description of the futile lifestyle of the lost. That's what we see around us every day—a lifestyle promising to satisfy, to bring happiness and pleasure and contentment. Yet it brings just the opposite. This lifestyle leads only to another hangover or another bout with guilt—if there is even enough conscience left for guilt. It's one "happy hour" (strange name!) after another. One high after another. One snort after another. One drug after another. One affair after another. One abortion after another. One partner after another. It's life lived for the highs, which are nothing more than temporary breaks in the lows. It's empty. It's hollow. It's miserable. It's exactly as Peter describes it: a "futile way of life."

And we've been redeemed from that, not with silver or gold, "but with precious blood, as of a lamb unblemished and spotless, the blood of Christ."

Techniques to Remember

When we're in the comfortable conclave of Christian fellowship, it's relatively easy to be holy, to conduct our lives in the fear of God, and to focus our minds on the Savior (at least externally). But when we're out in the world, when we're in the minority, it's different, isn't it?

If you want to stay clean, even when you're walking alone in the dark, low-ceilinged coal mine of the corrupt and secular culture, you need to remember a few practical things—four come to mind.

First, pay close attention to what you look at. This takes us back to verse 13, where we are told to gird our minds for action, keep sober in spirit, and fix our hope completely on the grace that's revealed in Jesus Christ.

Our eyes seem to be the closest connection to our minds. Through our eyes we bring in information and visual images. Through our eyes we feed our imaginations. Through our eyes we focus on things that are alluring and attractive and, don't kid yourself, extremely pleasurable for a while . . . *for a while.* Remember, the Bible says that Moses, by faith, gave up the "passing pleasures of sin" to walk with the people of God (Heb. 11:24–26). The cosmos offers pleasures, no doubt about it, but they are passing. . . .

If then you have been raised up with Christ, keep seeking the things above, where Christ is, seated at the right hand of God. Set your mind on things above, not on the things that are on earth. (Col. 3:1–2)

Second, give greater thought to the consequences of sin rather than to its pleasures. One of the characteristics of the cosmos is that nobody ever mentions the ugly underside of pleasurable sins. If you're thinking about having an affair, if you are getting caught in that lustful trap, I strongly suggest that you walk through the consequences in your mind. Stroll slowly . . . ponder details. Think through the effects of that act in your life and in the lives of others whom your life touches.

In a *Leadership* magazine article titled "Consequences of a Moral Tumble," Randy Alcorn says that whenever he is feeling "particularly vulnerable to sexual temptation," he finds it helpful to review the effects such action could have. Some of things he mentions are:

- Grieving the Lord who redeemed me. . . .
- One day having to look Jesus . . . in the face and give an account of my actions. . . .
- Inflicting untold hurt on . . . your best friend and loyal wife. . . . losing [her] respect and trust.
- Hurting my beloved daughters. . . .
- Destroying my example and credibility with my children, and nullifying both present and future efforts to teach them to obey God. . . .
- Causing shame to my family. . . .
- Creating a form of guilt awfully hard to shake. Even though God would forgive me, would I forgive myself?
- Forming memories and flashbacks that could plague future intimacy with my wife.
- Wasting years of ministry training and experience for a long time, maybe permanently. . . .

- Undermining the faithful example and hard work of other Christians in our community.

- Bringing great pleasure to Satan, the enemy of God and all that is good. . . .

- Possibly bearing the physical consequences of such diseases as gonorrhea, syphilis, chlamydia, herpes, and AIDS; perhaps infecting [my wife] or, in the case of AIDS, even causing her death.

- Possibly causing pregnancy, with the personal and financial implications, including a lifelong reminder of my sin. . . .

- Causing shame and hurt to my friends, especially those I've led to Christ and discipled.[2]

And that's just a partial list of the consequences! It doesn't even begin to factor in the consequences for the other person in the affair and the number of people affected by his or her sin.

Take a realistic look at the other side of a moral tumble. For a change, force yourself to give greater thought to the painful consequences than to the passing pleasures of sin.

Third, begin each day by renewing your sense of reverence for God. Start each new day by talking to the Lord, even if that early-morning talk has to be brief.

"Lord, I'm here. I'm Yours. I want You to know that I'm Yours. Also I want to affirm that I reverence You. I give You my day. I will encounter strong seductive forces that will allure me. Since I am frail and fragile, I really need Your help."

If you know of some challenges you'll be facing that day, rehearse the areas of need. If you know a real test is coming, talk to the Lord about it. Then trade off with Him. Hand over your fragility and receive His strength in return. Reverence Him as the source of your power.

Fourth, periodically during each day focus fully on Christ. In his book *Spiritual Stamina,* Stuart Briscoe cites a good example of this:

It's fun watching young men in love. It can be even more fun when the romance is long distance.

You can predict what will happen. There'll be hours of late-night, heart-pounding telephone conversations. The postal service will be overrun with love notes crossing each other in the mail. Pillows will be soaked with tears.

But the most telling symptom is the glazed, faraway look in Romeo's eyes. I'm sure you've seen it. You ask the man a question and you get a blank stare. He's not at home. He's elsewhere. He's in another land. He's with his sweetheart.

You might say his heart is set on things afar, where Juliet is seated right by the telephone.[3]

That's being focused fully on another person. I challenge you to do this with your Lord. Deliberately set aside a few minutes every day when your eyes glaze over, when you don't realize where you are, when a telephone ring means nothing because you are focusing fully on Christ. Imagine Him as he walks with His disciples, touching those who were sick, praying for them in John 17, going to the cross, sitting with His disciples at the seashore and having broiled fish for breakfast. Then imagine Him as He is thinking about you, praying for you, standing with you, living in you.

These four techniques will help you stay clean in a corrupt society—to be in the world but not of it.

A Prayer for Hope Beyond Temptation

Thank You, Father, for Your truth preserved through the centuries. Thank You for the careful concern of a man like Peter who knew both sides of life on planet Earth: what it was to live in this old world and what it was to walk with the Savior, Your Son.

Lord, since You don't save us then suddenly take us home to glory, hear our prayer this day as we ask You to bring to our attention those things that will assist us in staying clean in a corrupt world. Give us an intense distaste for things that displease You and a renewed pleasure in things that bring You honor and magnify Your truth. As You do this, we will have what we need so much, hope beyond temptation.

I ask this for the honor of Him who consistently and victoriously withstood the blast of the Devil's temptations without relief, Jesus our Lord.

AMEN

4

Hope Beyond Division

Reasons for
Pulling Together

BEFORE ANDREW JACKSON became the seventh president of the United States, he served as a major general in the Tennessee militia. During the War of 1812 his troops reached an all-time low in morale. As a result they began arguing, bickering, and fighting among themselves. It is reported that Old Hickory called them all together on one occasion when tensions were at their worst and said, "Gentlemen! Let's remember, the enemy is over *there!*"

His sobering reminder would be an appropriate word for the church today. In fact, I wonder if Christ sometimes looks down at us and says with a sigh, "Christians, your Enemy is over there! Stop your infighting! Pull for one another. Support one another. Believe in one another. Care for one another. Pray for one another. Love one another."

One of the most profound comments made regarding the early church came from the lips of a man named Aristides, sent by the Emperor Hadrian to spy out those strange creatures known as "Christians." Having seen them in action, Aristides returned with a mixed report. But his immortal words to the emperor have echoed down through history: "Behold! How they love one another."

How often do we hear such words today from those who don't know Christ but who have watched those of us who do? I'm inclined to think that it's much more likely that they say, "Behold! How they hurt one another!" . . . "Behold! How they judge one another!" . . . "Behold! How they criticize one another!" . . . "Behold! How they fight with one another!"

This is the generation that has given new meaning to the shameful practice of brother-bashing and sister-smashing. You would think we were enemies rather than members of the same family. Something is wrong with this picture.

The mark of the Christian should be a spirit of unity and genuine love for others, but the church today rarely demonstrates those qualities. We are looked on by the world as self-seeking and factious rather than loving and unified. You question that? Just step into a Christian bookstore and scan the shelves. What impression do you get? Do the books reflect love and unity within the body of Christ? Or do they reflect polarization, criticism, and judgment of one another? Better yet, sit back and observe what's going on in your own church. Are you overwhelmed with the love and unity that exudes from your local body of believers? Or are you saddened and disappointed by the political power plays and petty disagreements that block our ability to get along with one another?

Unity: An Almost Forgotten Virtue

To underscore this important quality, let's consider Jesus' words in John 13, where we find Him with His twelve disciples for the last time. They have met together for a meal in a second-floor room in the city of Jerusalem. Jesus notices that the men have come into the room with dirty feet—not surprising in that rocky, dusty land. What must have been disappointing was that none of the Twelve had voluntarily washed the others' feet. So during supper Jesus arose from the table and poured water into a basin and proceeded to go around the table and wash the disciples' feet.

What a scene it must have been! To this day, I shake my head when I imagine the Savior washing the dirty feet of His disciples.

> And so when He had washed their feet, and taken His garments, and reclined at the table again, He said to them, "Do you know what I have done to you?" (John 13:12)

Understand, He wasn't fishing for the obvious answer, "You've washed our feet, Master." He was looking for the answer He has to explain to them a few moments later:

> You call Me Teacher and Lord; and you are right, for so I am. If I then, the Lord and the Teacher, washed your feet, you also ought to wash one another's feet. For I gave you an example that you also should do as I did to you. (John 13:13–15)

I think most of Jesus' disciples would have gladly returned the favor and washed *His* feet. Peter out of embarrassment. John out of devotion. That would be easy to do. After all, they loved Him. Why wouldn't they take an opportunity to wash His feet—if only to make a good impression? But that is not what Jesus told them to do. Instead He said, *"Wash one another's feet."*

Then, a bit later, in their final hours together, He changed the subject from washing feet to showing love.

> A new commandment I give to you, that you love one another, even as I have loved you, that you also love one another. By this all men will know that you are My disciples, if you have love for one another. (John 13:34–35)

It's easy to love Christ for all He is, for all He's done. It's not so easy, however, to love other Christians. Yet that is the command we have been given. That compelling mark of the Christian will be a powerful witness to non-Christians. It has nothing to do with talking to the lost about their spiritual condition. It has everything to do with how we treat one another. If you want to make an impact on the world around you, this rugged society that is moving in the wrong direction more rapidly every year, He said, "love one another." That's how they'll know that you're different. Your love will speak with stunning eloquence to a lost world.

Then, as the oil lamps flickered away the last hour before His arrest and trial, Jesus prayed to the Father on behalf of His disciples.

> I do not ask in behalf of these alone [the disciples], but for those also who believe in Me through their word [that's you and me]; *that they may all be one*; even as Thou, Father, art in Me, and I in Thee, that they also may be in Us; that the world may believe that Thou didst send Me. And the glory which Thou hast given Me I have given to them; that they may be one, just as We are one; I in them, and Thou in Me, that they may be perfected in unity, that the world may know that Thou didst send Me, and didst love them, even as Thou didst love Me. (John 17:20–23, italics mine)

Look at that! Believe it or not, He was praying for us during those final hours. He was praying that you and I might make an impact on the world because of our unity with Him and with each other.

The margin notes of the New American Standard Bible gives this literal translation: "That they may be perfected *into a unit*." A unit is a team, folks. No more brother-bashing. No more sister-smashing. No more ugly gossip groups. No more sarcastic, judgmental put-downs. Jesus prayed that we would support and encourage and love and forgive each other until we are perfected into a unit.

Unity. That's what He desires for us. Not uniformity, but unity; oneness, not sameness. We don't have to look alike. We don't even have to think alike. The body is made up of many different parts. He doesn't even pray for unanimity. We can disagree. Every vote doesn't have to be 100 percent. But we must be a unit: our eyes on the same goal, our hearts in the same place, our commitment at the same level. And we must love each other.

If there is anything that would keep me away from Christ these days, if I were lost, it would be the attitude Christians have toward one another. That would do it. While there is much wonderful fellowship in the church where the fire of friendship warms and affirms us, there are still too many places where for the life of me I don't know how people stay in ministry. The conditions in which some men and women labor are occasionally beyond belief.

Paul wrote to the Philippians:

> Do nothing from selfishness or empty conceit, but with humility of mind let each of you regard one another as more important than himself; do not merely look out for your own personal interests, but also for the interests of others. (Phil. 2:3–4)

Selfishness and conceit and pride are the things that break down our fellowship and erode our unity. Everything you need to know about getting along well in a family, to say nothing of getting along well in a church, is right here in these verses.

If you're on a church board and you're wondering what's going wrong, what's missing, what's happened to the unity you once had, I'll guarantee somebody isn't abiding by these verses.

You want to pull together as the family of God? It's merely a matter of obeying Philippians 2:3–4. Stop looking for credit. Stop looking for what you can get out of it. Think about the other person instead of yourself. Don't be selfish. Sounds like something a teacher would say to a roomful of kindergartners, doesn't it? Yet how many adult problems could be solved if the elementary truths woven into these two verses were the driving force in our relationships with one another? How many committees could resolve their disputes? How many couples could reconcile their marital differences?

Love: A Never-to-Be-Forgotten Command

With the teachings of Christ and Paul as a backdrop, we are better able to understand and appreciate Peter's comments about love and unity. Remember, he was writing to hurting people. They were scattered, many of them far from home (see 1 Pet. 1:1). They were "distressed," living in extreme situations (1:6). They were being "tested" by "various trials" (1:6–7). Some of them were running for their lives. With the madman Nero on the throne in Rome, it was a dangerous time to be a Christian. Some, no doubt, were tempted to conform, compromise, or give up altogether.

When I was a kid and an argument broke out in our home, my dad always used to say, "We may have a few differences inside these walls, but just remember, we're family. If your brother or your sister needs you, you take care of 'em. You love 'em. You pull for 'em." Good advice for the church as well!

When people hurt—and we've all been there—it's easy to get a little thin on love. But that's what these people needed. They needed to pull together and support each other. They needed a community where they could find acceptance and unity. They needed to conduct themselves as members of the family of God.

Following his strong words encouraging fellow believers to live holy lives, Peter gives them a pep talk, explaining exactly how they have been freed to support each other. He says, in effect, "You have everything you need that makes it possible; you don't have to live in lonely isolation." Read his counsel carefully:

> Since you have in obedience to the truth purified your souls for a sincere love of the brethren, fervently love one another from the heart, for you have been born again not of seed which is perishable but imperishable, that is, through the living and abiding word of God. (1 Pet. 1:22–23)

As we read Peter's uplifting words, we see that he specifies three things that encourage mutual support. First, obedience to the truth. Second, purity of soul. Third, a lack of hypocrisy.

Being obedient to the truth means that we don't have to look at others through the distorted lenses of our own biases. We can see them as God sees them and love them as He loves them. This has a purifying effect on us. It purges us, not only from a limited perspective, but from prejudice, resentment, hurt feelings, and grudges. Such purity of soul helps us love each other without hypocrisy and with a sincere love. It doesn't blind us to each other's faults; it gives us the grace to overlook them.

The glue—the bonding element—that holds all this together is love: "Fervently love one another from the heart." Peter writes with a strong, emotional, passionate commitment that is difficult to pick up on in the English.

Two Greek words are used predominantly in the New Testament to describe love, and Peter uses both of them here. One is *philos*, which generally refers to a brotherly love or the love of a friend. That is the word he uses for "love of the brethren." The other is *agape*, a higher form of love, a more divine type of love, which is the word he uses for "love one another." Peter then intensifies both with passionate modifiers: "sincere," "fervently," and "from the heart."

> These Christians to whom Peter was writing already had a fondness and an affection for one another. . . . But if these Christians would blend the two kinds of love, saturate the human fondness and affection with the divine love with which they are exhorted to love one another, then that human affection would be transformed and elevated to a heavenly thing. Then the fellowship of saint with saint would be a heavenly fellowship, glorifying to the Lord Jesus, and most blessed in its results to themselves. There is plenty of the *phile* fondness and affection among the saints, and too little of the *agape* divine love.[1]

Maybe it's time to pause and take a look inside your own heart. Are you "fervently loving one another from the heart"? When I am snippy or negative, judgmental or ugly toward a brother or a sister, I look at myself with honesty, shining God's light of truth on my own attitude, and I invariably find that it's my heart that's not right. The old spiritual hymn says it well:

> It's not my brother nor my sister
> but it's me, O Lord,

Standin' in the need of prayer.
It's not the preacher nor the deacon
   but it's me, O Lord,
Standin' in the need of prayer.

Support: Four Much-Needed Reminders

What kind of love and support do we need? What kind of love and support do we give? What about a "love one another" support group, in which we offer—and receive from—our brothers and sisters in the family of God this same kind of love and lack of judgmental spirit, this true affection, this arm around your shoulder, saying, "I'm in your corner"?

Many churches have support groups of various kinds in which individuals are actively involved in each other's lives. Through the years I've talked with lots of individuals who say they couldn't survive without such support groups.

Some are struggling through the backwash of a divorce, trying to gain self-respect and a sense of dignity again. Aided by the support of others who are going through, or have gone through, the same turmoil, they work through their feelings of rejection, sadness, and loneliness . . . then emerge stronger and more stable.

Some attend support groups because they are in the grip of an awful addiction. Right now they're clean or dry, but they realize they're just a day away, just an hour away, from the same old habit. The support of others keeps them strong and helps them hope again.

Most of these groups are not highly visible, but they're there for those who need them, week in and week out. With consistent regularity people keep coming because they find refuge in this safe and supportive harbor. They find love, acceptance, and a lack of judgmental spirit. They find tolerance and accountability. They find care and encouragement—and a word of affirmation from a sincere heart and an arm of support around the shoulder mean more than a thousand words from some frowning preacher.

What is it about the family of God that gives us this sense of one-ness and support? Since we don't have to look alike and we don't all have the same temperament and we don't all vote the same way at election time, what is it that draws believers together?

We Are Children of the Same Father

> For you have been born again not of seed which is perishable but imperishable, that is, through the living and abiding word of God. (1 Pet. 1:23)

In the human family, there are various kinds of birth experiences. But in God's family, everybody begins the same way. We are all adopted. We all have the same Father. We all come to Him the same way—through His Son, Jesus Christ. We are all members of the same family. Our background, our education, our social connections, our job, or how much money we have in the bank—all these things are irrelevant. We've all been born anew. We're all brothers and sisters in the Lord.

We Take Our Instruction from the Same Source

> Not of seed which is perishable but imperishable, that is, through the living and abiding word of God. For,
> "All flesh is like grass,
> And all its glory like the flower of grass.
> The grass withers,
> And the flower falls off,
> But the word of the Lord abides forever."
> And this is the word which was preached to you. (1 Pet. 1:23b–25)

The seed is the Word of God, our reliable source of truth, and we all get our instruction from this source. But for that seed to grow and produce fruit in our lives, it must be embraced and applied.

There's nothing automatic about being exposed to the same source of truth. We may all hear the same Sunday morning mes-sage, but unless our ears are attentive and our hearts prepared, that seed will be picked up in Satan's beak and winged right out of our lives. You can sit and listen to truth being delivered, and it can change your life in a moment's time. Yet someone sitting right next to you, hearing the same insightful information, can go right on living against the will of God.

We have a responsibility, not only to hear the truth, but to apply it. Just being exposed to the truth will not change us. You can put me in a room with a dozen beautiful Steinway pianos and leave me there for hours, but I still won't be able to sit down and play. You could put an accomplished pianist at every one and expose me to hours of exquisite music, but even in that stimulating environment I wouldn't be able to sit down and play. Bringing beautiful music from those black-and-white keys takes work—commitment, dedication, private lessons, and untold hours of practice.

We Have the Same Struggles

> Therefore, putting aside all malice and all guile and hypocrisy and envy and all slander. . . . (1 Pet. 2:1)

In case you've ever wondered what breaks down the fellowship, what keeps us from pulling together, there's your list. Read each one slowly and form pictures in your mind: malice, guile, hypocrisy, envy, and slander. In weaker moments we fall back on them, but God says, "put them aside"—get rid of them. If you want to move beyond your divisions, beyond your differences, if you want to become one in the Lord, lose them. And, by His grace, let them go!

Let's return to this list and probe a little deeper.

Malice. The Greek word here is a general word for the wickedness that characterizes unbelievers entrenched in the world system. These are the sins that hurt and injure others.

Guile. The Greek word means two-facedness, deception, or trickery. In its earliest form, this word meant "to catch with bait." It refers to a deception that is aimed at attaining one's own end—a hidden agenda.

Hypocrisy. The Greek word here means to act a part, to hide behind a mask, to appear to be someone else. This is what happens when we try to be someone or something we are not.

Some family members have a tendency to be envious of those who are going through "good times." Others have a tendency to slander those who are going through a bad patch. The next two sins are kind of the flip side of each other, and we are told to put both aside.

Envy is not only hidden resentment over another's advantage, but wanting that same advantage for yourself. According to Webster, it is "painful or resentful awareness of an advantage enjoyed by another joined with a desire to possess the same advantage." In other words, someone has something you don't have and you long to have it yourself. Edward Gordon Selwyn comments on the Greek term, saying that this sin is "a constant plague of all voluntary organizations, not least religious organizations, and to which even the Twelve themselves were subject at the very crisis of our Lord's ministry."[2]

Slander is even more vicious. Literally the word means "evil speaking." It occurs most often when the victim is not there to offer a defense or set the record straight. Often disguised as rumor or bad news or just passing on information, slander is disparaging gossip that destroys one's confidence in another, discoloring or harming that person's reputation. It can be as mild as bad-mouthing or as vile as backstabbing. When the tongue is used for slander, it becomes a lethal weapon.

Peter commands us to "strip off" these five outdated garments that once belonged to our old natures! If all of us in God's family were mutually committed to such behavior, can you imagine the pleasure we could enjoy together? But it'll never happen until we "strip off" the old garments that keep us carnal.

We Focus on the Same Objectives

Like newborn babes, long for the pure milk of the word, that by it you may grow in respect to salvation, if you have tasted the kindness of the Lord. (1 Pet. 2:2–3)

What is the objective of all this? Maturity. "Grow up," Peter says. And our model? The Lord Himself.

For three and a half years Peter followed Jesus everywhere He went. Why? Because he had "tasted the kindness of the Lord."

Nourished by that kindness, Peter grew toward greater maturity, and so can we!

What do people think of after they have had a conversation or a meal with you? What do they think after they have worked alongside you? Do they think, "How kind he is. What a kind person she is"? Selflessly giving ourselves to one another is the key to unity. Our relationships with others are to be built upon the example of the selflessness Christ first demonstrated.

It's so basic, isn't it? It reminds me of Robert Fulghum's *All I Really Need to Know I Learned in Kindergarten*, which I read when it originated as an article in the *Kansas City Times*. In it he said, "Share everything. Play fair. Don't hit people. Put things back where you found them. Clean up your own mess. Don't take things that aren't yours. Say you're sorry when you hurt somebody. . . . And it is still true, no matter how old you are: When you go out into the world, it is best to hold hands and stick together."

Come on, let's pull together. Let's support each other. In doing so, remember Paul's closing words in Ephesians 4. I like the way Eugene Peterson paraphrases that final verse:

> Make a clean break with all cutting, backbiting, profane talk. Be gentle with one another, sensitive. Forgive one another as quickly and thoroughly as God in Christ forgave you. (Eph. 4:31 MSG)

Think of somebody in the family of God—just one person you know—who could really use a word of support. Then give it! Don't wait . . . give it this week. Don't just think about it or write it in your journal. Do it. *Do it today.*

Pray for that individual you were thinking about a moment ago. Ask God to give you just the right word, just the right method of approaching that person. Maybe you need to write a note. Maybe you need to make a phone call. Maybe you need to take the person out for a cup of coffee or invite him or her over for a meal. Who knows? Your action could be the catalyst that causes that individual to gain hope beyond division.

Remember, "The enemy is over *there!*" Behold! How we need to love one another!

A Prayer for Hope Beyond Division

Forgive us, oh, forgive us, our Father, for the hours we have spent in the wasteland of malice and guile, hypocrisy and envy and slander. What grimy garments we've worn! Show us the joy of kindness, the long-lasting benefits of unity, grace, and support. Remind us that it all begins with genuine love prompted by forgiveness. Start a work within us so that our love flows from a pure heart, not from a desire to win friends or impress people.

Most of all, Lord, make us like Your Son. Kind. Meek. Humble. Gracious. May we grow up into His kindness, may we model His meekness, may we walk with His humility. May we reflect His grace so that others gain new hope. What we're really asking is that You help us grow up!

We're so glad to be in Your family, so grateful for Your forgiveness. Use us this week, perhaps even today, to help someone else feel grateful that he or she, too, is a part of this family. Through Christ, who prayed for our unity.

AMEN

5

❖

Hope Beyond Guilt

Becoming
Living
Stones

FOR SOME STRANGE REASON, those of us who have known the Lord since we were young have a tendency to outgrow a close friendship with Him. When we were children, we felt free and open with our heavenly Father. But when we became adults, we seemed to take a few giant steps backward in that relationship.

When we were young, we talked to Him freely. With a child's faith, knowing He loved us, we trusted Him with the details of our life. Nothing was too small and, for sure, nothing was too big to ask of Him. In unguarded innocence, we prayed for *anything*!

The ease with which we once approached God can be seen in the letters written to Him by children. See if the ones below don't take you back to a time of innocence and openness in your own relationship with Him.

Dear Lord,
    Thank you for the nice day today. You even fooled the TV weatherman.

                                 Hank (age 7)

Dear Lord,
   Do you ever get mad?
   My mother gets mad all the time but she is only human.

Yours truly,
David (age 8)

Dear Lord,
   I need a raise in my allowance. Could you have one of your angels tell my father?

Thank you.
David (age 7)[1]

Dear God,
   Charles my cat got run over. And if you made it happen you have to tell me why.

Harvey

Dear God,
   Can you guess what is the biggest river of all of them? The Amazon. You ought to be able to because you made it. Ha, ha.

Guess who[2]

Wouldn't it be interesting to compile an assortment of adult letters to God? Undoubtedly the childhood innocence would be lost as well as the candor and ease of approach. The words would be more guarded. We would be sophisticated. Fear and feelings of worthlessness would underscore the halting sentences. Shame, guilt, and regret would punctuate the paragraphs. We have lost much, haven't we, on the road to adulthood?

We can learn a great deal from children about simple faith and simple hope. Yet we have had years to experience those truths. We can look back at the many times He has taken our brokenness and made something beautiful of our lives. Our greatest failures, our deepest sorrows, have offered opportunities for the operation of His mercy and grace. How can we forget that?

God's Appraisal of Us

The Bible is filled with reminders of how much God cares for us, His plans for our welfare, and what our relationship with Him should be. Take, for example, the familiar words of the psalmist. Though an adult, he writes of God with free-flowing delight.

> Bless the LORD, O my soul;
> And all that is within me, bless His holy name.
> Bless the LORD, O my soul,
> And forget none of His benefits;
> Who pardons all your iniquities;
> Who heals all your diseases;
> Who redeems your life from the pit;
> Who crowns you with lovingkindness and compassion;
> Who satisfies your years with good things,
> So that your youth is renewed like the eagle. . . .
>
> For as high as the heavens are above the earth,
> So great is His lovingkindness toward those who fear Him.
> As far as the east is from the west,
> So far has He removed our transgressions from us.
> Just as a father has compassion on his children,
> So the LORD has compassion on those who fear Him.
>
> For He Himself knows our frame;
> He is mindful that we are but dust. (Ps. 103:1–5, 11–14)

What a list! What a relief! Our Lord understands our limits. He realizes our struggles. He knows how much pressure we can take. He knows what measures of grace and mercy and strength we'll require. He knows how we're put together.

Frankly, His expectations are not nearly as unrealistic as ours. When we don't live up to the agenda we have set, we feel like He is going to dump a truckload of judgment on us. But that will not happen. So why do we fear it could? Because we forget that He "knows our frame; He is mindful that we are but dust."

What, then, is God's agenda for us? What does He want for us this afternoon, tomorrow morning, or next week? Well, His plans for us are clearly set forth. He wrote them originally to Israel, but they apply to us too.

> "For I know the plans that I have for you," declares the LORD, "plans for welfare and not for calamity to give you a future and a hope. Then you will call upon Me and come and pray to Me, and I will listen to you." (Jer. 29:11–12)

Isn't that wonderful? "I have plans for you, My son, My daughter," God says. "And they are great plans. Plans for your welfare and not for your calamity. Plans to give you a future and a hope." It is God's agenda that His people never lose hope. Each new dawn it's as if He smiles from heaven, saying, "Hope again . . . hope again!"

After the fall of Jerusalem, the prophet Jeremiah reminded himself of God's hope-filled plans.

> This I recall to my mind,
> Therefore I have hope.
> The LORD's lovingkindnesses indeed never cease,
> For His compassions never fail.
> They are new every morning;
> Great is Thy faithfulness.
> "The LORD is my portion," says my soul,
> "Therefore I have hope in Him."
> The LORD is good to those who wait for Him,
> To the person who seeks Him.
> It is good that he waits silently
> For the salvation of the LORD. (Lam. 3:21–26)

Right now you may be waiting for something from the Lord. Matter of fact, most people I meet are in some sort of holding pattern. (I certainly am!) They have something on the horizon that they're trusting God for. (I certainly do!) And their hope is not misplaced. He is good to those who wait for Him. He is good to those who seek Him. We have nothing to fear. And we certainly have no reason for living each day crushed by guilt or shame.

He has redeemed us, given us an inheritance, and shown us forgiveness. The most succinct summary of God's appraisal of our relationship as His children can be found in Romans 8:31–32. Many years ago I memorized the concluding paragraph in Romans 8, which begins with these two verses. I cannot number the times I have had my hope renewed by quoting these words to myself.

> What then shall we say to these things? If God is for us, who is against us? He who did not spare His own Son, but delivered Him up for us all, how will He not also with Him freely give us all things?

Contrary to popular opinion, God doesn't sit in heaven with His jaws clenched, His arms folded in disapproval, and a deep frown on His brow. He is not ticked off at His children for all the times we trip over our tiny feet and fall flat on our diapers. He is a loving Father, and we are precious in His sight, the delight of His heart. After all, He "has qualified us to share in the inheritance of the saints in light" (Col. 1:12). Think of it! He's put us in His inheritance!

Remember that the next time you think God is coming down on you. You have reason to give thanks. You don't have to qualify yourself for His kingdom. His grace has rescued you. He has already qualified you by accomplishing a great deliverance in your life. That brings to mind another verse I love to quote:

> For He delivered us from the domain of darkness, and transferred us to the kingdom of His beloved Son, in whom we have redemption, the forgiveness of sins. (Col. 1:13–14)

He has literally transferred us from the dark domain of the Enemy of our souls into the light of the kingdom of His Son. He considers us there with Him, surrounded by love, receiving the same treatment He gives His Son.

Sometimes it's encouraging just to thumb through the Scriptures and find all the promises that tell us what God thinks of us, especially in a world where folks are continually telling us all the things they have against us and all the things they see wrong with us.

God is not only "for us," according to Romans 8, He is constantly giving great gifts to us.

> Every good thing bestowed and every perfect gift is from above, coming down from the Father of lights, with whom there is no variation, or shifting shadow. (James 1:17)

Literally, that last phrase means "shadow of turning." In other words, there is no alteration or modification in His giving, regardless of how often we may turn away. No shifting shadow on our part causes Him to become moody and hold back His gifts to us. Talk about grace!

God is for us. I want you to remember that.

God is for us. Say those four words to yourself.

God is for us.

Remember that tomorrow morning when you don't feel like He is. Remember that when you have failed. Remember that when you have sinned and guilt slams you to the mat.

God is for you. Make it personal: *God is for me!*

Never ever, ever tell your children that if they do wrong, God won't love them. That is heresy. There's no grace in that. Grace says, "My child, even though you do wrong, God will continue and I will continue to love you. God is for you, and so am I!"

I thought of this the other day as I was humming the children's tune, "Jesus loves the little children, all the children of the world." I thought, well, what about all the grownups? So I changed the words of that little song.

> Jesus loves His adult children,
> All the grownups of the world.
> Red and yellow, black and white,
> We are precious in His sight.

Jesus loves all the teens and adults of the world.
[Just thought I should include the teenagers too!]

Why do we think His love is just for the little children, innocent and disarming as they are? He loves all of His people. Let me repeat it once more: God is for us.

In Peter's letter, we catch a glimpse of the delight God takes in us as the apostle paints six beautiful word pictures of us, vivid pen portraits of God's children.

And coming to Him as to a living stone, rejected by men, but choice and precious in the sight of God, you also, as living stones, are being built up as a spiritual house for a holy priesthood, to offer up spiritual sacrifices acceptable to God through Jesus Christ. For this is contained in Scripture:
"Behold I lay in Zion a choice stone, a precious
    corner stone,
And he who believes in Him shall not be disappointed."
This precious value, then, is for you who believe. But for those who disbelieve,
"The stone which the builders rejected,
this became the very corner stone,"
and,
"A stone of stumbling and a rock of offense";
for they stumble because they are disobedient to the word, and to this doom they were also appointed. (1 Pet. 2:4–8)

We Are Living Stones in a Spiritual House

The metaphor woven through the fabric of this passage is that of a building, Christ being the cornerstone and we, His children, being the living stones that make up the building. (The apostle Paul uses this same image in Ephesians 2:19–22.)

Each time someone trusts Christ as Savior, another stone is quarried out of the pit of sin and fitted into the spiritual house He's building through the work of the Holy Spirit. And carefully overseeing the construction is Christ, who is the hands-on contractor of this eternal edifice.

We are His living stones, being built up as a spiritual house.

Think of it this way. There's a major construction project going on through time as Jesus Christ builds His family. It's called the *ekklesia*, the "church," those who are called out from the mass of humanity to become a special part of God's forever family. And you, as a Christian—a follower of Christ—have been picked, chosen, and called out to be one of them.

He has quarried you from the pit of your sin. And now He is chiseling away, shaping you and ultimately sliding you into place. You are a part of His building project.

All kinds of prophets of doom wonder about the condition of God's building. They see it as condemned property, worn out, dilapidated, and derelict rather than as a magnificent edifice that is being constructed on schedule. The truth is, God is the master architect, and every stone is being placed exactly where He designed it to fit. The project is right on schedule. Never forget, even on those blue days, we are living stones in a spiritual house. But there's more. . . .

We Are Priests in the Same Temple

Peter refers to us both as a "holy priesthood" and as a "royal priesthood." It's true that we're not all preachers or evangelists or gifted teachers. But we *are* all priests, belonging to a kingly order that has been set apart by God.

The role of priest implies more than meets the eye, for priests have specific responsibilities delineated in Scripture. Priests offer up prayers, bring spiritual sacrifices, intercede to God on behalf of others, and stay in tune with the spiritual side of life. All this applies to every believer, regardless of age, regardless of sex, regardless of social standing. Perhaps you never thought of this before, but it's really true; we are priests in the same temple. But there's more. . . .

We Are a Chosen Race

Our heads might have a tendency to swell at being chosen to be on God's team, so it might behoove us to take a quick glance at exactly why God chose the Hebrews to be His people. This will help us put the whole idea of being chosen by God into perspective. Here Moses is addressing the nation Israel, preparing them to enter the Promised Land.

> For you are a holy people to the LORD your God; the LORD your God has chosen you to be a people for His own possession out of all the peoples who are on the face of the earth. The LORD did not set His love on you nor choose you because you were more in number than any of the peoples, for you were the fewest of all peoples, but because the LORD loved you and kept the oath which He swore to your forefathers, the LORD brought you out by a mighty hand, and redeemed you from the house of slavery, from the hand of Pharaoh king of Egypt. (Deut. 7:6–8)

Why did God choose Israel? Because of their strength? No. Because of their numbers? Because of their mental or moral superiority? No. He chose them not because they deserved it, but simply because of His grace—a kindness shown to them entirely without merit on their part. Simply "because the Lord loved you."

Why did God choose us? For the same reason. Not because we did anything that impressed Him. It wasn't the size of our faith . . . or the sincerity. It wasn't the goodness of our heart . . . or the greatness of our intellect. It certainly wasn't because we first chose Him. It was entirely by grace. Grace prompted by love.

The Lord chooses us because He chooses to choose us. Period. He sets His love upon us because out of the goodness and grace of His own heart He declares, "I want you to be Mine."

I love that! Not only because it exalts the grace of God, but because God gets all the glory in it. We won't walk around heaven with our thumbs under our suspenders outbragging one another. Instead, we'll be absolutely amazed that we are privileged to be there.

John 15:16 says, "You did not choose Me, but I chose you." We didn't hunt Him down. He hunted us down. He is the eternal Hound of Heaven. We didn't work half our lives to find Him; He gave His life to find us. Being chosen by God says a lot more about Him than it does about us! He is the Good Shepherd who gives His life for the sheep. When you find yourself slumping in shame or giving way to guilt, remind yourself of this: You have been chosen by the Good Shepherd. He wants you in His flock. But there is more. . . .

We Are a Holy Nation

Holy can be an intimidating word. Though meant to be sacred, it can seem scary. Remember, earlier we explained that the word means "to be set apart." But let's look at it another way.

I'm sitting in my study right now, and I'm wearing a suit and a tie because I'm going to an important meeting in a couple hours. This morning when I was getting dressed, I looked on my tie rack and I selected a tie. I had a number to choose from, but I chose this particular one. I pulled it off the rack, put it around my neck, and tied the knot, and at that moment the tie became holy. Doesn't look holy. I can assure you, it doesn't feel holy. (As a matter of fact, I can see a small spot on it. Must have gotten some gravy on it when I wore it last.) But it's still the tie I set apart for this particular purpose. In the broadest sense of the word, the tie I'm wearing is "holy." It's set apart for a special purpose.

You and I are a holy nation. We make up a body of people set apart for a special purpose: to be ambassadors for Jesus Christ, the King of the church. We are a people set apart for His special purpose and glory.

If we seem out of step with the rest of the world, it is because we march to the beat of a different drummer. We sing a different national anthem and pledge our allegiance to a different flag—because our citizenship, our true citizenship, is in heaven. You and I are parts of His holy nation. But there's more . . . .

We Are God's Own Possession

Possessions of the powerful, wealthy, or famous, no matter how common, can become extremely valuable, even priceless. Napoleon's toothbrush sold for $21,000. Can you imagine—paying thousands of dollars for someone's cruddy old toothbrush? Hitler's car sold for over $150,000. Winston Churchill's desk, a pipe owned by C. S. Lewis, sheet music handwritten by Beethoven, a house once owned by Ernest Hemingway. At the Sotheby's auction of Jackie Kennedy Onassis's personal belongings, her fake pearls sold for $211,500 and JFK's wood golf clubs went for $772,500. Not because the items themselves are worthy but because they once belonged to someone significant.

Are you ready for a surprise? We fit that bill too. Think of the value of something owned by God. What incredible worth that bestows on us, what inexplicable dignity! We belong to Him. We are "a people for God's own possession" (1 Pet. 2:9).

I love that expression—"a people for God's own possession." And I'm glad this verse is correctly translated in the version of the Bible I'm using. For the longest time I used a version that said, "We are a peculiar people." (Actually, I saw all kinds of evidence of that around me, as if Christians were supposed to be odd or weird or strange.) But the correct rendering is far more encouraging. Weird or not, we're His possession . . . owned by the living God.

The price paid for us was unimaginably high—the blood of Jesus Christ—and now we belong to Him. We have been bought with a price. That's enough to bring a smile to anyone's face. But there is more . . . one more.

We Are a People Who Have Received Mercy

Have you lived so long in the family of God that your memory has become blurred? Have you forgotten what it was like when you weren't?

> . . . for you once were not a people, but now you are the people of God; you had not received mercy, but now you have received mercy. (1 Pet. 2:10)

As a result of God's mercy, we have become a people who are uniquely and exclusively cared for by God. The fact that we are the recipients of His mercy makes all the difference in the world as to how we respond to difficult times. He watches over us with enormous interest. Why? Because of His immense mercy, freely demonstrated in spite of our not deserving it. What guilt-relieving, encouraging news!

Of all the twelve disciples, none could have been more grateful than Peter . . . or, if he had allowed it, none more guilt-ridden. Called to serve his Savior, strong-hearted, determined, zealous, even a little cocky on occasion, the man had known the heights of ecstasy but also knew the aching agony of defeat.

Though warned by the Master, Peter announced before His peers, "Even though all may fall away . . . I will never fall away" (Matt. 26:33). And later . . . "Lord, with You I am ready to go both to prison and to death!" (Luke 22:33). Yet only a few hours later he denied even knowing Jesus . . . three times!

What bitter tears he wept when the weight of his denials crushed his spirit. But our Lord refused to leave him there, wallowing in hopeless discouragement and depression. He found the broken man and forgave him . . . and used him mightily as a leader in the early church. What grace . . . what mercy!

Charles Wesley beautifully captures the theology of such mercy in the second stanza of his magnificent hymn, "And Can It Be?"

> He left His Father's throne above,
> So free, so infinite His grace!

Emptied Himself of all but love,
And bled for Adam's helpless race!
'Tis mercy all, immense and free,
For, O my God, it found out me.

Our Lives Are Being Watched

> Beloved, I urge you as aliens and strangers to abstain from fleshly lusts, which war against the soul. Keep your behavior excellent among the Gentiles, so that in the thing in which they slander you as evildoers, they may on account of your good deeds, as they observe them, glorify God in the day of visitation. (1 Pet. 2:11–12)

Peter begins his practical summary of this section with the words, "Beloved, I urge you." He feels passionate about this—and there's a warning here. Peter is telling us that in light of all that we are as God's children, in light of our roles as living stones in a building that will never be destroyed, and in light of our being these things he's described—a royal priesthood, a chosen race, a holy nation, a people for His own possession, those who have received mercy, we are to live in a certain way. Our earthly behavior is to square with our divinely provided benefits.

For unbelievers, earth is a playground where the flesh is free to romp and run wild. But for believers, earth is a battleground. It's the place where we combat the lusts that wage war against our souls. For the brief tour of duty we Christians have on this earth, we cannot get stalled in sin or, for that matter, incapacitated by guilt. To live the kind of life God requires, Peter offers four suggestions.

First, live a clean life. Don't think for a moment that it makes no difference to unbelievers how Christians live. We live out our faith before a watching world. That's why Peter urges us to abstain from fleshly lusts, "in order to get their attention" and to prove that what we believe really works.

You and I don't know how many non-Christians are watching us this very day, determining the truth of the message of Christianity strictly on the basis of how we live, how we work, how we respond to life's tests, or how we conduct ourselves with our families.

Every time I hear of a pastor or Christian leader or well-known Christian artist who has failed morally, it breaks my heart. Not just because it scandalizes the church and possibly destroys his or her family, although those are certainly tragedies enough. But I think of what it says to unbelievers who read it in the headlines or hear it joked about on television talk shows. Living a clean life isn't merely a nice option to consider; it's the least we can do to demonstrate our gratitude for God's deliverance.

Second, leave no room for slander. When the ancient Greek philosopher Plato was told that a certain man had begun making slanderous charges against him, Plato's response was, "I will live in such a way that no one will believe what he says."[3]

The most convincing defense is the silent integrity of our character, not how vociferously we deny the charges.

Third, do good deeds among unbelievers. It's easy for Christians to have such tunnel vision that we limit all of our good deeds to the family of God. But if you're driving along and see someone with a flat tire, you don't roll down your window and say, "Hey there . . . you with the flat tire! Are you a Christian?" . . . then determine if you should help. We would do well to extend our good deeds to those outside the family.

What makes the story of the Good Samaritan so compelling? The merciful deeds were done on behalf of a total stranger. That is how we win the right to be heard—not by a slick mass-advertising campaign but by our compassionate and unselfish actions.

Notice that Peter says, "on account of your good *deeds*," not your good *words*. The unsaved are watching our lives. When our good deeds are indisputable the unbeliever says, "There must be something to it." Chances are good that at that point the person will hear what we have to say.

Fourth, never forget—we are being watched. The world is watching us to see if what we say we believe is true in our lives. Warren

Wiersbe tells a brief but powerful story that illustrates this beautifully.

> In the summer of 1805, a number of Indian chiefs and warriors met in council at Buffalo Creek, New York, to hear a presentation of the Christian message by a Mr. Cram from the Boston Missionary Society. After the sermon, a response was given by Red Jacket, one of the leading chiefs. Among other things, the chief said . . .
>
> "Brother, we are told that you have been preaching to the white people in this place. These people are our neighbors. We are acquainted with them. We will wait a little while and see what effect your preaching has upon them. If we find it does them good, makes them honest and less disposed to cheat Indians, we will then consider again what you have said."[4]

Whew! That's laying it on the line. I wonder how many people are looking at us and saying to themselves, "I hear what he's saying. Now I'm going to watch how he lives. I'll see if what he says is what he does."

Let's Not Forget—God Is for Us

This has been a searching chapter to write. I've not attempted to soften Peter's words, lest we miss the punch in his points. For whatever it's worth, I've felt a few stinging reproofs as well. Sometimes an author has to swallow some of his own medicine . . . except in this case, God is giving the medicine through Peter's pen, not mine! And so, you and I both have taken it on the chin. Hopefully, it will make a difference.

But let's not forget the good news: There is hope beyond guilt! May I remind you of that oft-repeated line from Romans 8? "God is for us." In devoted love He chose us. In great grace He stooped to accept us into His family. In immense mercy He still finds us wandering, forgives our foolish ways, and (as He did with Peter) frees us to serve Him even though we don't deserve such treatment.

So . . . away with guilt! If you need a little extra boost to make that happen, read Eugene Peterson's paraphrase of Romans 8:31–19. Read it slowly, preferably *aloud*. As a good friend of mine once put it, "If this don't light your fire, you got wet wood!"

So, what do you think? With God on our side like this, how can we lose? If God didn't hesitate to put everything on the line for us, embracing our condition and exposing himself to the worst by sending his own Son, is there anything else he wouldn't gladly and freely do for us? And who would dare tangle with God by messing with one of God's chosen? Who would dare even to point a finger? The One who died for us—who was raised to life for us!—is in the presence of God at this very moment sticking up for us. Do you think anyone is going to be able to drive a wedge between us and Christ's love for us? There is no way! Not trouble, not hard times, not hatred, not hunger, not homelessness, not bullying threats, not backstabbing, not even the worst sins listed in Scripture:

"They kill us in cold blood because they hate you.
We're sitting ducks; they pick us off one by one."

None of this fazes us because Jesus loves us. I'm absolutely convinced that nothing—nothing living or dead, angelic or demonic, today or tomorrow, high or low, thinkable or unthinkable—absolutely *nothing* can get between us and God's love because of the way that Jesus our Master has embraced us. (Rom. 8:31–39 MSG)

A Prayer for Hope Beyond Guilt

Father . . . dear gracious Father, we're our own worst enemy.
We focus on our failures rather than on Your rescues . . . on
our wrongs rather than on Your commitment to making us
right . . . on our puny efforts rather than on Your powerful

plans for our good. Even our attempts at being devoted to You can become so self-centered. Turn our attention back to You.

- *Remind us of our exalted position in Christ.*
- *Refresh us with frequent flashbacks—"God is for us."*
- *Renew our spirits with the realization that we're your possession.*

Then, with those joyful thoughts to spur us on, slay the dragon of guilt within us so we might enjoy, as never before, your ultimate embrace. Through Christ I pray.

AMEN

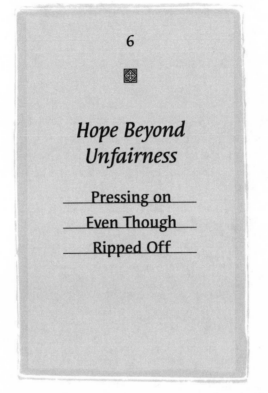

6

Hope Beyond Unfairness

Pressing on Even Though Ripped Off

EVER BOUGHT A LEMON of a used car? Ever sent away for some marvelous $16.95 gadget displayed on an infomercial and ended up with about 85 cents worth of plastic?

Who hasn't been hoodwinked by a smooth-talking salesman with styled hair and patent-leather shoes? Who hasn't been burned by a glitzy ad campaign that promises more than it delivers? Who hasn't, at some point, been taken advantage of or "ripped off"?

Yet we recover relatively easily and quickly from ripoffs like those. What's really difficult to endure is the kind of abuse or victimization that gets personal—when someone slanders our reputations, pulls the economic rug out from under us, or even threatens our lives. It's hard enough to deal with the consequences of our own missteps, miscalculations, and stupid mistakes. But it seems unbearable to suffer the consequences of something that wasn't our fault or that we didn't deserve.

If you've ever been treated like that, you're in good biblical company. David was ripped off by Saul, Esau was duped by Jacob, Joseph was mistreated by his brothers, and Job was victimized by the Sabeans and Chaldeans.

David, as a young shepherd boy, killed Goliath and helped rout the Philistine enemy. After that, David became overwhelmingly popular among the people. He also became the object of King Saul's rage. David had done only good for Saul and his people. Therefore, the people appropriately sang their praises to David: "Saul has slain his thousands, and David his ten thousands" (1 Sam. 18:7). That popular song sent Saul into such a revengeful rage against the young hero that for more than a decade David ran for his life while Saul hunted and haunted him. David didn't deserve this, but it happened.

Joseph didn't ask to be his father's favorite, but when Jacob showed favoritism to his youngest son, Joseph's brothers, in a moment of absolute hatred, sold him into slavery. Although Joseph triumphed over his circumstances, he was initially ripped off by his brothers.

Earlier, Joseph's father, Jacob, had cheated his own brother, Esau, out of his birthright. Admittedly Esau was rash and irresponsible, but Jacob took advantage of his brother in a vulnerable moment.

And what about that good man Job? According to the Scriptures, he was "blameless" and "upright" and had taken unfair advantage of no one . . . but because Satan used him as a guinea pig, Job lost all his land, servants, possessions, and above all, his ten children.

While God ultimately used all these circumstances for the believers' good and His honor, initially all of these men could have said, "What is happening here? This is unfair! I don't deserve this!"

So while we may be in good company—and misery does love company—company doesn't alleviate the pain of unfair treatment.

Natural Reactions to Unfair Treatment

It's been my observation that when we're treated unfairly, we respond with three common, knee-jerk reactions.

First, there is the aggressive pattern: we blame others. This reaction not only focuses on the person who ripped us off and keeps a running tally of wrongs done against us, it also engineers ways to get back. This reaction says, "I don't just get mad, I get even." In the process, aggression grows from simple anger all the way to rage. It starts with the seed of resentment, germinates into revenge, and in the process nurtures a deep root of bitterness that tenaciously wraps around our hearts. When allowed to grow to full size, it leaves us determined to get back at *every* person who has done anything against us.

It's like the fellow who was bitten by a dog and was later told by his physician, "Yes, indeed, you do have rabies." Upon hearing this, the patient immediately pulled out a pad and pencil and began to write.

Thinking the man was making out his will, the doctor said, "Listen, this doesn't mean you're going to die. There's a cure for rabies."

"I know that," said the man. "I'm making a list of people I'm gonna bite."

It is probable that a few who read these words are making lists right now of people you're gonna bite the very next chance you get. Some of you are already engaged in doing just that. The blame game may temporarily satisfy an aggressive inner itch, but it doesn't lead to a lasting solution. Small wonder God warns us: "Never take your own revenge . . . 'Vengeance is Mine, I will repay,' says the Lord" (Rom. 12:19).

Second, there is the passive pattern: we feel sorry for ourselves. We throw a pity party, complaining to anyone who will lend a sympathetic ear. "Life just isn't fair," we whine. But if we wallow in this slough of despondency too long, we become depressed and immobile, living the balance of life with the shades drawn and the doors locked. Like quicksand, feeling sorry for ourselves will suck us under.

Though you may be holding back, there's a lot of anger in this passive pattern as well. Give in to this temptation, and I can assure you, you'll not be vulnerable to anybody ever again.

Reminds me of some fellows in the military who were stationed in Korea during the Korean War. While there, they hired a local boy to cook and clean for them. Being a bunch of jokesters, these guys soon took advantage of the boy's seeming naiveté. They'd smear Vaseline on the stove handles so that when he'd turn the stove on in the morning he'd get grease all over his fingers. They'd put little water buckets over the door so that he'd get deluged when he opened the door. They'd even nail his shoes to the floor during the night. Day after day the little fella took the brunt of their practical jokes without saying anything. No blame . . . no self-pity . . . no temper tantrums.

Finally the men felt guilty about what they were doing, so they sat down with the young Korean and said, "Look, we know these pranks aren't funny anymore, and we're sorry. We're never gonna take advantage of you again."

It seemed too good to be true to the houseboy. "No more sticky on stove?" he asked.

"Nope."

"No more water on door?"

"No."

"No more nail shoes to floor?"

"Nope, never again."

"Okay," the boy said with a smile . . . "no more spit in soup."

Even in a passive mode, you can spit in somebody's soup.

Third, there is the holding pattern: we postpone or deny our feelings. We might call this the Scarlett O'Hara syndrome: "I'll think about it tomorrow." Every boiling issue is left to simmer on the back burner over a low flame. On the surface all seems calm—"Doesn't bother me"—but underneath, our feelings seethe, eating away at us like acid. This failure to deal with the problem forthrightly leads only to doubt and disillusionment and weakens the fiber of our lives. Furthermore, it's physically unhealthy to sustain feelings of resentment.

An Alternative That Honors God

Though they are all very common, don't expect to find any of these reactions in Peter's wonderful letter where he informs us how to have hope beyond unfairness. Expect instead an alternative reaction to unfair treatment.

The Command

> Submit yourselves for the Lord's sake to every human institution, whether to a king as the one in authority, or to governors as sent by him for the punishment of evildoers and the praise of those who do right. (1 Pet. 2:13–14)

It's important to understand the historical context of this command. The Roman Empire, throughout which the readers of Peter's letter were scattered, was not a benevolent monarchy. It was a dictatorship ruled by the insane demagogue Nero, who was especially notorious for his wickedness and his cruelty to Christians. Many of the believers who received Peter's letter had suffered persecution. The bodies of their friends and loved ones had bloodied the sand of the Roman coliseum. Their corpses, soaked in oil, had lit that vast stadium. So it was altogether natural and fitting that Peter would address the subject of unfair treatment. These believers had been the target of the grossest kind of mistreatment by government, by their fellow citizens, and by their neighbors.

Should these Christians pick up arms and resist a government with such a leader at its helm? No, said Peter. Incredibly, in the midst of all this, he had the audacity to say, "Submit."

God does not promote anarchy. Jesus said, "Render to Caesar the things that are Caesar's and to God the things that are God's" (Matt. 22:21). And Paul exhorts us to pray for those who are in authority over us (see 1 Tim. 2:1–2). Nowhere in Scripture is overt insurrection against the government recommended. The believer was not put on earth to overthrow governments but to establish in the human heart a kingdom not of this world.

There may be instances, of course, when we must stand our ground, when we must stand firm and disobey a law that is disobedient to the law of God. We are not to buckle under by compromising our convictions or renouncing our faith. But those are the exceptions, not the normal rule. Whenever possible we are to render unto Caesar the coin of civil obedience, pray for those in authority, pay our taxes, obey the laws of the land, and live honorably under the domain of earthly elected leaders.

The way to live honorably, Peter says, is to "submit." The Greek word is *hupotasso*, a military term that means "to fall in rank under an authority." It's composed of two words: *tasso*, meaning "to appoint, order, or arrange," and *hupo*, meaning "to place under or to subordinate." In this particular construction it conveys the idea of subjecting oneself or placing oneself under another's authority.

This recognition of existing authority, coupled with a willingness to set aside one's own personal desires, shows a deep dependency upon God. This submission to authority is not only in respect to God, the foremost human authority, but to lesser officials as well, such as kings and governors as well as law officers and teachers.

I'm convinced in my heart that if we were good students of submission we would get along a lot better in life. But I am also convinced that it is the one thing, more than any other, that works against our very natures, which argue, "I don't want to submit. I don't want to give in. I won't let him have his way in this." And so we live abrasively.

Let's get something very clear here. Our problem is not understanding what submission means. Our problem is doing what it says.

Because submission is so difficult, we need to look at the reason behind Peter's command.

The Reason

For such is the will of God that by doing right you may silence the ignorance of foolish men. (1 Pet. 2:15)

The Greek word translated "silence" here means "to close the mouth with a muzzle." You see, Christians in the first century were the targets of all kinds of slanderous rumors. "They're a secret sect," people said. "They are people of another kingdom." . . . "They follow another god." . . . "They have plans to overthrow us." Throughout the Roman Empire people gossiped about their secret meetings, their subversive ideologies, their loyalty to another kingdom, their plans to infiltrate, indoctrinate, and lead an insurrection. This kind of paranoia was common, all the way to Nero. To muzzle these rumors, Peter encouraged submission to the powers that be. By submitting, Peter said, by doing right before God, they would muzzle the mouths of those passing around such rumors.

Let's translate it into today's terms. We live in a city where the government is run by civil authorities. Our church building is located in that city. Now, those civil authorities have no right to tell us what to preach, what to teach, or which philosophy to adopt as a church. If they attempt to do that, we have a right—in fact, it's a duty—to rebel, because there is a higher law than their law, the higher law relating to the declaration of truth. However, they do have the right to say, "In this room you may put 150 people and no more. If you go beyond that you are violating the fire code and will be subject to a fine and possibly other penalties." It is neither right nor wise for us to break this civil law. It does not violate God's law and is, in fact, there for our protection. So we must submit to that law.

In the church I pastored in Fullerton, California, we had to abide by local laws, one of which stated that we could not use folding seats in the worship auditorium; the seats had to be fixed to the floor. Also, the local law mandated a certain predetermined ratio between how many cars were parked in a parking lot measured against how many people could sit in an auditorium. Any church that constructed a worship center had to provide parking for "X" number of people in the worship gathering. We agreed to cooperate with that.

By submitting to this civil authority, we muzzled any rumors that we were just a maverick group, that we did as we pleased, thank you. We would have gained nothing by rebelling against the civic authorities. In fact, we would have lost in many ways by doing so.

The Principle

> Act as free men, and do not use your freedom as a covering for evil, but use it as bondslaves of God. Honor all men; love the brotherhood, fear God, honor the king. (1 Pet. 2:16–17)

It's important that we keep the right perspective on the principle here. We do not submit because we necessarily agree. We do not submit because deep within we support all the rules, codes, and regulations. At times they may seem petty and galling, terribly restrictive, and even prejudicial. We submit because it is the "will of God" and because we are "bondslaves of God."

Now, you see, the principle comes to the surface: "Do not use your freedom as a covering for evil." Do not use or abuse grace so that your freedom becomes a cloak for evil.

In little staccato bursts, Peter gives us several commands in verses 16 and 17: act as free men; honor all men; love the brotherhood; fear God; honor the king. And wrapped around the commands is that main principle: "Do not use your freedom as a covering for evil."

We must forever be aware of the temptation to abuse liberty. It's so easy to stretch it; so easy to make it work for ourselves rather than for the glory of God.

An Example and *the* Example

Servants, be submissive to your masters with all respect, not only to those who are good and gentle, but also to those who are unreasonable. For this finds favor, if for the sake of conscience toward God a man bears up under sorrows when suffering unjustly. For what credit is there if, when you sin and are harshly treated, you endure it with patience? But if when you do what is right and suffer for it you patiently endure it, this finds favor with God. For you have been called for this purpose. (1 Pet. 2:18–21a)

To understand the full import of what Peter is saying we must understand something of the nature of slavery in the time of the early church. William Barclay sheds some historical light on this.

In the time of the early church . . . there were as many as 60,000,000 slaves in the Roman Empire.

It was by no means only menial tasks which were performed by slaves. Doctors, teachers, musicians, actors, secretaries, stewards were slaves. In fact, all the work of Rome was done by slaves. Roman attitude was that there was no point in being master of the world and doing one's own work. Let the slaves do that and let the citizens live in pampered idleness. The supply of slaves would never run out.

Slaves were not allowed to marry; but they cohabited; and the children born of such a partnership were the property of the master, not of the parents, just as the lambs born to the sheep belonged to the owner of the flock, and not to the sheep.

It would be wrong to think that the lot of slaves was always wretched and unhappy, and that they were always treated with cruelty. Many slaves were loved and trusted members of the family; but one great inescapable fact dominated the whole situation. In Roman law a slave was not a person but a thing; and he had absolutely no legal rights whatsoever. For that reason there could be no such thing as justice where a slave was concerned. . . . Peter Chrysologus sums the matter up: "Whatever a master does to a slave, undeservedly, in anger, willingly, unwillingly, in forgetfulness, after careful thought, knowingly, unknowingly, is judgment, justice and law." In regard to a slave, his master's will, and even his master's caprice, was the only law.[1]

That was the reality of the first-century world when Peter addressed slaves and told them to "be submissive" to their masters. It would have been easy for slaves who became Christians to think that their Christianity gave them the freedom to break with their masters. Peter, under the Holy Spirit's inspiration, stated that this was not so.

Centuries later, Christianity pervaded the culture and overcame slavery, but it didn't happen in the first century. This is a good lesson for us regarding God's timing versus our timing, even when it comes to adversity. While He certainly commands us to be salt and light and thus bring about justice and change in our culture, His ultimate priority is changing the individual human heart.

It's difficult for us in America to read some of these verses. Our frame of reference is so different—so Western, so twentieth century—that we sometimes try to rewrite God's Word to make it fit us. We can't do that. We must let it speak for itself.

"Well, that's great if you have a good master," you say. It's wonderful if you're a slave of Saint Francis of America . . . or Mother Teresa of your community. If you're working for some marvelous, saintlike boss, everything is cool. You're happy to submit. But what if your taskmaster fits the description in the last part of the verse—what if you work for "those who are unreasonable"?

Do you have an uncaring boss? Do you have a supervisor or a manager who isn't fair? Do you have to deal with unreasonable people? You may not want to hear this today, but there is a lot of truth for you in verses 18 and 19, none of which will ever appear in your local newspaper or on a television talk show.

The natural tendency of the human heart is to fight back against unfair and unreasonable treatment. But Peter's point is that seeking revenge for unjust suffering can be a sign of self-appointed lordship over one's own affairs. Revenge, then, is totally inappropriate for one who has submitted to the lordship of Jesus Christ. Christians must stand in contrast to those around them. This includes a difference in attitude and a difference in focus. Our attitude should be "submissive," and our focus should be "toward God." And how is this change viewed by God? It "finds favor" with Him.

Our focus, then, should not be consumed with getting the raise at the office but with getting the praise from God, not with getting the glory for ourselves but with giving the glory to Him.

> For what credit is there if, when you sin and are harshly treated, you endure it with patience? But if when you do what is right and suffer for it you patiently endure it, this finds favor with God. (1 Pet. 2:20)

The contrast is eloquent. There's no credit due a person who suffers for what he has coming to him. If you break into a house and steal, you will be arrested, and you could be incarcerated. And if you patiently endure your jail sentence, no one is going think you are wonderful for being such a good and patient prisoner. You won't get elected "Citizen of the Year."

But if you are a hard-working, faithful employee, diligent, honest, productive, prompt, caring, working for a boss who is belligerent, stubborn, short-sighted, and ungrateful, and if you patiently endure that situation—aha! That "finds favor" with God! (I told you this wasn't information generally embraced by the public!) Actually another meaning for the word translated "favor" is *grace*. So when you endure, you put grace on display. And when you put grace on display for the glory of God, you could revolutionize your workplace or any other situation.

Can you see why the Christian philosophy is absolutely radical and revolutionary? We don't work for the credit or the prestige or the salary or the perks! We work for the glory of God in whatever we do. The purpose of the believer in society is to bring glory and honor to the name of Christ, not to be treated well or to have life be easy or even to be happy, as wonderful as all those things are. Again, this is not promoted in today's workplace.

> For you have been called for this purpose, since Christ also suffered for you, leaving you an example for you to follow in His steps. (1 Pet. 2:21)

You are "called for this purpose." That's the reason you're in that company. That's the reason you're filling that role. That's the reason these things are happening to you. Why? So that you might follow in the steps of our Lord Jesus, who suffered for us.

I deliberately left Christ off the list of biblical examples at the beginning of the chapter because I wanted to mention Him here. No one was ever more "ripped off" than our Savior. Absolutely no one. Jesus of Nazareth was the only perfect Man who ever lived, yet He suffered continually during His brief life on this planet. He was misunderstood, maligned, hated, arrested, and tortured. Finally, they crucified Him.

And Peter says we are to walk in the steps of Jesus.

> Since Christ also suffered for you, leaving you an example for you to follow in His steps, who committed no sin, nor was any deceit found in His mouth; and while being reviled, He did not revile in return; while

suffering, He uttered no threats, but kept entrusting Himself to Him who judges righteously; and He Himself bore our sins in His body on the cross, that we might die to sin and live to righteousness; for by His wounds you were healed. (1 Pet. 2:21b–24)

In these verses Peter shifts from *an* example of unfair treatment to *the* example we should follow—from that of a servant to that of the Savior.

John Henry Jowett writes of Jesus' perfection.

> The fine, sensitive membrane of the soul had in nowise been scorched by the fire of iniquity. "No sin!" He was perfectly pure and healthy. No power had been blasted by the lightning of passion. No nerve had been atrophied by the wasting blight of criminal neglect. The entire surface of His life was as finely sensitive as the fair, healthy skin of a little child. . . . There was no duplicity. There were no secret folds or convolutions in His life concealing ulterior motives. There was nothing underhand. His life lay exposed in perfect truthfulness and candour. The real, inner meaning of His life was presented upon a plain surface of undisturbed simplicity. "No sin!" Nothing blunted or benumbed. "No guile!" Therefore nothing hardened by the effrontery of deceit.[2]

That's the sinless Christ. But still they mocked Him and bruised Him and beat Him and *crucified* Him. When Peter tells us He is our example, that's saying something!

Consider His focus. He "kept entrusting Himself to Him who judges righteously."

That's a good thing to do throughout your day. "Lord, this is a hard moment for me. I'm having a tough time today. Here I am again, dealing with this unreasonable person, this person who is treating me unfairly. Lord, help me. I entrust myself to You. I give You my struggle. Protect me. Provide the wisdom and self-control I need. Help me do the right thing."

We must understand that the purpose of Jesus' suffering was different from ours. I know there comes a point where subjection to certain situations can become absolutely unwise and unhealthy. No argument there. But most of us don't get anywhere near that. We are so quick to defend ourselves. We are a fight-back generation. We know our lawyers' phone numbers better than we know verses of Scripture on self-restraint. Quick to get mad! Quick to fight back! Quick to answer back! Quick to threaten a lawsuit! "Don't you DARE step across that line . . . I've got my rights!"

When was the last time you deliberately, for the glory of Christ, took it on the chin, turned the other cheek, kept your mouth shut, and gave Him all the glory?

A Benefit That Accompanies Such Obedience

For you were continually straying like sheep, but now you have returned to the Shepherd and Guardian of your souls. (1 Pet. 2:25)

Staring in horror at the cross, one can't help but become dizzy from a swarm of questions. Why? Why should this innocent man endure such unjust suffering? Why should we? Why shouldn't we resist the thorns and the lash we are forced to bear? Why should we submit to the hammer blows, to the piercing nails, to the cross of unjust suffering?

Because it causes us to return to our Savior for protection rather than defending ourselves or fighting for "our rights." That kind of reaction has become so much a part of our lifestyle and culture that we don't even realize it when we react that way. We don't even recognize that we should be different from those around us.

By the way, see the words, "by His wounds you were healed"? Talk about vivid! Peter had seen firsthand the yoke of unjust suffering placed upon Jesus' shoulders. No doubt he was remembering. He could see it as clearly as though it were yesterday—that moment when he saw his Master's bruised and bleeding body staggering along the narrow streets of Jerusalem on the way to Golgotha. And as he remembered that scene, he said, "by that He heals us."

Are you feeling the splinters of some cross of unjust suffering? Has a friend betrayed you? Has an employer impaled you? Has a disaster dropped on your life that's almost too great to bear? If so, don't fight back. Unjust suffering can be a dizzying experience. To keep your balance in those times when things are swirling around you, it's important to find a fixed reference point and focus on it. Return to the protection and guardianship of the Good Shepherd who endured the cross and laid down His life . . . for you.

It was because David refused to take vengeance on King Saul that we remember his story to this day. It was because Joseph was so willing to forgive his brothers that we admire him to this day. And it was because Job did not waver in his faith, in spite of all those unfair calamities, that we are impressed to this day.

If you'd just as soon be forgotten because you lived consumed with blame and self-pity, keep fighting back. Get even. Stay angry.

But if you hope to be remembered, admired, and rewarded, press on even though you've been ripped off.

A Prayer for Hope Beyond Unfairness

Dear Lord, find within us a yielded and quiet spirit of submission. To make that happen, we need You to come in like a flood. Occupy us as water finding empty spaces. Occupy reserved portions of our lives where anger is festering and the secret places where grudges are being stored. Sweep through our houses . . . don't miss one room or a single area—cleanse every dark closet, look under every rug. Let nothing go unnoticed as You take full control of our motives as well as our actions. Deep within our hearts we pray that You would sweep us clean of blame and revenge, of self-pity and keeping score. Enable each one of us to be big enough to press on regardless of what unfair treatment we've had to endure. Take away the scars of ugly treatment and harsh words. Forgiveness comes hard . . . but it's essential. Help us forgive even those who never acknowledge their wronging and hurting us! Give us peace in place of turmoil and erase the memories that keep us offended. We need fresh hope to go on! I ask this in the name of Him who had no sin and did no wrong, but died, the just for the unjust: Jesus Christ our Lord.

AMEN

7

Hope Beyond "I Do"

The Give-and-Take of Domestic Harmony

A WEDDING IS ONE thing. A marriage is another. What a difference between the way things start in a home . . . and the way they continue.

In his book *Secrets to Inner Beauty*, Joe Aldrich humorously describes the realities of married life.

> It doesn't take long for the newlyweds to discover that "everything in one person nobody's got." They soon learn that a marriage license is just a learner's permit, and ask with agony, "Is there life after marriage?"
>
> An old Arab proverb states that marriage begins with a prince kissing an angel and ends with a bald-headed man looking across the table at a fat lady. Socrates told his students, "By all means marry. If you get a good wife, twice blessed you will be. If you get a bad wife, you'll become a philosopher." Count Herman Keyserling said it well when he stated that "The essential difficulties of life do not end, but rather begin with marriage."[1]

Marriage begins like a romantic, moonlight sleigh ride, smoothly gliding over the glistening snow. It's living together after the honeymoon that turns out to be rough backpacking across rocks and hot sand. For two people to live in domestic harmony, it takes a lot of give-and-take. If you need any confirmation of this outside your own life, just look at the statistics. No, forget statistics. Just look about you. On the job. In the office. Around your neighborhood. At church. Broken marriages. Separations. Divorces. Fractured homes. Some children have so many stepparents they can't keep track of them.

A wedding is one thing. A marriage is something else entirely.

I am a realist, not an idealist. I've been married for forty-one years, and they have been years of learning and growth, years of difficulty and ecstasy, years of delight and discovery, years of heartache and hardship, years of having children and losing children (two miscarriages), years of growing together and, I must confess, some days in which it seemed we were growing apart.

At first, of course, deceived by the rose-colored glasses of romantic love, we didn't see any of this. And looking back through the fog of disappointment, we see very few things clearly.

In an essay on the theme of "arranged marriages," writer Philip Yancey offers these insights.

In the U.S. and other Western-style cultures, people tend to marry because they are attracted to another's appealing qualities: a fresh smile, wittiness, a pleasing figure, athletic ability, a cheerful disposition, charm. Over time, these qualities can change; the physical attributes, especially, will deteriorate with age. Meanwhile, surprises may surface: slatternly housekeeping, a tendency toward depression, disagreements over sex. In contrast, the partners in an arranged marriage [over half of all marriages in our international global village fit this description] do not center their relationship on mutual attractions. Having heard your parents' decision, you accept that you will live for many years with someone you now barely know. Thus the overriding question changes from "Whom should I marry?" to "Given this partner, what kind of marriage can we construct together?"[2]

Truthfully, that is the kind of attitude we need if we are going to move beyond romance into reality to build a strong and lasting life together. The apostle Peter gives us some helpful advice. He offers hope beyond "I do."

Tucked away in the heart of his letter is a little gem of truth, like a diamond in a ring. Without the right setting to enhance its beauty, this little gem would get lost; but viewed in its proper setting it becomes a sparkling delight. In the Bible, this setting is called the scriptural context.

The overall setting begins at 1 Peter 2:13 and continues through the end of chapter 3. These many verses challenge us to respond correctly, even in unfair circumstances. Some of those circumstances are briefly illustrated: citizens in various situations (2:13–17), slaves with unjust masters (2:18–20), wives with unfair husbands (3:1–6), and Christians in an unchristian society (3:13–17).

The key term in this context is the word *submit*, which we defined and analyzed in the previous chapter. You'll recall it is translated from a Greek military term meaning "to fall in rank under the authority of another . . . to subject oneself for the purpose of obeying or pleasing another." Some men have taken this word to the extreme in marriage, promoting cowering and servile behavior by women in the face of the worst kinds of abuse. Others have gone to the opposite extreme and labeled these passages dated and therefore culturally obsolete, saying that they apply only to the era in which they were originally written. The balance of the biblical position lies somewhere between these two poles.

Wise Counsel to Wives

The first six verses of our "gem of truth" passage refer to wives, and the seventh verse refers to husbands. One New Testament scholar gives a good explanation of this seeming inequity.

> It may seem strange that Peter's advice to wives is six times as long as that to husbands. This is because the wife's position was far more

difficult than that of the husband. If a husband became a Christian, he would automatically bring his wife with him into the Church. . . . But if a wife became a Christian while her husband did not, she was taking a step which was unprecedented and which produced the acutest problems.[3]

Despite that explanation, I know this passage is probably one of the hottest potatoes in Scripture, especially for women. Let me put some of you at ease. I do not believe this or any other part of Scripture admonishes a wife to stay in a situation where her health is being threatened or where her life—or the lives of her children—is in danger. That is not what submission is all about. So please don't run to that extreme and hide there, thinking you can avoid or deny the importance of submission in every other area or at any other level.

I find no fewer than three implied imperatives woven into the fabric of these important verses. They are reasonable and doable commands. They aren't culturally irrelevant. Best of all, they work!

Analyze Your Actions

In the same way, you wives, be submissive to your own husbands so that even if any of them are disobedient to the word, they may be won without a word by the behavior of their wives, as they observe your chaste and respectful behavior. (1 Pet. 3:1–2)

Many wives tend to view their roles as conditional; their behavior depends on the behavior of their husbands. "Sure, I'll be the kind of wife I should be if he's the kind of husband he should be." On the surface, that sounds great. Turnabout is fair play. There's only one problem: This passage isn't written just to wives who have husbands who play fair. Peter doesn't let us off the hook that easily. The passage is written to all wives, even those whose husbands are "disobedient to the word." In fact, by implication this paragraph is directed to women who live with disobedient husbands—husbands who are going their own way, husbands who care little about the things of God, husbands who would even mock the things of Christ. In short, these are husbands who aren't measuring up to God's standard.

Having to exhibit godly behavior under such circumstances can, however, cause wives to substitute secret manipulation for a quiet spirit. This may take many forms: pouting, sulking, scheming, bargaining, nagging, preaching, coercing, or humiliating. Wives who use this strategy are not trusting God to change their husbands' lives. They're trusting themselves.

You see, a wife is not responsible for her husband's life. She is responsible for her life. You cannot make your husband something he is not. Only God can do that.

I think it was the evangelist's wife, Ruth Graham, who once said, "It is my job to love Billy. It is God's job to make him good." I'd call that a wonderful philosophy for any wife to embrace.

Wife, it is your job to love your husband. It is God's job to change his life.

And wives who are truly obedient to Christ will find that He will honor their secure spirit. Yes, submission is a mark of security. It is not a spineless cringing, based on insecurity and fear. It is a voluntary unselfishness, a willing and cooperative spirit that seeks the highest good for one's husband.

"Well, that sounds like a dead-end street, Chuck," some of you might be saying. "If you only knew what I am living with, what a rascal, what a reprobate, what an ungodly man he really is."

But notice what Peter says: "they may be won without a word by the behavior of their wives, *as they observe your chaste and respectful behavior.*" The Greek term for *observe* suggests that this is a keen and careful observation, not a casual glance. As a "disobedient" husband observes his wife's godly behavior, his heart will eventually soften toward spiritual things. Such a lifestyle has been called "the silent preaching of a lovely life."

Watch Your Adornment and Your Attitude

And let not your adornment be merely external—braiding the hair, and wearing gold jewelry, or putting on dresses, but let it be the hidden person of the heart, with the imperishable quality of a gentle and quiet spirit, which is precious in the sight of God. (1 Pet. 3:3–4)

Obviously Peter is drawing a sharp contrast between inner beauty and outer beauty, or as Peter puts it, between outer adornment (verse 3) and inner adornment (verse 4).

It's easy in our shop-'til-you-drop culture to get carried away with the externals, ladies. Catalogs for every conceivable item of clothing pour into our homes, with their 800 numbers eager to take your order at any hour of the day or night. If that isn't convenient enough, we have entire television channels devoted to shopping and stores available on the Internet. Ready . . . set . . . *charge!*

The point of the contrast here is to restore the balance. Peter isn't prohibiting the braiding of hair or the wearing of jewelry any more than he's prohibiting the wearing of dresses. He merely wants to put those things in the background and bring the woman's character into the foreground. Perspective is the key.

Taken to an unrealistic extreme, you can really miss the mark in your external adornment. I have seen some women who think that it is a mark of spirituality to look like an unmade bed. That is not what God has in mind. On the other hand, if externals get overemphasized, appearance, cosmetics, and clothing take on too much significance. You can become preoccupied with your external adornment, and you can begin judging yourself and others solely by appearance, which is often what our culture does.

External beauty is ephemeral. Internal beauty is eternal. The former is attractive to the world; the latter is pleasing to God. Peter describes this inner beauty as "a gentle and quiet spirit." This might be paraphrased "a gentle tranquility." Without question, this is any woman's most powerful quality—true character. And such character comes from within—from the hidden person of the heart—because you know who you are and you know who you adore and serve, the Lord Christ. God values this kind of inner beauty as "imperishable" and "precious."

Outward adornment doesn't take a great deal of time. I've seen women do it in a few minutes on their way to work in the morning. (Ever been driving behind a woman putting on her makeup in the car as she's driving to work? It's an amazing process! And dangerous. I always cringe and wonder—what happens if she hits a pothole?) It may take only a few hours to prepare yourself for the most elegant of evenings, but it takes a lifetime to prepare and develop the hidden person of the heart.

Adornment is important but not nearly as important as attitude. If the internal attitude is right, it's amazing how much less significant one's external appearance becomes. Wise is the wife who watches both.

Evaluate Your Attention

> For in this way in former times the holy women also, who hoped in God, used to adorn themselves, being submissive to their own husbands. Thus Sarah obeyed Abraham, calling him lord, and you have become her children if you do what is right without being frightened by any fear. (1 Pet. 3:5–6)

The fact that Sarah called her husband her lord (Gen. 18:12) reveals much about their relationship. It shows that she respected him, was attentive to his needs, cooperated with his wishes, and adapted herself to his desires.

Wives, are you patterning yourself after Sarah's role model? Take a look at where you place most of your attention, where you spend your time, what the focus of your prayer life is. Is your husband at the top of your earthly list?

I would encourage you wives to evaluate where you place most of your attention, and this is especially true for women who are busy raising a family. It is so easy in the press of caring for the constant needs of your children to put the needs of your husband on hold. Experience has taught me that is often where a breakdown in a marital relationship begins.

Peter says, "Sarah obeyed Abraham." A good paraphrase might be, "She paid attention to him."

★

Strong Commands to Husbands

> You husbands likewise, live with your wives in an understanding way, as with a weaker vessel, since she is a woman; and grant her honor as a fellow heir of the grace of life, so that your prayers may not be hindered. (1 Pet. 3:7)

The final verse in this section turns the spotlight on husbands. It's short, but penetrating. I find that it is packed with three strong imperatives.

First, live with your wife. The Greek term here is a compound word composed of *sun* (with) and *oikeo* (to dwell/abide); put together they obviously mean "to dwell together." Now, you're probably thinking, "Well, certainly, I live with my wife. I'm *married* to her." But that is not what Peter is talking about. He's talking about a "close togetherness." *Sunoikeo* suggests much more than merely living under the same roof. There is a depth, a sense of intimacy, in the word. He is saying that husbands are responsible for that in the relationship. Providing a good living should never become a substitute for sharing deeply in life. The husband needs to be "at home with" his wife, understanding every room in his wife's heart and being sensitive to her needs. "Dwelling together" definitely means more than eating at the same table, sharing the same bed, and paying for the same mortgage.

Second, know your wife. Peter exhorts husbands to live with their wives "in an understanding way." That phrase literally means, "according to knowledge"—not an academic knowledge, but a thorough understanding of how your wife is put together.

"Oh, I know my wife," you may say. "Brown hair. Blue eyes. Weight. Height. I know what she likes for supper. Her favorite color is blue. I know where she likes to go for dinner." It's not that kind of knowledge either. Any man can know those things about her!

Your wife is a unique vessel, carefully crafted and beautifully interwoven by her Creator. To "know your wife" means you know the answers to those complex questions about her. What is her innermost makeup? What are her deepest concerns and fears? How do you help her work through them in the safety and security of your love? What does she need from you? Why does she respond as she does?

There's no handbook for those insights into her life. Even your father-in-law can't give you this inside information. You have to find it out in the intimacy of marriage and in the process of cultivating your life together. It takes time. It takes listening. It takes paying attention, concentrating, praying for insight, seeking understanding. Most wives long for that. Some of them die longing for it. Few things give a woman more security than knowing that her husband really knows her. That's what results in intimacy. That's what turns romance into a deep, lifelong love. That's what keeps her focused on and committed to you, longing to have you there, delighting in your presence, your words, your listening ear.

By the way, we need to address another phrase that occurs here: "living with your wife in an understanding way, *as with a weaker vessel.*" Now a word of caution: This has nothing to do with weakness of character or intelligence.

> The woman is called the "weaker vessel" (*skeuos*, lit., "vessel"); but this is not to be taken morally, spiritually, or intellectually. It simply means that the woman has less physical strength. The husband must recognize this difference and take it into account.[4]

Sometimes this is a bit difficult to comprehend when we consider what a woman goes through in bearing children. There's no doubt about the kind of strength women have within them when it comes to enduring pain. When my daughter gave birth to her second child, our fourth grandchild, she had natural childbirth. (Seemed strange to me—"natural" childbirth—and I was thankful I never had to go through that. I've never heard of anybody having a natural appendectomy or requesting a natural root canal!) What strength she demonstrated!

But when it comes to actual physical strength, Dr. Robert Kerlan, orthopedic surgeon and sports medicine specialist, says: "If the battle of the sexes was reduced to a tug-of-war with a line of 100 men on one side of the trench and 100 women on the other, the men would win." What makes the difference, he says, is muscle makeup.[5]

God's goal for us as husbands is to be sensitive rather than to prove how strong and macho we are. We need to love our wives, listen to them, adapt to their needs. We need to say no to more and more in our work so we can say yes to more and more in our homes . . . so we can say yes to the needs of our children and our families. (How else will your children learn what it means to be a good husband and father?)

Mind you, this is not to be a smothering kind of attention—the kind that says a husband is so insecure he cannot let his wife out of his sight. Instead, this is the kind of love that means your wife can't come back fast enough to your arms. Which brings us to the third imperative.

Third, honor your wife. To "grant her honor" is to assign her a place of honor. The same word translated "honor" here in 3:7 refers to the blood of Christ as "precious" in 1:19. I'd call that a rather significant analogy, wouldn't you?

Authors Gary Smalley and John Trent define this word well in their book *The Gift of Honor.*

> In ancient writings, something of honor was something of substance (literally, heavy), valuable, costly, even priceless. For Homer, the Greek scholar, "The greater the cost of the gift, the more the honor." . . .
>
> Not only does it signify something or someone who is a priceless treasure, but it is also used for someone who occupies a highly respected position in our lives, someone high on our priority list.[6]

That's how husbands are to treat their wives—to honor them by assigning them the top priority on their list of human relationships . . . in their schedules . . . and most importantly, in their hearts.

May I ask a few very personal questions? How do you treat your wife on an average day? Do you honor her? Do you give her a place of significance? Does she know she's your "top priority"? And do you communicate that in both actions and words? Honoring another is never something we keep to ourselves.

This is a magnificent truth, and you'll only get it from the Scriptures. It revolutionized my home. That's why I know it works. I didn't come from a model home and my wife didn't come from a home where her mother was honored. Cynthia and I knew that if we were going to make our marriage work, we had to go God's way, which meant we both had to be willing to change. We determined to do just that. And I'll freely admit, of the two of us, I have had to change more. About the time I think I've got things in good shape, another area emerges, and I have to deal with that! The journey toward marital maturity is a long one! And each year there are always some changes that must occur.

Let me summarize what Peter has written. Wives, your actions, your adornment, your attitudes, your attention are crucial in your marriage. Husbands, living with your wife, getting to know your wife, and honoring your wife are imperative if your marriage is going to be what it should be in God's eyes. Marriage is a two-way street. Both sides must be maintained.

A Promise to Both Partners

To seal this "heavenly bargain," Peter closes with a promise to both partners: "So that your prayers may not be hindered." This is an added incentive for husband and wife to live together in domestic harmony.

If you and your mate hope to cultivate an effective prayer life, the secret lies in your relationship with each other. Your prayers will not be hindered if you cultivate a close and caring relationship. Could that explain why your prayers are not being answered now?

A Project to Add Hope to Your Home

During the next week I'd like you to work on a very practical project. It will involve your doing two things. *First*, write down four qualities you appreciate most about your mate. After thinking them through, tell your spouse what they are and why they come to mind. Give examples. Take your time. Spell them out. Genuinely affirm your partner. *Second*, using this section of 1 Peter as your guide, admit the one thing you would most like to change about yourself. Don't be afraid to be vulnerable. Your mate will appreciate your willingness to be transparent.

Now don't get those two reversed. Don't mention four things you want your partner to change and the one thing you like most about yourself!

Talk truth. Refuse to blame. Guard against this becoming an evening of confrontation. Make it an evening of getting back together. Go ahead . . . be willing to risk.

You may be amazed to discover how quickly new hope for your marriage can return. The secret isn't that profound. A good marriage isn't so much finding the right partner as it is being the right partner.

And that starts with you.

A Prayer for Hope Beyond "I Do"

Lord, marriage was Your original idea. You hold the patent on this one. You brought the first couple together and gave Adam and Eve wise instruction on how to make their marriage flourish.

I believe You are still bringing men and women together . . . all around this big world. But today I pray specifically for those who read this chapter. For some, their hopes are dim. They don't know where to start or how to rekindle the flame that once burned brightly. For others, starting over seems too great a hurdle . . . too huge a mountain to climb . . . too much to face.

Somehow, Lord, break down the barriers. Bring back the "want to." Restore a glimmer of hope, especially in the lives of that one couple who think they will never make it. May Your Spirit miraculously renew their hope at this moment. I ask this in the name of Christ, in whom nothing is impossible.

AMEN

8

Hope Beyond Immaturity

Maturity Checkpoints

DURING MY MOST obnoxious years as a teenager I frequently received two admonitions. The first one was an abrupt, "Shut up!" The second was, "Grow up!"

Though I found it difficult on occasion, I usually managed to accomplish the first rather quickly. But I must confess, there are still days when I struggle with the second piece of advice.

En route to maturity, we all spill our milk, say things we shouldn't, and fail to act our age. At times we act like a two-year-old throwing a temper tantrum. At other times we pout like a pubescent child or go through sweeping mood swings like an awkwardly adjusting teenager.

This process is called "growing up." Let's not minimize the truth—it's painful. We struggle through it more by trial and error than by unfaltering charm-school grace. Consequently, every now and then we skin an elbow, bruise a knee, or bloody a nose from falling on our faces.

Growing up. Sooner or later we all have to do it. The sooner we do, the easier it will be to walk the uneven and sometimes uncertain sidewalks of faith.

Problem is, how do we determine whether we are grown up? Does it mean our hair starts to turn gray? No, that means we're growing older but not necessarily wiser. I've met people with snow-white hair who are still immature. Signs of aging do not necessarily mean we are showing signs of maturity.

If you think it's easier to tell from the inside out, forget it. How do you know that you are more mature this year than you were last year? Has living twelve months longer made any difference? We know we're growing older, but how do we know we're growing up? And is growing up something God even requires of us? Maybe He just wants us to live in His family, sort of exist between now and eternity, then He's planning to take us home. No, that's not the way it works. Growing up is a stated objective for every member of God's family. God says so in His Word.

The writer of Hebrews addresses this very matter when he takes his readers to task for their lack of maturity. They had grown older in the faith, but they had not yet grown up. Instead of building on the foundation laid by the apostles, they were still playing with blocks.

For though by this time you ought to be teachers, you have need again for someone to teach you the elementary principles of the oracles of God, and you have come to need milk and not solid food. For everyone who partakes only of milk is not accustomed to the word of righteousness, for he is a babe. But solid food is for the mature, who because of practice have their senses trained to discern good and evil.

Therefore leaving the elementary teaching about the Christ, *let us press on to maturity*, not laying again a foundation of repentance from dead works and of faith toward God, of instruction about washings, and laying on of hands, and the resurrection of the dead, and eternal judgment, and this we shall do, if God permits. (Heb. 5:12–6:3, italics added)

Do you notice the Lord's concern that some seem perpetually immature? "You have need *again* for someone to teach you the elementary principles of the oracles of God," says the writer (italics added). "You have come to need milk and not solid food." How interesting that he puts it like that. We would say, "You're back on baby food."

I've had grocers tell me that they sell more baby food to the aging than to the parents of infants in their community. As we get older, in many ways we revert back to childhood. Physically that can't be helped—as we age and grow infirm, our bodies deteriorate. But spiritually, immaturity is something we must not allow. God wants us to get beyond the elementary matters of the faith and set out on a life-long pursuit of maturity. He longs for us to grow up in the faith.

Leave behind elementary teachings, says the letter to the Hebrews. Press on to maturity.

By "elementary teachings," the writer is very likely referring to the Old Testament signs and sacrifices. "We've gone beyond that now," he says. In today's terms we could say, "Move beyond the gospel. You have heard the gospel, you have responded to the gospel, you have believed the gospel, now go on. Grow up. Get into areas of teaching and learning that probe much deeper into your life." That kind of solid food results in spiritual strength. In fact, I've heard it rendered, "We are to leave the ABCs of the faith." In other words, we need to quit playing blocks and sucking milk from a bottle and wanting to be entertained. Leave the things that characterize infancy and get on with a grown-up lifestyle.

Few things are more pathetic to behold than those who have known the Lord for years but still can't get in out of the rain doctrinally and biblically. To put it succinctly, they have grown old, but they haven't grown up.

Do you feed yourself regularly on the Word of God or must you have the teaching of someone else to keep growing? Now, don't get me wrong; I don't decry teaching and preaching. How could I? That's my job security! All of us have a need for someone to instruct and exhort us in the things of God. But it isn't because we have no way of taking it in on our own. Teaching and preaching are more like nutritional food supplements.

Let me ask you several penetrating questions. Are you digging into the Word of God? Are you truly searching the Scriptures on your own? Are you engaged in a ministry of concerted and prevailing prayer? Can you handle pressure better than you could, say, three years ago? Are you further along on your own growth chart than you were a year ago, two years ago, five years ago?

Checkpoints for Maturity

How can we know we're growing up? Outwardly we have various signs of physical growth and aging. But when it comes to spiritual maturity, we need another kind of growth chart, and Peter, in his letter of hope, offers us a series of checkpoints to help us know we're growing up and getting on in spiritual life.

In the past three years I have flown on more airplanes than ever before in my life, commuting from California to Texas and back again, plus dozens of other destinations. When people ask Cynthia and me where we live, I sometimes reply, "Seats 16C and D, American Airlines." We're now on a first-name basis with many of the airline personnel.

As a result of this unusual transitional lifestyle, I have had ample occasions to watch the procedure pilots go through as they prepare for an upcoming flight. You may have observed it as well. The next time you're taking a trip, stand in the terminal and look out the windows into the cockpit of the airplane parked at the gate. You'll see the pilot sitting there with a clipboard, checking off all the instruments and systems. He'll also get out and check the outside of the aircraft, walking all around it. This is a seasoned pilot, with perhaps tens of thousands of hours in the air. Still, every time, before he takes that airplane up, he runs through his preflight checklist. We're thankful he does!

Look at 1 Peter 3:8–12, and you'll find another kind of checklist—a checklist for spiritual maturity. It helps us evaluate how we're doing on this pilgrimage from earth to heaven.

To sum up, let all be harmonious, sympathetic, brotherly, kind-hearted, and humble in spirit; not returning evil for evil, or insult for insult, but giving a blessing instead; for you were called for the very purpose that you might inherit a blessing. For,

> "Let him who means to love life and see good days
> refrain his tongue from evil and his lips from speaking guile.
> "And let him turn away from evil and do good;
> let him seek peace and pursue it.
> "For the eyes of the Lord are upon the righteous,
> and his ears attend to their prayer,
> but the face of the Lord is against those who do evil."
> (1 Pet. 3:8–12)

If I count correctly, there are no fewer than eight checkpoints in this section of Scripture. They help us determine how we're doing in our growth toward maturity.

Unity

The first checkpoint is unity: "Let all be harmonious." This refers to a oneness of heart, a similarity of purpose, and an agreement on major points of doctrine.

Please remember, this quality is not the same as *uniformity,* where everyone must look alike and think alike, form identical convictions and prefer the same tastes. That's what I call a cracker-box mentality. Peter isn't promoting uniformity. Nor is he referring to *unanimity,* where there is 100 percent agreement on everything. And it is not the same as *union,* where there is an affiliation with others but no common bond that makes them one at heart.

The secret to this kind of harmony is not to focus on petty peripheral differences but to concentrate on the common ground of Jesus Christ—His model, His message, and His mission.

How mature are you in the area of unity? Are you at harmony with other believers in the family of God? Are you one who works well *with* others?

Mutual Interest

The second checkpoint is mutual interest: "Let all be . . . sympathetic." The Greek root gives us our word *sympathy*, meaning "to feel with."

This means that when others weep, you weep; when they rejoice, you rejoice. It connotes the *absence* of competition, envy, or jealousy toward a fellow Christian.

Romans 12:15–16 states it well: "Rejoice with those who rejoice, and weep with those who weep. Be of the same mind toward one another. . . ." Believers who are growing toward maturity share in mutual feelings—mutual woes and mutual joys.

This is one of the best benefits of being part of the body of Christ and a major reason why we need to be involved in a local church. In that local community we have a context in which we can rejoice with each other and weep with one another. Think what happens when you move to a new community, a new home. Sadly you leave the church that has been your home, your spiritual family, where God has used you and encouraged you. But then He leads you to another. When you move to a new town or city, as a Christian one of the first things you do is search for a new church home, one where your new brothers and sisters welcome you and receive you into their fellowship and life. Right away you're surrounded by a family.

How's your maturity level on this second checkpoint? Can you truly say you enter the feelings of the other person? When others hurt, do you hurt? When they enjoy life, do you really enjoy it with them? When God blesses them with material prosperity or some significant award or promotion, do you rejoice with them or do you envy them? When they lose, do you feel the loss with them, or do you feel just a tiny pinprick of satisfaction?

I've heard it said, "Maturity begins to grow when you can sense your concern for others outweighing your concern for yourself."

Maturing believers care very much about the things others are experiencing.

Affectionate Friendship

The third checkpoint is friendship and affection: "Let all be . . . brotherly."

The word translated here as "brotherly" is from the Greek word *philos*, which has in mind the love of an affectionate friend. The poet Samuel Coleridge once described friendship as "a sheltering tree." When you have this quality, the branches of your friendship reach out over the lives of others, giving them shelter, shade, rest, relief, and encouragement.

Much has been written about the importance of friendship. James Boswell said, "We cannot tell the precise moment when friendship is formed. As in filling a vessel drop by drop, there is at last a drop which makes it run over; so in a series of kindnesses there is at last one which makes the heart run over." Longfellow wrote, "Ah! How good it feels, the hand of an old friend." Isn't that true!

Friends give comfort. We find strength near them. They bear fruit that provides nourishment and encouragement. When something troublesome occurs in our life, we pick up the phone and call a friend, needing the comfort he or she provides. I think there are few things more lonely than having no friend to call. Friends also care enough about us to hold us accountable . . . but we never doubt their love or respect.

Are you cultivating such friends? Are you being a friend? Are there a few folks who will stand near you, sheltering you with their branches?

Jay Kesler, my long-time friend and currently the president of Taylor University, has said that one of his great hopes in life is to wind up with at least eight people who will attend his funeral without once checking their watches. I love it! Do you have eight people who'll do that?

As we mature, it is healthy for us to have a circle of friends who lovingly hold us close, regardless . . . who care about our pain, who are there for us when we can't make it on our own. The flip side of that is equally healthy—our being friends like that to others. Works both ways. As we mature our friendships deepen.

Kindheartedness

The fourth checkpoint is kindheartedness: "Let all be . . . kindhearted." The Greek term here can also be translated "compassionate," and it is used in the Gospels to describe Jesus.

And seeing the multitudes, He *felt compassion* for them, because they were distressed and downcast like sheep without a shepherd. (Matt. 9:36, italics added)

As a good shepherd, Jesus looked at humanity's lost sheep who were scattered, frightened, and hungry. What He saw pulled at His heartstrings. He was full of tenderness for them. He had compassion for them. Just as these hurting people touched the heart of the Savior, so should hurting people today touch our hearts. If they do, it's a definite sign of spiritual growth. No one who is mature is ever so important that the needs of others no longer matter.

I've just finished reading a fascinating volume, *Character Above All*. It is a compilation of ten essays on the ten United States presidents from Franklin Roosevelt in the 1930s to George Bush in the 1990s, each written by people who knew those presidents well—friends, speechwriters, fellow politicians, and other colleagues who worked alongside them.

My favorite was the chapter on Ronald Reagan, who served our country from 1981–1989. His speechwriter, Peggy Noonan, wrote the piece and captured the essence of his character in twenty-two pages. Wonderful reading!

She concludes with a story about, in her words, "the almost Lincolnian kindness that was another part of Reagan's character . . . everyone who worked with Reagan has a story about his kindness." Before I retell that story, go back and read those eleven words. Wouldn't it be great if that could be said about each of us? Wouldn't it be wonderful to be remembered for our kindness?

In highlighting this quality in Reagan's character, Noonan tells the story of Frances Green, an eighty-three-year-old woman who lived by herself on social security in a town just outside San Francisco. She had little money, but for eight years she'd been sending one dollar a year to the Republican National Convention.

Then one day Frances got an RNC fund-raising letter in the mail, a beautiful piece on thick, cream-colored paper with black-and-gold lettering. It invited the recipient to come to the White House to meet President Reagan. She never noticed the little RSVP card that suggested a positive reply needed to be accompanied by a generous donation. She thought she'd been invited because they appreciated her dollar-a-year support.

Frances scraped up every cent she had and took a four-day train ride across America. Unable to afford a sleeper, she slept sitting up in coach. Finally she arrived at the White House gate: a little elderly woman with white hair, white powder all over her face, white stockings, an old hat with white netting, and an all-white dress, now yellow with age. When she got up to the guard at the gate and gave her name, however, the man frowned, glanced over his official list, and told her that her name wasn't there. She couldn't go in. Frances Green was heartbroken.

A Ford Motor Company executive who was standing in line behind her watched and listened to the little scenario. Realizing something was wrong, he pulled Frances aside and got her story. Then he asked her to return at nine o'clock the next morning and meet him there. She agreed. In the meantime, he made contact with Anne Higgins, a presidential aide, and got clearance to give her a tour of the White House and introduce her to the president. Reagan agreed to see her, "of course."

The next day was anything but calm and easy at the White House. Ed Meese had just resigned. There had been a military uprising abroad. Reagan was in and out of high-level secret sessions. But Frances Green showed up at nine o'clock, full of expectation and enthusiasm.

The executive met her, gave her a wonderful tour of the White House, then quietly walked her by the Oval Office, thinking maybe, at best, she might get a quick glimpse of the president on her way out. Members of the National Security Council came out. High-ranking generals were coming and going. In the midst of all the hubbub, President Reagan glanced out and saw Frances Green. With a smile, he gestured her into his office.

As she entered, he rose from his desk and called out, "Frances! Those darn computers, they fouled up again! If I'd known you were coming I would have come out there to get you myself." He then invited her to sit down, and they talked leisurely about California, her town, her life and family.

The president of the United States gave Frances Green a lot of time that day—more time than he had. Some would say it was time wasted. But those who say that didn't know Ronald Reagan, according to Peggy Noonan. He knew this woman had nothing to give him, but she needed something he could give her. And so he (as well as the Ford executive) took time to be kind and compassionate.[1]

In our high-tech, cyberspace era it is so easy to become distant. We can live our lives untouched and untouchable. In a fast-lane world it isn't difficult to become uncaring and preoccupied with our own agendas. The freeway of life requires that we keep moving, no matter what we see happening around us. The pace at which we travel does not allow us to stop easily. And even if we could, we've seen the stories in the news about people who stopped to help and were rebuffed, mugged, or carjacked—even murdered. So we learn to keep our eyes straight ahead and keep going . . . fast! The homeless person on the sidewalk? The mentally disturbed stranger at the mall? Hurry past. Just keep looking straight ahead, moving past them, down the road of life.

Of course, we need to be wise; we must use discernment. Still, is there no place for kindheartedness and compassion in our world? Is there no time for tender mercies?

Read again the words that appear at the end of Ephesians 4:

> And be kind to one another, tender-hearted, forgiving each other, just as God in Christ also has forgiven you. (Eph. 4:32)

Maturing people are tender people. How valuable they are in a busy society like ours!

Humility

The fifth checkpoint is humility: "Let all be . . . humble in spirit." The phrase "humble in spirit" literally means "lowly" or "bowed down" in mind. It speaks of an internal attitude rather than an external appearance. Humility isn't a show we put on; in fact, if we think we're humble, we're probably not. And in our day of self-promotion, self-assertion, spotlighting "celebrities of the faith," and magnifying the flesh, this quality—so greatly valued by the Lord Jesus—is a rare commodity indeed. Oswald Chambers writes of this so insightfully:

> We have a tendency to look for wonder in our experience, and we mistake heroic actions for real heroes. It's one thing to go through a crisis grandly, yet quite another to go through every day glorifying God when there is no witness, no limelight, and no one paying even the remotest attention to us. If we are not looking for halos, we at least want something that will make people say, "What a wonderful man of prayer he is!" or "What a great woman of devotion she is!" If you are properly devoted to the Lord Jesus, you have reached the lofty height where no one would ever notice you personally. All that is noticed is the power of God coming through you all the time.
>
> We want to be able to say, "Oh, I have had a wonderful call from God!" But to do even the most humbling tasks to the glory of God takes the Almighty God Incarnate working in us.[2]

If you are blessed with abilities, if you are gifted, if you are used by God, it is easy to start believing your own stuff. Yet one of the marks of a truly mature life is humility of spirit.

> It can be said without qualification that no human being can consider himself mature if he narrows the use of his efforts, talents, or means to his own personal advantage. The very concept of maturity rests on the degree of inner growth that is characterized by a yearning within the individual to transcend his self-concentration by extending himself into the lives of others. In other words, maturity is a stage in his development when to live with himself in a satisfying manner it becomes imperative for him to give as well as to receive.[3]

A truly humble person looks for opportunities to give himself freely to others rather than holding back, to release rather than hoarding, to build up rather than tearing down, to serve rather than being served, to learn from others rather than clamoring for the teaching stand. How blessed are those who learn this early in life.

Carl Sandberg once related the story about a mother who brought her newborn son to General Robert E. Lee for a blessing. The southern gentleman tenderly cradled the lad in his arms then looked at the mother and said, "Ma'am, please teach him that he must deny himself."[4]

Forgiveness

Thus far, Peter has written about how maturity affects how we think and how we feel. In his last three checkpoints, found in verses 9 through 11, he tells us how maturity affects *what we do and what we say*. In verse 9 he tells us not to return evil for evil. In other words, be willing to forgive.

> . . . not returning evil for evil, or insult for insult, but giving a blessing instead; for you were called for the very purpose that you might inherit a blessing. (1 Pet. 3:9)

Isn't that a great statement? It touches all the important bases regarding forgiveness. Just look at the four steps in it; observe the process.

First, when we have true forgiveness in our hearts, we refuse to get back or get even.

Second, we restrain from saying anything ugly in return.

Third, we return good for evil, "giving a blessing instead [of evil or insult]."

And fourth, we keep in mind that we were called to endure such harsh treatment.

It's easy to miss that last one, isn't it? I thought at first I was misreading it, and then I went back to chapter 2 and found that's what Peter says over there too. So he must mean it. Do you remember his earlier comment?

What credit is there if, when you sin and are harshly treated, you endure it with patience? But if when you do what is right and suffer for it you patiently endure it, this finds favor with God. For you have been called for this purpose. (1 Pet. 2:20–21a)

What is a sure sign that I'm growing up? When I stop fighting back. When I take the chip off my shoulder. When I stop working on my clever answer so I can punch back with a sarcastic jab.

Whenever the urge to get even comes over us, it's important for us to realize that retaliation is a sign of adolescence while restraint is a mark of maturity.

A Controlled Tongue

"Let him who means to love life and see good days
refrain his tongue from evil and his lips from speaking guile."
(1 Pet. 3:10)

You knew we'd get around to this one, didn't you? The tongue . . . what a battle! Warnings about the tongue are threaded throughout the Bible. In fact, in this verse and the one that follows Peter is quoting from Psalm 34:12–16.

Here he says to "refrain" your tongue from evil. Actually the psalmist used a little more forceful language: "Keep your tongue from evil." The idea is to get control of your tongue, or, as James puts it, put a bridle on it. It's the idea of holding it back from galloping headlong into greater evil (see James 3:1–10). Control your tongue!

Show me a person who has learned to refrain from gossip, to refrain from passing on confidential information, to refrain from making an unverified comment, and I'll show you somebody who is well on his or her way to maturity.

You really want to love life? You want to see good days? Gain better control of your tongue. Life will be happier for you. It'll even be easier for you. You'll see better days.

Some never learn this lesson. Remember the classic grave marker from jolly old England?

Beneath this sod,
this lump of clay,
lies Arabella Young,
who, on the 24th of May
began to hold her tongue.

Will it take death to control your tongue? It need not! Pray that God will control your tongue, starting today! Pray that He will muzzle your mouth when someone says, "Please don't share this with anyone else." When someone speaks to you in confidence, seal the information in the secret vault of your mind.

Believe me, I'm a preacher, and I know how tempting it is to use real-life examples in my sermon illustrations, especially family-related examples. I heard recently about a preacher up in the Northwest who pays his kids a royalty of a dollar every time he uses them in an illustration! He asks permission, they approve, he tells the story, they get a buck. That'll curb a loose tongue real quick!

A mark of maturity is a controlled tongue.

A verse in Psalm 141 puts all of this so clearly. It's from the ancient writings of David, and I've often thought of it as a great prayer with which to begin each day.

Set a guard, O Lord, over my mouth;
Keep watch over the door of my lips. (Ps. 141:3)

How are you doing on the checklist so far? Unity. Mutual interest. Friendship and affection. Kindheartedness and compassion. Humility. Forgiveness. A controlled tongue. Pretty convicting list, isn't it? But if we wish to have hope beyond our immaturity, these qualities are worth our time and attention. And there's one more twofold checkpoint.

Purity and Peace

"And let him turn away from evil and do good;
let him seek peace and pursue it.
"For the eyes of the Lord are upon the righteous,

And his ears attend to their prayer,
But the face of the Lord is against those who do evil."
(1 Pet. 3:11–12)

Look again at Peter's counsel. "Turn away from evil and do good." That's purity. "Seek peace and pursue it." That's peace. And then he tells us that the Lord is watching us and listening to us. Why? Because He cares about our modeling these qualities.

The eyes and ears of the Lord are emblematic of God's providential care for His people. What a wonderful reason for pursuing purity and peace—the promise of God's providential care!

A Final Glance at the Checklist

That's quite a checklist, isn't it? Eight distinct notches to mark our Christian maturity. How do you measure up?

We're told to grow up. We're told to press on to maturity. But growing up is never easy. We all have areas of trouble, setbacks, stumbling points along the way. (I don't know of one item on this list that isn't a struggle for me at various times in my own life.) So those are the things that we pray about, for "His ears attend to our prayers."

Here's a practical suggestion. Go over that list at the end of every month. Write it out and stick it where you will see it. Put it under a refrigerator magnet. Tape it to your mirror. Ask God for strength in these eight areas.

As children of God moving toward maturity, let's be committed to harmony, to a spirit of unity. Let's engage in a mutual interest in each other's lives. Let's develop friendships marked by affection, by "touchable love"—love that is genuine and demonstrative. Let's be kindhearted and compassionate. Let's exhibit humility of spirit and a mind that is concerned about others instead of ourselves. Finally, let's forgive, control our tongues, and pursue purity and peace.

I am grateful airline pilots take the time to check their lists before we take off. I'm especially glad they don't shrug their shoulders when they see a bulge on one of the tires and say, "Well, we'll just hope for the best." I'm glad they don't ignore the smallest detail, even though they've gone down the same list hundreds of times in their careers. I'm glad they don't take my life and safety for granted. That's why they are willing to return to that list again and again and again.

We dare not take our Christian maturity for granted either. That's why we must return to God's checklist again and again and again.

We dare not do any less if we hope to get beyond a life of immaturity.

A Prayer for Hope Beyond Immaturity

Father, thank You for the reminder today of things that are such an important part of our lives. Though none of these qualities is new, we continue to need the reminder. How often we have come asking for help in one or more of these areas. You've heard our pleas on many occasions. We so want to be growing toward maturity . . . but the journey takes forever! And so, this very moment, we thank You for the Lord Jesus Christ, our model and our master, who fulfilled each of these marks of maturity and dozens of other character qualities to perfection, though fully man. Thank You for the hope we have that Your Holy Spirit will be with us each step of our way on our road to maturity. We certainly need His empowerment to keep us going and growing.

I would ask, finally, that You give us hope beyond our immaturity. Guard us from discouragement as we look back over the checklist and realize how far we have to go. Remind us that we've come a long way toward the goal, by Your grace. Through Jesus Christ I pray.

AMEN

9

Hope Beyond Bitterness

When Life
"Just Ain't Fair"

AN OLD FRENCH fairy tale tells the story of two daughters—one bad and the other good. The bad daughter was the favorite of her mother, but the good daughter was unjustly neglected, despised, and mistreated.

One day, while drawing water from the village well, the good daughter met a poor woman who asked for a drink. The girl responded with kind words and gave the woman a cup of water. The woman, actually a fairy in disguise, was so pleased with the little girl's kindness and good manners that she gave her a gift.

"Each time you speak," said the woman, "a flower or jewel will come out of your mouth."

When the little girl got home, her mother began to scold her for taking so long to bring the water. The girl started to apologize, and two roses, two pearls, and two diamonds came out of her mouth.

Her mother was astonished. But after hearing her daughter's story and seeing the number of beautiful jewels that came out in the telling, the mother called her other daughter and sent her forth to get the same gift. The bad daughter, however, was reluctant to be seen performing the lowly task of drawing water, so she grumbled sourly all the way to the well.

When the bad daughter got to the well, a beautiful queenly woman—that same fairy in another disguise—came by and asked for a drink. Disagreeable and proud, the girl responded rudely. As a result, she received her reward too. Each time she opened her mouth, she emitted snakes and toads.[1]

How's that for poetic justice!

There's something in each one of us that longs for circumstances to be fair, isn't there? Maybe that's why fairy tales are so appealing. Good people receive their rewards and "live happily ever after" while bad people are soundly punished. Life works out, justice is done, and fairness reigns supreme.

Unfortunately, real life doesn't usually turn out that way. Every child needs to be taught, "Fairness is rare." Every epitaph could read, "Life is difficult."

Our lives are haunted by unfairness when we want fairness. Instead of justice we are surrounded by injustice. We want deceit exposed, dishonesty revealed, and truth rewarded. But things don't work out that way. At least not as we perceive them.

Some families have been racked by unfairness. A mate leaves a loving, faithful partner. Disease steals a loved one prematurely. An unfair situation at work or at school keeps escalating.

Life just doesn't turn out fair for some . . . for most!

Truly, life *is* difficult. But therein lies some of life's best lessons.

I was reminded of those words when I read this astonishing statement by a well-known British writer and radio personality:

> Contrary to what might be expected, I look back on experiences that at the time seemed especially desolating and painful with particular satisfaction. Indeed, I can say with complete truthfulness that everything I have learned in my seventy-five years in this world, everything that has truly enhanced and enlightened my existence, has been through affliction and not through happiness. In other words, if it ever were to

be possible to eliminate affliction from our earthly existence by means of some drug or other medical mumbo jumbo . . . the result would not be to make life delectable, but to make it too banal and trivial to be endurable. This, of course, is what the Cross signifies. And it is the Cross, more than anything else, that has called me inexorably to Christ.[2]

Now it is one thing to read those words from a man like Malcolm Muggeridge and almost be moved to tears. It's another thing to embrace them in our own lives. I know there isn't a person reading this who hasn't, at some point, had reason to become bitter because of the way you were treated by someone or because of some "unfair" affliction or experience. Everyone can blame someone for something!

As Christians we know that, ultimately, good will triumph over evil and that our God is just and kind and fair. But what can we do with the injustices and unfairnesses in the meantime? How can we keep pressing on in spite of such mistreatment?

Two Different and Distinct Perspectives

Our response to unfairness, as with all other issues, is based on our perspective—the particular vantage point from which we look at life. Basically, in this case, we have two perspectives to choose from: the human perspective or the divine.

The Human Perspective

Our natural, human perspective contends, "Since life isn't fair, I'm going to get my share. I'm going to look out for number one. I'm going to spend my energy getting my own back or setting things straight or making it right. I'm not going to take it any longer."

Our world is full of literature and counselors who will help you carry out this agenda. The problem is, you may get even but you won't get peace. You may feel better for the short term, but you won't get lasting satisfaction. You may find a way to channel your anger, but if retaliation is your major goal, you will not glorify God. Those who live their lives from this perspective are more likely to end their lives as bitter, cynical, hostile people. Tragically, I have just described how the majority of Americans choose to live.

The Divine Perspective

Fortunately, we do have another option, and we find it clearly spelled out for us in 1 Peter.

> "For the eyes of the Lord are upon the righteous,
> And His ears attend to their prayer,
> But the face of the Lord is against those who do evil."
> (1 Pet. 3:12)

The principle that Peter gives us is this: God misses nothing. He's looking out for us. He's listening to our prayers. And He is completely aware of the evil that is happening to us.

Don't ever think He has missed the evil. He sees, and He remembers. He may be long-suffering, but He doesn't compromise His justice. Not only is His eye on the righteous, His face is against evil. Ultimately, good will overcome evil. In the end, God wins!

But if this is true, we wonder, why doesn't He do something about evil? Why does He let it go on so long? Because God's time line is infinite—He doesn't close His books at the end of the month. It may take a lifetime—or longer—before justice is served. But in the end, count on it, *God will be just*. In the end, He will "work everything together for good" and for His glory.

That thought gives us hope beyond bitterness. If we don't believe that and if we don't focus on that, we become the loser. We spend our years like a rat in a sewer pipe, existing in the tight radius of cynicism and bitterness. Ultimately, we become, in our aging years, angry old men and jaded old women.

★

Some Helpful Insights and Techniques to Keep Hope Alive

Building on this divine perspective, Peter gives us five ways we can live in an unfair and inequitable world. But first there's a general principle we need to underscore.

A General Principle

And who is there to harm you if you prove zealous for what is good? (1 Pet. 3:13)

If we were to paraphrase this verse, we could say that those who live honest lives will not usually suffer harm. *Usually.* There are exceptions, of course, to almost every rule, as we will see below. But as a general rule, if you live a life of purity and integrity, in the long run you usually won't suffer as much as those who habitually traffic in evil.

For example, if you pay your debts, chances are good that you won't get into financial trouble. If you pay all your taxes on time, you probably won't have the IRS on your case. If you take care of your body—get sufficient exercise and sleep, watch your diet and your stress level—chances are good that you will live a healthier life than those who don't. If you help others, chances are good that when you are in need someone will be there to help you. To paraphrase Peter's principle, those who do what is right are usually not in harm's way. *Usually* that's the rule.

Occasional Inequities

However, to return to reality, because life is difficult, there are times when life "just ain't fair." So there will be are times when, despite that general principle, despite your righteous life, despite your faithful walk with God, situations turn on you. And it's these exceptions to the rule that Peter is addressing in chapter 3, verses 11 through 17. He begins with a general summation of the condition.

But even if you should suffer for the sake of righteousness, you are blessed. (1 Pet. 3:14a)

Before going on, notice the words, "But even if you should." In New Testament Greek, there are four conditions introduced by the word *if*. Three were quite common. The first-class condition, meaning "assumed as true," was a common usage (see Matt. 4:3, 6); the second-class condition, meaning "assumed as not true," was also commonly used (see Gal. 1:10); the third-class condition, meaning "maybe, maybe not," was frequently employed by writers (as seen earlier in 1 Pet. 3:13). The fourth-class condition, meaning "unlikely but possible," is rarely used in Scripture. Interestingly, this is the condition Peter uses here in verse 14. It could be paraphrased, "It is unlikely that you should suffer for the sake of righteousness, but if you should. . . . " That, alone, ought to give us a boost of fresh hope!

Then Peter goes on to suggest five ways you and I should respond if this happens. Remember, this is not my advice; this is God's advice. Human advice says, "Kick 'em in the teeth. Get even." That's not good advice, but it's often heard. So we need to know what God has to say about how to respond when we have done what is right but wrong is done to us in return.

It might help if you wrote these responses down on a three-by-five card and keep them handy. I'd suggest that you look at the card at least once a day. You might want to stick it on your bathroom mirror or slide it under the glass of your desktop.

How are we to respond when the exception to the rule occurs?

First, consider yourself uniquely blessed by God.

As far as the injustice itself is concerned, Peter's surprising advice is, "Be happy! Consider yourself blessed!" James tells us something similar in the first chapter of his letter.

When all kinds of trials and temptations crowd into your lives, my brothers, don't resent them as intruders, but welcome them as friends! (James 1:2 PHILLIPS)

Sure sounds nice, you may say, but honestly now, how can we be happy and consider ourselves blessed when we've just been punched in the eye with the fist of injustice?

Well, we can do this by remembering two things: first, as we saw in chapter 6, we are called to patiently endure unfair treatment (see 1 Pet. 2:21; 3:9) so that when it comes we can know we're still experiencing God's plan and fulfilling our calling. Such treatment reminds us that God's hand is still on our lives. And second, someday we will be rewarded for our endurance of these undeserved trials (see Matt. 5:10–12; James 1:12).

Anybody can accept a reward graciously, and many people can even take their punishment patiently when they have done something wrong. But how many people are equipped to handle mistreatment after they've done right? Only Christians are equipped to do that. That is what makes believers stand out. That's our uniqueness. And, yes, there are occasions in life when we will be called for that very purpose. In the mystery of God's sovereign plan, we will be singled out. Then later, like Job, we will be rewarded for enduring those trials we did not deserve.

Remember Jesus' instruction?

"Blessed are those who have been persecuted for the sake of righteousness, for theirs is the kingdom of heaven. Blessed are you when men cast insults at you, and persecute you, and say all kinds of evil against you falsely, on account of Me. Rejoice, and be glad, for your reward in heaven is great, for so they persecuted the prophets who were before you." (Matt. 5:10–12)

Because of these promises (there are many similar ones throughout the Scriptures) Christians can do something different from all the rest of humanity. We can respond to injustice with a positive attitude. When we do, mouths drop open . . . and we're frequently given an opportunity to explain why we're not eaten up with revenge.

Second, don't panic and don't worry.

And do not fear their intimidation, and do not be troubled. (1 Pet. 3:14b)

It doesn't take a linguistic scholar to interpret that counsel. Peter puts his finger on two common responses. Panic and worry. I do both of those things when I operate in the flesh, don't you? But observe what Peter says.

First, look at the word *fear*. It comes from the original term *phobos*, from which we also get our word *phobia*. This kind of fear is the fear that seizes us with terror and causes us to take flight, running away from the pressure. Peter says, "Don't do that. There's no reason to run. Don't attempt to escape the trial. Don't panic."

In the second phrase he tells us that we don't need to "be troubled." The word *troubled* in Greek means "to be agitated, uneasy," the idea of feeling inner turmoil or agitation. Remember John 14:1, "Let not your heart be troubled"? Same root word here.

The energy and effort we expend worrying never solves a thing. In fact, it usually makes the situation worse for us, creating a terrible inner turmoil which, if allowed to intensify, can paralyze us.

Peter's counsel to us is that, even when trials are pressing in and people are trying to intimidate us, we can have a calmness of spirit. As far as the persecutor or instigator is concerned, we can be free from panic and worry. How? Why? Because we know that God is on our side.

Third, acknowledge Christ as Lord even over this event.

But sanctify Christ as Lord in your hearts . . . (1 Pet. 3:15a)

We often overlook the first phrase of this verse in our concentration on the second part:

. . . always being ready to make a defense to everyone who asks you to give an account for the hope that is in you. (1 Pet. 3:15b)

We usually apply those words to some public defense of the faith. While they may be used in that way, the verse actually appears in a context of wrong having come to us as a result of our doing what is right. And it says, "Do not fear . . . but in your hearts set apart [sanctify] Christ as Lord" (NIV).

You and I can do that in prayer. When we think a wrong has been done to us that we don't deserve, we can respond, "Lord, You're with me right now. You are here, and You have Your reasons for what is happening. You will not take advantage of me. You're much too kind to be cruel. You're much too good to be unjust. You care for me too much to let this get out of hand. Take charge. Use my integrity to defend me. Give me the grace to stay calm. Control my emotions. Be Lord over my present situation." In such a prayer, we "set apart Christ as Lord" in our hearts.

If I have prayed that sort of prayer once, I must have prayed it dozens of times. "Lord, there is no way I can set the record straight, it seems. It's getting more complicated and I find myself completely at Your disposal . . . at Your mercy. Take over, Lord. You be the sovereign Master over this moment. I can't change this person . . . I can't alter these circumstances. You be the Lord over this scene."

When our older daughter, Charissa, was in high school, she was on the cheerleading squad. One day at the church office I got an emergency call from her school. She had accidentally fallen from the top of a pyramid of the other cheerleaders during practice and landed on the back of her head. To her and everyone else's amazement, she couldn't move. It took me about fifteen minutes to drive from my study at the church to the school campus. I was praying that kind of prayer all the way. "Lord, You are in charge of this situation. I have no idea what I'm going to face. You be the Lord and Master. I am trusting You in all this."

When I got to the school, they already had Charissa immobilized on a wrap-around stretcher. I slipped to my knees beside her.

"Daddy, I can't move my fingers. My feet and legs are numb," she said. "I can't feel anything in my body very well. It's kind of tingling."

At that moment, I confess I had feelings of fear. But I leaned closer to Charissa and whispered in her ear, "Sweetheart, I will be with you through all of this. But more importantly, Jesus is here with you. He is Lord over this whole event."

Her mother and I were totally helpless. We had absolutely no control over the situation or over the healing of our daughter's body. She was at the mercy of God. I can still remember the deliberateness with which I acknowledged Christ as Lord in my heart and encouraged her to do the same. Cynthia and I waited for hours in the hospital hallway as extensive X-rays were taken and a team of physicians examined our daughter. We prayed fervently and confidently.

Today, Charissa is fine. She recovered with no lasting damage. She did have a fracture, but thankfully it wasn't an injury that resulted in paralysis. Had she been permanently paralyzed, we would still believe that God was in sovereign control. He would still be Lord!

A good example of someone who sanctified Christ as Lord in his heart is Stephen. When he gave an eloquent and penetrating defense of Jesus before the Jewish Sanhedrin, this infuriated many who heard him. Their hatred raged out of control. Do you remember his response?

> But being full of the Holy Spirit, he gazed intently into heaven and saw the glory of God, and Jesus standing at the right hand of God; and he said, "Behold, I see the heavens opened up and the Son of Man standing at the right hand of God." (Acts 7:55–56)

They wouldn't listen to him. They covered their ears and rushed upon him. They drove him out of the city and violently stoned him to death.

As Stephen died, "he called upon the Lord and said, 'Lord Jesus, receive my spirit!' And falling on his knees, he cried out with a loud voice, 'Lord, do not hold this sin against them!'" (Acts 7:59–60). And then he died.

Stephen didn't deserve their savage attack. He certainly didn't deserve death. Because of that, he could have died in bitterness and cynicism. He could have died with curses on his lips. Instead, he sanctified the moment to God and died with a prayer on his lips, asking forgiveness for those who so mercilessly killed him. When those men looked into Stephen's face, they didn't find their own hatred reflected back at them; they saw the reflection of the Savior's grace and love.

Like Stephen, we need to acknowledge Christ's control over our unfair circumstances and do our best to see that He is glorified in them. That is the only thing that will bring us lasting, peaceful satisfaction.

Fourth, be ready to give a witness.

> . . . . always being ready to make a defense to everyone who asks you to give an account for the hope that is in you, yet with gentleness and reverence. (1 Pet. 3:15b)

I'm intrigued by this. Some of us are so anxious to give a witness that we press it on others even when it isn't appropriate or when the timing isn't right. But this says we are to be ready *when they ask us* to give an account. And believe me, if you are handling mistreatment or unfairness or suffering for the glory of God, people will ask.

"How do you do it?" . . . "How do you handle this?" . . . "How do you live with it?" . . . "Why is it you haven't lost your joy?" . . . "What keeps you on your feet?" . . . "Why haven't you just turned tail and run?" . . . "Why haven't you fought back?" Common questions from curious onlookers.

"Be ready to make a defense . . . to give an account." The word *defense* comes from the term *apologia*. We get our word *apology* from this Greek word. It refers to making a verbal statement of defense. And *account* comes from the word *logos*, translated elsewhere in Scripture, "the word." At such times we are to be ready to give a verbal witness . . . a gentle and yet pointed declaration of the truth.

Stop and consider. Mistreatment is a perfect platform for a witness. Your neighbors will want to know how you stay calm in the midst of it, how you go through it without strongly reacting. Your friend at work will want to know, "How do you pull it off?"

Be ready to make a defense, to give an answer, to witness to anyone who asks. Seldom will there be a more opportune time to share your faith than when you are suffering and glorifying Him through it. Others who know what you are enduring will listen. You have earned the right to be heard. But don't miss the way you should testify: "with gentleness and reverence." Wise counsel from Peter, a man who had been broken.

William Barclay gives an excellent explanation of what our "defense" and "account" should be like.

> It must be *reasonable*. It is a *logos* [account] that the Christian must give, and a *logos* is a reasonable and intelligent statement of his position. . . . To do so we must know what we believe; we must have thought it out; we must be able to state it intelligently and intelligibly. . . .
>
> His defence must be given with *gentleness*. . . . The case for Christianity must be presented with winsomeness and with love. . . . Men may be wooed into the Christian faith when they cannot be bullied into it.
>
> His defence must be given *with reverence*. That is to say, any argument in which the Christian is involved must be carried on in a tone which God can hear with joy. . . . In any presentation of the Christian case and in any argument for the Christian faith, the accent should be the accent of love.[3]

And fifth, keep a good conscience.

Here Peter digs below the surface, turning up the rich soil of inner character. And what is the precious gem he is trying to unearth? *Integrity.*

> And keep a good conscience so that in the thing in which you are slandered, those who revile your good behavior in Christ may be put to shame. (1 Pet. 3:16)

Nothing speaks louder or more powerfully than a life of integrity. Absolutely nothing! Nothing stands the test like solid character. You can handle the blast like a steer in a blizzard. The ice may form on your horns, but you keep standing against the wind and the howling, raging storm because Christ is at work in your spirit. Character will always win the day. As Horace Greeley wrote: "Fame is a vapor, popularity an accident, riches take wing, and only character endures."

There is no more eloquent and effective defense than a life lived continually and consistently in integrity. It possesses invincible power to silence your slanderers.

The Underlying and Unwavering Principle

For it is better, if God should will it so, that you suffer for doing what is right than for doing what is wrong. (1 Pet. 3:17)

Simply stated, the principle is this: Unjust suffering is always better than deserved punishment. And sometimes—though we cannot fully explain why—it is God's will that His people should suffer for doing what is right.

An old Hebrew story tells of a righteous man who suffered undeservedly. He was a man who had turned away from evil, took care of his family, walked with God, and was renown for his integrity. But suddenly, without warning, and seemingly without reason, he lost everything he had: his flocks, his cattle, his servants, his children, and finally his health. This old Hebrew story is no fairy tale. It is the real account of a real person—Job.

Though he suffered terribly, and though he could never have foreseen it himself or understood it when it happened, Job has been remembered down through the ages and to this very day as a model of patient endurance. "The patience of Job" remains one of our axiomatic phrases.

I would not wish the life of Job on anyone. But, then, I'm not God. I've never been too good at directing anyone else's life. I have a hard enough time keeping my own on track. But I have observed a few "Jobs" in my years in ministry. They come under that fourth-class condition: "If He should will it so . . . it's unlikely but possible."

If you are one of those modern-day "Jobs," don't waste your time trying to figure out *why.* Someday all will be made clear. For now, follow the five responses outlined by Peter.

Dr. Bruce Waltke was my Hebrew professor during three of my years at Dallas Seminary. He has since become something of a mentor and friend. He is a brilliant man with a tender heart for God. When I was going through a very difficult time in my senior year in seminary and wanted some answers to the *whys*, Bruce said something like this: "Chuck, I've come to the place where I believe only on very rare occasions does God tell us why, so I've decided to stop asking." I found that to be very helpful counsel. From that point on, I began to acknowledge that I am not the "answer man" for events in life that don't make logical, human sense. I'm now convinced that even if He did explain His reasons, I would seldom understand. His ways are higher and far more profound than our finite minds can comprehend. So I now accept God's directions, and I live with them as best I can. And frankly, I leave it at that. I've found that such a response not only relieves me, it gives me hope beyond bitterness.

If God has called you to be a Job—a rare calling—remember that the Lord is not only full of compassion, He is also in full control. He will not leave you without hope. He offers us His promises:

> "For My thoughts are not your thoughts,
> Neither are your ways My ways," declares the LORD.
> "For as the heavens are higher than the earth,
> So are My ways higher than your ways,
> And My thoughts than Your thoughts." (Isa. 55:8–9)

> When a man's ways are pleasing to the LORD,
> He makes even his enemies to be at peace with him. (Prov. 16:7)

Listen to the counsel of Peter. Calmly and quietly let these five bits of counsel sink in.

- Consider yourself uniquely blessed by God.
- Do not run in panic or sit and worry.

- Acknowledge Christ as Lord even over this event.
- Be ready to give a witness.
- Keep a good conscience.

A Prayer for Hope Beyond Bitterness

Our Father, as we acknowledge Your Son as Lord, it is with a sigh, because we cannot deny the pain or ignore the difficulty of earthly trials. For some who read these words, the reality of this is almost unbearable. But being sovereign and being the One with full capacity to handle our needs, it is not beyond Your strength to take the burden and, in return, to give us the perspective we need.

Quiet our spirits. Give us a sense of relief as we face the inevitable fact that life is difficult and that there will be those rare moments when it will not be at all fair. Erase any hint of bitterness. Enable us to see beyond the present, to focus on the invisible, and to recognize that You are always there. Remind us, too, that Your ways are higher and far more profound than ours.

Thank You for the joy of this day. Thank You for the pleasure of a relationship with You and a few good, caring, loving friends. And especially, Father, thank You for the truth of Your Word that lives and abides forever. In the strong name of Him who is higher, Jesus the Lord.

AMEN

10

❖

Hope Beyond the Creeds

Focusing Fully
on
Jesus Christ

WHEN I WAS a little boy, my family moved to Houston, where my father had been hired to work at what was called, in those days during World War II, a "defense plant." Houston is a city of industry, and during those war years many of the industries retooled in order to manufacture implements, ammunition, and equipment for the war. The particular place where my father worked built transmissions for the rugged Sherman tank and landing gears for the powerful B-17 "Flying Fortresses."

We didn't see much of my dad during those five years because he was working ten to fifteen, sometimes even eighteen, hours a day, from six to seven days a week. Since our family had only one car, which Dad used each day to drive himself and several coworkers to the shop, the rest of our family had to walk to the grocery store, to school, and to church.

The closest church was a Methodist church at the end of our street. I still remember sitting in those wooden pews almost every Sunday. And every Sunday, as part of the worship-service liturgy of that particular Methodist church, we recited the Apostles' Creed.

I don't remember one sermon that was preached during those five years. I cannot recall any church-sponsored event that made an impact on me. But I clearly remember repeating the Apostles' Creed. In fact, I memorized that statement of faith in a matter of months simply because we repeated it Sunday after Sunday. You, too, may know these words well:

> I believe in God the Father Almighty, maker of heaven and earth;
> And in Jesus Christ, His only begotten Son, our Lord, who was conceived by the Holy Spirit, born of the Virgin Mary, suffered under Pontius Pilate, was crucified, dead and buried; He descended into hell; the third day He rose again from the dead; He ascended into heaven, and sits at the right hand of God the Father Almighty; from thence He shall come to judge the living and the dead.
> I believe in the Holy Spirit, the holy catholic church, the communion of saints, the forgiveness of sins, the resurrection of the body, and the life everlasting. Amen.

Even though I was only a small boy when I recited the creed, there were two statements in it that troubled me. My first concern was, "I believe in the holy catholic church." I knew our family wasn't Catholic, so how could I keep saying I believed in the Holy Catholic Church? Then, at some point, a youth worker explained to me that catholic (small "c") really meant "universal," so what we were really saying was, "I believe in the universal church." No problem.

More difficult to resolve, however, was the part where we said that Jesus Christ "descended into hell." That troubled me. There was nobody around who could answer that for me, not even my mother. Interestingly, it was almost twenty years later in a Greek class in seminary that I experienced a flashback to those days as a little boy in the Methodist church. We were digging into the text at the end of 1 Peter 3, and I came across the verse that described in Scripture what I had stated as a little boy but had never understood.

Let me remind you of the last five verses in 1 Peter 3:

For Christ also died for sins once for all, the just for the unjust, in order that He might bring us to God, having been put to death in the flesh, but made alive in the spirit; in which also He went and made proclamation to the spirits now in prison, who once were disobedient, when the patience of God kept waiting in the days of Noah, during the construction of the ark, in which a few, that is, eight persons, were brought safely through the water. And corresponding to that, baptism now saves you—not the removal of dirt from the flesh, but an appeal to God for a good conscience—through the resurrection of Jesus Christ, who is at the right hand of God, having gone into heaven, after angels and authorities and powers had been subjected to Him. (1 Pet. 3:18–22)

Isn't that a grand statement of faith? It's almost like another creed that we might recite in church from Sunday to Sunday.

Our Example

I have found in my study of the Bible that one of the best rules to follow if I'm going to understand any particular section of Scripture is to look at the whole scene (the context) before I try to work my way through each verse. Sort of like looking at the forest before examining the trees.

Following that rule, we first need to answer a primary question: What's the main subject of this paragraph? As you may recall from the subject we dealt with in chapter 9, it is unjust suffering. Remember the words of Peter?

For it is better, if God should will it so, that you suffer for doing what is right rather than for doing what is wrong. (1 Pet. 3:17)

If unjust suffering is the main subject, what's the point of the whole paragraph? Clearly, it is this: blessings follow suffering for well-doing.

Now at this point, immediately after Peter has written verse 17, the Spirit of God prompts him to mention the One who best exemplifies that truth. Who in every believer's mind would best exemplify blessing following unjust suffering? Obviously, Christ. And that's why Peter at verse 18 says, "For Christ." He doesn't say so, but we could insert in parentheses, "As an example."

> For Christ (as an example) also died for sins . . . the just for the unjust, in order that He might bring us to God . . . .

What is the blessing that came to us following Christ's unjust suffering? Our salvation. And what was the blessing for Him, personally, following His unjust suffering? His resurrection. That is stated at the end of verse 20.

The focus of attention here is Jesus Christ, not the recipients of the letter or those who would read it centuries later. It is Jesus Himself. He alone is the focal point. Look at this great statement of faith regarding the Lord Jesus.

Verse 18: He "died for sins." That's His *crucifixion*.

Verse 19: "He . . . made *proclamation*."

Verse 21: "through the *resurrection* of Jesus Christ."

Verse 22: "who is at the right hand of God . . . after angels and authorities and powers had been subjected to Him." That's *exaltation*.

What we have here, in brief, is a survey of the crucifixion, proclamation, resurrection, and exaltation of the Lord Jesus Christ. Peter is clearly and openly highlighting some major doctrines related to Jesus Christ. So far, so good. But the paragraph also includes a digression (see verses 19–21).

Sometimes while writing a letter you'll mention a subject that is important to you, which reminds you of something not as pertinent as the subject but since it completes the picture, you add it. It might take another paragraph to do so, or it might just take a sentence or two. In this instance, Peter completes the overall thought regarding Christ by adding some details . . . things seldom mentioned elsewhere in the Bible. In fact, there are two knotty issues here that every serious student of the New Testament struggles with. One of them has to do with Christ's "descent into hell" (see verses 19–20), and the other has to do with what appears to be an affirmation of baptismal regeneration, "baptism now saves you" (verse 21)—more about these later.

Our Entree

Having considered the overall context, then, let me come to the central theme of the passage. Look back again at verse 18. This is one of those all-encompassing verses that states the gospel in its briefest and most concentrated form. That concentrated statement concerning the Lord Jesus is beautiful: "Christ also died for sins once for all." We don't have to relive or redo the death of Christ. We don't have to anticipate His dying another time or several other times. He has died "once for all." It was the death of all deaths, permanently solving the sin problem.

When Christ came, He was the perfect substitute for sin. And as a lamb without spot and without blemish, He hung on the cross and died. His blood became the one-and-only, all-sufficient payment to God for sins. The anger of God was satisfied, because Christ's payment for sin settled the account, once for all. Furthermore, all the debt against us was wiped away as Christ's righteousness was credited to our account. It wasn't fair for Him to die. He was just. He died, "the just for the unjust."

You may not know it, but you're mentioned (by implication) in Scripture on a number of occasions. And here is one of those times. Your name could appear in the place of the words "the unjust."

Let me state it in my case: "For Christ also died for sins once for all, the just for Chuck Swindoll. . . ."

Or you could put *your* name there: "The just for [your name]."

Why did He do it? "In order that He might bring us to God." One very careful student of the New Testament calls this "an entree." Our Lord Jesus Christ, in dying on the cross, provided us with "an entree" into heaven. He gave us access. As a result of His death, the access to heaven is now permanently paved. It is available to all who believe in the Lord Jesus Christ.

He "was put to death in the flesh, but made alive in the Spirit." So what is He doing now? "He is at the right hand of God." Maybe you didn't know that—a lot of people don't know what Christ is currently doing. He has ascended from this earth, and He has gone back to the place of glory in bodily form. (He is the only member of the Godhead who is visible. God the Father is in spirit form. God the Spirit is in spirit form. The only visible member of the Trinity is the Lord Jesus Christ.) He sits at the right hand of God making intercession for us. He's praying for us. He is moved by our needs; He is touched with the feelings of our infirmities. He is there for us, His people, and He is interceding for us. Since He is at the right hand of God, there is no question of His place of authority.

The Apostles' Creed is correct when it says, "He ascended into heaven and sits at the right hand of God; from thence He shall come to judge the living and the dead." He will come to judge both, and that judgment awaits His return to this earth. What powerful truths are here! Peter knew his theology!

His Proclamation

All that is fairly clear . . . now the tough part. First of all, let's address the subject of Jesus' descent, as the creed calls it, "into hell." Referring to the Lord Jesus Christ, Peter tracks His itinerary following His crucifixion.

> . . . in which also He went and made proclamation to the spirits now in prison, who once were disobedient, when the patience of God kept waiting in the days of Noah, during the construction of the ark, in which a few, that is, eight persons, were brought safely through the water. (1 Pet. 3:19–20)

What in the world does that mean? When exactly did this occur? Who were these spirits that He visited? And what is the "proclamation" that He made? Good questions.

Let me draw upon your knowledge of the Scriptures and ask you to remember a scene back in the days before the Flood. It's recorded in the sixth chapter of Genesis. (When you have time, you may want to go back and read it.) We are told that during this period the depravity of men and women reached an all-time high. Their wickedness was so severe that it grieved the heart of God—He was sorry He had even created humanity!

> Then the LORD saw that the wickedness of man was great on the earth, and that every intent of the thoughts of his heart was only evil continually. And the LORD was sorry that He had made man on the earth, and he was grieved in His heart. (Gen. 6:5–6)

If you read this in the context of the first four verses of Genesis 6, you learn of an amazing and seldom-mentioned series of events that had happened. There was sexual cohabitation at that time between spirit beings and women on this earth. It is believed that during the antediluvian era—the time prior to the Flood—these spirits came in bodily form and somehow had intercourse with human women. As a result, a generation of supernatural beings were born—admittedly a strange phenomenon rarely mentioned by preachers and therefore seldom taught to Christians.

When the Flood came, it put an end to that heinous lifestyle and that freakish generation. Also, God's judgment fell upon those spirits who cohabited with women, and He placed them in a location called, in the original, *Tartarus*. It was a special place, described here as "a prison." It was there Jesus made His victorious proclamation.

What was this proclamation? I find it helpful to know that this is not the word used for proclaiming the gospel. Rather, it is a word, *kerusso*, used to describe someone "heralding" a statement. It denotes one who proclaims that the king has made a decision or that someone is declaring a certain edict—actually, it can refer to a proclamation of any kind. Jesus openly and forthrightly proclaimed that He had fulfilled His mission. He had died for the sins of the world. The work of salvation was accomplished.

When I put all of this together, I come to the following conclusion. I believe verses 19 and 20 describe the time immediately after Jesus died. His body was taken down from the cross and placed in a grave, but His inner being, His soul and spirit, descended into the shadowy depths of the earth, into the place of Tartarus (the creed calls it "hell"), where the antediluvian wicked spirits were imprisoned. Once there, He proclaimed to them His victorious death over sin and His power over the enemy, Satan himself. It was this proclamation that caused them to realize their work of attempting to corrupt and confuse the human race had been in vain. All of their attempts to sabotage the cross, to keep it from happening, were null and void. He went to that place to proclaim His victory at Calvary.

Our Faith

That brings us to the second question raised by verse 21, where we read: "Baptism now saves you." What does this mean?

Again, we can't ignore the context. First, we must understand that the Flood is in Peter's mind. He has just said so (verse 20). It was the Flood that brought death and destruction to those who didn't believe. It was also the water that brought deliverance to those who did—eight of them. Imagine that. Though there were multiple millions of people, only eight got in the ark. Along with the animals, only eight human beings believed and lived!

It was the ark floating on the water that got them through the Flood, which became a beautiful picture to the early church. In fact, the ark was frequently used to describe salvation. Today, we see the cross as our ark. It is our way to life. It is the way we get through the death-like world about us. Thus, baptism became another beautiful expression or picture of just such a deliverance from death—through the water.

Baptism symbolizes deliverance, just as the ark did. In fact, look at the words in parentheses, which in my Bible, the New American Standard version, are placed between dashes:

And corresponding to that, baptism now saves you—not the removal of dirt from the flesh, but an appeal to God for a good conscience—through the resurrection of Jesus Christ. (1 Pet. 3:21, italics added)

Baptism doesn't cleanse anyone, either literally or symbolically. It does not cleanse us externally, as a bath does; nor does it cleanse us within. But, indeed, it is our appeal to God for a good conscience. That which saves us is faith in the Lord Jesus Christ, and this is what is illustrated beautifully in baptism as we come out of the water. The Living Bible, in 1 Peter 3:21, offers a fine paraphrase of this parenthetical section.

(That, by the way, is what baptism pictures for us: In baptism we show that we have been saved from death and doom by the resurrection of Christ; not because our bodies are washed clean by the water, but because in being baptized we are turning to God and asking Him to cleanse our *hearts* from sin.)

Now you understand why in a baptismal service each candidate testifies personally to his or her faith in Jesus Christ. Nothing in the waters of baptism cleanses the flesh or the soul, but the water does illustrate what has already happened in the life of the redeemed.

Practical Principles

As we wrap up our thoughts here, let me mention a couple of very practical principles we can draw from this section of Peter's letter.

First, when unjust suffering seems unbearable, remember the crucifixion. I know you've heard that before, but it is something we cannot be reminded of too often. It can be a wonderful comfort. It is remarkable how focusing on the Lord Jesus Christ's body hanging on the cross as a payment for sin really does help alleviate the pain in my life. About the time I start thinking my suffering is terribly unjust I turn my attention to what He endured; that does a lot to ease or even erase any sense of bitterness or resentment within me. And so, when unjust suffering seems unbearable, remember the crucifixion.

Second, when the fear of death steals your peace, remember the resurrection. There is nothing quite like the hope we derive from our Lord's resurrection. Every Easter we celebrate it. In fact, every Lord's Day we're to be reminded of it. Certainly the Apostles' Creed reinforces it. Which brings us back to where we began.

I believe in God the Father Almighty, maker of heaven and earth;

And in Jesus Christ, His only begotten Son, our Lord, who was conceived by the Holy Spirit, born of the Virgin Mary, suffered under Pontius Pilate, was crucified, dead and buried; He descended into hell; the third day He rose again from the dead; He ascended into heaven, and sits at the right hand of God the Father Almighty; from thence He shall come to judge the living and the dead.

I believe in the Holy Spirit. . . .

Despite the all-encompassing truths contained in these concise words, the most personal and crucial part of the creed is the first two words, "I believe." Without them, it's just a statement someone originated—a statement many worshipers recite every week without ever having any kind of personal relationship with Christ. A body of bright, godly, religious-minded men honed that statement to put in simple form the salient features of our faith. But without our faith, it's still just a creed—a statement of *their* faith. What we need most is a firm hope beyond any creed we may recite.

The question is, do I *believe* the truth of that statement? Do you *believe* it? If you do, there is hope for you beyond it or any other creed. And that hope is a heavenly home reserved for you.

A Prayer for Hope Beyond the Creeds

Father, thank You for the truth of Your Word, for its clarity and its simplicity. And, Lord, because it is so exact, there isn't any reason to doubt. We do believe. Freely and willingly and gratefully, we believe.

But our belief goes beyond any creed . . . far beyond any statement originated by humans, no matter how godly or sincere. With great faith, our Father, we believe in the Lord Jesus Christ who died for us. We believe He suffered unjustly. We believe His payment was sufficient to wash away sins. Our sins. And now that He has been raised and ascended, our Father, we believe that He is alive, interceding for us, and is coming again.

Because of Christ's crucifixion, proclamation, resurrection, and exaltation, give us a sense of peace when we face death. Give us a sense of hope when we suffer unjustly. Remind us that heaven is our ultimate hope. I pray in His matchless name, with great anticipation.

AMEN

11

Hope Beyond
the Culture

How to
Shock the
Pagan Crowd

STEPPING ONTO FOREIGN soil and into the midst of another language and culture for the first time in one's life can be an uneasy experience.

It happened to me while I served in the Marine Corps in the late 1950s. Our troopship had carried us across the Pacific, and my comrades and I were about to step onto Japanese soil. We eagerly anticipated being on land after such a long time at sea. For many of us, it was our first visit to a foreign country. We were surging with excitement, imagination, and every other emotion you could think of due to those seventeen days on the same ship. We were ready!

Before we left the ship, however, our company commander called all of us together. He stood in front of us, looked around at the group, and then, staring deeply into our eyes, he said loudly and sternly, "I want all of you men to remember that for the first time in your lives, *you are the foreigners*. This is not your country or your culture. Now you are the minority. These are not your fellow citizens. They do not speak your language. They know nothing of your homeland except what they see in you."

It was one of those "behave yourself" pep talks, but it went beyond that. Our commander was also saying, "You, as individuals, are representing the entire United States. Don't blow it! Don't become another example of 'the ugly American.' Act in such a way that the Japanese people will gain a good impression of your country and what America must be like. Make us proud, not ashamed." Those words rang in my ears for many days.

As Christians, we face a similar situation. Since our citizenship is in heaven, planet Earth is really not our home. For us, it is foreign soil. We are citizens of another realm. We belong to the kingdom of God. Consequently, we need to be on our best behavior; otherwise, people will get a distorted perception of what our homeland is like. As a result of our behavior, they will either be attracted to or repelled by heaven, the place we call home.

The old gospel song is still right on target.

> This world is not my home.
> I'm just a passin' through.
> My treasures are laid up
> Somewhere beyond the blue.[1]

It's true! But it's easy to forget. Maybe this is a good time to be reminded . . . we live in a pagan culture, surrounded by people who embrace a pagan philosophy and a pagan way of life.

Just consider the latest Broadway fare being ecstatically hailed as "the breakthrough musical of the nineties" . . . "the most exuberant and original American musical to come along this decade." The play, *Rent*, is set "among the artists, addicts, prostitutes, and street people of New York City's East Village." The leading characters are "a drug-addicted dancer in an S&M club who is suffering from AIDS" and a rock singer who is HIV positive. "AIDS is the shadow hovering over all the people in *Rent*, but the musical doesn't dwell on illness or turn preachy; it is too busy celebrating life and chronicling its characters' effort to squeeze out every last drop of it." Those characters are a gay teacher, a transvestite, and a lesbian attorney, among others.[2]

A friend of mine would call that "being mugged by reality," but that's the world we live in. Our earthly culture is pagan to the core. Let's not forget that God has left us here on purpose. We're here to demonstrate what it is like to be a member of another country, to have a citizenship in another land, so that we might create a desire for others to emigrate. Our mission is to create a thirst and an interest in that land "beyond the blue."

In 1 Peter 4:1–6, the apostle gives some marching orders to Christian soldiers who are stationed on this foreign soil. He opens the subject by addressing a Christian's behavior before a watching world with the connective word, *therefore*.

> Therefore, since Christ has suffered in the flesh, arm yourselves also with the same purpose. (1 Pet. 4:1a)

Careful students of the Scriptures pay close attention to words, especially words that connect main thoughts. The word *therefore* is a word of summary that connects what the author is about to write with what he has just written. And what has he just written? Look back at 3:18 and 22.

> For Christ also died for sins once for all, the just for the unjust, in order that He might bring us to God, having been put to death in the flesh, but made alive in the spirit . . . . who is at the right hand of God, having gone into heaven, after angels and authorities and powers had been subjected to Him. (1 Pet. 3:18, 22)

Christ has suffered and died on our behalf, the just for the unjust. *Therefore* . . . Do you see how it all ties together? Since Christ has died for our sins, the just for the unjust, and since He has been seated at the right hand of God, and since all authorities have been subjected to Him, and since He has suffered in the flesh, *therefore*, we should arm ourselves with the same purpose He had when He was on this earth.

I like the way one scholar amplifies what was meant by "arm yourselves."

> [Peter] exhorts the saints to arm themselves with the same mind that Christ had regarding unjust punishment. . . . The Greek word translated "arm yourselves" was used of a Greek soldier putting on his armor and taking his weapons. The noun of the same root was used of a heavy-armed footsoldier who carried a pike and a large shield. . . . The Christian needs the heaviest armor he can get to withstand the attacks of the enemy of his soul.[3]

This word picture offers a blunt reminder that we Christians are not living on this earth as carefree tourists. We are not vacationing our way to heaven. We are soldiers on raw, pagan soil. Everywhere around us the battle rages. The danger is real, and the enemy is formidable. Christ died not only to gain victory over sin's dominion but to equip us for that fight—to give us the inner strength we need to stand against it. Therefore . . . we are to arm ourselves with the strength that Christ gives because our purpose in life is the same as His.

Martyn Lloyd-Jones's warning bears repeating:

> Not to realize that you are in a conflict means one thing only, and it is that you are so hopelessly defeated . . . you do not even know it—you are unconscious! It means that you are completely defeated by the devil. Anyone who is not aware of a fight and a conflict in a spiritual sense is in a drugged and hazardous condition.[4]

Transformation: Remarkable Difference in the Christian Life

Several years ago when I was preaching on First Peter, a man called me and said, "I just want to let you know, Chuck, that the message of First Peter is happening in my life." When I asked what he meant, he went on to describe some difficulties he'd been going through. As he did, he said, "The things you've been talking about recently came back to my mind."

He said he had felt a heaviness in his spirit . . . he called it "a dark oppression." We prayed together about his situation. A few days later when I saw him after the Sunday morning service, he said, "I just want you to know the cloud has lifted." He had sensed the beginning of deliverance from his private war in the realm of darkness.

Many of you live in the competitive jungle of the business world, and some of you may work for a boss who asks you to compromise your ethics and integrity. Pressured by the tension between pleasing your boss, who can fire you or demote you or just make your life difficult, and your commitment to Christ, you need the inner resources to stand firm. "Arm yourselves with the same purpose" is certainly applicable for you. The good news is this: you have it! The provision Christ gives will be sufficient for such a stress test.

> Therefore, since Christ has suffered in the flesh, arm yourselves also with the same purpose, because he who has suffered in the flesh has ceased from sin, so as to live the rest of the time in the flesh no longer for the lusts of men, but for the will of God. For the time already past is sufficient for you to have carried out the desire of the Gentiles, having pursued a course of sensuality, lusts, drunkenness, carousals, drinking parties and abominable idolatries. (1 Pet. 4:1–3)

Fortunately those who are "in Christ" have been transformed. This transformation brings with it at least four benefits that Peter mentions. We no longer serve sin as our master (verse 1b); we don't spend our days overcome by desires as we once did (verse 2b); we now live for the will of God (verse 2b); we have closed the book on godless living (verse 3).

We've sowed our wild oats. Most have had enough time to see the end result of this lifestyle of loose living. Peter calls that lifestyle "the desire of the Gentiles."

Before Christ entered our lives, we had no power to withstand sin. When temptation came along, we yielded. We were unable to do otherwise. When the weakness of the flesh appeared, we fell into its trap. Though we may have looked strong on the outside, we had no inner stability. But when Christ took up residence in our lives, He gave us strength so that we could cease serving sin as a master. (Romans 6 is a wonderful section of scripture on this subject.) Because Christ now lives within us, we have been released from sin's control. We are no longer enslaved to sin. We've been freed!

Observe how "the will of God" (verse 2) is contrasted with "the desire of the Gentiles" (verse 3). Notice, too, how "the desire of the Gentiles"—the old habits, practices, associations, places of amusement, evil motives, and wicked pastimes—are all scenes from the past. The list sounds like your average *Animal House* on some college campus:

- sensuality
- lusts
- drunkenness, carousals, and drinking parties.

The original terms are vivid. *Sensuality* refers to actions that disgust and shock public decency. *Lusts* go beyond sexual promiscuity and involve sinful desires of every kind, including the lust for revenge and the lust for money (greed). *Drunkenness, carousals, and drinking parties* describe a whole miserable spectrum of pleasure-seeking consumption, from wanton substance abuse to wild sexual orgies. And we thought these things represented twentieth-century wildness! When it comes to a shameless, pagan lifestyle, nothing is new.

What is so liberating about our relationship with Christ is that He fills the void in our lives that we once tried to fill with all that garbage. With the void filled, the gnawing emptiness that accompanied it is gone too. And with the emptiness gone, we no longer crave the things we used to crave.

That's where Christians are different from the world. That's where we stand out. That's where the light shines in the darkness. And invariably the darkness reacts to such a light.

*

Reaction: Angry Astonishment from the Unsaved World

While we may live in this foreign land, far from our ultimate home, we live for the will of God. As a result, there is a marked contrast between our lifestyle and the lifestyle of the pagans—people who do not know the Lord—around us. And when we don't partake of that lifestyle, we are considered "weird."

Make no mistake about it. If we don't participate in that lifestyle, you and I are weird. *We are really weird!* And they notice it. Again, Peter's words are as relevant as this morning's newspaper. Look how he describes the reaction of the unsaved world.

> And in all this, they are surprised that you do not run with them into the same excess of dissipation, and they malign you. (1 Pet. 4:4)

Talk about the relevance of Scripture! Peter sounds like he is alive today! Any lifestyle of restraint, no matter how tactful we try to be, makes unbelievers uncomfortable. Sometimes it makes them defensive and angry, causing them to lash out at us as though in living our lifestyle we were judging theirs. I experienced this among fellow marines on numerous occasions—those who spent their lives in a realm of lustful drives and carousals and one drinking party after another. We see the same thing today in the after-hours of the corporate world. It's all part of the so-called "happy hour."

Beyond their discomfort and defensiveness, of course, is the inner emptiness they live with, day in and day out, the natural result of a life of lust and debauchery. What emptiness there is when the party's over and everybody goes home! They're left with the horrors of the sunrise and a head-splitting hangover, the guilt and even some shame as they crawl out of somebody else's bed, wondering what disease they might have gotten this time. And there's always that dark-brown taste in their mouth.

It's a horrible lifestyle! I don't care how beautiful the commercials look, it stinks! It doesn't last an hour, and it's anything but "happy!" But if they haven't any power to overcome it, the only thing they have to look forward to is the next "happy hour." And if they play the music loud enough and if there's enough booze and drugs, they think they can drown their troubles. Another lie of the Enemy. He's got a thousand of them.

Do you get the picture? The time already past is sufficient for you to have had your fill of "the desire of the Gentiles." You've tasted it. You've known it firsthand. But when Christ transformed your life, He filled the void and took away a lot of that drive. It's borderline miraculous, in fact, especially if He's enabled you to quick-kick an addiction.

But when that happens, you stand out like a sore thumb in your neighborhood . . . in your university dorm . . . at the office party. You're noticed. Even without saying a word, you're noticed. Even if you very quietly and graciously request a 7-Up instead of a cocktail, the word gets out.

Why? Because you've been transformed. You're no longer a helpless slave to sin. You're not overcome by your glandular drives. You are now interested in God's will; you have closed the door on godless living. And the pagan sits up like a doberman, eyes open, ears perked. "What in the world is wrong with Sam? Remember when we used to run together? Now he's got religion." Or, "Suzy's gotten really weird . . . became a Bible-thumper. She was once a ton o' fun. Now she's Miss Goody Two Shoes. Next thing we know she'll become a televangelist!"

Brace yourself for such reactions if you're getting serious about Jesus and you've just broken off from a wild bunch of friends. The fact is, He is transforming you. Your old friends will not only be surprised, even shocked, at your new lifestyle, they might also actively ridicule and unjustly judge you for it as well. Expect it . . . it'll keep you from being "mugged by reality." You've just begun to experience hope beyond the culture.

Sometimes I wonder if they are really saying, "Look, misery loves company. If I'm gonna be this miserable, then you need to be miserable with me—like you used to. I don't want to do this alone."

The terrible irony of our unsaved friends' judgment is that they will themselves face the ultimate judgment . . . but that's the *last* thing they want to hear. Nevertheless,

> . . . they shall give account to Him who is ready to judge the living and the dead. (1 Pet. 4:5)

Some of you have discovered that your close friends have changed now that you're in Christ. Regarding that, let me first warn you, and then I want to commend you.

First, I want to warn you about spending all of your time with Christians. If your entire circle of friends and acquaintances is nothing but Christian people, you will really get idealistic and unrealistic about the world. You really will get weird! Furthermore, how are the lost going to hear the gospel if all the saved stay clustered, sipping their 7-Ups and reviewing Bible verses together? We need to guard against our tendency to be with believers exclusively. The lost, deep down, are curious . . . and we need to be nearby when they start asking questions.

Second, I commend you for changing your circle of close friends. Some of your former friends do you no good, especially if you cannot withstand the lifestyle temptations they bring your way. Most people who fall into gross sensuality do not do it alone. They're usually prompted or encouraged by other people. You need to be wise and tactful about it . . . but before long, your change in lifestyle needs to be communicated.

There's a line in a country-western song sung by Alabama, "I'm Not That Way Anymore," that says it well: "Time has closed yesterday's door."

That's the way it is with Christians. You're not like that anymore. The fact is, my friend, Christ has closed yesterday's door. The way you are is different from the way you *were*. You won't be able to hide it . . . nor should you want to. Hopefully, however, you'll become a magnet of understanding, drawing others to the Savior rather than an offensive porcupine, driving them away.

Ideally, we want to be a fragrant aroma of Christ, winsomely attracting the unsaved to Jesus, the Savior. But Scripture, as well as our own experience, teaches us that what is fragrant to some is occasionally fetid to others.

Live an Authentic Lifestyle

The point of all of this? Once again we're back to the theme of Peter's letter: finding hope beyond unjust suffering. Enduring hardship. Seeing the reasons behind unfairness. Simply because you desire to live for Christ you will have people who once really enjoyed your company now talking about you behind your back, wondering if you've lost it . . . gone over the deep end. That is tough to take, because you know they aren't representing you fairly. But it's to be expected, looking at life strictly from their pagan perspective.

In fact, the longer I live, the more I see the value of having a thick skin but a tender heart. If you do, their cutting comments won't get to you. Furthermore, you won't feel the need to "set the record straight." Those maligning and ugly words kind of glance off, freeing you from an attack-back reaction.

Let me tell you what's happening. The pagan crowd will never tell you this, but down deep inside, many of them envy you. They wonder, *How does she do that? . . . How can he no longer do these things? . . . I'm not able to stop. . . . What in the world has made the difference?* And when you get them alone, it's remarkable how many of them will really listen as you tactfully and graciously tell them what has transformed your life. That's the joy of being left on foreign soil. You get to acquaint them with a life that is now yours and can be theirs, if only they'll genuinely and completely turn their lives over to Christ.

But let me warn you: Don't beat them up for their lifestyle. Nobody ever got saved because he was rebuked for his drinking or shamed for taking drugs or sleeping around. To tell you the truth, I'm surprised more in the pagan world don't do more of that to fill the void. So don't make an issue of their lifestyle. They can't help it.

They have no power to stop. Let grace and mercy flow. Relax . . . and leave the rebuking to the Lord.

Admittedly, there will be times that it will get to you . . . and you'll find yourself reaching the end of your tether.

One of the Bible teachers who used to lecture at Dallas Seminary when I was a student on campus was as tough as nails yet pure in heart. On one occasion while he was in the city to deliver a series of lectures, he went to a local barbershop to get a haircut. (A friend of mine happened to work there and overheard this conversation.) The barber, who didn't have the faintest idea who the man was, began talking about various issues of the day, giving his opinion, as barbers usually do. He peppered every phrase with an oath or a four-letter word. The teacher bit his lip as long as he could. Finally, he grabbed the barber's arm, pulled him around to the side of the chair, and looked the man right in the eye. Quietly but firmly he pulled on his own earlobe and said to the barber, "Does that look like a sewer?" The rest of the haircut was done in absolute silence.

I realize that such a reaction may not win many friends . . . but I understand the frustration.

Sometimes I just get my fill of it, too, don't you? Especially something as prevalent as blasphemous profanity. Throughout my months in the marines, I listened to that stuff till I thought I'd scream, so it's not that I haven't heard it before or that I can't handle it. I just occasionally reach the place where I have to say something. If it's handled right, even *that* can result in an opportunity to witness.

But in the final analysis, you cannot clean up anybody's lips until you've cleaned up his or her heart. And, ultimately, that's Christ's job. He's a master at it. So you stand it as best you can, realizing these are all simply signs of being lost. Such habits make the inhabitants of this pagan culture appear rough and rugged, but down inside they're often frightened little children. And they're scared to DEATH of death and what it might mean—whether they believe that to be nothingness or judgment.

Thankfully, the believer doesn't have to fear any of that. Our judgment is behind us . . . but their judgment is in front of them. Christ took our judgment, and He bore it on a cross. And He's given us the power He had now that we're in Christ. Remember the words of Isaac Watts?

> Am I a soldier of the cross?
> A follower of the Lamb?
> And shall I fear to own His cause
> Or blush to speak His name?
>
> Sure I must fight if I would reign:—
> Increase my courage, Lord!
> I'll bear the toil, endure the pain,
> Supported by Thy Word.

It's a great hymn. Even though it is almost 275 years old it is really up to date! It applies to businessmen and women who are facing verbal from their fellow employees. It applies to athletes today who refuse to live the lifestyle of the others on the team. It applies to those in the military service who love Christ but serve alongside those who don't. You're a soldier of the cross. What more can you expect? You're not a martyr. You're just taking a few verbal punches. It's good for you and me to be talked about like that. It drives us back to our knees before Christ and reminds us of our dependence on Him.

All believers owe it to themselves to read at least a portion of *Foxe's Book of Martyrs*, which traces the martyrdom of Christians throughout the centuries and demonstrates how viciously the world can act in its attempt to extinguish the light of Christlike character. There are some scenes that will make you shake your head. Talk about paying a price for one's faith!

Do you, like the brave saints of old, want to stand out like a bright light against the darkness of your world? Do you want to shock the pagan crowd? You don't need flamboyance or fanaticism. You don't need to fly a giant JESUS SAVES flag over your house or to wag your finger and rail against others' lifestyles. You don't need put-down bumper stickers or T-shirts with big, bold messages. You certainly don't need to rely on sermons or shame. What you do need to do is live differently. And you need to be aware of the consequences of Christlike living. For some it may mean persecution; for others, it could mean death . . . as it did for John Hus, a Bohemian Reformer accused of heresy.

Prior to his appearance before the Council of Constance in 1414, Hus wrote to one of his friends,

> I shall not be led astray by them to the side of evil, though I suffer at His will temptations, revilings, imprisonments, and deaths—as indeed He too suffered, and hath subjected His loved servants to the same trials, leaving us an example that we may suffer for His sake and our salvation. If He suffered, being what He was, why should not we?[5]

I love that last sentence: "If He [Christ] suffered, being what He was [perfect, the ideal model], why should not we?"

You want to know how to really shock the pagan crowd? *Live an authentic Christian life*. No fanfare, of course. No need to wave John 3:16 signs at a ball game . . . or embarrass your colleagues by loudly spouting Bible verses to your unsaved friends at work. That's offensive, not winsome. They're lost, but they're not ignorant or beyond feelings. Just keep three things in mind—three simple but workable suggestions, not at all complicated.

First, continue living for Christ. That means being different on purpose. Let your integrity speak for itself. When opportunities occur for you to speak of your faith, do so graciously and kindly.

Second, expect to be misunderstood. Don't be surprised when ugly things are said or false accusations are made or twisted statements are passed along about your life. Your life will prove that they're wrong. Relax . . . and let the Lord defend you.

Third, keep your eyes fixed on Christ. Stay on a steady course. Keep on being different. Live an authentic godly life, and you'll blow the world away. This is especially true if you keep a healthy sense of humor! They will not be able to stay quiet about the difference between your life and theirs.

Never forget, this world is not your home . . . you're just passin' through.

A Prayer for Hope Beyond the Culture

Lord God, Your Son has closed yesterday's door, and we don't live like that anymore. Not because we've been strong and good and noble but because You have transformed our lives, Lord. You've changed our course of direction. Even though You've left us on foreign soil, we have a home in the skies. And sometimes we get pretty homesick!

Hear the prayers of Your people as we call out to You. Give us self-control on those occasions when we're tempted to moralize and put people down. Make us aware that a godly life, alone, preaches the most unforgettable message the unsaved can be exposed to. Help us remember that we're soldiers away from home, living in a culture that's lost its way and is in desperate need of Jesus Christ. Keep us easy to live with, strong in faith, unbending in our convictions, yet full of grace toward those who are bound by sin and captured by habits they cannot break. Enable us to shock this pagan culture with lives that are real, that still have fun, and that ultimately glorify You, O God . . . as Jesus did. In His name I pray.

AMEN

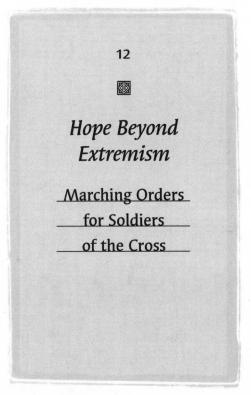

12

Hope Beyond Extremism

Marching Orders for Soldiers of the Cross

WHEN TIME IS short, things get urgent. And simplified. Something about the brevity of time introduces both urgency and simplicity to the equation of life.

When a friend or family member tells you he or she hasn't long to live, your time together becomes more urgent and your discussions return to the basics. When a hurricane is blowing in or the black funnel of a tornado looms on the horizon, you don't pull out a Monopoly game or begin preparing a gourmet meal. It's all about survival, and survival calls for simplicity. If you're driving to church and you see an accident happen and you are the only one there to assist, you don't worry about being late or about getting your Sunday clothes dirty or bloody. The situation is urgent. The mission is simple.

Jesus Himself modeled this for us. As long as there was time, He took time—to eat with His disciples, to train His disciples, to minister to individuals whenever and whatever their need. He would linger over a meal with friends. He would sit back and enjoy relaxed moments with close friends like Mary and Martha and Lazarus. But when the hour of the cross drew near, urgency gripped His voice and His attention focused on those few priorities that were in front of Him.

> From that time Jesus Christ began to show His disciples that He must go to Jerusalem, and suffer many things from the elders and chief priests and scribes, and be killed, and be raised up on the third day. (Matt. 16:21)

At that point, Peter—the same disciple who had just given a wonderful statement of faith—rebuked Jesus, saying, "God forbid it, Lord!" (v. 22), telling Him not to talk like that—that such things should never happen to Him.

Such audacity! Peter was planning on a kingdom. He was not planning on a cross.

But Jesus turned and said to Peter,

> Get behind Me, Satan! You are a stumbling block to Me; for you are not setting your mind on God's interests, but man's. (Matt. 16:23)

And then Jesus said to His disciples, in effect, "Let's get down to basics. Let's get down to the essentials, the simple requirements of discipleship."

> If anyone wishes to come after Me, let him deny himself, and take up His cross, and follow Me. (Matt. 16:24)

He was down to urgent, simple demands. Why? Because the hour was short.

During World War II, Winston Churchill encouraged and supported the people of Britain through endless dark hours. He made many memorable statements and speeches, but one rings particularly apt here. He was speaking to Parliament just after London had been bombed to smithereens, and he sensed the people were losing heart. It seemed as though Churchill never did. He must have had low moments, but his speeches don't reveal it. So he said to those people in Parliament, who were probably quaking in their spirits, "This is not the end. This is not even the beginning of the end. But it is, perhaps, the end of the beginning."

Jesus said the same sort of thing to His disciples, telling them, in essence, "When you see these things occurring, it isn't the end."

> And you will be hearing of wars and rumors of wars; see that you are not frightened, for those things must take place, but that is not yet the end. (Matt. 24:6)

If you live in the light of Christ's return each day of your life, it does wonders for your perspective. If you realize that you must give account for every idle word and action when you stand before the Lord Jesus, it does amazing things to your conduct. It also makes you recognize how many needless activities we get involved in on this earth. Sort of like rearranging the deck chairs on the *Titanic*. Don't bother! Don't get lost in insignificant details! He's coming soon! Recognize the urgency and the simplicity of the hour!

Peter seems to have gotten the message. He was a practical man. Prior to following Christ, his life consisted of very tangible, practical things: boats, nets, fish, supporting a family, hard work. And then he met the hard realities of the Master. Consequently, we should not be surprised that his personality and his prose followed suit.

Being neither scholarly nor sophisticated, Peter had little interest in theoretical discussions. Life was not meant to be talked about but lived out. If an urgent situation demanded action, Peter wasn't one to call for a committee to study the alternatives. He cut through the bureaucratic red tape and got down to business.

So when the big fisherman took up his pen to write about suffering saints, he cut to the chase. And when he addressed the reality of the end times, he summed up a game plan in a one-two-three fashion rather than waxing eloquent on the options. Pragmatic Peter at his best offers four commands and one goal to those of us who live nearer than ever to Jesus Christ's return. Simple. Direct. No beating around the bush.

Marching Orders for Soldiers of the Cross

Now remember, Peter is dealing with suffering saints, men and women who are being taken advantage of, men and women who can see no relief in sight. During days of suffering we often become even more intensely aware of the end—the final outcome, whatever that may be. And in writing to his brothers and sisters suffering in the trenches of persecution, Peter himself intensified his focus as he deployed the troops and briefed them for battle.

Observe the urgency and the simplicity in the words that follow.

> The end of all things is at hand; therefore, be of sound judgment and sober spirit for the purpose of prayer. Above all, keep fervent in your love for one another, because love covers a multitude of sins. Be hospitable to one another without complaint. As each one has received a special gift, employ it in serving one another, as good stewards of the manifold grace of God. Whoever speaks, let him speak, as it were, the utterances of God; and whoever serves, let him do so as by the strength which God supplies; so that in all things God may be glorified through Jesus Christ, to whom belongs the glory and dominion forever and ever. Amen. (1 Pet. 4:7–11)

Suddenly, with no relief in sight, Peter introduces the one thought that always helps people hope again: *the end of all things*. In doing so, he not only adds urgency to the moment, he also simplifies the game plan. He leaves his reader with four direct commands to obey and one clear goal to pursue in the midst of it all.

Four Commands to Obey

First, he says: *Use good judgment and stay calm in a spirit of prayer.*

> The end of all things is at hand; therefore, be of sound judgment and sober spirit for the purpose of prayer. (1 Pet. 4:7)

Be of sound judgment. Be of sober spirit. Be calm. Today we might say: Stay cool. Don't be filled with anxiety. Don't panic. Face life realistically. Realize God is in control.

Sober does not mean the opposite of *intoxication*. It means the opposite of living in a frenzy, in a maddening kind of extremism. For example, don't try to set dates regarding Christ's coming. That's an extreme reaction to prophecy. Here's another. Don't panic, as if things were out of control. And another. Don't be filled with anxiety. Don't quit your job, put on a white robe, and sit on some rooftop waiting for Christ to come back. That's extremism. And don't think you have to know every detail of the end times in order to feel secure, as Warren Wiersbe, in his book *Be Hopeful*, rightly notes.

> Early in my ministry, I gave a message on prophecy that sought to explain everything. I have since filed away that outline and will probably never look at it (except when I need to be humbled). A pastor friend who suffered through my message said to me after the service, "Brother, you must be on the planning committee for the return of Christ!" I got his point, but he made it even more pertinent when he said quietly, "I've moved from the program committee to the welcoming committee."
>
> I am not suggesting that we not study prophecy, or that we become timid about sharing our interpretations. What I am suggesting is that we not allow ourselves to get out of balance because of an abuse of prophecy. There is a practical application to the prophetic Scriptures. Peter's emphasis on hope and the glory of God ought to encourage us to be faithful today in whatever work God has given us to do (see Luke 12:31–48).[1]

The secret of maintaining the balance and calmness that my friend writes about is prayer. We don't need to parade through the neighborhood wearing a big signboard that says REPENT! THE END IS NEAR! Instead, Peter says, "Be calm, use sound judgment, and do it in a spirit of prayer." Such wise, reasonable counsel from a man who once was neither. Before, Peter would panic so easily. Now . . . he urges prayer.

We don't dream our way into eternity. We pray and watch. In fact, there is nothing quite like prayer to sharpen our awareness, to keep us alert, to make us more discerning, and yet to remind us who has the controls.

When I see a person who is all out of sorts, full of anxiety, on the ragged edge of extremism, I'm looking at a person who isn't spending enough time in prayer. Prayer calms your spirit, yet it doesn't make you indifferent. On the contrary, it reminds you: He has everything in control. Use sound judgment. Stay calm.

Let me go back, again, to yesteryear . . . a dark night in a garden near the edge of Jerusalem. Peter was one of the disciples who was told by the Lord in the Garden of Gethsemane to "Wait here and pray, while I go over there to pray." But when the Lord returned to them, he found Peter asleep. Sound asleep. And He said to Peter and the others, "Couldn't you have waited with Me for this hour?" That must have stung, especially since Peter was the disciple who, a few hours earlier, had bragged about his loyalty and commitment. You think Peter doesn't write with a sense of urgency and understanding here? You think he doesn't remember that rebuke? "I left you to pray, and you fell asleep." That's why Peter could add those words to his letter with a real sense of understanding.

Prayer was what allowed Jesus to submit to His arrest, and the lack of it was what made Peter resist.

The second command is: *Stay fervent in love for one another*.

Above all, keep fervent in your love for one another, because love covers a multitude of sins. (1 Pet. 4:8)

"Fervent" speaks of intensity and determination. It comes from the Greek word *ektene*, which literally means "strained." It's used to describe athletes straining to reach the tape at the finish line or stretching high enough to clear the bar.

When lean sprinters race around that last turn and are pressing for the tape, they'll get right to the end and then they'll deliberately lean forward. I've even seen runners fall on the track because they're pushing so hard to reach the tape before their competitors. That's "being fervent." It's the idea of stretching yourself. Those who do the long jump leap into the air and throw their feet forward as they stretch every muscle of their body to reach as far as they can. The same is true with the high jump or the pole vault. Athletes stretch to the utmost to reach the limit. All those actions describe "fervent." But here Peter applies it to love, not athletic events. He tells us to have fervency in our love for one another.

If there was ever a time when we needed to stay close, it is today. Don't play into the hands of the Enemy. This is the time to stick together. Don't waste precious time criticizing other Christians. Don't waste time criticizing another church or some pastor. Spend your time building up one another, staying fervent in love.

Look at how the verse begins: "Above all"—more than anything else. And then Peter gives them a compliment. He says, "Keep fervent." This implies that they already were fervent. Keep at it, he says. You're doing it already, so stay at it.

Because my schedule is already so full of regular responsibilities connected to both Dallas Seminary and our radio ministry, Insight for Living, I rarely accept invitations to minister elsewhere. But Cynthia and I have made an exception to this when it comes to the Christian Embassy in Washington, D.C., and a retreat they sponsor for many of the flag officers in the Pentagon and various members of Congress who serve on Capitol Hill.

On several occasions we have returned to this significant group of men and women to minister to them and spend some time getting to know their world better. Most of these generals and admirals are academy graduates who have spent many years in military leadership, some of which were during wars on land and at sea. The politicians are also seasoned veterans who have invested their time and effort serving the people of their states, standing for what is right and representing causes worth fighting for. Most who attend the retreat are Christians. They operate their lives on the cutting edge of our times. What amazing, admirable people they are!

As a result of our annual reunions, my wife and I have been able to see how these men and women have grown spiritually in their Christian walk (yes, there are *many* Christians in high places!). What stands out most eloquently to the two of us is their love for the Lord and their love for one another . . . as well as for us. Rather than being sophisticated and distant, these dear folks *fervently* express their love and *fervently* demonstrate compassion.

Peter would have been proud of them. They "keep fervent"—they stay at it, year after year.

If there's ever a time to stretch our love for one another to the limit, it's during the end times—*it's now*. And what is it that reveals this love? Forgiveness.

When Peter says that "love covers a multitude of sins," he's alluding to the principle in Proverbs 10:12:

> Hatred stirs up strife,
> But love covers all transgressions.

Nothing is a more compelling witness than the love and unity that Christians exhibit toward each other, and nothing is more disturbing or disruptive to the unity of the body than Christians who are stirred up against each other and experiencing strife. Nothing is a poorer witness.

Don't think the unsaved aren't watching when we bash our brothers and smash our sisters! They *love* it when we can't get along with each other. It makes news. They love to quote one Christian who is after another Christian. It's as if the journalist or pundit leans back and says, "Aha! Gotcha!"

Mahatma Gandhi, the Indian nationalist leader, once said, "I like your Christ but I don't like your Christians. . . . They are so unlike your Christ."[2]

What a rebuke. I deeply regret that his words are so often true!

And what is Christ like? He is characterized by love and forgiveness. An insightful person once said, "We are most like beasts when we kill. We are most like men when we judge. We are most like God when we forgive."

Let me repeat something I said earlier: I have never met a person who didn't have a reason to blame someone else. Every one of us can blame somebody for something that has happened in our lives. But don't waste your time. What we need most is a steady stream of

love flowing among us. Love that quickly forgives and willingly over-
looks and refuses to take offense.

Moffatt states that this passage "is a warning against loving others
by fits and starts. It is a plea for steady affection, persisting through
the irritations and the antagonisms of common life in a society recruited from various classes of people."

Some people are so easy to love that you just naturally fall into
their arms. But others are so hard to love, you have to work overtime
at it. There's something about their natures that's abrasive and irritating. Some are the opposite of magnets. They repel. Yet even they
need our love, perhaps more than the others. How very important
that we "stretch fervently" to love each other!

The third command Peter gives is: *Be hospitable toward one another.*

Be hospitable to one another without complaint. (1 Pet. 4:9)

Underscore the words "one another." It is the same phrase Peter
uses in verses 8 and 10, and it doesn't refer just to those who are lov-
able or friendly or fun to be with. It refers to all who are in the body
of Christ, even the unlovely and unfriendly.

Another little phrase tacked onto the end of verse 9 is a crucial
one when it comes to showing hospitality—"without complaint."

What do you complain about when it comes to hospitality? About
the time and trouble it takes? The energy it requires to invite someone into your home and entertain them? The expense? The mess?
The clean-up? It's true that hospitality takes effort and planning, and
it interrupts your privacy. But hospitality is never a problem when
our priorities are in place, when love opens the door.

"True love is a splendid host," said the famous English preacher
John Henry Jowett. In his excellent volume on the epistles of Peter,
he writes with eloquence:

> There is love whose measure is that of an umbrella. There is love
> whose inclusiveness is that of a great marquee. And there is love whose
> comprehension is that of the immeasurable sky. The aim of the
> New Testament is the conversion of the umbrella into a tent and the

merging of the tent into the glorious canopy of the all-enfolding heavens. . . . Push back the walls of family love until they include the neighbor; again push back the walls until they include the stranger; again push back the walls until they comprehend the foe.[3]

When was the last time you entertained someone who was once your enemy? There is something about hospitality that disarms a foe.

Since the former head coach of the Dallas Cowboys, Tom Landry, has served on our Dallas Seminary board for many years, I have had the opportunity to get to know the man. My respect for him has grown, not lessened, as time and our mutual roles have linked us together.

I was told a wonderful story about Coach Landry that illustrates the level of his Christian love for others. Years ago, the late Ohio State coach, Woody Hayes, was fired for striking an opposing player on the sidelines during a football game. The press had a field day with the firing and really tarred and feathered the former Buckeye coach. Few people in America could have felt lower than he at that time; he not only lost control in a game and did a foolish thing, but he also lost his job and much of the respect others had for him.

At the end of that season, a large, prestigious banquet was held for professional athletes. Tom Landry, of course, was invited. Guess who he took with him as his guest? Woody Hayes . . . the man everyone was being encouraged to hate and criticize.

The quality of our love is determined by its inclusiveness. At the one extreme there is self-love; but at the other extreme there is philanthropy! What is the "tense," the stretch, of my love? What is its covering power? . . . *"Love covereth a multitude of sins."* Not the sins of the lover, but the sins of the loved! Love is willing to forget as well as to forgive! Love does not keep hinting at past failures and past revolts. Love is willing to hide them in a nameless grave. When a man, whose life has been stained and blackened by "a multitude of sins," turns over a new leaf, love will never hint at the old leaf, but will rather seek to cover it in deep and healing oblivion. Love is so busy unveiling the promises and allurements of the morrow, that she has little time and still less desire to stir up the choking dust on the blasted and desolate fields of yesterday.[4]

Are you hospitable . . . I mean *really* hospitable? Do you make room in your life to be interrupted? Do you allow people to be drawn by the magnet of your love because of Christ's presence? One more question: Would you have done what Tom Landry did?

There's something about sitting down with someone over a cup of coffee or a sandwich. Something about taking time . . . making time. I am fully aware that there are times when we need to be alone. *But not all the time.*

Have you ever opened your home for a traveling college choir or other strangers who need lodging? Remember how Jesus and His disciples always stayed in private homes when they traveled and preached? Is your home open to those in need?

I can't tell you how many times people have told me what a blessing it has been to open their homes. Many of these were folks who felt a little uneasiness or apprehension at first, letting strangers invade their most private domain. But there's an unforgettable job connected with hospitality. Folks never forget the warmth of a home . . . the joy of kids around the table . . . the pleasure of meaningful conversation. A friend of mine traveled with a musical group during her college days, over thirty years ago, and she says she can still remember homes she stayed in and Christian hospitality demonstrated on her behalf. Such expressions of hospitable love gave her numerous opportunities to hope again during the three decades that followed.

From the perspective of the guest, however, hospitality is not something we should ever abuse. Apparently this was happening in the first century, largely by people who were living unbalanced lives in response to prophetic teaching. They reasoned, "Since Christ is coming soon, why bother working? Why not liquidate all assets and live off others?" The apostle Paul speaks directly to this heretical reasoning in 2 Thessalonians 3:6–15. Peter speaks to it more indirectly in the next two verses by promoting involvement in the local church and the exercise of spiritual gifts.

In fact, verses 10–11 contain his fourth command: *Keep serving one another*.

> As each one has received a special gift, employ it in serving one another, as good stewards of the manifold grace of God. Whoever speaks, let him speak, as it were, the utterances of God; whoever serves, let him do so as by the strength which God supplies. (1 Pet. 4:10–11a)

Do you know, fellow Christian, that you have at least one—perhaps more than one—spiritual gift? Several sections of the New Testament talk about these gifts—special abilities God has given the body of Christ with which we minister until He returns. Each gift we have needs to be used in serving one another. That is how we become good stewards of our gifts.

Here's a list of some of the places where spiritual gifts are listed. Look them up and examine your own life in the light of them.

- Ephesians 4:11–12
- 1 Corinthians 12:28–30
- Romans 12:6–8

Make a list of these gifts and then ask yourself, where do I best fit in this list? You might approach it the way you would approach applying for a job. If you don't find your spot right away, keep pursuing it. Keep thinking about it. Ask other Christians—those who know you and have been around you during various experiences—what they think your gifts are. Then try them out. Put them into action as you serve others. You'll discover what you do well . . . then do that throughout the balance of your life.

But note the warning in verse 11 that goes along with exercising our gifts.

> Whoever speaks, let him speak, as it were, the utterances of God; whoever serves, let him do so by the strength which God supplies. (1 Pet. 4:11)

When we speak, we shouldn't be voicing our own opinions and

philosophies about life; we should be speaking "the utterances of God." And when we serve, we shouldn't be doing so in our own strength but "by the strength which God supplies."

When you speak for Christ, base your words on the Scriptures, not on your own opinions. You will be forever relevant if you do. And you'll never lack for a message! When you serve, serve in His strength, not your own. That way, He gets the glory.

Many of you have the gift of teaching. You can teach children, teenagers, or adults. You can lead a Bible study at work or in your neighborhood.

Many gifted people also serve behind the scenes, doing vital but perhaps not-so-visible jobs. You help, encourage, and pray. The body would be crippled without the many parts that are able to serve, to help, to encourage.

Others have the gift of showing mercy, of ministering to those who are laid aside or suffering. You visit hospitals and nursing homes. You spend hours listening, caring.

Still others have the gift of evangelism. With ease they communicate the gospel and lead people to Christ. It's a natural part of their lives. God uses them again and again as He harvests souls for His kingdom.

But all of these gifts—there are many others—have one thing in common. They come alive in serving other people. So get out of your own tiny radius. It will do wonders for your depression, for your pity parties, for those times when you sit alone and want to sing, "Woe is me. Woe is me. Woe is me." (That's a very dull song.)

Think of it this way: When we employ our spiritual gift(s), others benefit. Others are encouraged. Others gain fresh hope. Interestingly, so do we!

A Goal to Pursue

Verse 11 ends with a purpose clause that reveals the logical reason we should obey these four commands. Why stay calm and pray? Why be fervent in love? Why demonstrate hospitality? Why serve one another?

. . . so that in all things God may be glorified through Jesus Christ, to whom belongs the glory and dominion forever and ever. Amen.

In everything, God gets the glory. How many church conflicts could be resolved if God's glory were everybody's goal? How many egos would be put in their place if God's glory—not human glory—were at stake? How much extremism would be avoided if we did all for the greater glory of God?

"But that's so basic," you may say. "Why even spend time on it?" Because without that, your teaching becomes drudgery, your helping leads to burnout, your evangelism becomes either frenetic or self-glorifying.

When we keep His glory uppermost in our minds, it's amazing how much else falls into place. Since He gets the glory, we're more comfortable leaving the results with Him in His time. Since He gets the glory, our umbrella of love expands to cover others. Since He gets the glory, it's easier for us to show hospitality to others, for we're ultimately serving Him. Since He gets the glory, exercising our gifts is not a pain but a privilege. The benefits are endless when the glory goes to God!

A Concluding Thought

Let me bring this to a close by returning to a comment I made at the beginning of the chapter: Time is short. You and I don't have forever to put these things into action. Whatever needs to be simplified, *let's simplify*! Whatever it takes to remind us of the urgency of the hour, *let's do it*! Time is short. That means we need to move the words off the pages and slide them into our lives—*now*.

Need a little boost? One of the most encouraging promises in all the New Testament comes to mind:

> For God is not unjust so as to forget your work and the love which you have shown toward His name, in having ministered and in still ministering to the saints. (Heb. 6:10)

Read that again, only this time *with feeling.*

Your effort is not in vain. Your love will not be overlooked. Your ministry—whatever it includes—will be rewarded. You will maintain a wonderful balance in the process. Keep your eyes on the Shepherd as you open your heart to His flock. And remember, He gets all the glory!

> The Bride eyes not her garment,
>   But her dear Bridegroom's face;
> I will not gaze at glory
>   But on my King of grace.
> Not at the crown He giveth
>   But on His pierced hand,
> The Lamb is all the glory
>   Of Immanuel's land.[5]

A Prayer for Hope Beyond Extremism

Our Father, keep us calm and cool in a spirit of prayer. Give us a fervency in our love for one another that has a way of covering a multitude of sins. Find us to be hospitable people who take time, who are accessible, available, and caring. And, Lord, as we put our gifts into action, use us to give a hope transplant to someone really in need. And may we do it all for Your glory.

May these words make a difference in the way we live, and may the difference be so significant that it is noticed, so that others have cause to give You praise . . . for You, alone, deserve all the praise and all the glory. I pray in Jesus' wonderful name.

AMEN

13

Hope Beyond Our Trials

"When through Fiery Trials . . ."

I am progressing along the path of life in my ordinary, contentedly fallen and godless condition, absorbed in a merry meeting with my friends for the morrow or a bit of work that tickles my vanity to-day, a holiday or a new book, when suddenly a stab of abdominal pain that threatens serious disease, or a headline in the newspapers that threatens us all with destruction, sends this whole pack of cards tumbling down.

At first I am overwhelmed, and all my little happinesses look like broken toys. Then, slowly and reluctantly, bit by bit, I try to bring myself into the frame of mind that I should be in at all times. I remind myself that all these toys were never intended to possess my heart, that my true good is in another world and my only real treasure is Christ. And perhaps, by God's grace, I succeed, and for a day or two become a creature consciously dependent on God and drawing its strength from the right sources. But the moment the threat is withdrawn, my whole nature leaps back to the toys.[1]

How eloquently C. S. Lewis's words from his penetrating book, *The Problem of Pain*, describe the role of trials in our lives. Such is human nature, and such is the nature of trials and tribulations.

Remember the words from the old hymn: "When through fiery trials my pathway shall lie, Thy grace all sufficient shall be my supply"? Well, fiery trials and painful ordeals aptly describe what most of us must pass through at one time or another in life . . . some, more frequently than that.

Peter addresses Christians who are going through just such desperate circumstances.

> Beloved, do not be surprised at the fiery ordeal among you, which comes upon you for your testing, as though some strange thing were happening to you. (1 Pet. 4:12)

Ever had anything like that in your life? Not simply trials, but what Peter calls "fiery ordeals"? If so, ever heard this kind of advice on how to handle such trials?

> . . . but to the degree that you share the sufferings of Christ, keep on rejoicing; so that also at the revelation of His glory, you may rejoice with exultation. (1 Pet. 4:12–13)

Probably not!

Practical Truths about Trials

Peter was not the only apostle who wrote to Christians who were strangers and aliens in a foreign land. James addressed his letter to those who were "dispersed abroad"—another group of people far away from home, and not by choice. This also applies to those of us who are strangers in this world below and those of us forced to live in the midst of circumstances that are not our choice. To all these, James wrote:

> Consider it all joy, my brethren, when you encounter various trials, knowing that the testing of your faith produces endurance. And let

endurance have its perfect result, that you may be perfect and complete, lacking in nothing. (James 1:2–4)

From these three verses we learn a great deal about trials. Four specifics stand out.

First, trials are common for Christians to encounter.

Don't ever let anybody tell you (and don't you dare tell anybody else!) that when you become a Christian your trials are over, from then on, "you can just trust Christ and fly away like birds toward the heavens." Get real! Notice that James says *"when* you encounter," not "if."

If you're experiencing trials, you're the rule, not the exception. If you have just gotten through one, take heart; there are more around the corner! Going through a trial is one thing that pulls us together. We've got that in common.

Second, trials come in various categories.

They may be physical, emotional, financial, relational, or spiritual. They may slip in unexpectedly and knock on the door of your business, your church, or your home. They may arrive at any time or at any season. They may come suddenly, like a car accident or a natural catastrophe. They may be prolonged, like a drawn-out court case or a lingering, nagging illness. Trials can be public in nature or very private. They can be directly related to our own sin, the sin of others, or not related to sin at all.

A trial can be like a rock hitting the water. You don't cause the jolt, but you're impacted by it. You're just standing there, and suddenly the smooth lake of your life surges into giant waves and almost drowns you.

Frankly, some trials seem to blow in absolutely without reason. My brother, Orville, encountered something like that when a hurricane named Andrew blew through the community where he lived in south Florida a few years ago. It tore and ripped and screamed its way through, tearing his house apart. He had a great attitude, though. He called and said, "What an experience! It really did a lot of damage. But the good news is it tore down everyone's fences, so now we'll get to meet our neighbors."

Third, trials put our faith to the test.

No matter what its source or intensity, there's something about suffering that simplifies life and draws us back to the basics. Invariably, especially during a time of intense trial, I go back to my theological roots. I go back to what I really believe. I return to the elementals such as prayer and dependence, like getting quiet and waiting on God. I remind myself, God is sovereign . . . this is no accident. He has a plan and a purpose. Those thoughts give us hope beyond our trials.

Trials put our faith to the test as well as stretch our confidence in Him. They force us back to the bedrock of faith upon which our foundation rests, and this becomes a refining and necessary process.

Fourth, without trials, there could not be maturity.

James says we experience trials so that we may be become "perfect and complete" (verse 4), like a plant that has matured to its maximum growth and fruitfulness. That, he says, is the "perfect result" of "endurance."

Most often, because of the discomfort, the pain, or the hardship, we try to cut our trials short—to put an end to them. Before long, we're resenting them to such an extreme that we'll try anything to escape, to run from them. Instead, James says, *endure* the trial; let it come to completion. When it does, you'll be a better person for it.

Remember the words of song writer Andrae Crouch? "If I'd never had a problem, I'd never know that He could solve them. I'd never know what faith in God could do."[2]

Few feelings compare with the joy of watching God step in and solve a problem that seems impossible.

Some trials are slight, brief, and soon forgotten. Others hang on and weigh heavily upon us. They leave us exhausted and sometimes bench us on the sidelines. The latter category is what Peter is talking about when he writes of "the fiery ordeal." This is no slight struggle Peter has in mind. It's an "ordeal" . . . one from which we cannot find relief.

Biblical Strength for Fiery Ordeals

What do you do when the rug is jerked out from under you? Do you panic? Do you doubt the Lord's love? Do you trust in God to get you through the tough times? Perhaps this is a good time to go back to God's truth and read His counsel written by Christ's closest companion while He was on earth.

We can learn a lot from Peter, a man who spent over three years with Christ and who, as we have seen, both pleased Him and failed Him. In fact, most of us should be able to identify with Peter. He'd been an eager disciple, defending his Master against all comers. He'd also been a failure, denying his Lord in the pinch . . . not once, but three times, back to back. Through all this, God reshaped him into a powerfully effective man of God. The vacillating, impulsive, overly zealous Simon was changed and broken, emerging as "Peter, the rock." Now, he writes out of his maturity and seasoned wisdom, under the guidance of the Holy Spirit. These are not theoretical terms the old fisherman tosses around but words shaped in the blast furnace of his own afflictions and pain. Read them again with that in mind:

> Beloved, do not be surprised at the fiery ordeal among you, which comes upon you for your testing, as though some strange thing were happening to you; but to the degree that you share the sufferings of Christ, keep on rejoicing; so that also at the revelation of His glory, you may rejoice with exultation. (1 Pet. 4:12–13)

He begins this section by addressing his letter to the "Beloved." This is truth directed to the beloved of God . . . in other words, truth for the believer only. This is information just for the Lord's people. It's got your name on it. Think of your name here in place of unnamed folks who were "beloved" to Peter.

He then goes on to tell us how to react to this more intense form of suffering.

How to React

Interestingly, our first response to an ordeal is usually surprise—"I can't believe this is happening." But Peter says, *"Don't be surprised."* The lack of surprise will enable us to remain calm.

Life is a schoolroom. In it, we encounter pop quizzes and periodic examinations. You can't have a schoolroom without tests—at least I've never seen one. I've never seen anyone earn a high school diploma or college degree without taking exams. The same is true in graduate school. Throughout the educational process our knowledge is assessed on the basis of examinations. The curriculum of Christlikeness is much the same. Our Christian maturity is measured by our ability to withstand the tests that come our way without having them shake our foundation or throw us into an emotional or spiritual tailspin.

The wonderful thing about God's schoolroom, however, is that we get to grade our own papers. You see, He doesn't test us so He can learn how well we're doing. He tests us so *we* can discover how well we're doing. So we can put our own benchmarks on our level of maturity.

Back in 1984, when you were tested, perhaps you didn't do too well. Maybe others didn't know that, but you did. In 1989, you did better. In 1993 an even tougher test confronted you, and you did rather well. As you grade your own paper, you can see the improvement. The testing of your faith reveals your increasing level of maturity.

Many years ago a good friend of mine, Dr. Robert Lightner, who is a long-time member of the theology department faculty at Dallas Seminary, was involved in a terrible plane crash. He was in a single-engine plane that flipped over during takeoff. He was badly injured and bruised beyond recognition. His wife, Pearl, said that when she first saw him at the hospital, "I looked at this black mass of flesh, and I didn't even know who he was." Thankfully, he did recover, and today he is a living testimony of the grace of God through that ordeal. "I learned things I didn't know I needed to learn," I heard him say on one occasion. Isn't that the way it usually is? What hope this should give us!

Don't be surprised when a test comes. Even though you don't know you need to learn certain things, God knows, and He sovereignly determines, "Now's the time." God is molding you into the image of His Son, and that requires trials. So, first off, don't be surprised.

But the second reaction Peter says we are to have is even more amazing: *"Keep on rejoicing."*

I hear some of you saying right now, "What! Are you kidding me? We're talking trials, right?" Right. "We're talking fiery ordeals, correct?" Correct. "And you're telling me to keep on rejoicing?" Wrong! I am not telling you this—*God* is telling you to keep on rejoicing. "To the degree that you share the sufferings of Christ, keep on rejoicing"

James put it another way: "Consider it all joy" (1:2). Why? Because trials enable us to enter into a more intimate partnership with Christ, and if we endure them faithfully, we will receive a future reward (see Phil. 3:10 and James 1:12). Along with that, our trials here give us at least a glimpse into the magnitude of Christ's suffering for us.

Trials, therefore, become a means to a greater end: a deeper relationship with Christ on earth and a richer reward from Him in heaven.

You and I would never know such fellowship were we not put to the test. Some of you are going through trials right now that have dropped you on your knees. At the same time those trials are pulling you closer to the Lord than you've ever been in your life. That ought to bring rejoicing. You'll be more closely linked to Him. Some of the mysterious themes threaded through His Word will become clearer because you have been leveled by some unexpected affliction or enduring persecution or facing misunderstanding.

Furthermore, you can rejoice because you will receive a future reward.

As I write these words, it happens to be getting close to graduation time, those days when diplomas, honors, and special awards are granted. Each year at Dallas Seminary we have a special chapel service near spring graduation during which we distribute special awards to those who have earned them. Our "Awards Chapel" is one of the highlights in our academic year.

Did you know that in the future when we stand before Christ our Lord, there will be special awards distributed by Christ Himself? They are called crowns. And did you know that there is a unique crown given to those who endure suffering? Read James 1:12:

> Blessed is a man who perseveres under trial; for once he has been approved, he will receive the crown of life, which the Lord has promised to those who love Him.

God has a crown reserved for those who endure the fiery ordeal. My brother, Orville, will have one. Bob Lightner will have one. My wife deserves one for living with me for over forty years! And many of you will have earned that crown as well.

In case you still are not convinced that trials can bring rejoicing, I want you to look at a classic case in point, recorded at the end of Acts 5. There we find that the apostles, including Peter, had just been flogged and ordered to stop preaching about Jesus. (Pause and imagine that bloody, brutal scene.) Look at what they did while they were still bleeding from the beating.

> So they went on their way from the presence of the Council, *rejoicing* that they had been considered worthy to suffer shame for His name. And every day, in the temple, from house to house, they kept right on teaching and preaching Jesus as the Christ. (Acts 5:41–42, italics added)

These men were people just like us . . . not super saints, but real-life folks. Only difference—they refused to let their "fiery ordeal" steal their joy or deter their objective. An attitude of joyful gratitude opens our minds to glean lessons from suffering we would not otherwise learn.

So much for how to react. Now let's focus on what to remember.

What to Remember

First: *Trials provide an opportunity to draw upon maximum power.*

If you are reviled for the name of Christ, you are blessed, because the Spirit of glory and of God rests upon you. (1 Pet. 4:14)

We must remember that we are never closer to Him, never more a recipient of His strength, than when trials come upon us. This is especially true when we are reviled for the name of Christ. One of the highest privileges on earth is to suffer for His sake. At those times the Holy Spirit draws near, administers strength, and provides an abiding presence of God's glory. If you recall the account of Stephen's martyrdom in Acts 7:54–60, which we read earlier, you'll see that's exactly what happened to him.

The second thing to remember is: *Sometimes our suffering is deserved.*

> By no means let any of you suffer as a murderer, or thief, or evildoer, or a troublesome meddler. (1 Pet. 4:15)

If our "fiery ordeal" comes as a result of our own sinful behavior, then we're not suffering for the glory of God; we're merely reaping the consequences of wrongdoing we have sown. As the prophet put it, when we "sow the wind" we "reap the whirlwind" (Hos. 8:7).

Sometimes we deserve the treatment we're getting. We deserve the punishment or the loneliness, the brokenness and pain. And notice that "troublesome meddlers" are listed right along with such reprehensible sinners as murderers, thieves, and other evildoers. That ought to get our attention! The term that is translated here as "troublesome meddler" literally means "one who oversees others' affairs." In other words, a busybody. Ouch! Suffering the consequence of being a busybody brings no one applause or affirmation, only a whirlwind of anguish.

The third thing Peter wants us to remember is: *Most suffering should in no way cause us to feel shame.*

> But if anyone suffers as a Christian, let him not feel ashamed, but in that name let him glorify God. (1 Pet. 4:16)

I have met folks who are ashamed that they are going through trials. Many apologize for their tears, almost as if they are embarrassed to weep. I've even known people who felt they needed to apologize because they had sought help from a professional to get through a very personal "fiery trial." Others feel ashamed because their walk of faith has caused a negative reaction. No need!

Instead of shame, we should feel honored when we suffer for our Lord. It is a privilege to bear wounds for the One who was "pierced through for our transgressions" and "crushed for our iniquities" (Isa. 53:5). That's the way Peter and the other apostles must have felt when they left the Sanhedrin, bloody but unbowed.

Self-imposed guilt and shame can be terrible taskmasters in our souls, whipping us down and keeping our spirits from soaring. Such guilt and shame have no place in our lives!

The fourth thing we need to remember is: *Suffering is usually timely and needed.*

For it is time for judgment to begin with the household of God.
(1 Pet. 4:17a)

One of the most difficult things to keep in mind is that we need to be purged and purified. After the fact we usually look back on the test or trial and say, "I really needed that," or, "The benefits that came from that are incredible," and we can name three or four insights we would not have gained had we not gone through the valley. Such perspective enables us to hope again.

Purging is not only needed among individuals in the household of God, but also in the church as a whole—locally, denominationally, or otherwise. Sometimes the "house of God" needs not only daily dusting but a thorough spring cleaning. Remember this the next time a scandal surfaces in the church. Don't get disillusioned. It's just God refusing to let us sweep the dirt in His house under the rug.

Sometimes we're rolling along happily, meeting our budgets, running our programs, yet there is no sense of zeal or revival among God's people. It's sort of sit, soak, and sour time for the flock. Congregations can get spoiled. With a smug shrug, they can be saved, sanctified, galvanized, and petrified. Church attendance becomes business as usual. What a miserable existence! About then God comes in and sweeps things clean as He works *through* the church in a timely and needed way.

Now look at the perspective Peter adds:

> If it begins with us first, what will be the outcome for those who do not obey the gospel of God? And if it is with difficulty that the righteous is saved, what will become of the godless man and the sinner? (1 Pet. 4:17b–18)

The latter part of that verse is a quotation from Proverbs, which the New International Version renders this way:

> If the righteous receive their due on earth,
>   how much more the ungodly and the sinner! (Prov.11:31)

In other words, if you think your testing is tough, imagine how tough it is for the person going through trials *without* the Lord. I'll be candid with you: I am absolutely at a loss to know how the lost person makes it when the bottom drops out of his or her life. This person has no Savior. No foundation. No borders. No absolutes. No reason to go on. Nothing to hold on to . . . no one to turn to . . . no way to calm his or her fears . . . no purpose for living . . . no peace in dying. Can you imagine that kind of hopelessness? If you can't, just look at what's happening in the world around you.

Imagine being without the Lord and hearing the worst kind of news from your physician or from the policeman who knocks on your door late at night. Though we, too, are rocked back on our heels by such things, as Christians we immediately turn to our sovereign absolute, our firm foundation, and we lean hard on Him. And if these earthly trials are hard for the lost to bear, imagine their having to face *eternal* judgment!

Which brings me to the fifth thing to remember: *There is no comparison between what we suffer now and what the unrighteous will suffer later.*

If we who are justified by faith have "fiery ordeals" in our walk now, imagine the inferno the lost will face in the literal fiery future that awaits them. Turn to Revelation 20:10–15 and take a few minutes to read and then imagine the horror. Talk about fiery ordeals. Talk about a reason to give your life to Christ.

Thus far, Peter has told us how to react and what to remember when we are going through fiery trials. Now he encourages us by telling us *on whom we are to rely.*

Therefore, let those also who suffer according to the will of God entrust their souls to a faithful Creator in doing what is right. (1 Pet. 4:19)

Entrust. What a wonderful word! It is a banking term in the original text, meaning "to deposit." One commentator has said, "The idea is that of depositing treasure into safe and trustworthy hands."[3] When it comes to trials, we deposit ourselves into God's safekeeping, and that deposit yields eternal dividends.

When you deposit money in the bank, there's a limit on how much the FDIC will insure under one account ownership; usually it's about $100,000. But our infinite God has no limits. Millions upon multimillions of Christians can deposit themselves in His care, and He will make every one of them good. He will hold every one of us securely. No one can declare Him bankrupt of compassion or care. God will never say to anyone, "Sorry. We're full up. That's the limit. We can't guarantee more." You can entrust your soul to this "faithful Creator."

Interestingly, the Greek word that is translated "entrust" here is the same one used by Jesus on the cross when He said, "Father, into Thy hands I *commit* My Spirit" (Luke 23:46, italics added). When we entrust our souls to God during our trials, we are following Jesus' example on the cross when He deposited His soul into the care of the Father. Again, I remind you, those without faith in Christ have no one in whom they can "entrust" their souls.

Personal Growth Through All the Heat

Tests are never wasted. God never says, "Oops, made a mistake on that one. I shouldn't have given you that. I meant that for Frank.

Sorry, Bob." It's as if the Lord has our name on specific trials. They are specifically designed for us, arranged with our weaknesses and our immaturity in mind. He bears down and doesn't let up. And we groan and we hurt and we weep and we pray and we grow and we learn. Through it all we learn to depend upon His Word. You see, there really is hope beyond our trials.

The furnace of suffering provides not only light by which to examine our lives but heat to melt away the dross. Just as famine and financial ruin brought the prodigal son to his senses, so our trials bring us to our senses and draw us into the embrace of our Father. The common response to trials is resistance, if not outright resentment. How much better that we open the doors of our hearts and welcome the God-ordained trials as honored guests for the good they do in our lives.

> Thus the terrible necessity of tribulation is only too clear. God has had me for but forty-eight hours and then only by dint of taking everything else away from me. Let Him but sheathe that sword for a moment and I behave like a puppy when the hated bath is over—I shake myself as dry as I can and race off to reacquire my comfortable dirtiness, if not in the nearest manure heap, at least in the nearest flower bed. And that is why tribulations cannot cease until God either sees us remade or sees that our remaking is now hopeless.[4]

As C. S. Lewis implies here, trials are not an elective in the Christian-life curriculum; they are a required course. Trials 101 is a prerequisite to Christlikeness. But sometimes the tests are so gruelingly comprehensive that our tendency is to drop the course entirely. Especially if we feel abandoned by God.

If that's how you're feeling in the test you are going through now, you need to consult the course syllabus for a few guiding principles. First, when trials come, it's important to remember that God is faithful and that you can rely on Him. Second, when trials stay, it's important to remember to do the right thing and to take refuge in Him. Rest in Him.

When the X-ray comes back and it doesn't look good, remember,

God is still faithful. When you read that heartbreaking note from your mate, remember, God is still faithful. When you hear the worst kind of news about one of your children, remember, God is still faithful. He has not abandoned you, though you're tempted to think He has.

At the height of one of his own personal tests, Hudson Taylor expressed his response in these words: "It doesn't matter how great the pressure is. What really matters is where the pressure lies, whether it comes between me and God or whether it presses me nearer His heart."

When we are pressed near the heart of God, He is faithful and He will hold us. He will hug us through it. We can entrust our souls "to a faithful Creator in doing what is right." But that doesn't mean things will calm down and start making better sense. Not necessarily! Our Lord's agenda for us is full of surprises, unexpected twists, and abrupt turns.

I like the way one fellow pastor put it:

> One of the most frustrating things about Jesus is that He just won't settle down. He is constantly moving us away from the places where we would prefer to stay . . . And moving us closer to . . . where we do not want to go.[5]

When you are tested, you will be tempted to resist such redirection, go your own way, fight in your own strength, and do what is wrong because it just comes naturally. It's called being streetwise (another word for *carnal*). You've fought your way thus far through life; you can fight your way through this test too.

But wait! Is that what God wants you to do? When trials linger on and you begin to wear down, the Enemy will be whispering all kinds of new carnal ideas. He'll even give you evidence that other people did those trials and got away with them. How much better to remember when trials *come* that God is faithful, still faithful. When trials *stay*, remind yourself to do what is right and take refuge in Him. Find your hiding place in Him.

"Suffering" and "glory" are twin truths that are woven into the fabric of Peter's letter. The world believes that the *absence* of suffering means glory, but a Christian's outlook is different. The trial of our faith today is the assurance of glory when Jesus returns . . . . This was the experience of our Lord . . . and it shall be our experience.

But it is necessary to understand that God is not going to *replace* suffering with glory; rather He will *transform* suffering into glory.[6]

When you and I take the long view, we should be grateful that Jesus just won't settle down. He's busy shaping us into His image . . . and for some of us, He's got a long way to go.

A Prayer for Hope Beyond Our Trials

Father, I pray today especially for those who find themselves in a dark place, who see no light on the horizon, who feel the hot blast from the fiery trials, with no relief in sight. Change this painful place into their hiding place where You are near, where You are real. Use this particular chapter to minister in a very special way to those chosen ones whom You are testing to prove their faith. Calm their fears. Quiet their spirits. Remind them that trials are essential if we hope to become Christlike.

This I pray through Jesus, who was, Himself, a Man of Sorrows, acquainted with grief . . . and who, though Your Son, learned obedience from the things which He suffered.

AMEN

14

Hope Beyond Religion

A Job Description
for Shepherds

OF ALL THE PREACHERS who ever lived, Charles Haddon Spurgeon was among the most colorful. He was also among the most prolific . . . and among the most controversial . . . and among the most eloquent . . . and on and on I could go. Spurgeon was one of a kind—if not the greatest preacher in the history of the church, certainly among the top ten, in my opinion. Any time the subject of preaching arises either in a classroom or among a group of pastors, the name Spurgeon will soon surface.

His works are both helpful and insightful. That is all the more remarkable because he lived over one hundred years ago, from 1834 to 1892. At the age of twenty, Spurgeon was called to the New Park Street Baptist Chapel in London, where he served his Lord until he preached his last sermon on June 7, 1891. He died the following January. During his years there, it was not uncommon for his congregation to number as many as 6,000. One biographer states that people would stand in the snow in the dead of winter waiting for the doors to open to assure themselves of a seat to hear this prince of the pulpit preach. During his thirty-eight years at the Metropolitan Tabernacle (five years after Spurgeon began his ministry there, they had to build a new building, which they renamed the Metropolitan Tabernacle), he was responsible for the swelling of the membership of the church to approximately 14,500. Remarkable, remarkable man. Although a Baptist, he was an evangelical Calvinist. Most of all, he was a man made for the pulpit. As one biographer put it:

> Preeminently he was a preacher. His clear voice, his mastery of Anglo-Saxon, and his keen sense of humor, allied to a sure grasp of Scripture and a deep love for Christ, produced some of the noblest preaching of any age.[1]

Despite all his strengths and noble accomplishments, however, a great deal of criticism was leveled against Spurgeon in his day. Like Martin Luther, he seemed to thrive in the storm. He was a man I would call *unflappable*. While he was criticized for a number of things in his preaching, the two things he was criticized for in his private life are curious.

First, he loved a good cigar. One of my favorite stories goes back to an occasion when a man called on him and criticized his cigar smoking. Spurgeon's response was classic: "When I take this to an extreme, then I will stop." When the man asked, "What is an extreme?" Spurgeon replied with a twinkle in his eye, "Two cigars at one time."

The other private criticism was leveled against him and his wife because, out of their own funds, they purchased and enjoyed an extremely large home on a sizable acreage. Predictably, the American press arrived on the scene and exaggerated the report of the home. This *infuriated* Spurgeon. But he pressed on, refusing to allow petty minds and exaggerated comments to deter him from his objectives. While many around him were "religious" and tried very hard to squeeze him into their proper religious mold, Spurgeon remained a maverick at heart, fiercely independent yet Christian to the core, thoroughly committed to Christ and His Word but unmoved by the pressure in Victorian England to fall in line and blend in with his peers.

The longer I live, the greater my admiration grows for this unique vessel so mightily used of God yet so vehemently criticized by others—especially other Christians. Though dead, he still speaks. His volumes continue to stimulate and instruct those of us in vocational Christian service. Anyone who enters the ministry owes it to himself or herself to read Spurgeon and to do so at least once a month. I especially recommend his book, *Lectures to My Students*. In it he writes:

> Every workman knows the necessity of keeping his tools in a good state of repair. . . . If the workman lose the edge . . . he knows that there will be a greater draught upon his energies, or his work will be badly done. . . .
>
> . . . It will be in vain for me to stock my library, or organize societies, or project schemes, if I neglect the culture of myself; for books, and agencies, and systems, are only remotely the instruments of my holy calling; my own spirit, soul, and body are my nearest machinery for sacred service; my spiritual faculties, and my inner life, are my battle axe and weapons for war. . . .
>
> [Then, quoting from a letter of the great Scottish minister, Robert Murray McCheyne, he concludes,] "Remember, you are God's sword, His instrument—I trust a chosen vessel unto Him to bear His name. In great measure, according to the purity and perfection of the instrument, will be the success. It is not great talent God blesses so much as likeness to Jesus. A holy minister is an awful weapon in the hand of God."[2]

There is every temptation for God's people (especially God's *ministers*!) to fall in line, get in step, and follow the cadence of our times . . . and in so doing, we will become unauthentic, boring, predictable, and, well, "religious." We need to be warned against that! While we cannot be Spurgeons (one was enough), there is much we can learn much from this model of clear thinking, passionate preaching, creative writing, and unbending determination. It is nothing short of amazing that a man of his stature and gifts remained at the same church almost four decades . . . especially since he was such a lightning rod, drawing criticism for so long from so many people.

One Practical Guideline for All to Remember

Let me begin with a few practical words of exhortation about sustaining a long-term ministry. My comments here have to do with unrealistic expectations—and they occur on both sides of the pulpit. A young minister comes to a church and has expectations of the flock. On the other side, the flock contacts and calls a man to pastor the church, and they also have their expectations. Both sets of expectations are so idealistic they're usually off the graph. This has the makings of early madness in any ministry.

One of the secrets of a long-term pastorate is clear-thinking realism on the part of both the pastor and the congregation. Let's understand, most churches will never be anything like a Metropolitan Tabernacle . . . and none of us in ministry will ever be a Spurgeon. My opening illustrations in this chapter are examples of the extreme. But the fact is, most of us are far down the scale from that, and we must learn to live with that, accept it, and be content with where and who we are.

The irony is, I think if Charles Haddon Spurgeon lived today, most churches would never even consider extending a call to him. They couldn't get over his style. And if they knew in-depth the whole story behind the Tabernacle, most pastors today would not want to serve in that place. (It's amazing what a hundred years' history will do to enhance our vision of a church or a man.)

The importance of two-way tolerance is extremely significant. A pastor needs to be very tolerant of the people he is serving. And the people who are being served by the minister need to be very tolerant of him. We need to give each other a lot of wobble room. Congregations need to give each other—and their pastors—room to be themselves. Religion, by the way, resists such freedom.

Please understand, I'm not saying anyone should live a lie; nor am

I promoting an unaccountable, sinful lifestyle. I'm simply encouraging grace here . . . giving room for others to be who they really are. All of us have quirks. All of us are unique in our own way. It's important that we adapt to a broad spectrum of personality types.

I smiled when I read this little sign recently:

Welcome to the Psychiatric Hotline!

IF YOU ARE OBSESSIVE-COMPULSIVE: Please press 1 repeatedly.

IF YOU ARE CO-DEPENDENT: Please ask someone to press 2.

IF YOU HAVE MULTIPLE PERSONALITIES: Please press 3, 4, 5, and 6.

IF YOU ARE PARANOID-DELUSIONAL: We know who you are and what you want. Just stay on the line so we can trace the call.

IF YOU ARE SCHIZOPHRENIC: Listen carefully—a little voice will tell you which number to press.

IF YOU ARE MANIC-DEPRESSIVE: It doesn't matter which number you press. No one will answer.[3]

If we're going to live together comfortably over a long period of time, we have to accept one another's idiosyncrasies and styles. This is an appropriate time for me to repeat something I wrote earlier: A good sense of humor is essential, especially if you hope to survive many years in church and/or the ministry.

Two Biblical Principles Regarding Ministry

I've expressed my concern about all this because we have come to a section in Peter's letter that sort of stands on its own as it deals with the pastor and the flock among whom he ministers. It's helpful because Peter's counsel doesn't have a religious ring to it. It's refreshingly insightful. The opening lines of the chapter offer a couple of effective and important principles worth mentioning.

> Therefore, I exhort the elders among you, as your fellow elder and witness of the sufferings of Christ, and a partaker also of the glory that is to be revealed, shepherd the flock of God among you . . . . (1 Pet. 5:1–2a)

The first principle is this: *The pride of position must be absent.* Remember who wrote these words: Peter the apostle, the spokesman for the early church, the one who saw Jesus with his own eyes, who literally walked with the Messiah for more than three years. What honor had been his . . . what privileges, and yet he never hints at his own position of authority. Any sense of pride of position is absent from Peter's opening remarks. He simply calls himself, "a fellow elder, a witness of the sufferings of Christ, and a partaker of the glory that is to be revealed."

I consider these very humble words. He says nothing about his authoritative apostleship. Nothing about the importance of the recipients of his letter being obedient to his advice. He simply identifies with the elders as a "fellow elder." And if you want to make the word "partaker" a little bit more understandable, think of the word *partner.* "I'm a partner with you in the same glory that's going to be revealed hereafter." He saw himself on the same level as the other elders.

A religious ministry is an easy place to secretly construct a proud life. Unfortunately, pride can consume a person in ministry. It not only can, it *has* for some.

Stop and think about why. We speak for God. We stand before large groups of people regularly. Most ministers address more people more often (without being interrupted) than most executives of large corporations do in their work. Those in ministry can live virtually unaccountable. We are respected and trusted by most. And throughout our careers, only rarely are we questioned. When we are, our answers are seldom challenged. We do our preparation away from the public eye as we work alone in our studies. All of that is fine . . . but it's like a mine field of perils and dangers. Because before you know it, we can begin to fall into the trap of believing only what we say and seeing only what we discover. This is especially true if your ministry grows and your fame spreads. When that happens, your head can swell and your ears can become dull of hearing.

If Peter, one of the original Twelve, the earliest spokesman for the church, an anointed servant of God, would not mention his role of importance, I think we can learn a lesson about humility. Mark it down. Don't forget it. The pride of position must be absent.

There is a second principle, equally significant: *The heart of a shepherd must be present.* Remember his opening imperative? "Shepherd the flock of God which is among you." The original root word means "to act as a shepherd, to tend a flock." And don't miss the flip side of the coin: He calls the people "the flock of God."

That is why I have never cultivated the habit of referring to any congregation I serve as "my people." The flock isn't owned or controlled by the under-shepherd; they are God's people! They must ultimately answer to Him. They live their lives before Him. They are to obey *Him.* It is His Word that guides us all, shepherd and flock alike.

I like this description: "By definition, the true elder is the shepherd of the flock in which God has placed him . . . who bears them on his heart, seeks them when they stray, defends them from harm, comforts them in their pain, and feeds them with the truth."

This is a good time to add that unless you have the heart of a shepherd, you really ought not to be in a pastorate. You might wish to teach. You might choose to be involved in some other realm of ministry, and there are dozens of possibilities. But if you lack the heart of a shepherd, my advice is simple: don't go into the pastorate. It soon becomes a mismatch, frustrating both pastor and flock.

This saying used to hang in the office of my good friend and former minister of worship, Dr. Howie Stevenson. "Never try to teach a pig to sing. It wastes your time, and it annoys the pig!"

I've heard some people say, "Well, I'll just learn how to be a shepherd." Sorry. There is more to it than that. Shepherding has to be in your heart. There isn't a textbook, there isn't a course, there isn't some relationship that will turn you into a shepherd. It is a calling.

It's a matter of gifting by God, as we saw in the previous chapter. You are not educated into becoming a shepherd. Seminary may help, for during their years in seminary, most students discover whether or not they have a shepherd's heart. If they do not, I repeat, they should not pursue the pastorate.

I've seen evangelists filling pulpits, and the church is evangelized. But it isn't shepherded. I've seen teachers, bright and capable teachers, filling the pulpit, and the church is carefully instructed and biblically educated. But it isn't shepherded. A shepherd's heart certainly includes evangelism, teaching and exhortation, but it must also include love and tolerance, servant-hearted patience and understanding, and a lot of room for those lambs and sheep who don't quite measure up. Pastoring a church isn't a religious profession, not really. It isn't a business decision but rather a call of God that links certain shepherds with certain flocks.

Religion speaks in terms of hiring qualified professionals to fulfill certain responsibilities. The result is "hirelings," as Jesus called them (John 10:11–15). But in God's flock, shepherds are gifted; they are called to serve and to give themselves, to love and to encourage, to model the Savior's style. When this occurs churches are blessed and they enjoy hope beyond religion.

Three Essential Attitudes for Non-Religious Shepherds

Shepherd the flock of God among you, exercising oversight not under compulsion, but voluntarily, according to the will of God; and not for sordid gain, but with eagerness; nor yet as lording it over those allotted to your charge, but proving to be examples to the flock. (1 Pet. 5:2–3)

I find at least three vital attitudes set forth in the verses you just read. Each attitude begins with a negative, followed by the positive side.

1. Not under compulsion . . .
   but voluntarily, according to the will of God

2. Not for gain . . .
   but with eagerness
3. Nor yet as lording it over those allotted to your charge . . .
   but proving to be examples to the flock.

Attitude number one is *an attitude of willingness.* "Not under compulsion, but voluntarily." *Compulsion* means "to be compelled by force." Like getting your teenager out of bed early in the morning to go to school. That is compulsion. Peter, however, isn't referring to a teenager at school but a shepherd with his flock.

This reminds me of a story I heard several years ago. A young man was sleeping soundly one Sunday morning when his mother came in, shook him, and said, "Wake up, son. You've got to get up . . . you've got to get out of bed." He groaned and complained. "Give me three good reasons why I have to get up this morning." Without hesitation his mother said, "Well, first of all, it's Sunday morning, and it's only right that we be in church. Second, because it's only forty minutes until church starts, so we don't have much time. And third, *you're the pastor!*"

Paul writes in his swan song that God's messengers are to "be ready in season and out of season" (2 Tim. 4:2). Faithful shepherds are to be willing "in season and out of season." . . . when we feel like it, when we don't . . . when the church is growing as well as when it's not.

One of the things that intensifies burnout in ministry is a lack of willingness. And willingness depends on resting when we should so we can give it our all when we must. That's why, each time I speak to them, I encourage ministers to take a day off every week—when possible, a day and a half or two days. Why? To replenish the soul, to refresh the spirit. Furthermore, it is also imperative to take sufficient vacation time, to get away. I encourage "mini-vacations" as well—to get away with your mate, to spend time in refreshment and romance and simply the enjoyment of one another. By doing so, we are better able to do our work willingly and "not under compulsion."

I see many a frowning face and weary body when I go to pastors' conferences. Candidly, of all the groups that I minister to, few are more depressed and exhausted than a group of pastors. They are overworked, usually underpaid, and almost without exception underappreciated, though most of them are doing a remarkable piece of work.

Mild depressions can come upon us unexpectedly that erode our willingness. Often we can't explain such depressions at the time. Later, perhaps, but not when they occur.

I was reading to Cynthia the other day from the book I mentioned earlier in the chapter, Spurgeon's *Lectures to My Students*. She was in the kitchen working, and I walked over and said, "You've got to hear this." Then I read her about three pages! (Talk about a willing spirit!) Though writing more than one hundred years ago, Spurgeon described exactly some of the reasons we suffer from "burn out" in ministry today. He even admitted to depression in his own life, often before a great success, sometimes after a great success, and usually because of something he couldn't explain. He called this chapter "The Minister's Fainting Fits" (great title!). Listen to his candid remarks.

> Fits of depression come over most of us. Usually cheerful as we may be, we must at intervals be cast down. The strong are not always vigorous, the wise not always ready, the brave not always courageous, and the joyous not always happy. There may be here and there men of iron . . . but surely the rust frets even these.[4]

Let me add one final comment here . . . for the flock of God. Be tolerant with your pastor. A better word is *patient*. Try your best not to be too demanding or set your expectations too high. Multiply your own requests by however many there are in your church, and you'll have some idea of what the shepherd of the flock must live with. Be very understanding. Remember, if you write a letter that will bring his spirit down, it could wound him for weeks. Sometimes a confrontation is necessary. But even then, be kind. Be tactful. Pray for him! Encourage him! When you do, you'll find him all the more willing to serve his Lord among you.

Now, look at the second attitude: *an attitude of eagerness*. This next phrase describes not just willingness but an attitude of enthusiastic eagerness. Look how Peter expresses this: "Not for sordid gain, but with eagerness." The old King James Bible called sordid gain (money) "filthy lucre." Make certain your ministry is not motivated by the monetary, external perks. Religious circles emphasize, think about, and make a big thing of money. Guard against that.

I challenge preachers—and I have done it myself through the years—not to do a wedding just because they may get fifty dollars (or whatever) to do that wedding. Be eager to serve, not greedy! And if you're invited to participate in a week-long conference, do it because you really want to, not because you'll get an honorarium. Money is not a healthy motivation, so watch your motives.

When I was in seminary, my sister made me a small black-and-white sign that I hung on the wall in front of my desk where I studied. It read simply, *"What's your motive?"* What a searching question. I looked at it, off and on, for four years. It's a question every shepherd needs to ask on a weekly basis. Motives must forever be examined.

There is nothing quite as exciting or delightful as a shepherd who emits enthusiasm. Such zeal is *contagious!* His love for the Scriptures becomes the flock's love for the Scriptures. His zest for life becomes the congregation's zest for life. His commitment to leisure and enjoyment of life becomes their commitment to leisure and enjoyment of life. His joyful commitment to obeying God becomes theirs. No wonder Peter emphasizes eagerness. His passion for the unsaved becomes their passion. How refreshing it is to be around shepherds who are getting up in years but still eager and enthusiastic!

There's a third attitude Peter highlights: *an attitude of meekness*. I think it was with an extra boost of passion that he wrote:

> . . . nor yet as lording it over those allotted to your charge, but proving to be examples to the flock. (1 Pet. 5:3)

I like the way Eugene Peterson paraphrases this:

Not bossily telling others what to do, but tenderly showing them the way. (MSG)

What concerns the old apostle here is a shepherd's exercising undue authority over others. We as shepherds must learn to hold our congregations loosely. We must watch our tendency to try and gain dominion over them, thinking of them as underlings. To avoid this, we must think of ourselves as servants, not sovereigns. Give the flock room to disagree. Assure them that they are to think on their own. But make no mistake. A shepherd who is "meek" is not weak. It takes great inner strength and security to demonstrate grace. He's willing to serve rather than demand. How beautiful, how marvelous it is, to witness one who is gifted and strong of heart, yet secure enough to let God's people grow and learn without having to fall in line with him at every point and march in lockstep to his drumbeat. The best shepherds are those who do their work unto the Lord, expecting no one to bow down before them.

While reading a recent issue of *Sports Illustrated*, I came across an article about Al Davis, owner of the Oakland Raiders football team. If you're a sports fan, you know that Davis is considered by many as one of the most greedy and proud of all owners in the business. He goes through more coaches in a decade than some owners do in a lifetime. This article reports that . . .

> Davis's abuses of power have become increasingly visible. For example, after practice it is customary for him to enter the equipment room, drop a towel on the floor and wait for an employee to clean his shoes. "I saw him make someone wipe his shoes in front of 75 people," says Denver Broncos coach Mike Shanahan, who coached the Raiders in 1988.[5]

When I read that, I thought—here's the *opposite* of servant-hearted leadership. Yet I've witnessed leaders in ministry positions who have abused their positions almost as blatantly.

I've just finished listening to a cassette tape. It's the voice of a man who has been in ministry for years, and it was as if I were listening to another Jim Jones as he preached. My heart ached for that flock who sat and endured his self-serving style. Here was a man who had gained the mastery; verbal abuse was commonly practiced. He snapped his fingers . . . they jumped. He cracked his whip . . . they bowed down. Friend, that is not "proving to be an example to the flock." That is religious abuse . . . the manipulation of a congregation . . . legalistic religion at its worst.

The pastorate brings an enormous amount of authority. Not even a board of elders or deacons, as powerful as they may be, can take the shepherd's place in the pulpit on Sunday. It is a place where he can wield incredible authority and, if he chooses to do so, pull rank. All the more reason not to abuse it. The shepherd is not a stand-in for the Lord!

What God's people need most in their minister is a model of the life of Jesus Christ. There is something convincing about a model. That's Peter's point here. The very best thing for the minister to do is live a life of authenticity, accountability, and humility. Few things win the hearts of sheep like a tender shepherd!

You may remember that Moses, toward the end of his life, was said to have been "very humble, more than any man who was on the face of the earth" (Num. 12:3). Here was a man who "pastored" millions of people, but he refused to pander to his fame. He cared nothing for the applause of the public. He would not manipulate the people. In fact, brokenhearted before God, he even said, "Just take me out of the way." This wonderful section of Scripture is a good reminder that as important as it is to be a decisive leader with strong convictions, accepting the responsibilities of the position, it is never appropriate for the shepherd to "lord it over" those in his care.

No extra charge for this little comment, but I want to underscore an earlier observation that taking control of others is a mark of insecurity. Those who must have absolute agreement from everyone are terribly insecure people. Isn't it interesting that Christ Jesus never demanded that His disciples write anything down, never once exhorted them to memorize things He said? What He told them most of all was, "Do not be afraid." That was His most frequent command. "Do not be afraid." And the other was given by implication, "Watch Me and follow My model." No one has ever had the authority over a flock like Christ, but only on the rarest of occasions did He even raise His voice . . . or rebuke His followers. Sheep do best when they are led, not driven . . . when they are released, not controlled . . . when they know they are loved, not shamed.

An Eternal Reward to Be Claimed

And when the Chief Shepherd appears, you will receive the unfading crown of glory. (1 Pet. 5:4)

I've mentioned crowns before in this book, but I've not mentioned *this* crown. Unlike the others, this is an exclusive crown. It is reserved for those who faithfully shepherd God's flock God's way. Only those who serve in this capacity will be able to receive the "unfading crown of glory." Notice, as a result of fulfilling these two principles and these three attitudes, the "crown of glory" will be awarded by "the Chief Shepherd" Himself.

Count on it, fellow shepherds. We have this to anticipate when we meet our Lord face to face.

Personal Suggestions for Both Sides of Ministry

To summarize, let me first address you who lead by saying, *keep a healthy balance.* If you teach, also be teachable. Read. Listen. Learn. Observe. Be ready to change. Then change! Admit wrong where you were wrong. Stand firm where you know you are right. You cannot win them all. And keep in mind, you're a servant of God, not a slave of the flock.

Since you are called to be a leader, when it's necessary, be a good follower—which takes us back to servanthood. When you lead, put yourself in the followers' shoes; think about what it would be like if you were sitting there listening to those things you are saying.

Neither underestimate your importance nor exaggerate your role. You are, admittedly, called of God. You represent Him, His message, His vision. You can become whipped by a congregation. (It happened to me once. It will never, by the grace of God, happen to me again.) Something tragic happens to a leader who has lost his drive and his determination. But you cannot do it all, so delegate. It's a big job to do, so invite others to help you do it. And when they do it well, give them credit.

Stay balanced. You are engaged in serious work, but (I repeat) keep a good sense of humor. Laugh often and loudly! And don't be afraid to laugh at yourself. My fellow laborers at Insight for Living make sure I do! On several occasions they have presented me with a tape containing all the "outtakes"—things they cut out of my taped messages during the year. Sort of my own private "bloopers." Some have even had the audacity to play this tape at a Christmas party for hundreds to hear and enjoy! As I listen, I cannot believe the dumb things I have said in any given year. It's enough to reduce even a strong-hearted shepherd to the size of a nit-pickin' termite!

Take God seriously, but don't take yourself too seriously.

Now, finally, to those of you being led, may I suggest that you *be a reason for rejoicing*. What a wonderful assignment!

Read the following slowly . . .

Obey your leaders, and submit to them; for they keep watch over your souls, as those who will give an account. Let them do this with joy and not with grief, for this would be unprofitable for you. (Heb. 13:17)

Think of ways to encourage your minister or leader. Pray often for him. Model gratitude and love. Demonstrate your affection with acts of generosity. Defend the shepherd whenever possible. And when you can't, tell him face to face, and tell no one else. Do it briefly, graciously, then forgive quickly. Try to imagine being in the shoes of the one who lives with the burden of the whole flock and is never free of that. And one more thought . . . think of how it would be if everyone else in the flock were *just like you*. C'mon, have a heart! The guy's not Spurgeon . . . and even if he were, you wouldn't agree with him either.

If you will do these things for your shepherd-leader, not only will you be rewarded, you will give him and yourself new hope . . . hope to press on, hope for the second mile, and everyone in the flock will enjoy hope beyond religion.

A Prayer for Hope Beyond Religion

Father, we consider it a priceless privilege to serve You, the living God. You've made all of us with different personalities, given us different gifts and responsibilities, and yet chosen to mingle us together in the same body, over which Christ is head. There are great temptations we face as shepherds and as sheep . . . to be in charge, to force others to get in line, to make things more uniform and rigid, to get narrow and demanding, to set our expectations too high . . . to handle ministry as if it were a secular enterprise. God, we need You to keep things fresh and unpredictable and especially to keep us authentic, servant-hearted people, and easy to live with.

So give us new hope . . . hope beyond religion, hope that motivates us to press on, serving You with pure motives and eager hearts. Thank You for Your grace, our only hope, dear Savior . . . in Your name.

AMEN

15

❖

Hope Beyond Dissatisfaction

A Formula That Brings Relief

OUR SOCIETY HAS gorged itself on the sweet taste of success. We've filled our plates from a buffet of books that range from dressing for success to investing for success. We've passed the newsstands and piled our plates higher with everything from *Gentleman's Quarterly* and *Vogue*, to the *Wall Street Journal* and *Time*. When we've devoured these, we have turned our ravenous appetites toward expensive, success-oriented seminars. We've gobbled down stacks of notebooks, cassette albums, and video tapes in our hunger for greater success.

The irony of all this is that "there is never enough success in anybody's life to make one feel completely satisfied."[1] Instead of fulfillment, we experience the bloated sensation of being full of ourselves—*our* dreams, *our* goals, *our* plans, *our* projects, *our* accomplishments. The result of this all-you-can-eat appetite is not contentment. It's nausea. How terribly dissatisfying!

"The trouble with success is that the formula is the same as the one for a nervous breakdown," says *The Executive's Digest*. If you find

235

yourself a little queasy after just such a steady diet, you don't need a second helping of success. You need a healthy dose of relief.

Interestingly, very few address that which most folks want but seldom find in their pursuit of success, and that is contentment, fulfillment, satisfaction. Rarely, if ever, are we offered boundaries and encouraged to say, "Enough is enough." And so we work harder and harder, make more and more, yet enjoy all of it less and less.

If we're hung up on any one subject in America today, we are hung up on the pursuit of success. Yet I don't know of another pursuit that is more deceptive—filled with fantasy dreams, phantoms, mirages, empty promises, and depressing disappointments.

Johnny Cash wasn't far off when he groaned, "If you don't have any time for yourself, any time to hunt or fish—that's success."

Today's Major Messages, Promising "Success"

The ad campaigns that come out of Madison Avenue promise much more than they can deliver. Their titillating messages fall into four categories: fortune and fame, power and pleasure.

Fortune says that to be successful you need to make the big bucks. Why else would the Fortune 500 list make such headlines every year? Anyone who is held up as successful must have more money than the average person.

Understand, there is nothing wrong with money earned honestly. Certainly there is nothing wrong in investing or giving or even spending money if the motive is right, if the heart is pure. But I have yet to discover anyone who has found true happiness simply in the gathering of more money. Although money is not sinful or suspect in itself, it is not what brings lasting contentment, fulfillment, or satisfaction.

Fame says that to be successful you need to be known in the public arena. You need to be a celebrity, a social somebody. Fame equates popularity with significance.

Power says that to be successful you need to wield a lot of authority, flex your muscles, take charge, be in control, carry a lot of weight. Push yourself to the front. Expect and demand respect.

Pleasure implies that to be successful you need to be able to do whatever feels good. This philosophy operates on the principle: "If it feels good, do it." It's just a modern version of the ancient epicurean philosophy, "Eat, drink, and be merry, for tomorrow you may die."

Fortune. Fame. Power. Pleasure. The messages bombard us from every direction. But what's missing in all this? Stop and ask yourself that question. Isn't something very significant absent here?

You bet. A *vertical* dimension. There's not even a hint of God's will or what pleases Him in the hard-core pursuit of success. Note also that nothing in that horizontal list guarantees satisfaction or brings relief deep within the heart. And in the final analysis, what most people really want in life is contentment, fulfillment, and satisfaction.

My sister, Luci, told me about the time she visited with a famous opera singer in Italy. This woman owned a substantial amount of Italian real estate, a lovely home, and a yacht floating on the beautiful Mediterranean in a harbor below her villa. At one point, Luci asked the singer if she considered all this the epitome of success.

"Why, no!" said the woman, sounding a bit shocked.

"What is success then?" asked Luci.

"When I stand to perform, to sing my music, and I look out upon a public that draws a sense of fulfillment, satisfaction, and pleasure from my expression of this art, at that moment I know I have contributed to someone else's need. That to me describes success."

Not a gathering of expensive possessions but a deliberate investment in the lives of others seems to be a crucial factor in finding fulfillment and contentment. Service. Help. Assistance. Compassion for others. Therein lies so much of what brings a sense of peace and true success.

In light of that, it seems, success is not a pursuit as much as it is a surprising discovery in an individual's life. All this brings us back to Peter's letter—old, but as we're discovering, ever relevant.

God's Ancient Plan: The Three A's

> You younger men, likewise, be subject to your elders; and all of you, clothe yourselves with humility toward one another, for God is opposed to the proud, but gives grace to the humble.
>
> Humble yourselves, therefore, under the mighty hand of God, that He may exalt you at the proper time, casting all your anxiety upon Him, because He cares for you. (1 Pet. 5:5–7)

The world's strategy to climb the ladder of success is simple: Work hard, get ahead, then climb higher—even if you have to claw and step on and climb over the next guy; don't let anything get in your way as you promote yourself. The goal is to make it to the top. It doesn't matter how many or who you push aside along the way, and it doesn't matter who you leave behind, even if it's your family or your friends or your conscience. It's a dog-eat-dog world, friends and neighbors, and the weak puppies don't make it. To survive, you have to hold on to the ladder for dear life. To succeed, you have to fight your way to the top . . . and never stop climbing.

I shook my head in disappointment when I read of Jimmy Johnson's decision to walk away from his wife and family several years ago when he became head coach of the Dallas Cowboys. He didn't deny it or hide it or apologize for his decision. He saw this major career promotion from the University of Miami to the Cowboys organization as his opportunity to make it to the top, big time. There was no way he would let anyone or anything get in his way; this was his moment to succeed, to move into big money. And things like home and family and kids (and grandkids!) were not going to stop him. He dropped all those responsibilities like a bad habit and split for Dallas like a hungry leopard searching for food.

In the world's eyes, he's now reached the pinnacle. A winning record, two Super Bowl rings, enormous amounts of money, fame, a yacht, several private enterprises, and now the Miami Dolphins with even greater hopes for more and more and more. As the public watches and reads of Johnson's accomplishments, most salivate. "The man's got it made!" would be the general opinion of athletes and sports fans and entrepreneurs and executives around the country. That, to them, represents success at its best.

God's plan, His ancient plan, is much different. We see it spelled out for us here in Peter's strategy for the right kind of success. In the three verses above, we see a series of contrasts to the kind of thinking I just illustrated. To keep everything simple, I call them the three A's: authority, attitude, and anxiety.

Authority

Peter's first piece of counsel advises us to submit ourselves to those who are wise and to "clothe" ourselves with humility.

> You younger men, likewise, be subject to your elders; and all of you, clothe yourselves with humility toward one another, for God is opposed to the proud, but gives grace to the humble. (1 Pet. 5:5)

The "clothe yourself" metaphor comes from a rare word that pictures a servant putting on an apron before serving those in the house. Perhaps Peter was recalling that meal in the upper room when Jesus wrapped Himself with a towel and washed the disciples' dirty feet (see John 13). Reclining at the table for their last meal with the Master, Peter and the other disciples had come to the table with dirty feet. The Savior, humbling Himself to the role of a servant, "clothed Himself" with a towel and, carrying a basin of water, washed their feet. I really believe the old fisherman was remembering that act of humility as he wrote these words in verse 5.

"Be subject to," he says—it's in the present tense here, "Keep on being subject to . . ." In other words, submission is to be an ongoing way of life, a lifestyle. We are to listen to the counsel of our elders in the faith, to be open to their reproofs, watch their lives, follow the examples they set, respect their decisions, and honor their years of seasoned wisdom. We must always remember that we need others. Their advice and model, their warnings and wisdom, are of inestimable value, no matter how far along in life we are.

I remember Dr. Howard Hendricks telling me years ago, "Experience is not the best teacher. *Guided* experience is the best teacher." The secret lies in the "guide"!

Bricklaying is a good illustration of this. As a novice, you can lay brick from morning to night, day in and day out, gaining several weeks of experience on your own, and you'll probably have a miserable-looking wall when you're finished. But if you work from the start with a journeyman bricklayer who knows how to lay a course of brick, one after the other, your guided experience can create a wall that is an object of beauty.

Proud independence results in a backlash of consequences, the main one being the opposition of God (see James 4:6). The original idea of God's opposing the proud is found in Proverbs 3.

> Do not envy a man of violence,
> And do not choose any of his ways.
> For the crooked man is an abomination to the LORD;
> But He is intimate with the upright.
> The curse of the LORD is on the house of the wicked,
> But He blesses the dwelling of the righteous.
> Though He scoffs at the scoffers,
> Yet He gives grace to the afflicted.
> The wise will inherit honor,
> But fools display dishonor. (Prov. 3:31–35)

In contrast to the humble, those who are proud in their hearts *scoff* at the Lord. This term expresses scorn and contempt. But God, not the proud, has the last scoff! As Solomon put it, "He scoffs at the scoffers."

When you submit yourself to those who are wise, instead of flaunting your own authority, you will have a greater measure of grace.

> But He gives a greater grace. Therefore it says, "God is opposed to the proud, but gives grace to the humble." (James 4:6)

And that is certainly what today's models of success could use a lot more of—a greater measure of grace. Isn't it noteworthy how rarely those who are on an aggressive, self-promoting fast track to the top even use the word *grace*. Grace, says Peter, is given by God to the humble, not to the proud.

Attitude

Peter's second strategy for success has to do with attitude. We must, he says, humble ourselves under God's mighty hand.

> Humble yourselves, therefore, under the mighty hand of God, that He may exalt you at the proper time. (1 Pet. 5:6)

In the Old Testament, God's hand symbolizes two things. The first is discipline (see Exod. 3:20, Job 30:21, and Ps. 32:4). The second is deliverance (see Deut. 9:26 and Ezek. 20:34). When we humble ourselves under the mighty hand of God, we willingly accept His discipline as being for our good and for His glory. Then we gratefully acknowledge His deliverance, which always comes in His time and in His way.

In other words, as we saw in the previous chapter, we don't manipulate people or events. We refuse to hurry His timing. We let Him set the pace. And we humbly place ourselves under His firm, steadying hand. As a result of this attitude—don't miss it!—"He may exalt you at the proper time."

I must confess there are times when God's timing seems awfully slow. I find myself impatiently praying, "Lord, hurry up!" Is that true for you too?

In today's dog-eat-dog society, if something isn't happening as quickly as we want it to, there are ways to get the ball rolling, and I mean *fast*. There are people to call, strings to pull, and strong-arm strategies that make things happen. They are usually effective and always impressive . . . but in the long run, when we adopt these methods, we regret it. We find ourselves feeling dissatisfied and guilty. God didn't do it—we did!

When I was led by God to step away from almost twenty-three marvelous years at the First Evangelical Free Church in Fullerton, California, and step into the presidency of Dallas Theological Seminary, Cynthia and I immediately faced a challenge . . . in many ways, the greatest challenge of our lives and ministry. What about our radio ministry, Insight for Living?

The seminary is in Dallas, Texas; IFL is in Anaheim, California. In order for Cynthia to remain in leadership at IFL and provide the vision that ministry needs, she has to be in touch with and available to our radio ministry, and she and I, both, need to be engaged in some of the day-to-day operations of IFL. Meanwhile my work at the seminary requires my presence and availability on many occasions. If I hope to be more than a figurehead, and I certainly do, then my presence on and around that campus is vital. But it's hard to be two places at once. I tried that several years ago, and it hurt!

Obviously, then, it makes sense for IFL to move to Dallas. But moving an organization that size (with around 140 employees) is a costly and complicated process. We have a continuing lease on our building in Anaheim, no property or building as of yet in Dallas . . . but she and I cannot continue to commute indefinitely. We have been doing that for well over two years—long enough to know we don't want to do that much longer! On top of all that, there's no money to move us.

So . . . we have two options, humanly speaking. We can run ahead, make things happen, manipulate the money needs, and get the move behind us . . . or we can "humble ourselves under the mighty hand of God" and pray and wait and watch Him work, counting on Him to "exalt us at the proper time" (answer our prayers, provide the funds, help us find a place in Dallas for relocating IFL, and end our commuting). And so we wait. We make the need known . . . and we wait.

We're still waiting. We're still praying. We *refuse* to rush ahead and "make things happen." Admittedly, we get a little impatient and anxious at times, but we're convinced He is able to meet our needs and He will make it happen! Meanwhile we must be content to humble ourselves under God's mighty hand.

What does it mean to humble *yourself* under the mighty hand of God in *your* job, vocation, or profession? What if you're not getting the raise or the promotion you deserve? What if you are in a situation where you could make things happen . . . but you really want God to do that?

Think of David, the young musician, tending his father's sheep back on the hills of Judea many centuries ago. He was a self-taught, gifted musician. He didn't go on tour, trying to make a name for himself. Instead, he sang to the sheep. He had no idea that someday his lyrics would find their way into the psalter or would be the very songs that have inspired and comforted millions of people through long and dark nights.

David didn't seek success; he simply humbled himself under the mighty hand of God, staying close to the Lord and submitting himself to Him. And God exalted David to the highest position in the land. He became the shepherd of the entire nation!

You don't have to promote yourself if you've got the stuff. If you're good, if you are to be used of Him, they'll find you. God will promote you. I don't care what the world system says. I urge you to let *God* do the promoting! Let *God* do the exalting! In the meantime, sit quietly under His hand. That's not popular counsel, I realize, but it sure works. Furthermore, you will never have to wonder in the future if it was you or the Lord who made things happen. And if He chooses to use you in a mighty way, really "exalt" you, you won't have any reason to get conceited. He did it all!

How refreshing it is to come across a few extremely gifted and talented individuals who do not promote themselves . . . who genuinely let God lead . . . who refuse to get slick and make a name for themselves! May their tribe increase.

Anxiety

Peter's third strategy for success tells us to cast all our anxiety upon God.

> Humble yourselves . . . casting all your anxiety upon Him, because He cares for you. (1 Pet. 5:6–7)

The original meaning of the term *cast* literally is "to throw upon." We throw ourselves fully and completely on the mercy and care of God. This requires a decisive action on our part. There is nothing passive or partial about it.

When those anxieties that accompany growth and true success emerge and begin to weigh you down (and they will), throw yourself on the mercy and care of God. Sometimes the anxiety comes in the form of people, sometimes it comes in the form of the media, sometimes it comes in the form of money and possessions, or a dozen other sources I could mention. The worries multiply, the anxieties intensify. Just heave those things upon the Lord. Throw them back on the One who gave them.

I love David's advice:

> Cast your burden upon the LORD, and He will sustain you;
> He will never allow the righteous to be shaken. (Ps. 55:22)

I have a feeling David wrote that one after he'd "made it," don't you?

If you've ever carried a heavily loaded pack while hiking, mountain climbing, or marching in the military, you know there is nothing quite like the wonderful words from the leader, "Let's stop here for a while." Everybody lets out a sign of relief and *thump, thump, thump, thump,* all those packs start hitting the ground. That's the word picture here. Release your burden. Just drop it. Let it fall off your back. Reminds me of John Bunyan's pilgrim when he came to the place of the sepulcher and the cross; the burden of sin fell off his back.

So here's the simple formula that will enable you to handle whatever success God may bring your way and will provide you with the relief you need while waiting:

SUBMISSION + HUMILITY − WORRY = RELIEF

Submission to others plus humility before God minus the worries of the world equals genuine relief. It will also provide hope and contentment without the pain of dissatisfaction.

Our Great Need: Effecting Change

Now I wish all this were as simple as just reading it and saying, "That's it. I'm changed. It's gonna happen." Believe me, it doesn't work that way. So let me suggest some things we need in our lives to effect these changes.

To grasp what true success really is and how to obtain it, we need to tune out the seductive messages from the world and tune in to the instructive messages from the Word. How? It occurs to me we need at least three things to make this happen.

First, we need direction so we can know to whom we should submit.

Let's understand . . . start trying to please everybody, and you're assured of instant failure and long-term frustration. We need God to direct us to those to whom we should submit.

Who are the people I should follow? Who are the folks I should watch? Whose writings should I read? Whose songs should I sing? Whose ministry should I support financially? Whose model should I emulate?

We need direction from God. So begin to pray, "Lord, direct me to the right ones to whom I should submit." Count on Him for direction.

Second, we need discipline to restrain our hellish pride.

Pride will keep rearing its ugly head. The more successful we get, the stronger the temptation to rely on the flesh. We've thought about that already in previous chapters. I use the words "hellish pride" because it is just that. Pride will whisper ways to promote ourselves (but look very humble and pious). Pride will tell us how and when to manipulate or intimidate others. We need discipline to keep ourselves from being our own deliverers. We need discipline to stay *under* the hand of God. Remember that—*under* His mighty hand. But pride hates being *under* anything or anyone. So ask God for discipline here.

Third, we need discernment so we can detect the beginning of anxiety.

245

Ever have something begin to kind of nag you? You can't put your finger on it. It's fuzzy. Sort of a slimy ooze. It's just growing in the corners, nagging you, getting you down. That is the beginning of a heavy anxiety. We need discernment to detect it, identify it, and get to its root so we can deal with it. When we see the beginning of anxiety for what it is, that's the precise moment to cast it on God, to roll that pack on Him. At that moment we say, "I can't handle it, Lord. You take over."

And how are these needs met? Through the Word of God. The principles and precepts of Scripture give us direction, discipline, and discernment.

Do you find yourself caught up in the success syndrome? Are you still convinced that the world's formula is best? Do you find yourself manipulating people and pulling strings to get ahead? Are you, at this moment, in the midst of a success syndrome you started, not God? No wonder you feel dissatisfied! That type of success *never* satisfies. Only God-directed success offers the formula that brings contentment, fulfillment, satisfaction, and relief.

God's success is never contrived. It is never forced. It is never the working of human flesh. It is usually unexpected—and its benefits are always surprising.

The hand of God holds you firmly in His control. The hand of God casts a shadow of the cross across your life. Sit down at the foot of that cross and deliberately submit your soul to His mighty hand. Accept His discipline. Acknowledge His deliverance. Ask for His discernment.

Then be quiet. Be still. Wait. And move over so I can sit beside you. I'm waiting too.

A Prayer for Hope Beyond Dissatisfaction

We are so grateful, Father, for the truth of Your Word—for the Old and New Testaments alike . . . the teachings of Jesus, the writings of Peter, the profound songs of David, the law of Moses. All of it blends together in a harmony, a symphony of theological and practical significance. You have us under Your hand, and in our more lucid moments we really want to be there. In times of impatience and wildness we want to squirm free and run ahead. Thank You for holding us, for forgiving us, for cleaning us up, for accepting us, for reshaping us, for not giving up on us. And at this moment, we give You the full right to discipline, to direct, to deliver in Your way and in Your time. Give us great patience as we wait. Humbly, I pray and submit to You in Jesus' name.

AMEN

Hope Beyond the Battle

Standing Nose-to-Nose with the Adversary

"AS YOU LOOK back over your life, at what places did you grow the most?"

Whenever I ask this question, almost without exception the person will mention a time of pain, a time of loss, a time of deep and unexplained suffering in his or her life. Yet when suffering rains down upon us, our tendency is to think that God has withdrawn His umbrella of protection and abandoned us in the storm. Our confusion during those inclement times stems from our lack of understanding about the role of pain in our lives. Philip Yancey is correct in his analysis.

> Christians don't really know how to interpret pain. If you pinned them against the wall, in a dark, secret moment, many Christians would probably admit that pain was God's one mistake. He really should have worked a little harder and invented a better way of coping with the world's dangers.[1]

Nevertheless, the pain rages on. With relentless regularity, we encounter hardship and heartache. We give ourselves to a friendship, only to lose that person in death. We grieve the loss and determine not to give ourselves so completely again . . . so loneliness comes to haunt us. Is there no hope beyond this? We find the answer to that age-old question, according to Peter, is a resounding YES!

Interestingly, the apostle never once laments the fact that the people he was writing to were suffering pain and persecution, nor does he offer advice on how to escape it. Instead, he faces suffering squarely, tells them (and us) not to be surprised by it, and promises that God provides benefits for enduring life's hurts. Even when life is dreary and overcast, rays of hope pierce through the clouds to stimulate our growth. In fact, without pain there would be little growth at all, for we would remain sheltered, delicate, naive, irresponsible, and immature.

Let's get something straight. Our real enemy is not our suffering itself. The real culprit is our adversary the Devil, the one responsible for much of the world's pain and danger. Although God is at work in the trials of life, so is Satan. While God uses our trials to draw us closer to Him, Satan tries to use them as levers to pry us away from Him. That tug-o'-war only intensifies the battle! Not surprisingly, Peter gives us some crucial advice on how to do battle with the Devil and how to keep him from gaining victory over our lives.

Battle Tactics

In his book *Your Adversary the Devil*, Dwight Pentecost compares the tactics of a physical battle to those of the spiritual one.

> No military commander could expect to be victorious in battle unless he understood his enemy. Should he prepare for an attack by land and ignore the possibility that the enemy might approach by air or by sea, he would open the way to defeat. Or should he prepare for a land and sea attack and ignore the possibility of an attack through the air, he would certainly jeopardize the campaign.
>
> No individual can be victorious against the adversary of our souls unless he understands that adversary; unless he understands

his philosophy, his methods of operation, his methods of temptation.[2]

This being the case, it should not surprise us that Peter begins by identifying the enemy and his general modus operandi. Whoever denies the fact that there is a literal enemy of our souls chooses to live in a dream world, revealing not only a lack of understanding but also a lack of reality. Throughout the Old Testament and the New we find ample evidence of a literal Devil, an actual Satan—a very real "adversary," to use Peter's word.

His Identity, Style, and Purpose

> Be of sober spirit, be on the alert. Your adversary, the devil, prowls about like a roaring lion, seeking someone to devour. But resist him, firm in your faith, knowing that the same experiences of suffering are being accompanied by your brethren who are in the world. (1 Pet. 5:8–9)

The original term translated *adversary* refers to an opponent in a lawsuit. This individual is a person on the other side. An adversary is neither a friend nor a playmate. An adversary is no one to mess around with—and no one to joke about.

Satan's constant relationship with the child of God is an adversarial relationship. Make no mistake about it; he despises us. He hates what we represent. He is our unconscionable and relentless adversary, our opponent in the battle between good and evil, between truth and false-hood, between the light of God and the darkness of sin.

"Your adversary, the devil," puts it well. That's the way Peter identifies the Enemy—boldly, without equivocation. "The devil" comes from the word *diabolos*, which means "slanderer" or "accuser." Revelation 12:10 states that the enemy of our souls is "the accuser of our brethren." He accuses us "day and night," according to that verse. Not only does he accuse us to God, he also accuses us to ourselves. Many of our self-defeating thoughts come from the demonic realm. He is constantly accusing, constantly building guilt, constantly prompting shame, constantly coming against us with hopes of destroying us.

Did you notice his style? "He prowls about." The Devil is a prowler. Think about that. He comes by stealth, and he works in secret. His plans are shadowy. He never calls attention to his approach or to his attack. Furthermore, he is "like a roaring lion." He is a beast, howling and growling with hunger, "seeking someone to devour"! To personalize this, substitute your name for "someone." When you do, it makes that verse all the more powerful. "Your adversary, the devil, prowls about like a roaring lion, seeking to devour _____ ." I find that has a chilling effect on my nervous system.

He isn't simply out to tantalize or to tease us. He's not playing around. He has a devouring, voracious appetite. And he dances with glee when he destroys lives, especially the lives of Christians.

A. T. Robertson wrote, "The devil's purpose is the ruin of mankind. Satan wants all of us." It's wise for us to remember that when we travel. It's wise for us to remember that when we don't gather for worship on a Sunday and we're really out on our own. It's wise to remember that when we find ourselves alone for extended periods of time, especially during our more vulnerable moments. He prowls about, stalking our every step, waiting for a strategic moment to catch us off guard. His goal? To devour us . . . to consume us . . . to eat us alive.

I hope you've gotten a true picture of your enemy. He's no sly-looking imp with horns, a red epidermis, and a pitchfork. He is the godless, relentless, brutal, yet brilliant adversary of our souls who lives to bring us down . . . to watch us fall.

Our Response

Peter's opening command alerts us to our necessary response: "Be of sober spirit, be on the alert."

Satan doesn't like chapters like this. He hates exposure. He hates being talked about. He certainly hates it when truth replaces fantasy and people are correctly informed. He especially hates having all of his ugly and filthy plans and destructive ways identified.

Be Alert. As his possible prey, however, our primary response should be to keep on the lookout for the predator.

Satan is a dangerous enemy. He is a serpent who can bite us when we least expect it. He is a destroyer . . . and an accuser . . . . He has great power and intelligence, and a host of demons who assist him in his attacks against God's people . . . . He is a formidable enemy; we must never joke about him, ignore him, or underestimate his ability. We must "be sober" and have our minds under control when it comes to our conflict with Satan.[3]

The Devil's great hope is that he will be ignored, written off as a childhood fairy tale, or dismissed from the mind of the educated adult. Like a prowler breaking into a home, Satan doesn't want to call attention to himself. He wants to work incognito, undetected, in the shadows. The thing he fears most is the searchlight of the Scriptures turned in his direction, revealing precisely who he really is and what comprises his battle plan.

> *Respect Him.* To defeat the Devil we must first be alert to his presence . . . respect him—not fear or revere him, but respect him, like an electrician respects the killing power of electricity.

One caution here, however.

A part of this soberness includes not blaming everything on the devil. Some people see a demon behind every bush and blame Satan for their headaches, flat tires, and high rent. While it is true that Satan can inflict physical sickness and pain (see Luke 13:16 and the Book of Job), we have no biblical authority for casting out demons of headache or demons of backache. One lady phoned me long-distance to inform me that Satan had caused her to shrink seven and a half inches. While I have great respect for the wiles and powers of the devil, I still feel we must get our information about him from the Bible and not from our own interpretation of experiences.[4]

Please be careful that you don't identify every ache and pain or every significant problem you encounter as being satanic in origin. My brother mentioned to me that he once counseled a woman who said she had "the demon of nail-biting." I've met a few who said they fought against "the demon of gluttony." (From their appearance, they were losing the war.) That is not a sign of maturity. I get real concerned about folks who blame the Devil every time something happens that makes life a little bit difficult for them. In fact, it can even become an excuse for not taking responsibility for your own life and your own decisions and choices.

So be alert and be sober. Be calm and watchful. Or, as Moffatt renders it, "Keep cool. Keep awake." We use that word *cool* very lightly today, but here it means a calm coolness. Like professionals in an athletic contest. The best in the game stay cool, calm, collected, and clear-headed, even in the last two minutes as they drive hard for the win, the ultimate prize. So be calm, but be on the alert. Satan's prowling around. This is no time for a snooze in the backyard hammock. He's silently maneuvering a brilliant strategy with plans to destroy us. This is serious stuff!

By the way, I've never seen a prowler who wore a beeper. I've never heard of a prowler who came honking his way down the street with a loudspeaker, saying, "I'm gonna slip in through the sliding door of that home at 7147 Elm at two o'clock in the morning." No, you know a prowler doesn't do that. He comes with stealth. He silently slides his way in. And you never even know he's in your house until he's robbed you blind.

Last fall Cynthia and I had the scare of our lives—literally. I was ministering at a hotel in Cancun—a nice, safe, well-equipped hotel. We turned in for the night around 11:30 or so and were soon in Dreamland. Shortly before 1:00 A.M. Cynthia's loud, shrill scream startled me awake. "There's a man in our room!!"

I looked toward the sliding-glass door that opened onto the patio . . . and there he stood, silent and staring into our room. A chill raced down my spine. The door had been slid open, and the curtains were blowing like sails into the room from the wind off the gulf waters. In fact, it was the surge of the surf that had awakened Cynthia, not the intruder. He had not made a sound . . . nor was he easily visible, since he was dressed in dark clothing.

I jumped out of bed and stood nose-to-nose with him . . . and yelled at the top of my lungs, hoping to frighten him away. For all I knew he had a gun or a knife, but this was no time to close my eyes and pray and lie there like a wimp. Slowly, he backed out of the room, jumped off the seawall, and quickly escaped. Hotel security never found a trace of him, except for a few footprints in the sand. He was a prowler who came, most likely, to steal from our room. Talk about a lasting memory!

Our adversary is a prowler. He comes without announcement, and to make matters worse, he comes in counterfeit garb. He is brilliant, and you and I had better *respect* that brilliance.

I've heard young Christians say things like, "This Christian life is thrilling. I'm ready to take on the Devil." When I can, I pull them aside and say, "Don't say that. It's a stupid comment! You're dealing with the invisible realm. You're dealing with a power you cannot withstand in yourself and a presence you have no knowledge of when you say something like that. Get serious. Be on the alert." Usually that's enough to wake 'em up. Every once in a while it's helpful to be knocked down a notch or two, especially when we're starting to feel a little big for our britches.

I heard a funny but true story recently about Muhammad Ali. It took place in the heyday of his reign as heavyweight champion of the world. He had taken his seat on a plane and the giant 747 was starting to taxi toward the runway when the flight attendant walked by and noticed Ali had not fastened his seat belt.

"Please fasten your seat belt, sir," she requested.

He looked up proudly and snapped, "Superman don't need no seat belt, lady!"

Without hesitation she stared at him and said, "Superman don't need no plane . . . so buckle up."

Don't be fooled by your own pride or softened by some medieval caricature of an "impish" little devil. Our adversary is a murderer, and except for the Lord Himself, he's never met his match. We may hate him . . . but, like any deadly enemy, we had better respect him and keep our distance. There's a war on!

Resist Him. After we are alert to him and respect him, we must resist him. Don't run scared of the enemy. Don't invite him in; don't play with him. But don't be afraid of him either. Resist him. Through the power of the Lord Jesus Christ, firmly resist him.

"But resist him, firm in your faith," writes Peter. Kenneth Wuest has a wise word of counsel on this.

> The Greek word translated "resist" means "to withstand, to be firm against someone else's onset" rather than "to strive against that one." The Christian would do well to remember that he cannot fight the devil. The latter was originally the most powerful and wise angel God created. He still retains much of that power and wisdom as a glance down the pages of history and a look about one today will easily show. While the Christian cannot take the offensive against Satan, yet he can stand his ground in the face of his attacks. Cowardice never wins against Satan, only courage.[5]

I like that closing line.

Once we have enough respect for Satan's insidious ways to stay alert and ready for his attacks, the best method for handling him is strong resistance. That resistance is not done in our own strength, however, but comes from being "firm in faith." An example of this can be seen in the wilderness temptations of Christ when He resisted Satan with the Word of God (see Matt. 4:1–11).

You know what helps me when I sense I'm in the presence of the enemy? Nothing works better for me in resisting the Devil than the actual quoting of Scripture. I usually quote God's Word in such situations. One of the most important reasons for maintaining the discipline of Scripture memory is to have it ready on our lips when the enemy comes near and attacks. And you'll know it when he does. I don't know how to describe it, but the longer you walk with God, the more you will be able to sense the enemy's presence.

And when you do, you need those verses of victory ready to come to the rescue. The Word of God is marvelously strong. It is alive and active and "sharper than a two-edged sword." And its truths can slice their way into the invisible, insidious ranks of the demonic hosts.

Although our own strength is insufficient to fend him off, when we draw on the limitless resources of faith, we can stand against him nose-to-nose, much like I did with that intruder at Cancun. And such faith is nurtured and strengthened by a steady intake of the Scriptures.

Furthermore, the strength that comes from faith is supplemented by the knowledge of that company of saints stretching down through history, as well as present-day believers joining hands in prayer across the globe. There is something wonderfully comforting about knowing that we are not alone in the battle against the adversary.

In spite of faith and in spite of friends, however, the battle is *exhausting*. I don't know of anything that leaves you more wrung out, more weary. Nothing is more demanding, nothing more emotionally draining, nothing more personally painful than encountering and resisting our archenemy.

The devil always has a strategy, and he is an excellent strategist. He's been at it since he deceived Eve in the Garden. He knows our every weakness. He knows our hardest times in life. He knows our besetting sins. He knows the areas where we tend to give in the quickest. He also knows the moment to attack. He is a master of timing . . . and he knows the ideal place.

But I have good news for you. Better still, Scripture has good news for you. When you resist through the power and in the name of the Lord Jesus Christ, the Devil will ultimately retreat. He will back down. He won't stay away; he'll back away. He will retreat as you resist him, firm in your faith.

Remember Ephesians 6:10–11: "Be strong in the Lord, and in the strength of His might. Put on the full armor of God, that you may be able to stand firm against the schemes of the devil."

This is where the Christian has the jump on every unbeliever who tries to do battle against the enemy. Those without the Lord Jesus have no power to combat or withstand those supernatural forces. No chance! They are facing the enemy without weapons to defend themselves. But when the Christian is fully armed with the armor God provides, he or she is invincible. Isn't that a great word? Invincible! That gives us hope beyond the battle.

It's a mockery to say to those who are not Christians, "Just stand strong against the enemy." They can't. They have no equipment. They have no weapons. A person must have the Lord Jesus reigning within to be able to stand strong in His might.

Our Rewards

Will there be suffering in resisting Satan? Yes. Will it be painful? Without a doubt. I have found that there are times we emerge from the battle a little shell-shocked. But after the dust settles, our Commander-in-Chief will pin medals of honor on our lapels. And what are they? Peter tells us.

> And after you have suffered for a little while, the God of all grace, who called you to His eternal glory in Christ, will Himself perfect, confirm, strengthen and establish you. (1 Pet. 5:10)

He will "perfect, confirm, strengthen and establish" us. Talk about hope beyond the battle! Here is the biblical portrait of a decorated war hero, a seasoned veteran from the ranks of the righteous whose muscles of faith have been hardened by battle. It is the portrait of a well-grounded, stable, mature Christian. Christ will make sure the portrait of our lives looks like that, for He himself will hold the brush. And His hand is vastly more powerful than our enemy's.

I remember one night when I was taking care of a couple of our grandchildren. It was late in the evening, but since grandfathers usually let their grandchildren stay up longer than they should, they were still awake. We were laughing, messing around, and having a great time together when we suddenly heard a knock at the door. Not the doorbell, but a mysterious knocking. Immediately one of my grandsons grabbed hold of my arm. "It's OK," I said. The knock came again, and I started to the door. My grandson followed me, but he hung onto my left leg and hid behind me as I opened the door. It was one of my son's friends who had dropped by unexpectedly. After the person had left and I'd closed the door, my grandson, still holding on to my leg, said in a strong voice. "Bubba, we don't have anything to worry about, do we?" And I said, "No, we don't have anything to worry about. Everything's fine." You know why he was strong? Because he was hanging on to protection. As long as he was clinging to his grandfather's leg, he didn't have to worry about a thing.

That happens to us when we face the enemy. When he knocks at the door or when he prowls around back or when he looks for the chink in your armor, you hang on to Christ. You stand firm in faith. You put on the "armor of God" (Eph. 6:11–20—please read it!). You have nothing to worry about. *Nothing.* For, as Peter reminds us, our Lord has "dominion forever and ever. Amen" (1 Pet. 5:11). He is the one *ultimately* in control, and that is something in which every believer can find strength to hope again.

Necessary Reminders

Now, I want to tie a couple of strings around your finger as reminders as we bring these thoughts to a close. This advice has helped me throughout my Christian life, and I think you may find it useful.

First, never confuse confidence in Christ with cockiness in the flesh.

Confidence and cockiness are two different things. When you're facing the enemy, there's no place for cockiness. There is a place for confidence, however, and it's all confidence in Christ. You tell Him your weakness. You tell Him your fears. You ask Him to assist you as you equip yourself with His armor. You ask Him to think through you and to act beyond your own strength and to give you assurance. He'll do it. I repeat, it's all confidence in Christ. It's not some sense of cockiness in the flesh. You're a Christian, remember, not Superman or Wonder Woman.

Second, always remember that suffering is temporal but its rewards are eternal. Paul's wonderful words come to mind:

> Therefore we do not lose heart, but though our outer man is decaying, yet our inner man is being renewed day by day. For momentary, light affliction is producing for us an eternal weight of glory far beyond all comparison, while we look not at the things which are seen, but at the things which are not seen; for the things which are seen are temporal, but the things which are not seen are eternal. (2 Cor. 4:16–18)

Our Lord set the example for us, "who for the joy set before Him endured the cross" (Heb. 12:2). We have all read the Gospel accounts that chronicle Christ's suffering on the cross. We have all heard the Good Friday sermons that recount the horrors of crucifixion. As we look up at Him there on the cross, we can sense His shame and feel the anguish of His heart as we stand at arm's length from His torn and feverish flesh. What we can't see is the joy that awaited Him when He surrendered His spirit to His Father. But He saw it. He knew.

Imagine for a minute how horrible that nightmare of the cross really was. Then imagine, if you can, how wonderful the joy awaiting Jesus must have been for Him to have willingly endured that degree of suffering and injustice. That same joy awaits us. But we have to stoop through the low archway of suffering to enter into it. And part of that suffering includes doing battle with the adversary.

There is probably no book, other than the Bible, that is as insightful or creatively written concerning the strategies of Satan than C. S. Lewis's *The Screwtape Letters*. Here is a sampling of Satan's strategy as articulated by the imaginary Screwtape, a senior devil, who corresponds with his eager nephew to educate the fledgling devil for warfare against the forces of "the Enemy"—that is, God.

> Like all young tempters, you are anxious to be able to report spectacular wickedness. But do remember, the only thing that matters is

the extent to which you separate the man from the Enemy. It does not matter how small the sins are, provided that their cumulative effect is to edge the man away from the Light and out into the Nothing. Murder is no better than cards if cards can do the trick. Indeed, the safest road to Hell is the gradual one—the gentle slope, soft underfoot, without sudden turnings, without milestones, without signposts.[6]

A Prayer for Hope Beyond the Battle

Almighty God, You are our all-powerful and invincible Lord. How we need You, especially when the battle rages! Thank You for standing by our side, for being our strong shield and defender. We have no strength in ourselves. We are facing an adversary far more powerful, more brilliant, and more experienced than we. And so, with confidence, we want to put on and wear the whole armor of God . . . and, in Your strength alone, resist the wicked forces that are designed to bring us down.

Give new hope, Lord—hope beyond the battle. Encourage us with the thought that, in Christ, we triumph! In His great name I pray.

A M E N

17

Hope Beyond Misery

Lasting
Lessons

I HAVE BEEN encouraged by the fact that in his writings Peter gets us beyond the misery part of suffering.

You have noticed, haven't you, how we all throw pity parties for ourselves when suffering comes? It's almost as though we capitalize on the downside rather than focus on the benefits that come from the hard times. How easily we forget that growth occurs when life is hard, not when it's easy. However, it is not until we move beyond the misery stage that we're able to find the magnificent lessons to be learned. The problem is, we almost delight in our own misery.

In keeping with that, Dan Greenburg has written a very funny book, *How to Make Yourself Miserable*, in which he says:

> Too long have you . . . gone about the important task of punishing yourself . . . by devious or ineffective means. Too long have you had to settle for poorly formulated anxieties . . . simply because this vital field has always been shrouded in ignorance—a folk art rather than a science. Here at last is the frank report you have been waiting for. . . . It is our humble but earnest desire that through these pages you will be

able to find for yourself the inspiration and the tools for a truly painful, meaningless, miserable life.[1]

The truth is, of course, that we don't need any help in this area. We have perfected the art of misery all by ourselves. We know very well how to capitalize on misery, how to multiply our troubles rather than learn—through the sometimes torturous and yes, humiliating experiences of life—the vital lessons that bring about true joy, true meaning, and true significance in life.

I think it was Charlie "Tremendous" Jones who said, "There is something wrong with everything." Have you found that true? No matter where you go or what you do, is there something wrong with it? Murphy's Law says, "If something can go wrong, it will." Another of Murphy's Laws says, "That's not a light at the end of the tunnel. That's an oncoming train." And then one wag adds, "Murphy was an optimist."

The problem is, when we're all alone, when we are feeling the brunt of the experience, when we are in the midst of the swirl, when we can't see any light at the end of any tunnel, it isn't funny.

As the apostle Peter so masterfully presents in his letter, however, suffering is not the end; it's a means to the end. Best of all, God's end for us is maturity. It is growth. It is a reason for living and going on.

Five Observations and a Set of Bookends

As we look back at the things we've seen in this book, a few broad-stroked observations stand out in sharp relief. Perhaps by reviewing where we've been, we'll be able to sharpen our perspective to an even keener edge.

First, Peter wrote the letter. Though it may seem simplistically obvious, this fact offers us a unique encouragement. Along with James and John, Peter was one of the inner circle of three confidants to whom Jesus revealed himself most fully. Of the twelve disciples, Peter was regarded as the spokesman. Never one to teeter on the fence of indecision, Peter was impulsive, impetuous, and outspoken. He often put his foot in his mouth. He knew the heights of ecstasy on the Mount of Transfiguration and the depths of misery and shame on the night of his denials. And yet, in spite of his flaws and his failures, he is called an apostle of Jesus Christ. What grace!

This is tremendous encouragement for all who fear that their flaws are too numerous or their failures too enormous to be given another chance.

I'm sure Peter looked back on many occasions and thought, *I wish I hadn't said that.* (Haven't we all?) But I'll tell you something else about Peter; he wasn't afraid to step forward—to put it all on the line.

Are you one of those people who never goes anywhere without a thermometer, a raincoat, an aspirin, or a parachute? Not Peter. He went full-bore into whatever he believed in. No lack of passion in Peter! What he lacked in forethought he made up for in zeal and enthusiasm.

Admittedly, that kind of lifestyle is a bit risky and unpredictable.

Do you ever envy some of the experiences of Peter kind of people—folks who are willing to say what they think or admit how they feel, even though they may be wrong? How much more fun it is to be around people like that than around those who are so careful and so closed-in and so protected you never know what they really feel or where they really stand. They're very, very cautious, ultra-conservative thinkers who wouldn't even consider taking a risk. And they get very little done for the kingdom because they are so busy guarding everything they do and say.

Not Peter. Peter says, in effect, "I wrote this. Yes, I'm the Disciple who blew it. I failed Him when He was under arrest. I spoke when I shouldn't have. But I write now as one who has learned many things the hard way, things about pain and suffering. I don't write out of theory; I write from experience."

Second, hurting people received the letter. They are not named, but their locations are stated in the first verse of the letter. Peter wrote "to those who reside as aliens, scattered throughout Pontus, Galatia, Cappadocia, Asia, and Bithynia."

These hurting people, scattered outside their homeland, were lonely and frightened aliens, unsure of their future. But though they were homeless, they were not abandoned; though they were frightened, they were not forgotten. Peter reminds them of that. They were chosen by God and sanctified by His Spirit, and His grace and peace would be with them "in fullest measure."

Whenever you find yourself away from home, whenever you find yourself feeling abandoned and frightened, overlooked and forgotten, Peter's first letter is magnificent therapy. I suggest you read it in several versions. The Living Bible, the New International Version, J. B. Phillips's paraphrase, and Eugene Peterson's paraphrase, *The Message*, will give you a good start. Read through without a break, if possible. Read it through sitting there in that hotel room or alone in your cell or apartment or home. It is excellent counsel for those who are hurting. It will assure you of your calling and reassure you that grace and peace are yours to claim in fullest measure.

Third, this letter came through Silas. The person to whom Peter dictated his words was Silas, one of the leaders in the early church (referred to in I Peter 5:12 as Silvanus).

Silas was a cultured Roman citizen, well educated and well traveled. Peter was a rugged fisherman, a blue-collar Galilean with little or no schooling, but apparently (beginning with 5:12) he took the pen in his own hand and wrote the final lines of the letter. We know that, not only because of the substance of verses 12–14, but because of the style. The grammar, syntax, and vocabulary become simpler in the Greek text.

The rest of the letter, however, came *through* Silas. If you're like most people, you don't know enough about Silas to fill a three-by-five card. Some people know him only as the guy who carried Paul's bags on long trips. Paul gets all the attention, yet it was Paul *and* Silas who carried the gospel. Silas was Barnabas's replacement on Paul's missionary journeys. Paul *and* Silas were the ones who sang in the jail there in Philippi at midnight. And Silas was the one alongside Paul when the man was stoned. Silas was one who really understood the hearts of Paul and Peter.

Look at Acts 15:22 in case your respect for Silas needs a little bolstering.

> Then it seemed good to the apostles and the elders, with the whole church, to choose men from among them to send to Antioch with Paul and Barnabas—Judas called Barsabbas, and Silas, leading men among the brethren.

Here is a man who was one of the "leading men" of the church in the first century, and at the writing of this letter, he remained alongside Peter. In fact, Peter calls him "our faithful brother (for so I regard him)" (1 Pet. 5:12).

God gives Peter the message, Silas writes it down, and the Spirit of God ignites it. There may have been times when Silas was the wind beneath Peter's wings. We all need a Silas . . . someone willing to stand alongside us.

Fourth, the letter concludes with a greeting from a woman.

> She who is in Babylon, chosen together with you, sends you greetings, and so does my son, Mark. (1 Pet. 5:13)

Now, obviously, everybody wonders who "she" is; who is the woman "who is in Babylon"? Most interpretations fall into two categories: Peter could either be referring to "woman" in the figurative sense, as the bride of Christ, or he could be using the word literally. If the latter is correct, the woman referred to may possibly be Peter's wife. We know Peter had a wife because Jesus healed Peter's mother-in-law. Then, in 1 Corinthians 9:5, Paul makes note of the other apostles' wives, which likely included Peter's wife. Clement of Alexandria states that she died as a martyr for the faith, so she may have been well-known among the early Christians. No doubt those who first received this letter knew who the woman was whether or not we do.

Fifth, the letter's final command is one of intimate affection. This old fisherman still has a lot of love left in him. He has not become jaded. Look how he expresses himself.

Greet one another with a kiss of love.
Peace [*Shalom*] be to you all who are in Christ. (1 Pet. 5:14)

The kiss of the Christian was called "the shalom," or "the peace." With the passing of time, the practice of the kiss of peace has disappeared from the church. It is fascinating to trace through church history how the kiss shared between people of the faith became less and less intimate. In fact, if you are a romantic-type person given to warm affection, it's enough to completely deplete all wind from your sails! In the first century, a kiss was placed on the cheek of believers as they arrived and as they left the fellowship of the saints. As time passed, people began kissing the precious documents rather than each other. And before long, a wooden board was passed among the people and everyone kissed that plank of wood. (That sounds exciting, doesn't it? "Let's go to church tonight. We'll get to kiss the board.") Anyway, through it all, the church lost the sense of affection and intimacy along with the embrace of peace.

Originally, as they kissed each other's cheeks, they would say to one another, "Peace be with you," or simply *Shalom*. And that's exactly what Peter does here. "Greet one another with the kiss of peace."

Augustine said that when Christians were about to communicate, "they demonstrated their inward peace by the outward kiss."

The formal kiss was the sign of peace among early Christians, demonstrating their love and unity. This outward sign reflected an inward peace between believers, a sign that all injuries and wrongdoing were forgiven and forgotten. Some traditions should be reinstated!

Personal Applications

Well, so much for the bookends that open and close Peter's letter. Now let's take a last look at the contents and how they can speak to us in our personal situations.

Three times in the letter Peter refers to the reader, which gives us a clue to the letter's structure. In fact, the letter falls neatly into three distinct sections, each one detailing the "how" of an important truth: a living hope and how to claim it (1:1–2:10), a pilgrim life and how to live it (2:11–4:11), and a fiery trial and how to endure it (4:12–5:11). An application of these three major messages should give us hope beyond our misery.

A Living Hope and How to Claim It

Blessed be the God and Father of our Lord Jesus Christ, who according to His great mercy has caused us to be born again to a living hope through the resurrection of Jesus Christ from the dead. (1 Pet. 1:3)

The idea of "living hope" occupies Peter's mind throughout this section of the letter. And how do we claim that living hope? By focusing on the Lord Jesus Christ and by trusting in "the living and abiding word of God." Living hope requires faith in the living Lord and His Word.

The grass withers and dies, flowers bloom and die, but the Word of God "abides forever."

That's a great image, isn't it? Especially in a culture like ours where people are so grass conscious. Just look at the commercials that start appearing on television in late winter, and the countless "garden centers" devoted to our yards and gardens that you can find across the country. We know what happens when we neglect our grass or our gardens—but the truth is, they will eventually wither and die anyway.

There is nothing tangible on this earth that is inspired but the Word of God, this book that holds God's counsel. It doesn't tell us about the truth; it *is* truth. It doesn't merely contain words about God; it *is* the Word of God. We don't have to try real hard to make it relevant; it *is* relevant. Don't neglect it. You can neglect your grass. You can neglect your garden. But you dare not neglect the Word of God! It is the foundation of a stable life. It feeds faith. It's like fuel in the tank. Don't wait till Sunday to see what the Scripture teaches.

We have a living hope, and Peter's words in this section tell us how to claim it—by faith in our Lord Himself and by faith in what He has written, His Word.

The Pilgrim Life and How to Live It

As Christians we live in a world that is not our home. We looked at this, in depth, in chapter 11. We live as pilgrims on a journey in another land. If you want to know how to live the life of an alien, a stranger, a pilgrim, Peter's letter will help.

We claim our living hope through faith, and we live the pilgrim life by submission. In fact, if there is one theme that stretches through this central section of Peter's letter, it is submission. We need to be reminded of it again and again and again because we are an independent lot. Especially here in America, we are so ornery and stubborn. It's come to be known as "the American way." It's the reason many sailed the Atlantic and later came west. It's built into our independent spirit to make it on our own, to decide for ourselves, to prove, if only to ourselves, we can do it! That may be the explorer's life or the pioneer's life . . . but it's not the pilgrim life. The pilgrim life is a life of submission, which works directly against our nature.

But where? When? To whom do we submit? As we saw earlier, Peter spells it out.

In government and civilian affairs. "Submit yourselves for the Lord's sake to every human institution, whether to a king . . . or to governors . . ." (1 Pet. 2:13–14). If you have a president, submit to the president. In Peter's case, they had an emperor. And what a monster he was. Nero. Yet Peter said, "Don't fight the system. Submit."

At work. "Servants, be submissive to your masters" (1 Pet. 2:18). My, that cuts cross-grain in our day of unions and strikes and lawsuits and stubborn determination to have it our own way. Peter says, in effect, "Submit to your boss or quit!"

Submit! Make the thing work or get out. Submit.

At home. "In the same way, you wives, be submissive to your own husbands." And in order for that to work, "You husbands likewise, live with your wives in an understanding way" (1 Pet. 3:1, 7). "Likewise" is a rope-like word that wraps itself around this chapter and part of the previous one, sustaining the thought of submission.

I remember talking with a young couple a few years ago when I observed a sterling example of this. He was a dentist in his mid- to late thirties, and he and his wife had come to a meeting where they found themselves rethinking their life plans for the future. Afterward, he said to me, "I'm thinking seriously about going into the ministry."

I said, "Really? Have you had any training at all?"

He said, "No, not formally. I'd have to go back to school. I'd like to have your suggestion about seminary and what you think would be best for me."

So we talked for a few minutes, and I concluded with this counsel. "If you are happy doing what you're doing, don't just jump into ministry because it seems fascinating or appealing to you."

The next day he came to me and said, "Your words really made me think throughout the night. To tell you the truth, I am very fulfilled in dentistry, and I find a lot of satisfaction in it."

His wife was standing beside him, and I turned to her and said, "And how do you feel about this?" She had a terrific answer. She said, "You know, Chuck, when I married this man I really gave myself to this marriage. And I determined that this man who is walking with God was worth working alongside of, no matter what and no matter where. However God leads him, I'm a part of that plan."

"How do you feel about going into ministry?" I asked.

"If he's convinced, I'm convinced," she said.

Now I know this woman. She's no dummy. She's no vanilla shadow, standing there sighing, "Whatever he wants is fine with me." She's not a beaten-down, doormat kind of wife. That's not the kind of woman she is, and that's not the kind of woman Peter is talking about here. There's vitality and zeal and strength of soul in her life. And she can say, "I am confident God is working in my husband. I wouldn't think of going some other direction." A harmonious blend of give and take is what Peter has in mind here.

In the church. "To sum up, let all be harmonious, sympathetic, brotherly, kindhearted, and humble in spirit; not returning evil for evil, or insult for insult, but giving a blessing instead; for you were called for the very purpose that you might inherit a blessing" (1 Pet. 3:8–9). Now isn't there a lot of submission at work there?

And a few verses later (3:22) we see that even the angels, the authorities, and the powers are subjected to Him. Just picture those magnificent angelic creatures bowing in submission to the risen Christ.

My suggestion on the heels of all this? Work on a submissive spirit. Don't wait for the media to encourage you to do this . . . it'll never happen. Ask God, if necessary, to break the sinews of your will so that you become a person who is cooperative, submissive, harmonious, sympathetic, brotherly or sisterly, kindhearted in every area of this pilgrim life.

Remember, ultimately we are not submitting to human authority but to divine authority. God will never mistreat us. Bowing before Him is the best position to take when we want to communicate obedience.

The Fiery Trial and How to Endure It

No matter how fiery the trial, the main thing is that you and I remember the temperature is ultimately regulated by God's sovereignty (see 1 Pet. 4:12–19). It's also important to understand that we don't suffer our trials in isolation; we are part of a flock that is lovingly tended by faithful shepherds (see 1 Pet. 5:1–5). Finally, we need to know that no matter how formidable our adversary, the power of God is available to help us endure (see 5:6–11).

And how do we endure the fiery trials that engulf us? By cooperation. We need to cooperate with God by trusting Him—with the leaders of the church by submitting to them, and with faith by standing firm and resisting the assault of the devil.

As you struggle with fiery trials, call to mind the sovereignty of God. Nothing touches you that hasn't come through the sovereign hand and the wise plan of God. It must all pass through His fingers before it reaches you. Ultimately He is in control.

As you endure the fiery trial, be in touch with and faithful to the flock of God.

And through it all, rely on the power of God. As we learned in the previous chapter, we must rely on that.

Four Lasting Lessons/Secrets of Life

We have finished his letter . . . but the ink from Peter's pen leaves an indelible impression on our lives. Along with everything else he tells and teaches us, I want to mention four lasting lessons, four secrets of life, that stand out in bold relief. All of these give us hope beyond our misery.

First, when our faith is weak, joy strengthens us.

> In this you greatly rejoice, even though now for a little while, if necessary, you have been distressed by various trials, that the proof of your faith, being more precious than gold which is perishable, even though tested by fire, may be found to result in praise and glory and honor at the revelation of Jesus Christ; and though you have not seen Him, you love Him, and though you do not see Him now, but believe in Him, you greatly rejoice with joy inexpressible and full of glory. (1 Pet. 1:6–8)

> Beloved, do not be surprised at the fiery ordeal among you, which comes upon you for your testing, as though some strange thing were happening to you; but to the degree that you share the sufferings of Christ, keep on rejoicing; so that also at the revelation of His glory, you may rejoice with exultation. (1 Pet. 4:12–13)

No matter how dark the clouds, the sun will eventually pierce the darkness and dispel it; no matter how heavy the rain, the sun will ultimately prevail to hang a rainbow in the sky. Joy will chase away the clouds hovering over our faith and prevail over the disheartening trials that drench our lives. In this regard I am often reminded of the promise from the Psalms.

> Weeping may last for the night,
> But a shout of joy comes in the morning. (Ps. 30:5)

Second, when our good is mistreated, endurance stabilizes us.

For this finds favor, if for the sake of conscience toward God a man bears up under sorrows when suffering unjustly. For what credit is there if, when you sin and are harshly treated, you endure it with patience? But if when you do what is right and suffer for it you patiently endure it, this finds favor with God. (1 Pet. 2:19–20)

The word *endure* in verse 20 means "to bear up under a load," as a donkey bears up under the load its owner has stacked high on its back. This patient bearing of life's cumbersome loads is made possible by love, made steadfast by hope, and made easier by example.

When we suffer, even though we have done what is right, there is something about endurance that stabilizes us. When our good is mistreated, endurance stabilizes us.

My hope for every one who reads these pages is that you will learn how to endure. Picture yourself as that little burro, abiding under the heavy load piled upon its back. Such quiet and confident endurance stabilizes us.

Third, when our confidence is shaken, love supports us.

Above all, keep fervent in your love for one another, because love covers a multitude of sins. (1 Pet. 4:8)

Love is the pillar of support when our world comes crumbling down around us. That's why, when warning about the end times, Peter puts love on the top of the survival checklist.

Fourth, when our adversary attacks, resistance shields us.

Be of sober spirit, be on the alert. Your adversary, the devil, prowls about like a roaring lion, seeking someone to devour. But resist him, firm in your faith, knowing that the same experiences of suffering are being accomplished by your brethren who are in the world. (1 Pet. 5:8–9)

When Satan stalks us like a roaring lion, we're not instructed to freeze, to hide, or to tuck tail and run. We're told to resist. And that

resistance forms a shield to protect us from our adversary's preda-
tory claws.

What Really Counts

And so we reach the end of Peter's letter that has endured the
centuries . . . and the end of my book that may not endure to the
end of this century, less than five years from now. But that is as it
should be. God's Word will never fade away, though human works
are quickly erased by the sands of time.

My concern is not about how long these pages remain in print but
how soon you will put these principles to use in your life. That's
what really counts in the long run. That's the important issue.
Frankly, that's why the old fisherman wrote his letter in the first
place. To help us hope again.

Hope to go on, even though we're scattered aliens.

Hope to grow up, even though we, like Peter, have failed and
fallen.

Hope to endure, even though life hurts.

Hope to believe, even though dreams fade.

A Prayer for Hope Beyond Misery

*Our Father, we thank You for sustaining us in Your grace
through times that absolutely defy explanation, times of
suffering and misery, times of mistreatment and
disappointment.*

*Thank You for being a Friend who is closer than a brother,
for meaning more to us than a mother or a father. Thank You
for Your mercy that takes us from week to week through a life
that isn't easy, dealing with people who aren't always loving*

and encountering battles that leave us exhausted. Thank You for strength that has come from a little letter written by an old fisherman who understood life in all its dimensions: failure and disappointment and victory and joy and intimacy. We commit to You, our Father, the truth of what we have read. Help us to find hope again as a result of putting these truths into practice. In the lovely and gracious name of Jesus Christ I pray.

AMEN

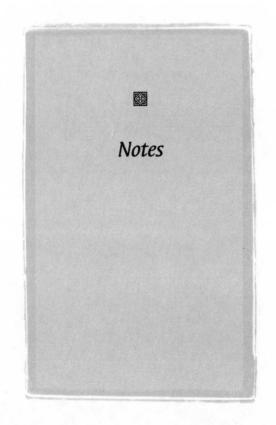

Notes

CHAPTER 1   HOPE BEYOND FAILURE

1   Eugene H. Peterson, *The Message: The New Testament in Contemporary English* (Colorado Springs, Colo.: Navpress, 1993), 486.

CHAPTER 2   HOPE BEYOND SUFFERING

1   Warren W. Wiersbe, *Be Hopeful* (Wheaton, Ill.: SP Publications, Victor Books, 1982), 11.
2   Julie Ackerman Link, "Fully Involved in the Flame," *Seasons: A Journal for the Women of Calvary Church*, Spring 1996, 1. Copyright Calvary Church, Grand Rapids, Michigan. Used by permission.

CHAPTER 3   HOPE BEYOND TEMPTATION

1   Kenneth S. Wuest, *In These Last Days*, vol. 4 in *Wuest's Word Studies from the Greek New Testament* (Grand Rapids, Mich.: Eerdmans, 1966), 125–26.
2   Randy Alcorn, "Consequences of a Moral Tumble," *Leadership* magazine, Winter 1988, 46.
3   Stuart Briscoe, *Spiritual Stamina* (Portland, Oreg.: Multnomah Press, 1988), 133.

CHAPTER 4   HOPE BEYOND DIVISION

1   Kenneth S. Wuest, *First Peter: In the Greek New Testament* (Grand Rapids, Mich.: Eerdmans, 1956), 48.
2   Edward Gordon Selwyn, *The First Epistle of St. Peter*, 2d ed. (London, England: Macmillan Press, 1974), 153.

CHAPTER 5   HOPE BEYOND GUILT

1   Quoted in *Dear Lord*, comp. Bill Adler (Nashville: Thomas Nelson, 1982).
2   Quoted in *More Children's Letters to God*, comp. Eric Marshall and Stuart Hample (New York: Simon and Schuster, 1967).
3   Quoted in William Barclay, *The Letters of James and Peter*, rev. ed., The Daily Study Bible Series (Philadelphia, Pa.: Westminster Press, 1976), 203.
4   Wiersbe, *Be Hopeful*, 57.

CHAPTER 6   HOPE BEYOND UNFAIRNESS

1   Barclay, *The Letters of James and Peter*, 210–11.
2   J. H. Jowett, *The Epistles of St. Peter*, 2d ed. (London: Hodder and Stoughton, n.d.), 92.

CHAPTER 7   HOPE BEYOND "I DO"

1   Joseph C. Aldrich, *Secrets to Inner Beauty* (Santa Ana, Calif.: Vision House, 1977), 87–88.
2   Philip Yancey, *I Was Just Wondering* (Grand Rapids, Mich.: Eerdmans, 1989), 174–75.
3   Barclay, *The Letters of James and Peter*, 218.
4   Edwin A. Blum, "1 Peter" in *The Expositor's Bible Commentary*, vol. 12, ed. Frank E. Gaebelein (Grand Rapids, Mich.: Zondervan, 1981), 237.
5   *Los Angeles Times*, 23 June 1988.
6   Gary Smalley and John Trent, *The Gift of Honor* (Nashville: Thomas Nelson, 1987), 23, 25–26.

CHAPTER 8   HOPE BEYOND IMMATURITY

1   Robert A. Wilson, ed., *Character Above All* (New York: Simon and Schuster, 1995), 219–21.
2   Oswald Chambers, *My Utmost for His Highest*, special updated

edition, ed. James Reimann (Grand Rapids, Mich.: Discovery House, 1995), November 16, n.p.

3 Alvin Goeser quoted in *Quote-Unquote*, comp. Lloyd Cory (Wheaton, Ill.: SP Publications, Victor Books, 1977), 200.

4 Cited in Jon Johnston, "Growing Me-ism and Materialism," *Christianity Today*, 17 January 1986, 16-I.

CHAPTER 9 HOPE BEYOND BITTERNESS

1 Retold from "Toads and Diamonds," *The Riverside Anthology of Children's Literature*, 6th ed. Boston: Houghton Miffiin, 1985), 291–93.]

2 Malcolm Muggeridge, *Twentieth-Century Testimony*, (Nashville: Thomas Nelson, 1988), 18–19.

3 Barclay, *The Letters of James and Peter*, 230–31.

CHAPTER II HOPE BEYOND THE CULTURE

1 J.R. Baxter, Jr., "This World Is Not My Home," © copyright 1946. Stamps-Baxter Music. All rights reserved. Used by permission of Benson Music Group, Inc..

2 Quotes from Georgia Harbison, "Lower East Side Story," *Time*, 4 March 1996, 71.

3 Wuest, *First Peter: In the Greek New Testament*, 110.

4 D. Martyn Lloyd-Jones, *The Christian Warfare* (Grand Rapids, Mich.: Baker, 1976), 41.

5 John Hus, quoted in John Moffatt, *The General Epistles: James, Peter, and Judas* (London: Hodder and Stoughton, 1928), 147.

CHAPTER 12 HOPE BEYOND EXTREMISM

1 Wiersbe, *Be Hopeful*, 107.

2 Mahatma Gandhi quoted in Brennan Manning, *Lion and Lamb* (Old Tappan, N.J.: Revell, Chosen Books, 1986), 49.

3 Jowett, *The Epistles of St. Peter*, 166–67.

4 Ibid., 167.

5 Anne Ross Cousin, "The Sands of Time Are Sinking."

CHAPTER 13   HOPE BEYOND OUR TRIALS

1   C. S. Lewis, *The Problem of Pain* (New York: Macmillan, 1962), 106.
2   R. C. H. Lenski, *The Interpretation of the Epistles of St. Peter, St. John and St. Jude* (Columbus, Ohio: Wartburg Press, 1945), 213.
3   Andre Crouch, "Through It All," © 1971, by Manna Music Inc., 35255 Brooten Road, Pacific OR. 97135. International copyright secured. All rights reserved. Used by permission.
4   Lewis, *The Problem of Pain*, 107.
5   M. Craig Barnes, *When God Interrupts* (Downers Grove, Ill.: InterVarsity, 1996), 54.
6   Wiersbe, *Be Hopeful*, 115–16.

CHAPTER 14   HOPE BEYOND RELIGION

1   J. G. G. Norman, "Charles Haddon Spurgeon," in *The New International Dictionary of the Christian Church*, rev. ed., ed. J. D. Douglas (Grand Rapids, Mich.: Zondervan, 1978), 928.
2   C. H. Spurgeon, *Lectures to My Students* (Grand Rapids, Mich.: Zondervan, 1962), 7–8.
3   Source unknown.
4   Spurgeon, *Lectures*, 154.
5   Michael Silver, "White Tornado," *Sports Illustrated*, 3 June 1996, 71.

CHAPTER 15   HOPE BEYOND DISSATISFACTION

1   Jean Rosenbaum, quoted in *Quote-Unquote*, 315.

CHAPTER 16   HOPE BEYOND THE BATTLE

1   Philip Yancey, *Where Is God When It Hurts?* (Grand Rapids, Mich.: Zondervan, 1977), 22–23.
2   J. Dwight Pentecost, *Your Adversary the Devil* (Grand Rapids, Mich.: Zondervan, 1969), Introduction.
3   Wiersbe, *Be Hopeful*, 138.
4   Ibid.
5   Wuest, *First Peter: In the Greek New Testament*, 130.
6   C. S. Lewis, *The Screwtape Letters* (New York, N.Y.: Macmillan, 1961), 3.

NOTES

CHAPTER 17   HOPE BEYOND MISERY

1   Dan Greenburg, *How to Make Yourself Miserable*, (New York: Random House, 1966), 1–2.

CHARLES R. SWINDOLL serves as president of Dallas Theological Seminary. He is also president of Insight for Living, a radio broadcast ministry aired daily worldwide. He was senior pastor at the First Evangelical Free Church in Fullerton, California for almost twenty-three years and has authored numerous books on Christian living, including the best-selling *Grace Awakening, Laugh Again,* and *Flying Closer to the Flame.*

Simple Faith

Publications by Charles R. Swindoll

Books:

Come Before Winter
Compassion: Showing We Care in a Careless World
Dropping Your Guard
Encourage Me
For Those Who Hurt
The Grace Awakening
Growing Deep in the Christian Life
Growing Strong in the Seasons of Life
Hand Me Another Brick
Improving Your Serve
Killing Giants, Pulling Thorns
Leadership: Influence That Inspires
Living Above the Level of Mediocrity
Living Beyond the Daily Grind, Books 1 and 2
Living on the Ragged Edge
Make Up Your Mind
The Quest for Character
Recovery: When Healing Takes Time
Rise and Shine
Sanctity of Life
Standing Out
Starting Over
Strengthening Your Grip
Stress Fractures
Strike the Original Match
The Strong Family
Three Steps Forward, Two Steps Back
Victory: A Winning Game Plan for Life
You and Your Child

Booklets:

Anger
Attitudes
Commitment
Dealing with Defiance
Demonism
Destiny
Divorce
Eternal Security
Fun Is Contagious
God's Will
Hope
Impossibilities
Integrity
Leisure
The Lonely Whine of the Top Dog
Moral Purity
Our Mediator
Peace . . . in Spite of Panic
Prayer
Sensuality
Singleness
Stress
Tongues
When Your Comfort Zone Gets the Squeeze
Woman

Simple Faith

CHARLES R. SWINDOLL

WORD PUBLISHING

NASHVILLE

A Thomas Nelson Company

SIMPLE FAITH

Unless otherwise indicated, Scripture quotations used in this book are
from the New American Standard Bible (NASB) © 1960, 1962, 1963, 1968,
1971, 1972, 1973, 1975, 1977 by The Lockman Foundation. Used by permission.

Other Scripture quotations are from the following sources:
The New English Bible (NEB), Copyright © the Delegates of the Oxford
    University Press and the Syndics of the Cambridge University Press,
    1961, 1970. Reprinted by permission.
The New Testament in Modern English (PHILLIPS) by J. B. Phillips, pub-
    lished by The Macmillan Company, © 1958, 1960, 1972 by J. B.
    Phillips.
The Revised Standard Version of the Bible (RSV), copyrighted 1946, 1952,
    © 1971, 1973 by the Division of Christian Education of the National
    Council of the Churches of Christ in the U.S.A., and are used by per-
    mission.
Scriptures identified as KJV are from the King James Version of the Bible.

Library of Congress Cataloging-in-Publication Data

Swindoll, Charles R.
    Simple faith / Charles R. Swindoll.
        p.   cm.
    ISBN 0-8499-0700-4
    1. Christian life—Biblical teaching.   2. Faith—Biblical teaching.
    3. Sermon on the mount—Criticism, interpretation, etc.   I. Title.
    BS2417.C5S85   1991
    248.4—dc20   91–28519
                                                              CIP

Printed in the United States of America

9   BVG   9 8 7 6 5 4 3 2 1

Just as you received Christ Jesus
the Lord, so go on living in
him—in simple faith.

Colossians 2:6 PHILLIPS

Early in the spring of 1971,
a handful of men acted in simple faith.
The result of their decision was life-changing
for my family and me. They had been given the task of
finding a senior pastor to lead the congregation of
the First Evangelical Free Church of Fullerton, California.

Through a series of events
which called for much prayer and patience,
discernment and persistence, warm hospitality,
seasoned wisdom, and great grace,
they became the catalyst that God used
to pry me from a comfortable, familiar place
and call me to a stretching and challenging ministry
with potential beyond our fondest dreams.

As my wife and I sat with these men recently,
reflecting over the past twenty years,
we realized how much we owe each person.

Except for one—Walt Herbst, who passed into the Lord's
presence in 1988—all are still actively involved in
the church, and all are still within the circle of our
faithful friends, whom we love dearly.

Because they have modeled the message
of this book so consistently,
it is a privilege to dedicate it to them.

Irv Ahlquist
Bob Bobzien
Walt Herbst
Hamp Riley
Emil Roberts
Ray Smith
Phil Sutherland
John Watson

On the twentieth anniversary of our relationship,
I give God praise for their remarkable vision,
undiminished integrity, and simple faith.

Contents

Acknowledgments

No book I write is the product of one man's effort. While I may be the only one who researches all the material and puts the original words together, the process that precedes and follows those disciplines is a team effort, I can assure you.

I have my friends at Word Books to thank for their continued enthusiasm over my writing. People like Roland Lundy, Kip Jordon, and Ernie Owen have remained supportive and affirming in too many ways to mention. David Moberg has been especially helpful in designing the cover and arranging the layout of the book. Byron Williamson has, once again, proven the depth of his friendship by giving creative ideas and suggestions that motivated me when the task of doing another major volume seemed formidable. His tireless efforts and excitement over the project prodded me on during the long hours when I worked alone, surrounded by nothing but stacks of books and papers, half-finished cups of coffee, and silence. All of these friends, plus so many others in the Word family, deserve much of the credit that, unfortunately, will be given to me. To these people who have been the wind beneath my wings, I express my heartfelt gratitude.

I also wish to acknowledge the valuable assistance of Judith Markham, my editor on this volume. I am grateful for her attention to detail, her insightful observations and suggestions, and her enthusiastic commitment to this project. Amidst an already full schedule she agreed to work with me in getting the material book-ready before its deadline. Under her careful eye the manuscript was reshaped and crafted.

Those who know me best, however, realize that the most significant individual engaged in the process of any book I write is my long-term executive assistant, Helen Peters. Since I first put pen to paper, she has been there to bridge the gap between author and publisher. It would be impossible to describe all she does to turn my primitive-looking, handwritten tablet pages into a readable, pristine manuscript. Her patience in researching all the footnotes, her expertise in making the word processor hum, and her diligence in staying at the arduous and thankless task of presenting the final manuscript to my publisher ahead of schedule deserves an enormous round of applause. Thank you, yet again, Helen, for slugging it out night after night, page after page, with no loss of cheer or enthusiasm.

To my wife, Cynthia, I also express true gratitude, especially for being so understanding of my intense love for writing. What began so many years ago almost as an afterthought has led to an addiction I cannot seem to break, nor do I try any longer. Instead of being jealous of it or selfish for my time, she is my most frequent source of encouragement. She listens as I read aloud one page after another. She interjects helpful hints when I cannot seem to get it said clearly. And she keeps on loving me and accepting my moods, even when my frustration mounts and I talk in my sleep . . . or jump out of bed at 2:30 in the morning when the ideas start flowing and my mind won't rest. Surely she must occasionally wonder if this isn't a bit more than she bargained for back in June of 1955 when we stood side by side and she said, "I do."

Finally, I am indebted to people like you, who pick up my book, thumb through its pages, and decide it is worth your effort to read it, and invest both your treasure and time to digest its content. Thank you sincerely. Just as music is meant to be played and sung, so a book is written to be read. Without your eyes and mind, my pen has little purpose, and apart from your trust, my writing is an exercise in futility. I suppose we could say that your decision to read this book is a matter of simple faith, for which I am grateful.

Introduction

When I completed my previous volume, *The Grace Awakening*, I felt as if I had written the final words I wished to publish. In fact, I told several family members and friends that if I were suddenly taken ill and died, I would leave this earth a satisfied man—certainly a fulfilled author.

That volume was the culmination of decades of growth, thought, and struggle. It represented "my message" to the world—if a man can have one main message—especially to my immediate sphere of influence, the Christian community. For many years I had wished someone would write boldly and biblically about our freedom in Christ . . . about the stranglehold legalism has on many (most?) Christians . . . about the delights and discoveries to be enjoyed if folks would only get beyond the petty, man-made demands and restrictions of the grace killers and enter into a life that is free of guilt and shame, intimidation and manipulation. To my surprise, I wound up writing that book myself.

The response I received from readers has only reinforced my assumption: A multitude of people in religious bondage long to be free, and they have nothing but gratitude for anyone who will help them break the chains so they can run for daylight. I know; I have a file folder full of grateful letters. In all candor, I expected much more denunciation than appreciation. Instead, the opposite occurred. Much to my amazement, those who have been most grateful are pastors and other leaders in Christian ministries. The overwhelming majority who responded have communicated two specific things: (1) "Thank you for writing on grace. . . . I have determined to make a change in my life and/or my ministry," and (2) "Please write more. I need help in knowing how to put these desires into action." In other words, "Where do we go from here?"

This book, in many ways, is the result of such urging. (Since it obviously wasn't God's plan to take me home as soon as *The Grace Awakening* was published, I guess He wants me to keep writing.) While this is not, by any deliberate design on my part, a sequel to *The Grace Awakening*, it grows out of a similar passion within me: to help those who were once held captive know how to live the life Christ taught and modeled. The difference is that the people I have in mind for this book are those who have become victims of tyranny, not legalism. That tyranny is the pressure and frustration and disappointment brought on by the never-ending demands of organ-ized religion. This kind of tyranny is intensifying because nothing in our world today is being simplified. In fact, everything in life has gotten complicated, including a life of faith. Instead of remaining a simple and meaningful relationship with God, the Christian life has evolved into a combination of big-time tingles, off-the-graph expectations, and borderline madness, which add up to voodoo religion.

Before you disagree, pause and ponder. Answer a few questions. Be painfully honest.

- Do you have a childlike trust in God?
- Are you comfortable with your prayer life?
- In a sentence or two, could you explain what it means to be a Christian?

- Does the word "satisfied" describe your feelings about your walk with Christ?

- Is "peace" the true condition of your inner being?

- Are you truly liberated from others' expectations?

- Have you been able to maintain a relaxed, contented, and joyful lifestyle in the midst of life's accelerated pace?

- If you were unable to attend your church for several Sundays, would you feel comfortable, mildly uneasy, or guilt-ridden?

- Do you think the Bible can be understood by people who have not been to a Christian college or seminary?

- Can a person who is not a missionary be as spiritual as one who is?

- When you sin, do you know how to find forgiveness and continue on in your Christian life?

See what I mean? Somehow, the complications of life in general have bled into our walk with Christ . . . and messed everything up. Ask the average believer a simple question like, "What does it mean to be a mature Christian?" and if you are lucky, about fifteen minutes later you'll get the complete, complicated answer. The list of qualifications does not end.

"Maturity? Well, for starters you need to be in church as often as possible, witness regularly, teach a Sunday school class, pray fervently, make hospital visits, write uplifting notes to the discouraged, tithe, memorize Scripture, attend a Christian seminar or two each year, go to your church's summer family camp, support and attend the week-long evangelistic crusade, send your kids to a Christian school—or, preferably, home school them—participate on several boards or committees, serve in the (pick one) nursery, church kitchen, neighborhood visitation outreach program, choir, summer missions project, or right-to-life campaign. In addition, if you are a *really* mature Christian, there is no place in your life for discouragement, no room for doubt, and no time for just plain fun. Faith is serious stuff. It's intense.

Enter: complications. Exit: joy.

How far we have drifted from Christ's original teachings on the simplicity of faith. I'll go a step further: How grieved God must be at our frenzied pace! We have turned a walk with God into a ruthless obstacle course, an exhausting marathon. We have added enormously heavy weights to the runners, and, as a result, many are opting not to enter the race at all. Frankly, I don't blame them. Who needs extra baggage when life is already too heavy?

All this reminds me of a funny story I heard recently about a man at Los Angeles International Airport who was worried about missing his plane. He had no wrist watch and could not locate a clock, so he hurried up to a total stranger and said, " 'Scuse me . . . could you give me the time, please?"

The stranger smiled and said, "Sure." He set down the two large suitcases he was carrying and looked at the watch on his wrist. "It is exactly 5:09. The temperature outside is 73 degrees, and it is supposed to rain tonight. In London the sky is clear and the temperature is 38 degrees Celsius. The barometer reading there is 29.14 and falling. And, let's see, in Singapore the sun is shining brightly. Oh, by the way, the moon should be full tonight here in Los Angeles, and—"

"Your watch tells you all that?" the man interrupted.

"Oh, yes . . . and much more. You see, I invented this watch, and I can assure you there is no other timepiece like it in the world."

"I want to buy that watch! I'll pay you two thousand dollars for it right now."

"No, it's not for sale," said the stranger as he reached down to pick up his suitcases.

"Wait! Four thousand. I'll pay you *four* thousand dollars, cash," offered the man, reaching for his wallet.

"No, I can't sell it. You see, I plan to give it to my son for his twenty-first birthday. I invented it for him to enjoy."

"Okay, listen . . . I'll give you *ten* thousand dollars. I've got the money right here."

The stranger paused. "Ten thousand? Well, okay. It's yours for ten thousand even."

The man was absolutely elated. He paid the stranger, took the watch, snapped it on his wrist with glee, and said "Thanks" as he turned to leave.

"Wait," said the stranger. With a big smile he handed the two heavy suitcases to the man and added, "Don't forget the *batteries*."

That's exactly what it is like when we tell folks about all the things Christ offers. We speak of one pleasure after another: this blessing and that benefit . . . sins forgiven . . . peace within, joy without . . . strength amidst trials, hope beyond the grave. I mean, who wouldn't want all that? But the killer is what we *don't* tell them. The package includes unexpected extra baggage, and it is only a matter of time before the added weight will turn a life of simple faith into a life oppressed by the tyranny of the urgent.

But what if being close to God were simple? What if this thing called faith isn't as complicated as it's cracked up to be? And while I'm asking the critical questions: What if you could be liberated—I mean really *set free*—from all those expectations that organized religion and even a few of your intense friends heap on you? What if I could show you how to get rid of all the excess baggage? What if you could return to a life that doesn't require running double-time or maintaining a superspiritual standard based on a hectic schedule?

I have the feeling you'd be interested. But you'd also be suspicious, right? You're sure that before I finished I would be handing you a couple of suitcases that are part of the deal, right? Wrong. The

life of faith was never meant to be complicated . . . and that's
what this book is about.

In a sentence: If Christ's life of *liberating grace* brings you hope
beyond the bonds of legalism, you dare not miss Christ's words of
simple faith to help you live beyond the harassment of expectations.
As you will discover in the following pages, the Christian life is not
based on high-level performance but on quiet faithfulness, not on
impressive works but on deep relationships. God came to our rescue while we were trapped in a dark dungeon of despair. He gave
us what we did not deserve and could not earn. He freed us. By
breaking the iron bars of sin, He opened the gates of hope. Grace
awakened us to a whole new world. But where do we go from there?
Having been set free, how do we live? What's next?

To the surprise of many, the life Jesus lived and taught so
clearly is neither demanding nor complicated. I like to think of it
as a life beyond the dungeon.

Charles Wesley's vivid description comes to mind:

> Long my imprisoned spirit lay
> Fast bound in sin and nature's night.
> Thine eye diffused a quick'ning ray:
> I woke, the dungeon flamed with light!
> My chains fell off, my heart was free,
> I rose, went forth, and followed Thee.[1]

Christ, who came to set captives free, still offers a life worth
living to those who have been liberated. It is a life that may not
always be easy or comfortable, but one thing is certain: It is not all
that complicated. As we shall discover from Jesus' own words, spoken on a mountain in the first century, it is a life of *simple faith*. To
make it more than that is heresy.

Charles R. Swindoll
Fullerton, California

1
Let's Keep It Simple

W HEN IT CAME TO CLEAR COMMUNICATION, Jesus was a master. Children and adults alike had no difficulty understanding His words or following His reasoning. This is remarkable because while He was on earth He lived in a society that had become accustomed to cliché-ridden religious double-talk. The scribes, priests, and Pharisees who dominated the synagogue scene in Palestine saw to that. They unintentionally made Jesus' simple style and straight-forward approach seem all the more refreshing. When He spoke, people listened. Unlike the pious professionals of His day, Jesus' words made sense.

This was never truer than when He sat down on a hillside with a group of His followers and talked about what really mattered. Thanks to tradition, this teaching session has come to be known as the Sermon on the Mount—in my opinion, an unfortunate title. His words were authoritative but not officious, insightful but not sermonic. His hillside chat was an informal, reasonable, thought-ful, and unpretentious presentation. He distilled an enormous amount of truth in an incredibly brief period of time, and those who had endured a lifetime of boring and irrelevant sermons sat spell-bound to the end.

The result was that when Jesus had finished these words, the multitudes were amazed at His teaching; for He was teaching them as one having authority, and not as their scribes.

Matthew 7:28–29

If we fail to understand the background behind that statement, we will not appreciate the depth of His listeners' gratitude. In short, they were fed up with the manipulation, the pride, and especially the hypocrisy of their religious leaders. Long years of legalism, mixed with the pharisaic power plays designed to intimidate and control, held the general public in bondage. Man-made systems of complicated requirements and backbreaking demands shut the people behind invisible bars, shackled in chains of guilt. They could not measure up; they could not quite keep their heads above water unless they dog-paddled like mad . . . and many were losing heart. But who dared say so?

Out of the blue came Jesus with His message of liberating grace, encouragement to the weary, hope for the sinful. Best of all, everything He said was based on pristine truth—God's truth —instead of rigid religious regulations. He talked of faith— simple faith—in terms anyone could understand. His "yes face" invited them in as His teaching released them from guilt and shame, fear and confusion. The Nazarene's authenticity caught them off guard, disarmed their suspicions, and blew away the fog that had surrounded organized religion for decades. No wonder the people found Him amazing! No wonder the grace-killing scribes and Pharisees found Him unbearable! Hypocrisy despises authenticity. When truth unmasks wrong, those who are exposed get very nervous . . . like the two brothers in a story I heard recently.

These brothers were rich. They were also wicked. Both lived a wild, unprofitable existence, using their wealth to cover up the dark side of their lives. On the surface, however, few would have guessed it, for these consummate cover-up artists attended the same

4

church almost every Sunday and contributed large sums to various church-related projects.

Then the church called a new pastor, a young man who preached the truth with zeal and courage. Before long, attendance had grown so much that the church needed a larger worship center. Being a man of keen insight and strong integrity, this young pastor had also seen through the hypocritical lifestyles of the two brothers.

Suddenly one of the brothers died, and the young pastor was asked to preach his funeral. The day before the funeral, the surviving brother pulled the minister aside and handed him an envelope. "There's a check in here that is large enough to pay the entire amount you need for the new sanctuary," he whispered. "All I ask is one favor: Tell the people at the funeral that *he was a saint.*" The minister gave the brother his word; he would do precisely what was asked. That afternoon he deposited the check into the church's account.

The next day the young pastor stood before the casket at the funeral service and said with firm conviction, "This man was an ungodly sinner, wicked to the core. He was unfaithful to his wife, hot-tempered with his children, ruthless in his business, and a hypocrite at church . . . but compared to his brother, *he was a saint.*"

The boldness of authenticity is beautiful to behold, unless, of course, you happen to be a hypocrite. That explains why Jesus' words, which brought such comfort to those who followed Him, enraged the Pharisees. Although He never called one of them by name during His hillside talk, He exposed their legalistic lifestyle as no one had ever done before. Count on it: *They* knew what He was saying.

On the surface, Jesus' words, recorded in Matthew 5, 6, and 7, may seem calm in tone and basic in their simplicity. We can read them in fifteen or twenty minutes, and at first glance they appear to be nothing more than a gentle tap on the shoulder. But to those who had twisted religion into a performance-oriented list of demands and expectations, they were nothing short of a bold exposé.

When Moses came down from Mount Sinai centuries earlier, he did not bring Ten Suggestions; likewise, when Jesus delivered His message from the mount, it was no humble homily. To legalists His words represented a howling reproach that continues into the modern age. Jesus' words may be simple, but they are definitely not insipid.

Jesus' Words: A Plea for True Righteousness

Behind Jesus' teaching on the Palestinian hillside was a deep concern for those who had surrendered their lives to the tyranny of pressure that was light-years away from simple faith. Of special concern to Him was the possibility that some had gotten sucked into the pharisaic model of substituting the artificial for the authentic, a danger that always lurks in the shadows of legalism.

That is what leads me to believe that the major message of Jesus' teaching in this setting could be encapsulated in these five words He spoke: "Do not be like them" (Matt. 6:8).

Our Lord wants His true followers to be distinct, unlike the majority who follow the herd. In solving conflicts, doing business, and responding to difficulties, Jesus' people are not to maintain the same attitudes or choose the priorities of the majority. And for sure, we are not to emulate pharisaism. When Jesus teaches, "Do not be like them," He really means it. Hypocrisy, He hates . . . authenticity, He loves.

Hypocrisy permits us to travel both sides of the path—to look righteous but be unholy, to sound pious but be secretly profane. Invariably, those who get trapped in the hypocrisy syndrome find ways to mask their hollow core. The easiest approach is to add more activity, run faster, emphasize an intense, ever-enlarging agenda. The Pharisees were past masters at such things! Not content with the Mosaic Law that included the Ten Commandments, they tacked on 365 prohibitions, as well as 250 additional commandments. But did that make them righteous? Hardly.

> For I say to you, that unless your righteousness surpasses that of the scribes and Pharisees, you shall not enter the kingdom of heaven.
>
> Matthew 5:20

No, you didn't misread it; He said *surpasses*. You see, a busier schedule mixed with a longer to-do list does not equal greater righteousness any more than driving faster leads to a calmer spirit. On the contrary, when we attempt to become more spiritual by doing more things, we do nothing but complicate the Christian life. Can you imagine the shock on the faces of the Pharisees when they heard that Jesus was telling His followers that their righteousness must *exceed* that of the Pharisees?

In fact, if we do a quick overview of Jesus' magnificent message, we find Him simplifying the walk of faith with four basic teachings, all of which were diametrically opposed to the pharisaic lifestyle. First of all, He says:

Out with Hypocrisy!

Even a casual reading through the forty-eight verses in the fifth chapter of Matthew leads me to believe Jesus is answering three questions:

1. What does it mean to have character? (vv. 3–12)
2. What does it mean to make a difference? (vv. 13–16)
3. What does it mean to be godly? (vv. 17–48)

Interestingly, in that third section, verses 17–48, He repeats the same statement no fewer than six times:

> "You have heard . . . but I say to you. . . ." (vv. 21–22)
> "You have heard . . . but I say to you. . . ." (vv. 27–28)
> "It was said . . . but I say to you. . . ." (vv. 31–32)

"You have heard . . . but I say to you. . . ." (vv. 33–34)
"You have heard . . . but I say to you. . . ." (vv. 38–39)
"You have heard . . . but I say to you. . . ." (vv. 43–44)

Why? What is Jesus getting at?

He is reminding the people of what they have heard for years, taught (and certainly embellished!) by their religious leaders; then He readdresses those same matters with an authentic life in view. And what kind of life is that? A life free of hypocrisy. Jesus' desire is that His followers be people of simple faith, modeled in grace, based on truth. Nothing more. Nothing less. Nothing else.

How easy it is to fake Christianity . . . to polish a superpious image that looks godly but is phony. Through the years I have come across Christians who are breaking their necks to be Mother Teresa Number Two or, if you please, Brother Teresa! Or Saint Francis of Houston or Minneapolis or Seattle . . . or wherever. Far too many Christians are simply trying too hard. They are busy, to be sure. But righteous? I mean, genuinely Christlike?

Sincere? Many of them. Intense? Most. Busy? Yes . . . but far from spiritual.

Several years ago I came across one of the simplest and best pieces of advice I have ever heard: "Be who you is, because if you is who you ain't, you ain't who you is."[1] Wise words, easily forgotten in the squirrel cage of religious hyperactivity.

Down with Performance!

If the early part of Jesus' teaching is saying, "Out with hypocrisy," this next section, recorded in Matthew 6, is saying, "Down with performance!" Quit placing so much attention on looking good. Quit trying to make others think you are pious, especially if beneath the veneer there are hidden wickedness, impure motives, and shameful deeds. In other words, don't wear a smiling mask to disguise sadness and depravity, heartache and brokenness.

8

In the area where I live, we would say, "Leave Showtime to the Los Angeles Lakers."

Jesus puts it straight: "Beware of practicing your righteousness before men to be noticed by them" (Matt. 6:1). In other words, "Stop acting one way before others, knowing you are really not that way at all." Then He offers three practical examples:

1. *Giving*

> When therefore you give alms [when you are in church and you give your money], do not sound a trumpet before you, as the hypocrites do in the synagogues and in the streets.
>
> Matthew 6:2

Today, we don't blow trumpets—not literally. But many who give sizable contributions like to see their names cast in bronze. They like it to be known by the public and remembered forever that they were the ones who built the gym. They are the ones who paid for the new organ. They are the heavy givers . . . the high donors: "A little extra fanfare, please." In contrast, when it came to giving, Jesus emphasized anonymity. No more hype, He said. When we live by simple faith, big-time performances that bring us the glory are out of place.

What a wonderful and welcome reminder—unless, of course, you are a religious glory hog. When we choose a life of simple faith, we keep our giving habits quiet.

2. *Praying*

> And when you pray, you are not to be as the hypocrites; for they love to stand and pray in the synagogues and on the street corners, in order to be seen by men. Truly I say to you, they have their reward in full. But you, when you pray, go into your inner room, and when you have shut your door, pray to your Father who is in secret, and your Father who sees in secret will repay you. And

when you are praying, do not use meaningless repetition, as the Gentiles do, for they suppose that they will be heard for their many words.

Matthew 6:5–7

Many words, even eloquent words, never caused anyone to be heard in prayer. My fellow preachers and I who are often called upon to pray in public would do well to remember that.

Dr. Lewis Sperry Chafer told a story on this subject.

> It seems that a certain minister was in the habit of profound prayers, oftentimes resorting to words beyond the ken of his simple flock. This went on week after week, to the dismay and frustration of the congregation. At last, a wee Scottish woman in the choir ventured to take the matter in hand. On a given Sunday, as the minister was waxing his most eloquently verbose, the little woman reached across the curtain separating the choir from the pulpit. Taking a firm grasp on the frock tail of the minister, she gave it a yank, and was heard to whisper, "Jes' call Him Fether, and ask 'im for somethin."[2]

Whatever happened to simplicity in prayer? And uncluttered honesty? Like the prayer of a child. Or the prayer of a humble farmer needing rain. Or of a homeless mother with two hungry kids. Down with performance-oriented praying! God honors simple-hearted petitions and humble-minded confession.

3. Fasting

> And whenever you fast, do not put on a gloomy face as the hypocrites do, for they neglect their appearance in order to be seen fasting by men. Truly I say to you, they have their reward in full. But you, when you fast, anoint your head, and wash your face so that you may not be seen fasting by men, but by your Father who is in secret; and your Father who sees in secret will repay you.

Matthew 6:16–18

10

This is a great place to stop and say a further word to fellow preachers. When it comes to piety performance, we can be the worst offenders! All preachers know there's a way to look and sound like The Reverend Supersanctified Saint of Ultrapious Cathedral or Dr. Dull Dryasdust with stooped shoulders, long face, and dark suit (an out-of-date tie also helps) . . . struggling to keep the tonnage of his world in orbit and its inhabitants in line. There's a great Greek word for that kind of nonsense: *Hogwash!* Jesus shot holes in that look-at-me-because-I'm-so-spiritual showmanship. If we choose to fast, fine. In fact, it's commendable. But if we fast (or counsel or study or pray) to be seen, forget it! These disciplines were never meant to be displays of the flesh. We are not in them for the grade others give us or the superficial impression we can make. Leave the acting to those who compete for the Emmys and the Oscars. As suggested earlier, "Be who you is. . . ." Let's keep it simple. Out with hypocrisy! Down with performance! And:

Up with Tolerance!

I believe that is what Jesus is saying in the first five verses of Matthew 7. What searching, convicting words these are!

> Do not judge lest you be judged. For in the way you judge, you will be judged; and by your standard of measure, it will be measured to you. And why do you look at the speck that is in your brother's eye, but do not notice the log that is in your own eye? Or how can you say to your brother, "Let me take the speck out of your eye," and behold, the log is in your own eye? You hypocrite, first take the log out of your own eye, and then you will see clearly to take the speck out of your brother's eye.

He is continuing His passionate, howling reproach against hypocrisy, isn't He? But have we taken Him seriously? Not nearly enough.

Christians are fast becoming "speck specialists." We look for specks and detect specks and criticize specks, all the while deliberately ignoring the much larger and uglier and more offensive logs in our own lives that need immediate attention and major surgery—in some cases, *radical* surgery.

May I get specific? Be tolerant of those who live different lifestyles. Be tolerant of those who don't look like you, who don't dress like you, who don't care about the things you care about, who don't relax like you, who don't vote like you. As my teenage kids used to ask each other, "Who died and put you in charge?" You're not their judge.

Let me go even further. Be tolerant of those whose fine points of theology differ from yours. Be tolerant of those whose worship style is different. Be tolerant even of those who have been turned off by Bible-thumping evangelicals—folks who are up to here with the pettiness and small-mindedness in many churches. Be tolerant of the young if you are older . . . and be tolerant of the aging if you are young. For those who are theologically astute (especially you who are gifted and trained linguistically), be tolerant of those who don't know Hebrew or Greek. There is certainly nothing wrong with knowing those languages, you understand. They can be extremely helpful. But they can also be misused and abused. People who don't know the original languages of Scripture can be taken advantage of by those who do.

My close friend and pastoral associate, Paul Sailhamer, tells a humorous story that perfectly illustrates what I am getting at. Though apocryphal, it is appropriate.

Jorge Rodriquez was the meanest, orneriest bandit on the Texas-Mexico border. The guy would often slip across the line, raid the banks of South Texas, and steal 'em blind. Before they could catch him, he would race back into Mexico and hide out. No matter how hard the law tried, they could never catch him.

Finally the Texans got fed up with this nonsense and decided to put the toughest Texas Ranger they had on the case. Sure enough, that got the job done. After only a few days of searching, the Ranger found the bandit in a dingy, dusty saloon south of the border. He bolted into the bar, pulled both guns, and yelled, "Okay, stick 'em up, Jorge; you're under arrest! I know you've got the money."

Suddenly a little guy over in the corner butted in. "Wait, wait . . . just a minute, señor," he said. "Jorge does not speak English. He's my amigo, so I'll translate for you."

The Ranger explained, "Look, we know he's the bandit we've been looking for. We know he's taken thousands and thousands of dollars—about a million bucks, actually. We want it back *now*. Either he pays up or I'll fill him full of holes. You tell him that!"

"Okay, okay! I'll tell him . . . I'll tell him." So the little fellow turned to Jorge and repeated in Spanish everything the Ranger had said. The Texas Ranger, not knowing a word of the language, waited for the bandit's reply.

Jorge listened, frowned, then responded in Spanish, "Okay, they got me. Tell him to go down to the well just south of town, count four stones down from the top of the well, then pull out the one loose stone. All the money I have stolen I've hidden behind the stone."

Then the clever little translator turned to the Texas Ranger and translated with a shrug, "Jorge says, 'Go ahead, you big mouth; go ahead and shoot 'cause I'm not telling you where the money is.'"

On with Commitment!

Jesus' words penetrate, don't they? When our faith is a genuine faith—a simple expression of our walk with God—tolerance comes more easily. But does this negate commitment? Does everything about faith become passive and mildly indifferent? Not at all. Take a look at the rest of Jesus' talk recorded in Matthew 7. Pay close attention to the commands. Here are a few of them:

> Do not give what is holy to dogs, and do not throw your pearls before swine, lest they trample them under their feet, and turn and tear you to pieces.

Ask, and it shall be given to you; seek, and you shall find; knock, and it shall be opened to you. . . .

Enter by the narrow gate; for the gate is wide, and the way is broad that leads to destruction, and many are those who enter by it. . . .

Beware of the false prophets, who come to you in sheep's clothing, but inwardly are ravenous wolves.

Matthew 7:6–7, 13, 15

Now that's commitment! We will examine these exhortations and others much more carefully later in the book; but for now, don't kid yourself that living a life of simple faith means a yawn in the sunshine of convenience and casual commitment.

As our Lord brings His teaching to a close, He tells the story of two houses, one built on rock and another built on sand. And with this He wraps up His words with one major statement: *People of simple faith mean what they say and do what they hear.* That, in essence, is the practical outworking of Christianity. That is simple faith in a nutshell.

Unfortunately, we neither mean what we say nor do what we hear. We substitute words for action and pious discussion for personal involvement. As one writer put it:

> I was hungry
> and you formed a humanities club
> and you discussed my hunger.
> Thank you.
>
> I was imprisoned
> and you crept off quietly
> to your chapel in the cellar
> and prayed for my release.
>
> I was naked
> and in your mind

14

you debated the morality of my
appearance.

I was sick
   and you knelt and thanked God
   for your health.

I was homeless
   and you preached to me
   of the spiritual shelter of the
   love of God.

I was lonely
   and you left me alone
   to pray for me.

You seem so holy;
   so close to God.
But I'm still very hungry
   and lonely
   and cold.

So where have your prayers gone?
   What have they done?
   What does it profit a man to page through his
      book of prayers when the rest of the world is
      crying for help?[3]

Jesus' words that day on the hillside were even more powerful.
When He finished speaking, nobody moved. Small wonder. Those
words were like spikes, nailing them to their seats.

As A. T. Robertson writes:

> They [the people] had heard many sermons before from the
> regular rabbis in the synagogues. We have specimens of these dis-
> courses preserved in the Mishna and Gemara, the Jewish Talmud
> when both were completed, the driest, dullest collection of disjointed

comments upon every conceivable problem in the history of mankind. . . .

Jesus spoke with the authority of truth, the reality and freshness of the morning light, and the power of God's Spirit. This sermon which made such a profound impression ended with the tragedy of the fall of the house on the sand like the crash of a giant oak in the forest. There was no smoothing over the outcome.[4]

Simply Put: My Response

We're only one chapter deep, but already I feel the need to make four statements of honest confession lest we "smooth over the outcome." If these represent *your* life, too, join me in admitting the truth. I believe it will stop us in our tracks and help us then take the first steps to a life of simple faith.

First: *I admit I am not completely free of hypocrisy.* I confess it, Lord, and I know I'm not alone.

> I am like James and John.
> Lord, I size up other people
>   in terms of what they can do for me;
>   how they can further my program,
>   feed my ego,
>   satisfy my needs,
>   give me strategic advantage.
> I exploit people,
>   ostensibly for your sake,
>   but really for my own sake.
> Lord, I turn to you
>   to get the inside track
>   and obtain special favors,
>   your direction for my schemes,
>   your power for my projects,
>   your sanction for my ambitions,
>   your blank check for whatever I want.
> I am like James and John.

> Change me, Lord.
> Make me a man who asks of you and of others,
>   what can I do for you?[5]

If you find yourself in those words, as I do, then you must admit there are often hidden agendas within you.

Second: *I admit I do not always search my motives.* I openly confess that I do not always ask myself *why*. Jesus' words never fail to force me to examine my motives. Do you find that true as well? As we get under way in this book, my hope is that God will search you and reveal to you whatever is impure yet remains hidden.

Third: *I admit I still occasionally judge others.* My intolerance is at times blistering; my pride, at times, rotten and putrid. My patience, so short. My acceptance, so limited. Is yours? Don't be afraid to say so. It is the truth that will set you free.

Fourth: *I dare not continue as I am.* That's a statement I need to make. Do you? We need help to change—to sift truth from error, essentials from incidentals.

Some years ago I was given a book of Puritan prayers called *The Valley of Vision.* I have worn out one copy and had to purchase another. Late this afternoon as I was putting the final touches on this chapter, which has become so convicting, I happened upon a page from the Puritan's pen. Because it says so well what I'm trying to say, I close with his words, not mine. Read them slowly, preferably aloud.

> O LORD,
> I am a shell full of dust,
>   but animated with an invisible rational soul
>   and made anew by an unseen power of grace;
> Yet I am no rare object of valuable price,
>   but one that has nothing and is nothing,
>   although chosen of thee from eternity,
>   given to Christ, and born again;

I am deeply convinced of the evil and misery of a sinful state, of
    the vanity of creatures,
  but also of the sufficiency of Christ.
When thou wouldst guide me I control myself,
When thou wouldst be sovereign I rule myself.
When thou wouldst take care of me I suffice myself.
When I should depend on thy providings I supply myself,
When I should submit to thy providence I follow my will,
When I should study, love, honour, trust thee, I serve myself;
I fault and correct thy laws to suit myself,
Instead of thee I look to man's approbation,
  and am by nature an idolater.
Lord, it is my chief design to bring my heart back to thee.
Convince me that I cannot be my own god, or make myself
    happy,
  nor my own Christ to restore my joy,
  nor my own Spirit to teach, guide, and rule me.
Help me to see that grace does this by providential affliction,
  for when my credit is god thou dost cast me lower,
  when riches are my idol thou dost wing them away,
  when pleasure is my all thou dost turn it into bitterness.
Take away my roving eye, curious ear, greedy appetite, lustful
    heart;
Show me that none of these things
  can heal a wounded conscience,
  or support a tottering frame,
  or uphold a departing spirit.
Then take me to the cross and leave me there.[6]

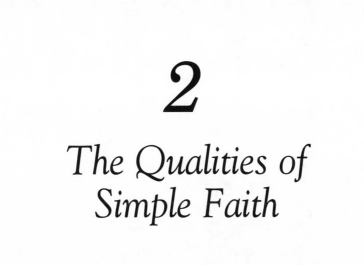

2

The Qualities of Simple Faith

GOOD SERMONS ARE RARE; GREAT ONES, almost unheard of these days. Of the hundreds—perhaps thousands—some of us have heard in our lifetimes, precious few fit the category of "great." Chances are good that those were preached by humble servants of God. Great sermons and godly servants usually go together.

Reminds me of the young, gifted minister whose preaching was a cut above the ordinary. As the ranks of his congregation began to swell, his head followed suit. After he had delivered his latest barnburner one morning, one of his loyal parishioners earnestly shook his hand and said, "You're becoming one of the greatest expositors of this generation, pastor."

As he squeezed his head into the car and slid behind the steering wheel, his weary wife alongside him and all the kids stuffed into the back seat, he could not resist sharing the story.

"Mrs. Franklin told me she thought I was one of the greatest expositors of this generation," he said proudly, caught up in the heady swirl of the woman's exaggerated compliment.

No response.

Fishing for affirmation, he glanced at his silent wife with a weak smile and prodded, "I wonder just how many 'great expositors' there are in this generation?"

Unable to resist the opportunity to set the record straight, she said quietly, "One less than you think, my dear."

No greater message was ever delivered than the one Jesus spoke from the Galilean mountainside. No more humble messenger ever communicated the life of simple faith than that thirty-something carpenter-turned-teacher from Nazareth. Twenty centuries have not come near exhausting its depths. With precision and courage He delivered one surgical strike after another, exposing the hypocrisy and legalism of first-century religion. As listeners followed His logic with mouths open in awe, they realized they were not sitting at the feet of another arrogant scribe but rather before the God-man, the Messiah Himself. Can you imagine the thrill of being there? To this day, His words strip away all the excess baggage many have added to the life of faith. It is a masterpiece of simplicity.

The Qualities of Jesus' Delivery

Having just read Matthew 5, 6, and 7 again, four general observations come to mind, each quite a striking contrast to the standard sermon preached today.

First: *He spoke these words outside rather than inside.* That means they were probably delivered extemporaneously and, for sure, without the aid of voice amplification. Perhaps that explains why He chose a hillside rather than a section of flat terrain in Palestine.

Second: *He was sitting down among His listeners rather than standing up before them.* His presence, while powerful, was not overpowering. By sitting with them, He remained approachable, touchable, believable.

Third: *He taught rather than preached.* His message had substance that called for action. Rather than relying on a series of emotional exhortations, He delivered teaching that was systematically and logically arranged. But make no mistake, His presentation was neither laid-back nor lacking in force. He taught them "as one having authority" (Matt. 7:29).

Fourth: *He blessed and encouraged rather than rebuked.* Most sermons are more negative than positive, more like scathing rebukes than affirmation. Not this one. With beautiful simplicity, using terms any age could understand, Jesus brought blessing rather than condemnation.

No fewer than nine times, back-to-back, He used the same phrase: "Blessed are those . . . ," "Blessed are you . . . ," "Blessed are these. . . ." Having endured a lifetime of verbal assaults by the scribes and Pharisees, the multitude on the mount must have thought they had died and gone to heaven. A pinch of positive blessing does more for our souls than a pound of negative bruising. When will we preachers ever learn?

The Qualities of the Blessed Life

As we dig deeper into these opening words from our Lord's message, we encounter one "blessed" comment after another. Here they are, exactly as Jesus delivered them. Though familiar, read them as if for the first time. Study His words with care. Notice the refreshing absence of clichés.

Blessed are the poor in spirit, for theirs is the kingdom of heaven.

Blessed are those who mourn, for they shall be comforted.

Blessed are the gentle, for they shall inherit the earth.

Blessed are those who hunger and thirst for righteousness, for they shall be satisfied.

Blessed are the merciful, for they shall receive mercy.

Blessed are the pure in heart, for they shall see God.

Blessed are the peacemakers, for they shall be called sons of God.

Blessed are those who have been persecuted for the sake of righteousness, for theirs is the kingdom of heaven. Blessed are you when men cast insults at you, and persecute you, and say all kinds of evil against you falsely, on account of Me. Rejoice, and be glad, for your reward in heaven is great, for so they persecuted the prophets who were before you.

Matthew 5:3–12

What is meant by *blessed*? Some say it is little more than a synonym for "happy," but it is much deeper than that. In extra-biblical literature, the Greek term that is translated *blessed* was used to describe two different conditions. First, it was used to describe the social stratum of the wealthy who, by virtue of their riches, lived above the normal cares and worries of lesser folk. Second, the term was also used to describe the condition of the Greek gods who, because they had whatever they desired, existed in an unbelievable state of well-being, satisfaction, and contentment.

To be sure, Jesus was speaking neither to the wealthy nor to the gods of the ancient world. But by repeating the same word to His band of simple-hearted, loyal followers, He reassured them that enviable qualities such as delight, contentment, fulfillment, and deeply entrenched joy were theirs to claim. In other words, He promised that by tossing aside all the extra baggage that accompanies religious hypocrisy and a performance-oriented lifestyle, we will travel the road that leads to inner peace. In doing so, we become "blessed."

But let's not think of these beatitudes as a collection of insipid, trite remarks or mild, sentimental platitudes designed to make everyone smile. Jesus didn't offer feel-good theology. A close examination reveals that His opening words pose a frontal challenge to virtually everything we assume about the way things are in our world. Or, as G. K. Chesterton remarked, "Most critics who are offended at the things Jesus says are offended precisely because Jesus does not utter safe platitudes."[1]

Though simple sounding and easy to read, each beatitude offers a radical rearrangement of our ordinary value system, daring us to be different. What we find here, in short, are guidelines for true Christian character. In a day like ours where acting has replaced authenticity and pretense gets the nod over inward reality, I know of no greater need than this dose of truth.

"Blessed are the poor in spirit."

Not poor in substance, but spirit. This first beatitude has nothing to do with being materially destitute or financially bankrupt. Jesus is placing value on a humble spirit, on those who acknowledge a spiritual bankruptcy in and of themselves. Where there is an absence of well-polished pride and personal conceit, there is a wholesome dependence on the living God. Instead of, "No problem, I can handle it. After all, look at the things I've accomplished already," there is quick confession, acknowledging one's own inadequacies.

Do you recall a contrasting scene Jesus created in one of His parables? Luke 18:9–14 records the account of two men, one a proud Pharisee, nauseatingly impressed with himself, and the other an unworthy, tax-gathering sinner, too aware of his transgressions to speak above a whisper. The Pharisee stood praying to himself, his words dripping with arrogance,

> . . . God, I thank Thee that I am not like other people: swindlers, unjust, adulterers, or even like this tax-gatherer. I fast twice a week; I pay tithes of all that I get.
>
> Luke 18:11b–12

Such pharisaic arrogance can be found in slick, proud-spirited, corporate-minded congregations . . . like the one in lukewarm Laodicea, a church in existence toward the end of the first century, mentioned in Rev. 3:14–18. Our Lord reproved the people of that church because they said, "I am rich, and have become wealthy, and have need of nothing" (v. 17a). But they did not realize that, spiritually speaking, they were "wretched and miserable and poor and blind and naked" (v. 17b).

In bold contrast to that whitewashed tombstone, the tax-gatherer described in Luke 18:13, painfully cognizant of his own lack of righteousness, was unwilling even to lift up his eyes to heaven. Instead, he pounded his chest as he muttered his simple, honest admission of need, "God, be merciful to me, the sinner!" The difference? The tax-gatherer was "poor in spirit."

Augustus Toplady captured the essence of this poor-in-spirit quality in several lines of his great hymn "Rock of Ages":

> Nothing in my hand I bring,
> Simply to Thy cross I cling;
> Naked, come to Thee for dress,
> Helpless, look to Thee for grace;
> Foul, I to the fountain fly,
> Wash me, Saviour, or I die![2]

And the promised blessing for such a humble, dependent, poor-in-spirit attitude? "Theirs is the kingdom of heaven," Jesus said. By living lives of such simple faith beneath our Father's sovereign, gracious care, we truly enter into what kingdom living is all about.

"Blessed are those who mourn."

This word translated "mourn" is the strongest Greek term the writer could have used to convey the idea of a passionate lament— the utter sorrow of a broken heart, a desperate ache of the soul. One who mourns enters into deep and intense anguish, whether mourning over something that is wrong and/or out of control in one's own life or in the world in general . . . mourning over some personal loss of possession . . . mourning over someone's death. In light of the context, it most likely refers to a passionate lament of the heart, something we might call a spirit of contrition. This is

vividly portrayed by Paul in his statement of unguarded vulnerability at the conclusion of his description of his own spiritual turmoil: "Wretched man that I am! Who will set me free from the
body of this death?" (Rom. 7:24).

In a time of extremes like ours, when the glorious grace of our
God is taken advantage of and misapplied to mean "live as you
please," it is easy to make too little of our sin. How seldom do we
find a contrite heart, or, as Jesus put it, how rare are "those who
mourn" over their own wretchedness. Rather than mourning, many
are "moaning" over the fact that other Christians don't look the
other way and shrug off their sinful behavior.

To "mourn" is to acknowledge the overwhelming sinfulness of
one's own sin, feeling indescribable sadness and brokenness over
the wrong that has transpired. Like Peter, who, after denying his
Lord on three separate occasions, felt the sudden weight, the enormity, of his transgression. His reaction? Scripture tells us, "And he
went out and wept bitterly" (Luke 22:62). A similar scene occurs
in Psalm 32 when David's sins associated with his Bathsheba affair
led to "groaning all day long," which, in turn, caused his "vitality"
to drain away (vv. 3–4). David mourned. Any attempt to rationalize or ignore wrongdoing only complicates matters. Simple faith
calls for swift and complete confession. Those who mourn, Jesus
promises, are blessed.

Sometimes our mourning is prompted by another's wrong.
Recently my wife and I watched a segment of the popular television program "60 Minutes." It featured several men and women—
mourners all—who are close relatives of some of Adolf Hitler's
highest-ranking henchmen. The relatives' grief-stricken faces,
their anguished tears, and their halting words told their own tragic
story. Humiliated, embarrassed, ashamed, and heartbroken over
their heritage, each expressed feelings of deepest lament. My heart
went out to those tormented men and women, several near my
own age, whose lives have been marked and marred by another's
sin.

And what is it Jesus promises those who mourn, who refuse to ignore their sin? "They shall be comforted," He says. Wonderful reassurance! Elsewhere in Scripture the Lord promises to bind up the brokenhearted, to give relief and full deliverance to those whose spirits have been weighed down by the realization of their failure and wrong. Read the following promise, then rejoice:

> For Thou dost not delight in sacrifice, otherwise I would
>   give it:
> Thou art not pleased with burnt offering.
> The sacrifices of God are a broken spirit;
> A broken and a contrite heart, O God, Thou wilt not
>   despise.
>
> Psalm 51:16–17

God does not expect or require months of misery-evoking penance or daily sacrifices to appease His anger. Christ's death on our behalf provided the once-for-all payment for sin. Nevertheless, a contrite heart that expresses itself in mourning over wrongdoing results in divine comfort. Count on it.

"Blessed are the gentle, for they shall inherit the earth."

Read that again, only this time think of that statement being made by some sales manager today. Or try to imagine the words coming from a competitive boss: "Just be gentle with your customer, okay?" You're probably smiling. In our high-pressured world of aggressive techniques, gentleness suggests becoming someone's doormat . . . sort of a cross between a wimp and a wallflower. What an unfortunate distortion of what Jesus taught.

Gentleness, in its genuine and original meaning, was used in various ways, all of them admirable:

- A wild stallion that had been ridden, broken, and brought under control was said to be "gentle."

- Words that calmed strong emotions were "gentle" words.

- Ointment that drew fever and pain out of a wound was a "gentle" medication.

- In one of Plato's works, a child asked a physician to be *tender* with him. He used the same Greek word translated "gentle."

- Those who were polite, treating others with dignity, courtesy, and tact, were called "gentle."

Even Jesus, when disclosing His personality, spoke of Himself as being "gentle and humble in heart" (Matt. 11:29). Obviously the word was used differently then than it is today. Rather than today's meaning of insecure, unsure, weak, or effeminate, back then it was a term denoting true inner strength under control. D. Martyn Lloyd-Jones adds this clarifying statement: "The man who is truly *meek* [gentle] is the one who is amazed that God and man can think of him as well as they do and treat him as well as they do" (emphasis mine).[3]

And what blessing did Jesus promise the gentle? "They shall inherit the earth," He said. That is not a reference to conquering and controlling the world. What it means is that, spiritually speaking, our needs will be met. As we trust the Lord to provide, we gain the "inheritance" He makes possible as He fights the battles and wins the territory. We don't have to roll up our sleeves and fight to the finish; He fights for us. We don't have to be preoccupied with protecting our rights or grappling for control; the Lord enables us to inherit whatever "land" we need. The greedy grab and lose, while the gentle inherit and gain.

What strange information in this era of demand for personal rights! Recently I saw a cartoon depicting a tiny baby only seconds after birth. The physician had the baby by the feet, holding him upside down and slapping him on the fanny. Instead of crying, the kid was screaming angrily, "I want a lawyer!" And so do most folks these days. The attitude is, "Who wants to wait for God to provide if I can sue someone's pants off and get what I want *now?*"

Are you serious about simplifying your walk of faith? Try gentleness. Allow your Lord room to be just that—the sovereign Lord in full control, capable of fighting for you and conquering whatever territory you need to inherit.

"Blessed are those who hunger and thirst for righteousness."

This beatitude reflects true spiritual passion, an insatiable hunger to know God intimately, to model His ways personally. Don't misread this. Jesus is not talking about merely increasing one's knowledge of biblical or doctrinal facts, though there is certainly nothing wrong with that. Instead, He's talking about aligning one-self with God's character: holiness, truth, goodness, and righteousness. Included in this "hunger and thirst" would certainly be the cultivation of the discipline of prayer and waiting on God, the submission of the will, and the desire to weave all that into everyday living. This is not to be pushed to unreasonable extremes that require a man to become a monk. Nor is Jesus interested in turning a mother into some sort of dreamy-eyed seraph who quotes Scripture instead of fixing meals. "Hungering and thirsting" means taking God seriously and finding how perfectly His truth fits into real-world existence. Best of all, as with both physical hunger and thirst, this spiritual appetite is an ongoing desire, needing to be frequently replenished on a daily basis.

And what will happen to those whose longing for God is so intense? Jesus promises, "they shall be satisfied." Wonderful thought! Rather than being perpetual victims of spiritual starvation, never getting sufficient nourishment to grow strong, "they shall be satisfied." One New Testament scholar suggests that the word "satisfied" was commonly used in reference to feeding and fattening cattle, since the root Greek term is the word for fodder or grass.[4] We have this hope: We will become so spiritually satisfied that we will be like hefty, well-fed livestock—strong, stable, able to handle harsh conditions and endure uncomfortable circumstances. Now that's a needed promise! God's pantry never runs low. His wells never run dry.

Interestingly, while the first four beatitudes focus attention on our relationship with the Lord—that vital vertical dimension of simple faith—the final four seem to emphasize the horizontal dimension, our *people-with-people relationships*.

"Blessed are the merciful, for they shall receive mercy."

Mercy is a concern for people in need. It has to do with assisting those less fortunate than ourselves, including those who suffer the consequences of disappointment, disease, and distress. One of my mentors used to say, "Mercy is God's ministry to the miserable." And it does not stop with compassion or sadness over someone in dire straits; it means identifying with those who are hurting and imagining the pain they are having to endure, then doing something about it.

When I think of mercy, I usually think of the Good Samaritan, the traveler who stopped to help a man who had been mugged, robbed, and abandoned by the road. Several religious leaders had already walked by the injured man. Perhaps they were preoccupied with practicing their sermons, repeating their memory verses, or going over their impressive "to-do" lists for the day. At any rate, not one of them gave the battered man the time of day. Then along came the Samaritan. He stopped and put himself in the broken man's place. He took time. He cleansed the man's wounds. He even loaded the man on his donkey and carried him to an inn for the night. And he said to the innkeeper, "Put it on my tab."

That's mercy at its best. It's not simply some feeling of sympathy or sadness over somebody in trouble, but really getting inside the other persons' skin, feeling what *they* feel, understanding *their* misery, and then helping them through it.

And whenever I think of the Good Samaritan, I also remember a couple of other Samaritan-like passages:

> If a brother or sister is without clothing and in need of daily food, and one of you says to them, "Go in peace, be warmed and be filled," and yet you do not give them what is necessary for their body, what use is that? Even so faith, if it has no works, is dead, being by itself.
>
> James 2:15–17

> But whoever has the world's goods, and beholds his brother in need and closes his heart against him, how does the love of God abide in him?
>
> 1 John 3:17

These verses pose some searching, probing questions: What good is unshared wealth? and, How does the love of God abide in such a person?

Shakespeare, in *The Merchant of Venice*, used these lines to describe mercy:

> The quality of mercy is not strained,
> It droppeth as the gentle rain from heaven.

Mercy is not reluctant. Force is not required to move it into action. No one has to hammerlock you and say, "Show mercy! Show mercy!" Mercy is voluntary. It flows like the gentle, falling rain.

What can we expect if we show mercy? Our Lord assures us in this beatitude that the merciful will, in turn, receive mercy. Those who live by mercy will die in mercy. You give to others in their misery, and they will give to you in your misery. God will see to it that your merciful investments today reap wonderful benefits tomorrow.

I know of no better setting in which to demonstrate mercy than in a marriage. Several months ago I sat behind a couple of newlyweds on a flight back to Los Angeles. How do I know they were newlyweds? Well, they were all over each other! He kissed her and she kissed him. She had left her purse in the overhead compartment, so she kissed him and asked if he would get it for her. He kissed her back as he stood up to get it. When he brought the purse down, it didn't look like it was worth all those kisses to me. But she kissed him again, and he kissed her back. I mean, they were so attentive to each other it was almost sickening! When the flight attendants served the meals, the bride kissed him before the meal . . . and he kissed her before, during, and after the meal. I had the same meal; it wasn't worth kissing over, I can assure you. It was just the usual "toy food" you get on an airplane—just another toy biscuit, toy meat, toy salad, and toy cake, plus a toy cup of coffee. Really, that stuff wasn't worth a kiss. As we arrived at the Los Angeles airport and everybody got up to leave, she reminded him with a kiss to pick up the things that were underneath the seat. After he pulled them out, he gave her a hug and another kiss! Soon they were walking out arm in arm. I confess, I was tempted to say in a booming voice, "I want to see you two in five years!"

It's not that you stop kissing; it's just that as life begins to unfold, things happen that require more than a quick kiss. You need to keep the fires of affection and tenderness stoked with something stronger. Heartaches happen, and that calls for mutual mercy. You are there for each other through the night. Both of you hang in there through the long haul. That's the kind of reciprocal give-and-take in the marriage commitment that calls for mercy. As one mate demonstrates it, God leads the other to reciprocate. As Jesus promised, the merciful will receive mercy.

"Blessed are the pure in heart."

Simplicity and purity fit together beautifully. A life of simple faith is linked to a pure heart. Perhaps the words "blessed are the utterly sincere" would be an appropriate paraphrase. If a film were made about someone who lived this kind of completely sincere life in both private and public, there would be no need to edit. You could videotape that person at church or at home, at work or at play, and you would catch no contradictions. The pure in heart live transparently . . . no guile, no hidden motives. How seldom we encounter anyone who lives anywhere near that standard!

What we all too often observe is what John R. W. Stott portrays in these tragic words: "Some people weave round themselves such a tissue of lies that they can no longer tell which part of them is real and which is make-believe."[5]

Rare though the "pure in heart" may be, this beatitude implies that life *can* be lived without masks. "Blessed are the pure in heart, for they shall see God." Meaning? They will see God work. They will see Him in their lives. They will feel His presence. There will be no waking up in fear that someone is going to find out the real truth. There is nothing to hide. There is just the living of a life before the all-seeing presence of God. That is the way our Lord lived, and He happily offers it to us.

"Blessed are the peacemakers."

Peacemakers release tension, they don't intensify it. Peacemakers seek solutions and find no delight in arguments. Peacemakers calm the waters, they don't trouble them. Peacemakers work hard to keep an offense from occurring. And if it has occurred, they strive for resolution. Peacemakers lower their voices rather than raise them. Peacemakers generate more light than heat. Blessed are such great-hearted souls! We need more of them in the ranks of faith. We have more than enough fighters, more than enough who are ready to pounce.

Make no mistake, however; *peacemaker* is not a synonym for *appeaser*. This is not peace at any price. There are limits. Just as Dietrich Bonhoeffer introduced the presence of "cheap grace,"[6] our Lord introduces the possibility of "cheap peace."

Cheap peace occurs when my brother (or sister) brings reproach to the name of Christ yet does not repent. For me to go right on as though everything is fine and dandy and, even worse, assure him he is forgiven and "all is well" cheapens peace. We are warned against that. Luke 17:3 says, "If he [your brother] repents, forgive him." It cheapens peace to ignore the gross offense, treat it lightly, and release him from accountability and responsibility if he doesn't have a contrite heart of repentance.

Churches are told to dwell together in unity, but not at the expense of sound doctrine. If a group is embracing heresy, you do not enhance the gospel by smiling and agreeing, all in the name of peace. Smiling at wrongdoing or erroneous teaching doesn't simplify life; it complicates it.

When Christ blessed the peacemakers, He was extolling the value of doing all we can to maintain harmony and support unity. His interest was in making peace where peace is an appropriate objective.

And what can peacemakers count on? "They will be called the sons of God," said Jesus. Was not Christ Himself called that by His followers? By our pursuing peace as He did, we shall be Christlike, sons and daughters of the living God, people with the Father's nature. So it is for those who choose to live in simple faith.

"Blessed are those who have been persecuted for the sake of righteousness, for theirs is the kingdom of heaven. Blessed are you when men cast insults at you, and persecute you, and say all kinds of evil against you falsely, on account of Me."

Now let's be careful with this one. Note again the *reason* these folks are being persecuted: "for the sake of righteousness." There is a kind of persecution we bring upon ourselves because we have been discourteous or needlessly offensive. There are certain reactions we can arouse simply because we adhere to some fanatical extreme that is based on personal taste or private opinion. But that is not what Jesus has in mind here. True persecution occurs when two irreconcilable value systems collide. When that occurs and you choose to stand on the principles of truth, you can count on it, *you will be persecuted.*

How will it happen? They will "cast insults at you," and "persecute you." The word translated *persecute* means "to pursue to the end." They will hunt you down. They will tell all kinds of evil lies about you. They will assassinate your character . . . and on certain extreme occasions, they may even attempt to take your life on account of Him. That has happened before, and it will happen again.

And how should you respond? "Rejoice, and be glad." Why? For two reasons. First, because "your reward in heaven is great." And second, because "so they persecuted the prophets who were before you." You are not alone. You are, in fact, in a long succession of very noble company. What a compliment!

When I go through this list of beatitudes, I am reminded all over again that God's ways are topsy-turvy to the world's ways. A few examples: God exalts the humble, but the world exalts the proud. God ascribes greatness, not to masters, but to servants. God is impressed, not with noise or size or wealth, but with quiet things . . . things done in secret—the inner motives, the true heart condition. God sends away the arrogant and the rich empty-handed, but He gathers to Himself the lowly, the broken, the prisoner, the prostitute, the repentant. The world honors the handsome and the gifted and the brilliant. God smiles on the crippled, the ones who can't keep up. All this makes the world nervous.

As Bonhoeffer once wrote: "And so the disciples are strangers in the world, unwelcome guests, disturbers of the peace. No wonder the world rejects them!"[7]

Simply Put: Applying Jesus' Words

How does all of this make sense for our daily lives? How do we develop this list of character traits with a view toward simple faith? In keeping with our theme, let's keep it simple. Here are two ideas.

Try this: Apply one beatitude a day. On Monday work on *dependence*, consciously focusing on being "poor in spirit." On Tuesday, apply *repentance*. On Wednesday, try *gentleness* as an attitude for the day. On Thursday, go after *righteousness*. Friday, let's make it a full day of *mercy*. Saturday, think on *integrity*. Sunday, deliberately be a *peacemaker*. And the next Monday? Cultivate *joy*. That will get you out of a repetitive cycle. Because there are eight beatitudes but only seven days in the week, you will have a new day with a new project on a regular basis. I challenge you: In place of a lifestyle that you have learned from the world's system, put these qualities into practice. Before you know it, your faith will begin to be simple again.

Here is another idea. Start listening for contrasts between the world's message and Christ's philosophy. You'll be amazed.

For example, instead of being a couch potato, start really "watching" television. Listen to what is being said. Better yet, notice what is *not* being said. Quit being gullible. How did the rich and famous get those lifestyles? Did they manipulate their way to the top? What about all those "honest," self-aware talk shows? Are they leading you to feed the flesh and encouraging you to fight selfishly for your own way? Think about the unending parade of award shows with their pride on display. Start paying close attention to what you are seeing and hearing. Keep in mind the Beatitudes and you'll witness many contrary messages emerging in seminars you attend and in magazines you read, as well as in the daily newspaper. But unless you're alert to these things, you'll be squeezed into the world's mold.

Ask the Lord to give you a redirection in life—to bring you back to simple faith.

I have often been grateful for the writings of J. B. Phillips, both his paraphrase of the New Testament and the volumes he authored. He has a way of capturing the essence of meaning in memorable words. He cleverly paraphrased the Beatitudes as the non-Christian world would prefer them. See if you don't agree that this version would fit rather well in today's media handbook:

> Happy are the "pushers": for they get on in the world.
> Happy are the hard-boiled: for they never let life hurt them.
> Happy are they who complain: for they get their own way in the end.
> Happy are the blasé: for they never worry over their sins.
> Happy are the slave-drivers: for they get results.
> Happy are the knowledgeable men of the world: for they know their way around.
> Happy are the trouble-makers: for they make people take notice of them.[8]

The Teacher from Nazareth offers a better way:

> How happy are the humble-minded, for the Kingdom of Heaven is theirs!
> How happy are those who know what sorrow means, for they will be given courage and comfort!
> Happy are those who claim nothing, for the whole earth will belong to them!
> Happy are those who are hungry and thirsty for goodness, for they will be fully satisfied!
> Happy are the merciful, for they will have mercy shown to them!
> Happy are the utterly sincere, for they will see God!
> Happy are those who make peace, for they will be known as sons of God![9]
>
> Matthew 5:3–10

These qualities of simple faith, when put into action, result in a life worth living. I dare you to try it.

3

A Simple Counterstrategy: Shake and Shine

ALMOST 275 YEARS AGO ISAAC WATTS asked three questions that need to be answered today. They appear in the lines of a hymn he wrote back in 1724, a hymn still sung in English-speaking churches around the world. Even its title is a question: "Am I a Soldier of the Cross?" But the questions I'm speaking of appear in the third stanza of that old hymn:

- Are there no foes for me to face?
- Must I not stem the flood?
- Is this vile world a friend to grace, to help me on to God?

Think about each of these, especially that last one; it's the clincher. Remove your rose-colored glasses. Toss aside your albums of dreamy love songs. Forget the motivational seminars and all those shoot-for-the-stars, positive-thinking, self-help paperbacks. Now then, looking at "this vile world" in raw reality, answer the question: *Is it a friend to grace?* Will this world help you to know

God? Love Him? Serve Him? As you sit at the feet of its professors, as you listen to its music and watch its films . . . as you take your cues from its philosophy and model its media, will the road narrow to the path that leads to God? No one in his or her right mind could ever answer yes.

Ours is a hell-bound, degenerate world and you know it. Isaac Watts's word is timelessly true: *vile*. Political corruption abounds. Academic pursuits, though temporarily stimulating, leave graduates empty and on futile searches that never satisfy. International peace, a splendid ideal, continues to blow up in our faces as war recurs with painful regularity. The crime rate escalates as domestic violence and gang wars and drug traffic and overcrowded jails continue to plague society. Pending legal cases choke the courts of our land with an endless litany of litigation. And even when cases are finally brought to trial, no courtroom or prison cell can remove madness from minds or hatred from hearts.

The Plain Truth About the Real World

The world is a war zone full of foes that must be faced. If it were not for the reliable promises God has given in the pages of His Book, a spirit of fatalism would reign supreme. The battle would already be lost.

Too bleak? An exaggeration? You decide after reading these words from the pen of the Apostle John: "We know that we are of God, and the whole world lies in *the power of* the evil one" (1 John 5:19). Three words—"the power of"—appear in italics in the text. The editors of the New American Standard Bible have added these words to make the passage clearer. Let me suggest a further variation: "The whole world lies in *the lap of* the wicked one" (italics mine).

Satan, our relentless enemy, has a game plan, and it's on the board. Knowing that his days are numbered, knowing that he has an appointed amount of time before the scoreboard counts him out, he holds the world in his lap and gives it directions, implementing his strategy day after day. On the surface, his plays are impressive and appealing and even very satisfying . . . for a while. So long as the adversary can keep earth's inhabitants believing his lies and blinded to his schemes, he will continue his subtle strategy. But the truth is, his ploys work against everything that is holy and just and good. I repeat Isaac Watts's question: "Is this vile world a friend to grace, to help us on to God?" Indeed, it is not.

To affirm the truth of that simple answer, read John's earlier words from the same letter:

> Do not love the world, nor the things in the world. If anyone loves the world, the love of the Father is not in him. For all that is in the world, the lust of the flesh and the lust of the eyes and the boastful pride of life, is not from the Father, but is from the world. And the world is passing away, and also its lusts; but the one who does the will of God abides forever.
>
> 1 John 2:15–17

Then who or what are we to love? Jesus' words come to mind: "This I command you, that you love one another. If the world hates you, you know that it has hated Me before it hated you" (John 15:17–18).

This raises another question: What can we expect from the world? We can expect *hatred* because the world hated the Lord Jesus Christ. And if we are in league with Him, it is going to hate us, as well.

Since this is true, what else can we expect from the world? *Persecution.* Jesus also warned of that during His earthly pilgrimage. "These things I have spoken to you, that in Me you may have peace. In the world you have tribulation. . . ." (John 16:33a).

What can we expect from the world? Hatred, persecution, tribulation. Those three reactions should never surprise us. They are not pleasant, for sure, but we have no reason to be caught off guard . . . or, for that matter, to feel abandoned or overwhelmed. Jesus went on to say, ". . . but take courage; I have overcome the world" (John 16:33b).

Why will the world treat us with hatred and persecution and tribulation? Two reasons: *generally* because the world lies in the lap of the wicked one, and *specifically* because we belong to Christ. It hated Him, so it will hate us. But therein lies the genius of our counterstrategy: By our being different, many in the world will realize what they are missing and will be drawn to Christ . . . a classic example of the old saying "opposites attract."

D. Martyn Lloyd-Jones is exactly right when he writes:

> The glory of the gospel is that when the Church is absolutely different from the world, she invariably attracts it. It is then that the world is made to listen to her message, though it may hate it at first.[1]

If our message is a mirror image of the message of the world, the world yawns and goes on its way, saying, "What else is new? I've heard all that since I was born." But if the Christian lifestyle and motivation and answers are different, the world cannot help but sit up and take notice, thinking:

- How come they live in the same place I live, but they are able to live a different kind of life?

- How is it that I cannot conquer this habit but he has?

- Why is their love so deep and lasting and ours so shallow and fickle?

- How is it that she can forgive and never hold a grudge, but I can't get over a wrong?

- Talk about kindness and courtesy! These people exude those things. I wonder why.

- Where did I miss out on mercy? They have so much more compassion and patience than anyone I've ever known.
- I've never seen such integrity. The guy wouldn't think of taking a dime that is not his.

Do you get the message? It is the difference that makes the difference. "Is this vile world a friend to grace, to help me on to God?" Of course not! It works the other way. The church is a friend to grace to get the attention of those who need God desperately.

Which brings us back to the words Jesus spoke from the hillside in Palestine . . . words full of surprise. Isaac Watts asked, "Am I a soldier of the cross?" Jesus described what a soldier of the cross looked like:

- poor in spirit
- mourning
- gentle
- hungry and thirsty for righteousness
- merciful
- pure in heart
- peacemaking

Talk about *different!* "But I thought we lived in a dog-eat-dog world," the world says. "I thought you had to be tough and rugged and selfish to make it. I mean, if you were to live like that, they would turn you into a doormat." It's true—

Blessed are you when men cast insults at you, and persecute you, and say all kinds of evil against you falsely, on account of Me. Rejoice, and be glad, for your reward in heaven is great, for so they persecuted the prophets who were before you.

Matthew 5:11–12

45

Because your life is a *rebuke* to those who are lost in the swamp of the system, they will put you to the test.

The Only Strategy That Works in the Real World

Jesus offered the only strategy that would counteract the world system:

> You are the salt of the earth; but if the salt has become tasteless, how will it be made salty again? It is good for nothing anymore, except to be thrown out and trampled under foot by men. You are the light of the world. A city set on a hill cannot be hidden. Nor do men light a lamp, and put it under the peck-measure, but on the lampstand; and it gives light to all who are in the house. Let your light shine before men in such a way that they may see your good works, and glorify your Father who is in heaven.
> Matthew 5:13–16

How in the world can soldiers armed with humility and contrition, gentleness and righteousness, mercy, purity, and peace ever make a lasting impact in a world that is so angry? The answer is found in the words you just read: by shaking salt and shining light. I repeat, to make a lasting impact on the world's system, one must be distinct from it, not identical to it. Jesus puts it so simply: "You are the salt of the earth. . . . You are the light of the world." Not just salt for your neighborhood or for the city where you live. There is enough salt to salt the whole world! Not just a local street light, but enough light to light the entire earth! Incredible statements. And so simple. But don't miss that emphatic "you" in both statements: "*You* are the salt of the earth. *You* are the light of the world."

I don't know if you have been to a basketball game lately, but nowadays one of the popular responses of many fans when a person fouls at a critical moment is to point and shout, "you, you, YOU,

YOU! YOU!!" The same applies to one of the referees when he makes a questionable call: "You, You, YOU, YOU! YOU!!"

Perhaps we need to move that chant out of the sports arena and into the arena of life. YOU, You, YOU, YOU! YOU!! are the light of the world. YOU, You, YOU, YOU! are the salt of the earth. Nobody else. You're on the spot; you're at the free throw line. Not somebody who has been to seminary. You. Not one of the ordained. You, YOU! All you who know the Savior. Every one of us in God's forever family is to be shaking salt and shining light.

Let's go further. It doesn't say, "You *can* be the salt," or "You *should* be the light." It says, "You *are.*" You don't even need to pray, "Lord, make me real salty. Lord, make me a bright light." You already are. Meaning what? Meaning, get at it. Shake the salt! Shine the light! Simple though it may seem, that is the game plan God has set up for counteracting a world that "lies in the lap of the evil one."

Slowly but surely our world is rotting from within. Not only are civilizations in the process of decaying, but morals are, as well. If Rip Van Winkle were still sleeping and awoke from his nap today, he would be shocked at the eroding standards of our time. What our culture accepts as the norm would have been considered scandalous back when he went to sleep.

The deadly erosion has plunged our world into frighteningly deep darkness. Some Christians have distanced themselves so far from the lifestyle of the unbeliever that they don't have a clue how dark the world system really is. They don't see its boredom, its flat tastelessness, its terror, and its stark hopelessness. There is the inescapable threat of AIDS, along with the abduction of children, alcoholism, and fears of growing old, of financial reversal, of marital infidelity, of emotional breakdown. Such darkness surfaces only briefly, then runs and hides its face in the valley of death.

One morning when I had a few extra minutes, I thumbed through a few pages of a local newspaper. Immediately I felt the edges of darkness closing in:

- A freeway shooter left a driver crippled, paralyzed from the neck down after he was shot in the neck. The gunman was sentenced to a maximum of ten years as the fellow in the wheelchair sat in the back of the courtroom and shook his head in amazement.

- In nearby Santa Ana a man was stabbed to death by two of his "friends."

- A wife and mother shot her daughter, then her husband, and then killed herself. All that happened in a quiet little home a few blocks south of where I live.

- Two men who swindled $9.5 million from several thousand people in telephone scams were sentenced to fifteen to twenty years.

- A wife was found guilty of killing her husband for insurance money.

- A restaurateur was convicted of arson conspiracy in the case of a fire in a neighboring community.

- Jurors convicted an El Toro man of manslaughter.

- During a hotel party, a man fell eight stories, but was not killed. His fall was broken when he struck a wooden lattice over a bar on the first floor. He was drunk.

- Twenty-two motorists were arrested in one day at checkpoints. All failed the sobriety test.

And all this didn't quite get me halfway through section 2 . . . but I had read enough!

Do you have any idea what that kind of news does to the average citizen? If it doesn't scare the life out of him, it can make him strangely apathetic. Then he gets hardened to it . . . shrugs it off, and says, "Who gives a rip?" So it goes in the darkness. But Jesus has devised a strategy that works.

A Better Taste of the Salt

> You are the salt of the earth; but if the salt has become tasteless, how will it be made salty again? It is good for nothing anymore, except to be thrown out and trampled under foot by men.
>
> Matthew 5:13

Before refrigeration, salt served a vital purpose. Fishermen, for example, knew its value. As soon as they got their catch, they packed the fish in layers of salt to preserve the meat until they could get it to market. Our forefathers who crossed the rugged plains and mountains in prairie schooners often layered their meat in salt or carried meat that had been soaked in brine to preserve it for as long as possible. Salt has a preserving effect. In other words, it arrests corruption.

Salt also adds flavor to food. Just a little shake of salt can dramatically change the taste of a dish. One of salt's most valuable contributions is the "bite" it adds to food. However, it can lose that bite.

I remember a course I took in chemistry in which I learned that sodium chloride is a very stable and resilient chemical compound. In reality, it never becomes "unsalty." Yet Jesus said that salt can become "tasteless." What did He mean? When salt becomes contaminated by dirt, sand, and other impurities, Jesus said it becomes "good for nothing." (Today if somebody is shiftless or lazy or does a poor job, we say that person is "good for nothing." That saying comes from Jesus' words.)

Look at a Christian who has absorbed the world system, and you will see salt that has lost its flavor—a tasteless, useless seasoning. The worse our world becomes, the greater is its need of salt because that's another important property: salt makes you thirsty.

In the case of the salty Christian, it makes the surrounding world thirsty for the very water of life. And, by the way, I'm not just talking about huge piles of salt (like big churches and evangelistic crusades) that make folks thirsty for the things of God. I'm talking about consistent, everyday, lifestyle things.

Earl Palmer, in a fine little book entitled *The Enormous Exception,* tells the story of a premed student at the University of California, Berkeley "who became a Christian after a long journey through doubts and questions." When Palmer asked the young man why he had chosen Jesus Christ, he answered that what had "tipped the scales" in his spiritual journey were the actions of a classmate who happened to be a Christian.

During the previous term the premed student had been very ill with the flu and, as a result, had missed ten days of school. "Without any fanfare or complaints," his Christian classmate carefully collected all his class assignments and took time away from his own studies to help him catch up.

The premed student told Palmer, "You know, this kind of thing just isn't done. I wanted to know what made this guy act the way he did. I even found myself asking if I could go to church with him."

God had used a salt-and-light Christian to tip the spiritual scales in this young premed student's life, and the Christian student proved to be a preservative influence "so that in that practical and what might appear quite small series of events his friend and fellow student had been able to find the way to an even more profound preservation of life."

Palmer says,

> I think the best tribute I ever heard concerning a Christian was the tribute spoken of this student. "I felt more alive when I was around this friend." It is this life that the disciples felt when they were near Jesus and it is what the world still feels when its people are near to those who know Jesus.[2]

Think about it: Do people feel more alive when they're around you? Do you create a thirst as you "shake the salt"? Does anyone ever wonder why you are so unselfish, so thoughtful, so caring? Do the neighborhood children want to be in your home because of the way you treat your children? And how about the teenagers? Is there some kind of "salty magnet" that draws them toward you?

People who live in darkness not only need salt, they also need light.

A Closer Look at the Light

What is the purpose of light? The answer is not complicated. Light dispels darkness.

Have you ever experienced complete, utter darkness? I vividly remember a couple of times when I have been in unbelievably thick darkness. The first time was when my family visited Carlsbad Caverns in New Mexico. It was in the early 1950s, back in the days when guides would lead groups far down into the bowels of the cavern. I can still remember how they turned off all the lights, and for some reason played a recording of a choir singing "Rock of Ages, Cleft for Me." As a teenager I was more concerned about getting the lights back on than singing along with some choir. It was *so* dark! When I put my hand in front of my face, just a few inches away from the end of my nose, I could feel the heat from my hand, but I could not even make out its silhouette. The cavern was absolutely *inky* black. Then someone struck a match—just one tiny match—and the light shown like a brilliant beacon.

I recall another scene. As a little boy I went flounder fishing along the Texas gulf shores with my father. If you have never floundered, you have missed half the fun of growing up. About the time it starts getting dark, you light a portable lantern and walk down to the edge of the bay; then you wade in until you're about knee deep. Next, you begin to walk very slowly, following the shoreline. By late evening the water has become calm, and the flounders (you hope) have come in close to shore. Using their wide fins, they settle down into the mud and sand and lie there with their mouths wide open, waiting for supper (some unassuming mullet or shrimp dancing in the shallows near the shoreline). What the flounder does not know is that it's going to be someone else's supper! Walking along, swinging the lantern, you peer into the water for the outline of a flounder lying absolutely still. When you spot one, down goes the gig, and, after a flurry of activity, you manage to get it onto your stringer.

Now when I was very small, I was much more concerned about getting back home in the dark than I was about locating flounder on the ocean floor. But I wanted to be with my dad, so I took the risk. If I asked him once, I must have asked him a dozen times, every time we went floundering, "Dad, in case the lantern goes out, do you know how to get back home?"

"Yeah, son. Don't worry . . . we'll get back. No problem. Just watch for the flounder."

"I know, Dad, but is there plenty of fuel in the lantern?"

"Yes, there's plenty of fuel. Now, watch for the flounder."

When we got to one point along the winding shoreline, we could no longer see our bay cottage—that was the point of no return in my little mind. I always feared that transitional moment. I can still remember rounding the point and craning my neck for one last look at the cottage light, because from then on the lantern's glow was our only hope of piercing the darkness.

On one occasion we had gotten a mile or so beyond that point when my dad gigged a flounder. Its fins and wide tail splashed the water up out of the bay in a furious explosion of water and sand. As the cold water hit the scorching-hot lantern glass—BOOM! —the light went out. It was suddenly pitch black! And I was scared spitless. My dad hadn't told me, but he always carried a flashlight in his hip pocket. What a relief when he snapped it on. I remember asking him, "Are the batteries in the flashlight good?" He reassured me they were new. There we were, miles from home, knee deep in water, and surrounded by thick darkness on a moonless night. That single ray of light was our only hope . . . but it was all we needed.

When you live in the darkness, you not only have no ray of light, you don't even know where home is. That is the way it is for the majority in the world. Some folks are born, raised, and die in cultures that have never seen their first flashlight of hope. Imagine it!

When the truth of that hits me, I find myself a little impatient with Christians who do nothing but shine lights for themselves. They even have what we might call flashlight parties where they just shine the light on each other. Lots of light! Too much light to be hoarded! Jesus says to shine for the world. Shine your light into the darkness; that's where it is really needed. Spend less time in your own little well-lighted all-Christian world and more time there in the darkness!

Years ago I came to appreciate this verse by C. T. Studd:

> Some wish to live within the sound
> Of Church or Chapel bell;
> I want to run a Rescue Shop
> Within a yard of hell.[3]

You say your environment is dark? What an opportunity! You're the only one in the company who knows the Savior? Now you're talking! You've got the light! Now be careful . . . don't shine a big blinding beacon right into your co-worker's eyes. He needs light, but just enough in the right places. And salt? Don't dump a truckload on him. Just a little, please. Too much salt ruins the food just as too much light blinds the eyes. The counterstrategy is simple: Shake, don't pour. Shine, don't blind.

Remember how Jesus put it? "A city set on a hill cannot be hidden." You couldn't hide it if you tried. Your light is on the hill.

"Good works" sound a clarion call. Just live a different life. That will drive them nuts, wondering why *you* don't do the things they do. They won't know why you have peace of mind. They won't know why you don't worry. They won't know why you smile more than you frown. But they'll sure be curious.

It is amazing how light attracts. When you're in a dark place with just one light, all eyes focus on the light. Light is what gives mariners a course to follow across the seas. They determine their direction by the stars, light-years away. The gleam of a lighthouse on the horizon gives a direction. It attracts attention.

"Don't make it complicated," says Jesus. "Simply let your light shine." Isn't that easy? Just let it shine. No need to add extra voltage. No need to make a giant public announcement, proclaiming "I walk in the light." Just shine.

Jesus never said to His disciples, "You know, fellas, we have to work on gathering a better crowd. They're getting pretty thin, especially on Sunday night." No, it was never like that. He just turned on the light and they came to Him. In the wilderness. Or in the city. On a hillside. At the lakeside. They came! He was so different! He was light. And so are we.

What will they see? They will see "your good works," Jesus said. Like what? They will hear your courtesy. They will detect your smile. They will notice that you stop to thank them. They will hear you apologize when you are wrong. They will see you help them when they are struggling. They will notice that you are the one who stopped along the road and gave them a hand. They will see every visible manifestation of Christ's life being normally lived out through you. They will see all that and they "will glorify your Father who is in heaven" (Matt. 5:16). John R. W. Stott writes:

> I sometimes think how splendid it would be if non-Christians, curious to discover the secret and source of our light, were to come up to us and enquire:
>
> > Twinkle, twinkle, little star,
> > How I wonder what you are![4]

Isn't it a pleasure when someone says to you, "Why are you like that?" And isn't it a natural thing to respond, "I'm glad you asked. Let me tell you what's happened"? And then you light their way home.

I love the way one man expressed much of what I've been describing in a profound prayer. Profound, yet simple:

> LORD, HIGH AND HOLY, MEEK AND LOWLY,
> Thou hast brought me to the valley of vision,
>> where I live in the depths but see thee in the heights;
>> hemmed in by mountains of sin I behold thy glory.
> Let me learn by paradox
>> that the way down is the way up,
>> that to be low is to be high,
>> that the broken heart is the healed heart,
>> that the contrite spirit is the rejoicing spirit,
>> that the repenting soul is the victorious soul,
>> that to have nothing is to possess all,
>> that to bear the cross is to wear the crown,
>> that to give is to receive,
>> that the valley is the place of vision.
> Lord, in the daytime stars can be seen from deepest wells,
>> and the deeper the wells the brighter thy stars shine;
> Let me find thy light in my darkness,
>> thy life in my death,
>> thy joy in my sorrow,
>> thy grace in my sin,
>> thy riches in my poverty,
>> thy glory in my valley.[5]

Simply Put: Suggestions for Shaking and Shining

When you shake and shine, you *influence* others, which Webster defines as "the act or power of producing an effect without apparent exertion of force or direct exercise of command."

As one writer says,

We who are married do not have to pretend we are living as Barbie Dolls on a wedding cake. We have struggles, and dashed expectations too. But if we offer the world a model of a reasonably good marriage, a reasonably good church, a reasonably good college fellowship, it will have radicalizing effects on the world.[6]

As I close this chapter, let me mention three "don'ts." First: *Don't overdo it.* Remember, don't call attention to the salt or the light, just live the life. If you are married, perhaps your best testimony in this dark world is little more than "a reasonably good marriage." Isn't that relieving? No need to walk on water.

Second: *Don't hold back.* When you live the life of faith fairly consistently, you will attract the attention of those in the darkness; you will cultivate a thirst in those who are living tasteless, hopeless lives. And when they come asking for information, you will have a perfect opportunity to tell them about the Source of the salt and light.

Take a risk. Take a risk with good works. They will make a difference in this "vile world."

Just consider a few of the specific ways that shake-and-shine Christians have made a difference in the world: abolition of slavery, prison reform, medical care, helping the addicts, world missions, alternatives to abortion, exposing child abuse, establishing orphanages, making a positive influence in the political world, holding leadership positions in large companies that are making an impact in this world—and much more.

Third: *Don't worry about the few who resist it.* Nobody bats a thousand. Some even walked away from the Master Himself. (Remember, He was the only perfect human being who ever lived, yet they crucified Him.) Even the great prophets and apostles were ignored, forgotten, and martyred. Don't worry about the few who reject the salt and resist the light.

"Is this vile world a friend to grace, to help me on to God?" In no way. Quite the reverse, in fact. People who are salt and light are the friends of grace. We are the ones who help the world on to God. What a counterstrategy! Best of all, it is simple. Just shake and shine.

4

Simplicity Starts from Within

SOME BIBLICAL SCENES WOULD BE absolutely great on a videocassette. Not the Cecil B. DeMille productions with all their phony costumes, lavish makeup, special effects, and plastic landscapes. I'm talking about the real thing—the original events—being captured on film for all to see.

How about that time when all those Hebrews crossed the Red Sea? Or when Elijah mocked the prophets of Baal, then called down fire from heaven? I would love to see that moment in Joseph's life when he was surrounded by his brothers and they didn't have a clue that he was their relative . . . and then he revealed his identity. What an ending! Another winner would be Noah's ark—from the inside: wall-to-wall animals cooped up together for weeks in that floating zoo. My long-time mentor and friend, Howie Hendricks, once commented that Noah's family in the ark reminded him of God's family in the church: "If it weren't for all the trouble on the outside, we couldn't stand the stench on the inside."

I suppose each one of us would have our favorite biblical film clips. Being a preacher, I can think of several original "preacher scenes" I would find extremely interesting—like when the prophet Jeremiah wept through a few sermons he preached, or when Jonah made that first amphibious landing and instantly hightailed it to Nineveh. Or imagine the epic adventure of John the Baptizer roaming the wilderness dressed in camel's hair, eating locusts dipped in honey, and shouting, "Repent, you hypocrites!" Classic moments. Watching Paul as he addressed all those eggheads on Mars Hill in Athens would be another scene worth viewing. The city's philosophical brain trust had just labeled him a "seed picker," then minutes later heard him spontaneously quote from one of their own poets as he spoke of Christ's miraculous resurrection! D. Martyn Lloyd-Jones, while delivering a series on preaching at Westminster Theological Seminary years ago, declared:

> What is preaching? Logic on fire! Eloquent reason! Are these contradictions? Of course they are not. Reason concerning this Truth ought to be mightily eloquent, as you see it in the case of the Apostle Paul and others. It is theology on fire! And a theology which does not take fire, I maintain, is a defective theology; or at least the man's understanding of it is defective. Preaching is theology coming through a man who is on fire.[1]

We still have the fiery words of great preachers of the past, but because we cannot literally hear their voices and actually watch their gestures, we miss much of the fire that originally burned in them and through them.

This is especially true regarding the message Jesus delivered on the mountain outside Jerusalem. Talk about a man on fire; the Master was ablaze! Full of passion and zeal, at the zenith of His human manhood, our Lord used the simplest of words to cut to the heart of the issues that mattered, so much so that His hearers sat spellbound. His theology-on-fire gripped their hearts. If you think His style was mild-mannered and passive, you owe yourself another reading of Matthew 5, 6, and 7. No question, He shook up the troops! And this message was one of the earliest in His ministry. It reminds me of a similar style that characterized George Whitefield, that brilliant, eighteenth-century, Oxford-trained proclaimer of truth. The very first Sunday after his ordination Whitefield preached with such fervor that a complaint was made to the bishop, "asserting that as the result of his sermon fifteen people had become insane."[2] That, friends and neighbors, is theology on fire.

The Authority of the Scriptures

Were we able today to witness Jesus' message in person, I have no doubt that it would stab us awake. Why do I say that? Because He spoke with authority—the all-powerful, invincible authority of the Scriptures. Human opinions no longer mattered, not even the longstanding, rigidly enforced pharisaic rules and regulations.

Are we talking about merely making an impression or being persuasive? No. Webster defines *authority* as "the power to influence or command thought, opinion, or behavior." I would use two additional words to describe authority: *convincing force* . . . a force far greater than any human can muster. Jesus' words were "living and active" (Heb. 4:12), eclipsing every man-made code of ethics or moral standard.

Why Is Authority Important?

Remove that standard and humanity is awash in this person's opinion or that culture's tradition or some group's regulations, or, most specifically, in pharisaic legalism. In the final analysis, it was when Jesus had the audacity to question those longstanding traditions that plans for His demise were put in motion. If we had a videocassette of His delivering this sermon and if the camera were panning His audience, we would detect a few astonished faces and, no doubt, a few frowns about the time He said the words recorded in Matt. 5:17: "Do not think that I came to abolish the Law or the Prophets; I did not come to abolish, but to fulfill."

Suddenly, for the first time, He—personally—is brought into focus. During the Beatitudes He spoke in the third person: "Blessed are those who," and "blessed are they." When He talked about shaking salt and shining light, He subtly shifted the pronouns from third to second person: "You are the salt . . . you are the light." But now? Now He speaks of Himself. Why does He do this? Because some must have wondered if He was speaking on His own behalf. Maybe one or two thought, *Who does He think He is? Is He above the Law? Sounds like He sets Himself up as judge and jury. Is He beyond the authority of Scripture?*

The Fulfillment of the Law

Let's not make Jesus' statement complicated. He gave it to simplify the issue, not confuse His hearers.

The Law and Christ

His initial remark stands on its own. He had not come to cancel out the Law or to remove its authority. Then how are we to interpret His second comment? "I did not come to abolish, but to fulfill." In what way?

Think about it. He brought the Scripture to completion in His person. Old Testament Scripture speaks often of the Messiah who was to come. "I am He," implies Jesus. Furthermore, He fulfilled Scripture when He gave it a literal point of reference. Periodically during His earthly ministry Jesus mentioned, "This fulfills what was spoken by the prophet." He also fulfilled Scripture by obeying its moral code and ethical commands. At every point, He obeyed. Never once did He compromise or hedge.

In fact, if you still wonder if Jesus was a little soft on Scripture, get a load of His next statement:

> For truly I say to you, until heaven and earth pass away, not the smallest letter or stroke shall pass away from the Law, until all is accomplished.
>
> Matthew 5:18

I can remember when the only Bible every Christian used was the King James Version. Because it renders this verse a little differently, let me quote it here.

> For verily I say unto you, Till heaven and earth pass, one jot or one tittle shall in no wise pass from the law, till all be fulfilled.

Study those two unusual words, *jot* and *tittle*. What is Jesus saying here? The word *jot* is literally a transliteration of a Hebrew character, *yodh*. It is the smallest letter in the twenty-two characters of the Hebrew alphabet. In the King James Version it is translated "jot"; in the New American Standard translation it is "smallest letter." It is a tiny character that looks a bit like an apostrophe.

But if you think that's tiny, the tittle is even more so. In Hebrew, two letters look almost identical. If it were not for an additional "tail" on the end of one of those letters, you would swear they were the same. In fact, they would be. The only difference is that tiny additional part of the letter. And that very small part of one letter is called the tittle.

It is as if Jesus were saying, "I so believe in the authority and the preservation and the inspiration of Scripture that not even the dot above an *i* or the cross on a *t* shall pass away until it has all been fulfilled." Jesus erased all questions regarding His commitment to Scripture or obedience to its command.

But the truth is, God was still in the process of revealing His truth as He spoke through His Son Jesus. In that process, God wanted His people to know more than the letter of the Law, but in no way were they to erase the truths of the Old Testament or take them lightly, which is why Jesus adds,

> Whoever then annuls one of the least of these commandments, and so teaches others, shall be called least in the kingdom of heaven; but whoever keeps and teaches them, he shall be called great in the kingdom of heaven.
>
> Matthew 5:19

The Law and the Christian

What is life in the kingdom of heaven? Generally speaking—simply speaking—it is a life lived under the authority of Scripture. If you take advantage of it, if you compromise it, if you fuss around and say it does not mean what it says or it means something other than what it actually says, you will miss much of what God has in mind for us in kingdom living.

Jesus goes on to say:

> For I say to you, that unless your righteousness surpasses that of the scribes and Pharisees, you shall not enter the kingdom of heaven.
>
> Matthew 5:20

Again, if we had a few video shots of some Pharisees when they heard these words, we would be looking at frowning stares, for sure. No one was more pious in appearance than the Pharisees. They wore certain garments that gave them an externally religious look. They conducted themselves in a publicly pious way. They said words that made them seem so holy and at the same time made others feel guilty. But don't misunderstand. Externally it seemed as though they fulfilled every letter of the Law, but what was missing was the spirit of the Law. Jesus says, in effect, "Unless your righteousness goes deeper than theirs, unless your genuine faith surpasses their external piety, you don't know what kingdom living is all about." It is the inner heart that God searches and rewards.

A quick trip to the animal world might help. You can take a pig out of the pigpen and you can wash that pig until it is spotless. You can then spray it with the finest perfume. You can even put a pink ribbon around its neck and teach it to snort for its food. But as soon as you turn that pig loose and allow it to be itself again, it will go back to the muddy pigsty and dive right into the slop for dinner. Why? Because you have not changed its heart—its "pigness."

Howie Stevenson, my dear friend and minister of worship and music at our church, has this saying framed and hanging on his office wall:

> Never try to teach a pig to sing.
> It wastes your time and it annoys the pig.

The Pharisees were big on external washings; they were good at perfume, great at pink ribbons and all kinds of public tricks, but they missed the heart. They cared little about that.

Jesus wasn't always tactful with the grace-killing Pharisees of His day. A little later in His ministry, as their attacks on Him intensified, He exposed them without mercy.

> You hypocrites, rightly did Isaiah prophesy of you, saying,
> "THIS PEOPLE HONORS ME WITH THEIR LIPS,
> BUT THEIR HEART IS FAR AWAY FROM ME.
> BUT IN VAIN DO THEY WORSHIP ME,
> TEACHING AS DOCTRINES THE PRECEPTS OF MEN."
> Matthew 15:7–9

Then in order to encourage His followers to live authentic rather than hypocritical lives, Jesus immediately called them aside and warned, "Not what enters into the mouth defiles the man, but what proceeds out of the mouth, this defiles the man" (Matt. 15:11).

Wow! That hit home, too. For the Pharisees not only talked about washing, they were very big on diet. The Jews had to eat certain foods a certain way or they broke the traditions. Now Jesus was saying, "It doesn't matter that much what goes into the mouth. What really matters is what comes out."

I love the next verse. It always makes me smile: "Then the disciples came and said to Him, 'Do You know that the Pharisees were offended when they heard this statement?'" (Matt. 15:12).

So? Big deal! They *needed* to be offended. One might hope the well-deserved rebuke would awaken them. Unfortunately it didn't, not even when Jesus dug deeper.

> Let them alone; they are blind guides of the blind. And if a blind man guides a blind man, both will fall into a pit. . . .
>
> Do you not understand that everything that goes into the mouth passes into the stomach, and is eliminated? But the things that proceed out of the mouth come from the heart, and those defile the man. For out of the heart come evil thoughts, murders, adulteries, fornications, thefts, false witness, slanders. These are the things which defile the man; but to eat with unwashed hands does not defile the man.
>
> Matthew 15:14, 17–20

I think the point is as simple as it is obvious: In the final analysis, what is significant is that which comes out of the heart. The Pharisees never got the message. Simply put, their faith had lost its simplicity.

The Law and Righteousness

Up to this moment, Jesus' message has been fairly general. From now on, however, He gets quite specific; in fact, He addresses six areas where what goes on in the heart is more important than what occurs on the surface.

To clarify what is coming, let me offer a simple overview. In each of the six popular topics He mentions in this section of Matthew 5, Jesus offers quotes either from the Law or from the traditional teachings of the day; then with each one He gives insight on how to model a righteousness that surpasses all the external stuff.

Subject	Traditional Teaching	New Insight
Murder (vv. 21–26)	"You have heard"	"but I say"
Adultery (vv. 27–30)	"You have heard"	"but I say"
Divorce (vv. 31–32)	"It was said"	"but I say"
Oaths (vv. 33–37)	"You have heard"	"but I say"
Retaliation (vv. 38–42)	"You have heard"	"but I say"
Love (vv. 43–47)	"You have heard"	"but I say"

No one can ever accuse Jesus of overlooking or dodging relevant issues. The list remains up-to-date, even though it is over nineteen centuries old. We shall consider only the first subject in the remainder of this chapter, then we will look at the other five later on.

First,

You have heard that the ancients were told, "You shall not commit murder" and "Whoever commits murder shall be liable to the court."

Matthew 5:21

Jesus begins the list of six issues by mentioning both the Mosaic Law ("the ancients") and the civil law ("the court") regarding murder. It is homicide He has in mind, a premeditated taking of another life, and the Law specifically condemned such: "You shall not commit murder." As time passed, "Whoever commits murder shall be liable to the court" was added. His listeners were especially familiar with that, since the Pharisees taught that rule almost to the exclusion of the initial commandment.

Because Jesus was urging them to attain a righteousness surpassing that of the Pharisees, He goes deeper than the surface—He goes to the heart with the words:

> You have heard that the ancients were told, "YOU SHALL NOT COMMIT MURDER" and "Whoever commits murder shall be liable to the court." But I say to you that everyone who is angry with his brother shall be guilty before the court; and whoever shall say to his brother, "Raca," shall be guilty before the supreme court; and whoever shall say, "You fool," shall be guilty enough to go into the fiery hell.
>
> Matthew 5:21–22

All right, let's wade into that statement. Clearly, Jesus is describing an anger that goes beyond proper bounds. Let me clarify this, because some will think Jesus is teaching that we should never express anger at all. But if that were the case, God would have been guilty of breaking His own command (remember reading about "the wrath of God"?). In fact, later on in the New Testament Paul teaches in Ephesians 4:26, "BE ANGRY, AND YET DO NOT SIN." So there is a place for appropriate anger. There is justified anger. But Jesus is not referring to that here in His sermon.

Go back and read verse 22 again. Occasionally in a musical score you will find a crescendo symbol. This verse is like that . . . the anger is seen as a crescendo that builds through three stages to the point of murderous statements and thoughts. To begin with there is anger at its basic level, "everyone who is angry with his brother."

Then comes the second stage: "whoever shall say to his brother, 'Raca.'" *Raca* is an Aramaic term that means "empty," most often used with reference to mental emptiness. Our colloquialism today might be "airhead," "nitwit," "bonehead," "numbskull," or "blockhead," any one of those slang expressions. It is an insulting term used in anger against a person. In other words, if someone gets so angry with another that he looks at him and either thinks, says, or shouts, "You mentally worthless idiot!" he or she has gone too far.

Finally Jesus moves to stage three: "and whoever shall say, 'You fool.' " In the original Greek the word is *moros*. Can you guess which term we get from that? Yes, of course: *moron*. It was used most often with reference to people who lived morally wasted lives. In other words, by calling someone this you take the position of a judge because you have determined that that person is morally wasted. And what happens? You "shall be guilty enough to go into the fiery hell." Be careful here. Do not put words into Jesus' mouth. He does not say you go to hell; He says it brings *enough* guilt to send one to hell. This third stage is verbal murder . . . long-lived, nursed anger that is sustained to a vicious point. It bursts out of the mouth in a rage. Remember, the tongue speaks from the heart. And in this case the heart has entertained degrading and insulting thoughts of contempt.

Anger can be difficult to control, and sometimes we fail. But when we get to stage three, we've gone too far. It is nothing less than a verbal stabbing from the heart. It murders the other person with a sharp, knifelike insult. Yet we will allow ourselves to get so completely out of control that we don't even think twice. In fact, we rationalize that, "she had it coming," or "he deserved to hear that." Whoa! If you and I are kingdom people, we don't let that happen.

Jesus mentions two examples that were probably imaginary cases. It is doubtful He had someone specific in mind, but they were certainly true to life. One took place at the temple and the other occurred in the courts. One is in a religious setting and the other in a legal setting. In verses 23 and 24 we have the religious scene, and in verses 25 and 26, the legal scene.

> If therefore you are presenting your offering at the altar, and there remember that your brother has something against you, leave your offering there before the altar, and go your way; first be reconciled to your brother, and then come and present your offering.
>
> Matthew 5:23–24

This is one of the few times in the Bible when we are instructed to interrupt our worship with something that is even more important.

The scenario might go something like this. You get up early Sunday morning and get ready, drive to church, locate a parking spot, and make your way inside. You sit down and begin to prepare yourself for worship. In doing so, you start to focus on the Lord. Beautiful music surrounds you as the organist begins to play some quiet strains of familiar hymns. People around you are talking about things that are joyful and encouraging. It is a peaceful scene, perhaps different from where you work or what you live with. Soon you begin to commune with your Lord. You start to pray. But your eyes haven't been closed sixty seconds when, suddenly, flashing across the back of your eyelids is a face or a name—not just any face, but an individual you offended. You remember it well. The Lord brings that person to your attention. He pulls up that face on your memory screen, and He won't let you forget it. You try to ignore the promptings . . . to go on in worship . . . to sing the words of the hymns; but you are blocked. The Lord is saying, in so many words, "You have to make that right." Maybe it's a former business associate, maybe your marriage partner. Maybe it's your ex. Maybe it's somebody on your ball team that you took advantage of recently, or somebody who is furious with you at school, or an angry neighbor. You are clear about one thing: There is an offense. And what eats your heart out is he knows or she knows that you are the offender.

So? Jesus says to "leave your offering there." To apply it literally, you excuse yourself, get up from the pew, walk out the door, get in your car, and drive away. You get in touch with that offended person.

Jesus doesn't say, "Wait a week and pray about it, then write a letter or make a quick phone call." He says, "Go and be reconciled first." That's an order.

Your goal is to turn enmity into amity. You have offended someone. This is not a passing offense or slight thing; it is a heavy weight on your mind. It won't leave you alone because you know the offense has not been reconciled. The best thing to do? Keep it simple—go and make it right.

This is a book on simple faith, and here is another example of how many people complicate their lives instead of simplifying them. You've done wrong? You've been offensive? Your actions or words have caused hurt? To do nothing is not only in direct disobedience to Jesus' teaching, it also complicates your life. It adds heavier mental weights than you are capable of carrying. It is like dropping an anchor and then cranking up your boat's engine and putting it in gear. The anchor keeps catching and snagging on the bottom, making for a terribly uncomfortable ride across the water. How simple the solution! Just pull in the anchor. (By the way, I've never been on a boat with an automatic return anchor. If you dropped it out . . . you need to pull it in.)

Are you nursing a lingering offense? That is, does someone have a lingering offense against you? Let me give you a simple tip: We cannot be right with God until we are right with others. That is the whole gist of this statement.

Here's another one. You might say, "Well, it's true I've had a problem with that guy, but, you know, he's not a Christian. He's more like an enemy, an opponent." Well, I'm glad you brought him up. Jesus adds this counsel regarding our opponents:

> Make friends quickly with your opponent at law while you are with
> him on the way, in order that your opponent may not deliver you

to the judge, and the judge to the officer, and you be thrown into prison.

Matthew 5:25

In other words, solve the problem before it gets to court—before it really gets serious.

Do you like defending your rights? Are you the type of person who always has an attorney ready to help you get your way? If you're not, you are unusual. As I mentioned earlier in this volume, this is the day for threatening each other with lawsuits. I've met folks who sit anxiously on the edge of their seats, just waiting for a chance to sue. Jesus' words stand squarely against that attitude. You want to be different? Jesus suggests, "Solve it out of court."

Simplicity starts from within. Is there so much pride in your heart that you are going to get your way, no matter what? That is nothing but anger, pure and simple, that has gotten out of control—which takes us back to the whole issue of murder. Jesus is concerned about estranged feelings that grow into a small sore. Then the sore festers, comes to a head, and fills with pus; then it bursts, with corruption oozing all over the relationship. The simple (not easy, mind you, *simple*) answer is to work it out between you. Jesus spoke with fire in His bones. We cannot be right with God until we are right with one another.

Simply Put: The Relevance of the Truth

As I reflect on these wonderful words of life, I find three principles worth pondering.

First: *The principles of Scripture go deeper than externals.* The Pharisees never learned this. If all you get from your church or from your Bible study is surface religion and the importance of superficial appearance, you are missing what true Christianity is all about. If your heart is not being convicted and moved to change, there is

74

something missing that is terribly important. There are unspoken motives that must be addressed. There are personal secrets that await your attention, perhaps a hidden agenda that you have not yet acknowledged. The authoritative Scripture penetrates far below the surface.

Second: *The potential of anger is greater than words.* You can be a killer yet never hold a lethal weapon in your hand. Don't ignore the murder in your attitude.

You may live in an argumentative family. You may have developed the habits of answering back, being defensive, sarcastic, caustic. You may have a violent temper. You are missing the best of kingdom living by letting that linger. Come to terms with those habits. Once you do, you will be amazed how much it will simplify your life.

Third: *The power of reconciliation is stronger than revenge.* It is amazing how forgiveness unloads the weapon in the other person's hand. When you reconcile with your brother or sister, it is amazing what it does in both hearts. It is like having your nervous system flushed out. It is like getting over a longstanding fever and cleansing the corruption that has been diseasing your mind. You don't need an attorney for that. You probably don't need a minister or a counselor, either. You just need humility. To put it straight, in the final analysis you need *guts*. Don't wait any longer . . . draw in the anchor.

It was said that in ancient days Saint Patrick, one of the early saints, had this prayer inscribed on his breastplate:

> God be in my head,
>   And in my understanding;
> God be in my eyes,
>   And in my looking;
> God be in my mouth,
>   And in my speaking;

God be in my heart,
And in my thinking;
God be at mine end,
And at my departing.[3]

Simplicity starts from within. Start!

5

Simple Instructions on Serious Issues

It is easy for those who speak in public to substitute length for strength. There is this mistaken idea that a talk needs to be long before folks will think it's important. Ministers are the most notorious when it comes to this strange logic. Somehow we feel the longer the sermon the more memorable its contents when, in fact, others know better.

One Sunday afternoon a preacher asked his wife, "Do you think I put enough fire in my sermon?" She answered, "To tell the truth, I didn't think you put enough of your sermon into the fire!"

If cleanliness is next to godliness in a home, brevity and clarity are next to accuracy in a sermon. Truth spoken to the point sticks, and anyone who makes a living with his or her voice will testify that preparing a short message is a much greater challenge than a long one. You really have to have a clear picture of what you want to say.

A sculptor was once asked by a group of visitors how he carved such a realistic lion when he didn't have a model. His response brought smiles, though he wasn't trying to amuse them: "I simply carve away anything that doesn't look like a lion."

Jesus was the best when it came to communication. He knew precisely what He wanted to say and how to say it so anyone could understand it. He was often criticized for *what* He said but *never* for how long it took Him to say it. He never wasted a word. Before long, people realized that, from start to finish, His words were worth their undivided attention. Paul O'Neil, a writer for *Life* magazine for many years, would surely have given Jesus an A for His ability to model "O'Neil's Law" to perfection: "Always grab the reader by the throat in the first paragraph, sink your thumbs into his windpipe in the second and hold him against the wall until the tag line."[1] Sounds so easy . . . until you try to do it.

A Brief Reminder of the Sermon's Beginning

Jesus didn't merely try to do it in His Sermon on the Mount, He did it. No message has ever distilled more truth in fewer words. In less than twenty minutes He left his audience reeling . . . thoroughly convinced. To this day great minds are still impressed with that command performance delivered on an ancient hillside. James T. Fisher, a seasoned psychiatrist, was correct in his observation:

> If you were to take the sum total of all the authoritative articles ever written by the most qualified of psychologists and psychiatrists on the subject of mental hygiene—if you were to combine them and define them and cleave out the excess verbiage—if you were to take the whole of the meat and none of the parsley, and if you were to have these unadulterated bits of pure scientific knowledge concisely expressed by the most capable of living poets, you would have an awkward and incomplete summation of the Sermon on the Mount.[2]

Blessings, Blessings!

Talk about coming to the point! Jesus bypassed all clichés and predictable preliminaries as He began His message. He didn't even say, "It's nice to be with you today." Like a fleet sprinter leaping from his starting blocks, Jesus offered a quick series of back-to-back blessings.

- Blessed are the poor in spirit . . .
  - Blessed are those who mourn . . .
    - Blessed are the gentle . . .
      - Blessed are those who hunger and thirst for righteousness . . .
        - Blessed are the merciful . . .
          - Blessed are the pure in heart . . .
            - Blessed are the peacemakers . . .
              - Blessed are those who have been persecuted . . .

His opening words grabbed everyone by the throat. Full attention was riveted on the Nazarene from that moment on.

Shake and Shine!

Next, He challenged His listeners to make a difference. How? "You are the salt. . . . You are the light, . . ."—single-syllable, easily understandable terms, familiar to everyone. The exhortation fit the symbols to perfection: "Since you are salt, shake it! Since you are light, shine!" In other words, "Be different!"

Watch Your Attitude!

After challenging them to demonstrate a righteousness that surpassed that of the scribes and Pharisees, He got specific. In fact, He dug beneath the surface of inappropriate actions and addressed two deep-seated attitudes.

Surface Action	*Deeper Attitude*
Murder (vv. 5:21)	Unrestrained anger (vv. 5:22)
Unresolved conflict (vv. 5:23)	Lack of forgiveness (vv. 5:24–26)

Then, as we shall soon discover, He goes on to deal with two more realms of righteousness that were ignored and rationalized by the religious teachers of that day: marital fidelity (vv. 27–32) and verbal integrity (vv. 33–37). Some preachers, then and now, avoid sticky issues as though they are sidestepping puddles of hot tar. Not Jesus. With a beautiful blend of courage, wisdom, and simplicity, He waded right in.

A Clear Declaration of Two Absolutes

I find it nothing short of amazing that the subjects Christ addressed in His century-one sermon are as relevant today as they were when He first spoke. Murder and conflicts. Divorce and lies. We've considered the first two; let's hear Him on the next two.

Marital Fidelity

You have heard that it was said, "YOU SHALL NOT COMMIT ADULTERY"; but I say to you, that everyone who looks on a woman to lust for her has committed adultery with her already in his heart. And if your right eye makes you stumble, tear it out, and throw it from you; for it is better for you that one of the parts of your body perish, than for your whole body to be thrown into hell. And if your right hand makes you stumble, cut it off, and throw it from you; for it is better for you that one of the parts of your body perish, than for your whole body to go into hell. And it was said, "WHOEVER SENDS HIS WIFE AWAY, LET HIM GIVE HER A CERTIFICATE OF DIVORCE"; but I say to you that everyone who divorces his wife, except for the cause of unchastity, makes her commit adultery; and whoever marries a divorced woman commits adultery."

Matthew 5:27–32

He begins by quoting the sixth commandment, which everyone in His audience knew painfully well. From childhood, all Jewish citizens had had the commandments drilled into their heads. With consistency, every synagogue service reminded the congregation of that moral code Moses brought down from Mount Sinai: No adultery! But Jesus goes further. Jewish ears all over that hillside must have perked up when He added, "But I say to you. . . ." Why go further? What more needed to be said? Surely "Do not commit adultery" was sufficient, right? Not if we are going to the heart of the problem . . . not if the goal is a righteousness that surpasses pharisaic righteousness.

Jesus never promoted a performance-oriented, surface-only religious lifestyle, but rather an authentic, true-to-the-core life of faith. So if that's true, then the subject of adultery must be traced to the origin of the problem: the inner person where thoughts find their root. To put it straight, long before adultery takes place in the bed, it has already been visualized in the head. Therefore, Jesus added, "but I say to you, that everyone who looks on a woman to lust for her has committed adultery with her already in his heart" (Matt. 5:28).

Those words are familiar to us today, but back then? Revolutionary. Absolutely and shockingly revolutionary. By going to the heart of the issue, Jesus' simplified instructions removed the gray areas related to adultery. He introduced an unheard-of equation: unbridled lust equals adultery.

Some have taken His subsequent words about tearing out an eye or cutting off a hand literally. With great zeal and little wisdom they have followed His words to the letter. Origen of Alexandria actually made himself a eunuch. In A.D. 325 at the Council of Nicea, self-mutilation was finally declared a barbarous practice and officially forbidden.

But Jesus said of the eye that makes us stumble, "tear it out." Should we take Him literally? I think not . . . otherwise, every man I know would be blind! On this issue of interpreting such Scriptures literally, I am often reminded of C. S. Lewis's words:

> There is no need to be worried by facetious people who try to make the Christian hope of "Heaven" ridiculous by saying they do not want "to spend eternity playing harps." The answer to such people is that if they cannot understand books written for grown-ups, they should not talk about them. All the scriptural imagery (harps, crowns, gold, etc.) is, of course, a merely symbolical attempt to express the inexpressible. Musical instruments are mentioned because for many people (not all) music is the thing known in the present life which most strongly suggests ecstasy and infinity. Crowns are mentioned to suggest the fact that those who are united with God in eternity share His splendour and power and joy. Gold is mentioned to suggest the timelessness of Heaven (gold does not rust) and the preciousness of it. People who take these symbols literally might as well think that when Christ told us to be like doves, He meant that we were to lay eggs.[3]

Well, then, how do we make sense of what He taught regarding marital fidelity? It helps me to go back to what our Lord actually said: "everyone who looks on a woman *to lust for her* has committed adultery with her already in his heart" (italics mine). He is not speaking of simply looking at another person, but looking for the purpose of lusting. Such looks obviously pass through the eye gate. Furthermore, lust can be intensified by wrong uses of our hands as well as allowing our feet to take us places where our sexual restraints are weakened. All these actions stimulate seductive and sensual feelings within us (in the "heart"), and when that happens it is as if we have actually acted out illicit expressions of sex.

So? So, do not look to prompt lust. Do not touch to stimulate lust. In today's terms, do not undress a man or woman in your mind as you stare at the physical appearance. Do not linger at the magazine rack or rent X-rated videos or watch films that stir your sensual desires. And, ladies, you can cooperate by refusing to wear seductive attire. By saying no to such things, you "tear out your eye" and you "cut off your hand." One of the best ways I have found to obey Jesus' instruction is simply to replace sensual thoughts with wholesome ones . . . to occupy my mind with things that are pure, lovely, healthy, and positive rather than lurid, provocative, and questionable. Scripture memory works wonders, frankly. I find it impossible to simultaneously lust and repeat verses on moral purity.

Issue of Divorce

Jesus builds on His words regarding lustful thoughts by turning our attention to divorce.

> And it was said, "WHOEVER SENDS HIS WIFE AWAY, LET HIM GIVE HER A CERTIFICATE OF DIVORCE"; but I say to you that everyone who divorces his wife, except for the cause of unchastity, makes her commit adultery; and whoever marries a divorced woman commits adultery.
>
> Matthew 5:31–32

He begins by quoting words from Moses' pen, written centuries earlier in the ancient book of Deuteronomy. Let me quote that original source:

> When a man takes a wife and marries her, and it happens that she finds no favor in his eyes because he has found some indecency in her, and he writes her a certificate of divorce and puts it in her hand and sends her out from his house, and she leaves his house and goes and becomes another man's wife, and if the latter husband turns against her and writes her a certificate of divorce and puts it in her hand and sends her out of his house, or if the latter husband dies who took her to be his wife, then her former husband who sent

her away is not allowed to take her again to be his wife, since she
has been defiled; for that is an abomination before the LORD, and
you shall not bring sin on the land which the LORD your God gives
you as an inheritance.

Deuteronomy 24:1–4

Originally, when "a certificate of divorce" was first used, it
came as a concession because of the hardness of the Hebrews'
hearts. It was not commanded; it was permitted, reluctantly and
rarely.

It may help you to know that when Jesus spoke of divorce, He
addressed a hot issue that was often debated among religious leaders in His day. Contradictory positions were taught in rival rabbinic
schools, Shammai and Hillel. Rabbi Shammai, the conservative,
took a rigorous approach. He founded his teaching on Deut. 24:1,
which he felt allowed divorce strictly on the basis of some grave
matrimonial offense or indecent act of unchastity. This austere position grew out of Shammai's extremely strict interpretation of
Scripture. Rabbi Hillel, on the other hand, adopted a much more
lax position. Josephus, a well-known Jewish historian, states that
Hillel applied the Mosaic provision to a man who "desires to be
divorced from his wife for any cause whatsoever."[4] We are talking
superliberal here. For example, a man could divorce his wife,

- if she spoiled his dinner by adding too much salt,
- if she were seen in public with her head uncovered,
- if she talked with other men on the street,
- if she spoke disrespectfully to her husband's parents,
- if she became plain-looking compared with another woman who seemed more beautiful in her husband's opinion.

Unbelievable! For the most insignificant and subjective reasons imaginable, a first-century divorce was justified by rabbis who

had been trained at the Hillel school. This explains why, a little later on, some Pharisees put Jesus to the test by pressing Him on His position regarding divorce:

> And some Pharisees came to Him, testing Him, and saying, "Is it lawful for a man to divorce his wife for any cause at all?"
>
> Matthew 19:3

Apparently they wondered if He agreed with the Hillel school of thought. In other words, "In which camp are you, Jesus, Shammai's or Hillel's?" His answer revealed He was in neither camp. In fact, His whole line of reasoning differed from theirs.

As I examine Jesus' teaching, both in Matthew 19 and here in His sermon on the mountain, I find three contrasts between His position and the Pharisees' position:

1. The Pharisees were preoccupied with grounds for divorce, but Jesus was much more concerned with the *institution of marriage*. They wanted to know how to get free from the commitment, while He emphasized the sanctity and permanence of the partnership.

2. The Pharisees called Moses' provision a command, while Jesus considered it a *concession*. This is not nitpicking at words. The former calls for obedience and seems to justify their desire for divorce. The latter holds much tighter reins on the issue, making divorce a reluctant and hesitant act of regrettable compromise.

3. The Pharisees regarded divorce *lightly*. Jesus always viewed it *seriously*. They were forever on a search for reasons to claim a marriage could end, while Jesus resisted such an attitude. He stood steadfastly for the bond that was sealed at the time of marriage.[5]

I am fully aware of the unhappiness in many marriages. Having served in the pastorate for almost thirty years (and having remained at the same church for over twenty of those years), there are not many stories I haven't heard. While I am certainly not one whose position is so rigid I would never see a reason for divorce, I must express my grave concern over the tragic erosion of marital fidelity I have witnessed during the past three decades. My plea is that couples take their marriage vows far more seriously . . . that they see their vows as a lifelong commitment to one another, "for better or for worse," because there is a lot of both! I realize my conservative position is not news to anyone who knows me well, but if it helps hold even one couple together, it will have been worth my repeating the obvious: Marriage is for life. Let's make it last!

If it will help, return to those initial beatitudes Jesus spoke and apply them to marriage. Remember those blessings our Lord gave to the gentle, the poor in spirit, the merciful, and several other groups of greathearted souls? Chrysostom, that ancient saint, offers this appropriate counsel:

> He that is meek and a peacemaker and poor in spirit and merciful, how shall he cast out his wife? He that is used to reconciling others, how shall he be at variance with her who is his own?[6]

Let's return to Jesus' final comment on marriage in His great sermon:

> But I say to you that everyone who divorces his wife, except for the cause of unchastity, makes her commit adultery; and whoever marries a divorced woman commits adultery.
>
> Matthew 5:32

The exception clause that appears in Jesus' statement here is probably the most popular exception clause in all the Scriptures, "except for unchastity." There is no need to complicate the issue. Simplicity, remember, is His style. I take it to mean what it says: that divorce may occur when there is sexual intimacy by a married partner with someone outside the marriage bond and it continues to occur as a habit or as a lifestyle. Why? Because that clearly destroys the bond. (This is not the only place where divorce is addressed in Scripture. In case you are wrestling with the subject and want to probe more deeply into the other Scriptures as well, I suggest you read chapter 9 in my book *Strike the Original Match*.)

An unfaithful mate may give you the right to seek divorce, but you are not obligated to exercise that right. Remember, divorce is a God-given concession, not a command. The laws of our land give us the right to sue whomever we wish, but most of us live our entire lives and never sue anyone. Instead, we swallow hard, take it on the chin, and occasionally live with mistreatment. Why? Because taking someone to court, like divorcing an unfaithful mate, is not an obligation, but a concession. Before you yield to a divorce, I suggest one simple exercise, taken seriously: Review what you vowed when you got married.

Verbal Integrity

Speaking of vows, Jesus deals next with verbal honesty.

> Again, you have heard that the ancients were told, "YOU SHALL NOT MAKE FALSE VOWS, BUT SHALL FULFILL YOUR VOWS TO THE LORD." But I say to you, make no oath at all, either by heaven, for it is the throne of God, or by the earth, for it is the footstool of His feet, or by Jerusalem, for it is THE CITY OF THE GREAT KING. Nor shall you make an oath by your head, for you cannot make one hair white or black. But let your statement be, "Yes, yes" or "No, no"; and anything beyond these is of evil.
>
> Matthew 5:33–37

I confess, I read that a dozen times before it began to make sense, so be encouraged if at first glance it seems confusing.

Let's not make it complicated. Obviously, the subject is people who speak the truth. Oaths have to do with taking vows for the purpose of adding veracity to a statement. When I borrow a book from you and say to you, "I'll give it back; I promise," that is a vow. To use the biblical term, it is an oath. Other illustrations come to mind. When our president takes office, he puts his hand on a Bible and makes a vow to uphold the Constitution of the United States of America. We even call that "taking the oath of office." Individuals who are ordained into ministry take vows that relate to being faithful to minister as they commit themselves to a life of purity and devotion to Jesus Christ and His Word. When you go to a courtroom to be a witness, you swear "to tell the truth, the whole truth, and nothing but the truth, so help me God." You make an oath. It doesn't keep you from perjury, but it makes you liable if you commit perjury, because you vowed to tell the truth.

When Jesus says, "Make no oath at all," is He disavowing all oaths? Is He telling our president not to put his hand on a Bible and swear that he will uphold the Constitution? I don't think so. Jesus' comment has to do with vows that are added to a statement, thinking that the additional promises will make the statement trustworthy. They don't. The point is, our word ought to stand. When a monosyllable will do, why waste our breath on polysyllables? Once again, keep it simple. Say yes or say no. Verbosity is no guarantee of veracity.

You say, "That's no big deal. My goodness, anybody could do that." Well, let me probe a little. Let's suppose you promised you would pay off a portion of a debt every month. Are you doing that? To go a step further, are your payments on time? Or let's say you needed a tool, so you borrowed it from your neighbor with the promise that you would return it soon as you were finished. Have you? You promised that you would be true to your mate. Are you? At a serious moment of conviction you promised your Lord you would stand up for Him. Have you been doing that? There's no need to add a lot of additional words or high-sounding oaths of reassurance; just do it.

Some people think that by adding words they will make their statements all the more believable. Not so. All that's needed is,

"I'll meet you here tomorrow afternoon at two o'clock," not "I'll meet you here, for sure, tomorrow afternoon at two o'clock. I swear to you, you can count on it. By the authority of heaven, I will keep my word." That doesn't add veracity to the promise. I just need to be sure I am where I said I would be at two o'clock. Yes ought to mean yes. No should mean no. Keep it simple.

Sometimes a simple statement of truth can be a strong motivation for those around you. Korean evangelist Billy Kim tells a wonderful story that beautifully illustrates my point.

After the war the communists swept down into South Korea from the North. One of the first things they did was to gather a group of Christians into their church building, where they demanded that the leaders deny their Lord. They backed up their demands with torture and threats to the lives of their prisoners. One by one the leaders succumbed. When their torturers handed them the Bible and told them to spit upon it, they did so. Until the communists came to one little girl.

Fearlessly she looked at her tormentors and said, "You can hammer me into a pulp. You can beat me into extinction, but I will never deny my Lord!" Then she began to sing, after turning to the leaders who had fallen to say, "May God have mercy on your souls." What was the result? The crowd with her in the church joined her in singing. She turned the tide of denial that had been begun by the leaders. What did the communists do? They executed the leaders who had denied Christ and set free the girl whose courage had been so clearly communicated.[7]

Jesus' counsel is clear: Let your yes be *yes*; let your no be *no*. In other words, be known as a person of verbal integrity. Special and sometimes surprising results await those who refuse to pad the record or add a lot of self-justifying remarks. God honors simple honesty.

In his work, *The Christian Century*, Lloyd Steffen writes of a time back in the eighteenth century when King Frederick II of

Prussia visited a Berlin prison. One inmate after another tried to convince the monarch of his innocence. Amazing! To hear them tell it, they were all being unjustly punished for crimes they never committed—all, that is, except one man who sat quietly in a corner while all the rest unfolded their lengthy and complicated stories.

Seeing him sitting there, oblivious to the commotion, the king asked the man why he was in prison. "Armed robbery, Your Honor."

The king asked, "Were you guilty?"

"Yes, sir," he answered, without attempting to excuse his wrongdoing.

King Frederick then gave the guard an order: "Release this guilty man. I don't want him corrupting all these innocent people."[8]

Simply Put: A Personal Commitment to the Savior's Words

This section of Jesus' sermon is not all that difficult to understand. He speaks in terms anyone can grasp, though admittedly all may not find His words easy to accept. He speaks about marital fidelity and verbal integrity. So let's summarize His teaching with a couple of practical suggestions.

The first has to do with marriage. *Marry for all of life or do not marry for all your life.* Whatever state you are in right now, make that a vow before God. Tell the Lord you want to do that: "For the rest of my life, Lord, I don't want to marry unless I can marry for all of my life." Keep it that simple and you may be surprised how that statement will uncomplicate your love life.

The second suggestion has to do with your words: *Say what you mean and mean what you say.* It is just that simple. No mumbo jumbo, no long, drawn-out, religious-sounding stuff is necessary. Just talk truth.

6

Simple Advice to the Selfish and Strong-Willed

Last week I heard about a traveler who, between flights at an airport, bought a small package of cookies. She then sat down in the busy snack shop to glance over the newspaper. As she read her paper, she became aware of a rustling noise. Peeking above the newsprint she was shocked to see a well-dressed gentleman sitting across from her, helping himself to her cookies. Half-angry and half-embarrassed, she reached over and gently slid the package closer to her as she took one out and began to munch on it.

A minute or so passed before she heard more rustling. The man had gotten another cookie! By now there was only one left in the package. Though flabbergasted, she didn't want to make a scene so she said nothing. Finally, as if to add insult to injury, the man broke the remaining cookie into two pieces, pushed one piece across the table toward her with a frown, gulped down his half, and left without even saying thank you. She sat there dumbfounded.

Some time later when her flight was announced, the woman opened her handbag to get her ticket. To her shock, there in her purse was her package of unopened cookies. And somewhere in that same airport was another traveler still trying to figure out how that strange woman could have been so forward and insensitive. Assumptions are shaky things to rely on; situations are not always as they appear.

It would be easy to assume that a nation as advanced and civilized as ours would be full of nothing but kind and courteous people. Furthermore, with roots that go back to God-fearing forefathers and freedom-loving ancestors, certainly those attitudes must prevail. How easy to assume that we are all a people of righteous zeal, respect for authority, uncompromising integrity, and a humble, submissive spirit. After all, anyone who reads the moving biographies of the great men and women who shaped our country and gave us our proud heritage could easily think that we still model those godly ways. As much as we may wish that to be true, it is an inaccurate assumption.

The wholesale breakdown in integrity and the national collapse of a high moral standard are now shamefully notorious in our land. In place of gentle grace and an unselfish willingness to share, it is not uncommon to encounter snarling defiance and strong-willed independence. Of course, there are exceptions, but therein lies the tragedy—they are the *exceptions*. Whoever assumes otherwise has taken up mental residence in Fantasyland.

Our Dog-Eat-Dog Mentality

Without wishing to come off as a doomsayer, I am convinced we are on a downward spiral. The slogans we have become accustomed to hearing are somewhere between disappointing and disgusting. To name only a few:

- "I've got my rights."
- "I'm looking out for number one."
- "Do unto others before they do unto you."

- "Shoot first . . . ask questions later."
- "It's none of your business."
- "I don't get mad, I get even."

I can still remember when the family I grew up in moved from the sleepy little South Texas town of El Campo to the sprawling industrial city of Houston. The Second World War had begun only a few weeks before we moved. My dad, a few years too old to qualify for the military draft, felt it was his duty to leave a successful career in the insurance business and work in one of the many "defense plants," industries that set aside their civilian products and retooled their shops to contribute to the national war machine. His patriotism eclipsed what little bit of greed he may have possessed, as all five of us left the safe, secure, and simple lifestyle of a small town and slipped quietly into the harsh and often ugly realities of the big city, which back then held the dubious distinction of being the murder capital of the nation. It was frightening, to say the least.

My folks had a few friends in Houston with whom they spent some of their leisure hours, rare though they were. On one occasion their conversation turned to the strong contrast between the easygoing, gentle life in tiny El Campo and the fast-lane, sometimes-brutal environment of huge Houston—especially East Side Houston, where we lived for many years. My mother frequently repeated the words of one particular lady who warned that we would never find in the big city what we had left in our little protected hometown, adding, "It's more of a dog-eat-dog mentality here . . . and heaven help you if you forget that it can eat you up. Be careful!" She couldn't have been more correct in her evaluation. What I find disturbing, some fifty years later, is that those things which once characterized only the larger cities of America are now woven through the fabric of our society. The laid-back style of yesteryear has eroded into the fight-back world of today. A few quiet pockets of peace and innocent contentment may still exist, but no one can deny they are few and far between. Horrible acts of violence are commonplace, and the crime rate is on the rise. A recent *USA Today* headline read, "7 cities lead violence 'epidemic.'" The article stated:

> Violent crime in the USA soared 10 percent in 1990—with seven cities accounting for more than a quarter of the slayings reported to FBI.
>
> The dramatic surge in violent crimes, 21 percent since 1987, continues to be driven by drug trafficking, experts say.
>
> "The nation has got to wake up to the fact that we're in an epidemic of violence," says Barry Krisberg, National Council on Crime and Delinquency.[1]

Ours is a selfish and strong-willed society. Law-enforcement agencies record it, the news media reports it, but our real need is to solve it . . . but how? Idealistic though my response may seem, I firmly believe the best answers are found in Jesus' words, which He spoke more than nineteen centuries ago. His simple advice to selfish and strong-willed humanity remains powerful and effective to this day. Be ready for a surprise, however. Most folks would never even consider following His instructions.

Christ's Countercultural Counsel

In my opinion, Jesus' words recorded in Matt. 5:38–48, are among the most unusual He ever uttered. The strange-sounding advice not only cuts cross-grain against our human nature, it also represents the antithesis of the advice most Americans are given. Nevertheless, His words are wise and His way is right. If we will only give them a chance, we will discover how true and—yes, once again—how *simple* His advice really is.

He begins by quoting one of the oldest laws in the history of civilization: "You have heard that it was said, 'AN EYE FOR AN EYE,

AND A TOOTH FOR A TOOTH'" (Matt. 5:38). At first glance it seems that Jesus is drawing that statement from the Mosaic Law. He certainly had the writings of Moses in mind, but that was not the first time such words had been heard by humanity. Jesus was citing the oldest law in the world—an eye for an eye and a tooth for a tooth. The original concept first occurred in the Code of Hammurabi, who ruled over Babylon from 2285 to 2242 B.C. To quote part of it:

> If a man has caused the loss of a gentleman's eye, his eye one shall cause to be lost. If he has shattered a gentleman's limb, one shall shatter his limb. . . . If he has made the tooth of a man . . . fall out, one shall make his tooth fall out.[2]

Progressing in time to the days of the Mosaic Law, we read similar words:

> But if there is any further injury, then you shall appoint as a penalty life for life, eye for eye, tooth for tooth, hand for hand, foot for foot, burn for burn, wound for wound, bruise for bruise.
> Exodus 21:23–25

> And if a man injures his neighbor, just as he has done, so it shall be done to him: fracture for fracture, eye for eye, tooth for tooth; just as he has injured a man, so it shall be inflicted on him.
> Leviticus 24:19–20

> Thus you shall not show pity; life for life, eye for eye, tooth for tooth, hand for hand, foot for foot.
> Deuteronomy 19:21

So when Jesus begins, "You have heard," indeed they had. What they had been taught was retribution of the first order. Don't misunderstand. God has never upheld senseless or unjust violence, certainly not mindless brutality. However, He did establish capital punishment as the means of dealing swiftly, firmly, and thoroughly with those who acted out their violence on the innocent. As I understand Scripture, it is still the correct method of dealing with murderers. But Jesus goes further as He addresses several of the "rights" that we, in our human nature, cling to. First, familiarize yourself with what Jesus actually said:

> But I say to you, do not resist him who is evil; but whoever slaps you on your right cheek, turn to him the other also. And if anyone wants to sue you, and take your shirt, let him have your coat also. And whoever shall force you to go one mile, go with him two. Give to him who asks of you, and do not turn away from him who wants to borrow from you.
>
> Matthew 5:39–42

Do you detect certain "rights" in His words? Let me suggest four:

- My "right" to dignity . . . to be treated without insult
- My "right" to comfort . . . to cling to what pleases me
- My "right" to privacy . . . to do only what I prefer
- My "right" to possessions . . . to keep all I wish

Release Instead of Resist

Look over the list. Pretty impressive, pretty important, I'm sure you would agree.

Let any of those so-called rights be threatened today, and I can assure you somebody will soon be talking to a lawyer. Interestingly, Jesus doesn't offer that as His game plan. To the shock of His hearers then and now, He urges all of His followers to release instead of resist.

Now let me clarify something before I go any further. Please do not misapply these principles and assume they are appropriate in a national context. They aren't. At no place in our Lord's message does He address the government of a nation. This is not counsel for our national defense. This is personal admonition for the Christian, not military strategy for combat-ready forces in the field. Government's job is not the same as the Christian's job. The Christian is to follow the teachings of Jesus Christ *as an individual*. Government has a basic law of protecting its constituency, its people, and thereby serving it well. Jesus is speaking to individuals on the mountain, not to the nation in general. If they claim to follow Him, He is telling them how to do that. This is to all Christians who claim to be followers of the Way, who wish to embrace Christ's will in their lives. In Jesus' words I find four specific things His followers are to release:

First: *Release your right to personal dignity.* Now look again at how He said it. "Do not resist him who is evil; but whoever slaps you on your right cheek, turn to him the other also" (Matt. 5:39).

Even back in Jesus' day there were words that meant punching someone in the mouth and knocking him into the middle of next week. Jesus does not use those words here. He chooses other terms deliberately and for a reason. A slap on the cheek was a first-century way of insulting someone. A slap on the other cheek was yet another insulting comment, especially true in the East, where the back of the hand was a statement of insult. It wasn't the same as a doubled-up fist thrown directly into the mouth of another person. Notice that Jesus deliberately refers to a slap on the cheek.

"That was a backhanded compliment if I've ever heard one," we say today. That's our way of saying someone has made an insulting remark.

Just as we did not take plucking out the eye and cutting off the hand in a literal sense, neither do we take the slap of a hand as a literal blow to the cheek. What Jesus is getting at is an insulting expression. If we are good at anything in our fight-back, get-even society, we are good at slapping others with insults.

None was better at insults than Winston Churchill, who had no love affair with Lady Astor. Actually, the feeling was mutual. It's reported that on one occasion she found the great statesman rather obviously inebriated in a hotel elevator. With cutting disgust she snipped, "Sir Winston, you are drunk!" to which he replied, "M'lady, you are *ugly*. And tomorrow I will be sober." That may be a classic example of how *not* to handle an insult.

Unfortunately, the more you do it, the better you get at it. And some of us are very good at it! We can make one person's sarcastic jab look mild compared to our back-of-the-hand insulting retort. Christ's simple advice? "Don't. Rather, turn the other cheek."

Insulting retaliations are not always verbal. Some of the worst occur in our driving when we are on the freeway and some self-appointed A. J. Foyt races in front of us, cuts us off, and misses hitting us by one coat of paint. The roadhog is reckless, careless, and thoughtless. What do we do? Our first thought is never, *Bless you, my son.* We usually wait for a tiny open space in the next lane so we can squirt up next to him . . . and what? *Cut him off!* (Or hope that some burly trucker in an eighteen-wheeler will cut him off before we get there.) That is just the way it is in human nature.

I think it is worth noting that our Lord suggested two cheeks . . . not dozens of them, lest we become a doormat to the abusive. I am not the first to notice that. A successful Irish boxer was converted and became a preacher. He happened to be in a new town setting up his evangelistic tent when a couple of tough thugs noticed what he was doing. Knowing nothing of his background, they made a few insulting remarks. The Irishman merely turned and looked at them. Pressing his luck, one of the bullies took a swing and struck a glancing blow on one side of the ex-boxer's face. He shook it off and said nothing as he stuck out his jaw. The fellow took another glancing blow on the other side. At that point the preacher swiftly took off his coat, rolled up his sleeves, and announced, "The Lord gave me no further instructions." *Whop!*

Charles Haddon Spurgeon said, "We are to be the anvil when bad men are the hammers." We are to take the blows of bad men's words. Let them glance off you. But be assured, nowhere in Scripture are we instructed to be submissive doormats to rapists, silent victims of sexual or physical abuse, or helpless pawns in the hands of a would-be murderer.

> Christ's illustrations are not to be taken as the charter for any unscrupulous tyrant, beggar, or thug. His purpose was to forbid revenge, not to encourage injustice, dishonesty, or vice. . . . True love . . . takes action to deter evil and to promote good. . . . He teaches not the irresponsibility which encourages evil but the forbearance which renounces revenge.[3]

Some have taken this verse to ridiculous extremes and promoted an indifferent pacifism. If they had their way, brutal bullies would dominate our lives and dictatorial tyrants would rule the land. Martin Luther described one such pacifist as "the crazy saint who let lice nibble at him and refused to kill any of them on account of this text, maintaining that he had to suffer and could not resist evil."

If you have roaches (or lice!), don't twist Jesus' words into a persuasive plea for letting them live on, untouched. Likewise, if you have rats, poison those suckers! Furthermore, if our nation encounters an enemy who would steal our liberty, there is nothing in this that even implies we should let that enemy conquer us.

But the slap on the face is clearly an insulting comment. Release your right to answer back. When you do, you not only simplify the conflict, you usually discover that the verbal conflict ends as quickly as it began.

Second: *Release your right to cling to comforts.* Jesus said, "If anyone wants to sue you, and take your shirt, let him have your coat also" (Matt. 5:40).

This is not modern-day courtroom counsel, remember; this is personal counsel to the Christian. In this case, the man was rather well off, since he had both shirt and coat. Many lived with only a shirt. The coat was actually a cloak that was worn around the body much like a blanket; at night it was used something like a temporary sleeping bag. The human tendency was to cling to one's coat. But Jesus says here, "Let him have your coat also."

We live in an era when we have our rights to have any comfort we wish and let the rest of the world eat cake! Jesus is saying, "Those are not My words. My followers are to be moved over the needs of others and to release whatever is needed without selfishness."

When you give someone your coat, most folks won't understand you. Christ says, "Why not share? Release your rights to cling to comforts. Nothing wrong with having comforts, just don't cling to them." As I've said for years, there is absolutely nothing wrong with owning nice things, but something is terribly wrong when those nice things own us.

Third: *Release your rights to your own private lifestyle.* In Jesus' day it was not uncommon for citizens to feel the flat side of a Roman spear on their shoulder and hear some gruff-voiced soldier behind them commanding, "Pick up this package and carry it. Carry it for the next mile."

Jesus says, "Whoever shall force you to go one mile, go the second." I would imagine that back then there was some kind of saying like, "Take it a mile if they require a mile—5,280 feet—*but don't go one more foot.*" But Jesus says, "Go the extra mile." (That's where we get the expression.) By the way, the same term, translated "force" is rendered "compel" later on when Simon of Cyrene is "compelled" to carry the cross of Jesus. Isn't that interesting? Aren't you glad he picked it up? Looking back in a few days, I'm sure *he* was! Jesus says, "Don't just go the required distance. Double it."

We need to remember that Christ does not limit this to church life and Christian circles. It also applies beautifully where you are employed, especially if you are in a people-related business. There is something more important than quitting time. There is something more important than your getting every little second of your lunch hour. There is something wonderfully Christian about someone who goes beyond what is expected just as a habit of life. I want to assure you that if you live a lifestyle like this, you won't need to send out a search warrant for an audience of unbelievers who are interested in the gospel. They will seek you out!

Christ never ordered an evangelistic campaign; the crowd came to Him, not so much because He did miracles, but because He was Himself miraculous. He lived a miraculously different life. He not only modeled unselfishness, He carried a cross. He took the blows and never answered back. And aren't you glad He did? You want to simplify your faith? Release your right to a lifetime of uninterrupted privacy.

Fourth: *Release your right to exclusive ownership.* Jesus said, "Give to him who asks of you, and do not turn away from him who wants to borrow from you" (Matt. 5:42). Do you have something someone else can use? Why not share it? I never knew how many friends I had till I owned a pickup truck. The books I have lost in letting people borrow them could probably make up a small library. And I'm sure a few of the books in my library have somebody else's name on them.

Sure, occasionally you may get ripped off. No doubt a few people will take advantage of you. I have never met a generous person yet who wasn't occasionally taken advantage of. But I've never met a truly generous person who kept score . . . or decided, "since a few don't play fair, I'm knocking this off." Every generous person I know is a person of relentless optimism. Don't let the few ripoffs make you bitter.

But is Jesus suggesting indiscriminate giving? I don't think so. William Barclay's answer to that question is probably the best I've ever read:

> The Rabbis loved to point out that loving-kindness was one
> of the very few things to which the Law appointed no limit at all.

Are we then to say that Jesus urged upon men what can only be called indiscriminate giving? The answer cannot be given without qualification. It is clear that the effect of the giving on the receiver must be taken into account. Giving must never be such as to encourage him in laziness and in shiftlessness, for such giving can only hurt. But at the same time it must be remembered that many people who say that they will only give through official channels, and who refuse to help personal cases, are frequently merely producing an excuse for not giving at all, and are removing the personal element from giving altogether.[4]

So then—to simplify the issue at hand, Jesus says to release instead of resist. As we do, He somehow takes up the slack.

There is one more piece of advice in this section of Jesus' message. It is:

Love Instead of Hate

Love has been called the most effective motivational force in all the world. When love is at work in us, it is remarkable how giving and forgiving, understanding and tolerant we can be. It is easy to assume that power is always at work within us, but it's not. It is there, ready to be put to use, but it gets blocked. Since this has always been true, the first-century scribes and Pharisees developed a "saying," sort of a slogan that was commonly repeated among the Jews. It sounded like one of Moses' commandments, but it was a distortion instead. Jesus quoted it here: "You have heard that it was said, 'YOU SHALL LOVE YOUR NEIGHBOR, and hate your enemy'" (Matt. 5:43). The first half of that saying did appear in the Law (Lev. 19:18), but the latter half was a pharisaical addendum. Now, those Pharisees knew better. They knew that Prov. 25:21 was in the Book:

> If your enemy is hungry, give him food to eat;
> And if he is thirsty, give him water to drink.

That and other similar statements appear in the Old Testament. But none of those statements concluded "and hate your enemy." So in order to correct the fallacy of such strong-willed reasoning, Jesus taught:

> But I say to you, love your enemies, and pray for those who persecute you in order that you may be sons of your Father who is in heaven; for He causes His sun to rise on the evil and the good, and sends rain on the righteous and the unrighteous. For if you love those who love you, what reward have you? Do not even the tax-gatherers do the same? And if you greet your brothers only, what do you do more than others? Do not even the Gentiles do the same?
>
> Matthew 5:44–47

It may help to simplify Jesus' revolutionary counsel by observing what He does *not* say. "Love the way your enemies live." No, He does not say that. How about, "Love their methods . . . defend their ways?" Again, no. None of that appears in His statement. We are talking about people, eternal souls, spiritually blind men and women who know nothing of Christ's power.

True love possesses the ability to see beyond. In that sense we might say that love has x-ray vision. It goes beyond mere words. It sees beneath the veneer. Love focuses on the soul. Love sees another's soul in great need of help and sets compassion to work. I think of the late Corrie ten Boom and her response to the Nazi guards who had brutalized her sister. She was able to forgive them. She refused to live the rest of her life brimming with resentment and bitterness. True love sees beyond the treatment that it endures. True love doesn't need agreement to proceed. True love goes on against all odds. That is why Jesus simply says, "Love them."

I am intrigued by the sentence construction in verse 45: "in order that you may be sons of your Father." Why doesn't He say, "in order that you may be Christians"? or "in order that you may be My followers"?

I imagine Matthew, who recorded this, was among the group who first heard Jesus' sermon. Naturally he would remember the words Jesus used, even the phrases. Since Jesus spoke Aramaic, His words were more akin to Hebrew than the Greek that became the basis of the New Testament. Hebrew is not a language rich in adjectives. Instead of saying, "He is a peaceful man," the Hebrews would usually say, "He is a son of peace." Instead of saying, "She is a kind woman," the Hebrews would often say, "She is a daughter of kindness." Here, notice that Jesus says, "in order that you may be sons of your Father." May I rephrase it? "In order that you may be Fatherlike." Very seldom do we use the word "Fatherlike," but it fits here. Those who love like God begin to model a Fatherlike response . . . even toward the unrighteous. And the most Fatherlike response of all? Love.

A driving rainstorm in an area suffering from drought does not discriminate. All receive the benefits. The same can be said for the sun. It bathes all homes alike with warmth and light. Why? Because God is love. Grace is His style. That is why Christ would minister so graciously to those who hated Him. Love and grace prompt the rain to fall on all the ground and the sun to shine on all the homes. For love to replace hate and grace to replace prejudice, playing favorites must cease. Love and grace befit those who are Fatherlike.

Next, consider the words Jesus spoke: "And if you greet your brothers only, what do you do more than others? Do not even the Gentiles do the same?" (Matt. 5:47). The Gentiles were considered the "dogs" of the human race; yet even they loved those who loved them. Likewise the tax collectors. (I won't even tell you what they called the tax collectors. There just wasn't a synonym for them that you could say in public.) Then how far do we take this love-your-neighbor stuff? Do we love atheists? Yes! Scoffers? Yes! Criminals? Yes! There would never have been a Prison Fellowship if a man named Chuck Colson had not seen beyond the bars and the hateful things men and women do. Love, remember, sees the soul and focuses on the heart.

As far back as 1880, A. F. C. Vilmar wrote:

> This commandment, that we should love our enemies and forgo [*sic*] revenge will grow even more urgent in the holy struggle which lies before us and in which we partly have already been engaged for years. In it love and hate engage in mortal combat. It is the urgent duty of every Christian soul to prepare itself for it. The time is coming when the confession of the living God will incur not only the hatred and the fury of the world, for on the whole it has come to that already, but complete ostracism from "human society," as they call it. The Christians will be hounded from place to place, subjected to physical assault, maltreatment and death of every kind. We are approaching an age of widespread persecution. Therein lies the true significance of all the movements and conflicts of our age. Our adversaries seek to root out the Christian Church and the Christian faith because they cannot live side by side with us, because they see in every word we utter and every deed we do, even when they are not specifically directed against them, a condemnation of their own words and deeds. They are not far wrong. They suspect too that we are indifferent to their condemnation. Indeed they must admit that it is utterly futile to condemn us. We do not reciprocate their hatred and contention, although they would like it better if we did, and so sink to their own level. And how is the battle to be fought? Soon the time will come when we shall pray, not as isolated individuals, but as a corporate body, a congregation, a Church: we shall pray in multitudes (albeit in relatively small multitudes) and among the thousands and thousands of apostates we shall loudly praise and confess the Lord who was crucified and is risen and shall come again. And what prayer, what confession, what hymn of praise will it be? It will be the prayer of earnest love for these very sons of perdition who stand around and gaze at us with eyes aflame with hatred, and who have perhaps already raised

their hands to kill us. It will be prayer for the peace of these erring, devastated and bewildered souls, a prayer for the same love and peace which we ourselves enjoy, a prayer which will penetrate to the depths of their souls and rend their hearts more grievously than anything they can do to us. Yes, the Church which is really waiting for its Lord, and which discerns the signs of the times of decision, must fling itself with its utmost power and with the panoply of its holy life into this prayer of love.[5]

What maturity for one to give that kind of counsel!

Can you begin to see how far we have drifted from Jesus' counsel? Don't you see why unsaved people are not really drawn to Christians? There is so little difference externally—sometimes, none at all.

Be "Perfect," Not Merely Human

As if all His other advice has not been tough enough, Jesus closes with this: "Therefore you are to be perfect, as your heavenly Father is perfect" (Matt. 5:48). Your first reaction might be one of exasperation: "Oh, give me a break!" But wait. The Lord never asks us to do the unattainable. So there must be something here we are missing. He certainly cannot mean "sinlessly perfect," an altogether impossible goal. Then what? Perhaps, "Don't be merely human; be perfect." In other words, don't operate from a faulty human philosophy, but from a divinely prescribed philosophy.

To return evil for good is devilish; to return good for good is human; to return good for evil is divine. To love as God loves is moral perfection, and this perfection Christ tells us to aim at.[6]

Jesus is urging: "Aim high—aim at perfection." But what is perfection? Perfect is from the word *telos* or *teleios*, which means not an abstract, philosophical kind of perfection, but rather *functional* perfection. In other words, to be perfect is to reach the full purpose of something or to complete the process.

If I am working on the engine on my boat and I need a certain wrench that will fit an unusual kind of nut, I may need to go to the hardware store and buy it. When I reach into the engine and the wrench fits into place, that wrench has become "perfect" in that it has fulfilled the purpose for which it was made. That is precisely what Christ's command means. Just as our heavenly Father fulfills His purpose, so should we.

Simply Put: Doing What's Right

Most of us have three major realms of relationships in which we live: an immediate realm of family, an intermediate realm of friends, and a broad general realm that certainly would include some enemies.

Thinking in terms of three concentric circles, let's go first to the center and think about the family. For this I have three words of advice: *Release your rights.* There are precious few family conflicts that cannot be settled by simply releasing rights.

I have never, never met a marriage conflict that is irreparable if both sides were equally willing to release all rights and both unhesitatingly say, "I will release my rights as I trust my God to pull us back together." If you are the selfish or strong-willed type, this will call for a radical change in attitude. I challenge you to make that change.

Second, within the intermediate circle of your friends, *look beyond the wrongs.* Every friend I have has disappointed me in one way or another. And I have done the same to him or her. But because there has been a willingness to overlook that, we still have a friendship. Love helps us stay at the task.

And finally, within the broad realm of relationships, even with your enemies, *fulfill your role.* Aim high. Be the vital wrench in their engine. Live in such a way that what you have to offer becomes a perfect fit for the things that they are missing in their lives. It is remarkable how the Lord will bring you together.

Now, for the sake of a few idealistic souls who could assume only the best and think, *I can hardly wait to live like this; this is going to be fun!* I want to bring you back ever so gently to reality. When you decide to live like Christ among the selfish and strong-willed, God will honor your decision, *but* . . . you will encounter misunderstanding and mistreatment. You will be taken advantage of. However, don't make another wrong assumption by thinking that if you are going through tough times, you are off target. Not so. Doing what is right is never a stroll through a rose garden. Jesus' plan for living may be simple, but it is not easy.

To mention only one particular area, think of confronting prejudice . . . standing for those who are objects of mistreatment. By doing so, we will please God, but we will also encounter those who hate us.

William Wilberforce stood virtually alone in England as he attempted to block slave-trading and set the blacks free. He demonstrated true Christianity, but do you know what his enemies did in return? They slandered him. They spread every kind of false rumor about him—all lies. They said he was a brutal husband. He was not. A wife beater. Never. Some passed the word that he was married secretly to a black woman. Another falsehood. He did right, but he suffered for it.

Abraham Lincoln also took up the torch against slavery during his years as our sixteenth president. The result? He became the object of hatred—and not just in the South. Some of the stories of the treatment he received from fellow Americans are beyond our comprehension. Prejudice ultimately killed him in the form of an assassin's bullet.

When Martin Luther King, Jr. began to promote his vision of nonviolence, many who were full of prejudice subjected him to incredible injustices. After King's assassination, Dr. Benjamin Mays listed some of the persecutions the man had endured. His home had been bombed. He had lived day by day, for thirteen years, under constant threats of death. He was publicly accused of being a communist. He was falsely slandered for being insincere. He was stabbed by a member of his own race. He was jailed more than twenty times. In fact, the man wrote most of his sermons in jail cells. "Love is the only force capable of transforming an enemy into a friend," he said, and he died believing that.

I'm not saying King or Lincoln or Wilberforce or any one of us who stands for something that is right but unpopular is anywhere near perfect. I'm just saying that when we live by a cause that is so different that it rebukes people, some will hate us for it. It is naïve to assume they won't. Nevertheless, let me exhort all of us to follow the teachings of Jesus Christ. No matter how painful it may be, let us trust Him to bring good from our living His way.

The Lord Jesus Christ is the model to follow—and you remember where He wound up! But think of all those who were once His enemies, now His friends. You and I would certainly be numbered among them. The force of love is absolutely unconquerable.

7

Beware! Religious Performance Now Showing

SINCE WE HAVE REACHED THE HALFWAY point in this book, you should know by now that I like things simple, especially the important things. I like simple instructions, not the kind that require a degree from MIT. I like simple meals. You know, the kind that not only taste great but also need no interpreter to analyze what you are sinking your teeth into. I also like simple evenings, preferably with members of my family or a small group of real close friends. Forcing small talk or trying to look happy while shuffling and stumbling among a couple hundred people in a crowded room is not my idea of a fun evening. Give me a fireplace, a bowl of popcorn, a little classical (or country-western) music in the background, and quiet conversation sprinkled with some laughter and even a few tears, and I'm one contented dude.

The same applies to my idea of genuine worship: Keep it simple. I much prefer quiet, reflective times in the Lord's presence to giant meetings led by professionals who know how to work the crowd and keep the show looking good. Give me a few grand hymns mixed with several choruses of worship and spontaneous moments of silence rather than all the religious hoopla where "guest artists" take turns and crowd-pleasing singing groups share color-coordinated microphones and try to get everybody to smile and clap along with the beat. No thanks. Something within me recoils when I sense that the program is choreographed right down to the last ten seconds and I am an observer of a performance instead of a participant in worship. Don't misunderstand: I have no problem with great entertainment or professional performances. Nobody screams louder than I do at a ball game or applauds with greater enthusiasm following an evening at the symphony, but when something as meaningful and beautiful as worship gets slick or bears the marks of a complicated stage show or starts to look contrived, I start checking out the closest exits.

Micah the Prophet Speaks

While thinking about this recently I got reacquainted with an ancient prophet named Micah. Not being one of the greater lights among the more popular prophets, Micah isn't exactly a household word. Too bad. Though obscure, the man had his stuff together. Eclipsed by the much more famous Isaiah, who ministered among the elite, Micah took God's message to the streets.

Micah had a deep suspicion of phony religion. He saw greed in the hearts of the leaders of the kingdom of Judah, which prompted him to warn the common folk not to be deceived by religious pretense among nobility. In true prophetic style, Micah comforted the afflicted and afflicted the comfortable. He condemned sin. He exposed performance-based piety. He championed the cause of the oppressed. He predicted the fall of the nation. And he did it all at the risk of his own life.

But Micah didn't just denounce and attack, leaving everyone aware of the things he despised but none of the things he believed. Negative, ultrazealous preaching can lead people to wonder what they should do, since they hear only warnings and tirades of condemnation. Not so with Micah. Like rays of brilliant sunlight piercing charcoal-colored clouds after a storm, the prophet saved his best words for a positive message to the people. Immediately on the heels of the Lord's indictment of His people—about the time many must have begun to wonder what they had to do to make things right—Micah told them, and I am pleased to say that he did it with simplicity.

Using the time-honored method of questions and answers, he asked not one but four questions, each with greater intensity than the previous one (Mic. 6:6–7):

> With what shall I come to the LORD
> And bow myself before the God on high?
> [That is precisely what many were and are still wondering.]
> Shall I come to Him with burnt offerings,
> With yearling calves?
> [Some surely asked that question: "Does God expect me to
> sacrifice one of my livestock?"]
> Does the LORD take delight in thousands of rams,
> In ten thousand rivers of oil?
> [Don't miss the crescendo of intensity—the possibility of
> pleasing God must be remote in the mind of some: "Is
> this what He requires?"]
> Shall I present my first-born for my rebellious acts,
> The fruit of my body for the sin of my soul?
> [The ultimate—the zenith of devotion! "Is it going to take
> sacrificing my oldest child . . . or is He demanding that
> I throw myself into the fire on the altar? Will *that* do it?
> Will *that* cause God to smile again?"]

Micah's words state exactly what many, to this day, wonder about pleasing God. Teachers and preachers have made it so sacrificial . . . so complicated . . . so extremely difficult. To them, God is virtually impossible to please. Therefore, religion has become a series of long, drawn-out, deeply painful acts designed to appease this peeved Deity in the sky who takes delight in watching us squirm.

Micah erases the things on the entire list, replacing the complicated possibilities with one of the finest definitions of simple faith:

> He has told you, O man, what is good;
> And what does the LORD require of you
> But to do justice, to love kindness,
> And to walk humbly with your God?
>
> Micah 6:8

At the risk of overstepping proper bounds by putting God's preference in my own words: *God Likes It Simple*. He does *not* look for big-time, external displays. He does *not* require slick public performances. He does *not* expect gigantic acts of self-sacrificial heroism, seventy-hour work weeks of ministry, a calendar of exhausting activities, an endless number of church meetings, massive dedication that proves itself in going to the most primitive tribe hidden away in the densest jungle of the world. STOP!

Go back three spaces on your monotony board of religious performance. Go back and look at how you have complicated what God said so simply. What is required? Slow down and read the list aloud:

- To do justice
- To love kindness
- To walk humbly with your God

Period.

Stop and let that sink in. Don't read one more word until you can say those three lines with your eyes closed. I'm going to test you on them later, so learn them well.

Faith is not a long series of religious performances. It is not doing a pile of pious things either to keep God from being angry or to impress others with how dedicated you are. The sooner we believe that and start living like that, the quicker we will understand the true meaning of the Christian life as God planned it—and the more contented we will be. All God asks is *simple faith*.

Jesus, Our Lord, Instructs

These things remind me of the message Jesus delivered on the mountain—a message so simple and to the point He must have sounded like Micah from centuries earlier. The times were different, as was the geography, but the basic message was the same: Jesus underscores doing justice, loving kindness, and, especially in the early part of Matthew 6, walking humbly.

Beware of This!

Beware of practicing your righteousness before men to be noticed by them; otherwise you have no reward with your Father who is in heaven.

Matthew 6:1

In prophetlike fashion, the Messiah introduces this section of His sermon with a strong warning: *Beware!* Of what? Had something gone wrong? Was there some danger on the loose? You better believe it! A humble, uncomplicated walk with God had been replaced by a prime-time performance of religion. It was righteousness on display . . . strut-your-stuff spirituality led by none other than the scribes and Pharisees who loved nothing more than to impress the public with their grandiose expressions of piety on parade.

Remember the Nazarene's earlier remark about righteousness?

For I say to you, that unless your righteousness surpasses that of the scribes and Pharisees, you shall not enter the kingdom of heaven.

Matthew 5:20

He is back on that same subject, only now He gets painfully specific with His warning. I'm always interested in seeing how a particular passage is translated in the different versions of the Bible. Here are three:

> Beware of practicing your piety before men.   RSV
>
> Be careful not to make a show of your religion.   NEB
>
> Beware of doing your good deeds conspicuously to catch men's eyes.   PHILLIPS

Walking humbly with one's God was never meant to be a theatrical performance, or, as we called it when I as a kid, "showing off."

Those of us who live in the Greater Los Angeles area have a vast choice of professional entertainment: theatrical performances, both live and on film; dinner theaters; theme parks like Disneyland, Knotts Berry Farm, Magic Mountain, and a half-dozen similar spots where we can spend a full day watching talented people entertain audiences. But when it comes to maximum excitement and a crowd-pleasing evening, I don't know of any place better than the famous Forum on a night when the Los Angeles Lakers are in town. The man who has announced their games for almost three decades is still at it: Chick Hearn. Every few years Chick's co-host changes—usually it's a former basketball player—but nobody ever upstages the man at the main mike. In a rapid-fire, staccato manner, Chick Hearn spits out his full-court commentary faster than any sportscaster I have ever heard. If you are stuck in your car and can't watch the game on television, no problem. Hearn's descriptions give the listener all that is needed to picture the game to a T. Every once in awhile, after a perfectly executed fast break that included several bullet passes and a basket-pounding slam dunk by one of the Lakers, Chick Hearn's voice drowns out the Forum roar as he shouts his familiar response, "*It's Showtime!*"

That's to be expected in the high-octane, upbeat world of professional basketball where fans gather for another loud and entertaining performance. The show is supposed to be spectacular; after all, there's Magic in the air!

But when it comes to the walk of faith, when the subject is righteousness and the object is to glorify God, beware of showtime. Or, as Micah put it, "walk humbly with your God." Jesus is not telling His followers to stop shining light. On the contrary, He said earlier, "Let your light shine." But that had to do with the kind of much-needed light that gives others hope and attracts them to the Savior so that "they glorify your Father who is in heaven." Here He is warning against displaying our devotion before others "to be noticed by them." Simple faith and showtime don't mix.

Once He sounds the warning, Jesus applies it to the three cardinal works of piety frequently paraded by the scribes and Pharisees: giving (Matt. 6:2–4), praying (6:5–15), and fasting (6:16–18). Let's consider the first two subjects in the balance of this chapter and save the third for chapter 8.

When You Give

> When therefore you give alms, do not sound a trumpet before you, as the hypocrites do in the synagogues and in the streets, that they may be honored by men. Truly I say to you, they have their reward in full. But when you give alms, do not let your left hand know what your right hand is doing that your alms may be in secret; and your Father who sees in secret will repay you.
>
> Matthew 6:2–4

"Giving alms" in the first century was considered synonymous with "righteousness." The ancient terms for both found their origin in the same root word, and those who were considered truly righteous were people who contributed to others' needs. But, said

Jesus, there's a way *not* to give alms (v. 2), and there's a right way to do it (vv. 3–4).

It may help to know that the Pharisees had a little ritual they went through when they gave money to the poor. Whether in the synagogues or the streets, as they proceeded toward the offering container they were preceded by trumpeters who literally blew a loud fanfare. If Chick Hearn had been living back then, it would have been appropriate for him to shout, "It's Showtime, folks!"

Perhaps the Pharisees excused their self-righteous action by saying it was to attract the attention of the poor and give them new hope. We're back to that old Greek word for such rationalization: *Hogwash!* On another occasion one of their contemporaries came right out and exposed their hidden motive, saying, "they loved the approval of men rather than the approval of God" (John 12:43).

And Charles Spurgeon's comment is classic: "To stand with a penny in one hand and a trumpet in the other is the posture of hypocrisy."

That last word, "hypocrisy," though often used, is not fully appreciated without an understanding of its etymology. In classical Greek, the root term *hypocrites* was first applied to an orator and then to an actor. Figuratively, the word was used to refer to anyone who treated the world as a stage on which he played a part. No longer himself, the "hypocrite" impersonated someone he was not. That was perfectly acceptable in theatrical performances where, in ancient days, the actor wore an mask. The trouble with the religious hypocrite, however, is that he or she deliberately sets out to deceive others.

So much for how not to give. What does Jesus say about how we should give? If I read His instructions correctly, I find three primary guidelines to follow.

- Give spontaneously (not letting your left hand know what your right hand is doing).

- Give secretly (that is, anonymously).
- Give with purity of motive, knowing your heavenly Father will reward you. Count on it!

Some would argue that this makes giving mercenary. I disagree. If it were, why would Jesus mention it? Furthermore, He does not tell us how we shall be rewarded, nor should we think all His rewards will be tangible. I think C. S. Lewis is on to something when he writes this about kinds of rewards:

> There are different kinds of rewards. There is the reward which has no natural connection with the things you do to earn it and is quite foreign to the desires that ought to accompany those things. Money is not the natural reward of love; that is why we call a man mercenary if he marries a woman for the sake of her money. But marriage is the proper reward for a real lover, and he is not mercenary for desiring it. . . . The proper rewards are not simply tacked on to the activity for which they are given, but are the activity itself in consummation.[1]

So then, what could be God's "reward" to us? Certainly the inner joy, the sheer delight in knowing that one's gift helped meet a need—someone hungry was fed, someone sick was given medical assistance, someone in vocational Christian work was encouraged to stay at the task. Great "secret joys" follow generous secret gifts.

Before Easter of 1991, several anonymous individuals in our congregation contributed to the refurbishing of our large worship center, including our adjacent chapel, choir rehearsal room, and a sizable room where we conduct adult classes and hold receptions for smaller weddings. We really needed new carpet, new pew coverings, new robes, new chairs, new paint work, and new hymnals. The congregation at large had no idea this plan was under way, nor did we ever announce either the names or amounts of money each contributor gave. Once the full amount was available, the color choices were made, fabric and carpet were selected, and the furnishings were ordered. Bright and early on a prearranged Monday morning our main building was swarming with workmen who began the project. As each day of the week passed, those of us in leadership smiled with excitement, knowing that on the next Sunday a very surprised congregation would walk into an entirely refurbished place of worship.

Sunday arrived . . . and did we have a great time! Best of all, there was no trumpet fanfare, no names were splashed up front in lights, no bronze plaques or sculptured busts on pedestals were displayed for all to see. No, there was only praise to God for the beautiful new "facelift" provided by fewer than a dozen folks who chose to give in simple faith, over and above their regular offerings. As I ministered on that delightful "surprise Sunday," I couldn't help but notice a special look of quiet delight on the faces of those who had given so generously. Because they refused to "sound a trumpet . . . that they may be honored by men," their heavenly Father had already begun to repay them.

When You Pray

And when you pray, you are not to be as the hypocrites; for they love to stand and pray in the synagogues and on the street corners, in order to be seen by men. Truly I say to you, they have their reward in full. But you, when you pray, *go into your inner room, and when you have shut your door,* pray to your Father who is in secret, and your Father who sees in secret will repay you. And when you are praying, do not use meaningless repetition, as the Gentiles do, for they suppose that they will be heard for their many words. Therefore do not be like them; for your Father knows what you need, before you ask Him.

Matthew 6:5–8 (emphasis mine)

As before, Jesus talks briefly about what *not* to do, then spends more time on what *to* do when we pray. Make no mistake here, Jesus was certainly not discouraging prayer any more than He was discouraging giving earlier. What He spoke against was playing the role of a hypocrite when going through the motions of prayer. Thanks to the professional show-offs of the day, prayer had become formal, repetitive, regulated, and overdone . . . another tragic practice of religion on display. Using their example, hypocritical to the core, we are able to discern what not to do when we pray:

- Do not be hypocritical
- Do not seek to be seen while praying
- Do not limit your praying to public places
- Do not use meaningless repetition

Putting prayer on display is one of the most obvious and obnoxious acts of hypocrisy we can engage in. If you have ever done so, determine from this moment on never again to make prayer a public performance. This intimate act of worship must never be abused. How often I hear (and occasionally participate in!) long, wordy, self-serving acts of intercession where prayer becomes the vehicle for transporting loads of theological jargon and eloquent, pious phrases uttered to impress. Let's stop it!

Then what should we do instead? Jesus tells us.

First: *Find a private place to be alone.* He is talking about private devotions here, not public prayers. Get away. "Shut your door." Deliberately do not let it be known that you are meeting alone with God. You have no quiet place? How about your car? When our busy family was growing up, my mother preferred the bathroom. That door even has a lock. Go in. Be quiet. Pour out your soul.

Second: *Pray to your heavenly Father in secret.* I love the words the psalmist wrote on prayer:

When Thou didst say, "Seek My face," my heart said to Thee,
"Thy face, O LORD, I shall seek."

Psalm 27:8

He who dwells in the shelter of the Most High
Will abide in the shadow of the Almighty.

Psalm 91:1

Do you have a place of shelter where you seek only His face? Do you spend time in that secret place? Have you given prayer the priority it deserves? When you pray, remember it is the Lord's face you seek. I am learning as I continue in ministry that it is possible to be engaged in the work of ministry yet be in secret very, very seldom. There is this great tendency to think my best work is done at my desk or on my feet . . . but it's really done on my knees. It is easy to become so caught up in people's needs (which are endless and usually urgent) and to be so preoccupied with meeting those needs that I miss "the shelter of the Most High." How easy to emphasize all the involvements of being with people, rather than being alone in a secret place with Him. And I do mean *alone* with God, as though there is not another care, another need, another person—only "the Almighty."

In the last year and a half, maybe two, I have begun to realize the value of this. As a result of time invested in the secret place we gain an invincible sense of God's direction and the reassurance of His hand on our lives, along with an increased sensitivity regarding iniquity in our own lives.

Being alone with God is not complicated, but it is tough to maintain. Nevertheless, we need secrecy, especially in this hyperactive, noisy, busy world of ours.

Paul Tournier, in his work *Secrets*, writes:

> Every human being needs secrecy in order to become himself and no longer a member of his tribe . . . in order to collect his

thoughts. . . . To respect the secrecy of whoever it may be, even your own child, is to respect his individuality. To intrude upon his private life, to violate his secrecy, is to violate his individuality. . . .

So therefore, if keeping a secret was the first in the formation of the individual, telling it to a freely chosen confidant is going to constitute then the second step in the formation of the individual. He who cannot keep a secret is not free. But he who can never reveal it is not free either.[2]

Consider the beauty, the wonder, the magnificence, the awe-inspiring times of praise in the secret place! There is nothing to be compared to it. As great as corporate worship may be, with a magnificent pipe organ and full orchestra and a congregation singing at full volume, it cannot compare to the secret place where our best work is done and where God's best work is accomplished in us. I am fully convinced that doing justice and loving kindness and walking humbly with our God simply cannot happen without sufficient time in the secret place.

Third: *Keep it simple.* God doesn't pay closer attention because we use more verbiage, nor does it take a continuous stream of repetitious words, like some mysterious mantra, to make Him sit up and take notice.

Jesus gave His listeners a simple prayer to use as a model; we call it the Lord's Prayer. Actually it is the disciples' prayer. We shall look at it in depth in the next chapter.

Simply Put: The Spirit Applies . . .

This is a good place to stop and put all that we have considered in this chapter into perspective. Admittedly, we have covered a lot of ground, but at the heart of everything has been Jesus' warning: "Beware of religious performances!" Why? Because God is not glorified in such extravaganzas . . . and because we suffer the consequences. Three "performances," in particular, come to mind:

- When our devotion becomes an act
  we lapse into hypocrisy.
- When our giving lacks secrecy
  we lose our reward.
- When our prayers turn into demonstrations
  we lack God's power.

Remember Micah's threefold answer to those searching questions he asked? What is it God requires? Extensive burnt offerings? Yearling calves? Thousands of sheep? Ten thousand rivers of oil? Our firstborn? Our own lives thrown into the fire? No.

Then what? See if you can you remember.

- To do _____.
- To love _____.
- To walk _____.

That's it. That's all. Really, that's everything.

Back in 1958 when I was a young Marine stationed on the island of Okinawa, I became closely associated with a man I deeply admired. His name was Bob Newkirk. I didn't know what it was exactly that first drew me to Bob. More than anything, I guess, there was something refreshingly unpretentious about him. He was devoted to the things of the Lord, no question, but it was never on parade, never for the purpose of public display. And I loved that. Perhaps it was his balanced Christian life that I admired most. He was serving back then with The Navigators, an international Christian organization committed to ministering to military personnel. However, he never tried to squeeze me into some Navigator mold. I liked that especially. When we worked, we worked hard, but when we played, we had a first-class blast. I never got the idea that Bob was interested in making big impressions on me or other people. He was what he was, plain and simple—far from perfect, but authentic. Real.

I remember dropping by his home late one rainy evening to pay an unexpected visit. His wife met me at the door and informed me that he was not home. She added, "You've probably noticed lately that he has been under some stress. I think he may be down at his office. I'm not really sure. But he told me he just wanted to get alone."

I decided to try the office, a little spot down in Naha. I caught the three-wheel jitney that took me from the village where the Newkirks lived down to the capital city of the island. It was still raining lightly, so I stepped around and over the puddles as I made my way down a street, across an alley, then another alley until I came upon his unassuming, modest office. Before I arrived, however, I could hear singing in the distance—

> Come, Thou Fount of every blessing,
> Tune my heart to sing Thy grace.[3]

It was Bob's voice; I'd know it anywhere. I stood outside in the rain for a few moments, listening. The simple hymn continued. I confess, I peeked in the window and saw a candle on a table, my friend on his knees, and not another soul around. He was spending time with the Lord . . . all alone. As I stood outside, the soft-falling rain dripping off my nose and ears, my eyes filled with tears of gratitude. Bob never knew I came by that evening, but without his knowing it, I got a glimpse of authentic Christianity that night. Not piety on parade . . . not spiritual showtime, but a man "in the shelter of the Most High."

In the back streets of Naha I learned more about simple faith than I would later learn in four years of seminary.

Prayer and Fasting Minus All the Pizzazz

THE ENEMY OF OUR SOULS IS THE EXPERT of extremes. It seems he will stop at nothing until we get out of the realm of balance and onto some lunatic fringe.

Take evangelism. Instead of adopting a lifestyle-evangelism approach where presenting the claims of Christ flows very naturally and appropriately, Christians seem to either clam up or get fanatical. If the truth were known, many believers never open their mouths regarding their faith. They are secret-service saints, not about to speak of the One who has transformed their lives. And then there are others who go temporarily nuts. They elbow their way in and offend more than they win. The problem is that neither category has learned the value of balance.

Bible study is another example. On the one hand there are Christians who virtually ignore the Scriptures all week long, then when Sunday comes they start the hunt to see where they left their Bible after church last week. And then there are those who become Bible *freaks*. They live for one purpose: to study the Scriptures.

Between Bible classes, home Bible studies, Bible correspondence courses, and going part-time to a Bible college, they hardly have time for work or family. Few sights are more pathetic than a Christian who has gone overboard and doesn't realize it. The family is embarrassed, especially the kids. The neighbors are turned off. The folks at work hate to see that person coming toward them.

Having said all this, I would also be the first to say that the things of the Lord are not only thrilling, they are downright fascinating. And because scriptural truth is so profound, a bottomless pit of inexhaustible and magnificent riches, the treasure hunt through God's Word is like nothing else on earth. Having spent about forty years of my life searching through the doctrines, the theological subjects, the biblical characters, the history, and the practical application of truth to life, I can vouch for the fact that it can easily become addictive. And those most addicted are often those most preoccupied. Their heads are so into the queen of the sciences, some can hardly match their socks.

I suppose every person who has studied at a theological seminary has a story or two about a preoccupied professor. I certainly do. Usually this character is balding, wears thick glasses and baggy pants, carries a beat-up briefcase, hasn't the foggiest idea who won the World Series last week, and cannot quite remember where he parked the car that morning.

One of my esteemed mentors, I understand, once traveled from his home in Philadelphia to Baltimore for a weekend of ministry. Late Sunday evening he caught the flight back to Philly, but his wife wasn't there to meet him. He gave her a call to see why.

"Dear, where are you? I'm back. I thought you'd be here to meet me."

"To meet you? Where are you?"

"I'm here at the airport. Just flew in from Baltimore, remember?"

"The airport! Honey, you *drove* to Baltimore."

It takes a special kind of mate to be married to someone who lives in a world all his (or her) own. But since such a malady is so innocent, I suppose God gives special grace.

When the addiction leads to personal preoccupation, that is one thing. But when it leads to public ostentation, that is quite another. Webster defines ostentation as "excessive display," and therein lies the dark side of the extreme. That is what Jesus attacked with a vengeance in His immortal sermon. As you may recall, He spoke directly against making an excessive display of things like giving and praying.

A Brief Review: Give Anonymously, Pray Secretly

Beware of practicing your righteousness before men to be noticed by them; otherwise you have no reward with your Father who is in heaven.

Matthew 6:1

You remember that warning, I'm sure. Jesus' passionate plea is not that we stop giving or praying in public, but that whenever we do either, we not make a show of it.

The Christian is to live in such a way that men looking at him, and seeing the quality of his life, will glorify God. He must always remember at the same time that he is not to do things in order that he may attract attention to himself. He must not desire to be seen of men, he is never to be self-conscious. But, clearly, this balance is a fine and delicate one; so often we tend to go to one extreme or the other. Christian people tend either to be guilty of great ostentation or else to become monks and hermits. As you look at the long story of the Christian Church throughout the centuries you will find this great conflict has been going on. They have either been ostentatious, or else they have been so afraid of self and self-glorification that they have segregated themselves from the world. But here we are called to avoid both extremes.[1]

Not wishing to leave us with a general warning but no specifics, Jesus addresses three very real areas of the Christian life: giving, praying, and fasting.

Specific Commands

"When you give. . . ." We examined this closely in the previous chapter, so there is no need to rehearse the scene again. Just keep in mind the importance of not calling attention to yourself. Give, and go on with your life.

"When you pray. . . ." Here again, no ostentation, please. Keep it quiet. Remember you are praying "to your Father," not to those who may be sitting near you. And lots of words or the same phrases used repeatedly will not get you anywhere with God. Repeated requests sound as monotonous to Him as they do to others—maybe even a little irritating.

I was at the grocery store down the street the other evening, and in a bit of a hurry. As usual, the lines were long and everyone, it seemed, was buying enough to feed the entire roster of the Los Angeles Rams. Right in front of me was a hassled mother with three small, active boys who appeared to be about ten or eleven months apart in age. The youngest was the busiest of them all. He was perched in the shopping-cart seat, leaning over toward the gum and candy bars with two outstretched arms and repeating the same line over and over again as Mama was trying to unload her cart. The other two were shoving and arguing with each other. She was trying to referee while junior kept up his pleading:

"Mama, I want some TicTacs . . . Mama, I want some Tic-Tacs. Mama, I want some TicTacs . . . Mama, I want some TicTacs."

By now most folks in all the lines were looking in his direction, but the little guy never let up.

"Mama, I want some TicTacs. Mama, I want some TICTACS. Mama, I WANT SOME TICTACS. MAMA, I WANT SOME TICTACS. MAMAIWANTSOMETICTACS!!!"

Even though I was not "Mama," I was about to unload the case of TicTacs on the kid when Mama reached her breaking point. "NO . . . AND STOP ASKING!" she screamed in a voice that carried six stores away, I'm sure. He never stopped. Suddenly, to my surprise, she grabbed a box of TicTacs and shoved them into his hands. I then realized why the kid kept asking. He had learned that it worked!

When I returned to Jesus' words in Matt. 6:7, it dawned on me that the mindless-repetition approach may work with pagans and hassled parents, but it doesn't work with God! Endlessly repeated words may wear some parents down and force them to give in, but God tells us "do not be like them; for your Father knows what you need, before you ask Him" (6:8). God takes delight in meeting His children's needs, but His response is not based on how often we ask or how many times we use the same words. All He expects is that we come in simple faith.

Further Instruction: When Praying . . . When Fasting

Only on the rarest of occasions did Jesus ever spell out some precise pattern to follow in any of the disciplines of piety. It is as though He left the nuts and bolts to each of His own, not expecting us to jump through a prescribed set of hoops. But here is one of the rare occasions.

"Pray, Then, in This Way"

What a model He has left us! A studied look at the whole prayer will be worth our effort.

Pray, then, in this way:
"Our Father who art in heaven,
Hallowed be Thy name.
Thy kingdom come.
Thy will be done,
On earth as it is in heaven.
Give us this day our daily bread.
And forgive us our debts, as we also have forgiven our
debtors.
And do not lead us into temptation, but deliver us from evil.
[For Thine is the kingdom, and the power, and the glory,
forever. Amen.]"

Matthew 6:9–13

As I glance over the prayer we are to pattern ours after, the first observation that jumps out at me is that the focus is on the Lord: His person, His name, His rule, His will. Next, attention is drawn to our needs.

- Give us . . . our daily bread.
- Forgive us our debts.
- Deliver us from evil.

So simple, so clear, so easy to follow. I hope I don't complicate things as I dig a little deeper for the next few lines. Much of the prayer is self-explanatory.

To begin with, the Lord would have us address Him as "Our Father." We are living in a time when more and more Christians direct their prayers to Jesus. I do not remember any occasion in the Scriptures where people prayed to the Son of God, so I suggest we follow His instructions stated here. When He taught His followers to pray, it was always to the Father. So if you wish to be absolutely biblical about it, pray to the Father and call Him that. It will help you in praying to picture Him in your mind as Father more than Friend, or more than just a distant Deity. But of all the titles we could choose to use, Father says it best. He is our heavenly Father. He cares for His children. He knows how to handle His family.

There is both respect and freedom in the title. When there is a healthy relationship between Father and child, there is freedom. There is also openness. You can relax as you speak, yet you respect Him. And the longer I spend in the Father's presence, the less I want to tell Him what to do, and the more I want to linger in His presence.

Notice how He would have us envision Him: "who art in heaven." Literally it reads "in the heavens," for the Greek uses the plural term. This speaks of the transcendence, the immanence of God. He is in the air that surrounds us. He is in the galaxies, the multiple thousands of galaxies removed from us. He encompasses the heavens. He is not contained in the letters G-O-D. He is everywhere and yet as close as my own breath.

"Hallowed be Thy name." Hallowed is one of those terms we rarely use these days. It means consecrated, holy, dedicated.

Perhaps the most eloquent time "hallowed" flowed from English-speaking lips was when Abraham Lincoln used it in his Gettysburg Address. Looking out over the Pennsylvania fields that had been littered with the remains of thousands of brave young Americans only five months before, Lincoln said, "But, in a larger sense, we cannot dedicate, we cannot consecrate, we cannot hallow this ground. The brave men, living and dead, who struggled here, have consecrated it far above our power to add or detract."

In a similar sense, we cannot "hallow" God, but we can acknowledge that He is holy. "Hallowed be Thy name," then, is a statement of fact rather than a request. "I acknowledge, by uttering Your name, Father, that Your name is hallowed, holy, absolutely separate from sin."

By merely reviewing the first few lines of the Lord's Prayer, we gain a renewed respect . . . a healthy and wholesome sense of reverence for our Almighty God and Father. Rather than causing us to run from Him and hide in fear, I find that such an awesome respect makes me want to come close to Him, to wait quietly for Him to work. And so I urge you to slow your pace, to approach His "hallowed name" thoughtfully. Take time! Give Him the respect He deserves. Wait on God. In return, He will give you a clearer vision. Furthermore, He will soften your will and make you want to know and do His will.

The prayer continues with these familiar words: "Thy kingdom come. Thy will be done." It is as if Jesus is saying, "Let it come to pass. May it one day transpire in that grand kingdom You promised for this earth. May it be the kind of kingdom where You rule over all. In the meantime, may Your will be done on earth as it is always done among the adoring angels about You." I detect here the willing submission of one's life to the will of God. "Let Your will be done in me, whatever it may take, Lord." Simple words to say, but terribly significant.

After focusing on His heavenly person, His name, His rule, and His will, there is an appropriate shift to earthly needs: "Give us this day our daily bread." Look closely. "Daily bread" means the basics. It's not, "Give us this day our daily cake," "our daily pie," or even "our weekly feast." All we need in order to live is bread, basic sustenance. "Just enough clothing to keep me warm, Lord, just give that. Anything above that is grace. I'll settle for bread, and I need it on a daily basis." Daily bread is a symbol for everything necessary for the preservation of life.

"And while You're giving, there is something I need just as much for my inner self, Lord . . . forgiveness." What bread is to the physical being, forgiveness is to the soul. Sin is like a lingering debt. Interest accumulates. If that debt is not paid, we must bear the consequences. We cannot cover our own sins all alone. We need help from above, and the help He provides cleanses us and washes our sins away. So when we pray, let's not forget to place our debt of sin before the One who forgives it.

The part that troubles most people in the Lord's Prayer is the request, "Do not lead us into temptation." How could He? His name is hallowed. He is holy. If temptation means the solicitation to evil, how could He do that? James says,

> Let no one say when he is tempted, "I am being tempted by God"; for God cannot be tempted by evil, and He Himself does not tempt anyone. But each one is tempted when he is carried away and enticed by his own lust. Then when lust has conceived, it gives birth to sin; and when sin is accomplished, it brings forth death.
>
> James 1:13–15

Clearly, God cannot tempt anyone. Holiness never solicits evil.

Some have suggested this means, "Do not lead us into a test." But why wouldn't He? Testing breeds endurance, and through endurance we develop character. So the Lord does grant testing.

Most likely the phrase "do not lead us" is a permissive imperative and could best be rendered, "do not allow us to be led into temptation." Or better, "do not allow us to be overwhelmed by temptation," which explains why He then adds, "but deliver us from evil." I think that is a reference to the enemy himself—Satan—the evil one and his host of demons. In other words, "Lord rescue us."

Could there also be a veiled reference to the Trinity in these three levels of requests? It is the Lord our Father, our Sustainer, who gives daily bread. It is the Son, our Savior, who makes the forgiveness of debts possible through His blood. And it is the Spirit of God who is our Indweller and Rescuer.

Are you aware of what our adversary hates most about you and me? He hates the pleasure we enjoy in our Father's presence. He once enjoyed it himself. But through a series of prideful acts, he was cast out. And he looks back with despicable envy on all who enjoy the pleasure in the presence he once enjoyed, but is now separated from forever.

Thomas Watson, the seventeenth-century Puritan, put it very well: "Satan envies man's happiness. To see a cloud of dust so near to God, and himself, once a glorious angel, cast out of heavenly paradise, makes him curse mankind with inveterate hatred."

And then comes that dramatic conclusion, which has inspired such grand music: "For thine is the kingdom, and the power, and the glory, forever. Amen." What an appropriate ending for the prayer!

While thinking through the themes of this prayer, my mind has often returned to the theme of forgiveness. Is there any greater relief on earth than that?

Dr. Earl Palmer, a good friend and the senior pastor at the First Presbyterian Church of Berkeley, California, does a masterful job of illustrating this truth as he likens it to the Golden Gate Bridge:

> I have often thought of the Golden Gate Bridge in San Francisco as our city's boldest structure in that its great south pier rests directly upon the fault zone of the San Andreas Fault. That bridge is an amazing structure of both flexibility and strength. It is built to sway some twenty feet at the center of its one-mile suspension span. The secret to its durability is its flexibility that enables this sway, but that is not all. By design, every part of the bridge—its concrete roadway, its steel railings, its cross beams —is inevitably related from one welded joint to the other up through the vast cable system to two great towers and two great land anchor piers. The towers bear most of the weight, and they are deeply imbedded into the rock foundation beneath the sea. In other words, the bridge is totally preoccupied with its foundation. This is its secret! Flexibility and foundation. In the Christian life, it is the forgiveness of the gospel that grants us our flexibility; and it is the Lord of the gospel who is our foundation.[2]

"And Whenever You Fast"

Just as Jesus dealt with giving and praying, He now deals with fasting—how not to do it, then, how to do it. Consider, first, the negative.

> And whenever you fast, do not put on a gloomy face as the hypocrites do, for they neglect their appearance in order to be seen fasting by men. Truly I say to you, they have their reward in full.
>
> Matthew 6:16

He tells us not to put on a gloomy face, not to neglect our appearance, and not to seek a superpious look. I believe He is saying that no one should ever be able to tell just by looking that we have been fasting. Great game plan . . . but not always followed.

Have you ever been around people who really wanted to look spiritual? They are gloom personified, apparently living out one of the unwritten laws in the ancient code of pharisaical ethics. Down through the centuries of Christianity many have cultivated that "seriously religious" appearance. It is especially popular among superpious missionaries who talk about the burden of the mission field, or among pastors who are weighed down with the burden of the pastorate. Burden? Whose burden? The ministry is *His* burden. Since that is true, what are we doing bearing His burden and trying to look so grim about it? We *ought* to be grim if we are attempting to carry what God is supposed to carry! But we are not made to carry out His role, so let's stop trying. Playing a false role promotes pride, which is easily detected.

I heard recently that a flight attendant once said to the then-heavyweight champion of the world, Muhammad Ali, "Please fasten your seat belt."

He replied with a sneer, "Superman don't need no seat belt."

"Superman don't need no airplane," she responded. "Buckle up, please."

Show-offs never miss a trick. In Jesus' day some religious show-offs even painted their faces a little whiter so they would look pale when they were fasting—not unlike an old marble statue of a saint might look standing in the dusty corner of a giant cathedral.

One of my best friends and a longstanding mentor has often said with a smile, "You can be a fundamentalist, but you don't have to look like one."

Some people think they will appear more spiritual if they look like an unmade bed . . . hair unkempt, no deodorant, no pressed clothes or shined shoes, and certainly no stylish fashions. After all, we are supposed to be citizens of heaven! That may be true, but until we get there, there are lots of folks who have to live with us on earth. Let's be considerate of them! Fasting or not, trying to look holy (whatever that means) won't cut it. In today's terms, Jesus says, "Knock it off!"

Fasting is good for one's health. Fasting helps bring perspective and break bad habits. Fasting is good for self-control. It encourages a protracted focus on Christ and a wholesome self-discipline. It gives time to let the silt of our lives drop to the bottom. It brings us back to basics. Fasting simplifies our faith. But that is also why we are never to promote it, brag about it, or display it. There should not be a conference on fasting, where everybody goes out and does it for four hours and then returns for a big supper that night.

There is an old rabbinical maxim that says: "A man will have to give an account on the judgment day for every good thing which he might have enjoyed, and did not."[3]

As the Apostle Paul put it, "God . . . richly supplies us with all things to enjoy" (1 Tim. 6:17). Yes, "all things."

Jesus Himself spoke against wearing a gloomy face and having an unkempt look to parade one's spirituality, which is not spirituality at all.

146

But you, when you fast, anoint your head, and wash your face so that you may not be seen fasting by men, but by your Father who is in secret; and your Father who sees in secret will repay you.
Matthew 6:17–18

What wonderful, balanced counsel! How often our Savior must have fasted, but never once did He make a show of it.

Simply Put: Personal Obedience

Jesus has touched on things that are so down to earth and so practical you would think the ink was still wet. They could have been written this very morning. In a sense they were . . . that's the way God's Word is, always alive and active and sharp.

Now, how do we make it happen—come alive—in our lives? Let me leave with you a couple of suggestions.

First, *make the heavenly Father, not people, your main focus.* Remember the prayer pattern? *"Our Father who art in heaven"* . . . we're not praying to all the people who watch us. "Hallowed be Thy name" . . . not the folks around us—none of their names are hallowed. *"Thy will be done . . . Thy kingdom come"* . . . not the will of our fellow church members.

Have you allowed yourself to fall under the thumb of somebody's will? No wonder you don't enjoy life! You are taking your cues from those who frown back at you. What do they know about what God is doing in your life?

I'll be candid with you. The older I get the less I worry about what people think and the more I concern myself with what God thinks. When I get His green light, I confess, I move in that direction and He and I have the time of our lives. But, invariably, there are some people who don't understand. (Many don't want to understand.) That is why I encourage others to focus on Him. I strongly suggest you do the same. But watch out . . . it will change your life.

147

Second: *Make the secret place, not the public place, your primary platform.* You want a safe place to spend more time? Choose the secret place. Spend more time there and less time seeking the public platform. In that secret place you will find a quiet depth and a courageous invincibility that is nothing short of contagious.

9

When Simple
Faith Erodes

LAST NIGHT WAS WONDERFUL. It was more than that; it was memorable. It had all the ingredients of a never-to-be-duplicated evening. Long-term friends. Nostalgic reminders. Laughter and a few tears. Words of gratitude. Authentic expressions of praise to God. Glorious music. Well-chosen remarks from sincere hearts. Choice comments in print . . . the works! Cynthia and I were treated to a delightful evening at our church where the congregation gathered to say, "Thank you for twenty years of ministry among us." It was hard to believe that twenty years had already passed.

We were urged to sit back, relax, and accept everything that was planned in our honor. And though neither of us feels all that comfortable in the center of such celebrations, we were reminded more than once that we needed to have "the grace to receive" (sound familiar?) what people wanted to do for us and say to us. To God went the glory—no question about that—but to my wife and me came the most overwhelming expressions of affirmation we have ever received. Because it was handled so appropriately, so lovingly, and because nothing said or done represented flattery, but rather respect and true gratitude, Cynthia and I left with misty eyes and joyful hearts.

The theme was "Thanking God for the First Twenty Years." I suppose there was a hint of job security in that phrase, so that alone was encouraging. But the best part of all was looking into the faces of many of the most significant and cherished people in our lives and realizing how interwoven our paths have been during these two decades we have journeyed together. I will never forget those faces. Each one reflected absolute honesty, genuine respect, and, yes, simple faith . . . but most of all a deep trust that has been building over the past twenty years.

I didn't sleep much through the night. Those faces kept passing in review, faces that smiled and said, "We trust you . . . We believe in you." Unless I miss my guess, those same faces were also saying, "Stay true . . . continue to give us reasons to trust you, to respect and believe in you . . . keep growing; but as the years of the future pass, don't drift, Chuck. As you have done for us in the past, give our children the memory of a minister they can trust. Stay strong. Remain pure, dear friend. Don't fake it . . . don't start covering up secret sins that will one day turn to scandal." Understand, no one actually said those words, but as I lay there awake, looking at the moonlit ceiling, that's what I heard.

It is an awesome thing to be trusted. Respect, though so very important, hangs on terribly thin wires. And what makes it all so fragile is that there is nothing in the mere passing of time that automatically strengthens the fiber of one's character. As a matter of fact, each day we live there are subtle opportunities inviting us to let up, to compromise. Nothing boisterous and bold, you understand, but little things, secret things, that wink and flirt and invite us in. It is like erosion—never obvious or quick or announced. One of my esteemed mentors of yesteryear, the late Dr. Richard H. Seume, had an eloquent description for it: "the lure of a lesser loyalty."

No guarantees accompany a minister's second twenty years in the same place. If anything, they are tougher. A maintenance mentality can emerge as zeal fades. Rationalization can accompany slight slips and within a matter of time secret sins, like undetected melanoma, begin to take their toll. The categories are legion. We usually think first of being lured into sexual compromise, a very real and common area of enemy attack, but it is only one of many possibilities. Greed is equally subtle. The same could be said of pride or unaccountability or lust for power . . . jealousy of the younger and more gifted, the tendency to become manipulative or overly dogmatic, negative or self-serving . . . or just plain slothful, relying on yesterday's study and last year's sermons. I dare not miss mentioning the hidden snare of cynicism or an attitude of presumption. The supple, teachable years of our youth can erode, leaving us brittle, boastful, or even bitter. And learning to cover all that up comes easier with the passing of time. Ever so slowly a life of refreshingly simple faith can become tainted and tortured within, before anyone knows it is happening.

The Tragedy of Settling for Less

None of the above is new. The roots of secret erosion go deep into the soil of humanity; some of these cases are so notorious they have found their way into the biblical record. Elisha's trusted servant comes to mind. Quiet, faithful, and loyal to the prophet, Gehazi entertained private thoughts of materialistic greed. Who would ever have guessed? Nothing external sounded an alarm . . . but when the test came, the once-trusted servant was trapped.

And then there was King David's own General Joab, tenacious in battle and a time-honored friend, who started strong but ended weak. This man of military might died in dishonor and was buried, not in Israel's equivalent to Arlington National Cemetery with full military honors alongside other national heroes, but by a cabin in the wilderness. What happened to Joab? How could he have done such a thing? Chalk up another one for erosion.

And Demas—we dare not omit his sad scriptural obituary from Paul's pen: "Demas, having loved this present world, has deserted me." A trusted friend, no doubt a traveling companion who once talked and prayed with Paul, who knew the hardship and heartaches of ministry as well as delightful moments of accomplishment shared together, was lured by a lesser loyalty. Tragic, indeed.

The path of the faithful is littered with the mute remains of those who once sang great songs of loudest praise before their simple faith slid into cynicism and spiritual defeat.

Oswald Chambers serves notice to all of us who tread the path of faith:

> Always remain alert to the fact where one man has gone back is exactly where anyone may go back. . . . You have gone through the big crisis, now be alert over the least things; take into calculation the "retired sphere of the leasts."[1]

I understand that one year when Dr. Will Houghton was still the president of Moody Bible Institute, he was addressing a packed auditorium during the school's Founder's Week. In the course of his message, he told of an experience he'd had some years earlier with his predecessor, Dr. James M. Gray. The two of them had been together in conference ministry, and as they parted company, they paused for a few moments of prayer. Dr. Houghton still remembered the vulnerable, unguarded petition that fell from Gray's lips that day. To his amazement, he heard his quiet and dignified colleague utter the simple prayer, "O God, don't let me become a wicked old man." There remains a warning in that to all of us: "Let him who thinks he stands take heed lest he fall" (1 Cor. 10:12). It is those "retired spheres of the leasts" that we cannot, we *dare not* ignore.

I have thought about all this a lot, not only in the last eighteen hours but for the last several years. The crucial question, I think, is this: *Why would anyone let this happen?* Nobody in his or her right mind gets up in the morning, sits on the side of the bed, and thinks, *Let's see, how can I ruin my life today? How can I break the trust of all who respect me and believe in me?* Of course not. What happens is far more subtle. Perhaps it originates with these alien thoughts: *Who will ever know? I'm absolutely safe. Furthermore, this is as far as I'll go . . . period. Not even God concerns Himself with such small things. He's much too involved with bigger issues than this; He hardly cares . . .* Wrong! Read and reason through the following:

> The LORD looks from heaven;
> He sees all the sons of men;
> From His dwelling place He looks out
> On all the inhabitants of the earth,
> He who fashions the hearts of them all,
> He who understands all their works.
>
> Psalm 33:13–15

> O LORD, Thou hast searched me and known me.
> Thou dost know when I sit down and when I rise up;
> Thou dost understand my thought from afar.
> Thou dost scrutinize my path and my lying down,
> And art intimately acquainted with all my ways.
>
> Psalm 139:1–3

For the eyes of the LORD move to and fro throughout the earth that He may strongly support those whose heart is completely His. You have acted foolishly in this. Indeed, from now on you will surely have wars.

> 2 Chronicles 16:9

And there is no creature hidden from His sight, but all things are open and laid bare to the eyes of Him with whom we have to do.

> Hebrews 4:13

While I am mentioning all this scriptural evidence, do you remember what we heard from Jesus' lips in the previous chapter? Several times He spoke of "your Father who sees in secret" (Matt. 6:4, 6, 18). A firm belief in the omniscience of God—His knowing all things at all times—will go a long way in restraining our tendency to rationalize or think we can operate in secret. God sees it all because He cares about every single detail of our existence. The life of simple faith is a life that is lived openly before God and in willing accountability before others. If you want to complicate your life, start thinking that you can divide your world into public and private realms. That is as erroneous as telling ourselves that life can be divided into the secular and the sacred. For the one who claims to be a follower of Jesus, nothing falls under the "secular" category. When we start believing that heresy, "the lure of a lesser loyalty" only intensifies.

The Impossibility of Serving Two Masters

Returning to Jesus' profound words, we come to one of the most penetrating paragraphs of truth in the New Testament. Read His words carefully.

> Do not lay up for yourselves treasures upon earth, where moth and rust destroy, and where thieves break in and steal. But lay up for yourselves treasures in heaven, where neither moth nor rust destroys, and where thieves do not break in or steal; for where your treasure is, there will your heart be also. The lamp of the body is the eye; if therefore your eye is clear, your whole body will be full of light. But if your eye is bad, your whole body will be full of darkness. If therefore the light that is in you is darkness, how great is the darkness! No one can serve two masters; for either he will hate the one and love the other, or he will hold to one and despise the other. You cannot serve God and mammon.
>
> Matthew 6:19–24

Talk about clear communication. As I have said several times, no one was ever better at it than Jesus.

Looking over His words, it is the contrasts that stand out. I see at least four:

- Treasures upon earth . . . treasures in heaven (vv. 19–20)
- Outer/visible treasure . . . inner/invisible treasure (v. 21)
- If the eye is clear . . . if the eye is bad (vv. 22–23)
- A body full of light . . . a body full of darkness (vv. 22–23)

We'll come back to those contrasts momentarily, but first, observe how Jesus begins His remarks in contrast to the way He ends them. At the beginning He gives a strong command: "Do not . . ." (v. 19), but at the end He states a simple fact: "You cannot . . ." (v. 24). Contrasts make things crystal clear, and since He spoke these words in a culture where the master-slave relationship was commonplace, we can be certain His audience got the point, especially when He declared, "No one can serve two masters." Dual lordship is an impossibility; when we attempt to do the impossible, the life of simple faith degenerates into maximum complications.

To put it in the simplest of terms: Jesus is emphasizing the folly of choosing the wrong way, the wisdom of choosing the right . . . and the impossibility of having both. It is an either-or proposition. I repeat, when we question that and attempt to travel both paths, keeping the wrong a secret, the life of simple faith erodes.

Now let's go back to Jesus' four contrasts. The first has to do with the *treasure* of our lives, which is what we have—our possessions. The rest have to do with the *focus* of our lives, which is what we are—our direction. Let's take them in that order.

Our Treasure: What We Possess

Our earthly treasure is not difficult to identify. It would include anything that is tangible and has a price tag. We can see it, touch it, measure it, and enjoy it. Our heavenly treasure would include the invisible, intangible, priceless possessions that belong to anyone who is numbered among God's forever family. The former, according to the Master, can corrode, age, deteriorate, and be ripped off. For the latter, however, none of that is true.

Exactly what is it He is prohibiting when He says, "Do not lay up . . ."? Possessions in and of themselves? No. Scripture does not condemn owning possessions. How about planning for the future? Is Jesus telling us not to buy insurance and not to face the future with some sort of strategy? No. Well, then, is our Lord condemning the enjoyment of things we own, even nice things? Again, no. In spite of all you may have heard or believed, none of the above is the point Jesus is making. Matter of fact, we are distinctly told that God gives us "all things to enjoy" (1 Tim. 6:17). Yes, *enjoy*. Paul found that he not only needed to learn "to be content in whatever circumstances" he found himself, but he also needed to learn "how to live in prosperity" as well as with "humble means" (Phil. 4:11–12). I know, I know. Some have taken this prosperity issue to such an extreme that they have learned how to rationalize ostentatious opulence, clearly an incorrect and unbiblical interpretation. But equally tragic are those who have not learned how to accept or enjoy anything above the lowest economic level, believing if they do so, they will be unspiritual. Few responses are more shame-based and guilt-oriented than that. Since I have already dealt with that issue in great detail in *The Grace Awakening*, there is no need to repeat those same things here.

What, then, is Jesus denouncing? Namely this: the selfish accumulation of tangible treasure to the point where enough is never enough . . . extravagant living to the exclusion of others in need. More specifically, it's setting our hearts on earthly things so much so that we don't own them, they own us. How easy in our materialistic age to be "lured into a lesser loyalty" by fixing our attention on things that have price tags.

This is a perfect moment to stop for a quick self-analysis. I am not interested in how much you make or what choices you make regarding your lifestyle. Who am I to judge another? My concern really has nothing to do with what you own but rather with why you own it. In light of what we have just read, can you honestly say that your heart is not fixed on tangible treasures? Is your giving generous? Do you readily help others, even as you enjoy God's gracious provisions? Are you genuinely unselfish, openhanded, greathearted, free from materialistic addictions? Selfishness evidences itself in the materialist who always wants more and in the miser who hoards needlessly.

Martin Luther wrote:

> Whenever the Gospel is taught and people seek to live according to it, there are two terrible plagues that always arise: false preachers who corrupt the teaching, and then Sir Greed, who obstructs right living.[2]

I do not know of a more pronounced idol in this generation than "Sir Greed." I'm convinced it is more powerful and certainly more popular than lust, especially in these United States. If you are determined to simplify your life, you will need to ask yourself some hard questions: Why do you want that second job? Why are you working such long hours? Why have you deliberately put your family on hold while you play Russian roulette with greed? When will you be able to say, "Enough"? Why is your occupation or your position so important to you?

Am I suggesting that if you are really a person of devotion you would leave your present occupation and go into the ministry? No way. I am just maverick enough to say that I think fewer Christians ought to be going into the ministry and more should be going into business and into occupations that have nothing to do with vocational Christian service. As I mentioned earlier, I don't see life divided into public and private, secular and sacred. It is all an open place of service before our God. My hope is to see this generation produce a group of Christians who will infiltrate our society—in fact, our entire world—with a pure, beautiful message of grace and honesty in the marketplace.

Recently I had a delightful talk with a keen-thinking young man following one of the worship services at our church. As we visited, I asked him about his future plans. "Well, I've just graduated from law school," he said. When I asked about how he hoped to use his training, he said, "I want to be a man of integrity who practices law." What refreshing words! They reflected the right priority. There is not a career worth pursuing where you *cannot* have integrity. Every vocation cries out for it.

Rather than placing all the emphasis on earthly, tangible treasures, our Lord instructs us to turn our attention to those intangible treasures that defy destruction and cannot be stolen—eternal treasures that keep the perspective clear.

Back in the spring of 1991 my wife and I were invited to Washington, D.C., as guests of the Christian Embassy. That trip proved to be one of the most eventful of our lives, as we had the opportunity to meet and spend time with some of the highest ranking officers in all the branches of our military services, many of whom are sterling Christians. I ministered to a group of them early one morning at the Pentagon. As we sat around a long table together, Bibles opened, they were anxious to hear what God's Word had to say about their lives. Though incredibly responsible, intelligent, and decisive men, they were as unassuming and teachable as schoolchildren . . . and far more attentive! Because they were men who were laying up treasures in heaven, their hearts were open and receptive.

Our trip included a visit to the Oval Office where we were privileged to meet the president and vice president—wonderful experience! We found our highest elected national leaders to be gracious and kind men. This was followed by my being given the opportunity to address a room full of greathearted people serving on the White House staff—another delightful occasion. We found these people to be teachable folks with servant hearts, not at all like the press often portrays them.

The climax of our East Coast trip occurred at a retreat center in the Blue Ridge Mountains of Virginia, a place called Wintergreen. There over one hundred Pentagon-based officers, plus senators and representatives from Capitol Hill, had gathered for spiritual renewal. We prayed, laughed, sang, spent time in the Scriptures, and shared that slice of life together in a relaxed setting. Most of these people had played significant roles in the Vietnam War as well as the victorious war in the Persian Gulf; yet there they sat, drinking in the truth of Scripture, grateful for a chance to receive insights from God's eternal and inerrant Word. As Cynthia and I flew back to California, though exhausted from our five-day investment of time and energy, we were over-flowing with gratitude. We had been with those who had every earthly reason to be full of pride and/or cynicism, but were neither. They had discovered over the years that the teachings of Christ were more significant than anything they dealt with professionally . . . and that glorifying Him was far more important than fighting wars or pleasing the public. Their hearts were right, therefore their treasures were in correct perspective. Putting together a strategy that would result in a successful military campaign was, of course, important, but not more important than their simple faith in God's dear Son.

Our Focus: What We Are

Let's take another look at Jesus' words here:

> The lamp of the body is the eye; if therefore your eye is clear, your whole body will be full of light. But if your eye is bad, your whole body will be full of darkness. If therefore the light that is in you is darkness, how great is the darkness! No one can serve two masters; for either he will hate the one and love the other, or he will hold to one and despise the other. You cannot serve God and mammon.
>
> Matthew 6:22–24

Jesus uses an illustration from basic human anatomy to illustrate the importance of the right focus in life. Just as the eye affects our whole body ("the lamp of the body is the eye"), so our focus (whatever we set our hearts on) impacts our whole life. Paul, a few years later, put it this way:

> If then you have been raised up with Christ, keep seeking the things above, where Christ is, seated at the right hand of God. Set your mind on the things above, not on the things that are on earth. For you have died and your life is hidden with Christ in God.
>
> Colossians 3:1–3

> Finally, brethren, whatever is true, whatever is honorable, whatever is right, whatever is pure, whatever is lovely, whatever is of good repute, if there is any excellence and if anything worthy of praise, let your mind dwell on these things.
>
> Philippians 4:8

Clearly, our minds determine the direction of our lives. Whatever we think on, we become. Right focus—good results; wrong focus—bad results. Or, as Christ describes it, clear eyes—light; bad eyes—"how great is the darkness!" In other words, "How far you can be lured from the right loyalty . . . how confused you can become, simply by false focus!" We can, in fact, be enslaved by the wrong master. Remember His words—"No one can serve two masters."

D. Martyn Lloyd-Jones, in his splendid work on the Sermon on the Mount, titles the chapter in which he addresses these words of Jesus, "Sin's Foul Bondage." And so it is. The "great darkness" that accompanies an out-of-focus life is nothing less than the foul bondage brought on by sin.

> According to the Scripture man was made in the image of God; and a part of the image of God in man is undoubtedly the mind, the ability to think and to reason, especially in the highest sense and in a spiritual sense. Man, therefore, was obviously meant to function in the following way. His mind, being the highest faculty and propensity that he possesses, should always come first. Things are perceived with the mind and analysed by it. Then come the affections, the heart, the feeling, the sensibility given to man by God. Then thirdly there is that other quality, that other faculty, called the will, the power by which we put into operation the things we have understood, the things we have desired as the result of apprehension.[3]

During the days of our innocence (that is, Adam's and Eve's innocence), things were in proper order. There was the mind, which gave facts to the body and prompted the emotions to respond correctly. In turn, the emotions signaled the will, which carried out the desires, and obedience followed. The mind learned, based upon the facts of truth, then dictated to the emotions the proper response, which gave the will the green light to move ahead and obey. When "sin's foul bondage" occurred (when Adam and Eve fell into sin in the Garden), the first two were reversed. The tragedy is this: We still live like that. Now what is considered of foremost importance is what "feels good."

D. Martyn Lloyd-Jones then defines the tragic results of sin in four ways.

- Sin causes an entire disturbance to the normal function.

- Sin blinds us in certain vital respects.

- Sin makes us a slave of the things that were originally meant to serve us. (The thing that would shock us and keep us from sin, the addiction of the thing, becomes our *drive*. And it is indeed an addiction.)

- Sin entirely ruins us.[4]

I have talked with individuals whose focus has gotten out of whack, and I have attempted to dissuade them on the basis of sheer logic, basic facts, evidence, scriptural truth—the whole nine yards. They may listen, but when I am through, it is like a stiff arm extends in my direction, saying, "Don't bother me. I knowwhat I'm doing." What they are doing is serving the wrong master. And their addiction has blinded them. Returning to Jesus' closing words, we can understand His reason for saying:

> No one can serve two masters; for either he will hate the one and love the other, or he will hold to one and despise the other. You cannot serve God and mammon.
>
> Matthew 6:24

You cannot! Let those words sink in. You cannot be a slave of two masters simultaneously. It cannot occur. When wrongly enslaved, simple faith erodes, which explains why Paul wrote so passionately to the Corinthians:

> But I am afraid, lest as the serpent deceived Eve by his craftiness, your minds should be led astray from the simplicity and purity of devotion to Christ.
>
> 2 Corinthians 11:3

A mind that is "led astray from the simplicity . . . of Christ" is one whose loyalty has been divided. When that happens, erosion has been set in motion.

Simply Put: The Security of Living in Truth

I have given a lot of thought to these things, not only because I have tried to figure out why some who once walked in "simplicity and purity" no longer do, but also because I realize I am vulnerable to the same temptation to drift. While pondering these things, two thoughts keep coming to the surface of my mind. Let me state and explain both.

First, *by living in truth our options remain open*. The secret is making the right choices. Here's what I mean. In the light of truth, you and I are able to see both truth and lie, both light and darkness— that which is simple, pure, and clear and that which is deceptive. But enslaved to darkness and plunged into the pit of the lie, we no longer see the truth. We have no other option but to believe the lie. We become victimized in our addiction—in "sin's foul bondage."

The secret, of course, is making the right choices every day. So? Watch those choices! Watch your decisions!

No married couple suddenly divorces. No home suddenly fractures. No church suddenly splits. Nobody becomes a cynic overnight. Nobody makes one leap from the pinnacle of praise to the swamp of carnality. Erosion is a slow and silent process based on secret choices. And isn't it remarkable? If you do not stop yourself in the downward process, last week's wrong choice doesn't seem quite so bad this week. In fact, in a month's time it seems like not that bad a choice at all! Thus simple faith erodes into a life of secrecy and complication.

Second, *by living in truth, our focus stays clear*. The secret here is serving the right Master. We need to keep asking ourselves, Does this honor the Savior? Does this exalt my Lord? Does this bring glory to His name? Does this lift Him up? How powerful is our focus!

Let me level with you. I know some of you are thinking, *I'm never going to become that wicked old man. I have had enough warning,*

Chuck. I have heard enough sermons on this theme. I've read the Scriptures. I know the verse that says, "Let him who thinks he stands take heed lest he fall." I'm safe. For you, especially, I close the chapter with this story.

Robert Robinson was born in England more than two hundred years ago. When he was just a boy, his father died, and his widowed mother sent him to London to learn the trade of barbering. In that great city Robert came under the persuasive influence of a powerful man of God, the great Methodist revivalist George Whitefield. Robinson was soundly converted and felt a call to the ministry; he began at once to study for a lifetime of serving Christ.

At twenty-five Robert Robinson was called to pastor a Baptist church in Cambridge, where he became very successful. But the popularity was more than the young minister could handle. It led to the beginning of a lapse in his life of simple faith. Ultimately he fell into carnality, another tragic victim of "sin's foul bondage." As the years passed he faded from the scene and few even remembered his earlier years of devotion to Christ.

Years later Robinson was making a trip by stagecoach and happened to sit next to a woman who was reading a book with obvious pleasure. She seemed to be especially interested in one page of the volume, for she kept returning to it again and again. Finally she turned to Robinson—a complete stranger to her—and held the page toward him. Pointing to the hymn she had been reading there, she asked what he thought of it.

Robinson looked at the first few lines:

> Come, Thou Fount of every blessing
> Tune my heart to sing Thy grace;
> Streams of mercy, never ceasing,
> Call for songs of loudest praise. . . .

He read no further. Turning his head, he endeavored to engage the lady's attention on the passing landscape. But she was not to be denied. Pressing her point, she told him of the benefit she had received from the words of that hymn and expressed her admiration for its message.

Overcome with emotion, Robinson burst into tears. "Madam," he said, "I am the poor, unhappy man who wrote that hymn many years ago, and I would give a thousand worlds, if I had them, to enjoy the feelings I had then."[5]

Robert Robinson was now many years older and light-years removed from his earlier commitment to Christ. His days of simple faith had eroded. How ironic that, at the end of the hymn, he had seemed to prophesy his own downward course:

> O to grace how great a debtor
> Daily I'm constrained to be!
> Let Thy goodness, like a fetter,
> Bind my wandering heart to Thee:
>
> Prone to wander, Lord, I feel it,
> Prone to leave the God I love;
> Here's my heart, O take and seal it;
> Seal it for thy courts above.[6]

That is precisely what he did. Robert Robinson died shortly thereafter at the young age of fifty-five, the victim of the lure of a lesser loyalty. He had left the God he once loved and had become "a wicked old man."

10

The Subtle Enemy
of Simple Faith

O<small>KAY, NOW THAT I HAVE YOUR ATTENTION,</small> what is it? Which sin is the subtle enemy of simple faith? In the previous chapter we spent a lot of time on materialism and greed. But neither of those is the enemy I have in mind. Furthermore, neither is all that subtle. Anyone who battles either materialism or greed soon telegraphs the struggle publicly. How about anger? No, that's not it. Or lust? Wrong again. We have already taken a long look at hypocrisy, as well as several of the commandments Jesus restated having to do with murder, adultery, divorce, and making false vows, but those would not qualify as *subtle* enemies.

Stop and think. Once you decide to trust God in simple faith and allow Him complete freedom to carry out His plan and purpose in you as well as through you, you need only relax and count on Him to take care of things you once tried to keep under control. From now on you won't step in and take charge. "God is well able to handle this," you tell yourself. But in a weak moment the adversary of your soul whispers a doubt or two in your ear, like, "Hey, what if—?" If that doesn't make you churn, he returns in the middle of the night and fertilizes your imagination with several quasi-extreme possibilities, leaving you mildly disturbed if not altogether panicked. No one can tell by looking (and you certainly wouldn't think of *telling* anyone), but in place of your inward peace and simple faith, you are now immobilized by . . . what? You guessed it, the most notorious faith killer in all of life: *worry*.

A Brief Analysis of Worry

For this reason I say to you, do not be anxious for your life, as to what you shall eat, or what you shall drink; nor for your body, as to what you shall put on. Is not life more than food, and the body than clothing?

Matthew 6:25

Being something of a wordsmith, I find the term "worry" fascinating, though the reality of this in our lives can be downright maddening. To begin with, the word used by Matthew (translated here as "anxiety" and "anxious") is the Greek term *merimnao*. It is a combination of two smaller words, *merizo*, meaning "to divide," and *nous*, meaning "the mind." In other words, a person who is anxious suffers from a divided mind, leaving him or her disquieted and distracted. Actually, our English word *worry* is from the German, *worgen*, which in that tongue means "to strangle." This ties in vividly with what Jesus taught when He spoke on another occasion of the farmer who sowed good seed among thorns. When interpreting what He meant in that parable, He explained:

And others are the ones on whom seed was sown among the thorns; these are the ones who have heard the word, and the worries of the world, and the deceitfulness of riches, and the desires for other things enter in and choke the word, and it becomes unfruitful.

Mark 4:18–19

Did you catch that? Those thornlike "worries of the world
. . . choke the word," making it unfruitful. Worry strangles the
good Word of God that has been sown, rendering it ineffective and
making those who once walked in simple faith unproductive
people.

Of all the biblical stories illustrating worry, none is more
practical or clear than the one recorded in the last five verses of
Luke 10. Let's briefly relive it.

Jesus dropped by His friends' home in Bethany. He was, no
doubt, tired after a full day, so nothing meant more to Him than
having a quiet place to relax with friends who would understand. However, Martha, one of the friends, turned the occasion
into a mild frenzy. To make matters worse for her, Martha's sister
Mary was so pleased to have the Lord visit their home that she sat
with Him and evidenced little concern over her sister's anxiety
attack.

> Now as they were traveling along, He entered a certain vil-
> lage; and a woman named Martha welcomed Him into her
> home. And she had a sister called Mary, who moreover was lis-
> tening to the Lord's word, seated at His feet. But Martha was
> distracted will all her preparations.
>
> Luke 10:38–40a

You've got the picture. To Martha, preparing a big meal was
the only option ("Nothing but the best for Jesus" must have been
in the back of her mind), so she became "distracted"—another colorful Greek term meaning "to draw around," like being mentally
knotted up in a network of frayed emotions. We can imagine the
dear lady scurrying around the kitchen, kneading dough, basting
the lamb, boiling the vegetables, trying to locate her best dishes,
hoping to match tablecloth and napkins, ultimately needing help
to get it all ready at the proper time. We have all been there, but

usually we've had a few extra hands to help. Martha didn't, and that was the final straw. Irritated, exasperated, and angry,

> . . . she came up to Him, and said, "Lord, do You not care that my sister has left me to do all the serving alone? Then tell her to help me."
> Luke 10:40b

Her boiling point led to blame: "Don't you even care, Lord? Tell her to get up from there and come in the kitchen and help me!" Martha was so upset that she commanded Jesus to do something about it. But Jesus was neither impressed at her busyness nor intimidated by her command. Graciously, yet firmly, He said:

> . . . Martha, Martha, you are worried and bothered about so many things; but only a few things are necessary, really only one, for Mary has chosen the good part, which shall not be taken away from her.
> Luke 10:41–42

Those two terms He used to describe her attitude are significant: *worried* and *bothered*. The first one, translated "worried," is the same term found in Matthew 6, translated "anxious" . . . *merimnao*. "Martha! You are so mentally torn, you are trying to do too many things at once"—that sort of thing. Worry occurs when we assume responsibility for things that are outside our control. And I love His solution—"only a few things are necessary, really only *one*." What a classic example of simple faith! This could very well mean "only one dish." We'd say today, "Just fix a sandwich, Martha." Martha had complicated things by turning the meal into a holiday feast. Not Mary. All Mary wanted was time with Jesus . . . and He commended her for that. Mary's simple faith, in contrast to her sister's panic, won the Savior's affirmation.

What is wrong with worry? It is incompatible with faith. They just don't mix.

How can we conquer worry? The story of Martha and Mary comes in handy here, for in it I find three helpful answers.

• *Realistic expectations.* Martha set her heart on many hopes and dreams. She was driven by idealism. Mary? Only one thing occupied her mind. She was content to sit and relax in the presence of her Lord.

• *Refusal to play God.* Martha had a game plan and she convinced herself that it was God's as well. That is why she rebuked Jesus for not cooperating. When Mary didn't move toward the kitchen, Martha assumed the role of the fourth member of the Trinity and told Jesus to get with it.

• *Remember God's character.* Is God good? Is He just? Fair? Reliable? Faithful? Worriers (like Martha) tend to forget that the Lord is imminently capable of handling *every* situation. Because He is God we can count on Him to come through.

It has been my observation that worriers are basically dissatisfied people. Something is never quite right. When one thing is fixed, something else is out of whack. Contentment with the way things are, even knowing that God could change them if He wished, is a mind-set that is foreign to the worrier. What *is* is not enjoyed because of what *could* be. Whoever chooses to live like that should be ready for a lifetime of dissatisfaction.

About a year ago I came across a piece written by fourteen-year-old Jason Lehman. Because it is such an apt description of what I'm trying to say, I will let it speak for itself.

Present Tense

It was spring
But it was summer I wanted,
The warm days,
And the great outdoors.
It was summer,
But it was fall I wanted,
The colorful leaves,
And the cool, dry air.

It was fall,
But it was winter I wanted,
   The beautiful snow,
And the joy of the holiday season.
  It was winter,
But it was spring I wanted,
   The warmth
And the blossoming of nature.
  I was a child,
But it was adulthood I wanted.
   The freedom,
And the respect.
  I was 20,
But it was 30 I wanted,
   To be mature,
And sophisticated.
  I was middle-aged,
But it was 20 I wanted,
   The youth,
And the free spirit.
  I was retired,
But it was middle age I wanted,
   The presence of mind,
Without limitations.
My life was over.
But I never got what I wanted.[1]

Jesus' Counsel to Worriers

I am so pleased that our Lord included the subject of worry in His message on the mountain. In fact, He devotes more space to this issue than any other. Those with keen eyes could have seen it coming. When He said, "Do not lay up for yourselves treasures upon earth," it was His way of saying, "Get your eyes off the horizontal!" And later when He warned, "You cannot serve God and mammon (money)," He was talking about living with divided objectives . . . having a "divided mind" *(meriomnao)*. So we shouldn't be surprised that He jumps right into the whole world of the worrier, a person enslaved to earthly perspectives.

I want to suggest a new outline of Matthew 6. It may seem a little elementary at first, but you won't forget it, guaranteed! You want things simple? Here's *simple!*

Matt. 6:1–18
  Warning against parading
  our acts of righteousness   *Do not brag!*

Matt. 6:19–24
  Warning against falling
  into the trap of materialism   *Do not sag!*

Matt. 6:25–32
  Warning against being preoccupied
  with wrong things   *Do not worry!*

Matt. 6:33–34
  Warning against anticipating
  all of tomorrow's concerns today   *Do not hurry!*

Jesus' Repeated Commands

Before going any further, we need to read Jesus' words about worry. Since this marks the core of His message, let's take our time. If you are in a place where you can do so, read the paragraph aloud.

For this reason I say to you, do not be anxious for your life, as to what you shall eat, or what you shall drink; nor for your body, as to what you shall put on. Is not life more than food, and the body than clothing? Look at the birds of the air, that they do not sow, neither do they reap, nor gather into barns, and yet your heavenly Father feeds them. Are you not worth much more than they? And which of you by being anxious can add a single cubit to his life's span? And why are you anxious about clothing? Observe how the lilies of the field grow; they do not toil nor do they spin, yet I say to you that even Solomon in all his glory did not clothe himself like one of these. But if God so arrays the grass of the field, which is alive today and tomorrow is thrown into the furnace, will He not much more do so for you, O men of little faith? Do not be anxious then, saying, "What shall we eat?" or "What shall we drink?" or "With what shall we clothe ourselves?" For all these things the Gentiles eagerly seek; for your heavenly Father knows that you need all these things. But seek first His kingdom and His righteousness; and all these things shall be added to you. Therefore do not be anxious for tomorrow; for tomorrow will care for itself. Each day has enough trouble of its own.

Matthew 6:25–34

If you like to mark the book you are reading, you will want to underscore the identical commands "Do not be anxious." Each time it is *merimnao*, "do not be divided in your mind—double-minded." Elsewhere in Scripture we are told that a person who is double-minded is unstable (James 1:8). Harassed and haunted either by what we think might happen or by something that has already occurred—neither of which we can control or change—we become fearful and unsure. Most worries not only haven't happened, they won't ever happen . . . and many worry over that! They are sure the other shoe will fall, and it is maddening to wait for that to happen. If we were to keep a record of our fears for fifty years of our lives, chances are good that 90 percent (or more) of those things we dreaded never came to pass.

Clarence Macartney's story about Thomas Carlyle is a good example.

In his house in Chelsea in London they show you the sound-proof chamber, a sort of vaulted apartment, which Carlyle had built in his house so that all the noise of the street would be shut out and he could do his work in unbroken silence. One of his neighbors, however, kept a cock that several times in the night and in the early morning gave way to vigorous self-expression. When Carlyle protested to the owner of the cock, the man pointed out to him that the cock crowed only three times in the night, and that after all that could not be such a terrible annoyance. "But," Carlyle said to him, "If you only knew what I suffer waiting for that cock to crow!"[2]

Again and again our Lord admonishes His people who wish to live lives of simple faith, "Do not be anxious!" This is not a series of mild suggestions, understand . . . but *commands*. Do not! In other words, stop it!

Pay attention to the three areas He identifies:

- Do not be anxious for your *life* (v. 25)
- Do not be anxious for your *needs* (v. 31)

  "What shall we eat, drink, wear?" Charles Spurgeon called these "the world's trinity of care."

- Do not be anxious for *tomorrow* (v. 34)

  "A mild recession is sure to come."

  "The unemployment rate will certainly rise."

  "The housing market is due to take a hit."

  "Money will be tight next year."

  "A huge earthquake—the big one—will probably hit this area within the next six months . . . certainly not more than nine months from now."

179

My family and I have been living in Southern California since the summer of 1971. Do you know how long we have heard doomsday warnings about "the big one"? *Since the summer of 1971.* Am I saying we should not be prepared? No, of course not. Never once did Jesus advocate an irresponsible or careless lifestyle. But worry? That is, live out our lives every day distracted by the dread of a possible quake that may reach 8.5 on the Richter scale? What good would *that* do? Think of all the energy I would have expended and all the time I would have wasted since 1971. Furthermore, think of what such hopeless dread would have done to my mind . . . and what a heavy toll it would have taken on my leadership. Worry is not only incompatible with faith, it also siphons hope from our hearts . . . and hope is our main fuel for the future. Take away hope and it is curtains.

Years ago an S-4 submarine was rammed by a ship off the coast of Massachusetts and sank immediately. The entire crew was trapped in a prison house of death. Every effort was made to rescue them but all failed. Near the end of the ordeal, a diver placed his helmeted ear to the side of the vessel and heard a tapping from inside. He recognized it as Morse Code. It was a question, forming slowly: "Is . . . there . . . any . . . hope?"[3]

If I may hitchhike on that true story, let's let the sub represent life and let's pretend we are the ones trapped inside. If Jesus were the diver, He would tap back: "Do . . . not . . . be . . . anxious . . . I . . . am . . . in . . . full . . . control."

Jesus' Penetrating Questions

Jesus' sermon does not provide the answers to all our questions, but it does address some of our most crucial questions. As I read through and ponder Jesus' statements, no fewer than five questions leap off the page:

- Isn't life more than food and the body more than clothing? The anticipated answer is "Yes, of course."

- After mentioning the tiny birds of the air and how faithfully the Father feeds them, another probing question occurs: Aren't you worth much more than they? Again, the clear implication: "Absolutely!"

- Then He asks a question regarding the ineffectiveness, the complete waste, of worry. Which of you by worrying about it can add even one inch to your height? (Or one day to your life?) Now there's something to think about!

- The fourth question strikes at the issue of motive: Why are you worried about what you wear? Those why questions—they *really* penetrate, don't they?

- The last question forces us to think theologically . . . and rare are those who do. Won't God do much more for you than He does, say, for the field lilies or the grass that grows wild in the meadow?

These five questions touch the tender nerve endings of our lives. They probe our temporal desires, our worth in God's estimation, our hidden motives, our theology, our perspective.

To live in simple faith is not to practice a head-in-the-sand theology. None of what I write is intended to suggest that we stop thinking and drift into Fantasyland, expecting God to cook our meals, set the table, serve the food, and do the dishes, while all we do is sit and eat. As responsible and thinking believers, we are to be engaged in the demands of everyday living . . . but free of the accompanying worry that plagues the pagans who have no God.

Jesus' Vivid Illustrations

While we are dissecting the sermon Jesus preached, two illustrations stand out in bold relief.

First, *when it comes to food,* "look at the birds of the air." Maybe a couple of Palestinian sparrows flitted by just then and He looked up and pointed in their direction. He carries it further by mentioning that those tiny rascals don't plant seed, neither do they harvest the crops nor store them in the barn. We have never seen a flock of "sparrow sharecroppers," yet they don't go hungry. He drives home His point by reminding everyone that those He created in His image are "worth much more" than those tiny creatures of the sky. As the old gospel song goes, "His eye is on the sparrow, and I know He watches me."

And while we are on the subject, this is a good time to allow our imagination to run free and compare the natural world to our material lives.

- No bird ever tried to build more nests or more extravagant places to live than its neighbor.

- No fox ever got ticked off because she had only one hole in which to hide and rear her young.

- No squirrel ever had a coronary because he failed to store enough nuts for two winters instead of one.

- No bear was ever envious of another bear with a larger cave in which to hibernate.

- No dog ever lost a good night's sleep over the fact that he had not laid aside enough bones for his declining years. And yet our heavenly Father takes wonderfully good care of all His creatures. What a waste is worry!

Second, *when it comes to clothing,* "observe how the lilies of the field grow." They don't compare or complain; they simply grow and bloom, grow and bloom, grow and bloom. Wherever they are planted, they grow . . . and whether they are appreciated or are not even noticed, they burst forth into brilliant blossoms. As Jesus put it, not even Solomon at the height of his prosperous career wore kingly robes or jeweled crowns more beautiful than the lilies that adorned the landscape surrounding his palace. And though his resplendent residences housed more anxiety and heartaches than we can imagine, those lilies outside grew and bloomed free of both.

From the tiny birds of the air and from the fragile lilies of the field we learn the same truth, which is so important for those who desire a life of simple faith: God takes care of His own. He knows our needs. He anticipates our crises. He is moved by our weaknesses. He stands ready to come to our rescue. And at just the right moment He steps in and proves Himself as our faithful heavenly Father.

Simply Put: Our Relief from Worry

But seek first His kingdom and His righteousness; and all these things shall be added to you. Therefore do not be anxious for tomorrow; for tomorrow will care for itself. Each day has enough trouble of its own.

Matthew 6:33–34

Do you really want to live a worry-free life? I mean, are you serious about getting rid of those mental distractions and emotional drains? If so, these concluding verses in Matthew 6 offer the two passwords for entering that new mode of existence: *priorities* and *simplicity*.

Priorities

Put first things first. Each morning as you get up to face the day, tell the Lord, "Today, my desire is to seek Your will, Lord . . . Your righteousness. Whatever happens, whatever I encounter, may I be sensitive to Your presence and depend on Your strength. May Your kingdom agenda be my top priority, the most significant thought in my mind. This day is Yours, Lord."

If I read verse 33 correctly, all the stuff you once worried about and fretted over will fall into place. As you care more and more about giving Him first priority, you will care less and less about the things that once "strangled" you emotionally and spiritually, thereby stealing your peace. Furthermore, who's to say that things are as bad as they may seem? I usually discover later on that good things were happening even when it seemed nothing was working out right.

That statement is illustrated perfectly in a story I heard recently that made me smile. It's about a farmer who wanted to breed his three sows. He had a friend who owned a few boars, so they made arrangements to get the sows and boars together. One afternoon the farmer loaded the sows into his pickup truck and hauled them over to the nearby farm. While the pigs were getting very well acquainted, he asked his friend how he would know if his pigs were pregnant.

"That's easy," said the man. "They wallow in the grass when it takes, but they wallow in the mud when it doesn't."

Early the next morning the farmer awoke, glanced out the window of his bedroom, and noticed all three sows wallowing in the mud. So he loaded them back into his pickup and took them for a second round with the boars. Next morning . . . same result. All three were wallowing in the mud. Disappointed but determined, the farmer once again took them back, hoping the third time would be the charm.

The following morning the farmer had to be away from the farm on business, so he anxiously phoned his wife, "Are they wallowing in the grass or the mud, dear?"

"Neither," she replied. "But two of them are in the back of your pickup and the third one's up front honking the horn!"

Maybe the farmer was worried about not getting his way, but the pigs were having the time of their lives. Things are seldom as bad as we think.

Simplicity

Live one day at a time. You've heard it before: Don't contaminate today by corrupting it with tomorrow's troubles. Refuse—yes, *refuse*—to allow tomorrow's lagoon of worries to drain into today's lake. Today is challenge enough! And since you will need fresh energy and new insight to handle what tomorrow throws at you, wait until it dawns before taking it on. Some of the things you do today may seem totally insignificant so far as tomorrow is concerned, but stay at it. Keep life simple. Do what you have to do today and, to your surprise, it may make an enormous difference in the world you wake up to tomorrow. And while I'm tossing out all this advice, never underestimate the importance of even the most menial of tasks you carry out each day. Don't think that some slight contribution you make on a given day is not worth the effort . . . or won't make any difference tomorrow.

In his book, *The Fall of Fortresses,* author Elmer Bendiner tells the remarkable story of a B-17 Flying Fortress that flew a bombing mission over Germany toward the end of World War II. The bomber took several direct hits from Nazi antiaircraft guns; a few actually hit the fuel tank. Miraculously, the crippled aircraft made it back without exploding or running out of fuel.

After landing, eleven unexploded twenty millimeter shells were carefully removed from the bomber's fuel tank! Each was dismantled and examined. To everyone's amazement, all eleven were empty of explosive material. Why? How could it be? Why would the enemy fire empty shells? The mystery was solved when a small note was found inside one of the shells, handwritten in Czech. Translated, it read, "This is all we can do for you now."

A member of the Czech underground, working in a Nazi munitions factory, had deliberately omitted the explosives in at least eleven of the shells on his assembly line. Not knowing if any of his sabotage efforts would prove effective, he slipped the note into one of the shells, hoping that someone who benefited from his efforts one day might discover why.

That same person may have died wondering if the quiet work he was doing to subvert the enemy war machine would ever make any difference to the outcome of the war. Nevertheless, he pressed on, doing what little he could each day, letting the future take care of itself . . . and indeed it did. There was a Flying Fortress crew who had him to thank for their lives and their future.[4]

"Each day has enough trouble of its own," said Jesus, urging us to do today only what must be done today. Those who learn to live like that have taken a giant step toward defeating the subtle enemy of simple faith.

11

If You're Serious About Simple Faith, Stop This!

SOME CHRISTIANS PLAY A LOT OF indoor games. Among their favorites is one we might call "Let's Label."

Here are some ground rules for starting. Find someone who is different. He or she may look different or sound different or think different. It works real well if the person holds to different opinions and/or reacts in a different way than the "acceptable manner," which differs from your religious group. This game is especially effective if someone has a mark on his or her past record that your group considers worth discussing, even if it is over and done with, fully forgiven, and none of your business (which is true over 95 percent of the time).

Here is how you play Let's Label. It involves at least six steps.

• *First step:* Find something you don't like about the person. That's not hard to do since most people are much more demanding of others than of themselves.

• *Second step:* Examine the externals. You have to do this since there is no way to know the "internals."

• *Third step:* Form negative and critical opinions.

• *Fourth step:* Jump to several inaccurate conclusions. This follows naturally, because there is always an inability to know *all* the facts.

• *Fifth step:* Mentally stick a label on the person in question. That saves time . . . keeps you from having to verify all the details.

• *Sixth step:* Freely share all findings and identifying labels with others . . . so everyone can "pray more intelligently."

Actually, there is another name for the game. It doesn't sound nearly as nice or inviting, but it is the term Jesus used in His mountain message: *judging.*

Judging: A Quick 'n' Dirty Analysis

Interested in cultivating people of simple faith, Jesus gave instructions that would help make that happen. He cut no corners. With the skill of a surgeon, He sliced near sensitive nerves to reach precise areas of the heart for the purpose of doing His corrective work. Occasionally, as we have seen already, He came across tumors that needed to be excised. When He did, He exposed them in all their ugliness. He was neither diplomatic nor sympathetic. It was His way of saying, "If you are serious about simple faith, this *has* to go!" In this case He said, "Stop it!"

What is so bad about judging? And why would Jesus have reserved some of the strongest words in His sermon for this? Four answers come to mind:

• We never know all the facts.
• We are unable to read another's motive.
• We are prejudiced people, never completely objective.
• We put ourselves in a position we are not qualified

to fill . . . namely, we play God.

Most of us are so unaware of these things that we overlook our limitations. We *think* we know more than we do, hence our judging continues out of habit. Because of this we jump to false conclusions. In one of the first books I wrote, I told a true story that's an example of this. I repeat it here because it shows how easily we could incorrectly judge another by not knowing all the facts.

A close friend of mine has an acquaintance who is a young attorney in a sizable Texas law firm. The head of this firm is a rather traditional kind of boss who enjoys a special kind of ritual at Thanksgiving time.

On the large walnut table in the boardroom of the office suite he sets out a row of turkeys, one for each member in the firm. At which point the members go through a rather involved ceremony.

Each man, in turn, steps forward and picks up the bird, announcing how grateful he is to work for the firm and how thankful he is for the turkey this Thanksgiving.

Now the young attorney is single, lives alone, and has absolutely no use for a huge turkey. But because it is expected of him, he takes a turkey every year.

One year his close friends in the law office replaced his turkey with one made of papier-mâché. They weighted it with lead to make it feel genuine, and wrapped it up like the real thing.

On the Wednesday before Thanksgiving, everyone gathered in the boardroom as usual. When it came his turn, the young attorney stepped up, picked up the large package, and announced his gratitude for the job and for the turkey.

Later that afternoon, he sat on the bus going home, the big turkey on his lap, wondering what in the world he would do with it. A little further down the bus line, a rather discouraged-looking man got on and took the vacant seat beside the young attorney.

The two men began to chat about the upcoming holiday. The lawyer learned that the stranger had spent the entire day job-hunting with no luck, that he had a large family, and that he was wondering what he would do about Thanksgiving tomorrow.

The attorney was struck with a brilliant idea: *This is my day for a good turn. I'll give him my turkey!*

Then he had second thoughts, *This man is not a freeloader. He's no bum. It would probably injure his pride for me to give it to him. I'll sell it to him.*

"How much money do you have?" he asked the man.

"Oh, a couple of dollars and a few cents," the man said.

"Tell you what. For that, I'll sell you this turkey," he said, indicating the package on his lap.

"Sold!" The stranger handed over the two dollars and a few coins. He was moved to tears, thrilled to death that his family would have a turkey for Thanksgiving.

"God bless you," he said as he got off the bus and waved goodbye. "Have a wonderful Thanksgiving. I'll never forget you."

The next Monday when the attorney got to work his friends were dying to know his reaction to the turkey. You cannot imagine their chagrin when he told them about the man on the bus—or when they told him what was really in that package. I understand, through my friend, that they all got on the bus every day that week, looking in vain for a man who, as far as I know, to this day still thinks a guy intentionally sold him a fake turkey for his last couple of bucks and some loose change.[1]

We can be certain of this: That man judged the young lawyer . . . and when you stop to analyze why, all four of the reasons I mentioned earlier apply. He didn't know all the facts, he didn't know the young man's motive, he couldn't be totally objective, and therefore he was not qualified to be the man's judge.

Jesus' Timely and Relevant Counsel

Enough of our own observations and analysis. It is time to see what Jesus taught.

Do not judge lest you be judged. For in the way you judge, you will be judged; and by your standard of measure, it will be measured to you. And why do you look at the speck that is in your brother's eye, but do not notice the log that is in your own eye? Or how can you say to your brother, "Let me take the speck out of your eye," and behold, the log is in your own eye? You hypocrite, first take the log out of your own eye, and then you will see clearly to take the speck out of your brother's eye.

Matthew 7:1–5

His opening comment is a strong imperative. In essence He is saying, "Stop this!" When He says, "Do not judge!" He leaves no wobble room. He didn't intend to.

Understanding the Command

It will help us to understand what Jesus means (and does not mean) by *judge*. The term *to judge* in Greek is *krino*, which really means "to separate," but it has a much broader range of possibilities. It is a term from the ancient courtroom where a judge separated the facts and discerned or decided the truth. Occasionally the judge came to his conclusion and condemned the person on trial.

Obviously, Jesus is not telling His followers to stop being people of discernment. Throughout His mountain message He has been encouraging discernment as it relates to the scribes and Pharisees . . . and He will soon warn them to "beware of the false prophets, who come to you in sheep's clothing." Elsewhere in Scripture we are admonished, "do not believe every spirit, but test the spirits to see whether they are from God" (1 John 4:1). Some judging is not only acceptable, it is mandated. We are never to suspend our critical faculties or turn a deaf ear or close our eyes to error. Few things will remove us from a walk of simple faith quicker than putting our discernment in neutral. A gullible spirit quickly leads to complications.

What, then, does His command mean? He is saying, "Do not be censorious . . . don't conduct your life with a judgmental or negative attitude." In that sense, *to judge* means:

- to assess others suspiciously,
- to find petty faults,
- to seek out periodic weaknesses and failures,
- to cultivate a destructive and condemning spirit,
- to presume a position of authority over another.

When we do these things, we have assumed an all-knowing role that suggests we are Lord and others are our servants—a position of enormous arrogance. Paul mentioned this practice to both the Roman and Corinthian believers:

Who are you to judge the servant of another? To his own master he stands or falls; and stand he will, for the Lord is able to make him stand. . . . But you, why do you judge your brother? Or you again, why do you regard your brother with contempt? For we shall all stand before the judgment seat of God. For it is written,

"AS I LIVE, SAYS THE LORD, EVERY KNEE SHALL BOW TO ME, AND EVERY TONGUE SHALL GIVE PRAISE TO GOD."

So then each one of us shall give account of himself to God.

Therefore let us not judge one another anymore, but rather determine this—not to put an obstacle or a stumbling block in a brother's way.

Romans 14:4, 10–13

For I am conscious of nothing against myself, yet I am not by this acquitted; but the one who examines me is the Lord. Therefore do not go on passing judgment before the time, but wait until the Lord comes who will both bring to light the things hidden in the darkness and disclose the motives of men's hearts; and then each man's praise will come to him from God.

1 Corinthians 4:4–5

No human—no matter how gifted or influential—is anywhere near Almighty God, possessing His omniscience and insight. The ability to read another's heart or correctly analyze all that goes into another's actions belongs to God, and to Him alone. When we act in that capacity, usurping the prerogative reserved for the Divine Judge, we play more than Let's Label; we play God. The right to give the final word about our neighbor has been denied us. Clearly, our Lord commands: "Condemn not!"

I have heard some people justify their judgmental attitude by rationalizing, "I'm not judging, I'm just inspecting fruit," which is no excuse. It is the "inspecting" part that Jesus attacks. More often than not, judging is an ego trip, prompted by pride. There are more than enough critics roaming the landscape. What we need to remember is the demoralizing impact judging has on individuals, especially those who struggle with a tender, fragile conscience. How much more wholesome and needed is a word of affirmation! William Barclay wrote that the early rabbis declared:

> There were six great works which brought a man credit in this world and profit in the world to come—study, visiting the sick, hospitality, devotion in prayer, the education of children in the Law, and *thinking the best of other people.*"[2]

That list, though old, is not a bad one to follow today.

Explaining the Reasons

As we meditate on Jesus' words, it soon becomes evident that He had reasons for such a strong command. To begin with, the attitude we demonstrate will be the one that returns to us. If we are good at verdicts and sentences against others, the same will return to us. If we pose as another's judge and jury, we cannot later plead that we are free of the standard we administered. If, however, we are greathearted and tolerant, forgiving and generous, we can expect the same to come back in our direction. As Jesus said elsewhere,

> Be merciful, just as your Father is merciful. And do not judge and you will not be judged; and do not condemn, and you will not be condemned; pardon, and you will be pardoned. Give, and it will be given to you; good measure, pressed down, shaken together, running over, they will pour into your lap. For by your standard of measure it will be measured to you in return.
>
> Luke 6:36–38

A second reason is that judging is hypocritical. To live a life of censorious suspicion filled with a condemning attitude is to choose the most hypocritical of all lifestyles. Why? Because it implies that the critic is free of similar (or the very same!) faults.

To communicate how ridiculous it is to operate as though the critic is above the possibility of wrong in his or her own life, Jesus chooses an illustration that is deliberately ludicrous and humorous: the speck-and-log analogy. Let's glance over it again:

> And why do you look at the speck that is in your brother's eye, but do not notice the log that is in your own eye? Or how can you say to your brother, "Let me take the speck out of your eye", and behold, the log is in your own eye? You hypocrite, first take the log out of your own eye, and then you will see clearly to take the speck out of your brother's eye.
>
> Matthew 7:3–5

Dr. James Moffatt, in his translation of the New Testament, calls this the splinter-and-the-plank syndrome. The whole idea is hilarious on purpose. It doesn't take long for the imagination to run wild! Here's a guy, puffed up in self-inflated arrogance, with a "plank" protruding from his own eyeball (which he completely ignores) as he comes up close to another and engages in "splinter inspection." No wonder Jesus pulls no punches. "You hypocrite!" He says.

Charles Spurgeon captures the essence of Jesus' warning:

> Fancy a man with a beam in his eye pretending to deal with
> so tender a part as the eye of another, and attempting to remove
> so tiny a thing as a mote of splinter! Is he not a hypocrite to pre-
> tend to be so concerned about other men's eyes, and yet he never
> attends to his own? . . . Sin we may rebuke, but not if we indulge
> it. We may protest against evil, but not if we willfully practice it.
> The Pharisees were great at censuring, but slow at amending.[3]

Understand our Lord's point, but don't misread it. He is not
saying it is wrong to help someone deal with a "speck" that needs
attention. What is hypocritical is to do so while denying the log(s)
in one's own life. Only people who keep short accounts of their own
failures, sins, and weaknesses have earned the right to assist others
with those things in their lives. Vulnerable, humble, transparent
individuals make the best confronters.

Most folks know the tragic failure of David with Bathsheba,
the darkest spot on the man's record. Many, however, are not familiar with how he was confronted by Nathan the prophet. Apparently no one had said a word to David about his sin before that
fateful day. When the king and the prophet finally stood nose to
nose, Nathan framed his concern in an imaginary story about a man
who possessed numerous sheep but who still took the one little ewe
lamb that was owned by another. Nathan then posed the question:
What should be done about this?

David, unaware that the story was a parable of his own careless and carnal life, spoke words of righteous-sounding anger against
the man who would take advantage of another like that. There
stood the hypocritical monarch, with "planks" of deception and
murder in his own eye, speaking with arrogant zeal and false piety—
to which Nathan replied, "You are the man!" I have no doubt that
at that moment tears rushed from King David's eyes as planks and
logs washed away in a flood of humiliation, allowing him to see
himself clearly.

Applying the Reproof

Before proceeding, pause and ponder the depth of our Lord's words regarding a judgmental spirit. Let's face it, most Christians may not openly cheat on their mates or carry a flask of hard liquor in their pocket or double up their fists and punch another's lights out, but we will hardly hesitate to speak judgmentally of a brother or sister in God's family. Strangely, we have placed that practice in the same category of "acceptable sins" as gluttony, worry, indifference, and sloth. In the swirl of such compromise, the life of simple faith gets lost.

Just in case you find yourself rebuked by Jesus' reproof, take the time to read His half-brother's lament. Referring to the strongest muscle in our body, the tongue, James writes:

> With it we bless our Lord and Father; and with it we curse men, who have been made in the likeness of God; from the same mouth come both blessing and cursing. My brethren, these things ought not to be this way.
>
> James 3:9–10

> Do not speak against one another, brethren. He who speaks against a brother, or judges his brother, speaks against the law, and judges the law; but if you judge the law, you are not a doer of the law, but a judge of it. There is only one Lawgiver and Judge, the One who is able to save and to destroy; but who are you who judge your neighbor?
>
> James 4:11–12

The fact is, God may wish to use us to "take the speck out of our brother's eye." If so, it is extremely important that we do so correctly.

First: We must be sure our own hands (and heart) are clean.

Second: We must be tender and gentle. We are dealing with a sensitive issue here. We are working with specks in eyes, not rocks in shoes or burrs on Levi's. Paul, the Apostle of Grace, put it this way:

> Brethren, even if a man is caught in any trespass, you who are spiritual, restore such a one in a spirit of gentleness; each one looking to yourself, lest you too be tempted. Bear one another's burdens, and thus fulfill the law of Christ.
>
> Galatians 6:1–2

I particularly like the counsel of Chrysostom: "Correct him, but not as a foe nor as an adversary exacting a penalty, but as a physician providing medicines."

Third: We must remember we are dealing with family members . . . our own brothers and sisters. They, like we, have enough people condemning, judging, and labeling them. What is really needed is tenderness and honesty mixed with compassion. What we are dealing with, bottom line, is an attitude, isn't it? Those who need help with their "specks" may be overwhelmed and blinded by their sin, but they still have feelings. They can tell immediately if we are coming to them in a spirit of gentleness or judgment. Simple faith and a sensitive spirit go hand in hand.

Very few people fully know the strength of another person's temptations. Those with mild and easily restrained temperaments cannot understand the struggles of one whose blood is afire and whose passions are controlled by a hair trigger. Those whose worlds have been protected and secure can scarcely imagine the harsh realities of life on the street. And those who have been blessed with loving, wise, and faithful parents know nothing of the temptations and battles endured by those from dysfunctional, abusive homes fractured by brutality, crime, and divorce. So? So have a heart. Apply a little grace. Correction . . . a lot of grace. Those who hope to minister deeply in others' lives must control and ultimately conquer the habit of judging fellow believers.

Simply Put: Conquering the Habit

Playing the Let's Label game can be addictive. In fact, judging can become such a habit we hardly know we are doing it. But that neither excuses it nor removes the consequences. What is needed most of all is that we stop it! The beast within us must be conquered. Here are four suggestions that may help you as much as they have helped me.

First: *Examine yourself before being tempted to inspect others.* Focus on your own areas of weakness and error. For starters, look at your own impatience, laziness, pride, intolerance, greed, lust, ingratitude, anger, careless tongue, indifference, gluttony, pessimism, and worry, to name only a few. Self-examination does wonders when we are tempted to find fault.

Second: *Confess your faults before confronting another.* I cannot explain why, but there is something therapeutic about admitting one's own weaknesses prior to facing someone you need to confront. It brings humility to the surface, sending pride to the pit . . . and humble, gentle confronters are the best confronters.

Third: *Try to understand the other person's struggle.* That will make you gentle rather than harsh and condemning. Want a helpful tip? Start at home. If you can resolve the log-and-speck tension there, you are qualified to do so elsewhere.

Fourth: *Remember, the goal is restoration, not probation.* We are to relieve a person's burden, not add to it. I wish there were a support group in every church called "Gossips Anonymous." It would be a great place for folks to go who cannot control the urge to judge . . . to malign . . . to put labels on those they criticize. Unfortunately, because Gossips Anonymous does not exist, self-appointed judges continue to run free, ignoring Jesus' command and making life miserable for many in their own spiritual family, which is really God's family. The pain they create is intense.

While I was awaiting my plane yesterday morning, a woman walked up and asked if I happened to be an author . . . the one who wrote *The Grace Awakening*. When I admitted I was the one, she very graciously expressed how thankful she was for the book, which, she said, played a part in saving her life as well as her marriage.

She had been reared in an extremely legalistic home and fell into the clutches of that negativistic, grace-killing lifestyle. The man she married became a preacher in the same religious system: long lists of taboos, exceedingly rigid expectations, unending requirements, judgmental suspicions—the works. They had a house full of children . . . and as time passed, she began to realize the collision course she and her entire family were on. She became increasingly discouraged, depressed, and overwhelmed. She could no longer ignore what all of this was doing to her husband, their children, *herself.*

Finally, she told her husband that she could not continue to live like that. The judging, the guilt, the blame, the shame-based religion . . . the whole scene was like a concentration camp from which she longed to escape. Enough was never enough. The legalism was killing the tiny bit of joy that still existed in her life. The growing hypocrisy left her even more guilty and defeated.

Courageously her husband, too, admitted many of the same feelings. Even though he knew that his career was on the line, he determined not to continue living a lie and promoting such a graceless and condemning message. Finally he resigned. My book proved helpful in the process of their change, she told me. I won't go into detail about that. Suffice it to say they quietly and bravely walked out of a dark, heavy, cultlike church setting and stepped into the sunlight of a whole new realm of grace-oriented freedom.

Their joy is returning. Their marriage has been restored. They have found a wonderful church that teaches the Scriptures and is full of encouragement, edification, genuine worship, and a balanced message of hope and obedience based on the Word of God and the life Jesus taught and modeled. The difference is that now their obedience is spontaneous, their love for God is genuine, and their relationship with others is free of binding legalism. She is virtually a new woman. Her husband is happily employed and continuing to grow in grace and the knowledge of Christ. He hopes to return to ministry as that door opens in the future.

Only one part of their story brings sadness. All their former church friends and even members of their own families have written them off. Though I felt I knew what she would say, I asked how their former friends viewed them.

She sighed, "Well, they have labeled us liberals, even though we are not that at all. Actually, we are walking closer to Christ than ever before."

I asked how it made her feel.

"In many ways we expected it," she replied. "For most of my life that is the way I handled anyone who did not agree with me. My husband and I judged them, plain and simple. We were right, and whoever was not in our group was wrong. Those are the rules of legalism."

The game goes on. Let's Label is still a favorite among many who call themselves followers of Christ. Judging continues in the name of Jesus, even though He is the One who commanded that we stop it.

12

The Most Powerful of All Four-Letter Words

A WORD FITLY SPOKEN," WROTE THE wise Solomon, "is like
gold in pictures of silver" (Prov. 25:11, KJV). Like Jell-O,
assume the mold of the words into which they are poured.
not been stabbed awake by the use of a particular word
combinations of words? Who has not found relief from a we
word spoken at the precise moment of need? Who has n
crushed beneath the weight of an ill-chosen word? And
not gathered fresh courage because a word of hope penetra
fog of self-doubt? The word *word* remains the most powerf
four-letter words.

Colors fade.

Shorelines erode.

Temples crumble.

Empires fall.

But "a word fitly spoken" endures.

Fitly spoken words are *right* words . . . the precise words
eded for the occasion. Mark Twain, a unique wordsmith, once
rote, "The difference between the right word and almost the
ght word is the difference between lightning and lightning
g." And what power those "right words" contain! Some
unch like a jab to the jaw, others comfort like a down pillow,
ll others threaten like the cold, steel barrel of a .38 Smith and
esson. One set of words purifies our thoughts, transplanting us,
least for an instant, to the throne room of God; another set of
ords ignites lust, tempting us to visit the house of a harlot.
me words bring tears to our eyes in a matter of seconds; others
ing fear that makes the hair on the back of our necks stand on
d.

Returning momentarily to the pen of David's greater son, we
d ourselves smiling one moment and frowning the next:

> As a ring of gold in a swine's snout,
> So is a beautiful woman who lacks discretion.
> > Proverbs 11:22

> When you sit down to dine with a ruler,
> Consider carefully what is before you;
> And put a knife to your throat,
> If you are a man of great appetite.
> > Proverbs 23:1–2

> Like a bad tooth and an unsteady foot
> Is confidence in a faithless man in time of trouble.
> > Proverbs 25:19

Did such power-packed verbal missiles just flash into Sol-
mon's mind or was he on a quest for them? He answers that
uestion in his autobiography, in which he calls himself, "the
reacher."

In addition to being a wise man, the Preacher also taught the people knowledge; and he pondered, searched out and arranged many proverbs. The Preacher sought to find delightful words and to write words of truth correctly.

The words of wise men are like goads, and masters of these collections are like well-driven nails; they are given by one Shepherd.

Ecclesiastes 12:9–11

I love that! The man deliberately sought out "delightful" words (the Hebrew here is colorful: words that find favor, are easily grasped, readily digested), knowing that they are like "goads" (prodding, pushing us on) and "well-driven nails." Beautiful . . . and so true. J. B. Phillips has correctly assessed the impact of such words:

If . . . words are to enter men's hearts and bear fruit, they must be the right words shaped cunningly to pass men's defenses and explode silently and effectually within their minds.[1]

The finest examples of that, I repeat, are the words and phrases of Jesus Christ—His choice of words, His placement of words, His economy of words, even His eloquent turn of a phrase. Never once retreating from His all-out assault against the scribes and Pharisees, He reserved His sharpest goads for them. I am thinking of the time He took them on before His disciples and many followers, a scene recorded in Matthew 23. Seven times He blistered them with words of condemnation by repeating, "Woe to you, scribes and Pharisees, hypocrites!" (vv. 13, 14, 15, 23, 25, 27, 29). Once He called them "blind guides" (23:16) and even said they were "like whitewashed tombs" (23:27) and "serpents . . . brood of vipers" (23:33). Just picture that: "You snakes!" He said. No one ever goaded like the Son of God, hence no one's words ever penetrated like His either. Every time I hear someone in a speech refer to Jesus as if He were some kind of meek 'n' mild, spineless wimp, I want to raise my hand and ask, "Ever read Matthew 23?"

The Power of Jesus' Penetrating Principles

Let's keep all this in mind as we get back to His message delivered from the mountain.

Dogs, Pearls, and Pigs

> Do not give what is holy to dogs, and do not throw your pearls before swine, lest they trample them under their feet, and turn and tear you to pieces.
>
> Matthew 7:6

Talk about shocking words! The One who earlier urged us to shake salt and shine light and not judge . . . the One who would later implore His own to take the good news to the ends of the earth here warns against giving what is sacred to "dogs" and "throwing pearls before swine."

His choice of words was designed to startle. While we are not to judge and condemn others without knowing all the facts, neither are we to be gullible fools. To borrow from Mark Twain, "the difference between the right word and almost the right word" is the difference between being people of simple faith and being simpletons. Our Lord neither extols the virtues of gullibility (there are none), nor does He wink at a lack of discernment. To walk with God in a quiet, uncomplicated manner, sharing our faith with non-Christians, in no way suggests that we keep hammering away at stony hearts and indifferent wills.

The life-changing message of Jesus Christ's death and resurrection is a treasure beyond price. While it is ours to claim and to share, we cheapen it by pressing the issue beyond sensible bounds.

Face it; some individuals are impervious to spiritual riches. They are so debauched, senseless, hateful, and closed that their continued resistance and cynicism is signal enough to encourage the discerning to turn elsewhere. There comes a point when persisting is a waste of time and energy. To quote the prophet, "Ephraim is joined to idols; / Let him alone" (Hos. 4:17). We are never to give up hope, but we are wise to move on.

All this brings us to the first of three penetrating principles implied in Jesus' words: *Discernment must temper our declaration.* I am aware that endurance and faithfulness are qualities to be modeled by God's people. No question, most of us were won over because someone didn't quit when we resisted the offer of eternal life with God through Christ. Nevertheless, Jesus is teaching here that there will be occasions when perpetually closed minds need to be left on their own. In fact, when instructing His twelve disciples, He reminded them of this principle as He released them to spread His message.

> And into whatever city or village you enter, inquire who is worthy in it; and abide there until you go away. And as you enter the house, give it your greeting. And if the house is worthy, let your greeting of peace come upon it; but if it is not worthy, let your greeting of peace return to you. And whoever does not receive you, nor heed your words, as you go out of that house or that city, shake off the dust of your feet. Truly I say to you, it will be more tolerable for the land of Sodom and Gomorrah in the day of judgment, than for that city.
>
> Matthew 10:11–15

More than once Paul modeled the same discerning style. Because he did, the Gentiles were given the opportunity to turn to Christ.

> And the next Sabbath nearly the whole city assembled to hear the word of God. But when the Jews saw the crowds, they were

filled with jealousy, and began contradicting the things spoken by Paul, and were blaspheming. And Paul and Barnabas spoke out boldly and said, "It was necessary that the word of God should be spoken to you first; since you repudiate it, and judge yourselves unworthy of eternal life, behold, we are turning to the Gentiles. For thus the Lord has commanded us,

> "I HAVE PLACED YOU AS A LIGHT OF THE GENTILES,
> THAT YOU SHOULD BRING SALVATION TO THE END OF THE EARTH."

And when the Gentiles heard this, they began rejoicing and glorifying the word of the Lord; and as many as had been appointed to eternal life believed.

Acts 13:44–48

But when Silas and Timothy came down from Macedonia, Paul began devoting himself completely to the word, solemnly testifying to the Jews that Jesus was the Christ. And when they resisted and blasphemed, he shook out his garments and said to them, "Your blood be upon your own heads! I am clean. From now on I shall go to the Gentiles."

Acts 18:5–6

Perhaps you find the idea of turning away from those who persist in their unbelief difficult to accept. You may be working with a stubborn individual who is closed . . . but in your heart you cannot release him or her. It is possible you should not; then again, maybe you would be wise to back away and let God take full charge. There is no hard-and-fast rule on this. There does come a time, however, when it is best (to borrow from a familiar saying) to "let stubborn dogs lie." Left alone, suffering under the consequences of an unbelieving, empty lifestyle could be what the stubborn one needs.

I have discovered over the years that hostile mates are seldom persuaded by a persistent, verbal witness from their believing partners. Also, those whose lives are complicated by substance abuse often must be given assistance in finding hope beyond that addiction before they can begin to grasp the gospel message. Furthermore, some folks, like Pharaoh in Moses' day, deliberately harden their hearts and become impervious to spiritual truth. In such cases, to keep pounding away is counterproductive. Simply gather up your precious pearls and move on. The soil of some souls is too hard for planting . . . which reminds me of an old Southern expression I was raised with: "You can't get sap out of a hoe handle." There comes a time when it is purposeless to persist.

But you and I *can* continue to pray. And that is exactly what Jesus addresses next in His message.

Asking, Seeking, Knocking, and Receiving

The following may sound both familiar and simple, but they are yet another example of powerful words:

> Ask, and it shall be given to you; seek, and you shall find; knock, and it shall be opened to you. For everyone who asks receives, and he who seeks finds, and to him who knocks it shall be opened.
>
> Matthew 7:7–8

"Ask . . . seek . . . knock," three powerful, monosyllabic words, all commands, urging us not to cave in with discouragement when facing the difficult or the unknown. They are all "present imperatives" in the language in which Matthew wrote them:

"Keep on asking!"

"Keep on seeking!"

"Keep on knocking!"

The implication is, "Whatever you do, don't quit; keep it up!" In childlike innocence we are to turn to our heavenly Father and trust

Him to do what we cannot. And whoever said we are to ask only once has not understood the Savior's instructions: "Keep on asking . . . seeking . . . knocking." Paul, the Apostle of Grace, later wrote, "Pray without ceasing" and demonstrated it by returning to the Lord again and yet again for relief from his "thorn in the flesh" (2 Cor. 12:7–8). This kind of earnest prayer is different from the mindless repetitions we discussed in chapter 8. "Pray without ceasing" doesn't mean to endlessly mumble a monotonous set of words that lost their meaning long ago. Let's take Jesus at His word. Let's be earnestly persistent.

Having reared four children, Cynthia and I have witnessed how our children did this very thing. If we were nearby, they asked—*and kept asking.* If we happened to be out of the room, they would seek one or both of us—*and kept seeking.* If we needed a few moments of peace and quiet, we occasionally would go to our bedroom and close the door to read or talk together. Do you think the kids gave up? You know better. They knocked . . . and knocked and knocked and *kept knocking!*

Our older daughter, Charissa, and her husband, Byron, have their hands full with their two busy little ones, Parker and Heather. Now a mother in her late twenties, Charissa made a statement that reminded me of something I had said when she was her children's age. "Dad, there are days I would enjoy just five minutes all alone and to myself . . . but it is impossible. These two are *omnipresent!*" She admitted that she slipped into her bedroom the other morning and gingerly closed the door—and *locked* it—so she might sit all alone for only a few minutes. Wouldn't you know it? Sixty seconds hadn't passed before she heard two little fists pounding away on her door: "Mom, Mom! . . . Mom, are you in there?" When she didn't answer immediately, they persisted—knock, knock, Knock . . . KNOCK . . . *KNOCK!*

She flung open the door and looked down into two little cherubic faces as both said in unison: "Hi!" They simply wanted to be where she was. Her heart melted.

Perhaps this is a mere sampling of the way God feels about His own children. Therefore, we are invited to persist in our quest for His presence, His assistance.

Don't miss the threefold promise that accompanies the commands. What happens when we ask and seek and knock?

- "It shall be given to you"
- "You shall find"
- "It shall be opened to you"

You wish to receive something you need? Ask! You desire to find something important? Seek! You long for a tightly sealed door to open? Knock! Simple faith calls for nothing more than that: *simple faith*. No mumbo jumbo, no voodoo, no need to bargain, beg, plead, or pay penance . . . no incantations, no secret password. Nothing but the most difficult thing for high-tech, superefficient, uptight, and overachieving souls to do. Just ask in simple faith.

The Western world is not characterized by prayer. By and large, to our unspeakable shame, even genuine Christians in the West are not characterized by prayer. Our environment loves hustle and bustle, smooth organization and powerful institutions, human self-confidence and human achievement, new opinions and novel schemes; and the church of Jesus Christ has conformed so thoroughly to this environment that it is often difficult to see how it differs in these matters from contemporary paganism. There are, of course, exceptions; but I am referring to what is characteristic. Our low spiritual ebb is directly traceable to the flickering feebleness of our prayers: "You do not have, because you do not ask."[2]

In my opinion, those last nine words (quoted from James 4:2) are among the most convicting words we will ever read, which brings us to the second penetrating principle we can draw from Jesus' words: *Persistence must characterize our prayers.* There is no place for reluctance or timidity or, for that matter, uncertainty. You have a need? Then do the simple thing (and the *best* thing!) first: Ask in simple faith.

Bread, Stones, Fish, and Snakes

Jesus concludes this section of His sermon with more words fitly spoken. As you read, feel free to smile. The words are purposely colorful, even playful:

> Or what man is there among you, when his son shall ask him for a loaf, will give him a stone? Or if he shall ask for a fish, he will not give him a snake, will he?
>
> Matthew 7:9–10

Are you a parent? If so, you have an inside track on understanding what Jesus is getting at.

Your child is hungry and doesn't hesitate to ask you for a piece of bread, perhaps a grilled-cheese sandwich. Would you ever go outside, look around the backyard, find a rock in the flower bed, and say, "Here, kid, munch on this"? Never! We would never consider doing that to our hungry children. If you're like me, you tend to give *more* than they request. "Let's hop in the car and go get a hamburger together."

I'll go a step further. Let's imagine that your kids really love to fish. I mean it is their all-time favorite thing to do with you when a holiday or vacation time rolls around. Would you—even in your worst moment—ever *think* of taking them to a swampy, snake-infested area, cruelly substituting something unpleasant and dangerous for their very favorite pastime? Never. You would do everything possible to provide a fishing trip they would never forget. That is

just the way parents are. We may be imperfect and sinful people
. . . but when one of our own really wants or needs something, we
do it up right. "You're hungry? How about a burger? . . . Go fishing together? I know a great spot, son!"

Now, the clincher:

> If you then, being evil, know how to give good gifts to your chil-
> dren, how much more shall your Father who is in heaven give what
> is good to those who ask Him!"
>
> Matthew 7:11

Isn't that magnificent? Our perfect Father in heaven outgives
all imperfect fathers on earth . . . again and again and again.

So? So persist in your prayers! So count on your Lord to answer in the best possible manner in *His way* and in *His time*. Don't
be discouraged, my friend. He is faithful and good and generous and
just . . . even though we are none of the above.

Others and Us

Being the ultimate wordsmith, Jesus has saved the most significant words until the last. What you are about to read is commonly called the Golden Rule.

> Therefore, however you want people to treat you, so treat them, for
> this is the Law and the Prophets.
>
> Matthew 7:12

What a classic example of "apples of gold in settings of silver."
That single sentence is perhaps the most universally famous statement Jesus ever made, "the Everest of Ethics," as one man put it.
In some ways it is the cornerstone of true Christianity, certainly the
capstone of Jesus' sermon. I appreciate the positive emphasis:

Instead of saying, "Don't do this," He says, "Do this." Study the statement. More importantly, live it. If you have wondered about how to get started in a lifetime of simple faith, here it is.

The principle? *Modeling must accompany our message.* You want to be forgiven? Forgive. You need affirmation? Affirm. You feel hurt, wounded, broken, and could stand a gentle touch? Be gentle with others. You have discovered the value of tact when something sensitive needed to be addressed? Be tactful. The examples are endless. Unfortunately, models of such greathearted behavior are rare. Is it any wonder the non-Christian world looks with suspicion in our direction?

The best part of the whole principle? It is so simple. Living by the Golden Rule prevents the need for laying down an endless list of little rules and regulations to govern conduct. Just put yourself in the other person's place and think, *What is it I would need if I were him or her?* And then? *Do it.* When you do, you will fulfill the essence of "the Law and the Prophets."

Simply Put: The Greatest Message We Can Deliver

It is time to turn the tables. Throughout the book I have been referring to Jesus' greatest message. Do you know the greatest message *we* can deliver? It is the message of Christlike character. No message on earth is more needed or more powerful.

You want to impact your family . . . your church . . . your community . . . your place of employment? You want to make a difference in the life of your mate, a family member, a friend (Christian or not), some person in the workplace? Demonstrate the characteristics of Christ. No need to drop gospel tracts from a low-flying airplane or display a bright red twenty-foot-square "Jesus Saves" flag over your house. No need to stick a fish-shaped symbol on your car or quote a lot of verses every day to your neighbor or rant and rave against all the ills of society down at city hall. Just take the distilled essence of the Christian message as contained in the words of the Golden Rule and live it out. Morning to night. Day after day. Week after week. Month in, month out. Spring, summer, fall, and winter. As the prophet Micah put it: Act justly, love mercy, and walk humbly. You will be *astounded* at the impact that kind of simple-faith lifestyle will make.

It has been said that the only Bible most folks ever read is the daily life of the Christian. If that is true, I believe the world needs a *revised version*. Our problem is not that too many of us are being ignored, it's that we are all being observed!

> You are writing a gospel, a chapter each day,
> By deeds that you do, by words that you say.
> Men read what you write, whether faithless or true.
> Say, what is the gospel according to you?[3]

If you think that words fitly spoken are powerful, they are nothing compared to the power of a life fitly lived.

13

Simple Yet Serious Warnings for Complicated Times

Are americans busy? do we have a lot of irons in the fire? Have we turned what was once a simple, quiet existence into a complicated maze of activity, a Rubic's cube of complex dilemmas? You tell me.

Every day in America . . .

- 108,000 of us move to a different home, and 18,000 move to another state.
- the United States government issues 50 more pages of regulations.
- 40 Americans turn 100, about 5,800 become 65, and 8,000 try to forget their 40th birthdays.

Every day in America . . .

- 167 businesses go bankrupt while 689 new ones start up—and 105 Americans become millionaires.

- the Smithsonian adds 2,500 things to its collections.
- Americans purchase 45,000 new automobiles and trucks, and smash up 87,000.
- 20,000 people write letters to the president.
- more than 6,300 get divorced, while 13,000 get married.
- dogs bite 11,000 citizens, including 20 mail carriers.

Every day in America . . .

- we eat 75 acres of pizza, 53 million hot dogs, 167 million eggs, 3 million gallons of ice cream, and 3,000 tons of candy. We also jog 17 million miles and burn 1.7 billion calories while we're at it.[1]

It doesn't require a Ph.D. from Princeton to assess that we are busy, busy, busy. Forever on the move, doing things, eating stuff, working, jumping, jogging, writing, marrying, divorcing, buying, biting . . . you name it, our country is doing it. And in no place in our land are people doing more of it more often than this hub of humanity where I live, Southern California. The pace is somewhere between maddening and insane. The freeways are choked with traffic, people are going or coming twenty-four hours every day . . . with no letup in sight. Faces reflect tension. The air is polluted. The earth shakes. The malls are crowded. Nerves are shot. Many of the streets are dangerous. Interestingly, the more I travel to major population centers, the more I find similar scenes everywhere around the globe, not just in California.

> This is the age
> Of the half-read page.
> And the quick hash
> And the mad dash.
> The bright night
> With the nerves tight.

The plane hop
And the brief stop.
The lamp tan
In a short span.
The Big Shot
In a good spot.
And the brain strain
And the heart pain.
And the cat naps
Till the spring snaps—
And the fun's done![2]

In the two-plus decades my family and I have lived out here, I have had scores of people who reside elsewhere ask me how we can stand living in such a hotbed of activity among wall-to-wall humanity. The conversation usually runs something like this:

"Don't you get tired of all the people?"

"Yes, occasionally."

"Isn't the speed of things enough to make you want to scream?"

"Often, yes, quite frankly."

"Aren't you concerned about the impact that hurry-up lifestyle and shallow-thinking mentality might have on families in general and your own kids—and grandkids—in particular?"

"Always."

"Then, haven't you given serious consideration to getting out of there and permanently relocating on some quiet, rural, wooded piece of land by a small lake . . . free of the hassle and demands of the city?"

"Never."

"Why?"

"Because there is no place I know of in America where the all-conquering message of Christ and the life of simple faith is needed more than *here*."

When God called the Swindolls to this sprawling metropolis, He put us smack dab in the nucleus of maximum human depravity and critical needs. When I speak and write of the truth Jesus offered and the remarkable life He modeled, the contrast is so obvious out here no one has difficulty detecting the difference. People in places like this are searching for something to ease the ache and quiet the heart, mainly to bring order out of chaos and peace in place of pain. Candidly, my wife and I cannot imagine what life would be like for us in some sleepy, slow community where people talk of things like the weather and the tide, and get all hot 'n' bothered over whether the pansies and petunias will bloom early or late in the spring. If that is the kind of stuff that turns your crank, fine. All I ask is that you not feel sorry for us because we are stuck out here in wild 'n' wooly Crazyland. We really are not stuck, we're *called*. If simple faith is put to the test anywhere, it is here! And if it passes the test here, friend, it will work *anywhere*.

In a world gone mad, full of frowning people who have lost their way, the calm, wise, and timeless truths Jesus spoke make more sense than ever. What a privilege it is to communicate them.

A Simple Outline

You may recall earlier in the book that I suggested a four-point outline for Jesus' great sermon:

- Out with Hypocrisy!   (Matt. 5)
- Down with Performance!   (Matt. 6)
- Up with Tolerance!   (Matt. 7:1–5)
- On with Commitment!   (Matt. 7:6–29)

Throughout His message the emphasis has continued to rest on the application of truth, not just its declaration. He wants His followers to be doers of the Word, not hearers only . . . to lift sterile, antiseptic theories from the yellowed pages of the Law and the Prophets and incarnate those precepts and principles before a world that doesn't have a clue. In effect, He is saying, "Enough of external religion!" What He pleads for is an authentic transformation of life based on what the living God has said in His Word. While scribes and Pharisees sat around splitting hairs over theological and theoretical minutia, the Son of God pressed for action, which is preaching at its best. No one walked away from that hillside discourse unsure of what to do about what had been said. The question each person then (and now) needed to answer was, "Will I do these things?" Great preaching does not stop with interpretation; exhortation always follows exposition as the preacher "stops preachin' and starts meddlin'." And that is never more obvious in Jesus' sermon than when He reaches His concluding comments.

The following words of D. Martyn Lloyd-Jones express my convictions perfectly:

> Here once more we are reminded that our Lord's method must ever be the pattern and example for all preaching. That is not true preaching which fails to apply its message and its truth; nor true exposition of the Bible that is simply content to open up a passage and then stop. The truth has to be taken into the life, and it has to be lived. Exhortation and application are essential parts of preaching. We see our Lord doing that very thing here. The remainder of this seventh chapter is nothing but a great and grand application of the message of the Sermon on the Mount to the people who first heard it, and to all of us at all times who claim to be Christian.
>
> So He proceeds now to test His listeners. He says, in effect, "My Sermon is finished. Now at once you must ask yourselves a question, 'What am I doing about this? What is my reaction? Am I to be content to fold my arms and say with so many that it is a marvellous Sermon, that it has the grandest conception of life and living that mankind has ever known—such exalted morality, such wonderful uplift—that it is the ideal life that all ought to live?'"

The same applies to us. Is that our reaction? Just to praise the Sermon on the Mount? If it is, according to our Lord, He might as well never have preached it. It is not praise He desires; it is practice. The Sermon on the Mount is not to be commended, it is to be carried out.[3]

Since officially entering ministry in the early 1960s, I have continued to emphasize the application of God's truth, not merely the explanation of it. Rather than stopping with ". . . and that is what Scripture teaches," how much better to continue with ". . . and this is how it is to be applied." Happily, I have found that such an emphasis is really the only way to cope with and cut through the complicated times in which we live, including life in always-on-the-move Southern California.

A Strong Reproof

Christ does not ask His followers to "make a few minor adjustments" or "try a little bit harder to be religious." His words call for a radical transformation—first in thinking, next in living. He leaves no third alternative, no middle ground, when He exhorts us to decide either for or against kingdom living. He expects (and deserves) our allegiance, our obedience, our very lives. When this finally becomes a reality in anyone's life, it is absolutely remarkable how many things are simplified.

Priorities that come from Him enable us to filter out the worrisome incidentals and focus only on essentials. Others' opinions pale into insignificance as we pursue His plan. Things like geography and culture and marital status and occupation are of little importance as we discern His will and walk in it. Rather than a hodgepodge of *both-ands*, the simple teachings of Christ offer us *either-ors*. How we need them!

Speaking of that, in the concluding words of Jesus' message, we find four "paired alternatives": two paths (Matt. 7:13–14), two trees

(7:15–20), two claims (7:21–23), and, as we shall see in the final chapter, two foundations (7:24–29). Each requires a choice. Either we go with Him or we walk away from Him; it is as simple as that. Simple . . . not easy.

Two Paths

> Enter by the narrow gate; for the gate is wide, and the way is broad that leads to destruction, and many are those who enter by it. For the gate is small, and the way is narrow that leads to life, and few are those who find it.
>
> Matthew 7:13–14

Let me ask you, is that difficult to understand? Compared with the philosophical meanderings of our times, including all the convoluted, abstruse opinions of various intellectuals representing a broad spectrum of human thought, Jesus' comment reads like a child's primer. And because it does, sophisticated intellectuals look down their noses and sneer. To them it lacks the mind-capturing nuances of deep thought they find stimulating. How could something as basic as a narrow gate interest broad-minded thinkers? It doesn't, quite honestly. Not if they are caught up in the quest for knowledge for knowledge's sake.

C. S. Lewis doesn't hesitate to admit as much in his stimulating autobiography, *Surprised by Joy*. He writes openly of the turning point in his own life when the wide gate and the broad way attracted him. While but a thirteen-year-old schoolboy, he found the taste of intellectualism delectable:

> I was soon (in the famous words) "altering 'I believe' to 'one does feel.'" And oh, the relief of it! . . . From the tyrannous noon of revelation I passed into the cool evening of Higher Thought, where there was nothing to be obeyed, and nothing to be believed except what was either comforting or exciting.[4]

At the risk of sounding terribly simplistic to all eggheads, let me call attention to Jesus' words regarding one's ultimate destination. To make the plain painfully clear, Jesus spoke of only two conclusions to one's earthly life.

- The wide gate/broad way leads to *destruction*.
- The small gate/narrow way leads to *life*.

The broad, wide path may seem the only way to travel; however, to do so without taking into serious account its ultimate destination is dreadfully shortsighted. All the mental stimulation and intellectual excitement of scholarship notwithstanding, if that is all there is, the end is disastrous. As Solomon the wise once wrote,

> There is a way which seems right to a man,
> But the end is the way of death.
>
> Proverbs 14:12

"Enter by the narrow gate . . . the way is narrow that leads to life." What, exactly, does that mean? Rather than relying on my own words, let's look at Christ's. Elsewhere, Jesus speaks in similar terms as He addresses the same subject of enjoying eternal life with God. "I am the door; if anyone enters through Me, he shall be saved, and shall go in and out, and find pasture." (John 10:9). Here Jesus refers to Himself as *"the* door." And in yet another context, Jesus told His disciples, "I am the way, and the truth, and the life; no one comes to the Father, but through Me" (John 14:6).

Again, don't overlook the thrice-stated definite article. Jesus is not *one* of the ways, or one among several truths, or a choice alongside others leading to life. In each case, He is *the* one and only.

Paul, a genuine intellectual who turned in simple faith to Christ, wrote, "For there is one God, and one mediator also between God and men, the man Christ Jesus" (1 Tim. 2:5). Interestingly, he also singles out Jesus Christ—not as one of several mediators, but as *the* one and only.

I take it that this means precisely what it says: If an individual hopes to spend eternity with God after death, faith in Jesus Christ's death and resurrection is the only way to make that happen. In other words, Jesus is the only option. All other alternatives are roads to destruction—broad, appealing, comfortable, popular, perhaps even logical, but *wrong*.

Going back to Jesus' sermon, the same "narrow" message could be summarized in a simple series of sentences:

- There are *only two* roads to choose—one seems easy, the other hard.
- They are entered by *only two* gates—one is broad, the other narrow.
- They are traveled by *only two* crowds—many and few.
- They end at *only two* opposite destinations— destruction and life.

I am fully aware that few facts are more unpopular or more offensive than the words I have just written. In our complicated times it is far more appealing to make easy choices and remain on neutral ground. Certainly this is true among philosophical types. Nevertheless, Jesus taught otherwise, and I would be an unfaithful messenger to fail to tell you so. If you really desire a life worth living—the kind of simple faith I have been writing about for all these pages—you need to start with Christ, placing your trust in Him and Him alone. There is no other alternative that guarantees you immediate forgiveness of sins and an eternal home in heaven.

Anyone who tells you that there are other ways to God besides Christ is misguided and falls into the category of a *false teacher*. We should not be surprised to see that Jesus warns His followers of such people next in His sermon.

Two Trees

Beware of the false prophets, who come to you in sheep's clothing, but inwardly are ravenous wolves. You will know them by their fruits. Grapes are not gathered from thorn bushes, nor figs from thistles, are they? Even so, every good tree bears good fruit; but the bad tree bears bad fruit. A good tree cannot produce bad fruit, nor can a bad tree produce good fruit. Every tree that does not bear good fruit is cut down and thrown into the fire. So then, you will know them by their fruits.

Matthew 7:15–20

Look closely. Think clearly. We live in such complicated times that wolves look and sound like sheep. They appear merciful, they seem genuine, they look beautiful, but all that is only fleece deep. Be warned! Jesus has our good at heart when He looks beneath all the externals of deceivers and exposes them for what they are— "ravenous wolves." Believe it! The problem is, you and I can't tell by a quick glance. Counterfeit Christians, like counterfeit twenty-dollar bills, are not easily detected. It takes a trained, discerning eye.

This is a good moment for me to encourage you to be a careful student of the Scriptures and a watchful follower of spiritual (perhaps a better word would be *religious*) leaders . . . in that order. The better you come to know God's truth, the keener will be your watchfulness. When Jesus spoke of checking the fruit of another's life, He was emphasizing the importance of paying attention to what is being taught—both what is said and what is left unsaid— as well as that which is taught as it is being lived out. In the final analysis, a tree cannot hide what it is. Take a close look. Slowly and carefully taste the fruit (if you can't tell by looking), get a respected second and even third opinion, and stay on the alert.

There are many who appeal to our senses and many who plead for our loyalty—and especially for our money. Discerning disciples of Christ are not fooled by all the externals: charisma and charm (or an accent!), seminary or university education, impressive résumés, beautiful facilities, large audiences, or even public appeal in the media. All those are externals that matter little. The blossoms in the spring may be lovely, but what does the fruit taste like in the fall? What matters is what is inside . . . what is being produced. Pay attention to doctrine, character, conduct, emphases, motives (if you listen and watch long enough, you can tell), and—of primary importance—how God's inerrant Word is handled. "All doctrines must be brought to the Word of God as the standard, and that, in judging of *false prophets*, the rule of faith [i.e., Scripture] holds the chief place."[5]

The difference between the genuine and the counterfeit is always subtle, never obvious. That is why so many are fooled. No one at a local department store would be deceived if I produced a twenty-dollar bill that was oversized, yellow, and had my wife's picture in the middle. But if it were a crisp, perfectly shaped, green piece of paper that bore all the marks of currency, felt like a twenty, and looked like a twenty with that distinguished picture of Andrew Jackson in the center, many would be fooled. And in comparison to counterfeit money, religious deceivers are often much more difficult to spot.

Keep in mind the "wide gate/broad way" feel-good message being promoted by the "false prophets." One of the telltale signs of these religious deceivers is their penchant to offend no one . . . to make everyone think that, no matter what, "anything goes." They use religious-sounding terms, never get specific about heaven or hell, soften the issues regarding faith in Christ alone for salvation, deliberately bypass what they consider to be "scare words" such as sin, obedience, wrong, doctrine, and repent, and promote the message that we are all in the family of God . . . regardless. Just believe, they say—it doesn't matter what you believe. Just be sincere. Just love, love, love. As a friend of mine who was saved out of that kind of nonsense said, "Those folks would have loved me right into hell."

Many years ago I was invited to attend a church with the family of a young man I had met in the Marine Corps. We drove up to the church buildings, which were immaculate in appearance. Beautiful lawn. Exquisite stained glass in the foyer. Elegant furnishings. Friendly people who greeted everyone as they arrived. Deep carpet. Original works of art in well-appointed rooms . . . the works. As we stood chatting with the greeters, I couldn't help noticing a long row of tastefully framed oil portraits hanging along the brick wall separating the narthex from the sanctuary. I studied each one. I cannot recall them all, but they included an ancient Greek poet, a British statesman, a famous composer, the late President John F. Kennedy, a renowned winner of the Nobel Peace Prize, Mahatma Ghandi, and Jesus of Nazareth. It was a real mixture of human greatness, fame, and achievement. But what stood out in my mind were the bronze, four-inch letters above the portraits:

FOR YOU ARE ALL SONS OF GOD
Galatians 3:26

After we made our way inside the almost-full sanctuary, I turned to that verse in my Bible. I learned a great deal about the teachings of that church when I observed what had been *omitted* from the quotation of that particular verse of Scripture:

THROUGH FAITH IN CHRIST JESUS.

Don't be sidetracked by other things as you attempt to discern truth from error. Certainly there is nothing wrong with fine buildings, elegant furnishings, works of art, and a well-manicured landscape. But when the name of Christ is deliberately omitted lest things appear "too narrow," it is time to wonder if there might be wolves in sheep's clothing on the loose. Simple faith, as I have said before, is not gullible faith.

Tragically, false teachers lead to false followers, a subject that Jesus addresses next in His discourse.

Two Claims

If you think it has gotten a little tight so far, hold on:

> Not everyone who says to Me, "Lord, Lord," will enter the king-
> dom of heaven; but he who does the will of My Father who is in
> heaven. Many will say to Me on that day, "Lord, Lord, did we not
> prophesy in Your name, and in Your name cast out demons, and
> in Your name perform many miracles?" And then I will declare to
> them, "I never knew you; DEPART FROM ME, YOU WHO PRACTICE
> LAWLESSNESS."
>
> Matthew 7:21–23

If you are the religious type who loves creedal affirmations
more than biblical application, those words Jesus spoke probably
make you nervous. Plenty nervous. They were spoken to get the
religious professionals off the fence of theory (where things sound
so right, so pious) and into the world of reality (where true Christianity is put into action). Christ, then and now, continues to look
for and affirm each person "who does the will of My Father." Not
talkers . . . *doers.* Not people who make all the public declara-
tions, but those who walk the talk by living the life. You see, simple
faith—a genuine, heartfelt, deep-seated relationship with Jesus
Christ, based on faith, not works—soon and often reveals itself in
Christlike actions. True believers ultimately do more than
believe . . . they demonstrate a life of obedience as their faith is
lived out on a day-to-day basis. They are not saved by works, but
works do follow their conversion. Works prove the validity of our
faith.

Let me go one step further here. The works I refer to are not
mere words, important though words are. Jesus Himself spoke
condemningly of those who say "Lord, Lord." He went further and
pointed out those who prophesy and perform religious deeds,
claiming they do them all in His name; yet He says of them, "I
never knew you." Telling us what? That there is a major difference

between mouthing the right words or carrying out impressive deeds and being men and women whose hearts have been invaded by the Lord Jesus Christ. The former is religion, the latter, a relationship; the former is surface talk and superficial deed, the latter, an authentic inner transformation brought about through vital faith in Christ.

In summary, Jesus has given us three warnings:

- Only one kind of gate leads to eternal life with God. It is the narrow one, not chosen by the majority.

- Only one kind of teacher deserves to be followed. It is the one who embraces the truth as set forth in Scripture.

- Only one kind of person can have the assurance of eternal life with God. It is the one whose simple faith in Jesus Christ leads to works of obedience.

Simply Put: A Personal Response

One—and only one—question ought to consume us at the close of a chapter this direct. *What about me?*

To determine the answer, the following questions may help:

- Have I chosen the correct gate?
- Am I traveling the right road?
- Does my tree bear the right fruit?
- Am I following those who teach the truth?
- Is my faith being demonstrated in good deeds?
- Do I truly know God through Jesus Christ?

I care too much to shield you from the harsh reality of choosing any alternative but Christ. You are free to reject Him and continue to live apart from Him . . . you know that . . . but if you die without Him, all hell will break loose. Literally. Immediately.

It makes no difference whether you have lived a busy life of empty religion full of nice-sounding God talk, or a life entirely devoid of spiritual things. Either way, Jesus declares you are lost. The issue is your lack of a faith relationship with Him.

I urge you, turn to Him now. As you have read, especially in this chapter, He is the only alternative God honors: "the way, the truth, the life."

> Without the way, there is no going
> Without the truth, there is no knowing
> Without the life, there is no living.[6]

Simple faith begins with Christ.

14

The Simple Secret of an Unsinkable Life

Few things are more enjoyable than a good story. It makes no difference whether the story is true or fictional, happy or sad, long or short; if it has enough human interest and if the surprise element keeps us dangling, our concentration doesn't waver.

It happened to me just this past week while I was talking with Joe Gibbs, head coach of the Washington Redskins, and he mentioned a funny story that had to do with one of his friends. Since it was true, my interest was immediately tweaked.

Joe's friend owns a fine Labrador retriever. The friend, whom I will call Frank (not his real name), looked out his window one morning and saw his faithful, obedient dog sitting on his haunches near the front porch. Frank thought he saw something hanging from the dog's jaws. Sure enough, a closer look revealed it was his neighbor's pet rabbit . . . now dead. Frank was stunned. Not exactly sure what to do, his brain clicked through several options until he landed on one that seemed the best, though it would require a rather tedious process.

He gingerly pulled the rabbit from the Lab's mouth, brought the thing into the kitchen, and washed off all the dirt and gunk. He then took it into the bathroom, pulled out a hair dryer, and spent several minutes blow-drying the dead creature until it was nice and fluffy. That night, after it was dark and quiet in the neighborhood, Frank crawled over the back fence, slipped across the neighbor's backyard, opened the door on the rabbit hutch, placed the dead rabbit back in the cage, and snapped the door shut. He then slithered back through the darkness, hopped the fence, and breathed a big sigh of relief.

Next morning there was a loud knocking at his front door. Frank opened it and, to his surprise, found his neighbor clutching the dead rabbit. He was steaming.

"Frank, we have a real sickie in our neighborhood."

"Really? Why do you say that?"

"Well, see . . . my rabbit here died three days ago and I buried it. Some guy just dug it up, cleaned it off nice 'n' neat, and *stuck it back in the hutch.* We're talkin' a *real sickie*, Frank!"

Stories stay with us, especially those that sneak past the defenses of the intellect and lodge in the soft, nostalgic places of our heart. We remember not only the people involved in them but the plot that held us in rapt attention the first time we heard the story.

Since my work involves the communication of biblical truth, I often rely on stories from the Scriptures to illustrate what I'm getting at or to drive a point home. They work like magic. I have witnessed one well-placed story from Scripture change the mood of a congregation in less than two minutes. Who wouldn't be interested in a story about true-to-life characters from biblical days whose situation matches today so perfectly? Among my favorites would be:

- David and Goliath
- Daniel in the lions' den
- Joseph forgiving his brothers
- Jonah in the great fish
- Elijah on Mount Carmel
- Samson and Delilah
- Naaman the leper being cleansed
- The plagues in Egypt
- Jacob wrestling with the angel
- Job's losses and suffering

- Jesus' feeding the 5,000
- The raising of Lazarus
- Paul and Silas in the Philippian jail
- Peter walking on the water
- Abraham almost sacrificing Isaac on Mount Moriah
- Moses at the Red Sea
- Cain and Abel
- Noah and the ark
- The crucifixion of our Lord
- The empty tomb

The list is endless, of course. Each story captures us with such captivating charm that we relive the account as if we had stepped into a time tunnel and walked where the ancients walked. Try though we may, it becomes impossible to remain aloof from such events.

A good story doesn't permit casual observation. It wraps you up in truth and recognition and won't let go. You are there, in the story; your imagination is kindled; you are involved; you interact with truth on a deep and personal level because you are in the story and now the story is in you. Then it's over, and you sit in the embrace of truth. The story is still resonating in the deepest part of you. For the moment, you are still because it simply takes some time to "get back." And once you emerge from the story, you are never the same again. That's what stories can do.[1]

Stories That Stay with Us

What is it that makes a good story "stick"? Why, with all the other things we have to think about, do they not get lost from our minds? I think we could boil it down to three reasons:

- People and personalities give a story interest. We soon forget abstract concepts, but never interesting characters.

- Life situations that we can enter into provide scenes with which we can identify. Similar circumstances draw us in. Often, the plot includes a struggle we are going through or a chain of events not unlike something that once happened to us.

- Good stories teach lasting lessons from which we gain new perspective. The best ones, of course, need no explanation. They stand on their own, leaving us pensive and riveted to the seat.

Jesus was a master storyteller. His favorites were parables. Interesting word, *parable;* it means, literally, "to cast alongside." In other words, a parable is a story in which some familiar situation is cast alongside the unfamiliar for the purpose of illustration—making the unfamiliar clear and easy to grasp.

I suppose we could say that the parables Jesus told were profound comparisons in story form. For example? The Prodigal Son. Or the farmer who sowed seed in different soils. Or the lost sheep. Or the Good Samaritan. Wonderful stories, all! He relied on such stories to underscore some particular truth He wanted people to understand, yes—but more importantly, to apply. A life of simple faith is built, I believe, on a reservoir of simple yet profound stories.

So we should not be surprised that when Jesus reached the climactic conclusion of His Sermon on the Mount, He relied on a story to clinch His final words and leave His listeners speechless. Did it work?

> The result was that when Jesus had finished these words, the multitudes were amazed at His teaching; for He was teaching them as one having authority, and not as their scribes.
>
> Matthew 7:28–29

For folks who had slept through many a long and boring sermon, that was saying a lot. To the end they sat spellbound, shaking their heads in amazement, astonished—another vote for profound stories that make the truth stick.

A Parable of Lasting Value

Even though the concluding story Jesus told has become familiar to many, let me encourage you to read it as if for the first time. By doing so you will see new vistas and feel a fresh touch from the scene Jesus verbally paints.

> Therefore everyone who hears these words of Mine, and acts upon them, may be compared to a wise man, who built his house upon the rock. And the rain descended, and the floods came, and the winds blew, and burst against that house; and yet it did not fall, for it had been founded upon the rock. And everyone who hears these words of Mine, and does not act upon them, will be like a foolish man, who built his house upon the sand. And the rain descended, and the floods came, and the winds blew, and burst against that house; and it fell, and great was its fall.
>
> Matthew 7:24–27

As I ponder the scene Jesus creates so colorfully with words, I detect at least three categories in the story.

First, *identical elements*. The two main characters are builders. They are building the same things in two different locations: two builders constructing two houses. Let me also hasten to point out that Jesus is not talking about building literal houses on literal rock and literal sand but about building lives—establishing values and determining priorities on contrasting philosophies or lifestyles.

Another set of identical elements in the story is the life situations of both builders. Each goes through a storm. Neither is able to escape it or ignore it. Both feel the downpouring rain that increases to flood level and the sting of the wind that hits with horrendous velocity. Such storms are inevitable. Clearly Jesus is not telling us how to find a safe, comfortable setting, an ideal atmosphere where life remains nonthreatening and where the climate is wonderfully supportive. On the contrary, His story is forcing us to face reality: life is difficult . . . storms are inevitable . . . pain and discomfort happen. As Earl Palmer says:

> We must prepare the houses we are building for wind, rain, and floods. We must prepare the child for the road, not the road for the child. There is a testing of all of the houses we are building, and that testing is built into the whole plan; no favorites are excused from the inevitable testing of the value systems and philosophies of life and dreams into which we invest our lives.[2]

There is no escaping life's calamities.

The second category is *contrasting factors*. The two builders may be constructing identical houses and the same storm may be blasting both places with similar fury, but the builders themselves are totally different kinds of men. That means they build their houses in totally different manners. One chooses to build on rock; the other, on sand. The first builder is the type who does more than hear what Christ has to say. According to Jesus' own words, he hears and acts upon the truth. Interestingly, the second builder hears the very same things . . . but he stops there. He deliberately does not act upon what he hears. Jesus called the first builder "wise" and the second builder "foolish." Curiously, no one can tell by looking at the builders which one hears and acts and which one merely hears. It takes a storm to reveal which is which.

A second contrast in the story is eloquent—the ultimate outcome of the two houses. One "did not fall"; the other "fell, and great was its fall." The wise builder has so constructed his life that no amount of testing, no extent of difficulty, is sufficient to bring him down. Why? The story line tells us it is because "it had been founded upon the rock." It takes no theologian to identify what the rock represents . . . Christ Himself. The wise builder has turned to the Lord Jesus Christ in simple faith and, acting upon the truth He teaches, has built his life on the principles of His instruction. This gives him a solid and secure foundation unlike his counterpart, whose life is foolishly built on sand. This, of course, is the story that gave birth to a gospel song the church has sung for over a century:

> My hope is built on nothing less
> Than Jesus' blood and righteousness;
> I dare not trust the sweetest frame,
> But wholly lean on Jesus' name.
>
> On Christ, the solid Rock, I stand;
> All other ground is sinking sand,
> All other ground is sinking sand.

The third category is *underlying principles*. As I think through the story, two enduring principles emerge:

1. If you are only hearing and reading the truth, you are not prepared for life's storms.

Throughout the pages of this book I have reiterated the importance of embracing truth, not just hearing it or thinking about it. In this information era it is easy for us to become fascinated by more and more words, interested in intriguing concepts—and making the process of gathering data an end in itself rather than acting upon the truth that is presented. The "foolish" builder heard everything the "wise" builder heard. The only difference was his refusal to do something about it. Small wonder Jesus frequently punctuated His remarks with the reminder "He who has ears to hear, let him hear!" To listen with no plan to act—to read with no interest in responding—is to miss the whole point of Christ's great message on the mountain. Divine truth is given not to satisfy idle curiosity, but to change lives . . . not to lull us to sleep in church, but to equip us for today and ready us for eternity.

Charles Spurgeon was gravely concerned about this over a hundred years ago:

> There are tens of thousands to whom the preaching of the gospel is as music in the ears of a corpse. They shut their ears and will not hear, though the testimony be concerning God's own Son, and life eternal, and the way to escape from everlasting wrath. To their own best interests, to their eternal benefit, men are dead; nothing will secure their attention to their God. To what, then, are these men like? They may fitly be compared to the man who built no house whatever, and remained homeless by day and shelterless by night. When worldly trouble comes like a storm those persons who will not hear the words of Jesus have no consolation to cheer them; when sickness comes they have no joy of heart to sustain them under its pains; and when death, that most terrible of storms, beats upon them they feel its full fury, but they cannot find a hiding place. *They neglect the housing of their souls*, and when the hurricane of almighty wrath shall break forth in the world to come they will have no place of refuge. In vain will they call upon the rocks to fall upon them, and the mountains to cover them. They shall be in that day without a shelter from the righteous wrath of the Most High.[3] (emphasis mine)

Be certain that you have *acted upon* the truth not just read colorful words and interacted with mentally stimulating concepts.

2. If your foundation is sure, no storm will cause your life to collapse.

The rains of adversity will fall, no question about it. That's life. The floods of misery and heartache will rise, for sure. No one can dodge such harsh realities. And the winds of pressure will howl, threatening both your security and your sanity. As one of my mentors used to say, "Hardship is part of the divine curriculum: Reality 101." But the good news is this: Your life will not collapse. Christ came to be believed in, not simply studied and admired.

There is a moving story of Steinberg and the gypsy girl. Struck with her beauty, Steinberg took her to his studio and frequently had her sit for him. At that time he was at work on his masterpiece "Christ on the Cross." The girl used to watch him work on this painting. One day she said to him, "He must have been a very wicked man to be nailed to a cross like that." "No," said the painter. "On the contrary, he was a very good man. The best man that ever lived. He died for others." The little girl looked up at him and asked, "Did he die for you?" Steinberg was not a Christian, but the gypsy girl's question touched his heart and awakened his conscience, and he became a believer in him whose dying passion he had so well portrayed. Years afterward a young count chanced to go into the gallery at Dresden where Steinberg's painting of "Christ on the Cross" was on exhibition. This painting spoke so powerfully to him that it changed the whole tenor of his life. He was Count Nikolaus von Zinzendorf, founder of the Moravian Brethren.[4]

The great sermon Jesus preached on the mountain has not been preserved simply because it is a literary masterpiece. It is here to be acted upon. We are to step into it, make its truths our own, and in doing so, discover the simple secret of an unsinkable life. That means building on the right foundation . . . the solid Rock of Christ rather than the sinking sands of a self-made life.

Simply Put: Two Lingering Questions and a Love Story

I have so enjoyed spending time with you in the pages of this book. We have shared similar emotions as we have pushed aside all the clutter of religious activity and returned to many of the basics of simple faith.

But as enjoyable as our time together has been, I must confess that I am concerned. Since I cannot sit down beside you, look at you, speak with you, and listen to you, I have no way of knowing whether these have been mere words you have read or truths you now embrace by faith. My hope, of course, is the latter.

Two lingering questions are yours—and only yours—to answer:

- Is the foundation beneath your life absolutely solid? If it is on Christ, the Rock, it is. If not, it isn't.

- Is the life you are building eternally reliable? Storms are sure to come, bringing a downpour of difficulties that will test the materials you are using. If your life is solidly and squarely resting on Christ, you will ride out the storm, not fearing the flood. If not, the sand will ultimately give way, your life will collapse, and you will sink.

Admittedly the last two chapters of my book have been direct and pointed. You may even think I have seemed a little too severe. You must understand that I write out of great passion . . . and perhaps in doing so, I have failed to communicate a dimension of the living God that makes His message so appealing. It is His love. He does not stand aloof from us, pointing and shouting words of condemnation. Rather, He reaches back to us with open arms, offering His strength in place of our weakness. He desires to help us in our struggles, to rescue us from sinking, and to bring us to safety. I repeat, it is His all-conquering love that refuses to let us sink and drown.

The truth of all this is brought home beautifully in one of Frederick Buechner's poignant volumes, *The Wizard's Tide*. There he writes of young Teddy Schroeder and his sister Bean, who grew up in the disastrous era of the Great Depression. It is the "mostly true story" (as Buechner puts it) of a family struggling to find harmony and love amidst those turbulent times.

Out of that story, one particular scene comes to mind. Teddy and his family, including his grandparents, were enjoying some time together at the beach. For Teddy, the best part of the day was his chance to go swimming in the ocean with his father. They rode the waves together for a while before his father told him he felt the boy was ready to swim out to the barrels. The barrels were a long distance from shore, and only the stronger, more experienced swimmers even attempted to go that far, since they were anchored out there to show that it was not safe to swim beyond them. To Teddy, they seemed frighteningly far.

Off splashed father and son through the salty ocean waves. When they were about halfway . . .

Teddy thought the barrels still looked a long way off, and the beach was so far behind he could hardly recognize his mother and Bean sitting on it. His arms were beginning to ache, and he was feeling out of breath. What if he started to drown, he thought? What if he called for help and his father, who was a little ahead of him didn't hear? What if a giant octopus swam up from below and wrapped him in its slimy green tentacles?

But just as he was thinking these things, his father turned around and treaded water, waiting for him.

"How about a lift the rest of the way?" Mr. Schroeder said. So Teddy paddled over and put his arms around his father's neck from behind, and that was the best part of the day for him and the part he remembered for many years afterward.

He remembered how the sunlight flashed off his father's freckly, wet shoulders and the feel of the muscles working inside them as he swam. He remembered the back of his father's head and the way his ears looked from behind and the way his hair stuck out over them. He remembered how his father's hair felt thick and wiry like a horse's mane against his cheek and how he tried not to hold on to his neck too tightly for fear he'd choke him.

His mother said bad things about his father. She said that he had no get-up-and-go and that he was worse than Grandpa Schroeder already though thirty years younger. She said he needed a swift kick in the pants and things like that. And Teddy knew that his father did things that he wished he wouldn't, like drink too many cocktails and drive his car up on the lawn and come to kiss him and Bean goodnight with his face all clammy and cold.

But as he swam out toward the barrels on his father's back, he also knew that there was no place in the whole Atlantic ocean where he felt so safe.[5]

It was while picturing that scene in my mind that the words of the old gospel song took on new life:

> I was sinking deep in sin, far from the peaceful shore,
> Very deeply stained within, sinking to rise no more;
> But the Master of the sea heard my despairing cry,
> From the waters lifted me, now safe am I.
>
> Love lifted me! Love lifted me!
> When nothing else could help,
> Love lifted me.[6]

All of us who now live in simple faith were once rescued from sinking sand.

Conclusion

AMONG THE MANY PLAYS AND MUSICAL performances I have attended, none has ever gripped me like *Les Misérables*. When these playwrights and composers decided to put Victor Hugo's classic novel on the stage in the form of a dramatic musical, a masterpiece was created for the public to enjoy. When my family and I saw the performance, we were moved to tears . . . literally. To this day, its scenes and songs often return to mind, bringing fresh delight.

As you may know *Les Misérables* is another story of a lifelong conflict between law and grace . . . between one whose hatred and bitterness drove him to despair and another, reclaimed by forgiveness, who chose to live in love and grace.

Jean Valjean, released on parole after nineteen years on the chain gang, soon learns that his wretched past has condemned him to the life of an outcast. Only a saintly bishop treats him kindly; and yet Valjean, scarred and hardened by his prison years, repays the bishop by stealing some of his silver. Caught and brought back by the police, Valjean is astonished when the bishop demonstrates mercy and lies to the authorities to save him. In addition, the kind man of God forgives him, extends love to him, and gives him two precious silver candlesticks. Seized with the significance of such an act of grace, Valjean declares that he will never be the same. He will become a man of simple faith and begin to live a worthwhile life.

From then on, however, Valjean is hunted and haunted by his enemy, the policeman Javert, who is determined to prove him guilty and get him back into prison. Valjean, nevertheless, stays with his commitment. In utter humility, he refuses to retaliate, which both infuriates and confuses Javert, the consummate legalist. In tender love, Valjean adopts the child Cosette and later risks his life for her fiancé. Again and again, he overcomes evil with good by turning the other cheek, loving his neighbor as himself, refusing to seek his own needs first, sacrificing for those in need, and doing unto others as he would have them do unto him. Consistently, he shakes salt and shines light, never bears grudges, continues to care for the dying, and, in the end, overpowers his enemy, Javert, with the love of Christ. In short, Jean Valjean models the Sermon on the Mount.

The last line of the theater production captures both the essence of the musical and the message of this book: "To love another person is to see the face of God."

In a busy, angry, complicated world like ours, I know of no greater need than an authentic display of simple faith. Surrounded by a jumble of activities being carried out by exhausted, joyless people—many of them claiming to be Christians—the presence of a life that demonstrates love and extends grace, a life that represents compassion, humility, and mercy, is long overdue. Because Jesus did so in His days on earth, the impact was astounding. It was, in fact, life-changing. The world awaits others, who, like Jean Valjean, will walk as He walked, forgive as He forgave, care as He cared, love as He loved.

Will you be one of them?

In the hurried lives of too many Christians there is a *peace* missing. We will not find it until we return to the only life worth living . . . a life of simple faith.

Notes

Introduction

1. From the hymn "And Can It Be That I Should Gain?" by Charles Wesley (1707–88).

Chapter 1 • Let's Keep It Simple

1. Larry Hein, quoted by Brennan Manning, *Lion and Lamb* (Old Tappan, N.J.: Chosen Books, Fleming H. Revell Co., 1986), 24.
2. Lewis Sperry Chafer, quoted in Richard H. Seume, *Shoes for the Road* (Chicago, Ill.: Moody Press, 1974), 44.
3. From *The Churchman,* Diocese of Dallas, quoted in Charles Allen, *You Are Never Alone* (Old Tappan, N.J.: Fleming H. Revell Co., 1978), 143–44.
4. Archibald Thomas Robertson, *Word Pictures in the New Testament,* vol. 1 (Nashville, Tenn.: Broadman Press, 1930), 63.
5. Robert A. Raines, *Creative Brooding* (New York: Macmillan Publishing Co., 1966), 94–95.
6. Arthur Bennett, ed., *The Valley of Vision* (Carlisle, Pa.: The Banner of Truth Trust, 1975), 91.

Chapter 2 • The Qualities of Simple Faith

1. G. K. Chesterton, *The Everlasting Man* (New York: Doubleday, 1974), 194–95.
2. From "Rock of Ages," Augustus Toplady (1776).
3. D. Martyn Lloyd-Jones, *Studies in the Sermon on the Mount,* 2 vols. (Grand Rapids, Mich.: William B. Eerdmans Publishing Co., 1959–62), 1:69.
4. Robertson, *Word Pictures,* 41.

5. John R. W. Stott, *Christian Counter-Culture: The Message of the Sermon on the Mount* (Downers Grove, Ill.: InterVarsity Press, 1978), 49.
6. Dietrich Bonhoeffer, *The Cost of Discipleship* (New York: Collier Books, Macmillan Publishing Co., 1963), 45ff.
7. Ibid., 121.
8. J. B. Phillips, *Good News: Thoughts on God and Man* (New York: Macmillan Co., 1963), 33–34.
9. Ibid., 34.

Chapter 3 • A Simple Counterstrategy: Shake and Shine

1. Lloyd-Jones, *Studies in the Sermon*, 1:37.
2. Earl F. Palmer, *The Enormous Exception* (Waco, Tex.: Word Books, 1986), 33–34.
3. Norman P. Grubb, C. T. *Studd: Cricketer and Pioneer* (Philadelphia, Pa.: Christian Literature Crusade, 1948), 166.
4. Stott, *Christian Counter-Culture*, 61.
5. Bennett, *The Valley of Vision*, 1.
6. Rebecca Manley Pippert, *Out of the Saltshaker* (Downers Grove, Ill.: InterVarsity Press, 1979), 162.

Chapter 4 • Simplicity Starts from Within

1. D. Martyn Lloyd-Jones, *Preaching and Preachers* (Grand Rapids, Mich.: Zondervan Publishing House, 1971), 97.
2. Ibid., 320.
3. Billy Graham, *Facing Death—and the Life After* (Waco, Tex.: Word Books, 1987), 174.

Chapter 5 • Simple Instructions on Serious Issues

1. Paul O'Neil, quoted in George P. Hunt, "Editor's Note: Attila the Hun in a Tattered Sweater," *Life*, 13 November 1964, 3.
2. James T. Fisher, quoted in Charles L. Allen, *The Sermon on the Mount* (Westwood, N.J.: Fleming H. Revell Co., 1966), 18.

3. C.S. Lewis, *Mere Christianity* (New York: Macmillan Co., 1958), 106.

4. William Whiston, trans., *Josephus' Complete Works* (Grand Rapids, Mich.: Kregel Publications, 1960), 99.

5. Stott, *Christian Counter-Culture*, 94–95. I am indebted to John R. W. Stott for his excellent development of these three observations.

6. Philip Schaff, ed., *Saint Chrysostom: Homilies on the Gospel of St. Matthew*, vol. 10 of *A Select Library of the Nicene and Post-Nicene Fathers of the Christian Church* (Grand Rapids, Mich.: William B. Eerdmans Publishing Co., 1983), 119.

7. Billy Kim, quoted in Stuart Briscoe, *Now for Something Totally Different* (Waco, Tex.: Word Books, 1978), 100–101.

8. Lloyd H. Steffen, "On Honesty and Self-Deception: 'You Are the Man,'" *The Christian Century*, 29 April 1987.

Chapter 6 • Simple Advice to the Selfish and Strong-Willed

1. Sam Vincent Meddis, "7 Cities Lead Violence 'Epidemic,'" *USA Today*, 29 April 1991.

2. William Barclay, *The Gospel of Matthew*, vol. 1 (Philadelphia: Westminster Press, 1975), 163.

3. Stott, *Christian Counter-Culture*, 108.

4. Barclay, *Matthew*, 171–72.

5. A. F. C. Vilmar, cited in Dietrich Bonhoeffer, *The Cost of Discipleship* (New York: Collier Books, Macmillan Publishing Co., 1963), 167–69.

6. Alfred Plummer, *An Exegetical Commentary on the Gospel According to St. Matthew* (London: Robert Scott Roxburghe House, 1909), 89.

Chapter 7 • Beware! Religious Performance Now Showing

1. C. S. Lewis, *The Weight of Glory* (New York: Macmillan Publishing Co., 1980), 4.

2. Paul Tournier, *Secrets* (New York: Pillar Publications, 1976), 22, 29.

3. Robert Robinson, "Come, Thou Fount," adapted by Margaret Clarkson.

Chapter 8 • *Prayer and Fasting Minus All the Pizzazz*

1. Lloyd-Jones, *Studies in the Sermon*, 2:13.
2. Palmer, *The Enormous Exception*, 145.
3. Barclay, *Matthew*, 236.

Chapter 9 • *When Simple Faith Erodes*

1. Oswald Chambers, *My Utmost for His Highest* (New York: Dodd, Mead and Co., 1952), 110.
2. Martin Luther, cited in Stott, *Christian Counter-Culture*, 155.
3. Lloyd-Jones, *Studies in the Sermon*, 2:98.
4. Ibid., 97–106.
5. David J. Beattie, *The Romance of Sacred Song* (London: Marshall, Morgan, and Scott, 1931), 216–17.
6. Robinson, "Come, Thou Fount," adapted by Margaret Clarkson.

Chapter 10 • *The Subtle Enemy of Simple Faith*

1. Jason Lehman, "Present Tense." Used by permission.
2. Clarence Edward Macartney, *Macartney's Illustrations* (New York: Abingdon-Cokesbury Press, 1946), 414.
3. Ben Patterson, *The Grand Essentials* (Waco, Tex.: Word Books, 1987), 35.
4. Ibid., 144.

Chapter 11 • *If You're Serious About Simple Faith, Stop This!*

1. Told in slightly different form in Charles R. Swindoll, *Three Steps Forward, Two Steps Back* (Nashville, Tenn.: Thomas Nelson Publishers, 1980), 25–27.
2. Barclay, *Matthew*, 261–62.
3. Charles Haddon Spurgeon, *The King Has Come*, ed. Larry O. Richards (Old Tappan, N.J.: Fleming H. Revell Co., 1987), 78.

Chapter 12 • *The Most Powerful of All Four-Letter Words*

1. J. B. Phillips, *Making Men Whole* (London: Collins, 1955), 75.
2. D. A. Carson, *The Sermon on the Mount: An Evangelical Exposition of Matthew 5–7* (Grand Rapids, Mich.: Baker Book House, 1978), 109.
3. From "The Gospel According to You" in *Poems That Preach*, comp. John R. Rice (Wheaton, Ill.: Sword of the Lord Publishers, 1952), 68.

Chapter 13 • *Simple Yet Serious Warnings for Complicated Times*

1. Condensed from Tom Parker, *In One Day: The Things Americans Do in a Day* (Boston: Houghton Mifflin Co., 1984).
2. Virginia Brasier, "Time of the Mad Atom," as quoted in Sara Brewton, John E. Brewton, and John Brewton Blackburn, *Of Quarks, Quasars, and Other Quirks: Quizzical Poems for the Supersonic Age* (New York: Thomas Y. Crowell Co., 1977), 2.
3. Lloyd-Jones, *Studies in the Sermon*, 2:218–19.
4. C. S. Lewis, *Surprised by Joy* (New York: Harcourt, Brace and World, 1955), 60.
5. William Pringle, trans., *Commentary on a Harmony of the Evangelists, Matthew, Mark and Luke*, vol. 1 (Grand Rapids, Mich.: Baker Book House, 1984), 365.
6. Merrill Tenney, *John: The Gospel of Belief* (Grand Rapids, Mich.: William B. Eerdmans Publishing Co., 1948), 215–16.

Chapter 14 • *The Simple Secret of an Unsinkable Life*

1. Reg Grant and John Reed, *Telling Stories to Touch the Heart* (Wheaton, Ill.: Victor Books, 1990), 9.
2. Palmer, *The Enormous Exception*, 143.
3. Charles Haddon Spurgeon, "On Laying Foundations," in vol. 29 of *Metropolitan Tabernacle Pulpit* (London: Banner of Truth, 1971), 49–50.
4. Clarence Edward Macartney, *Preaching Without Notes* (New York: Abingdon Press, 1946), 45.

5. Frederick Buechner, *The Wizard's Tide* (San Francisco: Harper & Row, 1990), 45–46.
6. "Love Lifted Me," James Rowe (1865–1935).

The author gratefully acknowledges the following writers and publishers for permission to quote from their works:

The Valley of Vision, a collection of Puritan prayers, ed. Arthur Bennett. Copyright 1975 by Banner of Truth Trust. Used by permission of the publisher.

Selections from Dietrich Bonhoeffer, *The Cost of Discipleship*, trans. R. H. Fuller, with some revision by Irmgard Booth (New York: Macmillan; London: SCM Press, 1959). Reprinted by permission of the publisher.

"Time of the Mad Atom," by Virginia Brasier, © 1949. Reprinted with permission of the *Saturday Evening Post*.

An untitled poem from Norman Grubb, *C. T. Studd, Cricketer & Pioneer* (Fort Washington, Pa.: Christian Literature Crusade; Cambridge: Lutterworth Press, 1933). Used by permission.

"Present Tense," a poem by Jason Lehman, 36 Old Quarry Road, Woodbridge, Conn. 06525. Used by permission.

Creative Brooding, by Robert A. Raines. Copyright 1966 by Macmillan Publishing Company, Inc. Reprinted by permission of the publisher.

"The Gospel According to You" in *Poems That Preach*, comp. John R. Rice (Wheaton, Ill.: Sword of the Lord Publishers, 1952), 68. Used by permission of the publisher.

Lloyd H. Steffen, "On Honesty and Self-Deception: 'You Are the Man,'" *The Christian Century*, 29 April 1987. Used by permission of the Christian Century Foundation.